"Uncertainty affects all of us and influences practically everything in our lives."

Brent Nelson Ph. D.

ABSOLUTE UNCERTAINTY

How uncertainty affects your life,
And what you can do about it.

BRENT NELSON PH. D.

H H

Heather Hill

Cover Art BNelson

Table of Contents

Preface

Throughout history, most of human activity has been motivated by uncertainty. Yet, never before have so many people experienced so much uncertainty.

The last hundred and fifty years have seen more advancement in our quality of life than ever before. Society has made great advancements to reduce uncertainty, but it has likely made us more vulnerable to uncertainty.

The most pivotal events in recent history were rooted in uncertainty and increased world-wide uncertainty to unprecedented levels. Events included Y2K, terrorism, wars, earth-quakes, hurricanes, tsunamis, oil spills, nuclear disaster, and the financial crisis with falling home prices, bank failures, bankruptcies, and the stock market crash.

Uncertainty is absolute because it affects all of us and is always present. It influences how we think and motivates our behavior. Understanding uncertainty can change how you think about practically everything in life. So, it is helpful to understand how uncertainty affects us and what you can do about it.

This book is about how uncertainty motivates our behavior and how we communicate with one another. It offers ideas on how to improve communicating skills in order to commu-nicate more effectively. It was first developed as a practical guide to communicating more effectively with people in a variety of situations. However, when describing practical ap-proaches, it is helpful to explain the rationale behind them. So, the elements, process, and laws of communicating are included.

This book takes the approach of examining the nature of how people actually communi-cate. Typical approaches to communication focus on topics or types of communication like interpersonal, family, or organizational communication. They characterize communication based on a sender or receiver using abstract terms.

These approaches are often organized by where the communication takes place rather than the nature of how people are actually communicating, which can create artificial divisions that may not accurately reflect real life circumstances.

Instead, this book utilizes a levels of interaction approach to cover practically all ways that we communicate. This provides a means to cover how we communicate in a comprehensive way to avoid duplication or omission of information.

This book is written in a casual, conversational style as if someone was talking with you. It is written for ease of reading using informal language with minimal technical jargon or academic terms. It is intended to be used by anyone without the need for any specific knowledge or skills.

This book is organized in the following manner.

Chapter 1. Rationale. The first chapter begins with an explanation of the rationale behind how we communicate to provide a foundation for the rest of the book. It describes elements of communicating that are applied to all levels of interaction in the other chapters.

It is recommended to read this chapter first. Then you can read any section that interests you. Key information is restated in each section, so it can be understood without having to read the entire book.

Chapter 2. Individual. This chapter begins with the first level of interaction. It is about how you as an individual communicate with yourself to develop a sense of identity and self-concept that is communicated to other people.

Chapter 3. Relational. This chapter describes the second level of interaction. It is about how you communicate with other people in a variety of relationships from superficial to intimate. It is about how many types of relationships are created, developed, and maintained.

Chapter 4. Professional. This chapter is about the third level of interaction. It is about how you communicate with other people in groups and organizations. It is about how to create, develop, and maintain professional relationships in a variety of situations.

Chapter 5. Societal. This chapter describes the fourth level of interaction. It is about how people communicate publicly within society. It looks at how you can communicate in public and how you are affected by what other people communicate through the media.

In order to characterize communicating as an active continuous process, this book uses the words "communicating" or "communicate" rather than "communication." This is meant to emphasize communicating as an active and dynamic process that occurs between people rather than communication, which can seem more passive or static. Communicating begins with one individual person and as the reader of this book that person is you.

Communicating is how we reduce uncertainty, share meaning, and invest in ourselves and others through the exchange of verbal and nonverbal information. Communicating is how we share our experiences, get to know other people, and learn about ourselves, others, and the world around us. Understanding how communicating works is helpful to improving our quality of life and is an essential skill for our career.

Communicating effectively is important because of the amount of time we spend communicating. It is how we gain information and new ideas, learn how to do things, and learn about ourselves and the world around us. It is how we develop our own sense of identity and self-concept, and facilitate personal growth. It is how we show that we respect and care about others, and create and maintain all types of relationships.

This book is written to help you to increase your awareness and provide you with options, so you can determine what works best for you. Since an author of a book cannot know your situation, they cannot know what is best for you. So, this book does not advocate a specific course of action because there is no best "one size fits all" approach that works for everyone all of the time. It is not intended to be a traditional self help style book. This book is not meant to provide legal, financial, psychological, relationship, or other types of professional advice like those that necessitate personal contact.

This book can be used as a course textbook, or supplementary resource for schools, businesses, groups, and organizations. Research in this book was utilized in new and creative ways to determine the effectiveness of how people communicate to share meaning with one another. It has no long examples, stories, illustrations, or cartoons, only information to make the most of your time.

Much of what we know comes from personal experience gathered through our five senses. If we want to know about something we may observe what others do, listen to them talk about their experiences, or participate ourselves. For instance, if we want to learn how to play tennis we might read about it or observe how others do it. We may take lessons from someone more experienced and we practice doing it to improve our skills.

This book utilizes scholarly research for the purpose of reporting, commentary, analysis, and criticism to create new knowledge and insights into behavioral communicating. The methods of gathering information utilized in this book include observation and experience through the process of naturalistic observation as a research methodology. Naturalistic observation is a scientific methodology that facilitates understanding of how things work through observation and participation in the natural environment. This allows analysis of communicative behaviors in naturally occurring groups subject to real life influences.

This method produces findings that can be more useful than forming artificial groups with contrived tasks that make universal generalizations problematic. This method ensures that participants behave in ways that are more applicable to actual situations and that the findings are not based on any particular individual, group, or set of behaviors.

This method of gaining knowledge is similar to how we learn much of what we know. We process and analyze information to look for findings that can be useful to us. Observation gives us an objective view as an outsider, whereas with naturalistic observation we can share experiences and gain the knowledge of an insider to better understand what we observe.

Naturalistic observation, interviews, focus groups, and seminars provided the basis of the knowledge utilized herein. This method provides a way that you can get to know more about yourself, others, and the world around you. This can be an ongoing process that continues throughout our lives.

The author of this book is the first person to develop and apply new and innovative methodologies to understand how people are motivated by laws that govern communicating and behavior. They are the first person to identify these laws, *The Nelsonian Laws of Uncertainty, Shared meaning, and Investing,* which comprise a *Grand Unified Theory of Behavioral Communication.* These laws have influenced people's behavior since the beginning of time.

Uncertainty affects all of us and influences practically everything in our lives. Uncertainty is difficult to cover in one book and could be studied indefinitely. So, this book focuses on how uncertainty affects how we communicate and our behavior. While this book is designed to be comprehensive, it is not meant to be all encompassing. Due to the nature of uncertainty, this book will likely be revised as circumstances necessitate. This book is not meant to be the last word on uncertainty. It is meant to increase awareness in order to provide a place to initiate a discussion of how uncertainty affects us all.

Chapter 1
Rationale

What if you found yourself in a place that was unfamiliar to you, that you knew nothing about? What if you were surrounded by people you did not know, who you could not communicate with or understand? What would you do?

While this is unlikely to happen, it is similar to what we experience when we are born. We are born with little understanding of ourselves, others, and the world around us. We are born into a world we did not create, and that we know nothing about. We are surrounded by people we cannot clearly communicate with or understand. We are totally dependent upon them for all of our needs to live. This motivates us to start a lifelong process of developing communicating skills, so we can better understand ourselves, others, and the world around us.

At some time in the distant past, humans began to explore a planet they knew little about. They encountered things and had experiences they sought to understand. They experienced a high degree of uncertainty that motivated them to try to reduce it in order to fulfill their needs and wants. They had to develop ways of communicating with one another to better understand themselves, other people, and the world around them.

This book is about the process by which we learn about ourselves, others, and the world around us. It is about how our needs and wants motivate us to communicate with others. It is about how we share our experiences to create meaning. It is about how uncertainty has motivated practically all of human activity throughout history.

This process of gaining understanding through communicating has worked over time to advance human society. Practically everything we do, everything we think, everything we learn, everything we experience, and everything we know is created and shared by communicating with other people. The history of human civilization is the process of gaining and sharing a better understanding of ourselves, others, and the world around us in order to reduce uncertainty.

Needs and Wants

Uncertainty begins with how we were created. As human beings we are all born with needs we cannot fulfill ourselves, so they must be fulfilled by others so that we can survive. When we are born our needs are fulfilled by our parents and family. From the time we are born, we try to communicate our needs to others who try to understand them. Having needs that must be fulfilled motivates a lifelong process of communicating with others.

As children, we develop additional needs and discover that we want more. Since we are still dependent on our parents and others to fulfill our needs and wants, we are motivated to develop ways of communicating in order to get what we want. For example, a young child may want a toy and if they do not get it, they may go to great lengths including crying and throwing a tantrum to communicate how much they want it.

As we get older we have an ever increasing number of needs and wants. What constitutes a need or want depends upon many things. It depends upon who we are, where we live, what we do, our family, our culture, our experiences, and our traditions. We might feel that we need to have what we see others have. While our basic human needs remain the same, other needs and wants are constantly changing over time. We may feel we need to have something and once we get it we may decide we no longer want it.

We can have unlimited wants that are constrained by limited resources. We can feel tension between competing needs because we may not have the resources to fulfill them. In relationships, competing needs can create tension and even conflict between people who have different ideas on how resources should be utilized. We have many needs and wants we cannot fulfill by ourselves, so we are motivated to communicate with others to fulfill them.

For example, in order to provide for ourselves and our family we need an income, which motivates us to find a job where we have to communicate with our boss and coworkers. This makes our ability to fulfill our needs and wants to some extent contingent upon our ability to communicate with other people.

We have many needs that can be grouped into the following types.

- Physical. These include everything we need to survive such as air to breathe, food to eat, water to drink, clothing and shelter for protection from the elements, and so on. Physical needs are universal because everyone needs them fulfilled in order to survive.

- Safety. We all have the need for safety and security, to feel safe and free from harm. Having safety and security creates stability that is essential to a well functioning society. This motivates the creation of institutions in society such as government, military, and police who help to keep people safe from harm.

- Material. We all have material needs and the most fundamental is money. In today's society it is difficult to live without it. Material needs include money and the many things we have that make everyday life possible. We need a certain amount of material things in order to survive.

- More. It seems that when people have needs or wants fulfilled, they may feel the need for more. They want new, improved, and better things. People can have virtually unlimited needs and wants, which can be restrained by limited resources.

- Spiritual. We need to know more about ourselves such as who we are, where we came from, and where we are going. We need to know more about God and why we were created. This can motivate us to believe in something greater than ourselves like religion and various forms of spirituality.

- Freedom. People need basic human rights like freedom of speech, movement, association, and religion.

- Emotional. Since we experience emotions, we have a need to express them. We need to share them with others and to seek out emotional support. We express our emotions because we need to feel connected to others. We need to feel cared for, to be supported, and to support others.

- Intellectual. We need to learn about ourselves, others, and the world around us. Throughout history people have been motivated to explore the unknown to learn new things out of a need to reduce uncertainty. Explorers, inventors, and scientists have taken great risks, even sacrificing their own needs like their safety and security in order to pursue their need to know the unknown. We pursue education out of a desire to learn, to gain knowledge, and to seek understanding. We do this out of the need to improve ourselves and our quality of life.

- Accomplishment. People may do things out of the need to feel a sense of accomplishment. We need to feel useful and that what we do matters to others. Achieving goals gives us a sense of accomplishment and a feeling of fulfillment. We need to contribute because we want to be part of something bigger than ourselves. We want to be respected and well regarded by others. We show concern for others or make sacrifices by forgoing benefits for ourselves to pursue something more meaningful. We want to support and help others not only because it is the right thing to do, but also so they will support and help us.

- Inclusion. We want to be part of a group and have connections with other people. This is why we seek out the acceptance and approval of others. We give up some of our own individual freedoms to others in order to be part of a group, so that we can feel connected to other people. When we are included, we feel like we belong, that we are accepted by others, and that we fit in. We like to be liked, so we seek out the approval and acceptance of others because it makes us feel good about ourselves. We feel the need to be close to others for friendship, affection, and intimacy. We want to love and be loved. We want to care about others and have them care about us.

- Escape. We need to be part of a group and have relationships, but we also need our own space. We feel the need to work, but we also need rest and leisure. We need enjoyment, pleasure, entertainment, fun, and to escape by getting away from our daily routines. This need can be fulfilled by pursuing our interests, hobbies, and other types of recreation. The need to work and the need to relax can be mutually exclusive, they cannot both be fulfilled at the same time. This conflict between opposing needs can create tension motivating us to resolve it.

- Power. There are many types of power. We tend to think of power in terms of financial or political power. Power can be the ability to control resources or have influence over others. It can be the ability to get things done or to get people to do what we want them to do. It can be getting what we want, making a difference, or being respected by others.

- Control. People need to have some degree of control over their own life. They want control over resources like money or other people. They may use control as a type of emotional release. When people become upset they may clean the house or rearrange the furniture even though it may not need it. They may do this to fulfill a need to control something in their lives.

- Self image. We have a need to present a positive image of ourselves to others. We do this because we have a need for prestige, status, respect, or to be held in high regard. When we have these things, we feel valued by others. This need motivates us to do things like joining groups and organizations that have the ability to fulfill them.

- Self expression. This is the need to be yourself by discovering who you truly are. It is knowing yourself and being able to communicate that clearly to others. While people might think about fulfilling this need through artistic or creative expression such as through the arts and music, we can express ourselves in practically anything we do.

- Self fulfillment. This involves becoming all that you can be, fulfilling your destiny, developing your talents, or following your calling. Often self fulfillment is looked at as developing your talents, rising to the top of your profession, or gaining status and recognition such as becoming a professional musician, athlete, artist, or actor. Sometimes it's climbing the corporate ladder, writing a novel, creating an invention, or building a business. However, self fulfillment can come from doing anything you choose to do. It can come from being anything you want to be like a farmer, truck driver, store clerk, carpenter, or practically anything else. Self fulfillment is not about what you do, it's about how you do it. It comes from doing what you enjoy to the best of your ability.

There are some needs that are required for survival, however, other needs are contingent upon each individual person. Some people need to be around others or be the center of attention, where others need time for themselves. Much attention has been given to how we organize or prioritize our needs. Some suggest that there is a hierarchy for everyone's needs that can be ranked by importance where they must satisfy one level of needs before proceeding to the next. However, this does not necessarily hold true.

Everyone is different with their own priorities for fulfilling their needs and wants, so there is no one way that everyone organizes or prioritizes their needs and wants. It all depends upon our individual priorities. Needs do not form a hierarchy like a video game where each person has to satisfy one level in order to proceed to the next. We choose which ones are important to fulfill and which ones are not. Self fulfillment or actualization is not fulfilling our needs in a predetermined order, but instead being able to pursue the ones that are important to us and being able to put aside others which are not.

We each have complementary and conflicting needs and wants that can motivate our behavior. So, it can be problematic to attempt to simplify how these work by creating a single, simplistic metaphor. Life cannot, and should not, be trivialized as a form of game playing with winners and losers. It is much more complex and sophisticated than that. These terms carry generalized stereotypical positive and negative connotations that can potentially limit their significance and application.

For example, some people might choose not to play or they make up their own rules. Not everyone benefits by winning and some benefit by losing. Even the definitions of these terms are relative based on individual interpretation making generalized comparisons or application problematic. How our individual needs and wants motivate behavior in order to reduce uncertainty cannot easily be generalized as there is no one best one size fits all approach that works for everyone in all situations. It is unlikely that people play individual separate games resulting in a winner and loser, or both winners or losers. More commonly, we participate in a series of interconnected situations were we may get some of what we want, motivating communicative behavior.

Our needs and wants have an important impact on our behavior. We communicate for a reason and our reasons are often based upon our needs and wants. Since we need the help of others to fulfill them, we are motivated to communicate with other people to do so. In order to better understand ourselves and our behavior, it can be helpful to know more about how our needs and wants motivate our actions to communicate with others. By being aware of our needs and wants, we can communicate more effectively to improve the quality of our relationships with other people. All too often we may not be aware of what those needs are or why they motivate our behavior. By understanding how needs and wants work to motivate our behavior and how we communicate with others, we can make choices about what we do rather than reacting without knowing why.

The nature of needs and wants.

We may feel frustration, depression, or tension in our lives and wonder why we are feeling this way. Tension is a natural part of everyday life because it arises out of our needs and wants. Unfulfilled needs and wants are uncomfortable, which creates tension. We often have more needs and wants than we have resources to fulfill, forcing us to set priorities that can be difficult because it can leave some of them unfulfilled creating tension. Some needs and wants are mutually exclusive and cannot be fulfilled at the same time creating tension between them. Balancing tension created by our needs and wants can be one of the most challenging things we do. By having an awareness of our needs and wants, and how they motivate behavior, we can reduce our feelings of frustration and tension.

We have many conflicting needs and wants. We need to feel close to others, but we also need our own space. We need to belong to groups like our family, but we also need our own individual identity. We need safety and stability, but we also need adventure and excitement. We need to share information about ourselves to develop relationships, but we also need privacy. We need to work and be productive, but we also like to take time off and have fun. When we have conflicting needs and wants, we might feel tension or guilt. For example, if our family wants us to spend time with them, but we need some time to ourselves, we may feel guilt or tension. By understanding how competing or conflicting needs and wants affect us we can find a balance to avoid unnecessary frustration or tension.

How we perceive our needs and wants could be characterized in the following ways.

1. Compelling needs and wants. These motivate us to take action.

2. Competing needs and wants. These create tension between which one to choose.

3. Conflicting needs and wants. These can hinder us from taking action.

In order to better understand what motivates your behavior, make a list of your needs in order of importance. Do the same for your wants. Next to each one, on a scale of 1 to 10 write down how well you feel they have been fulfilled. Doing this can help increase your awareness of your needs and wants and how they motivate you. Not fulfilling some needs and wants can lead to unhappiness and tension leaving us feeling frustrated and depressed, but we may not know why. Making a list can help you determine what is important to you, so that you can more effectively allocate your time to fulfill more of them. It can help you spend less time doing things that make you end up feeling frustrated and spend more time doing things that make you feel fulfilled.

We were created by nature with needs and wants we cannot fulfill ourselves. Unfulfilled needs and wants make us uncomfortable, and since we don't like being uncomfortable, we are motivated to take action to alleviate this discomfort by fulfilling them. Since it is difficult for us to fulfill all our needs and wants on our own, we are motivated to get assistance from other people. In order to do this, we must be able to communicate with them. This is how our needs and wants motivate us to communicate with one another.

When we communicate, people share stories about themselves with us which gives us a better understanding of others and adds deeper meaning to our own experiences. This process helps to create a shared understanding between people that can help to develop relationships. Developing relationships is fundamental to the formation of families, groups, organizations, and communities. These institutions help us to create a stable society that can provide predictability, so we can know what our lives might be like in the future. This gives us confidence to invest our time, energy, money, and other resources in ourselves, our families, businesses, and society.

The Laws of Communicating

As humans we were created by nature with needs and wants. Needs that must be fulfilled in order to survive and wants that motivate us to take action to fulfill them. We could have been created by nature to be simpler and less complicated with fewer needs and wants like other creatures on earth. We could have been created with the ability to satisfy all our needs and wants by ourselves, but this was not how nature intended us to be. We were created with complex needs and wants, so we have to take action and communicate with others in order to fulfill them. This means that the laws of communicating were created by nature because we were meant by nature to communicate and become involved with one another.

It is difficult to talk about communicating in and of itself because it is so closely linked with our behavior. Rarely do we just communicate with someone and that's the end of it. It is more common for us to communicate in the process of doing things. We don't often do things without communicating about them and we don't often communicate without taking some kind of action. How we communicate influences our behavior and the behavior of others. Our behavior has the ability to communicate information about us to others and the behavior of other people communicates information about them to us. So, when this book refers to communicating what is actually being described is behavioral communicating.

Communicating and behavior are virtually inseparable because our behavior communicates information to others. Behavior is better understood when we know why people communicate because it gives what they do meaning. Therefore, this process can be thought of as behavioral communicating. This consists not only of how people use behavior to communicate, but how communicating affects behavior. It is about what people say and do.

How we communicate is shaped by forces that originated in how the world was created. These forces are contained in laws that shape and motivate human behavior. They influence our behavior to comprise a *Grand Unified System of Human Behavior.* Like the laws of physics, these laws have governed human behavior and how we communicate since the beginning of time. By understanding these laws and the forces they create, we can better understand human behavior and how we communicate. The author of this book is the first person to identify and develop *The Nelsonian Laws of Uncertainty, Shared meaning, and Investing*, which comprise a *Grand Unified Theory of Behavioral Communication.*

These laws are analogous to the laws of nature, like the laws of physics, because they were created by nature. They apply universally to everyone, they do not change, and they cannot be altered by people. These laws shape human behavior and how we communicate. They can be used to help understand what motivates human behavior including how and why we communicate with one another. The three laws are *The Law of Uncertainty, The Law of Shared Meaning, and The Law of Investing*. These are in order of importance because the process begins with the first law and each preceding law is created by the ones before it.

The Law of Uncertainty

Life is uncertain. The world around us is chaotic. Things happen with no warning and for no apparent reason. We may know that things might happen, but do not know when or how. No one can predict the future or has the ability to control everything that might happen. Despite our best planning things do not go as we expect. We experience things we do not want such as illness, financial troubles, and natural disasters. We are aware of our own mortality, even though we do not know when or how it will happen. All these things create uncertainty.

Uncertainty is the first and most important law of behavioral communicating because it makes the other two laws possible. It is like the law of gravity because it affects everyone and cannot be changed by people. No matter how much people seek to reduce uncertainty, it cannot be totally eliminated. This is in part because we have needs and wants that must be fulfilled, because there are things about life we don't know, and because there are things that are out of our control. Even if uncertainty could be totally eliminated, it would be detrimental for us and society. The law of uncertainty provides critical functions that shape who we are as individuals. Without uncertainty we would not be motivated to do the things that need to be done for society to function.

The degree of uncertainty we each experience is based on our individual perspectives and experiences. What constitutes uncertainty for one person may be viewed as a challenge or adventure for another. Uncertainty is different for each person because it is based upon our past experiences, the degree to which our needs and wants are fulfilled, and the difference between our perceptions and expectations. Uncertainty can be viewed as the difference between how much security and stability we have in our life compared to what we need or want to have.

Uncertainty can affect our self-concept and how we interact with others based on the degree of confidence we have in ourselves and our abilities. It can be the difference between what we know and what we need or want to know. It can be the degree to which we feel we have some predictability about the future and having our expectations met. Uncertainty occurs when reality, or our perception of reality, does not meet our expectations. Uncertainty can be measured by the degree to which there is a gap between our expectations and our perception of reality.

Uncertainty should not be considered the same as confusion or inaction. Even though these words are sometimes used interchangeably, they are not the same. Confusion is a lack of clarity and indecision is the inability to make a decision. Uncertainty does not necessarily prevent us from thinking clearly or having the ability to act decisively. When we go through times where we feel uncertain about things around us, perhaps even about ourselves, it is not necessarily uncertainty. Rather, it may come from confusion or indecision about what we should be doing because we want to know that we are doing the right thing or that our life is going in the right direction. Uncertainty is not the same as doubt, which could be considered a lack of confidence in a person's competence or ability to affect a certain outcome.

Uncertainty is not the same as a risk. Uncertainty is created by nature whereas risk is generally created by people, and we have a degree of choice over how much we risk. For example, the stock market contains uncertainty because no one can predict what will happen to the economy or even to a particular company's stock. The market goes up and down, the economy has growth and recession, and individual companies go through good and bad times. The more money you invest, the greater your risk because the greater your potential is for loss. However, uncertainty is unaffected by how much money you invest. If you invest $100 in a stock you have a relatively low risk because you have little to lose. If you invest $100,000 in a stock uncertainty remains the same, however, your risk has increased because you have a much greater potential for loss. Some risk is good, we take risks to make life interesting. Greater risk often brings greater reward. Risk generally involves making choices about what is known, so we may have an idea of what we stand to lose. Uncertainty is different because it represents the unknown, we don't know what we might gain or lose.

Uncertainty reduction.

Uncertainty can be uncomfortable, painful, even intolerable. It can create feelings of tension, frustration, and even anger. When we are faced with something we do not like, that is uncomfortable, or painful we are motivated to reduce or eliminate it. This is how the law of uncertainty motivates people to reduce uncertainty through the process of uncertainty reduction. We reduce uncertainty to reduce tension, frustration, and discomfort. Uncertainty reduction can help us to create predictability, stability, and security improving our quality of life. When bad things happen, we seek to understand them in order to reduce uncertainty and its impact on us.

It is our need for uncertainty reduction that has motivated most of human behavior throughout history. Much of what we have created in society has been done to improve our lives by reducing the effects that uncertainty has on us. Exploration reduces uncertainty about the world around us. Science and medicine reduces uncertainty about our bodies and the illnesses that afflict them. Agricultural and technological advances have reduced uncertainty about the things we need to survive like food and shelter.

So, why don't we know everything we need to know? We may have been created by nature, but nature didn't reveal everything to us. We could have been created with all the knowledge we need about ourselves and the world around us from the time we are born. We could live in a world that we know everything about, inhabit bodies we fully understand, or have the ability to know what will happen in the future. If we lived in a world where there was no uncertainty, we would not have to solve many of the problems we face. But that was not the case, it was not what nature intended. If everything was created for a reason, then nature had its reasons.

Uncertainty motivates our behavior by forcing us to communicate with one another. It motivates us to take action to do everything that people have done since the beginning of civilization. If we had all the answers, we wouldn't have to look for them. Instead, we are forced to find them for ourselves leading to the creation of society as we know it today. Virtually everything that people have done since the beginning of time has been motivated by their need to reduce uncertainty in order to fulfill needs and wants.

By being unable to fulfill all our needs and wants, we are not always certain how they will be fulfilled. This creates uncertainty that can make us uncomfortable motivating us to take action. We want to know how our needs and wants will be fulfilled because we like stability and predictability, which it is comfortable. In order to reduce uncertainty we have learned to communicate with one another, we have learned how to find out more about the world around us, and we have learned how to better understand ourselves. From the moment we are born, as well as from the beginning of human history, people have been motivated by uncertainty to learn about themselves and the world around them, so that they could fulfill their needs and wants.

When we do not know about something we need or want we are motivated to create new knowledge through research, exploration, discovery, invention, or creation. We are motivated to learn and develop skills giving us a sense of purpose and facilitating personal growth. If we knew everything, we would not be as motivated to do these things. We would be deprived of the sense of wonder and amazement at the creations that surround us. We would not fulfill important needs like our need for accomplishment, to feel useful, to contribute, to help others, for self improvement, and to find our own sense of purpose. It would inhibit development of our self-concept and who we are as an individual.

So, what if there was no uncertainty? If all of our needs and wants were fulfilled and there was no uncertainty we would probably just sit around not doing much of anything. Without uncertainty we would not have the same motivation to communicate and work together with one another. This would make it less likely for people to have accomplished everything that has been accomplished throughout human history. Without uncertainty we would all likely have the same knowledge reducing individual differences. There would be no need to seek out new knowledge, facilitate change, and do the things that make our lives better. If we knew everything we would not be motivated to do the things that makes society work and we would miss out on some of the most important and rewarding aspects of life.

People often ask, why doesn't God tell us more? Since God knows everything, why hasn't he told us more? We pray for answers, but don't always get them. Think about what would happen if God gave us all the answers. What if your children knew how to do everything for themselves? Chances are they would think they didn't need you and not ask for your help. We want our children to need us, to ask for our help and advice. If God told us everything we wanted to know and bad things didn't happen to us, there would be little uncertainty so there would be little motivation for us to ask for help. Society and human advancement as we know it would probably grind to a halt because no one would have any need to do anything. By facing uncertainty and adversity, we are motivated to find ways to solve our problems for ourselves by communicating and working with others.

The origin of the law of uncertainty.

If uncertainty was created by nature, then where did it come from? Where did it first originate? Just as physicists look for the origin of the universe, what was the origin of human behavior? What started the chain reaction that has shaped human behavior throughout history? The origins can be found in a story that we all know.

The origin of uncertainty can be found in the Bible, Torah, and Koran. All three chronicle a similar story about how God created the heavens, the earth, and everything contained within. Then God created the first man and placed him in a garden that was full of food to eat and a river with water to drink. God saw that man was alone and needed companionship and created woman. All their needs were provided for so there was no uncertainty.

Then God made one condition, instructing them that they were not to eat the fruit of the tree of knowledge of good and evil. Since God has knowledge of everything, he must have known what was going to happen. Did God give man the free will to make a choice that would affect all humanity, so that man would take the responsibility for what God knew had to be done? With all their needs and wants fulfilled, God needed to motivate them to do what must be done to create society, but couldn't make them leave because they had been given free will. They had all their needs and wants fulfilled, but they wanted more. They had needs and wants they were willing to take a risk to fulfill, like gaining new knowledge.

When they ate the fruit of the tree their eyes were opened to good and evil. As a result, God cast them out of the garden for disobeying him. This constitutes the first account of a big bang type event in human behavior that introduced absolute uncertainty into the world because they no longer had stability, security, and predictability. They no longer had all their needs fulfilled, so they had to provide for themselves.

When they ate of the tree their eyes were opened and they saw clearly. They shared meaning about themselves and their surroundings. They made garments for themselves and were sent out to farm the land where they would have children. Now they had to invest in relationships with one another. From now on they would have to fulfill their own needs and wants. This event set off a chain reaction that has been the catalyst for human behavior and how we have communicated with one another ever since.

Other cultures and religions throughout history have told a similar story about the origin of uncertainty. Greek mythology tells the story of Pandora, the first woman on earth who was created by Zeus, the ruler of the Greek gods. She was given a vessel and instructed not to open it for any reason. Overcome by curiosity, she opened it and all the evils of mankind were released into the world. The world would now experience work, hardship, sickness, and the other evils of life creating absolute uncertainty. Whether we believe in these stories or not, there was a point early in history when humans appeared on this planet having to fulfill their needs and wants creating uncertainty.

Since the earliest times in history, the law of uncertainty has motivated human behavior. We all have needs that must be fulfilled in order to survive, however, there is uncertainty about how they will be fulfilled. This led to the pursuit of uncertainty reduction, which has dominated most of human behavior throughout history.

At one time people were hunter gatherers roaming the countryside looking for game to hunt and food to harvest in order to fulfill their need to eat for survival. They fulfilled this need by hunting and gathering food, which led to a nomadic lifestyle moving to wherever food could be found. They didn't always know for certain what they would find and if they did not find any food, they would probably go hungry. This way of life contained a high degree of uncertainty.

Motivated by the need to eat and the uncertainty of hunting and gathering, people took action to develop agricultural alternatives like farming and ranching. By growing their own crops and raising livestock, people fulfilled their need to eat by reducing uncertainty creating stability and predictability. No longer needing to move from place to place, they could now fulfill their needs by staying in one place for long periods of time. They were now able to invest their time and other resources in one place creating communities. So, uncertainty reduction to fulfill our basic needs led to the creation of many important institutions fundamental to developing society, making people's lives better by giving them security and stability.

As people developed the agricultural means to reduce uncertainty by providing adequate food for themselves, they had more time and energy to spend on other things. Since we were created not knowing everything about ourselves and the world around us, this time and energy could be channeled into fulfilling other needs and wants like the need for knowledge by making discoveries about the world around them, creating inventions to help make life easier, for self expression through the arts, and in many other areas that helped to develop society.

People could have been satisfied with what they had, however, as needs were fulfilled wants became needs and people developed new wants. The difference between perceived needs and wants and our expectations of their fulfillment creates uncertainty that motivates us to find ways to fulfill them. Since people have virtually unlimited wants, when some needs and wants are fulfilled, they develop additional ones that then in turn need to be fulfilled. This need to find something new and better motivates exploration, creation, innovation, and discovery. This is how uncertainty can motivate people to improve their quality of life.

People need change and excitement, they want new and better things. They have a need for more, to have more things and better things. This need motivated them to develop trade with other people in order to reduce the uncertainty of obtaining what they want. As society developed, new things became available. Imagine what it was like hundreds of years ago to experience eating corn, potatoes, or chocolate for the very first time having never seen them before. Instead of having to find what you need or want, the establishment of trade provided a more stable and secure means of getting things people wanted.

Fulfilling needs and wants motivated trade which necessitated communicating between diverse peoples and cultures. In doing so, people shared stories about themselves, their experiences, their traditions, and their history. They exchanged local foods and different ways of doing things. This increased the sharing of knowledge for their mutual benefit not only fulfilling needs and wants, but it also brought many different cultures together. Through trade, not only were goods exchanged, but also ideas that benefited society.

Uncertainty is created by nature, but it can be altered by our behavior and the actions of others. These are a few sources of uncertainty.

- Uncertainty in nature. We want safety and security in our lives. The world can be an uncertain and dangerous place that we do not understand. We face the possibility of unexpected events such as natural disasters, tornadoes, earthquakes, hurricanes, floods, or fires. Things can happen with little or no warning. This has motivated us to study what causes these phenomena, so we can understand them more fully to improve what we do about them. We have developed preventative measures, emergency response, and medical institutions to improve our safety and provide help when we need it. Nature has given us needs in order to survive and wants in order to live. This has motivated people to develop methods to reduce uncertainty to fulfill their needs and wants.

- Uncertainty about the future. We not only want safety and security in our lives, we want to know what to expect. We want to be able to make plans and have those plans become reality. No one has the ability to predict the future and not knowing what will happen creates uncertainty. We are aware of our own mortality, but we do not know the circumstances or what happens afterward. This can create uncertainty that can influence how we live our lives. Some of our oldest institutions and most deeply held beliefs help us to reduce these types of uncertainties.

- Uncertainty about knowledge. Uncertainty comes from our lack of knowledge about things that we want to know about or that are important to us. Since we are motivated to know how the world works, people have created ways to learn about these things. We have created methods of learning such as the scientific approach to gaining new knowledge to help fulfill our needs and wants. We have developed many fields of study and created an educational system. We have created professions dedicated to the pursuit of knowledge. We have done this so we can reduce uncertainty.

- Uncertainty about ourselves. We want to know how we think and why we act the way we do. Many things can happen to us that we do not want to happen like illness, accidents, or injury. Some happen unexpectedly and some can be brought about by our actions. We know that there are some things that can happen to us, we just don't know when. This uncertainty has motivated us to learn more about ourselves and how to improve our quality of life by developing fields of study like medicine. We have created religion and religious institutions to answer important questions about who we are and why we are here. People have created schools, hospitals, and research institutions to learn more about how our body works and how to cure ailments motivated by our need for health and well being.

- Uncertainty about society. People are a source of uncertainty because when we do not know anything about them, we do not know what to expect. People say and do things for their own reasons that may not make sense to others. They may be motivated to take advantage of other people and not act in the best interest of others. People need to feel safe and secure by reducing the potential for harm. Laws, law enforcement, and judicial systems were created to reduce uncertainty and create safety and security in society. People want to know what to reasonably expect in the future, so that they can do things that will improve their lives. Society needs to make decisions that promote the common good and keep its citizens free from harm. Systems of government were created to make collective decisions, provide for mutual benefit, and keep people safe from harm. Financial institutions were created to ensure financial stability. Many of our current systems and institutions were established because of our need to reduce all kinds of uncertainty.

- Uncertainty about people. Uncertainty is created by nature, however, it can be intensified by people. Uncertainty can be increased accidentally because people make mistakes or it can be used intentionally to get attention or gain power over others. While most people seek to reduce uncertainty to fulfill their need for stability and security, some people may seek to increase it to gain power or manipulate others to do what they want them to do. They may commit what seems like irrational acts, however, they are using the power of the law of uncertainty to fulfill their own needs, wants, or desired outcomes. This can be a powerful force because it allows a few people to change the behavior of large groups of people. If you want to motivate people to do what you want, increase uncertainty by making them fearful or angry.

We want to know what to expect from others in order to reduce uncertainty so that we can trust them. However, if we do not know what to expect, it will increase our feelings of uncertainty about them. The level of uncertainty we feel about other people can change because people do things that make us feel more or less comfortable with them. The degree of uncertainty we feel about others is often based on how closely our perception of them fulfills our expectations of them.

While uncertainty originates in nature, it is people who determine what to do about it. When we experience uncertainty we compare our perceptions to our expectations. If there is a noticeable difference between them, it can either diminish or intensify our feelings of uncertainty. People receive information that increases their apprehension and perception of uncertainty motivating them to take action to reduce it.

This can take intangible perceptions of uncertainty and create tangible consequences. For example, economic uncertainty can motivate people to cut spending even though they may not need to, which decreases economic activity creating a self perpetuating reality of its own.

Uncertainty can be helpful.

While we spend much time and energy to reduce uncertainty, having a manageable level of uncertainty is preferable to completely eliminating it because having some uncertainty serves important functions for us as individuals and for society. For example, uncertainty is created because we all know that we will get old, may become ill, and eventually die. This uncertainty has motivated us to develop our faith, religion, and sense of morality including our notion of right and wrong, without which the world would be a very different place.

Uncertainty is important because it can open our mind to new ideas. It makes us question our assumptions to ascertain their validity. It motivates us to adapt and rethink what we already know. It motivates us to look at what we know in new ways to come up with something better than we had before. It encourages us to change and try something new. And it motivates us to take action. However, we do not have to wait for difficulties caused by uncertainty to motivate us to look for new ideas and try new things. We can choose to open our mind and think about alternatives before we are forced to do so. While uncertainty may not always happen in positive ways, it does motivate us to look beyond what we already know.

So, why don't some things work out? When things work out for us the tension uncertainty creates is resolved. We feel more comfortable so there's less motivation to do something and we don't think as much about it. Our mind moves on to more pressing matters. If things don't work out, we need to think about them in order to work things through and look for alternative solutions.

When something doesn't work, it represents an unresolved state that creates tension making us uncomfortable motivating us to take action. It increases uncertainty motivating us to go beyond what we already know to gain new information and try new ways of doing things to resolve it. We have lots of things we need to do, so we have to prioritize what to do first and the more something doesn't work out making us uncomfortable, the higher priority it gets. If everything worked out for us, we would be less likely to challenge ourselves, gain new knowledge, or open our mind to new possibilities.

Change is uncomfortable because it takes time and energy. Since we don't know what might happen, it can create more uncertainty. So, in order for us to change, the current situation must become uncomfortable enough to overcome the discomfort it takes to change. When we are aware of how this process works, we do not have to let uncertainty frustrate us, we can use it to our advantage. We can be open to new information and ideas to initiate change in our own time and on our own terms rather than being forced to change by circumstances. Uncertainty can be ironic, when we fail to take the initiative to do these things ourselves life can have a way of making us do it.

While reducing uncertainty can generally be a good thing, too much uncertainty reduction may not be good. When we are sure about what we are doing and feel like we have everything figured out, we are not looking for new information or new ideas. In this frame of mind we can be less open to the possibilities that may be available to us. When we feel we have set goals, objectives, or a plan of action we may not consider that there may be better alternatives. This state of mind can create reduced awareness of the situation, which limits our possibilities and options. When we think we know what to do, we have less motivation to look at other options. When we are less aware of what is around us we might pass up opportunities by pursuing a steadfast single path.

When we reduce uncertainty it increases our confidence motivating us to take action. The danger is that when people feel reduced uncertainty, they may not be open to new information, so it can close them off from considering other ideas or alternative ways of doing things. It can cause them to filter out information and not listen to others who may have something to contribute. It can cause them to discount or filter out information that may be helpful. In extreme cases it can turn into arrogance creating an attitude that "I know what I'm doing." This can create the conditions that lead to bad decisions with potentially disastrous consequences.

This can happen when we are overly certain or when we think that we know what to do, so we do not stop and consider alternatives that might provide better choices. When we are certain, we are less likely to question our assumptions and the quality of our information. When we are certain, we do not look for flaws in our reasoning or test the validity of our solutions. When we are certain, we are in the frame of mind to get things done the way that we want, rather than considering the ideas of others. When we are certain, we know that we are right and do not stop to think that we might be wrong. When we are certain, we do not need to learn anything because we know what we are doing. When we are certain, we do not look at different ideas and people who have them are viewed as disruptive troublemakers.

Extreme certainty should not be considered the same as knowledge, expertise, experience, or confidence. Knowledge gives us information we can use. Expertise can provide us information and skills to handle uncertainty. Experience hones those skills in actual situations. And confidence gives us a belief in ourselves and our abilities. We can have all these things while still utilizing uncertainty to bring in new ideas in order to innovate and facilitate change. If everything was created for a reason, then uncertainty was created by nature for a reason, to provide us a means to motivate change and innovation. Having an awareness of how the law of uncertainty works helps us to avoid pitfalls, so we can use it to our advantage.

Uncertainty and the stop sign.

To illustrate how uncertainty affects our behavior think about what we do when we are driving and see a stop sign or stop light. We have to see the sign, understand what it means, and then act accordingly. The sign does not stop our car, so why do we really stop? We stop because of the law of uncertainty. Because there's a chance we might get hit by another vehicle or be pulled over and given a ticket that would cost us money. We stop because it reduces uncertainty by giving us reasonable expectations of getting safely across the road.

Uncertainty can serve as a form of social control by keeping people within the limits of acceptable behavior. By not knowing the future results of our actions, we are more likely to be careful and less risky in our behavior because there is a fear of potential negative consequences. The law of uncertainty motivates our behavior by keeping us within the rules of social reality and society. It inhibits us from taking too much risk or engaging in overly dangerous behavior. It motivates us to question ourselves and our actions, which is necessary in order to find the best solution and course of action.

All of our lives contain some degree of uncertainty. In order to reduce it, it is helpful to understand how it affects us in our own lives. What makes the difference is what we do about it. It is through increased awareness of how uncertainty works and how it acts in our lives that gives us the options that will help us to reduce uncertainty and its effects. One thing about life that is certain, there will always be absolute uncertainty.

The Law of Shared Meaning

The law of shared meaning is the second law of behavioral communicating. It is like the law of uncertainty in that it is created by nature, not by people. It is like the law of gravity because it affects everyone whether we want it to or not. It cannot be changed or eliminated. It affects how we communicate and share information with one another. It gives information significance to help make it useful to us. It helps us to understand and make sense of our experiences. It helps us to understand ourselves and develop our self-concept. When something contains meaning it helps us access additional information from our experiences that may be useful, so we don't have to get all the information we need every time we communicate about something.

We are motivated by the law of uncertainty to create and share meaning, so that we can understand others to work with them and form relationships. This helps us to make sense out of our experiences to help explain what has happened in the past and better understand what we can reasonably expect in the future. Sharing meaning helps develop feelings of security and stability because we have a better understanding of others and the world around us.

Our life consists of a series of experiences, some of which may not make sense motivating us to wonder why they happen and what we should do about them. In order to reduce the uncertainty that would be created if these were perceived of as just random events, we want to understand them better by looking for meaning in them. In order to do this, we may share our experiences with others to get their opinion about what happened to us and they may share their experiences with us in return. Sharing our experiences with others creates a mutual understanding, which gives us a deeper meaning reducing uncertainty that can help make similar situations more understandable in the future.

Shared meaning provides us a way to communicate with one another so we can share information about ourselves. Much of how our identity is created is through our experiences and sharing meaning about them. How we communicate our experiences helps develop our own sense of self-concept and identity. When we share our experiences with others they learn about who we are and we learn about them, which can help to reduce uncertainty so that we can develop relationships with them.

We all have needs and wants that necessitate help from others to fulfill and the law of shared meaning helps us to understand others so we can do this. It helps us to agree on the nature of what has to be done and how it is to be accomplished. In order to work together, we have to understand each other to know what things mean. Sharing meaning helps us to fulfill mutual needs such as safety, security, and stability, which in turn reduces uncertainty.

Throughout much of human history people have sought to know more about what was happening in the world around them. This motivated them to understand things like the changing of the seasons, how to grow crops, why they got sick, and their relationship with God. They looked for information to explain these things based on what was available to them at the time. Throughout history as people encountered uncertainty they looked for ways to understand what they experienced. Early Greek and Roman cultures sought to explain what they experienced by creating mythology. Later, people looked to religions and sacred texts. More recently people utilized science and empirical research methods to understand the world around them. These approaches helped them to create and share meaning to better understand themselves, others, and the world around them.

When people share stories with one another about their experiences it gives them deeper meaning. When these stories are shared they form a common bond between people creating a common culture. Often these stories have a deeper meaning sharing important information. Telling stories has become a part of society because by sharing experiences, people not only communicate information they share emotions, attitudes, values, beliefs, and a part of themselves. By sharing stories people communicate who they are, their history, and their aspirations which helps to reduce uncertainty and create trust enabling them to form relationships.

Shared meaning is often communicated in the form of stories told about people, events, and our own experiences. We tend to alter what really happened by editing events to emphasize some things, leave some things out, or add embellishments to others. This gives them a sense of drama to make them more exciting. We do this to make them more interesting to cut through the interference so people will listen to us.

The law of shared meaning affects how we interpret our observations, thoughts, feelings, and experiences to make sense of them. It shapes our view of practically everything. In order for us to reduce uncertainty, we need to know more about others, ourselves, and the things around us. We all have thoughts, feelings, and ideas, however, others cannot read our mind, so we need a way to share that information clearly and accurately with them. We can get information for ourselves, but that takes time and energy. This motivates us to seek it out from others, so we need a means to communicate information in a way that is useful to us. In order to do this, we need a shared understanding of what things mean.

This need motivated people to develop a common language as a means of sharing information by utilizing symbols which are invested with meaning. By giving symbols like letters and words meaning, we can communicate with others to share information in a way that we understand. However, this is not the only way we share meaning. We also utilize nonverbal information by investing practically everything around us with meaning. In order to reduce uncertainty about ourselves, others, and the world around us to help us fulfill our needs and wants, we need a means to share information by communicating. This is how the law of uncertainty creates the law of shared meaning.

How the law of shared meaning works.

You have likely experienced something that illustrates how the law of shared meaning works. Have you ever attended a party, wedding, or other event with a friend who knew everyone there, but you didn't know anyone? They probably talked, laughed, and shared stories about mutual friends with one another. If you didn't know anyone there you probably felt awkward, out of place, maybe even wanted to leave.

What you observed is how the law of shared meaning works. The others were able to take what they communicated and add additional information increasing its meaning and significance making it more useful to them, while you probably didn't know what they were talking about. What you experienced is what things could be like if there was no shared meaning.

The law of shared meaning can be illustrated by how we interpret information. To demonstrate how this works, find a book that has pictures of people you know and another book that has pictures of people you don't know, along with their names and some kind of other information about them like a school yearbook. Look at pictures of people you don't know.

You can see what they look like, read their names, and understand the information about them. You probably won't have much additional information about who they are other than what is printed. Now look at the book with pictures of people you know. Read their names and the information about them. You might recall things about them, things they did, perhaps even feelings or emotions. What you are thinking and feeling contains information that is beyond what is printed in the book.

When we see people we know, we recall things about them like the things that they did, perhaps even feelings or emotions. You might have feelings of warmth and affection or perhaps dislike or agitation. You might remember things that you did together that makes you laugh. What you are thinking and feeling contains information that is beyond what is happening in the present. It's like a connection is made and something opens up. It's a very different experience than when we see or talk to people we don't know.

If there were no law of shared meaning, what we communicate to others would be more like looking at pictures of people we don't know. We could communicate with one another, but there would be little additional information available making it more difficult to understand them. We would have to explain practically everything every time we communicated.

Having shared meaning gives us a reserve of information that we can call up without having to communicate it or have it explained to us every time we needed it. Shared meaning is how we make sense of the world around us. It is how we interpret our observations, thoughts, feelings, and experiences. It shapes our view of practically everything because it influences how we see ourselves, others, and the world around us.

The origin of the law of shared meaning.

The origin of the law of shared meaning can be found in the same places as uncertainty. God created the first man and saw that he was alone and needed companionship. So, God created woman and provided for all their needs. God instructed them not to eat the fruit of the tree of knowledge of good and evil. When they did eat from the tree, their eyes were opened and they both saw clearly and they knew good and evil. They now shared new meaning about themselves, each other, and the world around them originating the law of shared meaning. They were cast out of the garden, so they no longer had all their needs provided for, so now they had to provide for themselves.

Since our needs and wants motivate us to take action by communicating with others, sharing meaning helps us determine what actions to take. The meanings we share can determine our behavior. For example, we share meaning about things like the weather. At one time, people found meaning in the lack of rain and the failure of their crops to grow as God's displeasure with them or they made sacrifices to their gods. Today, when there's a lack of rain and failure of crops we interpret it as weather patterns brought by the jet stream and build irrigation systems. This means that the same set of circumstances, influenced by different shared meanings, motivates distinctly different behavior.

When we communicate with others we look for shared meaning not only in what they say, but also in what they do. We tend to interpret what people do, how they look, their facial expressions, and many other nonverbal elements by giving them meaning. Meaning is found not just in the words people say, but also in how they say them. We even find meaning in what people do not say. We look for meaning in these things so we can understand others better to reduce our uncertainty about them.

The nature of shared meaning.

Shared meaning gives us a sense of our identity as an individual and as a member of groups. Through the process of shared meaning when we communicate with others they respond with feedback that affects our perception of who we are. We share different meanings with others based upon the nature of our relationship with them such as our friends, family, or coworkers. We get a broader perspective about our experiences when we share them with others. When many people share their experiences, it creates a common history that develops culture. It is through shared meaning that we come to understand our relationships with other people.

We share meaning about what other people say and do in order to reduce uncertainty and to make them more familiar. When people are unfamiliar, we do not know what they might do and so we might be less willing to communicate or work with them. However, we need others to help us fulfill our needs and wants which motivates us to find meaning in what they do. So, we gather information by observing what people say and do. In order for that information to be useful, we interpret it by giving it meaning. Often we don't have enough information so we make inferences to fill in the gaps. This gives us an idea of what a person is like so that we know what we can reasonably expect from them to reduce uncertainty.

The law of shared meaning enables us to share knowledge so that we can learn from the experiences of others. As we all have things that we need to know and learn, we can gain information from others without having to figure everything out for ourselves. New information can be added to what people already know, growing the body of knowledge. This is the basis of our educational system. Many of the things we need or want have already been done by someone else, so we can benefit from their knowledge and experience through the process of shared meaning. We can take what is meaningful to others and make it useful to us without needing to have the same experiences. Without the law of shared meaning, developing and sharing knowledge would be more difficult.

The law of shared meaning makes possible many things that are essential to everyday life. Perhaps the most important is how it enables us to communicate with each other through a common language. Developing language is the process by which people create symbols, like letters and words, and invest them with meaning. Sharing meaning enables us to communicate with one another using a language that everyone understands. By giving symbols meaning, we can more easily and effectively communicate information and store it for future use.

Language often communicates other information about a person when they speak such as their culture, ethnicity, education, vocation, and how they view the world. Having a common language not only permits people to communicate and understand one another, it also creates a common bond giving them a sense of mutual identity that brings them closer together. The shared meanings that are in language reduce uncertainty because if everyone gave different meanings to the same things, we could not understand one another. Understanding is necessary for society to function and it occurs when we share meanings. When it doesn't, it can lead to misunderstandings, tension, conflict, and even hostilities.

We invest meaning in people we don't know as well as people we know like our family, friends, coworkers, or neighbors. We give meaning to our past experiences in order to add significance to our lives. We give meaning to the things that we enjoy such as art, literature, and music. We give meaning to geographic locations such as where we were born or where we live. We give meaning to our culture, ethnicity, nationality, and religion. Practically everything we do, everyone we know, and everything around us we invest with meaning and we share these meanings by communicating with others.

Traditions and rituals like holidays, celebrations, birthdays, anniversaries, and other occasions when people get together are an important way that we share meaning. We celebrate these events because of their significance and participate in them to share their meaning through our actions. Sharing traditions and rituals gives us a sense of who we are, where we have come from in the past, and our expectations for the future. It makes us feel closer to others and part of a group with whom we share the same experiences. It connects us to the past and our ancestors, as well as to future generations. This creates continuity across generations making us feel a part of something greater than ourselves, reducing uncertainty about ourselves and others giving us a feeling of stability and security.

The law of shared meaning makes society possible. By sharing meanings we communicate what our country stands for and what it means to be a citizen. We communicate our collective history and traditions, values and beliefs. This creates a set of shared meanings that can be easily understood by members of a society as well as by outsiders. These meanings shape the perception people have of a country and its citizens as well as who they are and what they stand for. It creates a sense of collective identity as people see themselves as a citizen of a country. How members of a nation or society share meaning can be a powerful force because it has the ability to motivate their attitudes and actions on a large scale.

The law of shared meaning leads to investing because when people give things meaning they also give them value. Giving something meaning gives it significance and significance increases its importance making it more valuable. This is because when something is important to us we are willing to do more or spend more to obtain it or keep it. We place value on people in relationships, on things and possessions, on intangible concepts such as skills or knowledge, and on practically everything we find around us. Value is often based on comparisons gained from our perceptions to create expectations. We use our perception based on currently available information and compare it to our expectations for the future. This can motivate us to rank things by their importance, which can help us to set priorities.

We often value things based on how useful they are to us in fulfilling our needs and wants. We place more value on relationships that fulfill important needs and wants. Shared meaning can determine what things we value based on our feelings about them. We place value on things that we feel an emotional attachment to or that are part of our past experiences. Sometimes how much we value something comes from what others think about it. Through the process of shared meaning, if people value something others are more likely to place a value on it. By sharing meaning we come to know how important, valuable, and useful things are. In this way sharing meaning has tangible and monetary consequences.

The Law of Investing

The law of investing is the third law of behavioral communicating. It is similar to the laws of uncertainty and shared meaning because it was created by nature, so it cannot be changed by people. It is like the law of gravity because it affects everyone whether we want it to or not. It was formed by the other two laws in order to make them work. We can reduce uncertainty and share meaning, but we need to take action for anything to happen. In order to reduce uncertainty and share meanings, we must invest our time and other resources in ourselves and others.

People may react to the first two laws by simply hunkering down and building a cabin in the woods. However, the law of investing forces them out into the marketplace of human activity. The law of investing regulates how we manage our resources and negotiate with others for our mutual benefit to fulfill needs and wants, so we can accomplish our desired outcomes. This creates a kind of behavioral communicative marketplace where people make and receive offers utilizing their resources to obtain their desired outcomes. Communicating is the currency of this marketplace because it enables us to invest these resources. This is the fundamental process that makes human behavior work by connecting us to others.

We all have needs and wants that we cannot fulfill ourselves, so we need help from others to fulfill them. Other people also have their own needs and wants that they cannot fulfill themselves, so they also need help. This puts everyone in the position of wanting things, but needing help from others to obtain them. Having our needs and wants fulfilled often comes at a cost. We have resources of value that others need and they have resources we want. The most familiar resource is monetary, but we more often utilize other resources like our time, attention, effort, energy, expertise, experience, and skills. When we have unfulfilled needs and wants it can be uncomfortable motivating us to communicate with others, so we can invest in relationships to achieve our mutual desired outcomes.

When this process goes smoothly everyone can benefit, however, it often does not. People can have virtually unlimited needs and wants to fulfill with limited resources. We often have conflicting needs and wants. We may feel we are contributing to others, but not receiving what we need in return. This can create tension and even conflict, which can force us to make choices about our relationships and how we communicate with others. For example, if we do not feel we are being fairly paid for the work we are doing, we might want to quit our job. If we feel we have been contributing to a relationship where the other person is only taking and our needs are not being met, we might want to breakup. This is how the law of investing can exert powerful forces that motivate our behavior, the decisions we make, and how we communicate with others.

In order to invest in others we need to reduce uncertainty. When we feel a great deal of uncertainty, we are reluctant to invest our resources because we do not know what to expect in return. When we reduce uncertainty, we are more likely to invest because we feel more safe and secure because we have reasonable expectations about what we will receive in the future. The less uncertainty we feel the more comfortable we are sharing our resources in order to help others fulfill their needs and wants. This also makes it more likely for them to help us fulfill ours.

Not only do we seek to reduce uncertainty to invest, but we also invest to reduce uncertainty. We invest our resources in relationships and activities that will benefit us now and in the future. For example, we invest time and energy in a job to receive not only a salary, but also for the safety and security that comes with it. This can help us to fulfill other needs such as buying a house, having a family, or retirement.

The law of shared meaning helps us to invest because it increases our mutual understanding of one another. When we share meaning with others, we feel we get to know them better so we know what to expect of them in the future. This can increase stability and security making us feel more comfortable investing our resources. The more we feel safe and secure, the more we are likely to invest ourselves and our resources in relationships without expecting an immediate return. This helps create the long term stability necessary for creating and maintaining meaningful relationships.

The origin of the law of investing.

The origin of the law of investing can be found in the same texts as the laws of uncertainty and shared meaning. When God created the first man and placed him in a garden, God saw that man was alone and needed companionship and so created woman. Then God instructed them not to eat the fruit of the tree of knowledge of good and evil. When they ate the fruit of the tree God cast them out of the garden. Now man and woman no longer had all their needs provided for, so they had to provide for themselves.

They no longer had stability, security, and predictability. After Adam and Eve left the garden they had children. From now on all people would be different because they would not be created directly by God, as were Adam and Eve, instead they would be created by people through reproduction. This meant that from then on people would be responsible for the creation of life, so they would have to invest their time, energy, and other resources in relationships including families, groups, and communities.

Nature created people with the ability to self replicate by having children for the continuation of humanity. However, nature provided only one method of human reproduction to create new life. From the moment they are born, a child is totally dependent on their parents and will need their family to fulfill their needs and wants for many years to come. Because of how we were created, we must invest in relationships with others not just for survival, but also for our well being.

Nature could have created us different. We could have been created to have children as an individual or by another process of reproduction as happens with other forms of life. We could have been created by nature to be more self reliant when we are born. We could have had the ability to care for ourselves sooner or to mature faster as do other living things. But that was not what nature intended. Nature intended for us to need other people. Our needs motivate us to create and maintain relationships with others such as our family. These relationships help us to fulfill our needs and wants making the law of investing a powerful force in our lives.

The marketplace of communicating.

When we communicate with others we often make verbal and nonverbal offers that are either accepted or rejected. This process works rather like the trading floor of a stock market. This happens in our daily activities like when we ask people for help, initiate relationships, negotiate family responsibilities, and get things done at work. This happens as we go about our daily activities, so it goes mostly unnoticed.

This marketplace is driven by how we communicate with each other so communicating could be characterized as its currency. In order to fulfill needs and wants, people enter the marketplace and negotiate with others by offering resources and seeking investments in return. It is through communicating that we negotiate what we are willing to do and what we might expect in return.

This negotiation may be overt and out in the open or it may be covert like when we try to cover up our intentions. We may be aware of what we are doing or we may do it by habit. Whatever the case, we are generally aware that we are doing something for someone else so they will do something for us. This negotiation is sometimes expressed when we say things like, "I owe you one."

People invest to reduce uncertainty, but how much they are willing to invest depends on their individual needs and wants, how much they think others have to contribute, and what they are likely to receive. Our perception can be affected by how well, or not so well, similar investments have gone in the past. This can be why we invest more in some relationships and less in others.

The level of investment is not only a matter of how much people are willing to invest, but also how long they are willing to wait before receiving a return. Sometimes we only do the basics to quickly get what we need in a relationship. Most impersonal relationships don't involve a great level of investment, like when we ask for help from a store clerk. Then there are more personal relationships that require long term investments like a spouse or family. The level of our investment can have less to do with our satisfaction with a relationship than it does with our perception of what needs and wants we have fulfilled.

We make many low level investments without even thinking much about them. For example, we might help a friend carry their groceries or a coworker fix a printer. Most things we do are low level investments, so we do them without thinking much about them. However, they do provide an indirect reward because doing them is the right thing to do. When we do the right thing, it shows that we are a good person so we feel good about ourselves.

Medium level investments are the things we do for others without asking for much in return. However, most of the time we expect to receive some benefit. It could be saying thank you or the expectation of them reciprocating in the future. For example, if we help a friend move or drive someone to the airport, there is the expectation that they would do the same for us in return. If a person does not reciprocate, we may become put off or offended even though we did not originally ask for anything. Even if we do not expect something in return for our investment, doing something selfless can give us a positive feeling and bolster our self-concept, which is in effect a positive reward.

Then there are high level investments that we make in relationships with others such as our family or our job. These are relationships in which we invest a great deal of time and energy with the expectation of receiving benefits that fulfill important needs and wants. Many times we are glad to do things because we feel we are contributing and making a difference without directly expecting a return. We make investments in our family because we are expected to do this and that's what families do. What we receive in return is fulfillment of many of our most fundamental needs and wants such as safety, security, stability, affection, or intimacy. At work we have the reasonable expectation of receiving a salary and other benefits. We are often willing to put in our time and other resources now with the expectation of future rewards such as a raise in pay or a promotion.

These are several other types of investments we make.

- The balance sheet. We often have a balance sheet in the back of our mind where we keep track of our investments and the return on them. If they are reasonably balanced we feel satisfied, however, if they are out of balance and we feel we are contributing more than we receive it can create unhappiness, tension, even conflict. When they are out of balance we are motivated to take action to establish economic equilibrium. We can have a portfolio of several balance sheets representing different relationships both personal and professional. This can show us what we really value, what is important to us, and how well our needs and wants are being fulfilled.

- The comparison. We want to know how our investments are doing and so we make comparisons with others we think are similar to see how they are doing. For example, if we feel we should be making more money at our job, we might look around to see how much other people are making or if we can get a better job. This is a natural tendency because we want to know if we are getting a fair return on our investment. We might look at how others are doing because it gives us more information. If we find that we are doing better, we may feel good about ourselves. If we are not, then we may look to change things.

- Return on investment. We look at needs and wants fulfillment in both the long and short term much like we look at monetary investments. The length of time we are willing to wait for rewards is often based upon our individual needs and wants. Short term rewards are generally smaller and more easily attainable. These involve things that are used to fulfill more immediate needs and wants such as food, clothing, and shelter. Long term rewards are generally more difficult to obtain making them more valuable. The longer the investment the higher the expectation for greater rewards. For example, people may make financial sacrifices so they can save money with the expectation of future financial security. Long term investments can include savings, home ownership, or self fulfillment. We are willing to wait longer for these rewards because they fulfill more important needs and wants.

- Profit taking. Everyone communicates for a reason and it is often to gain rewards, which are typically the fulfillment of needs and wants. They can be monetary, but they can also be social such as affection, prestige, respect, self-esteem, or being part of a group. Rewards can be professional such as a job or career. They can be material such as a nice house or car. They can be having good relationships with our friends, family, or spouse. When we feel that we have contributed enough, we tend to look to receive a benefit like when we make a profit from selling a stock. If we do not receive it, we may decide to increase our investment and stay the course or we may take what we can by getting out and cutting our losses. Whatever the case, there comes a point when we need some resolution.

- The money pit. We have all experienced a situation where a seemingly good investment turned into a money pit. If you haven't experienced this, don't worry you will. It may involve buying a house, a stock, a car, a boat, or something that seemed like a great deal, but turned into a money eating, time consuming nightmare. This happens when we get involved in something, like a relationship, which we reasonably expected would fulfill needs and wants or provide us with benefits. It can start out small, but then it needs increasingly more attention or resources like our time and energy until it reaches a point where we can't take it anymore. We may feel that we can't get out of it because we have too much invested, so we might feel trapped, even panicked. At this point there are basically two alternatives. We might stick with it to see what happens, but not expecting any return, which may increase uncertainty. Or, we might decide to cut our losses by getting rid of it as quickly as possible reducing future uncertainty.

Uncertainty and economic equilibrium.

Many times we evaluate our investments based on our perception of the return on those investments. For example, if we have a job where we feel we are working long hours and spending a lot of energy, we may feel that we are not getting the recognition we deserve or are not being treated fairly. This perception could make us upset and even angry to the point that we ask for a raise and if we don't get it, we might quit. Conversely, if we have a job where we feel we are working reasonable hours with reasonable demands, and are getting paid well for what we do, we feel valued and happy with our job. We are not likely to ask for a raise and we certainly would not want to quit. This is one way that the law of investing can affect our state of mind motivating our actions.

Communicating can be an indicator of value. People tend to communicate about things that are important to them, so you can determine what they value by measuring the amount of time and effort they spend communicating about something. We tend to not communicate about things that are not very important to us or things in which we have no interest. In order to connect with others and have them understand you, it's helpful to know what they value. This can be measured by the amount of time they spend communicating about it. By listening to others, we can know what is of value to them and determine what would make them more likely to invest. Since negotiation takes place through communicating, it's possible to analyze what is going on in any communicating marketplace by measuring its activity. This works rather like stock prices or economic indicators that can be used to explain what has happened in the past to provide some indication of what might happen in the future.

Conventional wisdom would suggest that in a marketplace people would seek to minimize costs and maximize rewards, in other words they buy low and sell high. However, when it comes to communicating with others, this is not usually the case. It may be more the exception than the rule because most people do not behave in this manner. This is because when one person seems to be benefiting much more than others, it creates an imbalance that can damage relationships. They may be seen as being self-centered and others may feel that they are not being treated fairly. No one wants to feel that they are being treated unfairly by being around a person who contributes as little as possible while seeking to gain as much as possible by buying low and selling high.

Everyone does not seek to maximize rewards, instead they look for rewards to fulfill their specific needs and wants. They look for balance by receiving a fair return based on fair investments. In this approach, a person may be the most satisfied by being slightly ahead, breaking even, or even having a small loss. This makes the breakeven point or achieving economic equilibrium an important factor in determining relational satisfaction, so everyone receives fair rewards and feels like they are being treated fairly.

Not everyone follows typical patterns when it comes to needs and wants fulfillment. Some people behave contrary to the conventional wisdom of investing to fulfill needs and wants. They may forgo their own safety and material comfort to live in arduous conditions so they can help others. They may give up lucrative careers to pursue endeavors that pay very little. While this behavior does not follow the convention of buy low sell high, it follows the laws of uncertainty and investing because people invest in order to fulfill their individual needs and wants, which can reduce their feelings of uncertainty.

However, under the law of investing, they are maximizing their investment based on their perception of what fulfills their needs and wants. This is because our needs and wants are more than just monetary, they can be spiritual, being needed by others, making a difference, feeling appreciated, or doing the right thing. When people want monetary rewards, what they may really need is recognition or status. For most people the rewards that are the most important to them are generally not material or monetary.

The law of investing can affect how happy we feel. All too often we find ourselves in relationships that aren't working and then wonder what's wrong. How we balance costs and rewards in relationships can be an indicator of several things. In order to better understand what these things are, you can create a balance sheet by listing your needs and wants in order of importance. For each one, ask yourself how well are each of them being met? When they are being reasonably met, it can make us feel good. When they are not being met, we can feel unhappy, even frustrated. When we understand how the law of investing works, we can use it to restore economic equilibrium by balancing rewards and costs. We are more likely to be satisfied and feel good about a relationship when we feel we are making fair investments and receiving fair rewards. When we feel that others are contributing to the relationship we are more likely to be committed and contribute to the relationship as well.

The Rules of Communicating

The laws of uncertainty, shared meaning, and investing were created by nature to motivate human behavior. In order for people to effectively utilize these laws, they developed rules for behavioral communicating. Rules govern human behavior by letting people know what is expected of them in just about every aspect of life. Rules tell people how to reduce uncertainty, they regulate how people share meaning, and they let people know what they can expect when investing in themselves and others. Rules are often developed by people over long periods of time. While they can be changed, this can be slow or difficult to do.

Rules help us to fulfill our needs and wants, so we generally agree to abide by them because if we did not life would be much more chaotic and it would be almost impossible to function. Rules allow the marketplace of communicating to function properly, so people can create relationships in order to fulfill their needs and wants. Nearly all human activities, groups, and organizations have their own set of rules which have been developed to meet people's needs and wants by regulating their behavior. Rules are necessary in order to reduce uncertainty so that people know what is expected of them and what they can expect from others enabling them to work with one another.

A good example of why rules were created and how they work is illustrated by those used in sports. Many of the sports that we are familiar with today, like basketball or football, at one time did not exist. They were created by people who got together to fulfill mutual needs and wants like having fun, to compete, or to be part of a team. In order for them to do this they had to create rules that governed their behavior, so that everyone knew what to expect. The rules changed over time to meet the changing needs of the sport and its participants. Without rules no one would know what to do and everything would breakdown into chaos.

Rules of society work much like the rules of sports. They were created by people so that they could function together in a mutual activity to fulfill their needs and wants. For rules to work everyone must agree to abide by them. They regulate behavior as a form of social control so people know what to do and what to expect. They tend to change slowly over time to accommodate changing circumstances while maintaining stability. They are mutually beneficial because without rules no one would know what was going on and there would be chaos.

Rules can be categorized into several types.

- Formal rules. Our behavior is governed by a specialized set of formal rules many of which are written down in laws. The purpose of these rules is to keep the peace and maintain order in society to reduce uncertainty. They tell people what they are supposed to do and provide penalties for violating the rules.

- Constitutive rules. These are the rules that constitute proper behavior. They are the rules of how to play the game. They can be written down like in sports, but often they're not. These rules govern our behavior in most aspects of our lives.

- Regulatory rules. These rules are used to regulate people's behavior. They are a means to enforce the rules by providing penalties when they are violated. The severity of the penalty depends upon the infraction and must be severe enough to motivate people to obey them. Without regulatory rules there would be no enforcement mechanism and eventually the rules would breakdown because no one would follow them.

- Practical rules. These are the general rules of everyday behavior that everyone is expected to know. Sometimes they consist of more formal rules that govern our behavior like manners or etiquette. Other times they are in the form of advice on how to accomplish something like how to play tennis or golf. These rules are developed over time based on practical experience and can be changed as needed.

- Rationale rules. In order to attract people to participate in an activity, they often have to be made aware of its importance. It is helpful to explain why the rules exist and why they are important so people will follow them. In many sports, rules provide for everyone's safety. Letting people know why the rules exist helps them understand why they need to follow them for their own benefit to encourage their compliance.

- Historical rules. Many activities have a history or traditions that are shared with others. Many groups and organizations are proud of their traditions as a part of their heritage or self-concept. These can be used to attract people to join them. Historical rules were developed in the past and are often maintained over time to keep customs and traditions alive.

Rules facilitate the process of shared meaning to reduce uncertainty in order to encourage investing in others, in groups, and in activities. They enable us to communicate more effectively with one another, which helps us to fulfill our needs and wants. It can be helpful to clearly communicate the rules because they create stability to reduce uncertainty by letting people know what is expected of them and what they can reasonably expect of others. Otherwise, they may try to circumvent rules they see as not in their own interest or that prevents them from getting what they want.

The Process of Communicating

The process of communicating provides a way to look at how we communicate by understanding individual elements in the process. It helps us to see how these elements work together so that we can be better understood by other people. We often communicate without thinking how things work so when they don't go as we want, like when we are misunderstood, we may not know how to fix them.

By understanding the process of communicating, you can develop skills to communicate more effectively with other people. How people communicate involves a number of elements that occur seamlessly so that we don't think much about them. Therefore, it can be helpful to break the process down into its elements to help understand how it works. How communicating works is often illustrated in a technical way using boxes, triangles, circles, arrows, and lines to connect things to other things. However, communicating is not about technical or abstract things, it is about living people who are active and dynamic. These human characteristics are reflected in the process of communicating.

You, your desired outcome, your Great Idea, others, connections, The Great Abyss, feedback, and effectiveness are all elements in the process of communicating. They provide a clear and accurate way to talk about specific parts of the process we use to communicate. Being aware of these elements and how they work provides a way to talk about how we communicate, so that we can communicate more effectively with others and improve our communicating skills.

The process of communicating consists of these elements.

1. You. You are the creator and communicator of your message, so the process of communicating begins with you. Everyone communicates for a reason because we have thoughts, ideas, and feelings we want to share with others. Since everyone is unique, you have your own unique way of doing things that includes your own style of communicating. These characteristics are what gives you your own unique personality. Many of these attributes affect how you communicate with others and can help or hinder you getting your message across to them. Some of these are changeable and some are not. Becoming more effective at communicating involves knowing your own individual style of communicating and being able to adapt your style to the situation, while still being yourself.

Everyone has a different style of communicating. Some characteristics that influence your style of communicating include your background, interests, and experiences. A person's first interactions are with their family, so this is where they first learn how to communicate with others. People may keep these ways of communicating throughout their life. A person's experiences affects how they communicate, so if they find a way of communicating with others that works they are likely to keep using it.

Everyone has a different set of communicating skills. This can affect how they communicate with others because people who have well developed skills tend to feel more confident, so they can be more likely to communicate with others especially in uncertain situations. People who feel they do not have communicating skills tend to hold back and may not participate as fully. This can give a false impression that they are not interested or are aloof. So, it can be helpful not to judge people just on their communicating skills, but on what they have to say.

2. Desired outcome. We communicate not only to share information and to understand each other, but also to get things done. We often determine what we want in terms of achieving goals and objectives, but desired outcome is different. Goals and objectives can be specific things we want to achieve, so we develop a plan and pursue a course of action that can put us on a single path leaving little room for alternative ways to achieve them. This can prevent us from noticing alternatives that may be preferable. There may even be the chance that the goal we are pursuing is not the best one for us. By pursuing goals and objectives we can lose out on potential opportunities that present themselves along the way.

We often characterize getting what we want as achieving a goal or objective. Using sports as an example, a goal or objective can be considered analogous to making a goal, basket, home run, or touchdown. It is a clear, definite action that is either accomplished or not. Since not every team can win every game, goals and objectives can be discouraging. They can even hurt your self-concept and sense of well being. A desired outcome approach would focus more on a general sense of well being such as personal growth and development, working better as a team, and enjoyment of the game regardless of winning or losing. While losing a game will not accomplish your objective, you can still achieve your desired outcome.

This concept can be applied to our careers and personal lives. For example, you may want to advance in your job. You may not get the promotion you feel you deserve, so you leave and move to another job. While this does not achieve your goals and objectives, the new job may be better for you by providing more opportunity in the future. Considering your desired outcome provides a more positive result than simply achieving goals and objectives because there could be things going on that you may not be aware of, which might affect your achieving them. For instance, your old company may have had underlying problems that might have prevented you from advancing or being happy there.

While losing a job is not necessarily a good thing, it may provide time for other more important activities you would not otherwise have time to pursue. It could motivate you to improve your education and other skills, to pursue important interests, and to develop better relationships with people who are close to you. Pursuing the desired outcome of increasing your job satisfaction and financial stability can put you on a different path helping you to achieve it in the long run.

Everyone communicates for a reason and desired outcome is a part of that reason. Desired outcome is what you want to happen after others get your message. It is more general in nature and considers the big picture, which gives you more ways to achieve what you want. Desired outcome encourages you to consider multiple paths to select the most effective one and to switch them as needed or if you run into difficulties. This enables you to pursue opportunities that may present themselves along the way. Desired outcome focuses less on achieving specific goals or objectives and more on fulfilling needs and wants which provides more flexibility in how you fulfill them.

While your desired outcome is about what you want to happen after you communicate with others, rather than looking for something specific to happen, take a big picture approach focusing on your general state of well being. This increases the number of ways to reach your desired outcome providing you with more flexibility. Increased flexibility can improve your effectiveness and the likelihood that you make it happen. It can reduce competitive pressure to win by reducing the prospect of losing by not achieving your goal. If one approach doesn't work, there may be other ways to achieve your desired outcome. This helps to create a more positive climate that can encourage others to work with you to achieve your desired outcome.

When you know your desired outcome you can spend time on what really matters. Everyone has tasks to accomplish, but desired outcomes are more than that. Simply accomplishing tasks themselves may not achieve our desired outcomes. This can be why we might feel that we are working all the time, but not getting anywhere. This could be one reason seemingly successful people may be frustrated, because they focus on accomplishing tasks or achieving goals and objectives, while neglecting their desired outcomes.

Focusing on achieving your desired outcome can be a more positive approach because it is less discouraging when what you want to happen does not happen. It helps us avoid making judgments about things being good and bad or feeling like a failure. It allows us to find partial success in what we do because pursuing a desired outcome considers the big picture in the long term as a general state of well being.

There are times when we try to achieve our desired outcome and things don't go the way we would like them to go. These situations could be characterized as resulting in unintended or undesired outcomes. An unintended outcome is a result that we did not expect, it can be positive or negative or a little bit of both. We may have asked for a raise, but instead we were given a promotion or had a pay cut. One was positive and the other was negative, however, we did not intend either to occur. An undesired outcome is when we get a result we do not want. We may want to get a raise, but end up being fired. We never wanted to be fired and if given a choice would have stayed at the same salary. Because it is undesired, it is generally considered negative.

While we can never be certain what other people will do or how they might act, we can utilize our knowledge of the process of communicating and our own skills to avoid unintended or undesirable outcomes. It can help to look at your desired outcome from the point of view of the other person and to consider how they might react. All too often we concentrate on what we want to happen instead of thinking about what others might do in response. No matter how effectively we communicate, there is always the possibility that instead of achieving our desired outcome we might get an undesired or unintended outcome.

3. Your Great Idea. Your Great Idea is the message you want to communicate. It is the part of the process of communicating that consists of the information you communicate to others. It begins with the message, which is what you say or write, but it can also consist of many other elements such as nonverbal information including facial expressions and gestures. It usually starts with an idea that exists in our mind not just in words, but also in pictures.

In order to communicate Your Great Idea to others, it has to be in a form that they can understand. This usually involves putting ideas into words that are spoken or written. The words and letters themselves are just symbols that have no inherent meaning. The meaning is given to the symbols by people who translate them into words in order to communicate them to others. When they receive the message, they translate the words back into ideas to understand them. We use the law of shared meaning to go through this process of investing symbols with meaning and translating that meaning into ideas. We do this so often it happens naturally without much thought. When we speak, our mind automatically translates our ideas into words and when we read or hear words they are automatically converted into ideas. This means that the meanings are in the minds of people and not necessarily in the symbols themselves.

For example, when you see the word TREE, you don't think oh, that's four letters. In your mind you see a picture of a big green plant with a trunk, branches, and leaves or needles. This is because everyone who understands English has learned that these four letters are symbols that represent a big green thing. The word TREE is not actually a living tree. Using symbols is critical to communicating because if every time we wanted to communicate the idea of a tree, we would have to describe it or show one to others and that would take a lot of time. Instead, we take the symbols T R E E and invest them with meaning so the letters become a shorthand reference that refers to the real big green thing.

4. Others. Others are the people with whom you communicate. In the process of communicating, everything begins with you so anyone else you communicate with whether it's just one person or a large number of people are referred to as "others." Just as you communicate with others for a reason, others listen and communicate with you for reasons of their own.

Since every person is unique, other people have their own way of doing things, which includes their own style of communicating. This can include their own individual characteristics that give them their own personality. These characteristics can affect how they communicate with you. This can help or hinder the communicating process and how well your message comes across to them. To communicate effectively, it is helpful to know and recognize the unique communicating styles of others to help adapt your own communicating style to them, while still being you. The same things that influence your style of communicating such as family, culture, education, religion, and geographic affiliation also influence how others communicate with you.

How others communicate is based upon their own background and experiences. No two people have the same experiences, even those who grew up in the same family. Even people who experience the same events have different perceptions of them. Others are more likely to communicate about things that they are interested in or things that they have strong feelings about. They are more likely to communicate about something they are interested in or that they like. Being aware of this can help you to communicate more effectively with others.

Everyone has different levels of skills to communicate with others. This can make it easier or more difficult for them to express and share ideas. Their skill level can make them feel comfortable with others or more uncomfortable. It's helpful to be aware of the communicating skills others have to avoid misunderstandings. Awareness of their skills and how comfortable they are communicating with others can help you to communicate more effectively with them. Sometimes a perceived unwillingness to communicate with you is not about you, but rather about the other person's comfort level with their communicating skills.

In order to effectively communicate with others, it's helpful to be aware of what things might influence how and why others communicate with you. By knowing this you can avoid perceiving their lack of communicating as personal because it may be due to some other factor. No matter how much we may want to, we cannot change how other people communicate and what they do. However, we can change the way that we communicate with them. By having an awareness of how the process of communicating works and how it affects others, we can adapt our own style to communicate more effectively with them.

5. Connections. Once you have created your Great Idea you need a connection to get it to others. A connection is the means by which you connect to others so that they can hear or see your message. Creating a connection is essential to effectively communicating with others. If there is no connection, they cannot get your message. Some common connections include speaking face to face, telephone calls, writing a letter or email, public speaking, or through the public media.

We make connections with others through our five senses. When we speak or listen to someone, we make an auditory connection. We use gestures and facial expressions such as smiling to communicate nonverbally, so others see us through a visual connection. Shaking hands or patting someone on the back makes a connection using touch. Wearing perfume or cologne or offering them food makes a connection using our sense of smell. Sharing food or drink, like dinner or coffee makes a connection utilizing taste. Most of the time making a connection involves using more than one of our five senses.

We all have different ways that we obtain and retain information. When you use multiple connections appealing to more than one sense, you increase the chance that people understand and remember your message. For example, if you want your children to be on time for dinner, you could utilize multiple connections through different senses. You can use an auditory connection by telling them. You can use a visual connection by leaving a note on the refrigerator where they will see it. You can use smell to make a connection by having food that smells good to attract their attention. On a romantic date we can make several connections to communicate including visually with our appearance, auditory by playing music; with the smell of cologne, perfume, or flowers; taste with food; and by touch. Increasing the number of connections can make an experience more intense.

Just as we make connections with others we also can become disconnected. We can become disconnected intentionally by no longer talking with someone such as the result of a disagreement. We can become disconnected unintentionally when a relationship drifts apart over time. It can be interrupted by interference and the things that get in the way when people are busy. We can lose touch with coworkers when we change jobs or neighbors when we move to a new community. This can happen for no apparent reason and can leave us feeling frustrated, depressed, or a sense of loss. By being aware of how the process of communicating works, we can make choices about how we connect or disconnect with others rather than letting it just happen and then end up wondering why it did.

6. The Great Abyss. In the process of communicating, you communicate your Great Idea to others by making connections with them in order to achieve your desired outcome. In an ideal situation they would receive and understand your message, however, in reality other things can get in the way. Making a connection with others does not necessarily mean that they will understand your message. Sometimes when we communicate with others, there is a huge chasm that separates you from them. In order to effectively communicate with others, you must make a connection to get your message across this chasm without it getting lost. This chasm can be characterized as "The Great Abyss."

The Great Abyss can alter how others perceive your message and even stop it from getting through to them. It can be thought of like a swamp or chasm that has to be crossed in order to make a connection with others. It characterizes everything that can potentially get in the way of you effectively communicating with others so that they don't get your intended message. Instead, they may get a different idea, the wrong message, or nothing at all which could result in undesired or unintended outcomes. This is why understanding what is in The Great Abyss can be helpful to effectively communicate with others.

The Great Abyss consists of interference that prevents others from understanding your Great Idea. You can interfere with your own message when it is unclear, confused, or disorganized. This can be overcome by using methods of organization, clarifying information, and seeking feedback from others to make sure they clearly understand your Great Idea. Interference cannot only create uncertainty, but can also increase it. Interference can come from others because they have their own ideas that may interfere with what you want to communicate to them. By being aware of how interference works, you can cut through it by emphasizing important points, repeating important information, seeking out feedback from others, or asking them questions. It can be helpful to cut through interference to help others better understand your message.

These are some of the types of interference in The Great Abyss.

- External interference. This includes things that people hear in their physical surroundings that can interfere with your message. Depending upon where you are, this can include things like an air conditioner, radio, television, traffic, or other people talking. This interference can mask or distract others from hearing and fully understanding your message.

- .Internal interference. This includes things that occur in people's minds that interferes with how they perceive your Great Idea. They may have a short attention span, their mind wanders, or they think about other things. Interference may also be physiological, others may be tired or not feeling well causing them to be unable to concentrate on your message. It can come from their lack of understanding of your Great Idea because they may not have the same background, education, experience, or expectations as you. By being aware of potential sources of interference, you can communicate in ways that minimize their impact by eliminating as many sources as possible. Using repetition, emphasizing important points, and soliciting feedback can help to cut through this type of interference.

- Point of view. This is how people see things including themselves, others, and the world around them. Everyone has their own unique point of view which is often based upon their past experiences. A point of view influences how people communicate with one another and affects what they pay attention to or ignore. It affects how they interpret and understand what you communicate to them. By being aware of other people's point of view, you can communicate more effectively with them.

- Frames of reference. A frame of reference is like the frame of a window or the viewfinder of a camera. It frames what a person can see or wants to see and everything outside the frame is blocked out or ignored. People can choose what things to let through their frames and what things to keep out. This can also happen subconsciously, so a person may not be aware that they are doing it. A person's frame of reference can be based upon their individual characteristics such as their background, interests, ethnicity, culture, religion, education, groups they belong to, and their past experiences. By being aware of how frames of reference work, you can create messages to get through them.

- Preconceptions. People tend to block out information that is contrary to what they feel they already know. For instance, if they have one political point of view they may block out information from other political points of view that contradict their own even if they know that the information is accurate. Because people tend to be more receptive to messages that fall within their preconceptions, it can be helpful to know what they are to shape your message to fit within them.

- Filters. Every day we are inundated with so many messages we block out many of them. These can come from people around us or the media. There is so much information out there in order to protect ourselves we filter much of it out. This is one reason why people generally tend to pay attention to only a small amount of information that is communicated to them. They pay attention to what they feel is important and filter out everything else.

- Attention span. The length of our attention span is contingent on many factors such as being tired, overworked, bored, or having too much to do. When we are driving we do not pay attention to all the signs we pass because we see so many. If we paid attention to all of them it would hinder our driving. Have you ever been in a car with someone who felt the need to read every sign out loud as you pass? Was it helpful or annoying? That's what it would be like if we paid attention to everything that is communicated to us. However, if we are almost out of gas we pay attention to every sign looking for a gas station. So, if we need or want something we are less likely to filter it out. By knowing how this process works, we can communicate more effectively with others to get and keep their attention.

7. Feedback. So, you have your Great Idea, made a connection, and crossed The Great Abyss to communicate it to others. How do you know if they got your message? Utilizing

feedback is the best way to find out how effectively your Great Idea has been received. Feedback can happen in a variety of ways. It can happen informally by asking questions or having others restate your ideas to determine if they fully understand them. Feedback can happen in formal ways such as surveys, interviews, polls, or focus groups that can be used to determine the effectiveness of media messages like an advertising campaign.

It is important that feedback be accurate and honest. A face to face conversation is the best means of feedback because it is instantaneous and offers the widest variety of channels to communicate. Other types of feedback such as customer comment cards, surveys, and polls can be helpful, but may be less accurate as people may not be motivated to participate, may provide incomplete information, or give the answers they think makes them look the best.

8. Effectiveness. Effectiveness is the degree to which others receive your Great Idea and you achieve your desired outcome. We might characterize some ways of communicating as good and some as bad. For example, if someone doesn't understand us, we might think that we did a bad job of communicating with them. If we speak in front of a group and it doesn't go well, we may feel that we are not a good speaker. Thinking about communicating in these terms does not permit us to look at what happened in a way that helps us to improve our skills, which can be discouraging. If we feel things didn't go so well, it can increase our anxiety making us reluctant to do it again. A speech that might have been considered bad could in fact have been somewhat effective in getting your message across. In this way, you can now look at how to make it more effective.

Rather than thinking in terms of good or bad, think of communicating effectively. Effective communicating is the degree to which you achieve your desired outcome. The more you understand others and the more they understand you, the more effectively you can communicate with them. Looking at how you communicate in terms of effectiveness rather than good or bad, can help you to determine what works and what could be improved. It can give you a more realistic idea of your skills so that you can feel better about what you can do and work on developing what could be done better.

Styles of Communicating

When people create their Great Idea they may use a particular style of communicating to make a connection with others. In order to communicate more effectively, it is helpful to recognize these styles and be aware of their strengths and weaknesses. How people communicate with others can be characterized by three basic styles.

The first style, the arrow approach.

This style of communicating is similar to shooting an arrow into the air and hoping it hits the target. In this approach, a person creates their Great Idea, they construct a message, send it to others through a connection, and then wait for the result. They hope it hits its target and is understood. The people who receive it may not fully understand the message or may interpret it differently than it was intended. While this sounds like an ineffective way to communicate that can easily create misunderstandings and increase uncertainty, it is how people have been communicating for a long time. Much of the news and information we receive that influences our perceptions and expectations, and shapes social reality is communicated through the media using this approach.

This method of communicating is based on a military model where a commanding officer sends a message down the chain of command to the troops in the field who are expected to follow orders. Then the commander waits for the result. This style was considered successful so it was adopted by businesses. A CEO could be considered a kind of commanding executive officer who sends orders down the chain of command to each level of management telling employees what to do. This style lacks an effective means to provide feedback to know if a message was received or understood.

The second style, the tennis approach.

This style of communicating resolves some of the problems with the first style. People needed to know if their Great Idea was accurately received, so they added a way to get feedback from those receiving the message. This approach encouraged the person receiving the message to communicate back to the person who sent it to determine how well it was understood. The original sender could then decide if additional information was necessary to clarify it.

This approach works like tennis where one person creates their Great Idea and then hits it over the net hoping the other person will get it. If the other person returns the ball it's a success. We use this style when we send emails, memos, and phone messages. This style offers some improvement over the first method because there is a mechanism to provide feedback to clarify the original message. It is commonly used even though it can be awkward and time consuming.

The third style, the conversational approach.

This style of communicating fixes most of the problems of the first and second styles. It is more realistic and effective because it takes into account all aspects of the process of communicating. It works like having a conversation where the people involved are talking to one another. They are communicating information and providing feedback simultaneously to facilitate understanding. It is the most effective approach, however, it can take the most energy. It is often preferred because it takes into account the individuals involved and the context of the situation.

This style is referred to as a conversational style because it is like having a conversation where people both speak and listen as well as provide information and ask questions simultaneously. Rather than being a process of one side against the other, it provides a collaborative process for people to work together to achieve a common understanding. This style works well in situations where instantaneous feedback is useful to help the process. For example, if you are trying to fix a computer it can be difficult reading a manual and could take forever to get the information you need using email. Having a conversation provides direct feedback to make the process easier.

We use this style when we see someone face to face and have a conversation or when we speak to them over the telephone. This style is a more effective means of communicating because we can get results immediately rather than waiting for feedback, which saves time. For example, a short conversation can accomplish more than dozens of emails because we can communicate exactly what we want, clarify information, answer questions, and resolve things much more quickly. However, people may avoid it, using the other two styles by texting and emailing because they can be reviewed and edited before sending. They may feel conversation is too spontaneous or risky increasing their anxiety and uncertainty.

In order to communicate more effectively, it is helpful to recognize when to use each of these styles of communicating and why. While the third style is the most effective, consider just how often people use the first two. We tend to get in the habit of using the first two styles because they can be easier and quicker. They save us time and allow us to make a connection, while still keeping a distance. Each of these styles can be useful depending on your desired outcome, but they also have their limitations.

The Nature of Reality

The laws of uncertainty, shared meaning, and investing were created by nature and the rules of communicating were created by people. Everything created by nature is governed by the laws of nature, like the laws of physics. Everything created by people has one thing in common, at one time it did not exist. It first existed as an idea in a person's mind who then, following the process of communicating, had to make a connection to communicate their Great Idea to others who had to understand it for it to become reality. This process of developing ideas and communicating them to others works not only for tangible things people create, but also for concepts and ideas. Often these ideas shape how people think and motivates their behavior creating physical reality. When people use this process to communicate their ideas to others, it helps to create social reality.

When we think of reality, we think of things like tangible objects that actually exist as opposed to something that exists in our mind. We don't necessarily consider concepts that exist in our mind as reality. However, communicating the thoughts and ideas that exist in our mind can become as much a reality as the tangible things all around us. What we think about and communicate to others can create a reality of its own.

Consider the following types of reality.
1. Physical reality.
2. Social reality.
3. Group reality.
4. Individual reality.

1. Physical reality.

Everything around us can be divided into two basic categories: everything created by nature and everything created by people. Physical reality includes everything that exists in nature such as all living things and naturally occurring phenomena. Some physical reality is created by people including tangible material objects like houses, clothing, and furniture. When we invest physical reality with meaning motivated by the law of shared meaning we create social reality.

2. Social reality.

Social reality is how we make sense of the world around us. It is created by people through the process of communicating with one another. People are motivated to create social reality by the law of uncertainty in order to reduce uncertainty. Social reality reduces uncertainty because it provides the information, structure, and rules people need to function in society. It shares meaning because it is an organized collection of people's experiences and behaviors. It allows investing because it creates stability so people know what to expect. It can be seen as an organized collection of rules, shared meaning, and the common expectations we have of ourselves and each other.

Social reality can create physical reality. While social reality primarily exists in our minds, it can become as real as physical reality because of its power to motivate people's behavior. Social reality is how we interpret the information we gather creating our perspective of how we see ourselves, others, and the world around us. Often the events that happen to us and the things we see around us are open to different interpretations. Social reality tells us which interpretations are acceptable and which ones are not. It can determine how we react to events and what we do about them. It influences how we interpret our experiences and the experiences of others.

Social reality manifests itself in the tangible objects that we create. This can change over time affecting our physical reality. Even though people's needs have remained much the same throughout history, how they fulfilled them has changed considerably. We need to wear clothes, but the way we dress is determined by what social reality tells us is acceptable. It once motivated women to wear corsets and men to wear tights.

Social reality can determine what ideas are considered acceptable and how they should be implemented. This can be illustrated by how people have interpreted the nature of government. Throughout history, people have formed governments motivated by similar needs for security and stability, but have created very different physical realities. In ancient times, rulers claimed they were descended from the gods or ruled by divine right. Later, monarchs were chosen by birthright. More recently, elected leaders are chosen through democratic means by the will of the people. Different social realities based on different cultures and time periods manifested themselves in different physical realities.

How social reality creates physical reality can also be seen in how people breed plants and animals. All living things including plants and animals were created by nature, which over time made changes in their characteristics. People considered some of these characteristics more desirable than others, so they intentionally bred changes in these species. This brought out specific traits that changed their physical reality. Some of these characteristics included hunting skills in dogs, appearance in cats, new colors in flowers, or increased yield in food crops. People are motivated to do this in order to add value by making these things more socially accepted or useful to them in fulfilling their needs and wants to reduce uncertainty.

Social reality is attractive because it answers many of the most fundamental questions about life for us. We don't have to figure everything out for ourselves if we choose not to do so. Instead, we do what social reality tells us to do. We do this because figuring everything out for ourselves takes time and energy, which can motivate us to invest in a particular social reality. We might try to work things out for ourselves, however, we run the risk of being perceived as being wrong. So, we go along with others because we feel they are knowledgeable and the details are taken care of for us, so we don't have to work everything out for ourselves.

Social reality can be analogous to having your taxes done. Everybody has to do their taxes and if you don't there are penalties. To do this we have two choices; to do it ourselves or to have somebody do it for us. Doing it ourselves takes time and energy, but we have a better understanding of what we did and may have learned something in the process. Having somebody else do it is easier because they fill in all the blanks and all we have to do is sign on. However, we may not understand everything we are signing. The same could be said of social reality. We join groups and organizations so someone else will fill in all the blanks to answer some of life's important questions. All we have to do is join and go along because we may increase uncertainty if we try to come up with the answers on our own.

Social reality is created by people to reduce uncertainty found in physical reality, so they can better understand and find meaning in the things that they perceive around them. It fulfills several needs including our need to create order out of chaos, our need to organize things around us, and our need for control. It tells us how we should act and what to do in various situations. It influences our behavior and keeps us in line with what is considered acceptable. These are all important functions for society because they reduce uncertainty and create stability. We know what is expected of us and what we can expect from others. However, it has the potential to give enormous power to those who create it.

Social reality gives us the ability to create and share meaning. We use it to interpret and invest physical reality with meaning. It helps us to take the unfamiliar and make it familiar. It takes chaotic events and makes them understandable by giving them meaning so they can be useful to us. It is an important mechanism we utilize to deal with the unpredictable and chaotic events of life. We create and share social reality so we can invest in ourselves, others, and society.

Social reality works because it fulfills many of our most fundamental needs including our need to know more about ourselves, others, and the world around us. It fulfills our need to exert control over a chaotic world by explaining how it works. It exerts social control over people to create a stable society. It enhances our understanding of things around us because it fills in the gaps in our knowledge and understanding. We cannot possibly experience everything, so we rely on social reality to fill in what we do not know.

The power of social reality is in its ability to motivate behavior by altering how we interpret our physical reality. For example, at times people have interpreted the lack of rain that made for a poor harvest as God's displeasure with them. Some cultures responded to this physical reality with human sacrifices, others sacrificed animals, and others felt they needed to atone for their sins by praying more.

Today, we explain the lack of rain as being due to weather patterns, so we develop drought tolerant crops and build irrigation systems. In each of these societies, differing social realities explained the same physical reality in different ways motivating people to take different actions. This makes social reality very powerful, even potentially dangerous because it motivates what people do about what they perceive.

Social reality can be a form of social control because it motivates and shapes our behavior by telling us what is socially acceptable and unacceptable, including what we can and cannot say or do. So, it not only serves to motivate our behavior, it may constrain it as well. In this way it can limit our choices exerting a kind of social control over us. People make choices and decide how to act based on the rules and expectations of social reality. While this sounds restrictive, and it can be, without social reality everyone would behave differently and no one would know what to do or what to expect from others. People behave differently enough as it is, imagine what life would be like without having social reality to regulate behavior. This would add to the level of uncertainty making life even more chaotic.

Social reality helps to bring our intangible thoughts and ideas into existence in physical reality. Everything created by people existed first in someone's mind who, through the process of communicating, shared it with others. As more people shared the idea it became a part of social reality. Even though social reality exists primarily in people's minds, it manifests itself in their behavior, actions, and how they communicate with others. Through their actions, it can create its own reality that can be as real as physical reality.

3. Group social reality.

Groups and individuals can create their own specialized version of social reality by adding their own ideas to meet their specific needs, wants, and desired outcomes. Group social reality often includes stories about how the group began, its founder, well known members, its history, significant events, and what it means to be a member. It can develop slowly through people sharing meaning over time or be created intentionally in a comparatively short period of time. Some types of groups that develop their own specialized social reality include educational, religious, political, military, and cultural groups. Tension between differing social realities can be a source of conflict, even violence or war.

A group social reality is often created to fulfill the needs and wants of the group. It can be used to encourage commitment to the group. It may be communicated to the public in order to gain outside support or recruit new members. For most of these groups their shared group reality fits in with the larger social reality. Artificial social realities can be developed by groups like political parties in order to promote a specific political agenda or to support candidates for public office.

Religion is an example of how social reality reduces uncertainty, shares meaning between people, and encourages them to invest in themselves and others. All religions serve a similar function and have similar elements, but these can be manifested in distinctly different ways. They answer some of life's most perplexing questions like who we are, why we are here, and where we are going. They interpret events and invest them with meaning. They have a history, traditions, and rituals that create and maintain connections between people. Their power is in how they take ideas and manifest them in physical reality, motivating the behavior of large numbers of people. How they accomplish these things is often contingent on their place of origin and the time period in history when they were established.

4. Individual reality.

An individual social reality is how we as an individual organize and make sense of the world. Not everyone subscribes to every aspect of the larger societal social reality, nor do they have to in order to function in society. However, this flexibility can manifest itself in differences that can create tension and even conflict between people and within society. These differences and disparities enable us to create our own individual reality that can fall within the larger social reality, but can also deviate from it in certain aspects.

We may subscribe to part of it, but then alter or change other parts to fit our personal needs and wants. We do this because it helps us get through everyday life. Without it things would be more difficult. Since we created it we can change it when it suits us. However, like our self-concept, an individual reality develops slowly over time so that we may not even be aware of it. Our individual reality includes how we see ourselves, others, and the world around us. Awareness of this type of reality is important because of the influence it has on how we communicate and how it motivates our behavior.

At times different social realities can compete and even come in conflict with one another. This is because they may be based on different cultures, countries, religions, or political social realities that may not be compatible. Some people may belong to different groups that have conflicting social realities that can create confusion or tension. To resolve this tension we could develop our own version that combines elements from several other social realities.

Alternate individual reality.

There are times when a person's individual reality can become an alternate individual reality. This can happen if they emulate real people or characters that they have seen in the media or in works of fiction. They become interested in these characters as much or even more than other people in their own life. This might happen when the physical reality or social realities fail to meet their needs and wants. When people have needs and wants that go unfulfilled, they may seek to create an alternate reality that provides a different means to fulfill them. It may be to fulfill needs for fun and adventure, for escape or excitement, to have something in common with others, or it could be to live vicariously through the actions of others. The alternative personal reality they create can be as real to them as physical reality.

Dramatic Narratives.

It could be said that forms of communicating fall into two basic types, fact and fiction. If fact comprises those things that are verifiably true and fiction is an imaginative creation that is not actual reality, then there are times when people may do neither. Instead, they take an inherent reality, choose a few pertinent aspects, and then present their own version of events that carries an emotional or persuasive quality. This approach falls between fact and fiction into the realm of dramatic narratives. This serves to explain events by investing them with shared meaning that makes a connection with others to help create and maintain their version of social reality. Much of how social reality is constructed happens through dramatic narratives.

When people come together, they often tell stories, but instead of giving an accounting of events, they may embellish what transpired. When people tell stories that have meaning to others, others may join in and share their own similar experiences. These stories can be emotional and might motivate people to take action. Dramatic narratives often consist of a story about people or the retelling of events characterizing them from a particular point of view, giving them an emotional quality to make them more interesting or exciting. They are created to have a desired effect on people like informing, entertaining, or persuading them. So, they are invested with shared meaning by the people who create and share them.

This process can take place face to face as well as through the media. When people share dramatic narratives they have the same understanding of events, so they share meaning. Examining dramatic narratives can provide a way to understand the shared meanings embedded in what people say, as well as the underlying motives for their behavior. Much of how we understand reality is communicated through dramatic narratives because of their power to reduce uncertainty.

Changing social reality.

While the larger social reality must change, once we adopt a particular social reality it may be difficult to change because it provides us with stability and security. We might react negatively to others who try to change it because change represents increased uncertainty. This is because social reality becomes a part of who we are and our self-concept, so we may see attempts to change it as threatening. We may resist change because if one part of what we believe is wrong, other things we believe could potentially be wrong as well. This can make us feel uncomfortable because it could undermine our feelings of safety and security increasing uncertainty. This motivates people to defend their version of social reality.

Change is inevitable and unavoidable because if social reality never changed we would still think the earth was flat and the sun revolved around the earth. In the past, people have resolved the tension created by conflicting social realities through various means including violence, war, and revolution. For example, the American Revolutionary War was about more than independence from England, it was to legitimize the changing social reality about the nature of self determination in government.

Having the ability to create a mechanism that allows social reality to adapt and change is essential to growth. Maintaining a constant social reality may be comfortable, however, without change to reflect changing needs and wants it would be nearly impossible for us to function in a constantly changing world. This may be one reason why young people can be more adaptable to some things than older people because their individual social reality has not yet been fully developed for as long a period of time. It has likely undergone change more recently, so change is more familiar.

While social reality governs how society works, in order for society to develop it needs a mechanism that allows for change while maintaining stability. One way this happens is through creative expression. Some groups and individuals such as artists, writers, fashion designers, actors, and musicians differentiate from accepted social reality by creating a specialized individual or group reality. This allows new ideas like artistic tastes and fashion trends to be tested and accepted before they become part of the larger social reality. For instance, there was a time when rock music and impressionistic painting were considered scandalous, but today they are considered part of our culture. This mechanism allows for new shared meaning to be created without excessively increasing uncertainty.

The Perception Process

Perception is how we gather information and give it meaning, so that it can be useful to us. We gather information through our five senses: sight, sound, taste, touch, and smell. We also gather information through other means such as our feelings, emotions, intuition, and impressions. Perception is much more than just receiving information, it is about what we do with this information. Perception is the means by which we get to know what we know. It is how we make sense of the world and influences how we communicate with others. Everything we know and think including how we view ourselves and others is created through perception.

Perception is important because it is not only the process by which we gather information, it is the process by which we come to understand it. It is how we make sense of ourselves, others, and the world around us. It is through perception that we create personal and social reality. It is how we learn by observing and doing to create new knowledge. Perception gives meaning to our experiences. It provides us with the information we use to solve problems and make decisions. It is how we develop our attitudes, formulate our beliefs, and establish our values.

By understanding how the perception process works, we can become more aware of our choices and have more control over how we utilize the information we receive. The perception process may provide information, but the information we receive can affect how we perceive things. When people get information that is not current, accurate, valid, or is biased it can create perceptions that are not accurate. This can result in unrealistic expectations altering their view of social reality. We perceive information all the time without thinking much about it, however, effectively utilizing it takes effort. Having an awareness of how the perception process works enables us to take control of the information we perceive rather than letting it control our thoughts and actions.

The perception process is motivated by the law of uncertainty. It is through our perceptions that we gain information and knowledge in order to reduce uncertainty about ourselves, others, and the world around us. The perception process is how we share meaning with others. It's how we gather, organize, and give information meaning so that it is useful to us now and in the future. We use our perceptions to determine whether or not to invest our resources in others and in relationships. The perception process provides the basis for how we make decisions and solve problems.

Like the process of communicating, perception begins with you. Perception makes the process of communicating work. How we think up our Great Idea is based upon our perceptions of what is around us. How we choose to organize our ideas and communicate them to others is based upon our perception that they will be interested. We make choices based upon our perceptions about how to make connections with others across The Great Abyss.

Interference can hinder our perceptions blocking out potentially important information. Our filters and frames of reference determine what information we actually perceive. Our perception is affected by the filters we use to remove information we don't consider useful and frames of reference that help form our point of view. By being aware of the perception process and how it works, we can improve our own process of communicating to communicate more effectively with others to reduce uncertainty.

Everyone has their own point of view that makes them perceive things differently. This is why several people can see the exact same event, yet they can give distinctly different accounts of what happened. The individual nature of the perception process can make eyewitness testimony one of the most unreliable forms of evidence. This occurs because perception is a complex process of selecting, interpreting, and organizing the information we perceive through our five senses. Often there is more information than we need, so we select what is important or interesting to us and discard the rest.

Sources of information.

- Firsthand. This is the information that we gather from what we experience ourselves through our five senses. This makes it the most real and the most memorable type of information. We use this information to form the basis of our own social reality, so it can motivate our behavior and how we communicate with others.

- Secondhand. This is the information we gain from communicating with others about their experiences. This is important because we cannot learn everything we need to know firsthand, so we have to depend on secondhand information for much of what we know.

- Third person. This is information that has been processed or edited from sources like the media. This information does not come directly from the original source so it is subject to the interpretation of the person communicating it. This kind of information is generally not utilized under circumstances where validity is essential such as academic research or legal proceedings. Despite its flaws, in our mass media society much of the information we depend upon comes to us through intermediaries like reporters. This information can have a significant impact on our lives because we often base our decisions on it. However, because of its nature, it can be the least reliable or accurate..

How the perception process works.

Perception is the process of listening, speaking, tasting, touching, and smelling as well as our intuition or gut feelings. We select and organize information to file away for when it may be needed at a later time. We retrieve what we feel we need in order to understand something or reduce uncertainty. We use this information to make comparisons between new information and our experiences in order to understand them better to give them meaning. How we make sense of what is around us is based upon the choices we make about how we use this information. Because it is important how we act around others, it helps to understand how the process of perception, selection, organization, and interpretation influences our behavior and how we communicate with others.

1. Selection. Selection is about what information we choose to perceive. We make choices about what information is important to us and what is not. There is often more information available to us than we can utilize, so we must select what we feel is useful and filter out the rest. Selection is making choices about what information to keep and what to discard. It's a natural process so we generally don't think much about it.

We select information based upon our personal preferences, experiences, and what we feel will fulfill our needs and wants. We are more likely to pay attention to information that is about things we like or that we find interesting. We have a tendency to look for and select information that fits in with what we already know because it fulfills our expectations reducing uncertainty. When we feel we know and understand things, we feel more confident and better about ourselves.

We tend to filter out or discard information that is unfamiliar or contradicts what we already know because it can be uncomfortable. If it is unexpected, it might not fall within our frame of reference. If it doesn't fit in with our current perceptions, we are likely to filter it out. This is a naturally occurring process because new information can create tension with what we already know which increases uncertainty and reduces stability. We tend to block it out because if we are wrong about one thing, we may be wrong about others, which can undermine our social reality. This is why we may filter out information we might need.

The process of selection is important because in order to communicate effectively we need to be aware of how interference like frames and filters affect our selection process. Since they develop slowly over time, they become second nature so that we are practically unaware of them and how they affect us. It is helpful to be aware of how interference affects other people, so we can be sure our information is communicated clearly and that they accurately perceive it.

Much of the perception process happens instinctively and subconsciously, however, there are times when we make conscious choices. We can choose to filter out information by withdrawing or not listening to others. We can choose to avoid unwanted information by excluding people, things, and situations we may find uncomfortable. We make choices to be around or listen to some people, but not others. We make choices about what to watch on television, listen to on the radio, and what to read in newspapers or look at on the internet. We select what information to allow in and what to block out. Even if we listen to someone, we may not be mentally engaged by thinking about something else that blocks them out.

2. Organization. After we select information to perceive, we have to organize it so it can be useful to us. Organization is how we arrange, sort, categorize, and fit together the informa-

tion that we perceive. Information rarely comes in a clearly organized way, so we need to arrange it in a way that's meaningful to us. How information is organized directly affects its meaning and how we utilize it. We do this because when information is organized it reduces uncertainty and we can give it meaning. This makes it easier to recall making it useful to us in the future.

Much of the information we receive comes in bits and pieces. The perception process has to put these pieces of information together, so that we can better understand them. How we choose to organize information determines how things fit together rather like a puzzle. However, this process doesn't always go easily and the puzzle may be missing pieces, so we have to fill in the gaps of missing information in order for them to make sense. Sometimes we only have fragments that do not seem to fit, so we need to find a way to utilize them. This can make us look for information so we can complete the picture. We may fill in the gaps by using inferences and other information that may not be true or accurate.

We utilize organizational methods to arrange information to make it easier for us to understand and remember. We can use methods like appearance, proximity, or similarity. We might create our own methods to categorize information by labeling things based upon our past experiences. When we come across something new we tend to organize it based upon our existing categories. If something doesn't fit into our categories, we are more likely to discard it. This is because grouping information together makes it easier for us to organize and recall it later.

Information comes to us in a steady stream often without a clear beginning or end. In order to make sense of it we have to cut it up into understandable pieces like punctuation does for words in forming sentences. A page of words without punctuation is difficult to understand because we don't know where ideas begin and end. Adding punctuation groups words together in order to give them meaning. We do the same with the information we perceive by grouping it together to give it meaning.

The perception process works a bit like books in a library. The books are organized by topics making it easy for us to find and use them. There is an established method to how they are organized so that new books can be added whenever they come in and we can find the one we want whenever we want. If the books were not organized this way and instead were put on the shelves in the chronological order they arrived at the library, like how we experience things in life, it would make finding the one we wanted almost impossible. This is why we may need time to process new information, so we can organize our experiences to make them easier to understand and retrieve them when we need them in the future.

3. Interpretation. The law of shared meaning motivates us to interpret the information we receive by investing it with meaning, so that it can be useful to us now and in the future. When we interpret information we can make comparisons between the new information and the information we already have. This helps us to determine the validity of the information and its usefulness. This process happens primarily subconsciously, however, there are times when we become aware of it such as when something doesn't seem right. Interpretation is very subjective because it is based upon an individual's experiences, point of view, and personal social reality. Understanding how we interpret information is essential to understanding how we communicate.

Interpretation of information is important because it has the potential to not only change our perception, but our individual social reality as well. This can affect how we communicate with others, our behavior, and how we see ourselves. Generally, our perceptions do not suddenly or significantly change our social reality because we need consistency. Consistency increases stability and reduces uncertainty, which makes us better able to function. However, there must be a way to change and adapt our perceptions in order to utilize new information. This creates tension between what we know and what we may need to know or what we perceive, which can lead to internal conflict.

How we interpret the information we perceive is influenced by many factors including our culture, ethnicity, family, education, age, gender, values, attitudes, beliefs, geographic affiliation, and past experiences. It is also influenced by our needs and wants, likes and dislikes, and the perceptions we have already interpreted. The factors that influence our interpretations of what we perceive is important because we make judgments that affect us and how we view everything around us based upon these interpretations. It also determines what information we use to create or change our own personal social reality.

Our past perceptions and interpretations have a significant influence on how we perceive and make sense of new information. We tend to look for things that are familiar to us because they fit in with the old information more easily. For instance, we might look for relationships with people that we have something in common or that we perceive to be like us. This helps reduce uncertainty and lets us reasonably make assumptions about them. If these perceptions hold true, it can give us confidence to experience new situations.

Interpretation of new information can take time and energy. This is why when something unexpected, shocking, or traumatic happens to us we may need some time to come to terms with it. We need time to process the new experience or information because it may not easily fit in with our past experiences or what we already know. This can be difficult when it challenges what we already know, our values, or our beliefs. Knowing how this process works can help us understand why we may have feelings like frustration or anger, so we can better deal with them. It is helpful at these times to allow yourself the time to process information or experiences to deal with them as well as possible.

Our mood or emotional state can affect how receptive we are to new information as well as how we interpret it. We have a tendency to be more perceptive when we are experiencing uncertainty because it motivates us to look for something new or different to improve our circumstances. When uncertainty is reduced, we tend to be more content or satisfied with our situation and less likely to look for something new as there is less motivation to change. Alternately, people who are overly dissatisfied such as being upset or angry might reject new information because they are not able to handle it at the time.

Perception causes us to form impressions of people. Since everyone communicates for a reason, we infer that there are motives behind a person's behavior and what they communicate. When we meet someone we have limited information about them. The perception process compares what we observe to our past experiences and then we fill in the gaps to form an impression of others.

This first impression may or may not be accurate, but it can be difficult to change because we have a tendency to categorize people and experiences by grouping them together based on similar characteristics and our past experiences. We do this because it enables us to fit new information in with what we already know. This gives us an idea of what to expect in the future by reducing uncertainty, so we are more comfortable getting to know them.

Improving perception skills.

Perception is a communicating skill that can be improved. These techniques can be helpful.

- Reduce uncertainty with feedback. We can ask others for feedback to check the accuracy of our perceptions. In the process of communicating, feedback is important to determine how well our message was understood by others. We can ask questions to determine how well the messages we communicate to others are received.

- Share meaning by questioning assumptions. During the perception process we often base our selection and interpretation of information on assumptions in order to come to conclusions so it will be useful to us. Sometimes these are inaccurate leading to faulty assumptions and wrong conclusions. Instead of clinging to first impressions and current assumptions, be open to the possibility that they might not be accurate.

- Invest by checking the facts. All too often opinion and inference are treated as fact. Having accurate information results in more accurate perceptions and better decisions. Information can be confirmed by checking the source or testing it for validity before using it. We don't usually do this because it takes time and effort, however, it is worth it because we will have more accurate perceptions.

- Be objective. We select and interpret information based upon our personal preferences because it's comfortable to confirm what we already know. However, if we didn't look at things from other people's perspectives we would never learn anything new. Just because we look at things from other people's perspective does not mean we have to agree with them.

- Keep an open mind. One of the biggest obstacles to perceiving new information is being closed minded because considering new ideas can increase uncertainty. Keeping an open mind allows us to consider a wide variety of sources increasing the likelihood that we get correct and accurate information. It allows us to consider new ideas and learn new things. Being open to new ideas does not necessarily mean we have to accept them.

- Reduce uncertainty with increased awareness. It's helpful to be aware of our own assumptions, perspective, and opinions as well as how they affect the perception process. Be aware of what kinds of information you perceive and how you interpret them. Think of ways to improve your perception process in order to communicate more effectively. Be aware of your own strengths and limitations that may be affecting your perception.

- Things change. One of the purposes of perception is to help us create stability and reduce uncertainty, however, it is important to be able to adapt to change because everything changes. It's helpful to develop your own ways to adapt your perception process to accommodate new information and changing circumstances.

There are many factors that influence the perception process. Consider what factors influence your perception. Doing this can be helpful to increase your awareness of not only how the perception process works, but how you observe, interpret, organize, and use that information. This can help you to improve your perception in order to communicate more effectively with others.

Expectations

Since no one can predict the future, we create expectations in order to reduce uncertainty because it can give us an idea of what the future might be like. Without them life would be more uncertain. We have expectations about ourselves, others, and practically everything around us. Without expectations, we could not function in daily life because they allow us to do things without having to think about them.

Everyone communicates for a reason and many of those reasons help to form the basis of our expectations. We communicate with others in order to achieve desired outcomes, which are based on our expectations. Expectations consist of something that we reasonably believe will happen or a mental image of what something will be like.

We are motivated to develop expectations by the law of uncertainty in order to have a reasonable idea of what things will be like in the future. Expectations reduce uncertainty by providing a measure of how well we are doing. If our perception of reality matches or exceeds expectation, we feel good about things. If they do not, it can make us feel frustrated, upset, or even angry.

Expectations fulfill the law of shared meaning because they give things additional meaning. Without having expectations, it would be nearly impossible to make investments in ourselves and others for the future. Expectations make the law of investing work because without having reasonable expectations of getting a return, we would be reluctant to invest our time and energy in anything. This means that expectations often represent benefits we would like to receive in the future.

Expectations may be realistic or unrealistic, accurate or off base, but we could not function without them. When we do something for others, we cannot be sure what they will actually do in return. Without reasonable expectations of some type of reciprocation or reward, people would not be as willing to invest their time, energy, money, and other resources in the things that are important for society to function.

We have expectations about practically all aspects of our life including what we do, what others do, our family, our friends, our job, our coworkers, and what life should be like. We have expectations not only about extraordinary events that may happen in the future, but also about everyday life. We have lots of small expectations without which we could not function.

We could not function on a daily basis without having expectations. There are many things that we need to do to get through everyday life that would not be possible without expectations. For example, we expect to wake up in the morning and get out of bed. We expect to get ready for work and arrive there without incident.

At work we expect everything to be as we left it and to get certain tasks done. After work we expect to go home, have dinner, and go to bed. Our day is full of many of these small expectations. We don't think much about them because most of the time they are fulfilled. However, when our expectations are not realized, it can be a source of dissatisfaction, tension, and even conflict.

We need to have these expectations in order to get through daily life because if we had to stop and think about each thing, it would take an inordinate amount of time and we would not get very much done. The vast majority of the time everything goes well, so we become accustomed to having these expectations met. We get so accustomed to this that when they do not go as we expect, it can throw us making us feel frustrated or angry. The smaller the expectation, the more we might expect it to happen. This can be one reason why people blow up over small, seemingly insignificant things.

We obey the rules of society because we have the expectation of receiving rewards that fulfill our needs and wants if we do. If we did not have these expectations, we would be less likely to accept the rules of social reality and focus on fulfilling our own needs and wants first. Instead, we may delay gratification for ourselves and contribute to society without expecting to receive something immediately in return. This promotes acceptance in others by having reasonable expectations of future benefits.

The perception and expectation gap.

Our feelings of satisfaction or dissatisfaction can have a lot to do with the gap between our perception of reality and our expectations. Success can be seen as the difference between our expectations of need and want fulfillment and our perception of what we receive. For example, when our perception of reality exceeds our expectations we are likely to feel happy, even elated at our accomplishments.

Conversely, when our perception of reality is below our expectations, we can feel upset, unhappy, or even angry. In each case the gap between our perceptions and expectations creates tangible feelings and emotions that can affect our behavior and actions. Our behavior can be markedly different depending upon if we feel successful or not based upon our perceptions and expectations.

Everyone's perception of reality is different and so are their expectations. A person with a seemingly high degree of success might be dissatisfied based upon the gap between their perceptions and expectations. This may be one reason why people who seem very successful, wealthy, or famous can be unhappy, dissatisfied, even suicidal. It may be because their perception of reality does not meet their expectations. Conversely, people who may not be considered as successful can be happier, because their perceptions meet their expectations.

Managing expectations.

We all want to improve our quality of life. We have expectations that things should get better over time. If our perceptions don't meet our expectations, it can be frustrating or debilitating. It can even make us quit trying altogether. If our perceptions exceed our expectations, we may feel that everything is fine and may not do anything to improve ourselves.

In order to facilitate improvement, it can be helpful to have expectations slightly above current perceptions to help motivate sustained improvement. When expectations are slightly above perceptions they can seem more achievable. If our expectations are too big it can become discouraging and if they are too small there won't be much improvement. So, in order to use perceptions and expectations to motivate behavior, set your expectations just enough above your perceptions to motivate you to improve without being discouraging.

What expectations do you have about yourself, your family, your job, your coworkers, or your life? It can be helpful to think about your perceptions and expectations. You might write them down and how well you feel they are being fulfilled. Ask yourself if your expectations are realistic or not. Ask yourself if your perceptions are accurate or not. Tension, unhappiness, and even conflict can come from inaccurate perceptions and unrealistic expectations. By understanding your perceptions and expectations, you can determine how accurate they are and if they are a source of unnecessary unhappiness. Sometimes clarifying perceptions and expectations can make them more realistic improving your outlook on life.

We all have expectations and make judgments based on our perceptions. It's a natural part of how we reduce uncertainty. We do this so often they become second nature, so we don't think much about them until they become a problem. By being aware of our expectations, we can be more realistic about what we expect of ourselves and others.

In relationships with others, such as with our family, it can be helpful to talk about our perceptions and expectations so that we know what others expect of us and they know what we expect of them. Sometimes we feel that others just know this or will just get it. The reality is most of the time other people don't just get it, creating unnecessary tension. By communicating our mutual expectations of one another, we can reach an understanding of how those expectations can be managed improving our relationships.

Communicating Skills

Awareness and options, competence and confidence, and range and repertoire are some of the skills that can be helpful to effectively communicate with others.

1. Awareness is about how we gather information through the perception process, and how we use that information gives us options. Awareness is much like communicating, it is something we all do naturally without thinking much about it. We feel that we are aware of what's around us because we notice things every day, however, awareness is a skill that can be developed. It involves developing our perception process so that we notice more of what is around us. It helps us to be more in control of the process of how we interpret and organize the information we perceive. It is the ability to look at what you know and use it in new ways.

Awareness includes self-awareness, which is knowing what we are communicating both verbally and nonverbally to others and how they perceive us. Awareness includes being aware of our own style of communicating including how our perceptions and expectations influence our behavior. It is understanding how well our needs and wants are being met. It is understanding how others communicate, their communicating style, their perceptions and expectations, their needs and wants, and what we can do to communicate more effectively with them.

Increasing self-awareness can be difficult because we don't know what we don't know. In order to effectively communicate with others, it can be helpful to see yourself as others see you. In the process of communicating, the interference of The Great Abyss can limit or constrain our awareness of ourselves. People in many professions increase their self-awareness by monitoring and reviewing how they communicate with other people. For example, public speakers or musicians might record themselves and then listen to their performances. Professional athletes may analyze videos of their games.

Everyone has a different level of self-awareness. Balance is important because a high level of self-awareness can be self indulgent and a low level can make us seem indifferent. Everyone can improve their awareness skills utilizing everyday activities. For example, if you are sitting in a restaurant, coffee shop, at work, or just about anywhere, take a minute and close your eyes. Try to remember everything you can about your surroundings. What people are in the room? What do they look like? What is the room like? What kind of furniture is in it and where is it located? Then open your eyes and see how accurate you were.

Try keeping a small notebook with you to write down your observations and perceptions. For instance, after a meeting, a lunch, or going someplace like shopping, take a moment to write down everything you can remember. Write it down in as much detail as you can. Once you are done, if you can, look around and check your accuracy.

The purpose is to train your mind to be naturally aware of your surroundings. This can help you to communicate more effectively, have a greater understanding of yourself and others, and in extreme situations might save your life. For example, could you describe someone to the police if you had to identify them? Could you find your way out of the room or building if you could not see, if the electricity went out, or there was smoke from a fire? Developing these skills can give us confidence and competence in our own abilities.

2. Options. Increasing our awareness can provide us with more options. Since there is no one right way to communicate in any given situation, having options helps us communicate more effectively. Having options is not just about having choices, but having the ability to choose the best one in a given situation. It helps us to not fall into the habit of doing the same things over and over when they may not be effective. It helps us to evaluate our ways of doing things to see what can be improved to be more effective. The more options you have, the better your chances of achieving your desired outcome.

However, options are good up to a point, because having too many can be as problematic as too few. When we have too many options, we can become paralyzed with an inability to choose one. Most of the time we need only a few good choices. Awareness helps us to look at what works and why it works. Having awareness and options makes it possible for you to change or add new ideas and skills, so you can choose what works best for you.

3. Confidence. In effectively communicating with others it is helpful to have confidence and competence. Confidence is about our believing in ourselves, our skills, and our abilities. It is the ability to develop our own self image and control how we present it to others. It is the ability to choose how we communicate with others so that they will understand us and respond positively to us. It is the ability to communicate effectively to achieve your desired outcomes.

People who speak clearly and with authority, who are knowledgeable, and are aware of themselves and others as well as the situation are often perceived as being confident. People are more likely to be receptive to someone who shows confidence because it makes them feel safe and secure by reducing uncertainty.

4. Competence. Competence is having a variety of skills and the ability to use them effectively. It is having an awareness of our own skills and knowledge of the options that are available to us. These skills can be based upon our experiences, education, and expertise. Practicing these skills not only makes us better at them, it makes us more confident so we will be perceived by others as being more competent. People who are competent are seen as being more likable, organized, and professional. Having competence gives us the confidence to use our knowledge and skills to the best of our ability.

5. Range and repertoire. Range is the variety of notes produced by a musician, the area in which something can operate, or the distance something can travel. In communicating, range is the variety of skills you have to communicate effectively with people in many different types of situations.

In music, repertoire is the body of artistic works a musician is able to perform. In communicating, it can be the variety of resources, techniques, or skills available to communicate effectively with others. This gives you options and having options gives you the flexibility and freedom to make choices rather than reacting to the actions of others. Having range and repertoire provides a variety of choices so you can select the best one for your particular situation.

6. Adaptability and Performance. Adaptability is having the expertise and capability to apply a variety of options and select the one that works best in a given situation. It's having the flexibility to move from one option to another if one doesn't work until a successful one is found.

Performance is having the expertise and capability to use communicating skills in real situations to communicate more effectively. Performance skills are developed through practice and experience. People who are effective communicators have the ability to adapt and hone their approach to communicate differently based on the situation and individuals involved. To do this it's helpful to break out of familiar patterns, to try new approaches, and to be aware of the feedback we receive from others.

Uncertainty and Communicating Rationale

Uncertainty is something that affects us all. Rather than letting uncertainty control us, we can increase our awareness and have options so that we can do something about it. This book applies the laws of communicating, the process of communicating, and the elements of communicating described in this chapter to the many ways that we communicate. It utilizes a levels of interaction approach to cover how we communicate with ourselves and others in a comprehensive way.

The next chapter is about how we communicate with ourselves to form our self-concept. Chapter 3 is about how we create and maintain relationships with other people. Chapter 4 applies communicating skills to how we work with other people in groups and organizations. And finally in Chapter 5 these concepts are applied to how we communicate in society.

These elements work together to reduce uncertainty and help us fulfill our needs and wants. The remaining chapters explain how these laws, skills, and elements work in many kinds of situations. Each section covers a specific topic to provide not only options to communicate more effectively, but also the rationale behind those options to increase awareness of how they work. These are meant to help you know how absolute uncertainty affects your life and what you can do about it.

Chapter 2
Individual Communicating

What if you were on stage in a play, but didn't know your lines or even what play you were in? What would you do? What if you were in front of an audience to give a speech, but didn't know what to say or why you were there? What would you do?

While this would probably never happen, these situations are similar to how we learn to communicate. From the time we are born, we encounter unfamiliar situations where we may not know what we should say or do. So, we learn as we go by communicating with others, often without intentionally developing or practicing communicating skills.

Communicating can be considered similar to acting or musical performance. Your audience needs to clearly understand you, which requires a certain amount of skill. Since communicating is something we do every day, we may give little consideration to developing these skills. However, like acting or music, in order to effectively communicate with others it is helpful to develop communicating skills and abilities. Effectively communicating with others begins with having an awareness of how we communicate with ourselves.

Many professionals like musicians and actors study fundamentals and basic techniques of their craft in order to develop skills essential for a successful performance. A similar approach can be taken to communicating. There are fundamental skills that can be developed to help us effectively communicate with others.

Do you ever talk to yourself? We communicate with ourselves in many ways. It may be out loud, it may be listening to our inner voice, or simply thinking inside our head. However it happens, we are constantly communicating with ourselves sending messages like, "I feel good today," or "Why did I say that," or "I feel so embarrassed." These messages are often about how we feel about ourselves and our perceptions about what is happening around us. We do this in order to help understand what we perceive.

Individual communicating is about you. It is the first level of interaction because it is about how we communicate with ourselves. Our self-concept is in part developed based on how we communicate with ourselves and the kinds of messages we send. We send ourselves so many messages we may not be aware of what we are telling ourselves. This is why it can be helpful to increase our awareness of the messages we send ourselves, so we can be in control of them in order to improve our self-concept. Individual communicating skills are important because how we communicate with ourselves can affect how we communicate with others.

So, why do we communicate with ourselves? Doing this helps us to organize our thoughts and sort out the information we receive. We do it to reduce uncertainty and learn more about ourselves, to help understand our experiences by giving them meaning, and to invest in ourselves. It is how we process information to make it useful. It helps us to make good decisions by weighing our options and thinking things through. Communicating with ourselves helps us to increase our awareness of things that we feel are important, to work out problems, to remind us of things we need to do, or remember things we have done well.

Life can be chaotic and there are lots of things happening around us. We might even have to overcome The Great Abyss to communicate with ourselves. How many times have you thought, "If only I had listened to myself?" Interference can affect the messages we send ourselves just like those we send to others. However, there are times when we don't listen, don't do what we know we should do, get distracted, or forget about it. Understanding the importance of utilizing this process can make it work more effectively for us.

In most situations we encounter it's helpful to have skills to effectively communicate with others. Developing personal communicating skills helps us to reduce uncertainty about ourselves and our own abilities. The more we are sure of ourselves and have developed our skills, the more we can effectively utilize them to achieve a successful desired outcome.

Sharing meaning is essential to understanding others as well as ourselves. Much of what we communicate carries meanings that we intend as well as some we do not. Developing individual communicating skills helps us to understand not only what we mean when we communicate, but also how others perceive us. It also helps us to better understand what others mean. Utilizing the law of shared meaning to develop our individual communicating skills helps us to communicate more effectively to create a common understanding with others.

The law of investing motivates us to invest time and resources in others. However, we also need to invest time and resources in ourselves. All too often we neglect our own needs and wants by putting ourselves last behind everyone else. Developing individual communicating skills can help us to invest in ourselves and in our abilities by improving how we communicate with others.

We have many needs and wants that we cannot fulfill ourselves. So, we need to communicate with others in order to fulfill them. Individual communicating skills can help us to communicate our needs and wants more effectively to achieve our desired outcomes. We can develop our individual communicating skills, like musicians develop skills in order to perform for an audience.

We communicate with others based upon the information that we have gathered through the perception process. We determine what information to select and how to organize and interpret it. This means that we can have the same experiences as others, but interpret them differently. By developing individual communicating skills, we can better understand the process of how we select, organize, and interpret the information we receive.

Our perceptions can create expectations. We often develop expectations by what we tell ourselves we should be doing, should be communicating, and should be receiving. For example, you may tell yourself that you should have better relationships, better pay, or more time to yourself. Eventually, you may begin to believe these expectations and act based upon them whether they are accurate or not. So, our perceptions and expectations can be based upon the messages we send ourselves, which can influence our behavior.

Social reality is constructed when people communicate with one another. The messages they send create shared meaning based upon their perception of themselves and the world around them. We can develop our own individual social reality based upon the messages people send us and the messages we send to ourselves. By developing individual communicating skills, we can have a better understanding of how social reality influences how we think and behave. This helps us make choices about how to communicate and act, rather than being influenced by others.

By understanding how we communicate with ourselves and the nature of the messages we send, we can increase our awareness of them. We can learn to critically evaluate them to determine their validity and effect on us. For example, we might send ourselves messages like, "That didn't go well," or "I feel stupid" without being aware we are doing it. When we are aware of the messages that we send ourselves, we can separate those that are true from those that are just an emotional response to a situation. When we have a chance to stop and think about it, we may realize that it isn't true.

By increasing our awareness of the messages that we send ourselves, we can make choices about what types of messages to send and which types to avoid. This gives us options to make choices in communicating with ourselves instead of falling into the same patterns. We can then choose to send ourselves more positive messages that can help improve how we perceive ourselves.

Self-Concept

Our self-concept is how we think about ourselves based on our perceptions and expectations. We develop our self-concept by communicating with ourselves and others. Our self-concept can be positive or negative depending upon the types of messages we receive. For example, if we tell ourselves that we feel we did a good job, it can bolster our self-concept and people may perceive us as more confident. When they do, they may treat us in a positive way reinforcing this self-concept. When other people like our friends, family, or co-workers tell us we've done a good job, it can bolster our self-concept so we see ourselves in a positive way. This is how perception can affect how we act, if others perceive us as more confident it can make their perception a reality.

Conversely, if we tell ourselves negative messages like we don't feel that we know what we are doing, others may pick up on our lack of confidence. They may perceive us as lacking ability, which can have a negative impact on our self-concept. In this way, how we communicate can have real and tangible consequences, so perceptions can become a reality. Sometimes if we hear messages long enough, we may eventually come to believe that they are true becoming a part of how we see ourselves.

When we are first born, we know very little about ourselves and the world around us. This motivates us to communicate with others in order to reduce uncertainty and find meaning in our experiences. One of our most basic needs is to know who we are as a person. This question is about how we develop a sense of ourselves and how we come to know who we are. We communicate with ourselves to find meaning in our experiences in order to understand ourselves more fully.

Communicating with ourselves helps to give us a sense of who we are. We are motivated to do so by the law of uncertainty because we might feel uncertainty about ourselves. When we feel that we do not know everything there is to know about ourselves, it gives us a desire to find out more. We want to reduce uncertainty about ourselves so that we are more able to fulfill our needs and wants, meet our expectations, and have satisfying relationships with others. This question gets at the core of who we are as a person and what it means to be human.

Developing your self-concept is about getting to know yourself, which can be one of the great adventures in life. People often take time to find themselves or to get to know themselves better. We do this because of the uncertainty we may feel about ourselves, about who we are, about our abilities, and about our future. We are born with little self awareness or self-concept, so we develop it as we get older. If we had a total understanding of ourselves there would be little motivation for self discovery, personal growth, or self improvement, which would make life less interesting. A lack of understanding motivates us to know more about ourselves by looking for meaning in ourselves and in our experiences. When we understand ourselves better, we are perceived by others as being more confident and stable making them more willing to invest in relationships with us.

We want to have a positive self-image. We want others to have a positive perception of us as well. This can motivate us to present a positive and confident image to others whether we feel it is true or not. We might have problems and shortcomings, insecurities and faults that we do not want others to see, or perhaps even want to look at ourselves. Instead of ignoring them, it can be helpful to be aware of them and work to improve them.

By increasing our self-awareness we not only know our skills and abilities, we also know our shortcomings. By knowing ourselves we can learn from others facilitating change and growth. By recognizing our shortcomings, and that there are things we do not know about ourselves, we can be motivated to improve our skills.

When we are born we know little about ourselves including why we are here. This can create uncertainty motivating us to look for meaning in our experiences to create a sense of purpose or reason for being here. One of our most basic needs is to have a sense of purpose in our lives by understanding why we were put on this earth. By knowing ourselves better, we can learn more about our purpose in life.

The nature of self-concept.

We develop our self-concept through communicating with others, however, there are other elements that may influence who we are. Part of who we are comes from our parents through our DNA and some comes from how we are brought up including our experiences. This is the question of whether it is nature or nurture that determines who we are. However, consider how a third factor could contribute to our self-concept.

Many believe that we all have a soul that is the essence of who we are as an individual and the basis of our personality. This is what makes each of us unique and distinctly different from every other person. If we believe that our soul leaves our body after we die, then it is reasonable to believe that our soul existed before we were born. If this is the case, it is also reasonable to believe that we have an essence of a personality in our body from the moment we are born.

If this element of our personal essence existed before we were born, it would constitute neither nature nor nurture because neither has come into play yet. It could to some extent predetermine our personality influencing our destiny. It is this third element that develops into our own unique self-concept influencing who we are as a person.

If we are born with a soul containing a personality, we can still be influenced by nature including our parents DNA, as well as nurture including the way we are brought up and our experiences. We are born with individual personality traits, however, it is through our experiences communicating with others that some of these characteristics come to the surface and develop, while others may not. By having free will, we can choose which characteristics to pursue and how to express them. For example, siblings who share the same parents and grow up in the same house may turn out to be very different. This can neither be attributed to nature or nurture, but to their personal essence or destiny.

The notion of destiny is an example of how the law of shared meaning can be used to reduce uncertainty because it can give meaning to our experiences and future expectations. People throughout history have believed that they had a destiny to fulfill and devoted their life to fulfilling that destiny. It has been a motivating force that has driven events throughout history, inspired individuals, motivated social and political movements, and even advanced the making of nations.

Some cultures and religions believe in not only destiny, but in predestination where our future is predetermined. Others believe in free will, that we have the power to determine our own destiny. While these two concepts may seem diametrically opposed, they can work together for us. While we may have a destiny or purpose, we have the free will to determine how to fulfill it. It is up to us to make the choices and take action to realize it.

For example, there once was a politician who was quite a colorful character. When he was asked if he had not entered politics what would he have done instead, his answer was not what you might expect. He said he would have liked to become an opera singer. While opera and politics seem very different, they have some similarities. Both involve performing in public, being around people, having an outgoing personality, and involves an element of drama. This is an example of how destiny and free will can work together giving us a sense of purpose and fulfillment. The politician's destiny was for being in the public eye, but how he fulfilled that destiny was determined by choice and free will.

We may feel that we have always had a sense of who we are or it may take a lifetime to figure that out. Determining our own destiny may be difficult because we do not see ourselves as others do. However, not knowing our destiny can give us the chance to try things out, explore possibilities, and have new experiences. It gives us time to develop our own self-concept and sense of identity. If we knew everything there was to know about ourselves, there would be little motivation for self exploration and we would miss out on some of the most meaningful experiences in life.

We are motivated by the law of uncertainty to reduce uncertainty. We are motivated by the law of shared meaning to understand ourselves and others. We are motivated by the law of investing to develop connections and relationships with others. However, we want to know more about the motivation for our own behavior. People are motivated to do what they do in order to fulfill their needs and wants, reduce uncertainty, and gain rewards.

So, why do people do what they do? People do what they do for the most part simply because they can. They are often able to do whatever they want given the opportunity and the ability. However, human behavior is generally limited by three factors.

1. Behavior is limited by physical reality. There are things people cannot do like fly unaided.

2. Behavior is limited by other people. When people do things that others do not want them to do, they may stop them. Our legal system was developed to limit people's behavior to what is considered acceptable.

3. Behavior is limited by themselves. This includes a person's individual social reality and rules of behavior. People are motivated to do the right thing and what they perceive is in

their best interest. Very few people commit crimes or fall off cliffs trying to fly even though they can. Everyone understands what is expected for reasonable behavior in a civil society and for the most part people abide by those rules for their own benefit.

How self-concept is created.

Our self-concept is the picture that we have of ourselves in our mind consisting of our perceptions and expectations. It develops slowly over time and as we get older becomes more stable and resistant to change. It is an important part of our own individual social reality motivating our behavior. We develop a self-concept because it fulfills our need to be a unique individual. We use it to fulfill the need for prestige, respect, status, and self-esteem. It helps us to answer the question of who we are by reducing uncertainty about ourselves. It motivates us to communicate with others to gain knowledge about ourselves.

We develop our self-concept partially based on the process of reflective communicating. This happens when we create our Great Idea and communicate it to others through connections across The Great Abyss and they communicate back to us. We use this feedback like a mirror to determine how we are being perceived by others because we cannot see ourselves as they see us. The perception process helps us to gather, select, organize, and interpret information other people send us to construct a picture of how we look to them. Some of this information we keep and some we discard. We are more likely to keep information that fits in with how we perceive ourselves and discard things that contradict our perceptions, whether they are accurate or not. The information that we keep becomes a part of our self-concept and how we see ourselves.

This is one reason why the way others respond to us can be helpful or hurtful to our self-concept. If we receive positive feedback, we feel good about ourselves. Conversely, if we receive negative feedback it can hurt our self-concept and make us feel bad about ourselves. This is why we seek out the approval or acceptance of others. It is why we want to be liked. If others like us then we must be likable. That is why it's important to be around people who are supportive of us and to avoid those who are overly negative because of the effect it can have on us and our self-concept.

While reflective feedback has the potential to influence our self-concept, by being aware of how it works we can decide how we want to use it. We can determine what is useful to us and what is not. We can let others know if their perception does not fit how we see ourselves. When people provide reflective feedback they may consciously or subconsciously wait to see if we accept it or not. If we accept it, it may confirm how they perceive us. If we reject it or correct their perception, they may be open to changing their perception of us.

For example, at work we may have been late once, but people may communicate the perception that we are never on time. If we do nothing to change that, it may confirm that impression whether it's true or not. It's up to us to correct that perception by letting them know that it is not accurate. Most of the time people will be open to changing their perception if you let them know in a positive manner. However, some people can form their own opinions and refuse to change them whether they are accurate or not, and so should be avoided.

While we really shouldn't care what other people think about us, the reality is that we do. We care because if people like us then we must be a good person because people like other people who are good. Instead of using reflective feedback, we could develop a more accurate self-concept through more effective self-awareness. We could utilize objective criteria based upon the things that we do. However, that would be more difficult and time consuming. So we use feedback from other people because it's easy to do and it happens so naturally we often don't notice it.

There are things in life that give us energy and make us feel rejuvenated. These include doing things that we like to do, being places we like to be, and being around people we like. However, we may feel full of energy and then for no apparent reason feel drained. This is because there are things that drain our energy making us feel tired and frustrated. There are people who give us energy and those that take it from us. Because we are busy, we may not be aware of this. We may have these feelings, but do not know why. It can be helpful to increase our awareness by writing down those things that both give and take energy from us. This can provide options on how we could maximize those things that give us energy and reduce those that take it from us.

Communicating with others and receiving feedback is not the only means by which we develop our self-concept. We also do this by comparing ourselves to others such as family members, friends, coworkers, neighbors, even famous people. We consciously and subconsciously compare ourselves to these people to measure how we think we are doing. We might look for others who have similar traits such as age, experience, education, or career. We might develop criteria based on what is important to us and what we think we should accomplish at certain times in our life. We are motivated to do this by uncertainty because we may not be sure we are doing what we are supposed to do and so we look at what other people are doing for comparison.

People utilize the following methods to form their self-concept.

- Self-concept from significant people. We are more likely to listen to feedback from people we know and who are important or significant to us because we are comfortable with them and what they have to say. This is because there is a low degree of uncertainty and a high degree of trust. We value their opinion and feel that they have our best interests at heart. These are people who are close to us like family and friends. We may seek out and ask for feedback from them when we need it.

- Self-concept and societal comparison. We look at other people to compare ourselves to in order to reduce uncertainty about ourselves. We might look at our coworkers to see how our job or salary compares to theirs. We might look at our friends and neighbors to compare the possessions they have such as their house or car. Society has a degree of influence over our self-concept because it creates social reality, which can communicate what constitutes success. Since we want to be successful, we look to others to see how well they are doing and then compare ourselves to them. Social reality communicates what is important, what is valued, what possessions to have, and how to behave. Rather than comparing ourselves to others, we can develop our own concept of success.

- Self-concept and expectations. The expectations people have of us can alter our self-concept because we have to cooperate with them to fulfill needs and wants. We may feel that we have to change our behavior to meet their expectations in order to reduce uncertainty, so that they will be willing to invest their time and resources in us. This means that we may have to change how we see ourselves in order to fit in. However, if their expectations are strong enough, and the rewards are great enough, we may end up behaving in ways we might not normally consider.

- Self-concept and media comparison. The media can have an influence over how we perceive ourselves and develop our self-concept. We might use what we see in the media as a gauge to evaluate ourselves to determine if we are successful. The media can create unrealistic expectations because what we see is often perfected by professionals for maximum impact. What we see can be distorted, edited, and may not reflect reality creating standards that may be unachievable.

- Self-concept and advertising. Advertising has the ability to influence social reality because it exploits our natural tendency for social comparison. It seeks to persuade us that in order to be successful, well liked, or to have a positive self-image we need to do or have certain things. Messages are designed to cut through the interference of The Great Abyss to get our attention. The purpose is to provide information to alter our perception that affects self-concept motivating us to do what they want.

The process of how we form our self-concept is an example of how we compare our perception of reality to our expectations. This creates a picture of ourselves where we might measure up or fall short. It can be based upon accurate as well as unrealistic information. This process is significant because it can motivate our actions and how we behave around others. If our perceptions and expectations are realistic and are fairly close to each other, we can feel more confident helping us to be successful in what we do. Conversely, if our perception is unrealistically negative, when we compare it to unrealistic expectations, we may feel inadequate so we act in ways that are less likely to be successful in what we do. In this way perceptions can create social reality.

Our perception is based upon the information we receive from others, society, and the media. This means the information we have that forms our perceptions may not accurately reflect reality. This can give us unrealistic expectations of ourselves, which if difficult to fulfill, may create unnecessary unhappiness. For example, our perception may be that we do more work and make less money than our coworkers resulting in dissatisfaction with our job motivating us to ask for a raise or quit. Conversely, if our perception is that we are getting fair rewards for our work we are more likely to feel good, bolstering our self-concept motivating us to do more for others.

Using comparisons as a basis for self-concept can lead to dissatisfaction because there will always be somebody who we will perceive as more successful. This can occur when we make judgments based upon a few specifics and ignoring others giving us a distorted image for comparison. We may pay attention to a person's salary without considering other factors such as the hours they work or the stress they may be under. We tend to look for information that confirms our existing perceptions and filter out other information that might be contrary to what we think we know.

Self-concept and expectations.

Our self-concept can also be affected by how well our expectations match our perceptions based upon feedback from others. Perceptions and expectations are intangible qualities that exist in our mind that can create physical reality. They can influence how we communicate with ourselves affecting our behavior. Our perceptions can differ from actual reality creating an inaccurate, even distorted view of ourselves. Part of our self-concept can be based upon the difference between our perceptions and expectations because we all have expectations about ourselves and how we want others to perceive us.

If the feedback we receive meets or exceeds our expectations it can create a positive self-concept, feelings of self worth, and increased confidence. If the feedback does not meet our expectations we may become frustrated, upset, and even angry. This can be influenced in part by our perception of reality being significantly different from the actual reality that others perceive. We may have unrealistically high or low expectations of ourselves, and when we do not receive the feedback we expect, it can create a distorted perception of ourselves. If we did not get the feedback we expect or think we deserve we may become frustrated, angry, or lash out at others.

Perception of our self-concept can be self perpetuating because we communicate with others based upon how we see ourselves. This can affect our behavior and how we communicate with them. Others perceive this behavior and may interpret it similar to how we perceive ourselves. They respond appropriately based upon their perception and interpretation of our behavior. Then the response we receive can verify our perception of ourselves.

Most of the time these perceptions are close to reality, but if they are not the positive ones can cancel out the negative creating a balance. However, we can get into cycles where we have an inaccurate self-concept that others perceive and reflect back to us reinforcing our distorted perspective. If we are unaware that this is happening, it could cause our self-concept to inflate unrealistically or diminish needlessly giving us a false sense of who we are.

If we have an overly negative perception of ourselves, we may send overly negative messages that are then reflected back to us. We may receive both positive and negative messages, but only pay attention to the negative ones. Positive messages might be filtered out by The Great Abyss or we may not even look for them as we do not expect them. This creates a negative cycle that can be difficult to break. Through awareness, we can check the messages that we are getting and use other information to develop our self-concept in order to take control of the process and break the cycle.

Our perceptions can also create a reality that affects our self-concept. We constantly form expectations based upon our perceptions in order to function in everyday life. We have expectations that we may communicate to others. We look for information to fulfill expectations through the process of communicating. We may filter out information that does not support our expectations because we are not necessarily looking for it. Our perceptions are based upon the information we perceive, so our expectations now become a part of our set of perceptions.

This information can confirm our expectations and become part of our perception of reality. If we believe these perceptions to be true, we can take action based upon them whether they are accurate or not. By taking action we may actually make these perceptions a reality. For instance, if we are in a relationship and have the expectation that a person will breakup with us, we look for evidence to support that expectation. If we do not look for evidence to the contrary, everything we perceive may be interpreted as supporting our expectation because we might filter out anything that contradicts it. This can turn our expectations into perceptions. It could motivate us to take action and breakup with them when the reality is they never intended to do so.

Self-concept development.

Think back to your earliest memories. Think about when you first became aware of yourself and when you started forming perceptions about who you are. It may be difficult to pinpoint a specific time because self-awareness develops gradually from the time we are very young. We go through several stages in the development of our self-concept as children, adolescents, and adults.

As children we communicate primarily with our parents and family because we are dependent on them to fulfill our needs and wants. Much of our early self-concept comes from our parents and family because these are the people who are most influential in our lives. This is because they help us to reduce uncertainty and share meanings, so we invest the majority of our time in relationships with them. Our family establishes boundaries, structure, routines, rules, and protects us from harm. It is a place where we first learn language skills, learn about culture, our history, and the world around us. We communicate with them and receive reflected feedback from them in return. This means that our first sense of self-concept is developed primarily from interaction with our family.

As we get older, we become more self-aware motivating us to develop our own self-concept as an individual separate from our family. While we are still dependent on our family for many of our needs and wants, we have an increasing need to fulfill them on our own. This motivates us to start making our own decisions, so we can assert more control over our lives. If our family's perception of us is resistant to change it might increase uncertainty potentially creating tension and conflict.

As a young adult, our self-concept is shifting from being based upon reflected communicating with our family to communicating with our peers. As our self-concept changes we may seek validation and support from others. If we don't get it from our family we might seek it from others outside the family. If our family resists this change, it could motivate us to disengage from them in order to develop an independent self-concept. If our family is supportive and open to our need for change, a new self-concept can develop that combines both the new and old identity.

As we become an adult, we have more experiences communicating with others that contribute to our self-concept making it more fully developed. As an adult our self-concept tends to stabilize and can be relatively constant for the rest of our lives giving us a feeling of security. While this helps to give us a sense of who we are, it can also make us resistant to change even when it may be beneficial. We may stay with our self-concept even if it is negative because it's comfortable and change can be uncomfortable increasing uncertainty.

Our self-concept undergoes change from the time we are young until we become an adult. After that, it remains fairly stable making it more difficult to change. However, there are some aspects of our self-concept that are more susceptible to change based upon changing circumstances.

- Self-respect is the degree to which we respect ourselves, believe in ourselves, and value ourselves as a person. Our experiences can change how we feel. For example, if we make a mistake or hurt someone we may blame ourselves and lose some self respect. In order to protect our self respect we may blame others to avoid taking responsibility.

- Self acceptance is the degree to which we accept ourselves and feel comfortable with who we are. If our self acceptance is high, we may feel comfortable with who we are and resist change. If our self acceptance is low, it may lead to dissatisfaction with ourselves. There may be a difference between our perception of acceptance and how we are actually accepted by others. This can create tension if we have a high self acceptance, but don't feel accepted by others. This disconnect can leave us wondering why people are not more accepting of us because we know that we are a really good person with a lot to offer.

- Self-esteem is the degree to which we value ourselves as being a worthwhile person. While our self-concept is fairly consistent, self-esteem is more flexible fluctuating up and down based upon how we feel about our circumstances. We may have a reasonably positive self-concept, however, our self-esteem may be particularly low from recent events like the loss of a job or relationship. Our self-esteem can be affected by our perceptions and expectations. If our perceptions do not meet our expectations, it can lower our self-esteem whether or not it is actually true.

Having an awareness of how we create our self-concept can help us to avoid distorted information that can be harmful to us. If we receive feedback that is negative or overly critical, it can contribute needlessly to a poor self-image. If we receive information that is overly positive, it can give us an inflated sense of ourselves encouraging arrogance. Since our self-concept is to some degree subjective it can easily become distorted. An overly high or low self-concept can be caused by inaccurate perceptions or unrealistic expectations. Sometimes people overcompensate to cover feelings of inadequacy or insecurity by becoming arrogant or abusive. Being overly confident can be harmful because it makes us resistant to feedback that could be beneficial to us.

It's helpful to be aware of this process because having a positive self-concept has many benefits. People who have a positive self-concept are generally more respectful of others, work harder, and strive for higher standards. They look realistically at their abilities and want to improve themselves. They are not overly critical of others and take criticism without feeling a need to defend themselves. They are comfortable trying new things and taking risks. They are comfortable complementing others and giving them credit for their accomplishments. People who have a negative self-concept tend to think less of others and themselves. They tend to do less and do not try to meet higher standards. They may have a tendency to defend themselves against criticism and are uncomfortable sharing ideas with others who may not agree with them. They may take the safe approach by being unwilling to take risks or try new things.

We can have a natural tendency to focus on the negative more than on what is positive. This is not because we are overly pessimistic, it's because negativity increases uncertainty making us uncomfortable, so it gets our attention. We may pay less attention to things that are positive because they are less likely to get through the interference of The Great Abyss than something negative. When something goes well the tension is resolved making it more comfortable reducing uncertainty, so it is less likely to get our attention. When something is negative it is generally not resolved, so it creates tension that gets our attention. Because it is uncomfortable it cuts through the interference, so it can motivate us to take action.

When it comes to our self-concept, we are more likely to be motivated to look for information that confirms how we already perceive ourselves. We might put ourselves in situations and spend time around other people who will confirm our self-concept. We do this because their confirmation is a form of acceptance that is a social reward. When others confirm what we already know, we feel that we are right and we would rather be right than wrong.

When we come across information that contradicts what we feel we already know, it can create tension increasing uncertainty that can make us uncomfortable. This tension must be resolved by either changing what we already know or dismissing the new information.

It can be easier to dismiss new information than to change what we know because it feels safe and secure.

We have a natural tendency to seek out information from relationships with others who confirm our current self-concept. We might reject others who have a different perception of our self-concept even if it is more accurate or more positive. We do this because we develop a mindset that information contrary to what we already know will not make a difference because it will not change who we are. It can be easier to rationalize or justify the current situation than to change it. It can sometimes be easier to attack anyone who challenges our perceptions then to change them.

It can be difficult to break out of a negative self-concept because we are motivated to confirm what we think we already know. It can help to understand how this process works to get more accurate feedback from others and take advantage of naturally occurring change. We can seek out feedback from people who are positive and supportive of us, and avoid being around those who are negative. We can increase our awareness and seek out more accurate information for a more realistic view of ourselves. Doing this can help us develop a desire to change and a willingness to work at it.

Developing an awareness of how we create and maintain our self-concept can help us to have control over how we perceive ourselves rather than having it control us. Most of the time this process works without having to think too much about it making it easy for negative and inaccurate information to become part of how we see ourselves. Not all feedback we receive should be considered when it comes to our self-concept. We should protect ourselves from others who are overly negative or critical and information that could damage how we see ourselves.

We should seek out feedback from people we trust, who are honest, and who are supportive of us. We can reduce or eliminate relationships where we receive negative feedback that can damage our self-esteem. We can develop a process of awareness and self monitoring so that we can form our own criteria for evaluating ourselves to rely more on our own perceptions and less on the opinions of others. By utilizing awareness and options we can create a more realistic and balanced self image that is acceptable to us. This can help us to have better self-esteem and a more accurate self-concept.

Evaluating self-concept.

It can be helpful to evaluate your self-concept and how you developed it by making an inventory of your strengths, weaknesses, accomplishments, and areas you would like to improve. Writing it down helps to validate the information you have to see how accurate or relevant it is. You might discover that your self-concept is based on outdated information and experiences that happened long ago. Negative experiences tend to stay longer in our memory even when they may no longer be relevant. This is because they represent unresolved tension, which is uncomfortable so it gets our attention.

The purpose of doing this is to create a more accurate and realistic picture of yourself. Doing this can help to form your own self-concept relying less on information from other people. By having realistic expectations based on clear perceptions of yourself, you can recognize your strengths while putting your weaknesses in perspective. Doing this can help to change an outdated or negative self-concept, which can help you feel better about yourself and improve your relationships with others.

We all have a picture in our mind of the person we want to be. We want to improve ourselves to reach that ideal picture, however, we often get sidetracked by everyday responsibilities such as work, family, and the hundreds of other things that use up our time and energy. This can make it difficult for us to find time for self improvement.

People change for basically one of two reasons, they want to change or they have to change. Most of the time we do the things we need or have to do. All too often we never get to the things we want or ought to do. Good intentions like making plans are no substitute for actually doing something. It's important to have the resources and support to make necessary changes. Change is difficult because it involves hard work, even though it can be rewarding. Meaningful change must come from within ourselves by deciding that we are going to change. And isn't it better to change because we want to, rather than waiting until we have to change?

In order to reduce uncertainty we need to be able to open our mind to new ideas, new ways of doing things, and think about what we already know in a new or different way. This can be one of the most challenging things we do because the law of uncertainty creates tension between change and stability. Just as there is no one right way to communicate, there is no one right way to do this. We can find our own way to balance these tensions in order to consider new ideas.

We can do this by developing a means to add new information to what we already know without undermining it. This can be difficult to do because we are busy doing everyday tasks that need to be done, so we don't always have the time or energy to think about new things. By setting aside some time to process the information we take in, we can consider possibilities we might otherwise overlook or discard.

Typically, when we have something we need to do we set out to do it. Along the way opportunities may present themselves, but we may not be open to them. We might reduce uncertainty to the point where we become focused on just getting things done. This prevents us from perceiving new information that may be around us. We may not consider other options until something happens to increase uncertainty motivating us to do so.

By utilizing the power of the law of uncertainty, we can develop ways to initiate this process when we want to, before we are forced to do it. By increasing awareness, we can understand how the perception process works in its normal state in order to be receptive to new information. We can utilize the process of communicating by understanding how others communicate their Great Idea making connections with us, so that we can make choices about our frame of reference and what to filter out. By being aware of how we use the perception process, we can develop more options on how to approach the information that's available to us so we can effectively utilize it to make it useful to us.

A common way to clear our mind and relax is by getting away. When we are around familiar surroundings, we tend to fall into familiar patterns and habits. Familiar surroundings can be a constant reminder of what we have to do, which can keep our minds thinking in the same way. Getting away can be like pressing a reset button for our mind motivating us to break out of old habits and do things differently, which can help us to think differently. If we can't physically get away, we could mentally get away. Some methods to do this include using yoga to relax, meditation for reflection, or prayer to seek answers. These methods can increase our awareness to help us see familiar things in a new way giving us more options.

Listening

The words listening and hearing are often used interchangeably, however, they are two separate processes that are not the same. Hearing is a natural physiological process where someone or something does something that produces sound waves that are transmitted through the air making vibrations on our eardrums creating sound. Hearing is passively receiving sounds, whereas listening is communicating.

Listening includes the process of receiving sound waves, but it also involves perceiving, understanding, organizing, interpreting, remembering, and responding to what we hear. Listening is like communicating, we do it all the time. We have done it for so long that it has become second nature, so we don't think about it very much. However, listening is like other communicating skills, we can develop these skills to reduce uncertainty to communicate more effectively with others. This makes listening an important individual communicating skill to help us better understand ourselves and others.

Listening is one of the most important ways we reduce uncertainty because the law of uncertainty motivates us to listen so we know what is happening around us. It provides us with the information we need to make decisions in order to function on a daily basis. It is necessary not only for survival, but also for enjoyment, gaining information, and understanding others.

When we share meaning we not only communicate with one another, we need to listen to one another. Listening can communicate many things such as consideration, concern, empathy, friendship, and respect. We interpret not only what people say, but also the sounds we hear in the environment around us by investing them with meaning. We give meaning to words, the sounds around us, music, noises, and many other things we hear.

We are motivated by the law of investing to listen to others so that we can invest our time and resources in relationships with them. We place a value on listening and when we listen to others we show that we value them and what they have to say. When others listen to us we feel closer and more connected to them. Because listening takes time and energy, when we listen to others we may expect to receive something in return. We expect that they will reciprocate and listen to what we have to say.

Listening is what makes the process of communicating work because it is an important connection by which we communicate our Great Idea to others and they provide us with feedback. When we communicate our Great Idea to others, we expect them to listen to us. Conversely, when they communicate with us to provide feedback, they expect that we will listen to them.

Listening is an important part of getting feedback from others because it is how we know if our message has been received and understood. By listening, we adjust our frame of reference to focus on what others have to say. We avoid filtering out information by paying attention to them. It is the means by which we understand and comprehend the feedback they provide.

Just as everyone communicates for reason, everyone listens for a reason. So, when you communicate with others, give them a reason to listen to you. When you listen let people know that they are important to you, that you respect their ideas, and that you are willing to consider what they have to say.

These are several reasons why listening skills can help us to communicate more effectively with others.

- Time. We spend a majority of our time communicating with others and much of that time is listening. Effective listening skills can save us time and energy.

- Information. Listening is the primary means by which we gain information. The better the information we have, the better decisions we can make.

- Learning. We learn how to do things by listening to others, so we don't have to figure everything out for ourselves saving us time and energy.

- Feedback. By listening to feedback we know if our messages are being understood by others, so we can communicate more effectively.

- Growth. By listening we learn about ourselves and the world around us in ways that help facilitate growth.

- Relationships. Listening is essential to creating and maintaining all types of relationships. It is how we learn about others and how they get to know us. Listening shows that we respect and care about others.

- Support. By listening we strengthen our relationships showing others that we support them.

- Likeability. People who listen to others are generally considered more likable because they are seen as considerate of others.

- Career. Listening is an essential skill for our career because it helps us to do our job better. Listening to others who are more experienced can help us improve our skills benefiting our career.

- Self-concept. Listening to others is part of the process by which we develop our own sense of identity and self-concept.

- Awareness. Listening increases our awareness of ourselves, others, and what's going on around us. Increasing awareness makes us more informed and better able to communicate with others.

- Options. Listening to others can provide a source of new ideas giving us more options on how to do things improving our chances of success.

Listening interference.

In the process of communicating, there is the interference of The Great Abyss that prevents our message from getting to others. This interference can prevent us from listening to what others communicate to us.

Even though we know it's important to listen, there are times when we do not. It's helpful to be aware of the reasons why we don't listen, so that we can make conscious choices about what we listen to and how we listen.

Why we unintentionally don't listen.
- Physiological. There may be physical impairments that hinder the ability to listen.
- External. This is external noise that is around us which affects how we listen like air conditioners or the traffic outside.
- Prejudgments. We might not listen to things that we feel we have heard before or that have no value to us.
- Wandering. We think faster than we speak, so our mind can wander and we stop listening.
- Overload. There are times when there is too much to listen to, so we block things out.
- Difficult. We are less likely to listen to things that are complex or difficult to understand.
- Unfamiliar. When messages are abstract or unfamiliar, we don't listen because we don't comprehend them.
- Preoccupation. We don't listen because we are thinking about other things that are more interesting or that we need to do.

Why we passively don't listen.
- Time. Listening takes time and we get busy or have more important things to do.
- Effort. Listening takes effort and there are times we don't have the energy to listen.
- Selection. We do not have the time to listen to everything, so we have to select what we listen to and filter out everything else.
- Interests. We listen to things that we find interesting and filter out things that are boring or that we have heard before.
- Usefulness. We listen to things that we feel will be useful to us or provide a benefit and filter out things that we do not.
- Style. We decide if we are going to listen to something based on the style in which the information is presented.

Why we actively don't listen.
- Critical. We don't listen to information that we do not agree with, approve of, or support.
- Different. We don't listen to things that are a different from what we already know or that challenges what we know.
- Social reality. We don't listen to information that contradicts our perception of social reality because it can be uncomfortable.
- Attitude. We don't listen because we know better or the other person does not know what they are talking about.
- Assumptions. We don't listen because we assume it is not important or we have heard it before.
- Entertainment. We don't listen to things that are not entertaining enough to keep our interest.
- Appearance. We don't listen based on a person's appearance or nonverbal behaviors.

Why we intentionally don't listen.
- Content. People might act like they are not interested in what others have to say.
- Value. People might act as if they have nothing to gain, as if what others have to say has no value or benefit to them.
- Domineering. People might try to monopolize or dominate the conversation by talking about themselves.
- Diversions. People might use diversionary tactics like changing the subject to stop others from speaking.
- Defensiveness. People might act like it's a legal proceeding, listening to gather evidence to defend themselves or to prosecute others.

Listening levels of engagement.

Just as we have our own style of communicating, we have our own style of listening. Our style of listening is based upon our past experiences, preferences, perceptions, expectations, needs and wants, and desired outcomes. By increasing our awareness, we can approach each situation based upon its unique characteristics to determine the best approach. Increasing our awareness gives us options, and when we have options to choose from we have a greater variety of skills giving us a greater chance for a successful desired outcome.

Effective listening involves more than just hearing. It is a general term that covers a wide variety of activities. We can listen to the radio, our boss at work, or to our friends and family. Each of these situations involves different types of listening because they each have a different desired outcome.

We have different expectations of what we hope to gain by listening. We may want to gain new information, show someone we support them, learn a new skill, improve our career, develop a relationship, or be entertained. Our reasons for listening create levels of engagement. These levels are based on the degree to which we are engaged in what we are listening to based on our desired outcome for listening. Levels of engagement help us to determine the appropriate approach for communicating in each situation.

Level I. Listening for hearing. We listen to the background noises around us to tell us information about our surroundings. We listen to traffic sounds, a ringing telephone, or an alarm. This type of listening fulfills our need for information to help us get through the day. Some sounds can warn us of danger. Most of the time this level of listening takes little effort and we do it without thinking much about it.

Level II. Listening for enjoyment. We listen to fulfill our need for enjoyment, relaxation, appreciation, and entertainment. This includes listening to music, the radio, television, or other forms of entertainment. Most of the time we listen passively rather than listening for content or to remember what we heard.

Level III. Listening for awareness. We listen to fulfill our need for information and increase our awareness about what is going on around us. This involves listening to news and information, as well as other people.

Level IV. Listening to understand. We listen not only to gain awareness, but also to understand and comprehend the information we hear. We use this type of listening at work and in our relationships.

Level V. Listening to remember. We listen not only to gain and understand information, but also to retain it so that it is useful to us in the future. When we listen to remember, we need to actively concentrate on what we are hearing and understand it. We may write things down so that we can look at them later to reinforce our memory.

Level VI. Listening to others. We listen to other people's thoughts, feelings, problems, and concerns to show that we support them. We change our point of view from our own to the other person's perspective by concentrating on their desired outcome instead of our own. This level of listening is essential to building relationships by making others feel valued and important.

Level VII. Listening to respond. There are times when people want us to listen and support them without giving them feedback. Other times, they want us to respond to what they have to say. It's important to know the difference because if feedback is given when it is not wanted, it can be perceived as criticism. Our response should be honest, but tactful and considerate of the other person.

Level VIII. Listening to evaluate. We listen not only to understand, but also to evaluate the information we hear. This involves comprehension and analysis to determine the accuracy and validity of the information we receive. We consider the credibility and motives of the originator of the message to help us from being manipulated or persuaded to do something we don't want to do.

The listening process.

Listening is a process that is comprised of several stages that we go through without thinking much about them. By being aware of how these work, we can listen more effectively. Listening works very similar to the perception process described in Chapter 1.

1. Hearing. Listening is a physiological process. It is how we receive sound waves transmitted through the air.

2. Receiving. Listening is not only auditory, it is supported by our other senses to complete the message. We hear the words people are saying, but we also see nonverbal behaviors such as facial expressions and gestures to tell us how to interpret what we hear.

3. Attention. To listen effectively we need to pay attention to cut through the interference of The Great Abyss. It helps to be aware of our filters and frames of reference that edit what we hear. Messages get through to us depending upon our needs and wants, interests, and desired outcomes. This part of the process is motivated by the law of uncertainty to reduce uncertainty.

4. Selection. We select information by evaluating what we hear to determine its usefulness because we cannot possibly listen to or use everything we might hear. Selection is when we choose what we will listen to and what we will ignore. It is based upon our needs, wants, and desired outcomes.

5. Organization. When we listen, information does not necessarily come in any particular order. It can seem chaotic, coming in random bits and pieces that we need to organize into recognizable patterns so we can understand and use them. If it fits in with something we already know it is more easily understood. Organization makes information easier to recall so it can be more useful to us in the future because it reduces uncertainty.

6. Understanding. In order for information to be useful to us, we need to give it meaning. We are motivated to do this by the law of shared meaning. We make sense of the information we hear by comparing it to our past knowledge. If it does not fit in with what we know we may discard it.

7. Interpreting. By interpreting information we give it meaning beyond what is actually contained in the message. We use it to draw conclusions and determine what it means for us. This is why even when people have the same information, they might interpret it differently based on their own individual perspectives.

8. Remembering. Information is more useful to us when we are able to recall it at a later time. We tend to remember only about half of what we hear and after awhile only about half of that. We can utilize techniques to help us remember information such as acronyms, mnemonics, and other word tricks or by taking notes. Remembering is important because it makes information useful to us long after we have received it. The more important and useful information is to us, the more likely we are to remember it. How we use this information is influenced by the law of investing.

9. Responding. There are times when we listen to others that it is important to respond appropriately to what they say. This shows consideration for their ideas, respect for them, and provides them with feedback. This can take the form of reviewing what they said, asking questions, and relating information from our own experiences. Responding can be both verbal and nonverbal using verbal expressions such as "yes" or "no." We can respond with affirming nonverbal behavior including eye contact, head nodding, and facial expressions like smiling. We can use responding to determine the accuracy of our understanding and to clarify information. Responding provides feedback to show support without necessarily agreeing or disagreeing with them. When we do not respond it can be perceived as rejection not only of what they have to say, but also of them as a person.

Listening skills.

We assume that everyone knows how to listen because we may have the perception it doesn't take any particular skill. Listening skills are like other communicating skills that can be developed and improved.

These are some options to help develop effective listening skills.

- Consider the desired outcome of others. Whenever we listen to someone consider their desired outcome or purpose for speaking. Determine if they want help, to share information, persuade us, or to self-disclose. By understanding their desired outcome, we can avoid misunderstandings that can make communicating more difficult. If this is not clear, ask them because people may frequently talk about one thing when it is really something else bothering them. As an effective listener you can tactfully draw them out.

- Consider your desired outcome. We listen to others for a reason, so what is your reason for listening? We are motivated to listen to reduce uncertainty, to share meaning with others, and to invest in relationships. Listening is an important means by which we understand ourselves, others, and the world around us. So, being clear about why we are listening to others helps us to know what to listen for and how to listen.

- Avoiding misunderstandings. By knowing both our own and the other person's desired outcome, we can avoid misunderstandings. For example, someone may want your support and when you try to be helpful and fix their problem it could be a source of tension. Consider that the other person may not actually want you to do anything, so trying to do something could make things worse.

- Work together. Listening can be a collaborative process where both people work together to come up with something new rather than competing to see who gets their way. Looking for common ground shows that you are considerate of their point of view. This does not necessarily mean you have to agree with them, you are still free to have your own ideas or disagree.

- Time. In order to listen effectively, it's helpful to make the best use of everyone's time. Establish a time when everyone can listen and give yourself enough time so that they can express themselves thoroughly, so they don't feel like they are being rushed. Take time to prepare to listen. Avoid bad timing when people are in a bad mood or are rushed for time. By establishing a time that is mutually acceptable you give yourself enough time to listen. Have a definite ending time so the other person focuses on what's important and things don't go on indefinitely.

- Place. Choose an appropriate place that is conducive to listening where you can be comfortable. Avoid discussing important issues in an inappropriate place like in public or in front of others. Having a place to listen that is free of distractions and interruptions can help you focus your attention and energy on what they have to say. The best setting for listening is a room free of external noise, that is comfortable, and provides privacy.

- Respond. Providing feedback and appropriate responses shows that you are interested and engaged in what they have to say. Provide verbal responses like saying yes, and nonverbal responses like smiling and nodding. Without interrupting, ask open ended questions that draws them out. Clarify information because people do not always say what they mean. Use nonverbal behavior to focus your attention by orientating yourself toward them. Wait until the other person has had a chance to finish what they are saying before responding.

- Emotions. People may want us to listen so they can express their feelings and emotions. When we care about someone it's easy to get caught up in the moment and absorb their emotions as our own. This can motivate us to respond with the same emotional intensity making things worse. It's helpful to stay calm, don't tell them how they should be feeling, and don't characterize their feelings as right or wrong. It's easy to tell them they shouldn't be feeling bad and should be happy because we care about their well being. However, this can make things worse because it discounts how they feel. If it seems like they are getting mad at you chances are it's not really about you.

Reasoning

Analytical reasoning is the process by which we use an established set of rules to make an argument or come to conclusions. It helps us to evaluate the claims people make and to improve the effectiveness of how we communicate with others. This can be considered the highest level of listening because it utilizes the other elements of the listening process. Analytical reasoning is the process of evaluating information, solving problems, and making decisions.

Analytical reasoning consists of the following elements.

1. Rules. Analytical reasoning utilizes a set of rules and methods for obtaining and analyzing information to reach a conclusion. The purpose is to set aside personal preferences to objectively discover the truth. For example, our judicial system uses analytical reasoning and an established set of procedural rules and laws that govern the process of presenting and utilizing evidence in a court of law to make a determination of guilt or innocence.

2. Claim. Analytical reasoning begins with a claim you want to prove. For example, a lawyer wants to prove that their client is innocent. A claim asserts what facts are relevant to the case and what evidence can be used. It can determine values such as whether something is right or wrong, good or bad. It can affect how to proceed in order to reach a conclusion.

3. Criteria. We hear people making claims about all kinds of things every day. Instead of using objective criteria to make a claim, people may present their own opinions as fact. Analytical reasoning utilizes clearly defined criteria that consists of a preestablished means to evaluate the claim. For example, criteria to evaluate a new building might include energy efficiency or cost effectiveness. The criteria must be universally recognized, objective, and based on the evidence instead of on opinion or emotion.

4. Evidence. Information must be presented to support a claim and its validity or truthfulness. Evidence can include facts, statistics, illustrations, observation, experience, comparisons, descriptions, and expert or individual testimony. Evidence needs to be accurate and objective, it must stand up to scrutiny, and be based on fact rather than inference or personal opinion. It can be evaluated using established criteria to determine its validity and credibility. It should be clear, easily understood, and support the claim otherwise it may undermine the argument. Building an argument is like building a wall with evidence as the bricks and reasoning as the mortar to hold them together.

5. Source. In order to evaluate the claim, the source of the information should be evaluated using the same criteria. Information does not simply just exist on its own, it must come from somewhere and where it comes from can make a difference. A source should be trustworthy and credible, honest and reliable. There are many types of sources like research institutions, associations, universities, government, companies, organizations, groups, and individuals. The credibility of a source can come from expertise, experience, education, training, credentials, and reputation. Knowing the source is important because the more credible the source, usually the better the information.

6. Organization. This is the order in which evidence is presented to support the claim. Organization involves what information is selected to use and the method in which it is presented. We can use different methods of organization to help find solutions to problems, as well as determine their causes. Several methods are described in Chapter 5.

7. Findings. The purpose of this process is to establish findings that support the claim. The findings include a conclusion or summary of your argument. It includes new knowledge that has been gained in the process. It can be used to determine if the initial claim is true or false. For example, evidence that is presented in a court trial uses reasoning to reach a finding of guilt or innocence. However, most of the time findings are not as straightforward.

Fallacies.

In the process of communicating, interference can keep others from understanding your Great Idea. In the process of analytical reasoning, interference can prevent you from coming up with valid findings. The purpose of analytical reasoning is to come up with the best possible solution, however, there can be flaws in the process that creates interference leading to faulty conclusions. There can be flaws in each step of the process including the validity of the evidence, the manner of reasoning, the nature of the source, and the determination of the findings.

Flaws in reasoning are called fallacies and increasing your awareness of how they are used can help you to avoid using them in the arguments you make and in evaluating the claims other people make. These claims can be found in the media, in advertising, organizations asking for support, elected officials and government policies, or a journalist reporting a story. These methods of reasoning can be applied to determine the validity of the argument.

In order to evaluate a claim, it is helpful to be aware of these commonly used fallacies.

- False evidence. Evidence may be distorted, faulty, slanted, or personal opinion presented as fact.

- False generalizations. Making generalizations based on too few examples that are not applicable to a larger group.

- False crisis. People can be motivated by crisis and a fabricated crisis can motivate people to do things they might otherwise not do.

- False history. You may hear someone say, "This is the way we've always done it." They are claiming that doing something for a long period of time makes it valid. Because times change, what has been done in the past may not be valid today.

- False analogy. Analogies compare two things that are similar to transfer the characteristics of one to another. A false analogy compares two things that are not really similar.

- False causation. Claiming that one event causes another or that a series of events will conclude in a specific result without establishing that there are any actual relationships between them.

- False connection. Making a claim that does not follow from its basic premise by creating a connection when none exists. Organizing evidence in a way that is not consistent with established methods of organization.

- False choice. Presenting a choice between several possibilities knowing that all except one are undesirable or unworkable. Or presenting several choices that are just restatements of the same thing.

- False authority. Utilizing someone who is not an authority or expert in the field in which they present evidence. A common fallacy of this type is that being well known or a celebrity constitutes expertise or credibility.

- False conclusion. Presenting valid information and reasoning that does not support the findings or conclusions.

- Missing information. Presenting only a portion of the information that supports the claim while leaving out other information that discredits it.

- Diversion. Creating a false issue to divert people's attention from another issue. When an argument doesn't have merit on its own, an alternative argument on a more pressing issue diverts people's attention so they don't examine the first argument as closely.

- Circular reasoning. Presenting a claim as the findings without offering supporting evidence. The reasoning goes in a circle because no new information is added, so the claim is used as its own evidence.

- Ambiguity. Purposeful ambiguity is being unclear in order to confuse others so they won't follow your reasoning. This can be done by using language that is overly technical, ambiguous, or confusing so that flaws in an argument won't be noticed.

- Incomplete. This approach is used when only parts of an argument hold true. It is used when an entire argument or claim does not have validity or enough evidence to support it.

- Emotion. Rather than appealing to reasoning or evidence, this approach uses emotional appeals to motivate people to take action. Some of the most effective emotional appeals utilize the law of uncertainty by appealing to fear or anger. Other methods include appealing to sympathy, nostalgia, or guilt.

- Herding. This is based on the concept of herding cattle by reasoning that people will do something because others are doing it. This works because people may follow others thinking that they know something they do not. They are motivated to follow because they don't want to miss out on something. A variation on this is stampeding the herd, motivating people to take action by creating fear or a false crisis.

- Assumptions. Much of what we do is based upon assumptions. We could not function if we had to question the validity of everything we do every day. However, assumptions are all too often treated as if they are facts or evidence, which they are not. It is common to take one assumption and then pile on another and another until they are taken as fact. When one of the arguments does not hold true, everything falls apart.

- Accusations. This involves undermining a person's credibility for the purpose of discrediting their argument. If an opponent cannot discredit a person's argument, they may attack the person in hopes that people will not listen to their argument or anything else they may say. While source credibility is important, an argument may still have validity and should be evaluated on its own merit.

- Repetition makes right. This is a common method of utilizing repetition of information in place of reasoning. Information is repeated over and over until it begins to take on a validity of its own.

- Correlation used as causation. This is a commonly used fallacy where people claim that one event is the cause of another when they only exist at the same time. A correlation is when two or more things have an interdependent relationship or they may occur simultaneously. Causation is when one event or action causes another having a direct effect on it.

Creativity

Creativity could be considered an inverse approach to analytical reasoning. It involves more than just our ability to evaluate existing information, it is about our ability to use our imagination to make something new and original. It helps us to use our resources in new and different ways to solve problems and make decisions. Like other aspects of communicating, there is no one best way to be creative. Regardless of how creative or not creative we might consider ourselves, it is a skill that can be developed because we can be creative in practically anything we do.

Creativity can both reduce and increase uncertainty. We use creativity to reduce uncertainty because it fosters innovation, develops new ideas, and creates new things. It is a means to find new ways to understand the world around us. We use it to reduce uncertainty about ourselves through self expression. Because creativity often involves things that are new and unfamiliar, it has a certain amount of inherent uncertainty that could make some people reluctant to be creative or accept the creativity of others.

Creativity is a means by which we share meaning about ourselves, others, and the world around us. Creativity utilizes the many types of connections we make with others. It helps us to share meaning that transcends language and culture in ways few other things do. For instance, we can understand music and appreciate art created by people from other cultures, as well as from other periods in history even if we know little else about them. We don't necessarily have to understand them to appreciate their creativity. We use creativity to invest things with meaning by investing our time, energy, and self-concept in them. Often when we create something such as a work of art, it represents an investment of ourselves and our self-concept that we communicate to others. When people share meanings with others through creativity they may add to social reality.

We use creativity to fulfill many of our needs and wants. The creative expression of others helps us fulfill our need for entertainment, excitement, adventure, and something new. We have a need to communicate our unique individuality through creative expression. When we are creative it fulfills our need for self expression, self fulfillment, to earn an income, and to make life more enjoyable. Creativity is a means to make connections with others to communicate our Great Idea. How others respond through the process of communicating works as reflective feedback that can affect our self-concept. This may be why we are at times reluctant to share our creativity due to uncertainty about how others will receive it. If they like it, it bolsters our self-concept. If they do not, it can hurt our self-concept undermining our confidence.

Just what we consider creative can depend on our perceptions and expectations. We perceive things as being creative based on our past experiences, culture, education, and other factors. What is creative to one person may not be to others. Our perceptions create expectations about what it means to be creative. When we think of creativity we often think of the arts. However, creativity doesn't have to be just artistic expression, it can be part of any aspect of our lives. Creativity is less about what we do and more about how we do it.

To be creative, start with what you like, what you are interested in, or what you feel passionate about. Creativity is like other communicating skills, it can be developed over time. By developing your ideas, increasing your awareness, and exploring options for self expression you can foster your creativity. Ask for feedback from people you trust, who will provide objective feedback, and who will be supportive. While it is nice to have people tell us how wonderful we are, it's more useful to have them give us specific information we can utilize to improve our skills.

Creativity involves seeing and doing things that are familiar in new and different ways. By going beyond normal traditional ways of thinking we can create innovation, increase productivity, and improve our quality of life. We might feel reluctant to be creative for fear others may judge or reject us. We might feel that others are better than we are and we will not look good. But that shouldn't stop you from being creative because creativity is expressing your unique individuality, and only you can be you.

Problem Solving and Decision Making

Imagine it's a typical day and your three children are fighting over the same toy. The fighting has been going on for some time now and it's getting quite loud, so you have finally had enough. What do you do? A natural tendency might be to go over and take the toy away from them. Congratulations, you made a decision. Unfortunately, the problem has not been solved. You still have three unhappy children.

Using problem solving skills you might have looked at why the children are fighting in the first place to determine how to best solve their predicament, instead of only resolving yours. Perhaps you could find a few other toys to take their mind off this one. Perhaps there was an activity they could do or a game they could play instead. Perhaps the toy could be shared with each one having it for a specific amount of time. You could sit down to play with all of them and the toy together until they got tired of it. Or, perhaps they are hungry or tired and need a nap. Considering what approach to take is problem solving, doing something about it is making a decision.

Decision making and problem solving are often used interchangeably because they are similar in nature. However, there is a distinct difference between making a decision and solving a problem. It is possible to make a decision without solving a problem. Solving problems often necessitates making a series of decisions including choosing information, establishing evaluation criteria, selecting solutions, and implementing them. Fortunately, methods and approaches for problem solving also apply to decision making. They give you options that can be adjusted to meet your specific needs and situation.

Like other communicating skills, there is no one best, one size fits all problem solving approach to use in all situations. Just as everyone has their own style of communicating, they have their own style of decision making and problem solving. To be more effective at problem solving, it's helpful to have an awareness of the different types of problems and their source. It helps to know as much as possible about the problem to be solved and have a variety of approaches to choose the one that works best for you.

Why we might avoid solving problems.

When faced with a problem, people might do things that are not helpful. They may deny the existence of a problem or ignore it hoping it will go away. They may distort the problem or minimize it because they do not have the resources to resolve it. They may try to avoid the problem by blaming someone else or only addressing part of the problem, then ignoring the rest. They may go from one problem to another to give others the impression they are doing something about it. If the problem is too overwhelming, they may just deny that it exists or simply give up on solving it altogether. People use these approaches because there are times when they work and because effective problem solving takes time and energy.

Some of the most commonly used methods of solving problems are not necessarily the best. These include trial and error, which is trying things that may or may not work. Sufficing, by choosing the easiest solution that suffices for now. Breaking something down into small pieces and taking them one at a time can mean only a few things get done and the larger problem goes unresolved. We can avoid responsibility by making excuses to explain what happened, or blame others for it. Other common approaches include ignoring it, running away from it, or claiming there really isn't any problem after all.

All too often problems are solved based upon what is cheapest, easiest, quickest, or closest to us. We are motivated to solve problems in this way because we have limited resources like time and energy to solve them. A common approach is to procrastinate or ignore the problem and hope it works itself out or goes away. We may do nothing and hope that some-one else will make a decision, so we can sit back and criticize them. Or we might just flip a coin. While these approaches might seem ineffective, it is surprising just how often they are used.

We can easily fall into the habit of approaching all problems the same. This is because we have a natural tendency to replicate past success. If one approach is successful, we are more likely to apply it to other problems even if it doesn't work very well. We may even persist in taking the same approach even when it doesn't seem to be working because we are comfortable with it.

We do this because trying something else can increase uncertainty making us uncomfortable. So, we keep doing what we are familiar with even though it may not work. This is why people can sometimes keep making the same mistakes over and over in hopes that this might be the time it works. Having several problem solving methods gives you more options to avoid falling into the habit of approaching all problems the same, which can increase your chances of success.

We solve problems and make decisions every day. We do it so much we don't think about most of them because there is not much at stake. Fortunately, most of the time we do not need detailed problem solving methods to make a decision. However, at times we attempt to take the methods we use to make simple everyday decisions and apply them to complicated important decisions where something is actually at stake. We may find that what works for everyday decisions does not work for more important ones. This can be a source of unnecessary frustration and unhappiness.

Decisions can be thought of as implementing solutions to problems. When we solve a problem, a decision has to be made on how to implement that solution. Sometimes decisions are made that do not actually solve the problems they are meant to solve. Conversely, not every decision represents a problem that needs to be solved. For example, what to wear to work or what to have for lunch is normally not a problem, but involves making a decision. Problem solving generally involves coming up with possible solutions whereas decision making is selecting one of them to implement.

These are options for effective problem solving.

- Have an awareness of the source of the problem and then consider the full range of options to find a solution.

- Have a clear understanding of the problem and separate what needs to be addressed from what is not important.

- Have good, clear, accurate, and up to date information from credible sources.

- Limit the scope of the decision and don't try to fix everything all at once.

- Have logical reasoning that is well organized.

- Remove the emotional elements and look at the issue in an objective way.

- Implement a solution and then follow it up by evaluating its effectiveness in achieving your desired outcome.

Whenever we have a problem it creates tension because there is something that is unresolved or out of balance creating uncertainty making us uncomfortable. This can motivate us to take action to solve the problem. When the problem is resolved the tension is diminished reducing uncertainty. When things are going well there's very little tension and consequently very little motivation to do anything. This can result in becoming complacent and not doing things that we probably should be doing. Instead, this is an opportunity to take advantage of a time of relative calm in order to get things done.

When we have little or no tension we feel comfortable and have little motivation to change or look for something new. Instead of being motivated to change, we are motivated to keep things the same to preserve our state of stability. This can keep us from being open to new information or ways of doing things that might benefit us. Tension can be beneficial because it irritates us so we will do things we normally might not do. It motivates us to look for new ideas, new ways of doing things, and to look at what we know in a new way. Since tension is uncomfortable, we are motivated to resolve it and that can be beneficial for us.

However, we don't have to wait for problems in order to take advantage of the benefits of tension. By being aware of how this process works we can utilize it whenever we want by asking questions, looking for information, increasing our awareness, and creating more options. It seems that whenever we fail to do what we need to do on our own, life has a way of giving us difficulties that make us do it.

Decision inhibiting inertia.

Inertia can inhibit both taking action as well as preventing the stopping of an action. It can prevent us from doing something or from doing something else. Tension can motivate us to take action to make decisions, however, there are circumstances when it can inhibit us from making decisions as well. We are all faced with making many decisions every day and some are more important than others. We make many of them without even thinking much about it, while others take a great deal of time and effort. Then there are times when we make large important decisions very quickly and easily, while small seemingly insignificant decisions can seem insurmountable.

What makes some decisions more difficult than others? When faced with a decision where there are two or more potential outcomes, we may experience inertia preventing us from choosing one. This can happen when the outcome is uncertain and choosing one precludes the others. As long as we haven't made a decision, all potential outcomes are still possible. Once we make a decision we have only one outcome, the one we chose. For instance, we know making a decision will result in either success or failure, but we don't know which one it will be. We want success, but there is the potential for failure. Since making a decision results in either one or the other, as long as we do not decide success is still possible.

This can create an inertia preventing us from making a decision because as long as we have not made it, in our mind there is still the potential for achieving our desired outcome. Once we make a decision the other alternatives are excluded. So, we might feel pressured to put off the decision until we feel we have a better chance of success. The fear of not achieving our desired outcome becomes a force that can inhibit us from making a decision. The intensity of the inertia can be a factor of the degree of uncertainty of the outcome. By reducing uncertainty, the inertia should be reduced.

This inertia can occur in situations where there are two mutually exclusive outcomes. Typically, one outcome is desired and the other is undesirable. As long as we do not make a choice, there is still the possibility of achieving our desired outcome. If we make a choice we achieve one, but not the other. Once the decision is made the other choices are gone.

An example of how inertia may inhibit us can happen in dating. When we meet someone we find attractive we have to decide whether to ask them on a date or not. Once we ask them out they either say yes, which is our desired outcome or, they say no, and it's all over. Even though we could ask them again we are less likely to do so. Rather than risk them saying no, which could hurt our self-esteem, we might experience a kind of paralysis that prevents us from asking them out because in our mind, as long as we don't ask them there's still the possibility that they will say yes. This can result in an inhibiting inertia because the possibility that they say no overshadows the likelihood that they may say yes.

It is good to have a number of options to choose from in making decisions so we do not fall into reoccurring patterns that reduce effectiveness. Having too many options can also create paralysis. This is because we only need so much information to make an informed decision. Too much information can overload the process creating confusion by increasing uncertainty. We can become sidetracked by useless information that only serves to make the decision process more difficult. Developing effective communicating skills can help us to determine what information will help us make a decision while filtering out what does not.

The following is a general process to solve problems and make decisions.

1. Determine the scope of the problem. Our perception of a problem might not match reality. Problems can appear to be larger than they actually are. Or we may downplay them to avoid them. Determine what the problem really is, its source, and the facts of the situation so you have a better idea what to do, because many problems are not as bad as they seem.

2. Determine your desired outcome. Considering the big picture will help to avoid spending time and energy on small issues that may not accomplish much. Determine if the problem is worth the effort to resolve it. The time and effort needed to resolve a problem should be proportional to its importance. Have realistic expectations that can actually be accomplished because we can create more problems by having unrealistic expectations or trying to accomplish too much.

3. Gather information about the problem and potential solutions. We might think we have all the information we need, but if we did the solution would be more obvious. Good solutions need current, accurate, and relevant information. We need resources like time and energy, so we don't simply choose the easiest solution even though it may not be the best simply because it saves time.

4. Gather resources. We like to feel that we can resolve our problems ourselves and asking for help might be admitting that we can't handle them. In order to find the best solution we need the best resources. We can benefit by getting help and advice from others who have expertise and experience, who can provide information, and who may give us a hand. We often solve problems by thinking about them, but explaining things out loud to someone else can help us to clarify and organize our thoughts.

5. Gather solutions. By this time, we should be thinking of possible solutions. We have a natural tendency to choose just one, but it's helpful to have a few potential solutions. This gives you options that provides some flexibility to determine which is the best one and if it doesn't work, you have a backup plan.

6. Select and implement the best solution. After implementing the solution determine how effective it was to improve your problem solving skills in the future.

Problem solving and decision making approaches.

The following are several approaches that are described in more detail in Chapter 4. These methods can be organized on a spectrum from the analytical scientific to the intuitive creative approaches. They are meant to be guidelines because only you can determine what methods work best for you. They can be followed, combined, or adapted to fit your needs.

- The scientific approach applies methods used in scientific research to problem solving and decision making. It consists of an established set of steps to reach resolution. These include identifying the problem, determining your objective, identifying and evaluating solutions, then selecting and implementing the best one.

- The analytical approach is a more flexible version of the scientific approach utilizing additional steps including defining the problem, determining the scope of the problem, identifying its cause, establishing criteria to evaluate solutions, and implementing the best one. It can include analytical reasoning covered earlier in this chapter.

- The creative approach is on the other end of the spectrum from the scientific and analytical approaches. It is more flexible because it develops solutions using creative methods before evaluating their viability. This approach emphasizes creativity by thinking about things in a new way. Ideas are not critically evaluated until as many as possible have been generated. Then, the best one is selected based on your criteria.

- The intuitive approach is based on the premise that we often get wrapped up or too close to a problem to see what may be right in front of us. After determining the scope of the problem and looking at possible solutions, we take a break and get away from it by doing something else. The rationale is that thinking about something else clears our mind so that we can look at the problem from a fresh perspective. This can give our mind time to interpret, organize, and process information to make it useful to us, similar to the perception process, described in Chapter 1. During this time our mind processes information and when it comes up with a solution, it will occur to us.

- The medical approach looks at problems similar to how a doctor would diagnose an illness that has symptoms that need a treatment to cure. It can take a holistic approach as found in Eastern medicine by looking at problems as interconnected systems. It can also take a Western approach by breaking issues down into components that can be analyzed separately.

- The participatory approach encourages participation by many people to contribute ideas for possible solutions. Each person contributes their ideas, which are then evaluated by everyone who together develop another set of alternatives. This encourages them to work together to find new ideas that might otherwise not have occurred to them if they were working alone as individuals. In this process everyone contributes to the solution.

- The long distance approach is a variation of the participatory approach. When people cannot meet together, everyone provides possible solutions by mail or email based on established criteria. These are organized and sent out to everyone and they select the best solutions from the compiled list. The most popular solution gets implemented.

- The reverse approach takes an opposite perspective on problem solving by beginning with the preferred solution and working backward to the present situation. It begins with the desired outcome and determines what has to be done preceding it. Then it works each step back to the current situation to develop a plan. This works like having blueprints when building a house.

- The external forces approach. When other methods of problem solving have not worked or we are not sure of the right solution, we might look to external forces outside ourselves to help resolve the problem. We may be afraid of making the wrong decision or want confirmation that we chose the correct one. We may feel high levels of uncertainty and need reassurance that we are doing the right thing especially under difficult circumstances. We look for a solution from forces we consider to be greater than ourselves. This can take the form of looking for a sign, listening to our conscience, or the little voice inside us. It can be intuition, premonition, or a gut feeling. We may look to God or other spiritual sources for inspiration and advice through prayer or meditation.

These represent a variety of problem solving approaches to help improve awareness of your alternatives. They are more fully detailed in chapter 4. These approaches are not meant to be inclusive of all possible approaches to solving problems, but rather to provide a variety of options to give you choices. There is no one right, one size fits all approach for all situations. Having options empowers you to try different approaches under different circumstances to determine which one is best for you.

Language

Language is the system of spoken and written words we use to communicate with one another. It is a specific means of communicating where symbols, that are invested with meaning, are shared by a group of people. In order for language to work, everyone has to agree on what the symbols mean and how to use them. Language is one of the single most important human creations. While language is something all people have in common, all people do not share a common language. Different groups of people have developed their own specialized ways of communicating based upon their ethnicity, culture, profession, or geographic affiliation.

The advantage of language is in its ability to convert everything we know and experience into symbols that can be easily shared by large numbers of people over vast distances. It gives us the ability to share, store, and transmit large quantities of information relatively easily. The power of language is in its ability to affect how we think and how it motivates our behavior. It enables us to work with one another to accomplish things and achieve our desired outcomes. It is the means by which we define ourselves, others, and everything around us. It is how we learn about and make sense of ourselves and the world around us. Without language, life as we know it would not be possible.

The law of uncertainty motivated people to develop language as an effective way to communicate with one another to reduce uncertainty about themselves, others, and the world around them. We use language to share information about ourselves in order to reduce uncertainty, to get to know other people, to create relationships, and to work together to get things done. It is how we share information and knowledge enabling us to learn from one another as well as about one another. Without language, life would have more uncertainty making society as we know it virtually impossible.

Language is a physical manifestation of the law of shared meaning because it provides people a means to share their ideas with others. It allows people to share information and ideas that cannot be done in any other way. While pictures or drawings allow us to share some meaning, it's difficult or impossible to effectively communicate abstract and complex ideas using anything other than language. Language allows us to share meaning one on one or with large audiences. It allows us to transcend boundaries by sharing meaning with people across great distances and over time.

Language enables the law of investing to work because it is the means by which we take symbols and invest them with meaning. This gives us the ability to communicate and to invest in relationships with one another. It provides a means to measure everything around us and communicate its value. Language can create power because it enables us to exercise control over resources and people. We can take large complex ideas and condense them into relatively small amounts of space, creating virtually unlimited numbers of copies, and distribute them to as many people as we like in order to send and receive information effectively and economically.

How we use language tells us what is important and what is not, what we value and what we don't. How we label things influences our perceptions and expectations of their past, present, and future value. Language creates many kinds of value; historical value, social value, cultural value, and monetary value. We use language to make value judgments about things by describing them as good or bad, rare or common, and expensive or cheap. This means that how we use language can have tangible results.

Language is the means by which we create and share social reality. When we communicate with one another and share stories about our experiences, we create a common culture. We use language to communicate our self-concept including our nationality, ethnicity, culture, and geographic affiliation. It is how we take ideas and communicate them to others in order to make them a reality. It is how we create and enforce the rules of society. It provides a means by which we make sense of ourselves, others, and the world around us.

Language has the ability to create and change people's perceptions and expectations. We use language to label things in order to shape perceptions and expectations. Language is an important part of the perception process that helps to create our expectations. We use language to share information about ourselves in order to influence people's perception of us. What we tell people affects their expectations about us in the future. This helps us to create and maintain relationships with one another.

Language is symbolic.

In the process of communicating, we take our Great Idea and convert it into language comprised of symbols that we invest with meaning. We use language to make connections with others so that they can understand us. Others use language to give us feedback, so that we know how well they understand our Great Idea.

Language is significant because it can be both spoken and written. If you think this is no big deal try communicating with others without language by using only pictures, drawings, photographs, or gestures for a day. Language can communicate information in many different forms including auditory by speaking, tactility in Braille, and visually in both writing and sign language.

Even though we use the same language, there's a difference between spoken and written language. When we speak to individuals, such as our friends or family, we tend to use a very informal, conversational style of speaking. Since most of what we say is spontaneous, we don't think much about it before we say it. We add additional information to the words we say with nonverbal information that lets people know how to interpret them.

When we speak in public before an audience, we generally use a more formal style of language. We most likely write down what we are going to say and edit it beforehand. When we speak directly to others we are able to utilize instantaneous feedback to know if they understand what we are saying. If we can see them, we look for their nonverbal reactions to help us understand how they perceive our message, so we can make changes as we go along.

When we write, we tend to use a more formal style of language. We take time to think through our ideas and edit them before sending them to others because once they have been sent, they cannot be changed. Writing tends to be a more deliberate formal style than speaking, however, in some forms like emails, the language we use can be very casual, including using abbreviations. When we write it can take some time to receive feedback as the reply is usually in the same format.

We use symbols in the form of letters and words to represent objects and ideas. The symbols we use have no real connection to what they represent. For example, T R E E are symbols that represent a big green plant with branches and a trunk. The letters have nothing to do with a tree, they don't even look like one. The rules of language determine that we use these symbols when communicating about a tree. Through shared meaning we understand what the symbols T R E E mean as individual letters as well as the word they comprise. Without the law of shared meaning motivating us to invest these symbols with meaning, they would just be marks on a piece of paper.

In language, each symbol has its own individual meaning which can be combined with other symbols to create longer meanings, like words and sentences. Symbols can be easily separated and rearranged to give them different meanings. The symbolic nature of language allows T R E E to become R E T E, which consists of the same symbols or letters rearranged to make the word rete. (Rete refers to an anatomical network of veins, arteries, or nerve fibers in the body.)

This flexibility allows us to communicate large amounts of information using relatively few symbols that can be arranged in potentially infinite combinations while still maintaining their meaning. Using symbols allows us to create, change, store, retrieve, transmit, and reproduce information in ways that would otherwise not be possible.

Language works because it is regulated by a structured system of rules that govern how symbols are used. Language works because everyone knows and abides by the same rules of usage. Rules are essential for language to function because if everyone created their own rules, no one would be able to understand one another. These rules involve how symbols are used, how they are structured, and what they mean.

Language provides us with a shorthand way of communicating our Great Idea using symbols to understand and share information. It allows us to communicate complex ideas easily and quickly with large numbers of people. It allows us to communicate not only about tangible things, but also about abstract concepts and ideas. It allows us to communicate not only about the present, but also the past and the future. Language allows us to do things that cannot be done in other ways.

We use these different types of language when we communicate.

- The formal form of a language. Formal English is based upon British English.

- The more commonly used form of a language. Standard American English is the common form of English spoken primarily in the United States, as well as in other countries.

- Vernacular. The ordinary, everyday spoken language that reflects how language is commonly used.

- Colloquialisms. Informal words and phrases more often used in conversation.

- Slang. Shorthand references to communicate more complex concepts that reflect current culture.

- Dialect. Regional or local variations of language that reflect its history or culture.

- Grammar. The formal rules that govern how language is used.

- Semantics. This is how meaning is created in language through use.

- Syntax. How words are organized in order to communicate, as some words have different meanings based upon word order.

- Jargon. Specialized technical language used by professions to increase precision and accuracy in communicating.

- Denotative language. Language that has literal common dictionary definitions. A word denotes its meaning.

- Connotative language. The words carry additional implied meanings beyond their literal dictionary definition.

In the process of communicating, you create your Great Idea and make connections with others who receive your message and hopefully understand it. The problem with this is interference can change the meaning of your Great Idea, so that it is not clearly understood by others.

In order to communicate more effectively, it's helpful to have an awareness of the following potential problems with language to avoid them.

- Ambiguity. This is a lack of clarity that creates confusion about what you say. Increasing uncertainty about your message can happen by not being specific or using words that can be interpreted in more than one way. It can be overcome by being specific and using precise language.

- Vagueness. This is not being specific about what we say or mean. It can be intentional or unintentional. We may be vague intentionally, so we do not offend others or to protect their feelings. This can be overcome through clarity, using precise language, and soliciting feedback.

- Interpretation. People can have their own personal interpretations of language and we may not realize how others interpret what we say. This can be overcome by using easily understood language and clarifying our message by soliciting feedback.

- Multiple meanings. There are words that have similar or multiple meanings that could cause confusion. We can clarify what we mean through explanations or by understanding the context in which they are used.

- Comparative language. These are words that have meaning only in comparison to something else. This includes words like larger, smaller, faster, slower, above, below, later, or earlier. Understanding what these words mean relies on knowing the basis for comparison. Using definite and precise language such as numerical references can make these meanings more clear.

- Euphemisms. We might use these terms to protect other people's feelings because we feel that they are more socially acceptable. However, since we have heard these before and know what they mean, they can be perceived as not being straightforward. A better approach is to avoid using them by being truthful, but tactful.

- Abstract language. We use this type of language to describe things, ideas, and concepts that are new or do not physically exist. Abstract language can be clarified by comparing the unfamiliar to something that is familiar.

- Clichés. These are common patterns that we substitute for what we really want to say. We can fall into the habit of using these phrases because they don't take much thought or effort. However, they can undermine a person's credibility by making others less likely to listen. Instead, think about what you really want to say and then say that.

- Addictive language. It is easy to get into the habit of using words that have no meaning including like, yet, you know, kind of, or I guess. Using them can undermine a person's credibility and reduce the effectiveness of what they have to say. People can become annoyed and are less likely to listen. Instead, say what you mean and cut these out.

- Throwaway language. We can get into the habit of using modifiers that have no meaning. These include words such as literally, very, actually, or whatever. Sometimes these words are useful, but most of the time you can do without them. You can tell if a word is necessary by removing it and if the meaning doesn't change, don't use it.

The nature of language.

What if each of us had our own unique language? Communicating and understanding one another would be nearly impossible. If we had to learn every person's unique language communicating would be time consuming and difficult. In order to understand one another, the law of uncertainty motivates us to create a common means to communicate with large numbers of people, including people we don't know.

A common language is like a common method of measurement. Imagine what would happen if how we measured things was arbitrary with every person having their own method. Building just about anything would be next to impossible. Similarly, it would be almost impossible to build a society without common agreement on language because people who share a language often share a similar social reality.

Language is more than just a means to communicate, it represents nationality, ethnicity, culture, religion, and geographic affiliation. Language can reflect the culture of the people who speak it. In order to understand a culture it helps to understand the language because it's a part of its history and traditions. However, language has to reflect changing circumstances. This creates a tension between change and stability. Some languages, like English absorb words from other languages. Many culinary terms come from French, Italian, and Spanish.

Many countries recognize the need for an official national language that everyone is required to learn. Speaking different languages, or not having a common language within a nation, could potentially create schisms in society. Some cultures discourage the use of foreign words by developing their own words in their place. Some countries have organizations to maintain the integrity of their common language by keeping out foreign words. Others require teaching of additional languages like English, so they can communicate with the larger world outside their own borders.

Language can shape traditions and rituals. We use it to keep traditions alive by repeating familiar texts and established patterns of behavior that give us a sense of common identity and culture. We use specialized language to celebrate holidays like Christmas and Hanukkah by telling familiar stories. People give speeches for significant national events like the Fourth of July and Memorial Day. We use language to share traditions and celebrate rituals within our family, community, and culture.

Language allows us to share meaning that makes traditions and rituals more meaningful. This can make us feel closer and more connected to others, even with people we do not know. When we practice them we often say the same words and phrases as our ancestors who practiced them in the past. Doing this gives us a sense of purpose, togetherness, and connectedness with a larger community. When we go to Christmas services, they may have the same program that has been performed for many years, which can give us a sense of security and stability. When we hear the same language spoken during celebrations at important times of the year it can help give us a feeling of support for one another and comfort.

Understanding a specialized language can identify who is a member of a group and who are outsiders. It can help insiders communicate in ways that can be difficult for outsiders to understand. People who understand a common language feel connected to others whether they know them personally or not. A common language can give a group a sense of collective identity and can be used to show commitment to the group.

Many professions and businesses have developed their own specialized language or technical jargon to communicate more accurately. Professions such as medical, legal, academic, and others have developed their own specialized common language and technical terms. This helps people within a profession to communicate more effectively with greater precision. Other groups have developed a common language based upon having a common nationality, culture, ethnicity, community, or religion.

Language can shape our behavior. Think about the last time you heard a passionate speech, read an inspirational poem, watched an emotional movie, or heard the lyrics to a sad song. It probably created feelings that affected your emotions. Language can create emotions that move people to take action to do things. Throughout history, language has been used for gaining political, economic, and social power. It has been used as a means to persuade people to accept new ideas and to be motivated to take action. We use language to shape people's perceptions and expectations. It is used to influence, motivate, and persuade us to take action. It has the power to shape how we perceive ourselves, others, and the world around us.

Language can shape our thoughts. It is flexible enough to enable us to think abstractly about things we can't see or that don't exist in reality. However, language can limit our ideas to the words that are available for us to use. For instance, do you think about things using words or pictures? If we think in words, they could constrain our thoughts and ideas because we have to use the words that are available to us. The words available to us may or may not accurately express our ideas. If we think in pictures or concepts, it may be difficult to put those ideas into words to communicate them to others. This brings up the problem of limitations with language. How do you use language to communicate about something that does not exist when there may be no words to describe it?

Language is a means of creative expression. It is not just a means to communicate ideas, it is also used as a means of entertainment and artistic creative self expression. It fulfills our need to express ourselves artistically and creatively. Language is used as a means of entertainment through comedy, drama, mystery, and suspense. Language makes drama, film, television, theater, music, opera, poetry, literature, and many other types of creative artistic expression possible. Language has the power to make us feel a wide variety of emotions. It can influence and inspire us. Language can engage our minds and touch our hearts.

Language can affect our emotions. Since words have meaning and meanings create emotions, words create feelings within us. If we listen to an inspirational speech or a sad song, we might feel emotions based upon the words we hear. We use language to describe our innermost feelings and emotions in order to share them with others. Just as language can shape or influence our thoughts, it can affect our emotions or inspire them in others. We have all experienced extreme emotions where we were at a loss for words. We may even have said something like, "Words cannot express how I feel." Language can have a cathartic affect because it allows us to talk about how we feel providing an emotional release to make us feel better. Conversely, we can also use language to hide how we really feel.

Language can communicate who we are. It can communicate information about who we are as an individual. It can be a source of confidence, competence, attitudes, and preferences that can help to develop our self-concept and sense of identity. We use it to create our identity and manage how others perceive us. It can communicate the groups that we belong to including our profession, ethnicity, education, and geographic affiliation. We use it to share information about ourselves including our experiences, interests, thoughts, and emotions. It is the means by which we think thoughts in order to develop our ideas. It enables us to think abstractly outside the limitations of time and space. It has the power to influence and persuade others how to think about things and motivate them to take action.

These are options to help use language skills to communicate more effectively with others.

• Use language that is plain, clear, and easy to understand.

• Use the language of your audience. Know the language that they speak so that they will understand you.

• Use language correctly and accurately. Be specific to avoid ambiguity that can create misunderstandings.

- Use language that is familiar. When talking about the unfamiliar, connect it to something others already know.

- Use imagery to create a picture in the mind of your audience, so they will better understand and remember your idea.

- Use descriptive words that explain your idea by giving details of its characteristics to facilitate understanding.

- Use examples and illustrations to clarify ideas by including experiences and situations that people find familiar.

- Use emotional language to make a connection with others, so your message is more engaging.

- Use language that describes events as if they are happening in the present to make them more interesting.

- Use language that appeals to the five senses. Let people know how things look, sound, feel, taste, or smell to make your message more real.

- Use language that is appropriate for your audience and the situation to meet their expectations. It should fit their level of understanding of the topic.

- Use figurative language like figures of speech or metaphors to help explain something the audience may be unfamiliar with by comparing it to something familiar.

- Use precise language by choosing the right word and using it correctly. People may use words inaccurately or try to coin a new word or phrase creating confusion or misunderstanding.

- Use modifiers sparingly including actually, very, or literally.

- Use language without meaningless fillers including like, yeah, whatever, or you know because they make you sound unsure of yourself.

- Use the word "but" sparingly because it can be used to divide two distinct ideas that can cancel or contradict everything that has been said up to it, by substituting what is said after it. For example, in a relationship a person might say, "You're a wonderful person, but I think we should just be friends." The bottom line is the relationship is over.

- Use of personal pronouns. When we use the personal pronoun "I" we take responsibility for ourselves and our feelings. We might use statements with the pronoun "you" to blame or shift responsibility to others. When we use the words "we" or "us" it creates a common bond with a common identity. When we use the word "they" we often refer to an unidentified person or persons we don't know. These words can be used as a method of inclusion or exclusion as a shorthand reference rather than using a specific name or description.

- Use directive language to give others directions. This could be driving directions, how to do something, or how something works. First, give people the big picture so they know how all the pieces fit together. When giving directions or describing a process, give the beginning and ending points for reference. Let others know where they are, when they began, and what things look like at the end. Second, agree on common terms you will use and be consistent in using them. For example, in giving directions use north-south, left-right, or inches and feet depending upon your purpose. Third, use familiar markers to let people know where they are, where they have been, and where they are going. This is so everybody is in the same spot because it's easy to get lost on the way. Fourth, let people know potential problems like where they might get lost or go the wrong direction.

Language is about making choices and the choices people make communicate who they are as a person and how they want to be perceived by others. Increasing your vocabulary gives you options to use language appropriately. Inappropriate use of language can undermine a person's desired outcome and credibility that can result in undesired or unintended outcomes. While we cannot always be certain of how others will interpret what we say, it's a good idea to avoid language that might be interpreted as offensive, demeaning, malicious, abusive, or harmful.

Some people may resort to offensive language when they are under pressure, to make a joke, or to get attention. However, this language can make a person appear ignorant, lazy, inarticulate, or even vulgar. Having a good vocabulary helps avoid offensive language and commonly used euphemisms or clichés by giving you the ability to clearly and accurately express your own thoughts to communicate what you really mean to say.

Vocabulary.

We all have our own vocabulary that consists of the number of words we know and use. Having a larger vocabulary can give us more options to express ourselves and to communicate with others. Employers look for people who have good communicating skills including a good vocabulary. Our personal relationships can be more fulfilling when we clearly express our thoughts and feelings. Since language is the means by which we make connections to communicate with others, being able to clearly express ourselves is an important skill. A good vocabulary is analogous to a musician having a large repertoire of music they can perform. This makes having a good vocabulary essential to communicating effectively with others.

Having a good vocabulary is not about trying to impress others by using long obscure words that no one understands. It's having the ability to use common words to accurately express yourself. It's about having an awareness of what words mean, which gives you options to choose the best word to convey your ideas. Effective communicating is not about using extraordinary words in common situations, it's about using common words in extraordinary ways.

Developing a good vocabulary is like any other communicating skill, everyone has an ability that can be developed. To develop your vocabulary, read about things that interest you where words are used in context rather than learning a list of words and their definitions. This helps develop a vocabulary that you will actually use. If you want to increase your vocabulary in a particular field or profession, look for articles written by experts in that field or in professional journals. Invest in several reference books like a good unabridged dictionary, a thesaurus, and a manual of style and grammar to help you use language more effectively. Pay attention to how others around you use language including the words they use and how they use them. When you hear a new word that you don't know, write it down and look it up to see what it means.

Names.

One of the most common ways we use language to reduce uncertainty and share meaning is by using names. People have named everything they have encountered in order to understand and communicate about them. They have named all kinds of living beings and inanimate objects in order to define them and give them a sense of identity.

Names are a specialized form of language created by people motivated by the laws of uncertainty and shared meaning. We name things in order to make them more familiar and give them a deeper meaning. This can personalize and humanize things reducing uncertainty. When we name something it becomes more familiar and we can communicate more easily about it. Names give us an easy way to communicate about things that would take too much time if we had to describe them. They serve to group things together as well as providing an individual identity.

There was a time when everything in the world around us did not have a name. As people learned more about the things around them, they named them in order to understand, organize, control, and communicate about them. This includes places, inanimate things, living things, ideas, concepts, and many others. When people discovered something new or came up with a new idea they named it so they could share it with others.

We are motivated to name people and things that are meaningful to us because it shows that we have a relationship with them. Naming things gives them a sense of identity and creates value. It can give us power and influence over them. Names influence our perception and expectations of objects as well as other people.

Every person has a name that was given to them by their parents. Our name gives us a sense of identity, personality, and uniqueness. It combines our own individual name with our family name to give us an individual identity, while connecting us to our family, culture, and nationality. Names give us a sense of who we are affecting our self-concept because we identify with it. We use it when presenting ourselves to others, so it influences how they perceive us shaping their expectations. It can communicate information about who we are including our gender, ethnicity, religion, or geographic affiliation.

Names give us a legal identity that we use on official documents such as the deed to a house or a driver's license to identify and differentiate us from everyone else. We might have a different social name or nickname that we use with family and friends to demonstrate a close personal relationship with them. Names are also used to indicate familial relationships such as mom and dad, status or rank such as president or general, and a person's profession such as reverend or doctor.

Nonverbal Communicating

Verbal communicating consists of both spoken and written language. Nonverbal communicating consists of practically everything else. While it is not the words we speak, it is how we say them. It includes our facial expressions, body language, and appearance. We are constantly communicating information nonverbally including how we look, how we act, and how we use our time, space, and money. Practically everything we create around us and everything we do has the potential to communicate nonverbally. If it communicates something to others and does not use words, it can be considered nonverbal communicating.

When we communicate our Great Idea to others we communicate with them by making a connection. Verbal connections are the words we use to communicate. Nonverbal connections include practically everything else that we interpret and invest with meaning other than the words themselves. Spoken words are partially verbal and partially nonverbal. The words are verbal, but how we say them is considered nonverbal because the meanings communicated are separate from the words themselves. We can change their meaning by how we speak using vocal variety, pitch, volume, pacing, intonation, and pauses or silence. We also use nonverbal body language like gestures or facial expressions to make a connection. Nonverbal communicating for written words can include typeface, color, size, punctuation, and format. Written words can be made to look different to give them different meanings. For instance, bold type or an exclamation mark indicates importance.

Since everyone communicates for a reason, we are motivated to look at the nonverbal behavior of others because we don't intentionally communicate nonverbally the same way we intentionally communicate verbally. We tend to give nonverbal behavior more significance than verbal because it provides us with information that cannot be obtained in other ways. It helps us to interpret the words others say by reducing uncertainty, so we can better understand them. It helps us to more fully understand their motives so that we can invest in relationships.

Nonverbal communicating is important because it is the most basic way that we communicate. It occurs at the most basic levels of communicating because it involves our behavior, demeanor, and emotions. We may take time to think about what we are going to say, however, we usually don't think much about what we communicate nonverbally. We interpret nonverbal information more intuitively, so we can be less aware of what we are communicating. People tend to put more importance on nonverbal information believing it over the words people say because it is considered more genuine. People are more likely to be deceptive with their words than with their nonverbal behavior. So, we use it to get information to fill in the blanks telling us how to interpret what people say by how they say it.

We learn nonverbal behavior early in life before we learn to speak. As an infant we cannot speak, so we communicate through our facial expressions, movements, and making noises like laughing or crying. Nonverbal behavior communicates emotions through body language like facial expressions and gestures. This is one reason why we often trust them more than words because they are seen as being more difficult to control or manipulate. When we speak we add vocal intonation and inflection to convey additional information like emotion.

There are times when words alone are not enough to express your Great Idea. In order to facilitate understanding, we add nonverbal information to convey additional meaning. The same words can have different meanings depending upon nonverbal information like how they are said. For example, "I'm fine," can mean that I am actually fine, I'm angry, or that I am not fine, I just don't want to tell you.

Nonverbal behavior is similar to what it represents. If we say we feel happy the words represent the feeling, but a smile is a nonverbal expression of happiness. Nonverbal behavior is continuous without a clear beginning or ending. We communicate nonverbally practically all the time even if we don't want to communicate anything. Some nonverbal behaviors are understood regardless of language or culture like a smile or a handshake. However, there are other nonverbal behaviors that can be interpreted differently depending on a person's experience or culture.

Verbal communicating consists of words that are distinct and separate from one another and are governed by a clearly organized set of rules. We understand individual words and know when a sentence begins and ends. If we don't want to communicate verbally, we stop speaking. Words are symbolic because they have nothing to do with what they represent. Whereas, nonverbal behavior is natural and spontaneous, so we don't usually think much about it. We are more likely to think about the words we are going to say before communicating them to others.

While verbal communicating involves listening and reading, nonverbal communicating uses all of our five senses with each making a connection. We see things visually like reading words, seeing objects, and observing behavior. We hear auditory messages like spoken words, vocal inflections, music, and the noises around us. Touch communicates what things are made of or the nature of our relationships with others. Smell tells us when things are good, fresh, and clean or when they are bad for us. Taste communicates different types of food and drink. Each of these is a nonverbal connection that provides us with information.

Life is chaotic and people often do things we do not understand, so the law of uncertainty motivates us to want to know more about them. We use nonverbal information to help us reduce uncertainty, to understand their motives and actions, and to make them more safe and predictable. We do this so that we can trust them enough to invest in relationships. When we want to know more about others, we look for meaning in the nonverbal information they communicate. This includes their appearance, demeanor, gestures, actions, behavior, and facial expressions. We look at how they use their resources such as how they spend their time, how they utilize their space, and the personal choices they make. All of these have the potential to communicate information nonverbally.

How we utilize nonverbal behavior is a practical application of the law of shared meaning. Uncertainty motivates us to invest nonverbal behavior with meaning so that we can better understand it. We use nonverbal behavior to convey meanings that language cannot adequately communicate. We use it to add additional meaning to what we say. For example, if someone says, "Love you," the nonverbal information that accompanies it tells us how to interpret it. A smile may indicate friendship, a hug may indicate a family relationship, and a kiss may indicate a more intimate relationship.

We invest nonverbal behavior with meaning because there are many aspects to a person that we cannot directly observe. We cannot see their attitudes, experiences, motivations, desired outcomes, needs and wants, or view of social reality. If we do not have a complete picture of them, we might add information to fill in what is missing, which may or may not be accurate. This is why people often make assumptions about others that they know little about that may not be true.

In order to invest in relationships with others, we need to reduce uncertainty to create trust. In order to do this, we observe and interpret a person's nonverbal behavior to give us information about them. This includes not only what they say, but how they say it. We also look at other nonverbal characteristics like their behavior, appearance, clothing, possessions, and how they organize their space at home and at work. We invest meaning in the things created by people such as clothing, furniture, art, music, literature, and architecture as well as others.

The more we invest in a relationship, the more kinds of nonverbal behavior we use to communicate. We use nonverbal communicating to signify our investment in relationships such as the use of facial expressions to indicate friendship or touch to express affection. We can use spatial relationships to indicate the nature of our relationships. We use food to welcome friends and family. We surround ourselves with objects we enjoy looking at to create a pleasant atmosphere.

At a very early age we learn to express our needs, wants, and emotions through nonverbal behavior. When we are first born, we cannot talk so we learn to communicate nonverbally when we smile, laugh, or cry. Our parents and family spend time learning what these sounds and behaviors mean in order to fulfill our needs. When a baby cries it could mean that they are hungry, need changing, feel cranky, or are experiencing something more serious. Parents are looking to make a connection by spending time talking and smiling at their baby, so when their baby smiles back, it's very rewarding.

We gain nonverbal information through the perception process of selecting, organizing, and interpreting information in order to give it meaning. Much of our perception of others comes from their nonverbal characteristics, which we use to develop expectations about their behavior in the future. We use our own nonverbal characteristics to influence the perception and expectations of others to achieve our desired outcome. For instance, if we are applying for a job we intentionally dress professionally and act with confidence in order to give them the perception that we are competent to reduce uncertainty so they will hire us.

In the process of communicating, we send our Great Idea to others and they provide us with feedback. Some of the feedback is nonverbal information based upon the behavior of others when they communicate with us. We often look for nonverbal feedback while we are talking with others to know if they understand what we are saying. We look for facial expressions such as smiling or behavior like head nodding that indicates their approval. If we see negative feedback such as avoiding eye contact or negative facial expressions, we may not feel good about what we are saying and may stop to ask them what's the problem.

Nonverbal feedback we receive from others can have an impact on our self-concept because we view it as more instantaneous and honest. People have time to think about what they're going to say and so they may not be as forthright. They usually don't have time to think about how to act. People may say that they agree with us, but their nonverbal body language may say otherwise, so we are more likely to believe that. People may hold back and not say anything in response to us. However, they cannot hold back communicating nonverbally. This is why we often look for nonverbal feedback as an indicator of how we are being perceived by others. Through the process of communicating, reflected feedback has the potential to have an effect on our self-concept. For example, if people say nice things to us, but they avoid us we may wonder what's wrong.

Our nonverbal behavior communicates information in addition to the message that we send to others. So, in order to communicate more effectively, it can be helpful to be aware of how nonverbal communicating can affect us.

• Nonverbal information can be used to support the verbal message by giving it additional meaning. It can be used to complement and emphasize the message or it can be used to alter it. We might gesture, point, or pound our fist to reinforce what we are saying.

• Nonverbal information can be used to substitute for verbal information by replacing what we might say verbally such as nodding yes or shaking our head no. We may do this when we are reluctant to say what we really think or feel.

- Nonverbal information can be used to contradict verbal information. We do this when we say things we don't really mean, when we don't want others to know what we are really thinking, or when we don't want to talk about something. This can create misunderstandings by communicating contrary messages.

- Nonverbal information can be used to hide the verbal message. There are times when we don't want others to know what we really think or feel, so we communicate something different using nonverbal behavior to cover our true feelings. We do this to protect ourselves, but it can also be done to manipulate others.

Nonverbal behavior can communicate the nature of a relationship between people. We can use it to observe others in order to understand their relationships. These are some relationships that can be communicated nonverbally.

- Authority. People in positions of authority often use dominant or aggressive nonverbal behaviors such as direct eye contact, posture, close proximity, and the loudness of their voice to assert their authority over others. People often assert dominance, status, prestige, and power through their nonverbal behavior. Their use of voice, distance, stance, posture, and eye contact can be used to assert power over others.

- Affiliation. Relationships are expressed through nonverbal behavior. We communicate warmth, closeness, friendship, and intimacy through our nonverbal behavior. The closer the relationship the more people tend to look at each other and make eye contact. They change the tone of their voice and facial expressions. We use touch to indicate the nature of our relationships from friendship to intimacy. Generally, the more people touch one another, the closer the relationship.

- Attraction. We can be attracted to others by their nonverbal behavior. We respond to positive eye contact, close proximity, facial expressions like smiling, and touch as a sign of attraction. Attraction can vary from professional to personal. We may be attracted to work with people who act professional or to form friendships with people we enjoy being around.

Nonverbal behavior.

Everyone communicates for a reason and that reason is often driven by their motivation. Sometimes we are aware of what motivates us and other times we are not. We generally do not share our motivation with others, but we are curious about what motivates them. We are motivated to protect ourselves by the law of uncertainty. We don't share the motivation behind what we do for fear that others may reject us. However, we want to know the motivation behind others behavior to reduce uncertainty so that we can trust them. When we know what to expect from others it gives us a feeling of predictability and stability that reduces our feelings of uncertainty.

If we don't have enough information about others to reduce uncertainty, we evaluate their nonverbal characteristics to make inferences about them and the motivation for their behavior. We make inferences about their behavior based upon our own because we like to be around people who we perceive as being similar to us. This is because it provides us a method to reduce uncertainty. Since we see ourselves as a good person, if they have similar nonverbal characteristics, then they must be a good person as well. When we reduce uncertainty, it can help us develop a relationship with others because they seem less risky.

Voice.

How you say the words you speak are considered nonverbal characteristics. This is the extra information that is added to our words and messages that tells others how to interpret what we say. We rarely speak without adding additional nonverbal information. If we didn't, we would speak in a monotone voice.

We change how we speak naturally without thinking much about it. We talk faster or slower, raise or lower the pitch of our voice, speak louder or softer, and add different intonations depending up on what we are saying. This is one way that we express our emotions. Our vocal intonation tells people if we are happy, sad, frustrated, angry, or depressed as well as many other emotions. These characteristics help others know how to interpret what we are saying.

We each have our own unique distinctive sounding voice. We often recognize people we know, as well as famous people, by the sound of their voice. Our voice is an important part of how others perceive us. While distinctive qualities of our voice are created by our physiology, we have some control over how we sound. We use our voice differently when we are sad, sincere, stressed, or sarcastic. How we use our voice tells people how to interpret the words that we say. Sometimes we do this intentionally and other times it's spontaneous. We can communicate more effectively when we are aware of how we speak and how we are coming across to others. Developing speaking skills gives us options to choose from so we can use our voice more effectively.

These are some vocal characteristics to be aware of because they affect how people interpret what we say.

- Pitch. This is the high or low tone of your voice, which can be similar to the notes on a musical scale. If we are nervous or stressed our voice tends to have a higher pitch. If we don't want people to know we are nervous, we can consciously lower the tone of our voice to sound more confident.

- Volume. This is how loud or soft we speak. When we are angry we might let people know by speaking loudly or shouting at them. If something is more personal we might whisper to emphasize privacy.

- Pacing. This is how fast or slow we speak. If we aren't sure what to say we may speak slower. If we are nervous we might speak faster. If we feel nervous and don't want others to know, we can speak at a more average pace.

- Inflection. These are the changes that we make in the intonation or sound of our voice in order to emphasize important points or to differentiate between different topics.

- Timbre. This is the quality or fullness of our voice. Sometimes we speak with the full resonant voice and other times we may have a nasal or airy quality. When we speak more resonant we sound more confident. We convey emotion through the timbre of our voice such as when it cracks or waivers with emotion. It can sound rich, energetic, or lively. Conversely, it can sound thin, flat, nasal, or raspy.

- Pronunciation. This is correctly saying the words we speak. Articulation is speaking clearly so that we are understandable.

- Vocal variation. Combining several vocal elements together creates variety. This helps to cut through the interference of The Great Abyss. Vocal variations add interest so that others are more likely to listen to what we have to say. Variation is a matter of balance. Too much vocal variation can be annoying making us difficult to listen to and too little makes us sound monotonous or boring.

- Pauses. What you don't say can be as important as what you do say. Pauses work much like breaks between paragraphs or chapters on a written page. They emphasize important points, transitions between ideas, and gives people time to think about what you said so they can catch up to you. We often use a dramatic pause for effect before and after a significant word or phrase setting it apart, such as using boldface type or an exclamation mark on a written page.

- Silence. This can communicate many things. Silence can be uncomfortable, pressuring us to say something. It can be considered rude or an expression of anger or rejection. We may have a moment of silence as a way of showing respect or reverence. It can be a way of expressing extreme emotion. It's what we might do when we don't know what to say. The meaning of silence is based upon the context of the situation and the people involved because it can have many interpretations.

Typefaces.

It has been said that it's not just what you say, it's how you say it. So, it could be said it's not just what you write, but how you write it. Typefaces are the visual equivalent of vocal expressions and gestures. Before communicating their Great Idea to others, people may spend a great deal of time designing how they present their message, and choosing the appropriate style of the lettering helps their words communicate the right message. Typefaces are important because we see written words practically everywhere. How we present our message can communicate information in addition to the words nonverbally to others.

There are basically two kinds of typefaces, serif and sans serif. A serif letter has spikes that are lines at the ends of letters that make them look older or elegant. Sans serif letters do not have those spikes making them look clean and modern. Serif fonts are often used in printed materials like books and newspapers because the eye naturally picks up on the short lines to help make reading pages of text easier. Sans serif letters are used when legibility is important such as for building and road signs. Modern letters with clean lines are frequently used by business to communicate professionalism, which can create a feeling of confidence to reduce uncertainty.

A typeface communicates something beyond the actual words, it communicates the nature of who originated the message and what people should think about it. We have all seen creative highly embellished, even wacky typefaces. Some look like calligraphy with lots of swirls, some look like The Old West wanted posters. Some lettering looks like it was written by children and others like they are from comic books. An office building might have very straight Roman looking letters to communicate authority. Each of these different typefaces communicates a message through the law of shared meaning.

The style of typeface can communicate many different kinds of messages. It can let people know that something is old or new, serious or humorous, formal or informal, professional or casual. When choosing a typeface, consider what it communicates to others, so that they will be more likely to invest in your message to achieve your desired outcome.

Emotions

Emotions are the psychological and physiological responses to our experiences, perceptions, and expectations. They are often spontaneous reactions to our interactions with others or our own thoughts. They can affect how we communicate with others. They can motivate our behavior and actions. They can bolster or hurt our self-concept. They are an unavoidable and inevitable part of life that can make it fun and exciting, or sad and overwhelming.

Sometimes we feel emotions that we would rather not feel. We may feel that we have little control over our emotions. By understanding how emotions can be a nonverbal expression of our thoughts and feelings, we can utilize them to communicate more effectively with others. Understanding our emotions helps us to better understand ourselves. While we can't always control how we feel, we can have more control over how our emotions affect us.

Emotions are a means by which we make connections with others. Emotions are part of how we communicate nonverbally with others. They let people know how to interpret what we communicate with our voice or body language. Emotions can share meaning in ways that words cannot. There can be times when we are not able to put our emotions into words. Sharing our emotions with others is not always easy because we're not always sure of what they are ourselves. We may try to suppress our feelings or put them aside until they become overwhelming and we have to deal with them.

Many of our emotions are the psychological and physiological manifestations of uncertainty. Uncertainty can bring out emotional responses that affect our state of mind and motivate our behavior. What emotions we feel can be based upon the degree of uncertainty we experience. For instance, moderate levels of uncertainty can create feelings of anxiety because we may not know what to expect. Increased levels of uncertainty can make us feel frustration or tension. If uncertainty increases too much, we may become fearful, frustrated, or even angry. When uncertainty is reduced we are more likely to feel better.

We are motivated by the law of uncertainty to understand our feelings and emotions to better understand ourselves. We want to understand how we feel because we trust our emotions when making decisions. Or we might follow our intuition or gut feeling. Since emotions can motivate behavior, understanding emotions can help us better understand our own behavior.

It can be helpful to understand how uncertainty can affect our emotions because of how much it can affect our thoughts and actions. How we feel can influence how we are perceived by others. If we feel good about ourselves, other people are more likely to feel good about us as well. Conversely, people do not want to be around someone who is frequently in a bad mood. We often express emotions through our nonverbal behavior. Sometimes we are aware of our behavior and other times it can take us by surprise. It is easy to feel emotions without being aware of the effect they can have on others. With increased awareness, we can choose what nonverbal behaviors we communicate regardless of how we feel.

We are motivated by the law of shared meaning to find meaning not only in our emotions, but in the emotions of others in order to reduce uncertainty. We want to know how other people feel about us, so we try to read their emotions to find out what they think. We might look for meaning in their emotional responses to better understand them and what they think about us. We look for meaning in emotions because they can communicate information in ways that other forms of communicating are unable to do. So, it can be helpful to be aware of what emotions mean and that they are open to differing interpretations.

Emotions are a means to protect ourselves. When we meet someone we don't know, we may feel apprehensive and interpret that feeling as meaning that we need to be cautious of them. When we are in a place that is unfamiliar, we may feel scared or fearful and interpret that to mean we could possibly be in danger, motivating us to be more careful or leave. We feel this way often due to the higher level of uncertainty.

We look to find meaning in the emotions of others, but we also look to find meaning in our own emotions. When we invest feelings and emotions with meaning, we do this to reduce uncertainty about them. When we have emotions, particularly strong emotions, we look to find meaning in them to better understand them and ourselves. One of the ways that we do this is to share them with others. We interpret how we feel based on our past experiences, but also on the experiences of others. Sharing meaning can give our emotions a deeper significance and help to reduce their intensity. This can make us feel better about our circumstances as well as ourselves.

We can be motivated by the law of investing to share our emotions with others. This is because sharing emotions can be a means of investing in ourselves and in relationships with others. When we do something well and we feel good about ourselves, it can be a means of investing in our own self-concept. When other people share positive emotions with us, it can serve as a means of reflected feedback through the process of communicating to make us feel better about ourselves. We can also make others feel good about themselves by sharing positive emotions about them.

What emotions we choose to share with others depends upon the nature of the relationship. We may feel comfortable sharing our feelings in some relationships, but may be reluctant in others for fear that it may undermine our investment in the relationship. Therefore, the level of emotional expression can be a reflection of our commitment and the degree to which we are invested in a relationship.

When we invest in relationships with others, we also have an emotional investment. The degree to which we invest emotionally in someone is based upon the nature of our relationship with them. The closer the relationship, the more emotions we invest. The more superficial a relationship, the less we are likely to emotionally invest in it. How much we invest emotionally in a relationship often depends on how much the relationship helps to fulfill our needs and wants. We do this because we share experiences over a period of time that involves emotional responses. We share emotions as a means of self-disclosure to let people know more about us in order to reduce uncertainty, so that they can trust us enough to invest in a relationship with us.

Emotions help us to fulfill many of our needs and wants. They fulfill our need to express ourselves to others. They can serve as a type of catharsis to release tension. Our emotions can be a result of tension created between competing or conflicting needs and wants, which can lead to feelings of uncertainty, frustration, or even anger. Understanding our needs and wants can help balance these tensions to reduce emotional intensity.

We express our emotions to help fulfill needs and wants to achieve desired outcomes. We do this to get support and validation from others so we know that they care about us. We want to tell others how we feel in order to reduce tension and stress. We want to strengthen our relationships to become closer to others. Sharing emotions can have healthy benefits by reducing tension and stress, because suppressing them can have negative consequences like anxiety, hypertension, and high blood pressure.

Emotions can have a physical and psychological effect on us such as an elevated heart rate or increased adrenaline. This can heighten our senses and give us energy to get things done. It can help us to do things we might not otherwise do. We can be more motivated to do something when we are feeling extreme emotions. The more intense the emotion, the more motivated we can become, like when we are fearful or angry. But by being aware of how emotions can motivate our behavior, we can make choices and how to best utilize them. We can separate useful emotions that help us from debilitating emotions that could hinder us.

Emotions can fulfill our need for safety and security by providing warnings to keep us safe from harm. We may have a feeling or premonition that increases our awareness of someone or something around us, so we pay more attention to it. For instance, if we are alone at night we may feel apprehensive which heightens our sense of awareness to help us protect ourselves. We use emotions to interpret what other people communicate. We tend to trust them more than the words they say because they are perceived as being more genuine. We often trust emotions because they are a spontaneous psychological response to a situation.

The emotions we feel often come from our perceptions and expectations. The difference between our perceptions and expectations can affect our state of mind, which can determine the emotions we feel. When our perceptions do not meet our expectations, it can make us feel bad or upset. Conversely, when our perceptions meet or exceed our expectations, it can help us feel positive emotions like being happy or elated. Since the perception process provides us information we use to create our expectations, how we use it can affect how we feel. Since our perceptions are often based upon how we interpret information, gathering new information or reinterpreting it can change our expectations. So, if we feel bad, we might improve how we feel by reevaluating our perceptions and expectations.

There are times when we may feel emotions without knowing where they came from. A consequence of the law of shared meaning is that we can absorb emotions from others by being around them. We might do this because we are concerned about them and want to be sympathetic. If someone we care about is sad, they can make us feel sad too because we feel for them. If someone is angry, we may respond by matching their emotional intensity. We can feel emotions caused by the actions of others and may not be aware of it. So, it is helpful to be aware of how easy it is to absorb other people's emotions because this can affect our behavior. We can avoid this happening by being aware of what we are actually feeling and by protecting ourselves from letting the emotions of others affect how we feel.

While it can be helpful to share emotions with others, most of the time we don't. This is because most of our emotions are relatively low in intensity, so we don't think or say much about them. When we feel more intense emotions, we may have difficulty understanding them. We may not be sure exactly what we feel because some emotions are difficult to put into words. Sharing our feelings with others isn't always easy because of the rules of social reality. We may not communicate our emotions because we might be afraid that others may no longer like or respect us. We may feel that others could perceive our emotions as a sign of weakness. We may be afraid that they might think less of us and will not want anything to do with us. So, instead we give others the impression that everything is fine.

Some people might not share emotions with others because they do not want to be a burden or inconvenience them. They may fear how others might react based on previous experiences when they got hurt. They may feel that sharing personal information will make them more vulnerable by giving others information that might be used against them. Some people may feel that sharing some types of information is not appropriate because private or personal information is not anyone else's business. They may feel that sharing feelings is a waste of time because it won't really change anything anyway. Sometimes it's easier to just deny how they feel by ignoring it, so they concentrate on how they should feel rather than how they actually feel.

It can be helpful to be aware of how the following circumstances can affect our emotions.

- Extreme emotions. These emotions can come on all the sudden or they can build up over time. We may get carried away in the heat of the moment and end up saying or doing things we do not intend to do. We may react instinctively to defend ourselves escalating the situation. We might do this out of a need to protect ourselves. It's helpful to get in the habit of understanding our emotions because of the potential impact they have on us and on others.

- Multiple emotions. We can have things happen to us that cause us to feel several different emotions simultaneously. Sometimes they can be complementary such as feeling happy and excited. However, when they are conflicted it can be a source of tension or unhappiness. For instance, someone close to us may land a great job, get married, or have a child. These may be things that we want, but have not obtained, so we are happy for the other person while also being upset that it hasn't happened to us. This can create conflicted emotions creating tension because we want them to be happy, but we want to be happy too.

- Past emotions. We all have had past experiences where we felt strong emotions. While that was in the past, we can have new experiences that make us feel the same emotions. For instance, we might have had a relationship end badly that left us feeling sad or angry. Some time later, we might have another relationship end that, under other circumstances would make us feel bad for only a short time. However, because of our past experience, we have a recurrence of the emotions from the past making this breakup more intense. The effects of emotions can accumulate over time, so if similar situations keep reoccurring, emotional feelings can become more intense.

- Negative emotions. We tend to remember negative emotions longer because they can be stronger. They represent something that is unresolved making them uncomfortable, so we spend time thinking about what we could have done to resolve them. They can be more significant because they change our physiology like our pulse or blood pressure. We can be more likely to be motivated to take action when we feel negative emotions because they are uncomfortable. If they are extreme enough, we may do things that under other less extreme circumstances we would not do. It can be helpful to have an awareness of how emotions affect our behavior to avoid falling into habits that could make the situation worse. Strong emotions can be a very powerful motivator. One of the most effective ways to motivate people to do something is to make them angry.

- Defensiveness. If people are feeling very strong emotions we may react to them with strong emotions of our own. Often in a disagreement or conflict, emotional levels can escalate with each person matching the emotional level intensity of the other. We do this to defend ourselves from what we perceive as a potential threat. For example, if someone is very angry we may become angry to defend ourselves. We may feel that we have to match their emotional intensity in order to get through to them, so if they yell we are likely to yell back. We should never become angry just because someone else is angry because it only serves to escalate the situation making it worse. In order to defuse the situation, it's helpful not to take the bait and absorb other people's feelings, but rather stay calm and in touch with your own emotions by considering your desired outcome.

- Emotional control. Emotions can motivate us to say and do things we would never do under other circumstances or they can paralyze us into doing nothing. Both situations can be debilitating and damaging unless we do something to control them. While we cannot control what others say or do and we may not be able to help how we feel. Improving awareness of our emotions can help us to know what we are communicating to others and how they perceive us. If you find yourself in an emotional situation, take a moment to consider your desired outcome. Doing this can help you to not let circumstances control you. It can stop the emotional momentum giving you time to consider your options and keep emotional control to choose the best approach for the situation.

Expressing emotions.

In order to deal with our emotions it's helpful to have an awareness of what they are. All too often when someone asks us how we are feeling we simply reply, "I'm fine." We say this to fit just about all emotions except perhaps the most extreme. We do this because we may have difficulty expressing our emotions or we simply may not be able to come up with the right words. Having a good vocabulary can help us to get in touch with our emotions and accurately express them. Developing your vocabulary can help you avoid always saying, "I'm fine." Instead, you can communicate precisely how you feel when appropriate.

These are some options to consider in expressing emotions.

- Reduce uncertainty by increasing awareness. We can deal more effectively with the uncertainty of our emotions by increasing our awareness of their cause and effect. Think about what things motivate which kinds of emotions. Think about what makes you feel good or happy and what things make you upset or depressed. Increased awareness gives you the ability to make choices about what to do. If you know a certain situation or person is the source of negative emotions, you could limit your contact or eliminate it altogether. Do things that make you feel good and spend time with people who are positive. While it is not always possible to avoid negativity all the time, having an increased awareness can make us more prepared for dealing with bad situations and keep us from absorbing the emotions of others.

- Consider how we share meaning through our emotions. When someone is experiencing extreme emotions we might think they are acting irrational, however, everyone feels that they act rationally. Asking them to talk about what is going on may cause them to realize what is happening when they hear themselves describing it. When someone experiences extreme emotion we have a natural tendency to tell them to relax. This might make them more upset because people do not like to be told what to do. It discounts how they are feeling by implying that their emotions do not matter. Instead, ask them about their emotions and why they are feeling the way they do. They may simply want to be heard by someone.

- Invest in relationships by talking with someone. It can be helpful to talk about our emotions with someone we trust to get feedback about how they perceive us. We tend to internalize our emotions and hide them from others, even from ourselves. We may act happy when in reality we are not. We do this because people prefer to be around others who are happy and upbeat. Social reality can discourage us from being too open, so it can be helpful to find someone we trust who will be honest and supportive. Talking about our feelings can make us feel better because it relieves stress and reduces tension by getting it out of our system. Having someone listen to us can be cathartic making us feel better. Sharing emotions with someone shows them that we trust them. When others share emotions with us, it shows that they care about what we think. By investing in relationships we connect with others and show them that we appreciate, value, and respect them.

- Know your desired outcome. Determine what emotions to share with whom. Choose an appropriate time and place to talk about emotions with others so that they will feel comfortable listening. Be sure the other person understands your reason for talking about your feelings. Do you want to vent your feelings, have them support you, give you feedback, or do something? While it can be good to be honest about how you feel, the reality is that not all emotions should be shared, especially if they could be hurtful to others. It's always good to be tactful to see how they are accepted because not everyone will accept all types of feelings, especially if they are about them.

- Decide to be happy. Given a choice between feeling good or bad, which would you choose? While we cannot turn our emotions on and off it's helpful to have an awareness of what makes us upset so we can do more to be happy. Emotions come from our state of mind, so if our state of mind can make us upset, it should also be able to make us happy. By doing this, we take something bad and turn it around to make it better. There are times when that is not so easy because other people do things that make us upset. But if someone does something bad to us why should we feel bad about it, because they probably don't feel bad about it. Feeling bad does not make anything better for you.

- Be realistic by checking your perceptions and expectations to see if they are accurate. We may become emotional based upon faulty perceptions or unrealistic expectations. Determine the scope of the situation because things are often not as bad as they seem. Understanding the source of what causes emotions can help to address or resolve them. Developing an awareness of the things that cause extreme emotions can help you prepare for them and know what to do when they happen. It's helpful to understand how we interpret information and give it meaning because of how it can affect how we feel.

- Choose an appropriate time and place to express your emotions. Most of the time we express our emotions when we feel them without thinking about the consequences. This is because emotions can happen without warning so we respond right away when it may be better to wait until later. While it is generally good to be honest about our emotions, the reality is that there are times when we should not let others know how we feel. By expressing our emotions in the heat of the moment we may say things we don't mean. While it's not good to suppress our emotions, it's not good to dump everything we are feeling on someone either. It's better to choose a time and place when others would be more receptive to them.

- When we use the term constructive criticism, all people generally hear is criticism. Is any criticism ever perceived as constructive? It's helpful to keep emotions, even negative ones, in a positive light. For example, rather than saying, "You made me angry," you might say, "When this happens, I feel angry." Sharing emotions follows the rules of self-disclosure because sharing information about ourselves can build trust, however, it should be done incrementally and appropriately. It can be helpful for others to share their experiences, but it should not become a contest to see who has had it the worst.

Uncertainty and stress.

Stress is an inevitable and unavoidable part of our lives caused by unresolved tension. It is an emotional and physiological expression of uncertainty that comes from unresolved problems, decisions, or unfulfilled needs and wants. Tension and stress can lead to medical problems, but if kept in perspective it can be helpful because it can give us a boost of energy when we need it. It can heighten our perception and motivate us to take action.

While we cannot totally alleviate stress, having an awareness of its sources and effects makes it easier for us to do something about it. By increasing awareness we can look objectively at what causes stress because we may have the perception that something is stressful when in fact the stress may be coming from somewhere else. By knowing the source of stress as specifically as possible, we can isolate the situations and people who cause it. When we know this we have a better chance to make changes, to keep it in perspective, or to eliminate it altogether.

These are some options to help manage stress.

- Reduce uncertainty by communicating. When faced with a stressful situation, we may instinctively react in a way that can make the stress worse. How we communicate in times of stress can determine how we feel about it affecting its outcome. It's helpful to communicate in a clear, accurate, and positive way that will help us and others cope with stress. Communicating in negative, unrealistic, and confusing ways can make the situation worse and more stressful. While that may sound obvious, we have a natural tendency to make things worse because it's easy to do. Identifying the source and scope of the stress, coming up with options to deal with it, and then following through can be a more difficult, but more effective approach.

- Awareness can help give us a realistic perspective on the nature and scope of the problem. It can help us determine what is actually causing stress and how it is affecting us. It gives us a clear picture of our skills in order to choose the best approach to resolve stress. Having options gives us a variety of approaches to resolve the stress in order to choose the best one for success. These can be prepared ahead of time, so that when stress happens you can respond appropriately before it gets out of hand.

- Confidence helps us to stay in control of the situation, to focus on the task at hand, and to evaluate our options. It helps us to have realistic perceptions and expectations about what we can do and what can be achieved. We can improve our confidence by developing a plan of action for stressful situations and practicing that plan so we are familiar with it. Confidence comes from experience and belief in our own abilities. By preparing beforehand for stressful situations, we can be more confident when they happen.

- Competence. Since stress is a natural part of life, we can be prepared for things that we know will happen to us that can be stressful. We know there's a good chance that we will face stressful situations like medical issues, work problems, and financial difficulties. We know that we may have unpredictable stress such as accidents, acts of nature, or illness. We can prepare for these things by having a plan to deal with them. We can reduce stress by instilling confidence when we feel prepared to handle stressful situations.

- Be positive. While it sounds cliché, it helps to remain positive during stressful situations. Concentrate on the issue at hand and avoid bringing in other things. State the positive when it is truthful and realistic. Don't make assumptions or jump to conclusions about what is happening or what might happen because these may not be true and could cause unnecessary stress. Show confidence by using positive facial expressions, open posture, self assured gestures, and definite movements. Lack of confidence is too often communicated through nonverbal behaviors like confusing facial expressions, excessive gestures, fidgeting, pacing back and forth, or tugging on hair or clothing. If you act confident others will pick up on your confidence and are more likely to reflect it back to you, making you feel more confident about yourself.

Uncertainty and risk.

Life is full of risks, but we take them because we are motivated by the laws of uncertainty and investing. We take risks to fulfill needs and wants as well as achieve desired outcomes. Risk involves an element of choice created by people as opposed to uncertainty that is created by nature so it is unavoidable. We take risks based upon our perception of the potential loss compared to our expectations of potential gain. We might overlook the potential harmful aspects of risk in order to fulfill needs and wants like fun, excitement, adventure, or material gains. Most of the things we do every day entail some degree of risk. When we drive to work, we risk an accident. When we are involved in a relationship, we risk the pain of rejection. We take risks because it helps us to fulfill our needs and wants to achieve our desired outcomes because most of the time we don't come to any real harm.

Different types of risks are invested with shared meaning. Some can be seen as foolhardy while others are perceived as noble. People who take risks can be perceived as being more interesting, exciting, or attractive. We can be attracted to them because they can be perceived as exciting, confident, or successful. We take risks to gain the attention of others, to obtain prestige or status, to make money, to bolster our self-concept, or just for the thrill of it to get an adrenaline rush. Taking risks can give us additional perspective by looking at the familiar in a new way.

When we reduce uncertainty life becomes more stable and secure, but it may also become boring and uninteresting. Risk can be stressful, but we take risks to gain an emotional response. Our need for excitement and adventure encourages us to take risks. For example, we might take up rock climbing because it is more exciting than staying at home. However, it entails more risk and potential harm. In many activities we may ignore the potential risks focusing more on the potential rewards.

In order to fulfill our need for excitement and adventure we might take part in activities that provide us the emotions of taking a risk when there is little actual risk involved. We might like to go on rides at a theme park because they give us the rush of being in seemingly dangerous circumstances when we are really in a controlled situation that is relatively safe. We like to see scary movies because we can feel emotions like the excitement and danger associated with taking risks.

As we become more experienced with risk we develop confidence in our abilities. However, overconfidence can create an attitude of arrogance where warning signs are discounted or ignored leading to excessive risk. Success can encourage people to take ever increasing risks giving them a feeling that they can handle it, they deserve it, or they know what they are doing. They may seek bigger and bigger rewards despite the increased risk or danger, even though it could result in undesired or unintended outcomes like a crisis.

Uncertainty and fear.

Fear is an emotional response to heightened uncertainty. It is an intangible mental state that has tangible consequences. People can use fear to achieve their desired outcome because it is a powerful emotion that can be used to motivate others to take action. This is why it is effective in advertising and political campaigns because it motivates people to do things they might otherwise not do. It can be used to manipulate people for personal gain. We are told to face our fears, but fear can be good because it can be a natural survival mechanism to protect us from things that could cause us harm.

By being aware of our fears, we can put them into perspective separating the rational from the irrational. By increasing our awareness we can reduce the potential consequences from things that can make us fearful. By gaining information these things become more familiar reducing uncertainty, so our fear does not have as much control over us. For example, we may fear flying on an airplane. The noises in a plane can make us apprehensive because it increases uncertainty. Learning about how an airplane works and what those noises mean can help make us less apprehensive because we know what to expect reducing uncertainty.

A helpful approach to facing fear is to separate those that are psychologically based from those that pose a real threat because both can be just as frightening or debilitating. Sometimes people talk about having irrational fears, but no fear is irrational to the person who has them. Any fear can seem very real with real consequences. Since fears are based upon an individual's perceptions and expectations, different people will fear different things to different degrees for different reasons.

Fears are sometimes based on our perception of a situation that comes in contrast with our expectations. For instance, we may have heard things around work that makes us fear losing our job. It can help to obtain more information directly from the source. If that's not possible, other information may be gathered to help clarify the situation. Alternatives could be explored such as managing our finances better or looking for another job, just in case you loose yours. In each of these situations, fear can be reduced by identifying it and taking action to reduce uncertainty.

Having awareness and options helps us to understand what we fear and the source of that fear, so that we can take action to mitigate its effect. Gathering information helps us understand the situation, so that we can put our fears in perspective. Fear can be analogous to a smoke detector. We should not try to disable it, but rather we should understand how it can be beneficial to us and what to do when is sounds an alarm. Fear can function as a gauge of uncertainty. It can be helpful if utilized appropriately because it is nature's warning system that can keep us from doing imprudent, thoughtless, irresponsible, shortsighted, foolish, or rash things. Rather than overcoming our fears, we can develop skills to take the appropriate action when we feel them.

Uncertainty and anger.

Despite our best intentions and communicating skills, situations can escalate beyond our capacity to handle them. Feelings of frustration can turn to conflict and anger. Once this process gets going it may be difficult to stop. Anger is often the result of conflicts going unresolved due to extreme levels of uncertainty. Anger is an emotion that is communicated to get attention or to motivate others to fulfill a person's desired outcome.

Expressing anger can provide emotional release for the moment, but it can have unintended and undesirable outcomes. It can lead to defensiveness and provoke retaliation from others. Anger can damage your health by contributing to higher blood pressure, a weakened immunity to illness, and increased levels of cortical that could increase the potential for artery blockage or heart attack. People don't want to be around others who are angry regardless if they are right or not.

When you feel angry it can be helpful to stop and ask yourself, what is your desired outcome? This may provide a moment to defuse the situation preventing it from escalating. Rarely is our desired outcome to get angry at someone, to yell at them, to retaliate, or to make an enemy out of them. If someone is angry at us and we do not respond in kind, if they are still angry then that's their problem. If we respond angrily, then it has become our problem. It's not that we don't want to get angry, it's just that it usually doesn't do any good.

To prevent anger, it can be helpful to know the sources of what makes us angry. Once you know what they are, you can decide what to do about them. Try avoiding them if possible or change the circumstances in order to work out other approaches to lessen their effect. We might try telling people who make us angry how we are feeling without casting blame or being judgmental. However, there are times when it may be better to keep them to yourself.

If they truly care about us they will be concerned and want to help us out. If we blame them, they are less likely to want to help us and will be more interested in defending themselves. However, there can be people who feel that they have no responsibility and are unwilling to help whatever the circumstances. Since we cannot control everything it's helpful to be prepared, have a plan, and avoid falling into unproductive behaviors.

It can be helpful to utilize the following options to reduce anger and its effects on us.

- Identify the real issues. We often get angry before actually understanding the issues and scope of the problem.

- Identify the source. Knowing what causes feelings of anger helps to better deal with them.

- Consider the potential consequences. Consider what it might do to your relationships with others and what it could do to you.

- Distance yourself from the source of the anger. Avoid people and situations that create anger when possible.

- Make changes to avoid repeating circumstances that create anger.

- Look at what you know in a new way in order to change the situations and relationships that make you angry.

- Consider avoiding or eliminating situations and relationships that cause anger.

- Get support from people who you feel comfortable talking with and who you trust.

- Tell someone you trust about your feelings to release built up emotions. Chances are they have been in similar situations and have had similar feelings. You may learn how to better cope with your feelings from their experiences.

Uncertainty and forgiveness.

There are things people do that creates tension by increasing uncertainty, so conventional methods of conflict resolution may not work to reduce it. The other person may be unwilling or unable to help. In these circumstances forgiveness is one way to resolve this tension with others by reducing the uncertainty we may feel.

Forgiveness is one way we can reduce uncertainty in our relationships with others. When people do something bad to us we may have to forgive them in order to let go of negative emotions like anger. If we hurt someone and expect them to forgive us, we should be able to forgive others. Religion encourages us to forgive others and seek forgiveness for our transgressions. However, when someone has done us wrong the last thing we probably think about is forgiving them. Our first impulse might be to get even or retaliate even though this rarely benefits us or resolves anything.

Forgiveness can be beneficial because it gives us, not the other person, a fresh start. It's a chance for us to show a spirit of generosity and compassion even if the other person doesn't warrant it. Forgiving others is for your benefit, not theirs because you stop dwelling on something you can't change that makes you upset. When something is unresolved it creates tension, which is uncomfortable motivating us to resolve it. Forgiveness is one way that we can resolve the tension we feel so we can forget about something someone did to us. It can be a substitute for actually resolving a situation when the other person is unable or unwilling to do so. In this way forgiveness can be a means to reduce uncertainty.

We may be reluctant to forgive because we feel that it absolves the other person of responsibility for what they have done. You can forgive someone without agreeing with them or condoning their actions. It does not mean that the other person should not have to pay the consequences or receive the justice they deserve. They should still have to account for their actions, but making them do that should not necessarily be up to you. Forgiveness does not mean doing nothing, we can still take action to protect ourselves to see that it doesn't happen to us again.

Forgiveness is about you, not the other person. It's about helping you to get over your bad feelings about the other person and what they did to you so that you can move on. We communicate in part based on our past experiences, so by continuing to think about how others have wronged us we are giving them power beyond what they deserve. The purpose of forgiving them is to take their power over us away.

How we approach forgiveness depends on the nature of the relationship. If we wish to continue a relationship after someone has hurt us, we need to find a way to come to terms with what happened and resolve the emotions that have been created, so that we can move on to restore normality. If someone hurts us who actually cares about us and maintaining the relationship, they should be willing to do what it takes to make things right. If they are unwilling to do this, you might reconsider the relationship.

When we are angry at someone or have a conflict with them, consider your desired outcome. At first it may be to hurt them, make them pay, or to get revenge. But that approach does nothing to benefit anyone. If we try to get even with everyone who has done us wrong, that's all we would have time to do. One purpose of forgiveness is to resolve the tension and have closure to end it in your mind, not necessarily to resolve it for the other person. If someone hurts you, why keep on hurting yourself?

Health and Uncertainty

It's been said that, it's what's on the inside that counts. While this generally pertains to who we are as a person, it could also pertain to our state of well being or health. Our health can have an important impact on our behavior and appearance. When we feel good we look good because we have a better self-concept, so we act more confidently. While we all want to have good health, our well being is often subject to the law of uncertainty.

We can reduce uncertainty about our health by communicating more effectively with others. Developing effective communicating skills can help us gain useful information to make important decisions. As the nature of healthcare changes, we are going to be increasingly responsible for maintaining our own health. This can motivate us to increase our awareness of health issues and our options to improve our well being. We will need knowledge and skills to better understand ourselves and our health needs. We can benefit by developing effective communicating skills to communicate with medical professionals. By knowing how to do research, we can be better informed. By knowing how crisis works, we can be prepared for what might happen in order to mitigate its effects. This can help us to reduce uncertainty, so that we can invest in ourselves, our health, and our well being.

Communicating effectively with others can help to create and maintain positive relationships to improve the quality of our health. This helps reduce uncertainty, which can lower blood pressure, reduce hypertension, and lower the risk of heart disease. When we share meaning with others it can make us feel needed and appreciated. This helps to create and maintain relationships that provide us with support and nurturing. By developing communicating skills, we can gain many health benefits from uncertainty reduction.

The laws of uncertainty, shared meaning, and investing can help to diagnose and treat physical and mental health issues. For instance, in diagnosing illness we look for the cause or symptoms in order to find a treatment. However, there could be a deeper, underlying cause. Increased uncertainty has the potential to be an underlying cause, so when we treat the symptoms it could help to look for ways to reduce uncertainty, share meaning, and encourage investing.

Increased uncertainty can lead to stress, anxiety, and depression that can in turn affect our health and well being in many ways. Our mental state can affect our physical state. Many of the emotions we feel like anxiety, fear, and anger can have health consequences. So, uncertainty has the potential to be an underlying source of medical and psychological conditions because social reality can create physical reality. For instance, someone may have a sleep or digestive disorder that is caused by stress or anxiety. Their mental state may be manifesting itself in a physical malady caused by uncertainty at home or work. So, in diagnosing medical problems, it can be helpful to look at how the law of uncertainty may be affecting them.

The law of shared meaning can affect our relationships with others, which can affect how we see ourselves, our self-concept, and how we relate to others. So, the nature of our relationships can affect our health. For instance, if we have a good communicating network and support system, it can improve our confidence and self-concept, which can help us feel better. If we share little meaning with others, we might feel alone, withdrawn, or depressed. If we are having difficulties in our relationships, it could diminish our confidence and self-concept. These can affect our health because psychological perceptions can have physical consequences.

The law of investing motivates us to invest in relationships with others to fulfill needs and wants we cannot fulfill ourselves. We invest in relationships because they can make us feel good about ourselves bolstering our self-concept, which can improve our health. We also need to invest in ourselves, which includes both our physical and mental well being. While we maintain our possessions like a car or house, it is all to easy to neglect taking care of our most important asset, ourselves. We insure our possessions in case of problems, so we should also insure ourselves. However, attempts to change healthcare can have the undesired outcome of increasing uncertainty, when it should be reduced to provide stability and security.

Good health is one of our most important needs and we want to feel good. Health and well being needs and wants can motivate behavior, however, the need to be healthy and wanting to feel good can be one of the most challenging set of conflicting needs and wants we have, making it difficult to find a balance. We enjoy eating food that tastes good, but we also need to eat healthy, which may not be as satisfying. A person may feel depressed or stressed due to increased uncertainty or if their perceptions do not meet their expectations. This can motivate them to eat, drink, or smoke to feel better even though it is harmful to their health.

Our perceptions and expectations can also have an effect on our health. When our perceptions are accurate and our expectations are reasonable, we can feel good. However, if our perceptions are not meeting our expectations it can make us feel sad, depressed, or even angry, which can affect our mental as well as physical health. Treating health issues can include addressing psychological issues that can originate in uncertainty, perceptions and expectations, and needs and wants fulfillment.

Improving our awareness can help us to know more about our current state of health and what might happen in the future. Our health care is one source of uncertainty because everyone will likely face health issues at sometime in their life. Increased awareness can help give us more options to prepare for and deal with them. It can help reduce the likelihood of having a health crisis because we can be better prepared for what might happen. Having options can also help us to find the best possible solutions to potential health problems in order to improve our quality of life.

Body Language as Nonverbal Communicating

Body language refers to how we use our body to communicate with others. It is a form of nonverbal communicating that we not only use to support the words we say, but also to communicate information without saying anything. Practically anything we do with our body has the potential to communicate something. Body language includes how we carry ourselves including our posture, demeanor, and bearing. It includes how we move parts of our body including our head, arms, hands, and legs. It includes gestures, facial expressions, and eye contact. We use body language to communicate messages to others that can support, substitute, contradict, or hide our verbal messages.

Our nonverbal behavior creates impressions in the minds of others even before we speak a word. Others use their perceptions of us to determine if we are approachable or not. This can determine whether they talk to us or not based on how they interpret our nonverbal behavior. We make these judgments based upon our perceptions of other people's behavior that we invest with meaning in order to reduce uncertainty about them. These judgments are important because they affect our behavior whether they are accurate or not.

We are motivated to observe and understand body language by the law of uncertainty. We do this to learn about others in order to reduce uncertainty. We do this when we don't have a lot of information, so we try to fill in the missing pieces, which can create an inaccurate picture. Nonverbal body language is open to interpretation, so we may misinterpret the information we have. These things can lead to inaccurate generalizations or stereotypes. So, it's helpful not to make judgments or come to conclusions until obtaining accurate information.

In order to reduce uncertainty, the law of shared meaning motivates us to invest meaning in other people's behavior including their nonverbal body language. For some behavior the meaning is universal such as a handshake or a smile. For others it is open to interpretation. While we invest behavior with meaning, there's always the possibility of misunderstanding what is meant. For example, a typical inference is that people who sit with their legs crossed or their arms folded are closed off to others. The reality may be that they are just more comfortable sitting that way and are really very open. When it comes to nonverbal body language we may think we know what something means, however, there may be other interpretations of this behavior. This can make it difficult to accurately ascertain what is meant without obtaining additional information.

The law of investing motivates us to look for meaning in nonverbal body language. When we meet someone, we want to know more about them in order to reduce uncertainty, so that we can invest in a relationship with them. Because we don't know them very well we may not have much information. We use the information we have, which is often gained by observing their nonverbal behavior. This information is often incomplete, so we fill in the blanks from our past experiences. We do this because in order to get to know someone and invest in a relationship with them we need to know more about them. Observing nonverbal body language is an important way that we do this. Once we get to know them, we rely less on nonverbal information and more on what they say or who they are.

Body language serves an important function by providing information that shapes our perception of others. The law of shared meaning motivates us to interpret what people mean by how they move. Much of what we perceive about others we gain through observing their behavior. We use the perception process to interpret what we observe in order to form expectations about how others will behave. It would be difficult to have relationships without these expectations because they reduce uncertainty to provide stability and a degree of predictability.

These are several functions that nonverbal body language fulfills.

- First impressions. When we first meet someone we use the perception process to form an impression of them based upon their nonverbal body language. We reduce uncertainty by observing a person's appearance, demeanor, mannerisms, and manner of speaking because we generally don't have much other information. While first impressions are often inaccurate because of lack of information, they can be difficult to change once formed.

- Likeability. When we meet someone we want to like them and want them to like us. We rarely meet people we want to dislike nor do we want them to dislike us. We make appraisals of likeability based upon nonverbal body language. For example, we can be perceived as more likable if we smile, lean slightly towards others, make appropriate eye contact, and shake hands. People can be perceived as more distant if they avoid eye contact, don't smile, or have little movement.

- Balance. We look for balanced nonverbal behavior that is not too extreme one way or the other. For example, people who speak with a slight lower pitch, even pacing, and a variety of intonation are perceived as more confident than those who have a high pitch, fast pacing, and uneven intonation. Too little eye contact can make others uncomfortable as well as having too much eye contact. To find the right balance, we use self awareness and feedback to determine how we are being perceived.

- Feedback. We use the nonverbal behavior of others as a kind of feedback to let us know how we are coming across to them. Positive feedback includes a smile, nod, leaning forward, or pat on the back. The nonverbal feedback others provide lets us know how they perceive us, which can affect the future of the relationship.

- Credibility. Much of what we perceive as credible is communicated nonverbally through body language and appearance. People are perceived as credible when they make appropriate eye contact, have proper posture, speak with a clear voice, use even pacing, have proper pronunciation, and enunciate words clearly, because these things reduce uncertainty. People are perceived as less credible if they don't make eye contact, look around or at the ground, have poor posture, shift from side to side, speak with a high pitch, use rapid pacing, or don't pronounce words properly or enunciate clearly.

- Control. We use nonverbal behavior to communicate control, dominance, or authority over others. This is done through posture, demeanor, gestures, and eye contact. Standing in close proximity, lowering the pitch of our voice, speaking louder, and steady pacing can give the perception of authority. Using extreme eye contact can he perceived as exerting dominance or intensity. People may be perceived as being submissive if they avoid eye contact, speak in a low volume or tone, shift their posture, or move away. What is perceived as submissiveness could actually be nervousness or simply being uncomfortable because of the mannerisms of others. Through awareness we can use nonverbal body language to assert ourselves and stand up to people who may try to dominate us without being overly aggressive. We can tell the difference between someone actually having authority or just acting like they do.

- Aggressiveness. People may use nonverbal techniques to pressure others to get them to do what they want them to do. By understanding how nonverbal body language works you can protect yourself so you are not as susceptible to them. If you feel like someone is pressuring you by being aggressive, you can stand your ground and not accept their control without escalating the situation into a conflict. Remain calm, but confident. Speak slowly in a clear, firm voice to assert yourself. Look them in the eye indicating that you do not accept their demeanor, but in a way that will not challenge them. This gives them the perception that you are secure in yourself and are in control, so they should back off.

Elements of nonverbal body language.

- Posture. One of the first things people notice about others is their posture. They make judgments based upon how a person stands and how they move. This includes their posture, stature, and bearing. Good posture involves standing with your back straight, shoulders back, head up, and feet at approximately a 45 degree angle about the same distance apart as your shoulders. Bearing is the way a person moves or stands. Having good bearing means that you move at a moderate pace with confidence, avoiding sudden or jerky movements.

We can perceive people who use good posture as more competent, educated, affluent, likable, and as having a more positive attitude. People who slouch, lean against walls, shift their weight, or have rounded shoulders can be perceived as sloppy, lazy, untrustworthy, incompetent, or having a low self-concept. People make judgments about our posture because it can be perceived as a reflection of our pride and confidence in ourselves.

- Gestures. When we communicate, we gesture by moving parts of our body including our hands, arms, fingers, head, legs, and feet. Gestures can be used as a kind of language to emphasize important words and phrases. They add interest to what we say when we are speaking. We can use gestures in place of words like when we wave hello or goodbye. They can be used to express feelings and emotions. They are used to show directions or demonstrate how something works. Gestures can be deliberate, however, we often use them without thinking or out of habit. We are motivated to use gestures by the law of uncertainty because they help to clarify what we mean when communicating with others.

Gestures should appear natural, be used sparingly and appropriately. People who use gestures appropriately are generally considered more interesting and engaging. They give the impression of having more confidence, which makes them likable. People who do not use gestures can be perceived as being withdrawn or not interested in others. Excessive gesturing can be perceived as being nervous, lacking confidence, unstable, or even aggressive making people distance themselves from them. If people feel nervous a common habit is to avoid gesturing by putting their hands in their pockets. Being aware of how gestures are perceived helps improve communicating skills so that we are perceived as being more self assured and confident to others.

- Facial expressions. Our face is the most noticed and expressive part of our body. It is our most distinctive and individually unique characteristic. Facial expressions involve all aspects of our facial movements including our eyes, mouth, lips, chin, forehead, and eyebrows. While many of our facial expressions are intentional, others can be involuntary based upon what we are saying, thinking, or feeling. We are motivated by the law of uncertainty to look for meaning in facial expressions to provide us more information about others.

Facial expressions are a practical application of the law of shared meaning, we look at a person's face for meaning to understand more about them. We look at a person's face to gain many different kinds of information. We use it to ascertain what kind of person they are. We use it to interpret the words they are saying. We use it to determine if they are being honest or not. We use it as an indicator of their emotions, moods, or how they are feeling. We use it to diagnose a person's health and if they are feeling well or not. We use it to express emotions with what we are saying or as a substitute for words. We use it to show approval such as smiling or nodding. We use it to show disapproval by frowning or shaking our head. We might even use it to avoid communicating by turning away.

We tend to trust facial expressions more than words because they are perceived to be more honest since they are spontaneous, even though sometimes people might try to use them to their advantage. Most of the time we use facial expressions to support what we are saying, however, there are other ways we can use them. We can use them to make what we are saying more intense like when we are surprised. We can minimize our reactions to show that something doesn't bother us. We might cover up our expressions in order to hide what we are thinking or feeling. We can use expressions that have little or no meaning so others won't know how we really feel.

- Eye contact. There's an old adage that says the eyes are the window to the soul. We look at people's eyes because of the kinds of information that can be communicated with them. They can be used to express many emotions including sympathy, surprise, affection, intimacy, or anger. While eyes are part of our facial expressions, they can take on a characteristic of their own. We look into people's eyes to determine if they are telling the truth, their motivation, their credibility, or how they are feeling. We use eye contact to express affection or intimacy, to emphasize important points, or to threaten others.

If we want to meet someone new or talk to someone we know, we use eye contact to get their attention to make a connection. We use it to regulate how we communicate with others, or to initiate and maintain relationships. We use it to get people's attention, encourage them to talk to us, or discourage them by turning away. When we speak to a group of people we make eye contact to create a connection with them. We observe the eye contact of others when we are speaking as a means of gaining feedback to let us know how we are coming across to them.

How people make eye contact can be an indication of the nature of their relationship. We tend to make more eye contact with people we like or with whom we have a close relationship. We make less eye contact with people we do not know well or who we do not like. When two people have a secret intimate relationship like having an affair, they might give themselves away by how they make eye contact with each other. It can be considered rude not to look at someone you are talking to as well as to stare at them. Using eye contact is a matter of balance because both excessive and lack of eye contact can make others uncomfortable.

Touch as Nonverbal Communicating

Touch is not only part of our nonverbal body language, it is one of the five senses we use to make a connection to communicate with others. It can be one of the most powerful ways to communicate because touch can be very personal in nature. It can communicate the nature of our relationships, not only between ourselves and others, but it can be observed by others outside the relationship. We make assumptions about others based upon our perception of touch. If we are watching two people engaged in a conversation, but cannot hear what they say, we can make inferences about the nature of their relationship based on how they use touch.

How we utilize touch is governed by the rules of social reality. It communicates how we feel about ourselves and others. It is a way to communicate our feelings and emotions, develop and maintain relationships, and express our thoughts when words may not be adequate. It is the way we show support and affection. It can be the most powerful form of nonverbal behavior.

The degree to which we use touch can be seen as an indicator of the level of uncertainty in a relationship. If we do not know someone there is a high degree of uncertainty, so we keep our distance and do not touch them because we do not know what to expect from them or how they will react. As we get to know someone, uncertainty is reduced so we are more comfortable using touch.

When we don't know someone we follow the rules of social reality by shaking hands. As we get to know them we may give them a hug. If the relationship becomes closer we may kiss or use other forms of touch.

Touch is a physical expression of the law of shared meaning. Practically all forms of touch carry some meaning. These meanings are governed by the rules of social reality, some of which are changing making them open to differing interpretations. Some meanings can be universal, while others differ based on culture, ethnicity, religion, and an individual's past experiences. If you are uncertain what something means, it's best to ask. Meaning is conveyed not just by how we touch someone, but where. For example, a pat on the back has a different meaning than a pat on the head or a pat on the bottom.

When we meet people we welcome them with a handshake. We express our friendship and affection with a hug. Touch can be a powerful social reward that affirms another person's value. It can make us feel accepted, attractive, or valued. It helps us to develop trust so that we can invest in relationships with others improving and strengthening them.

We use touch to express our feelings and emotions such as friendship, affection, and love. Generally, the longer the duration of the touch the greater the intimacy. We use touch to communicate our investment in relationships. This means that it can be used as an indicator of a person's investment in their relationships with others. The relationships where we have the greatest investment often involve the most use of touch.

Touch fulfills needs we cannot fulfill ourselves. We use it to communicate our needs and wants to other people. It fulfills our needs for closeness, friendship, affection, and intimacy. This makes it a powerful social reward. Babies need to be held in order to feel nurtured and to be healthy. We use touch to heal people and make them feel better.

How touch is perceived can be interpreted with different meanings based upon our experiences and social reality. It is subject to a wide variety of perceptions and expectations. What may be comfortable for one person may not be for another. We develop expectations about touch depending upon the nature of our relationship. It's helpful to communicate our perceptions and expectations about touch in relationships to avoid misunderstandings.

Not all touch is the same. Different types of touch have different meanings. These are a few of the most common types

- Public. In most of our daily activities we don't usually touch other people. Sometimes touch is accidental and unavoidable such as in crowded spaces like elevators or public transportation. Since the rules of social reality motivate our behavior in these situations touch can be awkward, so when it happens we tend to pull away.

- Professional. Many professions use touch. A doctor touches a patient to examine them, a massage therapist touches a client, and a hairstylist touches a person's head. They use touch in ways that under the circumstances are considered appropriate because they are necessary for them to do their job.

- Health. Touch is essential to good health and well being. Infants need to be held in order to properly develop. Lack of touch can result in increased tension or illness. Physical therapy and massage are based upon touch to promote healing.

- Social. There are certain types of touch that are expected in social circumstances. We shake hands, hug, or kiss on the cheek to say hello or goodbye. These rituals are regulated by the rules of social reality and not following them may be perceived as a rejection or being rude. These vary depending on the culture and geographic affiliation.

- Affiliation. People who belong to the same group or organization often use touch to communicate their affiliation. Members of a sports team or people who work together may pat each other on the back or hi five one another to communicate support. Groups like religions use rituals that involve touch like baptism, laying of hands, and group prayer because they believe touch has a special significance.

- Friendship. Touch is used to communicate friendship between people. The degree of touch can communicate the degree of closeness and nature of the relationship. Coworkers may pat each other on the back. Close friends or family members hug one another to communicate friendship, affection, or love.

- Aggression. People may use touch as a means of manipulating, dominating, or threatening others. The level of intensity can vary from grabbing someone by the arm to gain their attention to aggressive or violent behavior. In these situations aggressive use of touch can be symptomatic of larger problems.

- Affection. Touch is an important means of showing affection to others. How we use touch can vary depending upon the closeness of the relationship. Friends or family members show affection by hugging or kissing each other on the cheek. A couple in an intimate relationship uses touch to express their affection for one another. Generally, the closer or more intimate the relationship, the more ways people use touch to show affection.

- Intimacy. Touch is one of the ways we express affection and intimacy. An intimate relationship utilizes a high degree of touch to show the other person that they are loved and valued. The kinds of touch used are specific to the relationship indicating that the relationship is special.

Appearance as Nonverbal Communicating

There's an old adage that goes, you can't judge a book by its cover. Yet, publishers devote considerable resources to designing book covers. Appearance is about how we look, our attractiveness, how we do our hair, the clothes we wear, and what all those things communicate to others. Ideally, our appearance shouldn't matter. What should matter is who we are on the inside as a person. However, our appearance does matter because of the law of uncertainty. A person's appearance can be the most information we have about someone, especially if we don't know them very well.

Society invests personal appearance with meaning. People judge others by their appearance because it can be perceived as an outward manifestation of their inner qualities. Since people cannot see who we are on the inside, they look for information from our appearance. They perceive our appearance and compare it to their expectations based on other people they know. They do this in order to make inferences about what a person is like without having to get to know them.

The law of uncertainty motivates us to gravitate toward people who we perceive are like us because they seem familiar. The rationale is if they seem similar to us, they must be like us and we will have something in common with them. This is why people often associate with others who they perceive are like them and share similar characteristics like their age, culture, ethnicity, profession, or geographic affiliation. It's not necessarily a matter of discrimination, it's a means of uncertainty reduction.

We invest many characteristics of a person's appearance with meaning including their clothing, accessories, and hairstyle. This is because appearance can communicate a person's personal preferences and professional affiliations. For example, a dark suit conveys a different meaning than a T-shirt and jeans, a uniform, or overalls. We attribute meaning based upon the perception process where we take information and give it meaning, then compare it to other people from our past experiences. Appearance can convey a variety of meanings about a person's attitudes, values, preferences, education, profession, ethnicity, culture, and personal preferences.

In order to invest in relationships with others, we look to reduce uncertainty enough so that we feel comfortable with them. We are more likely to trust people whose appearance is familiar to us or similar to our own, making us feel more comfortable because it reduces uncertainty about them. This can motivate us to associate with those we perceive are like us who have the same background, interests, or culture. We might use appearance in place of other types of information as a means of determining if we are willing to invest in someone to get to know them. We are often willing to take greater risks getting to know someone we perceive as attractive, confident, or competent because they seem safe and stable.

Our appearance can work like our Great Idea in the process of communicating. It communicates information through connections to others who provide us with feedback about how they perceive us. If they like us, it has a positive effect on our self-concept. If they don't, it can be damaging particularly if it's from a person whose opinion we value. It's helpful to be aware of what our appearance communicates to others because it can support or override what we want to say, undermining our desired outcome.

We use our appearance to fulfill the need to express our individual personality and identity. Conversely, we may be motivated to dress the same as others to show group affiliation or camaraderie because it fulfills the need for inclusion and to be connected to others. We change our appearance depending upon what particular needs or wants we are looking to fulfill. Sometimes we use our appearance to persuade others to fulfill our needs and wants. For example, if we want a job or to get a promotion, we dress professionally. If we are going on a date to start a romantic relationship, we dress to be attractive to the other person.

Our appearance is important because it provides the first bits of information others perceive about us to form a first impression. We use our perceptions as the basis to make important initial decisions such as if we want to talk to someone and how to approach them. Even before we speak to them we develop expectations based on our past experiences. If a person looks closed off or threatening, we are less likely to approach them. If they appear open and engaging, we are more likely to go up and talk to them.

We use our perception of people's appearance to make judgments about them like their profession, education, economic status, and geographic affiliations. We do this by comparing our perceptions to people we have known in the past. These past experiences help to form our expectations about people's behavior. They can be based upon age, gender, ethnicity, clothing, hair, and nonverbal characteristics. Doing this can help us to form expectations about them by comparing our perceptions to our past experiences.

Clothing.

There's a saying that goes, clothes make the person. While they don't make you who you are, they communicate information about you to others, especially to others who may not know you very well. Clothing serves to reduce uncertainty by communicating information about you like your job, economic status, and credibility. It can be used to find help in a time of crisis, such as finding a police officer, EMT, or doctor. Clothing shares meaning about the person who wears it. Groups often have unwritten dress codes that are a part of their social reality. We make determinations about how to invest in others based on how they present themselves in public and in private.

Our appearance is created by the choices that we make. It is part of identity management and how we choose to present ourselves to others. Clothing fulfills some of our most fundamental needs in life. Sometimes those needs are dictated by our job based on the tasks we perform. We wear certain types of clothes to reduce uncertainty about ourselves and inspire confidence in others. We invest practically all types and styles of clothing with meaning and make judgments about people based on the clothing they wear. We consider some clothing more desirable or valuable than others. We make inferences about who a person is and what they do based upon what they wear. We do this because it helps us to reduce uncertainty so we can invest in relationships with others.

How we share meaning about clothing is determined by the rules of social reality, which have changed considerably over time. At different times in history people wore distinctly different types of clothing. At one time men wore tights and wigs, and women wore corsets and bustles. Fashion was often influenced by the materials that were available at a particular time and place as well as the perceptions and expectations of the people based upon their social reality.

Different styles of clothing are associated with people's history, culture, heritage, traditions, rituals, and geographic affiliations. How clothing looks and what it is made from is often based upon the geographic area and climate in which the people who wear them live. It is often designed and made based on the traditions and materials that were available locally to people at the time. Before widespread trade and manufacturing, people utilized raw materials that were indigenous to their geographic area. Growing the raw materials and making them into clothing helped give each geographic area its distinct culture and became part of its traditions. When we see different styles of clothing or types of fabric they can communicate a particular culture and geographic region like British wool, Chinese silk, or Egyptian cotton.

Clothing has the ability to communicate through multiple channels based on our senses. We see how it looks and its colors. We can feel the texture of a fabric, which can be rough or smooth, thick or thin, and course or soft. We can feel it from the outside as well as how it feels on our skin. We can hear fabric rubbing together or against something, or the sound of a snap or zipper. Clothing can smell good like when it is warm and clean out of the dryer or it can smell bad telling us it needs to be washed.

We have expectations about how people dress based upon the rules of social reality. These expectations are based upon our perceptions of what is considered functional, attractive, and appropriate. Sometimes there is a history, tradition, or practical reasons why we are expected to dress in a particular way. Some clothing is designed for its practical application such as to meet specific needs for safety. Some clothing is designed to meet public expectations or to communicate information to others. Some professions utilize specialized clothing because of what it communicates to others. For instance, some professions wear uniforms because they convey authority and can be easily recognized by the public. We don't have to know the individual person in order to know what they do.

What we wear has the potential to change our behavior and how we act. Self-concept is affected by reflective communicating which is the feedback we receive from others. When we wear certain types of clothing people can treat us differently, which can make us feel different about ourselves affecting our behavior. For example, when we dress up in a suit, people may treat us more serious, so we are motivated to act more dignified. When we dress scruffy in old clothes, people might treat us less formally causing us to act more casual and relaxed. We tend to treat people who wear uniforms like a police officer, minister, or doctor with respect. Because of how reflected feedback works, when people are treated in a particular way based upon their clothing they can change how they behave so that they can fulfill people's expectations.

Clothing can affect our emotions and how we feel. Sometimes we wear clothing for work that is uncomfortable, so when we get home we change our clothes into something more comfortable. This can reduce stress helping us to relax changing our mood. We wear some clothing because it makes us feel cozy, safe, or secure. If we are feeling stressed or depressed, putting on our favorite sweater or robe can improve our mood making us feel better. When we buy new clothes, we can feel excited in anticipation of wearing them. The feelings that clothing gives us can motivate people to shop to feel better. Dressing up can make us feel happy, excited, or sexy. Our clothes can make us feel better about ourselves by bolstering our confidence and self-concept, which we communicate to others.

Certain types of clothing and accessories can serve as a form of social control to motivate appropriate behavior. We reward some people for they way they dress. People are more likely to get promoted who fit in with the expectations of their job. Clothing can communicate messages within groups and organizations. Young people can assert their individuality by not dressing like their family, but like their friends or peers. Some people communicate their solidarity by dressing alike, sometimes outside societal norms. Ironically, some groups that reject societal norms often have stricter norms within the group by dressing more alike with less individual freedom than a typical member of society.

People with a similar cultural background or who belong to the same group may have symbols or emblems of their group affiliation. For example, some schools, organizations, and the military have specific colors and emblems that identify them. They may have awards that they wear on their clothing such as metals in the military or badges in the Scouts so that others can recognize their achievement. When schools have uniforms, it creates pride in the school and a feeling of being a part of a larger community. It puts all students on an equal footing so they are seen for their individual personality rather than for the type of clothes they wear.

Hairstyles.

Perhaps few things illustrate changing social reality being manifested in physical reality as much as hairstyles. What is considered fashionable or attractive one year may be considered outdated or unattractive the next. Different types of hairstyles are associated with a particular time period in history or specific culture. It's perhaps the one feature of our appearance that people notice the most that we can change the most. We invest a great deal of meaning in how people style their hair, so much that people spend a lot of time and money on it. How we style our hair can communicate information about our age, ethnicity, economic status, profession, and personality. People may use it as a basis of determining other people's credibility, competence, values, or professionalism.

Accessories.

A part of our appearance includes the accessories we wear or carry with us. People wear accessories that can communicate information to others including jewelry, watches, shoes, glasses, belts, scarves, handbags, and purses. They also carry items that create an impression like briefcases or electronic devices. They spend time choosing the right objects because these things can reflect their personality. People make inferences about others based upon the things we have in order to gain more information about us and who we are. For example, we make inferences about the wristwatch a person wears or the handbag a woman carries based on the brand and how expensive or fashionable it is. How we select the personal objects we have is often influenced by the rules of social reality.

In addition to clothing and accessories, people wear adornments like tattoos, piercings, or nail polish. For example, if a person's fingernails are rough and discolored it communicates that they might do manual work. If a person's fingernails are manicured they most likely do not. Tattoos and piercing can be used to show individuality as well as group affiliation.

It's helpful to be aware of what we communicate to others through the personal objects we have and the accessories we wear. Personal objects can communicate information about our age, gender, social status, income, culture, ethnicity, education, occupation, group membership, or geographic affiliation. Some objects communicate a specific message like a wedding ring tells others the wearer is married. We might buy an object with a specific desired outcome, but it may result in unintended and undesired outcomes. For example, we may buy an expensive watch to feel successful, but it may communicate extravagance.

We often use personal objects to communicate to others that we are successful, attractive, fashionable, or tech savvy. We might also use them to communicate that we are sensible, conservative, thrifty, or independent. While this may be our intent, people might perceive them as cheap, pretentious, or unattractive which is an undesired outcome. We use them to both fit in with others by having the things they have as well as to assert our individually by personalizing them. By using the perception process, we utilize information based upon our possessions to form impressions of who we are, which may or may not be accurate. By having an awareness of what our possessions can communicate to others, we can use our options more effectively to achieve our desired outcomes.

Possessions as Nonverbal Communicating

Possessions comprise all the material things we own. Since our possessions represent personal choices they communicate information about us to others. They can communicate our income, profession, ethnicity, education, attitudes, personal taste, priorities, values, and other aspects of who we are. Since we make choices about the possessions we own, others may use that information to make inferences about who we are.

For example, we all have perceptions about different types of automobiles. This is probably the most expensive possession we will buy outside of our home. A car is basically a means to get from here to there. A basic vehicle to fulfill our needs can be purchased relatively inexpensively, however, people often want more than just that. There are a wide variety of vehicles that give us different perceptions and expectations about the people who own them. These can potentially communicate much information about a person including their income, values, occupation, and family situation. An inexpensive minivan communicates a different impression than an expensive two seat sports car, SUV, or pickup truck.

We form our impressions about people from their possessions based upon our past experiences, what we see in the media, and our perceptions and expectations. Some possessions communicate luxury while others are more economical. Since we choose our possessions to fulfill needs and wants, what we choose can communicate what needs and wants we have. This gives people information to make inferences about our personal characteristics such as if we are extravagant or conservative, adventurous or reserved, or having a high or low income even though these inferences may not necessarily be true.

In order to reduce uncertainty, we form impressions of others based on our perceptions of their possessions. These can include everyday objects as well as larger possessions like their house. Our possessions can reflect who we are because we select them based on our interests, values, activities, ethnicity, and culture. They are significant because each item represents an expenditure of time, energy, and money. Our possessions reflect our personality because they have meaning to us, so we can learn much about a person by learning about their possessions, how they acquired them, and what they mean to them. People may be motivated to collect or hoard possessions as a response to a loss of something important or lack of control in another area of their lives as a means to reduce uncertainty.

Our possessions are a physical manifestation of the law of shared meaning. We accumulate things because they have meaning to us. We don't usually keep things around that have no meaning. We like to have things that have meaning to us because they can make us feel better about ourselves and bolster our self-concept. We like to have things that make a connection to others and the groups we belong to because it makes us feel close to them. We use things as a form of identity management to shape how others perceive us. It can help them perceive us as fun, sophisticated, or successful. Possessions can have more value if there is a good story about them. Antiques are an example of the law of shared meaning, they can have great value or be worthless based on their meaning. People often keep possessions because of what they mean to them, regardless of their monetary value.

While we accumulate possessions to fulfill our needs and wants, we have many options. We choose things that help us reduce uncertainty to make life easier and more secure. While we may feel that we own our possessions, there are circumstances where our possessions can end up owning us. Many possessions cost time and money to maintain, which can drain our resources.

Our possessions can be a means of investing in ourselves and others. We like something that is a good value. We might look for things that will be worth more in the future or will pay off by providing a social or monetary reward for having them. We use possessions as a means to grow the economy by motivating people to own things. Businesses like manufactures and retailers can become more effective by understanding how shared meanings motivate people to have the possessions they do.

It can be helpful to be aware of potential unintended and undesired outcomes that our possessions might communicate about us and how we live to others. Our possessions and practically everything we do results in some form of rubbish. When archaeologists study ancient civilizations, they often gain knowledge about people by excavating where they discarded their rubbish. Since we don't want others to know our personal or financial information, it can be helpful to look at what you throw away to see what it may communicate about you to avoid unintended and undesirable outcomes. Then you can develop options to securely dispose of it.

We may feel that what we communicate with others is private or secure, but we may be unintentionally communicating information about ourselves to others. The telephone, cell phone, or emails should never be considered secure. The mail is generally considered more secure than other forms of communicating, but once it's opened and put in the trash it might be legal to read it. Consider what you communicate or discard as a potential source of information others could use. In order to protect yourself, your identity, and your privacy it's helpful to have an awareness of what you might unintentionally communicate to others that you do not want them to know.

Space as Nonverbal Communicating

Space consists of everything that is around us. There are many types of space and there are many ways that we utilize it. We have the physical spaces we occupy like where we live and work, including our homes and workplaces. We create emotional space in relationships with others. We have space that we seek to control such as areas of influence and expertise like our turf or territory. While we want to share space with others, we also need our own space that we can control. Space may have been created by nature, but people have developed many ways to divide and change it to make it more useful to them. How we utilize space fulfills many of our most important needs and wants. How we use space can communicate information about ourselves to others.

Life is chaotic, the world around us is full of uncertainty. In response, people throughout history have used space to help reduce uncertainty. We explore it, define it, name it, divide it, conquer it, and remake it to fulfill our needs and wants. We explore the vast spaces in which we find ourselves in order to increase our understanding of them. We define spaces by establishing boundaries and creating structures within those spaces. We name spaces to make them familiar and to help us communicate about them. We divide them up in order to make them more useful to us. We create our own spaces in which to live and work to protect us from the elements and keep us free from harm. We use space in many ways to reduce uncertainty by creating structures both physical and psychological to increase stability and security.

How we create, design, divide, and utilize space is a practical application of the law of shared meaning. We find meaning in the spaces around us based upon their history, characteristics, style, purpose, and how we use them. Some spaces have historical significance because they may have had notable people associated with them or significant events took place there. We find meaning in how space is constructed such as architectural styles. Many of these are characterized by a particular historical or cultural style. Many cultures have distinct styles and ways to utilize space based upon their social reality, technology, and materials that were available at the time they were created.

When we see things in nature like mountains, a sunset, or a waterfall we may feel exhilarated or a sense of awe. This is because space can motivate an emotional response affecting how we feel. We can have similar emotional responses to the physical spaces we occupy like our homes and workplaces. When we find them attractive or inspiring it can give us a warm, positive feeling. When we find them bland or dull it can have a negative or depressing influence on how we feel. The nature of our space can have an emotional impact on how we feel that can affect our behavior.

Ambience affects the feelings and emotions we get from our physical environment. It can communicate a message to ourselves and others. We all know how the psychological effects of lighting candles or having a fire in the fireplace can change how we feel helping us to re-lax or set a romantic mood. Similarly, we utilize things like lighting, color, music, furniture, artwork, floor coverings, and wall coverings to create spaces that have a particular mood or feeling. We have possessions in our spaces that are familiar to us because they make us feel good. We do this to create a space in which we feel safe, secure, and comfortable.

We invest space with many different types of meanings because it is such an important part of our lives. We often see it as an extension of ourselves and our self-concept. Places where we spend much of our time like our homes and workplaces have more meaning for us. We assign meaning to space based upon how we utilize it. We inhabit public and private space, personal space, and shared space. We often inhabit spaces we did not create, so we make them more meaningful to us by personalizing them to make them uniquely our own. We personalize our space by how we design it and fill it with our possessions. When we feel ownership of a space like our home, it gives it a deeper meaning because it is ours. We form emotional attachments with many types of spaces such as homes, communities, or geographic areas. When we feel a connection to a specific place that has meaning to us it can be referred to as a geographic affiliation.

When we invest spaces with meaning it gives them value. We invest our time, energy, ef-fort, and money in them to make them more useful or attractive to us. The more we spend time in a space, the more we invest ourselves in it, so the more we feel connected to it. This makes some places more special to us than others. There are places that we are willing to protect and even defend with our lives like our homes and country. When many people find meaning in a particular space and want to be there, it can create competition that increases its value. The more people share meaning about a space and the more they are willing to do to get it, the more attractive it can become increasing its value including its monetary value.

Space can fulfill many of our most important needs and wants. It provides shelter from the elements, safety from harm, and a feeling of security. It can fulfill our need to have control over our lives and where we live. It can fulfill our need for status, prestige, or pride of ownership. It can fulfill our need to express ourselves and our sense of identity in how we decorate our spaces. It can fulfill our need for stability and predictability when we know where we will eat, sleep, and live now and in the future. We need our own emotional and psychological space by having time for ourselves to think and relax. When we share space with others we can have a feeling of closeness and connectedness fulfilling our need for inclusion and affection. We use space as a means to develop and maintain relationships. It helps to create and maintain connections by being close to others because we want to be around people we care about.

How we utilize space can be influenced by our perceptions and expectations. We spend most of our time in some kind of space, which affects our preferences. Our preferences create expectations about how to use our space as well as how others utilize theirs. We have expectations about how space is used based upon our social reality. For example, if we visit another person's house we have expectations about what it will be like. We would not expect to see only one room inside it, with an open bonfire. However, many cultures con-structed one room houses with a fire in the middle. Many of our expectations about space and how we use it are culturally based depending upon our background and where we live.

There was a time when all the spaces that have been created by people did not exist. The idea of how to utilize a space first existed in someone's mind who then had to communicate it to others through the process of communicating. They had to develop their idea on how to utilize a space like building a house, designing a building, or planning a city. They had to make connections with others and communicate their Great Idea across The Great Abyss. How we use space is not just an individual activity, but it is a cooperative venture with others influenced by social reality. This is because we have to get other people to agree to our idea to make it a reality. For example, a person cannot just build whatever building they want. They have to get permits, contractors, financing, and cooperation from the community. So, their Great Idea had to be communicated to many other people who had to support it in order for it to become a reality.

We define our space by establishing boundaries. We use boundaries in practically every area that we use space including physical, emotional, psychological, and relational. We use walls to create physical boundaries. We take time for ourselves to create emotional boundaries. We have responsibilities defined by psychological boundaries. We create rules in relationships that serve as relational boundaries. We do this to reduce uncertainty by exerting control over areas that we feel are ours. For instance, we give our physical spaces a sense of identity by filling them with our personal items as an extension of our own self-concept. This is why if we perceive that others invade our territory we might take action to defend it because we perceive it as an intrusion on who we are.

Our attitudes and behaviors can be affected by the spaces we inhabit. For instance, we feel differently when we are in a large public building, at a bar, at church, or at home. Large public buildings communicate authority, but they can be cold and impersonal. A cozy restaurant can be inviting and relaxing. A cathedral can give us a feeling of reverence to inspire us. Our emotional state can be affected by our perception of our surroundings creating feelings and emotions. It can be helpful to have an awareness of the affect that our space and surroundings have on us so that we can control them rather than they control us.

Physical space consists of the physical environment that has been created by people such as our homes, workplaces, public buildings, and other places where we spend time. The spaces that we inhabit like our homes and workspace can nonverbally communicate information about us to others. Our own physical space communicates information to others nonverbally because of the choices we make and what it reveals about us. How we arrange or decorate our space can be an extension of who we are as an individual and our personality. We seek to make this space safe and secure, so we mark our territory to show others that it is ours.

How we utilize our spaces can be a physical manifestation of our identity including how we perceive ourselves. We spend most of our time in spaces that have mostly been created by others so they do not necessarily reflect who we are, which can increase uncertainty. The more we feel uncertainty about a space the less comfortable we might feel, and if we spend a lot of time there, we can be motivated to change it to reduce uncertainty. We change the spaces we occupy to put our own personal imprint on them communicating a sense of our own identity. We do this by decorating and renovating our spaces to serve our own taste. We communicate who we are with our furnishings, artwork, use of color, and possessions. How we use our space communicates our creativity, values, and what's important to us. For example, we might bring personal items from home to decorate our workplace like pictures of our family to reduce uncertainty, so that we can work more effectively because we feel more comfortable.

When we visit another person's home or workspace we have perceptions about how it is decorated. We get a feeling of it being warm or cold, personal or impersonal, or casual or formal based on the use of color, style of furniture, and personal possessions. We make inferences about their status, background, income, and other factors based upon the type of space they occupy and how they use it. For instance, we might assume that the more expensive a home and its furnishings, the higher a person's income.

One of our needs is to have our own physical space that we can call our own. A place where we can feel safe, secure, comfortable, and in control. We are motivated by the law of uncertainty to reduce uncertainty by having control over our own space. This is why when life is chaotic and difficult things are happening to them, people may clean the house, organize a desk, or rearrange the furniture. They might do this to assert control over what they can to compensate for what they feel they cannot control.

Our need for a space of our own can create feelings of territorialism, so we exert control over both our physical and psychological space. We can use territorialism to mark our space by decorating it and with our possessions to make it more personal, more familiar, and more comfortable for us. When we feel a sense of ownership, we will defend that space over intrusions by others. At home we might have our own room, desk, side of the bed, or our own chair in the dining room or at the kitchen table. We can even feel ownership of space that is not ours. For instance, we might like to sit at the same table in a restaurant, the same seat on a bus or at the movies. If someone else is in our spot, it can make us feel uncomfortable, even upset. Depending on the circumstances, we may try to get them to move. We do this because it reduces uncertainty giving us feelings of safety and predictability.

These are some of the ways that we define physical space between ourselves and others.

- Public space is the largest space we utilize. It consists of the spaces we occupy when we are out in public. We have little control over them, so they can have a higher degree of uncertainty.

- Social space involves every day interactions with others like going to the store or work. It allows us to directly communicate with others, but keeps them out of our personal space because there is some degree of uncertainty.

- Personal space is being close enough to have a private conversation or to touch the other person. We use this distance in more personal relationships with friends and family. It communicates that we are comfortable with them because uncertainty is reduced. If someone we do not know very well enters this space we might feel uncomfortable.

- Intimate space is the closest we get to another person indicating a more intimate relationship. We are close enough to communicate verbally and physically, so we only allow a few people to get this close.

Psychological and emotional space.

Space is not just about physical space, there is also psychological and emotional space. Our use of this type of space is important in how we create and maintain relationships. The kind of space we have is often an indicator of the nature of a relationship. When we do not know someone very well we generally keep our distance and maintain appropriate space because of increased uncertainty. If we get too close it can make us uncomfortable and we may pull back. As we get to know someone, uncertainty is reduced so we feel more comfortable with them. The space between people can often indicate the type of relationship they have. Generally, the closer the distance, the closer the relationship because there is less uncertainty.

In personal relationships we can have competing needs, like being close to others as well as having our own space. We often live with others in the same space, which can lead to tension or conflict. When one person feels they want to do something and the other person doesn't, it can lead to tension or conflict because we feel they are invading our space. Sharing space with others can lead to tension and conflict over competing needs and wants based on how each person wants to utilize their space. It is helpful to have an awareness of how perception of the ownership of territory works to avoid unnecessary tension or conflict.

We not only need physical space, we need emotional space as well. A good example of two conflicting needs is our need to spend time with others and to spend time by ourselves. We might express this need by saying that we need our space. What we are referring to is a need for our own mental or emotional space so that we can have some time to ourselves to think or relax. We need a physical space to call our own and psychological space for our mental well being. We may need time to process new information such as in the case of a crisis or other distress. While others may think we should be with them, we may just want space to ourselves to work things through. It's helpful to be aware that people have these needs and when they say they need their space it is for their own well being and not a rejection.

We have a similar need to have control over areas where we feel we have knowledge, expertise, or responsibility. For example, at work we may be the person who writes the reports or schedules the meetings. We feel comfortable in that role because it allows us to interact with others. If someone else does it, even though they may be well intentioned, we may feel put out or even angry at them. We all have areas of responsibility or expertise that we feel is our territory, which belongs to us and we will defend what we perceive as our turf to prevent others from invading it. We can create tension or conflict when we invade other people's space and may not even be aware of it.

Shared space.

We have all gone through the experience of sharing space with others, whether it's with our family, roommates, or a spouse. Sharing space can create tension because of conflicting needs and wants. We manage this tension by staking out territory to create our own spaces we can control within a larger space. The closer we are in proximity to others and the greater the perceived threat to our space, the more likely we are to defend that space if necessary.

One way that we defend our space and mark our territory is by leaving our personal items there. For example, siblings or roommates may leave their clothes and other personal articles lying around to claim their space. In relationships, we may leave items such as a toothbrush or clothing at the other person's place. Because of the law of shared meaning, when people leave personal items lying around they may be staking claim to territory that they perceive as theirs. We are motivated to assert control over our spaces to let others know that it belongs to us.

The spaces we occupy at work can communicate our status, importance, and position. In organizations there are some spaces that are considered more prestigious than others and the competition for them invests them with meaning which gives them value. When spaces are valued by many people they can be used as a reward for achievement. For example, in a business the executives often occupy the largest offices in the most desirable locations with better furnishings and more space for support staff. This communicates their importance and prestige as well as serving as an incentive for others to work hard and follow the rules so someday they can occupy those spaces as well.

How space is arranged can have a significant influence on our behavior. People with private offices may communicate that they do not want to interact with employees or customers. It can discourage spontaneous conversation and sharing of ideas. Businesses with open floor plans or where people are easily accessible invite interaction and spontaneous conversations that encourages the sharing of ideas. We are more likely to talk with someone at a nearby desk then someone a long distance away. People use space to put barriers between themselves and others to create the perception of status or superiority.

We like to personalize our workspaces by displaying things like artwork, books, plants, or photographs to make it an extension of ourselves that reflects our personality. This communicates information about ourselves as well as letting others know that it is our space. We do this to reduce uncertainty for ourselves by making our space feel more familiar and comfortable. It makes our work more enjoyable helping us to be more productive. We tend to work better and get more done when we are in a space that we find enjoyable. It gives us a sense of pride in ownership encouraging our commitment to the organization.

Before putting out your personal items, look around to see how others personalize their spaces. You may want to emulate what other people do, at least until they get to know you. Other people's perception of your space is motivated by the law of uncertainty. Every organization has its own culture so if your space looks too unfamiliar, it may increase uncertainty about you and they may be less likely to get to know you. If other people perceive you as not fitting in they may expect you to either change or leave. If your space looks familiar it helps to reduce uncertainty, so they may be more likely to get to know you.

How space is utilized is important for children because they occupy spaces predominately controlled by adults, like their parents. As they grow older and develop their self-concept, children seek to communicate their identity in part by exerting control over a space that they consider their own. Having ownership of a particular space can be important to a child's development. We exert control over our spaces because it is an extension of our individual identity. A violation of a person's space can be seen as a violation of who they are as a person. They might perceive others not acknowledging their space as not showing respect for them.

When we exert control over a space we can come into conflict with others who may also use that space. In order to alleviate these tensions it can be helpful to give them a space that they can call their own along with the responsibility that goes along with it. For instance, having children be responsible for managing their own space teaches them responsibility as well as helping them to develop their own sense of identity.

Geographic affiliation.

Another way we share meaning with others to reduce uncertainty is through geographic affiliation. Geographic affiliation refers to any place that we may feel a connection to like a neighborhood, community, city, state, region, or country. This could be where we were born, where we grew up, where we spend time, or where we live now.

We may feel a connection with places we have only visited or have never seen in person such as where our ancestors came from. We may feel a connection to places through our family history, heritage, culture, ethnicity, religion, or personal interests. A geographic affiliation can become a part of our self-concept and how we see ourselves.

Geographic affiliation utilizes the law of shared meaning because it communicates information about people, whether it is accurate or not. It reduces uncertainty because we use it to know more about others, so we can make connections with them. When we introduce ourselves to others we might talk about where we were born, where we grew up, or where we live now. If they have been somewhere we have been, we might talk about it because it's something we both have in common. We do this to reduce uncertainty because it gives others information about who we are based upon our geographic affiliation.

Architecture as Nonverbal Communicating

People define and divide space to fulfill their needs and wants to reduce uncertainty and share meaning. Architecture is about how people design and build the structures they use and occupy. It utilizes a combination of art, science, and technology. While all people need shelter, how they design and build it can be distinctly different based on their individual identity, culture, social reality, and geographic affiliation. Architecture is not just about how we design our spaces, but also about what they communicate, how they influence people's perceptions, and how they affect behavior.

Architecture is a human creation motivated by the law of uncertainty because it reduces uncertainty about where we live and work, about our communities, and about ourselves. We all need shelter, but we want more than just to get out of the elements. We want to live in a place that makes us feel safe and secure by reducing uncertainty. Architecture reduces uncertainty because when we see a building it is designed in an architectural style that communicates information about the building. Different architectural styles share meaning with the public about the building, its history, and the people who built and occupy it.

Architectural styles are a physical manifestation of the law of shared meaning. How people arrange and design the spaces they inhabit are a means by which they share meaning about their culture, history, and traditions. Different geographical regions have different architectural styles based upon their artistic expression, social reality, and building materials that are locally available. Many geographic areas have signature architecture that has become a symbol for their community as well as their country, like the Eiffel Tower or the Empire State Building.

We share meaning about architecture in order to reduce uncertainty. We can easily tell the difference between a house and a courthouse, as well as many other kinds of structures by how they look. Each structure communicates its own meaning based on how it is designed and the material that is used to build it. The homes we live in are designed for comfort. They are designed to provide a feeling of warmth and intimacy. Businesses create buildings that reduce uncertainty and inspire confidence in their customers and the public. Government buildings are designed to communicate authority.

How space is designed can affect how we feel as well as our health and quality of life. The design of our physical space can affect our mental state of mind and productivity. Architectural design can help or hinder how we feel and how well we are able to get things done. Architectural styles have the ability to affect our feelings, emotions, state of mind, and well being. Whenever we enter a building whether it's a person's home, an office building, or government building we get a feeling about it whether we are aware of it or not. It can affect our emotions and how we feel. For example, a warm and comfortable space can uplift our mood. Having comfortable places to sit invites us to stay for a while. A cold impersonal space can make us feel depressed. Uncomfortable spaces compel us to move on. Architecture can have a significant impact on the people around it by making them move and interact within the space in particular ways.

In the process of communicating, our self-concept can be affected by reflected feedback from others. Utilizing this process, architecture can be an expression of our self-concept. We feel good about ourselves when we feel good about the places we live and work. When we look for a place to live, we often choose architectural styles that we like and that are a reflection of our self-concept. If it is well received by others, it can bolster our self-esteem.

Architecture can be used as identity management by the organizations and people who build and occupy them. It can be used to influence the perceptions of the public similar to how individuals use their appearance to influence the perceptions and expectations of others. They can use architecture to convey stability and power to engender trust so people will invest their resources in them. For example, government and financial institutions build large distinguished structures to portray authority and stability so people will have confidence in them.

Architecture helps fulfill some of our most basic individual, group, and community needs and wants. Structures not only fulfill our need for shelter, but they also fulfill needs such as educational needs with schools, spiritual needs with churches, health and safety needs with hospitals, and community needs with libraries.

We need shelter to live, but we want more. We want to live in a place that is aesthetically pleasing. Architecture fulfills our need for creative expression, prestige, status, achievement, and monetary gain. While all people have similar needs and wants for shelter, how they fulfill them can be vastly different resulting in the variety of architectural styles we have today. Throughout history people in different geographic areas have had different ideas about what architectural styles were desirable and how buildings should be built. Many of these architectural styles have a long tradition that represents various times in history and geographic regions.

Real estate comprises an important source of wealth creation that encourages people to invest their time, money, and other resources in it. People invest themselves in architecture by designing, constructing, maintaining, and restoring buildings. We put different values on different types of architecture and different kinds of space over others. So, architecture can be used to communicate what we value about ourselves and our community.

Architecture creates perceptions about a community in the minds of people. We have expectations about what buildings should look like, so when we see a community the nature of the architecture gives us an impression of what a town is like as well as the people who live there. We get different feelings when we are in a small town, a suburb, or a big city. Each of these utilizes different styles of architecture and different ways of arranging public space that communicates shared meanings about the people who live there and their community.

Architecture and public spaces give a community a sense of its collective identity just as a person's appearance communicates their identity to others. Different architectural styles represent different ideas about how space should be utilized based upon the perceptions of what was aesthetically pleasing and expectations of how architecture should be influenced by social reality. How a community designs their public spaces could be considered a form of community identity management.

Color as Nonverbal Communicating

Color is an important part of everything we see around us. It communicates many things, which helps us to reduce uncertainty because we recognize many things by their color. It can be used to cut through The Great Abyss in order to communicate information more effectively to others than without it. For instance, red communicates emergency such as a fire engine. We associate green with the environment, blue with loyalty, and purple with royalty.

Color is an important part of how we share meanings because we invest multiple meanings in practically every color. These meanings can affect our mood as well as our state of mind. We make choices of what colors to use in decorating our spaces like our home. We use color to communicate our self-concept in the clothes we wear. Color is a means for motivating investing as people can feel more confident when they see some colors, but can feel less confident as some colors can increase uncertainty.

Color is used by businesses as part of their public image to communicate a message. It is used by nations in their flags and other insignia to communicate what a country stands for and what it means to its citizens. In our society, we associate colors with different functions. Color is used to improve functionality of things. For instance, Interstate road signs are in muted green to make them easier to read. Fire trucks and fire hydrants are generally red to be seen at a distance. Police cars are black and white to make them easy to differentiate from other vehicles.

Products and advertising use color to communicate, to get our attention, and to cut through The Great Abyss to make them sell better. We use bright colors to get people's attention and muted colors to communicate tradition. Color is used to identify product brands encouraging customer loyalty. Some colors are more accepted by consumers than others. For example, clear soda is often packaged in green bottles because it sells better than in clear ones. Color has a psychological effect on us as well. Blue is considered calming and relaxing because we associate it with the sky or water. Red is considered exciting because it's the color associated with fire. Colors can be characterized by temperature. Warm colors are red, orange, and yellow. Cool colors are blue and green.

We choose colors based upon our personal preferences and often we have a favorite color. Some color combinations are pleasing to the eye, while others are not. Just as we communicate for a reason, we choose colors for a reason. We choose them because they have an emotional quality that can make us feel good, confident, relaxed, or give us energy. For instance, we might buy a red car because it feels exciting, a black car because it looks elegant, or a blue car because it's our favorite color.

Art as Nonverbal Communicating

Some of our needs and wants include entertainment, excitement, enjoyment, escape, relaxation, and self-expression. While these are a wide variety of needs, they are often fulfilled through artistic expression. We have a need to creatively express our individuality as well as to enjoy the artistic expression of others. The arts represent an important form of communicating. We do this in many different ways through art, music, drama, and literature. We do this as a means of entertainment and creative expression to communicate with others.

Artistic expression is motivated by the law of uncertainty because it can reduce uncertainty about ourselves and others. Different artistic styles are often associated with a specific culture, country, religion, or ethnicity. However, artistic expression can transcend culture because it can be universally understood. Art provides a means to get to know others by reducing uncertainty about them.

Art utilizes the law of shared meaning by giving artistic expression a deeper significance. Paintings, sculptures, musical compositions, and other forms of art are created not only for enjoyment, but also to share ideas, communicate a message, or commemorate important events. The arts are used to share meaning about individuals, cultures, ethnicity, religion, geographic affiliations, and other characteristics. Artistic expression can bring people together because it has the ability to transcend cultural and language barriers. As a society we invest in promoting arts and in arts education. People invest themselves in creating, expressing, and teaching the arts. Artistic expression has the power to affect our emotions, influence how we think, and motivate our behavior.

Artistic expression utilizes the process of communicating. Through artistic expression, our Great Idea is not only in what we say or write, it can also be communicated to others in artistic forms like music, drama, or art. We communicate our Great Idea in an artistic form to make connections with others through its display, print, or performance. Feedback can come in the form of applause at a concert, reviews, or critical and commercial success. Art has the potential to reach the individual as well as large audiences.

Throughout history people had the same needs and wants, but have fulfilled them in different ways. Artistic expression illustrates how people fulfill needs and wants in different ways by developing many different artistic styles based on their history, traditions, culture, and social reality. Artistic expression can have different meanings based on different cultures and their social reality. They can also have different meanings to the people who experience them based on their own perceptions and expectations.

Artistic communicating fulfills many of our needs and wants. It fulfills the need to express ourselves and communicate with others. It can fulfill the need for prestige, status, and to gain respect from others. It's a part of our identity and who we are. How people react to our artistic expression can affect our self-concept and how we see ourselves. Enjoying artistic expression fulfills our need for entertainment, relaxation, and enjoyment. We can enjoy art by ourselves or share it with others to make connections and develop relationships.

Food as Nonverbal Communicating

Imagine what it would be like at a family gathering, celebration, or special occasion without having anything to eat or drink. Think about what kinds of food and drink we share with others when we gather together for a birthday, wedding, holiday, or on a Sunday afternoon.

Communicating is about making connections between people and few things make connections better than food. However, food is not usually included in traditional approaches to communicating. Food is unique because it is a necessity of life, we cannot live without it. While food sustains and nurtures us, it is also a means to communicate with one another. The meaning of food is universal. It transcends culture, nationality, and language. We do not have to understand a culture or their language to appreciate their food.

Food brings people together to communicate friendship, affection, traditions, and culture in ways few other things are able to do. Food communicates who we are as an individual, who we are collectively as a culture, our ethnicity, and geographic affiliations like where we were brought up or where we live now. Food may fulfill our basic human need for sustenance, but we want more, so it has been elevated to an art form. Food not only feeds our body, it sustains our soul.

Food can be used as a means to reduce uncertainty about ourselves, others, our family, and society. We can reduce uncertainty about ourselves by sharing food with others. We can learn about others by what foods they like. Holidays, celebrations, rituals, and traditions would not be the same without food. Special occasions give food a deeper meaning than just something to eat for survival because they are often based on cultural and historical traditions. We use food to celebrate events in our lives like birthdays with ice cream and cake, a Thanksgiving turkey, and hot dogs on the Fourth of July. Many traditional foods originated during times of hardship or to commemorate important events. Future generations carry on these traditions because this food creates a connection with the past.

How we perceive food is a practical application of the law of shared meaning. Food brings people together, it helps us to develop relationships with others because we use it to meet people to make connections with them. Many events in our lives are frequently accompanied by food giving them a deeper significance because they have special meaning. Food can be a form of self-disclosure to communicate information about ourselves. When we want to develop relationships with other people, we may share a meal or go for coffee. Food provides us a means of emotional support, nurturing, comfort, and gives us a feeling of security. It is an expression of our community, traditions, and culture. It can be used to show respect, affection, appreciation, and acceptance of others.

Food is not only a basic need, it is also a want. We need food to survive, but we also use food to fulfill many of our needs and wants. We want food that is healthy, exciting, satisfying, and tastes good. It can fulfill our needs for enjoyment, fun, excitement, adventure, and emotional support. Nature could have created us with the ability to fulfill all our needs and wants for food by ourselves, but that was not what nature intended. Many other creatures are able to provide for themselves, but we need others to help grow, provide, and prepare the food we need and want. This has made food a means to reduce uncertainty, share meaning, and invest in others.

We use food to invest in relationships with others. When a couple dates, they might go out to dinner and when they begin to cook for one another, it can signify the relationship moving to the next level. Families spend time together around the breakfast or dinner table. Coworkers may go out for lunch or have coffee breaks together. These rituals based around food encourage self-disclosure, so people will share their experiences to get to know one another better which builds trust to help them create relationships. Food and agriculture is the basis of our economy, it adds value and creates wealth. It is the basis of economic organizations from small family businesses to large multinational corporations.

Food can be an intense means of communicating because it utilizes multiple connections. It can be colorful and looks good to us. We know many foods by their smell, which can be wonderful. Food has texture and some foods are eaten because of how they feel. Food can have sounds like when it has a crunch or sizzles while it's cooking. Food tastes good to us giving us a feeling of contentment, fulfillment, and well being. Without any of these connections food would not be the same. Perhaps this is why food can be so satisfying, fulfilling, and even sensual, because it is one of the few things that makes a connection using all of our five senses.

When we welcome people into our home, we offer them food as a sign of friendship. In many cultures when we are invited to somebody's home or when we travel and meet people, they show friendship and hospitality by offering us food. They may serve traditional food that represents their culture to make us feel welcome. We use food to celebrate collective gatherings such as a convention where there may be a dinner or banquet. Food is used to celebrate important events in our lives such as birthdays, anniversaries, and weddings. Imagine what these occasions would be like without food and drink.

It is often said you are what you eat. Perhaps this is true in the sense that food is part of our identity and self-concept. We grew up on certain foods and when we have them now they give us a feeling of comfort and nurturing. We express our individuality through the food we like and cook. Many foods are identified with a specific geographical region such as French, Italian, or Mexican. These foods were created with available local ingredients and have become a part of our history and culture.

Food is one of our most basic needs and for the first part of our life is fulfilled by our family. Food is a central part of what it means to be a family. Families use food to celebrate holidays and important events as well as share their traditions. Food provides a means for family members to get together to spend time with one another. This can help to reduce uncertainty, share meaning, and invest in other family members. Many of our fondest memories with our family were when we prepared or shared food together.

Remember when you were a child and had a bad day at school or didn't feel well? Your parents probably gave you milk and cookies or soup and a grilled cheese sandwich to help you feel better. We often eat food to make ourselves feel better because we associate it with caring, closeness, and nurturing. Since food involves making an emotional connection, we can use it when we are feeling bad or depressed. Food makes us feel better because it is fun, enjoyable, and satisfying.

Our family is where we first learn about food and how to prepare it. It brings families together over the breakfast and dinner table, which can help them to communicate with one another. It is a way they connect to communicate about things other than food. It is a chance to share the happenings of the day or their thoughts and feelings.

Whether it's having a meal or preparing food, cooking is a way to spend time together. Cooking encourages people to communicate when they are preparing a meal and when they are enjoying it. It gives people something to do together that does not take all their attention, so they are still able to have a conversation.

Parents teach their children how to cook because it provides many benefits. Preparing food is a means to learn valuable life skills besides just cooking. Preparing food teaches children how to make a plan and implement it, how to shop, how to work on a budget, how to use tools, how to work with others, and how things are made.

It teaches children how to take care of themselves to fulfill their own needs and wants. This benefits the family because the children are better able to take care of themselves. It may even become a future career. When we learn to cook, we learn where the things that sustain us come from and the amount of work it takes to get them to us. Being able to prepare food makes us more likable to others, it helps us to take better care of ourselves, and it can improve our relationships as well as our quality of life by reducing uncertainty.

Smell as Nonverbal Communicating

Remember when you were a child and came home from school, perhaps your mother or grandmother was baking cookies, bread, or apple pie. Wonderful smells filled the kitchen making you feel good, safe, and secure. Even today, when we smell baking cookies, bread, or apple pie it can make us feel good bringing back fond memories. Our sense of smell is closely related to our sense of taste. It enhances our enjoyment of food and drink. So, if we cannot smell something we may not be fully able to taste it.

Smell communicates many different kinds of information. We use smell to reduce uncertainty because it tells us what something is, its freshness, and even warns us of danger. We use it to provide information about others and our surroundings. It is a way to share meaning because we invest many smells with meaning. We consider some smells good and desirable, so we seek to create them. Other smells we consider bad so we avoid them and if they occur we are motivated to get rid of them.

Smells send a message that we invest with meaning to reduce uncertainty. We use our sense of smell to tell us many things. It not only helps us to recognize different kinds of food, it also tells us if it's good or has gone bad. It warns us of danger like if something is burning or rotten. It tells us if something is clean or dirty. We tend to trust our sense of smell because smells can communicate important information.

Smell can be a powerful motivator, it makes things more pleasant, attractive, and desirable for us. We can be attracted to some things and even other people because they smell good. Good smells make other people more attractive and bad smells can repel them. It makes products more appealing by making them smell better or fresher. Companies add scents to their products ranging from soaps to food products to make them more appealing to consumers. Advertisers include scents in magazines to encourage us to buy their products.

When we clean our homes or do our laundry, we have a feeling of satisfaction because of the clean smell. Clean clothes out of the dryer smell comforting. We enjoy the smell of the outdoors after the rain. Smells like perfume, cologne, or candles are often used to set a romantic mood because they have an effect on our emotions and state of mind.

We often remember things based upon the smells associated with them. When we smell something it can bring back past memories of when we smelled it before. Because smells can be closely related to our emotions, when we smell something from our past it can bring back the emotions connected to it. For example, smelling some foods, like baking cookies, can trigger childhood memories of when our family made them for us.

Time as Nonverbal Communicating

Time is our most valuable resource because it is our most limited one. While we all have different amounts of resources available to us like money or space, we all have the same twenty four hours each day. We can make more money, but we cannot make more time. So, managing time effectively is an important skill. Everyone communicates for a reason and everyone spends time the way they do for a reason. How we spend time communicates a great deal about us, our interests, our priorities, our values, and who we are.

People have divided and labeled time because of the law of uncertainty. We use time to reduce uncertainty by measuring it and dividing it into smaller segments making up clock and calendar time. Time as we define it is linear and does not exist in nature, it is a function of social reality created by people. Nature operates in endlessly repeating cycles that return to the same point, like day and night, the seasons, and each year. How we view time can be a manifestation of how our shared meaning of physical reality creates social reality

People have developed many ways to measure time to enable us to plan events with a degree of certainty creating expectations and a degree of predictability about the future. This creates structure and stability by having things happen at specific times during a day, week, month, and year. For example, we have meals at the same time of day, religious services at the same time of the week, and celebrate holidays the same time every year. This provides predictability reducing uncertainty because we know what to expect at certain times.

We invest time with meaning. Time, as we define it, is a human creation derived from the law of shared meaning based on the rotation of the earth. It may be based on physical reality, but how people interpret it is based on shared meaning as a part of social reality. People share many meanings about different times of the day, week, month, and year. Ever since the earliest civilizations, time was invested with meaning that was shared by people. This is because it was important to know when to do things like planting and harvesting crops. These shared meanings served as the basis of rituals and traditions that celebrated important times of the year such as the spring planting of crops and vernal equinox, the fall harvest and autumnal equinox, the winter and summer solstices, and the new year.

These traditions serve useful functions for society by sharing meanings about our history and culture. We look forward to rituals and traditions so that we can spend time with others, which is important to creating shared meaning, community, and culture. These rituals allow us to connect to one another creating common bonds and traditions that give us a sense of purpose and self-concept reducing uncertainty.

Since time is our most limited resource it creates value. We might judge the value of things by the time that we put in to them. We value relationships where we spend time and we spent time in relationships we value. We describe time in monetary terms such as spending time, saving time, investing time, and time is money. Because our time is limited we cannot spend it on everything we want to, so we have to make choices and set priorities. These choices communicate what is important to us.

What we do with our time is an observable way to measure values and priorities. We might say something is important, however, we may spend little or no time on it communicating a different message. We consider time an investment, so we look to get a return on that investment. When we spend a lot of time on something, we have expectations of what we want to get in return. For instance, we spend a large amount of time at our jobs so we expect to be compensated fairly for it.

Social reality contains rules that tell us how to use time. Some cultures view time as highly structured, dividing it up into precise increments stressing punctuality and timeliness. Other cultures view time as more flexible and relative. For example, if you were invited to a dinner party, in one culture you would be expected to arrive precisely at the time you are invited. In another culture, you might come fashionably late. In another culture you would come when you could. Time can be viewed in terms of specific days and times or viewed in terms of cycles and seasons. We can reduce uncertainty by increasing our awareness of how others view time, so we can communicate more effectively to fit in with their expectations.

Punctuality is about being on time and it is important because of what it communicates about us and what we think about others. Being punctual can be perceived as a sign of respect and courtesy. Not being punctual can be perceived as being rude and inconsiderate of others. When someone is late, people may become offended because they think you are wasting their time whether it's intentional or not. Perception of time is not only based on individual expectations, it can also be a function of culture and social reality.

Effective communicating is a matter of having appropriate timing to reduce uncertainty. There are times when people are more receptive to your message and times when they are less receptive. By increasing your awareness you can use timing to tactfully communicate information. There is no one best way to choose the best time, however, it helps to be considerate of the other person, their situation, their willingness to listen, and how receptive they are to your message. Timing can make the difference between being accepted or rejected, and being perceived as being respectful or rude. Timing can be based on the perception of urgency, necessity, and importance. It is important to choose an appropriate time and place to communicate to achieve your desired outcome

Everyone communicates for a reason and they decide when to do so for a reason. By paying attention to the timing of events and looking at what events preceded someone's actions, we might be able to determine the motivation for their behavior. If two events occur at a similar time, we can look for connections to see if they are in some way related, if one caused the other or if it was just a coincidence. This is the difference between causation or correlation.

We structure and measure time in order to enable us to work together, to know when to do things, and to know what to expect in the future to reduce uncertainty. When we do this we communicate our perceptions and expectations. It can be helpful to take an assessment of how you are spending your time to increase your awareness of what you may be communicating to others. We might think that we are spending a lot of time on some things, but in reality we are spending very little time on them at all. Often perception can be different than reality. For instance, we may feel that we may be spending enough time with our family when in reality we are not meeting their expectations. In order to communicate effectively with others, it's helpful to have an awareness of just how we are actually spending our time and what that communicates to them.

It seems that we never have enough time to fulfill all our needs and wants. This means we have to make choices and set priorities, which can create tension between conflicting needs and wants. This motivates us to spend most of our time on more pressing short term needs putting off long term wants because we feel that we will find time for them later. This can leave us feeling frustrated or unhappy and wondering why. By understanding how we spend our time and what that communicates to others, we can increase our awareness to give ourselves more options to balance how we use our time relieving tension and reducing frustration. The first step can be to understand how accurately your perceptions and expectations reflect reality.

Do you feel that you have enough time each day to get everything done you need to do? Do you feel that your time could be better spent on things you want to do? In order to more effectively utilize your time, from memory write down on a piece of paper everything you have done in the last month. Next to each item write down how much time you think you spent doing each one. Now take your calendar and look to see how much time you actually spent doing these things. This will tell you how accurate your perception of how you use your time is, because perception can be different than reality.

On another piece of paper, write down what you want to do during the next month and how much time you want to spend on each one. Then put that list away where you won't see it. For the next month, keep a detailed calendar of what you do and how much time you actually spend on each item. After the month is over, compare your calendar to the list you wrote at the beginning of the month to see how it compares. This will tell you how accurate your perceptions and expectations are so you can adjust your time to how you want to spend it.

In organizing your time it can be helpful to consider these four kinds of needs and wants.

1. What you need to do. These are things you must do in order to live.
2. What you have to do. These are everyday things you do, but could live without.
3. What you want to do. These are fun things to do that make you feel good.
4. What you ought to do. These are the things you know you should do.

Life would be much easier if we could do all of these tasks all the time. Since we have limited resources, making choices can be a source of conflict because doing one thing can preclude us from doing others. For instance, imagine it's Sunday morning and you need to get groceries, have to clean the house, ought to go to church, and want to sleep in. You must be at work by noon, so you cannot do all of them. Which one do you choose?

By increasing your awareness, you can see how you are actually spending your time. It's easy for time to get away and be spent in ways you do not want or intend to do. So, doing an audit and creating a budget of your time, like is done with finances, can help to organize the things that you do based on both short and long term priorities. This can help you to use your time more effectively in order to achieve your desired outcomes.

Once we are aware of how we spend our time and how we want to use it, we can take action to make changes to use it more effectively. While we may think about doing this, actually writing it down on paper helps to clarify our perceptions, so we can have realistic expectations. By evaluating how we are actually spending our time, we can reduce uncertainty to have more control over how we spend it.

Money as Nonverbal Communicating

After time, money is most likely our second most valuable and limited resource. There is the saying that money talks, so what does it say about you? How we spend our money communicates our values, interests, and priorities. It communicates information about what our priorities are and what is important to us. We develop perceptions and expectations about people who have money and how they use it. Everything created by people was made possible because they invested their time and money.

There are two ways to get something done; we can take the time to do it or we can spend money and have someone else do it. Most things that are created by people are a factor of time or money or both. We spend our time to make money and we spend money to save time. This makes money a form of concentrated time.

Money serves to reduce uncertainty by creating stability and security because it can be used as a form of social control to reduce uncertainty about people's behavior. If we want benefits like a house, car, and possessions we have to get money to pay for them, so we have to work. At work, if we want to earn money, we are expected to conform to the rules of our workplace, the larger organization, and social reality.

Money is a practical application of the law of shared meaning. How we value it is based on the meanings people share. While possessions and objects don't change, how we value them changes based on the meanings people share. The currencies of countries can change value based on shared meanings. Even money itself is a manifestation of shared meaning because paper money itself is worthless, it is our belief in it that invests it with value. At one time money was minted out of gold and silver that had value outside of being currency. Today paper money and coins are based on the shared meaning of its value because they have little actual value.

There is an inherent tension between our needs and wants when it comes to money because most of us have limited resources. We want to save it to have financial security, but we also want to spend it now for the things we want. These conflicting and competing needs can be the source of tension and conflict. Lack of money increases uncertainty because it is difficult to get along without it. Money is a means by which you can get things done and make things happen. It gives us the ability to care for ourselves and our loved ones.

Money and economic equilibrium.

Money could be compared to other forms of communicating. There is no one right, one size fits all approach to how we use money. Experts tell us what we should do with our money, but they cannot know your individual situation and they could be wrong. We can improve how we utilize money by increasing our awareness and options. Keeping track of how we spend our money can increase our awareness of where it goes to utilize it better. We have a much better chance to save it or use it more effectively when we know where it goes. Keeping a ledger of income and expenses like businesses do can help to get a handle on exactly where every dollar goes.

To effectively manage money, it can be helpful to separate essential from nonessential costs. Essential costs represent fulfillment of basic needs that we all must pay. Essential costs include food, housing, utilities, and taxes. Nonessential costs represent the things we want, but could live without, so we have more choices how we spend our money. These costs are different for each person. When budgeting, start with essential spending and follow with nonessential spending. This can help us use our money more effectively.

We work hard to make money and so we want tangible benefits from it. When we save money it goes into an account and we don't see it. When we spend money we get tangible possessions, which is rewarding. These are attractive because they fulfill many of our needs and wants like enjoyment, excitement, fun, prestige, and material rewards. This can motivate us to spend rather than save because it produces tangible rewards. This is why there should be more incentives for saving money to make it more attractive.

The law of uncertainty ensures that there will always be good and bad years ahead. In good years it is important not to spend money just because you have it, but to put some aside in order to get by when times are bad. It can be helpful to use money more effectively by separating income from spending. While we all want a higher income, what is more important is cash flow. If we spend all we take in we will never get ahead no matter how much money we might make. Spending according to your income may cover expenses now, but can create problems if the cash flow runs dry. The secret to financial success is to reduce economic uncertainty by living beneath your means spending less than you make creating a cash reserve.

That doesn't mean living like you don't have anything, it means making smarter choices. To do this it's helpful to disconnect income from expenditures because the key to financial security is to improve your cash flow by living beneath your means, spending less than you make. Determine how much you need to spend to be comfortable rather than determining how much to spend based on how much money you make. Otherwise you may be tempted to spend money just because you can. If you spend more than you take in, you will quickly run out of money. If you spend less, you should build up a cash reserve that can get you through difficult times.

When it comes to managing money, it can be helpful to utilize a business approach. While we don't think of ourselves as a business, there are several things that businesses do that can work for you. These include making monthly income and expense statements, a year end summary, a budget for the next year, and future financial projections. You might have separate accounts to pay different expenditures. For example, set aside money for fixed monthly costs that cover needs we can't live without like housing, taxes, and insurance. This way all the money is not spent on things we want, but could live without.

Set aside a separate work space like a desk and a filing cabinet to keep records in an organized, professional fashion. By having a separate space, you keep business from interfering with family time so you don't feel like you are in a never ending stream of paying bills. Have separate file folders for the bills that are paid each month and one for unpaid bills to keep them organized. Conduct business only during the business hours you establish, so you're not getting up at 11 o'clock at night to pay a bill. Do not discuss business, finances, or pay bills after hours. This sets aside time to relax.

Build a financial firewall to reduce uncertainty and protect you investments. We have a smoke detector to protect our home and family, software to protect our computer, but we may put our finances at risk. For example, our homes are our largest asset, but when people need money they are tempted to refinance taking the equity they earned out of their home. When everything goes well things can work out, but if it doesn't they end up losing their most valuable asset that fulfills one of their most fundamental needs. Consider having a financial firewall against difficult economic times. This contains three basic elements to increase financial security reducing uncertainty that can be harmful to you.

First, your home is your most important asset and despite some contentions is still your best investment in the long run. Shelter is a need we all have that we can't live without, which creates wealth. If you take out a thirty year mortgage and take all thirty years to pay it off, you are likely doubling the cost of your home. Pay the mortgage off early, so that you own your home free and clear as soon as you are able. Get a mortgage that lets you pay more than a minimum payment, then pay as much as you can afford, to pay it off sooner. Even a few years can make a big difference in the interest you will pay.

Second, put money aside as a cushion in case of unemployment and deposit it in a government insured account. Third, have home, car, health, and liability insurance to protect you from unforeseen financial losses.

By separating these finances you create a financial firewall to increase your financial security by protecting your most important assets. The law of uncertainty can motivate you to protect yourself, your family, and your well being because some kind of financial difficulties are sure to happen. Planning ahead and being prepared reduces uncertainty and insulates you from unexpected and undesired outcomes.

Uncertainty and Individual Communicating

There are times when we say something that makes us wonder why we said it. There are times we behave in ways that make us wonder if we really know who we are. We may feel tension or frustration and not really understand why. By understanding how communicating works, we can more fully understand the forces that affect what we say and do. By understanding how we communicate with ourselves, we can make informed choices rather than letting uncertainty control us.

By understanding our needs and wants, we can know what motivates us. This can help us to simplify our life by focusing on the things that are important while discarding those that are not. By increasing our awareness of our perception process, expectations, and desired outcomes we can better understand why we feel the way we do. By understanding how the process of communicating works, we can develop skills to communicate more effectively with others improving how we see ourselves and our self-concept.

We can utilize the laws of uncertainty, shared meaning, and investing to better understand the forces that motivate us. These elements can be utilized as a diagnostic methodology to provide insights into ourselves. We can identify sources of uncertainty in our lives to determine which ones we can do something about and what to do about them, as well as those that we can do little about in order to mitigate their effect on us. We can increase our awareness of the meanings that we share with others and how they develop our social reality, as well as how they create our perception of ourselves, others, and the world around us.

Chapter 3
Relational Communicating

What if you had to move away from where you live now to a place where you didn't know anyone? What if you had to leave behind everyone you know including your family, friends, neighbors, and coworkers, and not have any contact with them? What would you do?

Throughout our life we are constantly meeting new people and developing new relationships while others fade away. While we will probably not have to make all new relationships at the same time, thinking about this possibility can help us better understand how we have developed the ones we have now. This process is such a natural part of life we usually don't pay very much attention to it because we are constantly going through the process of forming, maintaining, and ending relationships. So, what would you do if you had to form all new relationships?

Relational communicating is the second level of interaction because it is about how you communicate with others to create and maintain relationships. We use the word relationship to characterize the connections we make with others like our friends, family, spouses, coworkers, and business associates. We might refer to a passing acquaintance as a relationship. We may talk about having a good relationship with a neighbor, coworker, or store clerk. However, when we do this we are referring to the positive climate of the interaction rather than making an ongoing reciprocated connection. We make connections and communicate with others all the time without creating an actual relationship.

Most of the communicating we do with others never develops into an actual relationship. In order to create a relationship both people must have a mutually similar perception that there is a relationship and have a similar understanding of the nature of that relationship. There are often shared expectations of having ongoing future contact. This can be as simple as seeing someone at work on a regular basis or as complex as a family member. For the purpose of this book, relationship refers to the connections we make directly with others, which they reciprocate by communicating with us on an ongoing basis.

Think about how many people you communicate with each and every day. Who are they? Where did you meet them? What do you talk about? Perhaps you know them socially as friends, professionally as coworkers, or intimately as family members. Each of these is a different type of connection that varies from impersonal to intimate. The ongoing patterns of communicating through connections that are recognized by both people determine the nature of the relationship.

We are motivated to form relationships to help us fulfill needs and wants we cannot fulfill ourselves. We enjoy being around other people like our friends and family. However, there can be times when we feel like we are struggling or working harder in the relationship than we should. There can be times when things don't feel quite right and we're not sure why. By understanding how we create, grow, and maintain relationships, we can increase our awareness of what is happening in them. This can give us options to improve them, so we can feel better about them. We can reduce uncertainty to help us share meaning, so that we can invest in relationships with others and they will invest in us.

We are motivated to form relationships by the law of uncertainty. When we don't know someone there is a high degree of uncertainty because we don't know what to expect from them. They probably feel the same because they do not know what to expect from us. We may perceive them as uncertain because we do not know if they will help or harm us. When we reduce uncertainty we create security and stability making it easier for us to communicate with them. This builds trust making it easier for us to develop relationships with them. This process is necessary in order for society to function because if we didn't get to know people and develop trusting relationships with them, it would be nearly impossible to work together to get things done.

Relationships can create their own specialized social reality facilitated by the law of shared meaning. When two people make a connection to communicate with one another they often tell stories about themselves, talk about their experiences, and share their perceptions and expectations of themselves, others, and the things around them. Sharing these things helps to promote increased understanding between them. Relationships do not exist in isolation. We have relationships with other people who in turn have relationships with others. This creates multiple connections that comprise networks of information that are communicated by people throughout society.

We are motivated by the law of investing to invest our time and other resources in others in order to gain rewards such as fulfilling our needs and wants. By getting to know others we can reduce uncertainty to help us trust them. The more we get to know someone, and the more they get to know us, the more likely we are to be comfortable investing in relationships with them. This is because when we get to know them we have reasonable expectations of their future behavior creating stability and predictability.

In relationships, we get to know what to reasonably expect from others and they get to know what they can reasonably expect of us. We are willing to make fair investments with the expectation of receiving fair rewards. We invest in relationships based upon our future expectations. If we have reasonable expectations of fair rewards that will fulfill our needs and wants, we can be willing to invest in a relationship even if it means putting off receiving benefits until sometime in the future. However, if our perception of what we are receiving does not meet our expectations it could undermine the relationship.

In the process of communicating, you create your Great Idea and communicate it to others across The Great Abyss. You do this by making connections with them. When you make a connection directly with another person, it may constitute the beginning of a relationship. This is because you have established your place in "relation" to the other person. If the connection is reciprocated, a relationship can be created. However, not all communicating through connections will result in creating a relationship. If we do not make an ongoing connection with another person, then no relationship is created. Relationships are about the connections we make with others and the type of relationship is based upon the type of connection.

Relationships and the process of communicating can affect our self-concept because when we share meaning with others about our experiences, we also share meaning about ourselves. Our self-concept is created in part through reflective communicating. When we communicate our Great Idea to others they respond through feedback. The nature of their response can work like a mirror to communicate how they perceive us. Since we cannot see ourselves as others see us, we utilize their feedback like a mirror to see ourselves. The information we receive can affect our self-concept. The closer the relationship and the better we know someone, the more likely we are to be aware of their feedback and utilize it. If we don't know someone very well, or the information we receive is too different from our own perception, we are more likely to brush it off or reject it.

We communicate the nature of our relationships with others not only by what we say, but how we say it. Everything we do in a relationship, whether it is verbal or nonverbal, has the potential to communicate a message that can be given meaning by the other person. Even if we choose not to say anything, such as not returning a phone call or email, it potentially sends a message. This may be perceived as rejection or disapproval when in reality it may not be.

Messages can contain two components. First, we communicate our ideas in the content of the message, which is made up of the words we say. Second, we communicate the nature of our relationship with others by how we communicate those words. This includes our nonverbal behavior, body language, facial expressions, and tone of voice because they tell the other person how to interpret what we say. We use it when we create, develop, and maintain relationships. We use it to indicate our investment in relationships with others through the process of shared meaning. How we say what we say communicates how much we value and care about the other person in the relationship. We may do this to exert control or power over others, to bolster or diminish our self-concept, or to persuade others to do what we want.

Relationships not only help us achieve our desired outcomes, but the relationship itself may be one of our desired outcomes. Whenever we meet someone we form an impression of the type of relationship we want with them. We usually do this within a relatively short amount of time. However, there are some relationships that can develop slowly over longer periods of time. In each of our relationships, and whenever we meet someone, we may take a moment to consider our desired outcome. One of the most common desired outcomes people have when meeting someone is to become friends.

Relationships are a natural and unavoidable part of life. We were created by nature with needs and wants, many of which we cannot fulfill ourselves. Without relationships, every time we had a need or want to fulfill, we would have to start over from the beginning. We would have to look for a way to fulfill it and find someone to help us do it. This motivates us to communicate with others in order to create and maintain relationships.

We create relationships with others based upon our perceptions of them and expectations of their future behavior. In relationships we have a perception of our own behavior including what we want to contribute as well as receive from the relationship. We have a perception of the other person's behavior and expectations, of what they contribute as well as what they receive from the relationship. These perceptions and expectations may or may not accurately reflect reality. These perceptions are important because they can create satisfaction or dissatisfaction with the relationship. If we perceive that we are contributing more than the other person and they are receiving more benefits, we may feel we are being treated unfairly and become dissatisfied. Conversely, if we perceive that we are fairly contributing and receiving in a relationship, it can increase our relational satisfaction.

We have perceptions and expectations about all of our relationships whether we are aware of them or not. We may have realistic or unrealistic perceptions and expectations that can affect how we feel about our relationships and motivate our behavior. It can be helpful to be aware of our expectations and how they may be creating feelings of satisfaction or dissatisfaction. This is because how we feel about our relationships can determine the commitment that we have to the other person and the relationship. This can happen whether we are aware of it or not, but by understanding how this process works, we can control it rather than let it control us so we can have more satisfying relationships.

Having expectations helps us to invest in relationships because if we did not have any expectations we might be reluctant to invest because we would perceive them as too uncertain. We often take our perceptions and expectations for granted and do not communicate them clearly to others. In a relationship, it is easy to assume that the other person would just know what we want. For example, in a romantic relationship one person might think that if the other person really loves them, they would know what they want. Since no two people have precisely the same perceptions and expectations, there is a good chance they might not know what you want. This can set up unrealistic expectations creating unnecessary unhappiness that can be resolved by clearly communicating your perceptions and expectations.

In order for relationships to function they need to be governed by a set of rules. If relationships did not have rules people would do whatever they wanted and things would become chaotic increasing uncertainty. These rules are often based upon a combination of the rules we get from our family, culture, ethnicity, religion, and geographic affiliation. These rules are important because they help people to know what is expected of them and what they can expect of others. Rules can do this because they govern how people in a relationship communicate with one another as well as regulating their behavior. When others fulfill our expectations, we are more likely to reciprocate and follow the rules because they enable us to fulfill our needs and wants. When our perceptions of others do not meet our expectations, we are more likely to challenge or reject the rules because we may feel that they inhibit us from achieving our desired outcome.

When we first meet someone our relationship is governed by the rules of social reality. As we get to know them, the relationship begins to develop its own rules. Our behavior and how we communicate is determined by the nature of the relationship. As our relationship progresses we develop specialized rules that are more applicable to the nature of the relationship. Conversely, the more impersonal the relationship, the more likely we are to continue to follow set patterns of communicating determined by social reality. For example, we often greet people by asking, "How are you?" The standard reply is to say that we are fine. When we get to know someone better, we might tell them how we really feel.

We develop rules in relationships based upon our past experiences. It is not uncommon for us to try to replicate what we perceive as a past success while avoiding past mistakes or repeating a bad experience. However, instead of helping a relationship, this could hinder or even undermine its success. For example, in a romantic relationship, one person may not want to move too fast toward intimacy because they have done so in the past and that relationship did not work out. Since they want this relationship to work out, it is their perception that if they go slow it will help the relationship. Instead, the other person may perceive this behavior as apprehension, rejection, or even manipulation motivating them to pull back or even end the relationship, which is the opposite of what was intended.

We are attracted to relationships when we know the rules. We are likely to be more attracted to relationships with others who we perceive as being similar to us because they share a similar set of rules, perceptions, expectations, and social reality. While this may be interpreted as being aloof or prejudicial, it is a natural response to uncertainty. This is because sharing a similar social reality or set of rules helps to reduce uncertainty about others.

Since a relationship is something that people create together, we are more likely to create relationships with others who share a similar social reality because it reduces uncertainty. If two people have conflicting social realities it can create obstacles that may be difficult to overcome impeding the establishment of a stable relationship.

Society places value on conformity because it creates stability, predictability, and reduces uncertainty, which is necessary for people to form a relationship. Each person is expected to communicate and behave in certain ways, complete specific tasks, and follow the rules of the relationship if they want to receive its benefits. While this may seem restrictive, without rules uncertainty would be increased making it more difficult to maintain a relationship.

When we first meet someone and begin to develop a relationship the rules have not yet been fully established. This creates a sense of uneasiness or awkwardness we often experience when we first meet someone. In order to get things started, we rely on familiar patterns of communicating determined by the rules of social reality. If we did not do this a high level of uncertainty would maintain feelings of uneasiness and awkwardness. This could prevent the relationship from functioning properly because no one would know what was expected of them or what to expect from others. While a high degree of uncertainty can create excitement in a new relationship, it can also become tiresome over time.

As we get to know others, we negotiate our own rules to govern the relationship. Most of the time these rules are communicated indirectly. We may only become aware of them after we have violated a rule and the other person gets upset with us. In order to avoid this, it is helpful to communicate perceptions and expectations about the relationship and its rules.

We form relationships because they can be fun and enjoyable. They can fulfill our need for affiliation and companionship because we like being around others. People can be interesting and entertaining fulfilling our need for excitement and variety. However, after a while a relationship may become more mundane so it feels like hard work leaving us wondering what happened. This is because relationships are not just fun and enjoyable, they have tasks that must be accomplished and needs that must be fulfilled to function properly.

The social aspects of a relationship are important because nobody wants to work all the time, we want to enjoy things as well. Relationships help us to fulfill important social needs such as relaxation, escape, and pleasure. They help us to reduce tension and to share interests with others. Even in work situations where the focus is on getting tasks done, having social time is essential to healthy working relationships. People need to take time off to get to know one another, to relieve stress, or just have fun. This is one reason why coworkers will socialize by going to lunch or out together after work. Regardless of the type of relationship, the functional aspect of getting things done and the social needs of the individuals should be addressed for the health of the relationship.

Behavioral reinforcement.

Have you ever felt like you acted in one way when you were with one person and in a distinctly different way when you were with someone else? We might change our behavior depending upon who we are with because of the effect that they have on us. This happens because we all have variable and nonvariable characteristics. Nonvariable characteristics include the things we cannot change about ourselves such as our gender, ethnicity, or age. These are the things about us that do not change when our circumstances change and they are the things that people are most likely to notice about us.

Variable characteristics include those things about us that we can change depending upon our circumstances. They can include things such as how outgoing we are, our sense of humor, or what we like to talk about. Variable behavior is important because it allows us to act differently when we are out with friends, at work, or in church. Our behavior with others changes appropriately depending upon the nature of our relationship with them. There are characteristics of our personality that become dominant or regressive depending upon who we are with, the nature of the relationship, and the particular situation. We can do this in ways that we may not even notice. We may be outgoing and have a sense of humor when we are with our friends and act more subdued or serious with our coworkers at work.

How we communicate depends upon the nature of the relationship. What is acceptable in one relationship may be considered inappropriate in another. We may feel comfortable telling jokes or colorful stories with our friends, but not with our coworkers. This negotiated collective shared meaning that we develop with others can influence and motivate our behavior. How we accomplish this depends on our past experiences, the nature of the relationship, and our desired outcome for forming the relationship. It is likely influenced by the perceptions and expectations that we have of ourselves and that others have of us. We do this to manage our identity and present ourselves in a manner that encourages development of the relationship.

We often behave differently in different relationships because they are created by the people involved in them. Every relationship has its own unique qualities that give it a distinctive character or personality. This means that it is possible for a relationship to become something that we do not want or do not intend it to be. This is why we may feel that a relationship is not going the way we want or that we don't have any control over it.

How this works can be illustrated by imagining two musicians playing on the same street corner. If each of them are playing their own song it would be difficult to hear either one of them and it would probably sound awful. If they play the same song together it would sound much better. However, neither one has complete control over what the people passing by hear. They hear a combination of the two that neither can create by themselves. When people in relationships behave as individuals, like the musicians, it can become hard work that can increase uncertainty. When people are aware of how relationships work they can work together to make the relationship less stressful, less work, and more beneficial to both.

Since every relationship is a separate entity created by the people involved, it can develop its own unique personality. This is because we manage our identity based upon our perceptions of how others are perceiving us and our expectations in the relationship. Through the process of reflective feedback, other people can have an affect on our variable characteristics, which can change our behavior. Different people have the potential to bring out different parts of our personality. This is why we may act one way in one relationship and in an entirely different way in another. We may even act in ways we do not expect.

Since a relationship is a separate entity with its own unique characteristics it can develop its own rules, structure, and norms of behavior which may be the same or different than we have in our other relationships. We may find ourselves with one set of behavioral norms in one relationship and a different set in another, motivating us to exhibit different behaviors and communicate in different ways. We manage our identity in our relationships, and in each relationship we make different choices how to do that. Since a relationship is a combination of the people who created it, even though it involves us, we might feel like we have little control over it and may be surprised by the direction it is going.

Why we form relationships.

When we are born, we begin to form relationships with others who are close to us such as our parents and family. As we get older, we become more independent and are able to form relationships more by choice than by necessity with people like friends and classmates. As our self-concept develops, we look for relationships that support how we see ourselves or how we would like to be perceived. As we are able to fulfill more needs and wants for ourselves, we move farther away from our home and family to form relationships with others based on other characteristics such as similar interests.

Just as everyone communicates for a reason, everyone forms relationships for a reason. The reasons we form relationships can be as different as the individuals who form them. We commonly form relationships in order to fulfill needs and wants, and to achieve desired outcomes. We have a natural curiosity about others and the world around us, so we create relationships to learn more about ourselves and others. By forming relationships, we are able to communicate less superficially with others and interact with them on a deeper, more meaningful level. We can communicate with them in a way that would be considered uncomfortable and inappropriate if we did not have a relationship with them. This is necessary in order to more fully understand ourselves, others, and our experiences. It helps us to know more about ourselves and others to reduce uncertainty. It provides useful information in order to enable self-improvement and personal growth.

We are motivated to form relationships in order to achieve desired outcomes we cannot achieve on our own. These can include things like being on a sports team, finding a job, or getting married. We develop professional relationships to earn income necessary to help us fulfill our monetary needs. We develop personal relationships to help fulfill our social needs such as being part of a group. We develop intimate relationships to help fulfill our needs for closeness and intimacy. When we form relationships it provides benefits for others as well as ourselves.

Relationships help us to fulfill our needs and wants. When we are born, our family provides for all our needs. As we get older, we develop our own relationships to help us to obtain the things we need like a job, family, home, and even a positive self-concept. Without relationships, achieving these outcomes would be more difficult, if not impossible. Relationships can be used to gain power, status, and respect. Developing relationships can be used to elevate a person's status so they are perceived as being important to others. This can help to provide them with resources to achieve their desired outcomes. Relationships can help us to exercise control not only over our lives, but also over resources and the actions of others.

We are motivated to form relationships in order to fulfill needs and wants we cannot fulfill ourselves. Relationships provide a stable ongoing means of needs and wants fulfillment. They motivate us to take action and get to know others rather than living by ourselves in a cabin in the woods. We do this because if we had to negotiate with someone every time we needed something it would take too much time and energy. Relationships provide us with connections on an ongoing basis making a more efficient use of our time and resources.

Relationships help provide us with feedback. When we develop a relationship with others, we may feel comfortable sharing our thoughts and feelings with them. This is because we feel comfortable being ourselves so we can more easily talk about things without having to worry about what we say or how they will react. We communicate our thoughts and feelings in order to gain new insights into ourselves from others that we cannot gain by ourselves. This is because when we share ideas with others they add their perceptions and experiences that give our ideas additional meaning. They can also give us advice on how we can improve because they see us from a different perspective that we cannot see ourselves.

In a relationship, we can gain feedback by using the other person as a sounding board to test our ideas. We feel comfortable doing this because we know that they will not reject us because of our ideas, but rather provide us with honest and objective feedback. Relationships help to create an atmosphere of trust so that we can express ourselves and communicate our true thoughts and feelings. We do this because showing consideration for one another helps us to share ideas more open and honestly.

Relationships contribute to the development of our self-concept. Our self-concept is partially constructed by reflective communicating with others. We utilize feedback from others to create a picture of how they perceive us. This can be helpful in managing our identity and communicating more effectively with others. This makes it important to create relationships with others who we know will be honest with us, so that we can trust their perceptions and feedback. This information is useful to help us improve ourselves and our communicating skills. However, we can be motivated to seek relationships with others who will simply confirm our own perception of ourselves, which may or may not be accurate.

We tend to like people who we perceive are like us and who tell us good things about ourselves because it can bolster our self-concept and increase our confidence. However, in some instances people may be overly complementary to achieve their own desired outcomes, which may not be in our best interest. They may be reluctant to tell others the truth because others won't like them if they do. When this happens in extreme cases, it can lead to overconfidence or arrogance. So, it can be helpful to be aware of who is providing the feedback and the nature of that feedback in developing a realistic self-concept.

We form relationships to provide support because life can be challenging, discouraging, and difficult. We form relationships to help make life easier and the workload lighter. Relationships make us feel that the problems of life are not so difficult because they provide us with both tangible and emotional support. We look for relationships with people that can help us fulfill our needs for nurturing and support to give us a positive self-concept to make us feel valued and worthwhile. We look for relationships that make us feel like we make a contribution and that what we do matters. We look for relationships to share mutual interests and participate in mutual activities to make them more meaningful. We look for relationships so that we feel appreciated and loved.

Relationships make us feel valued because others invest in us by contributing their time and other resources. We feel valued because we are part of someone else's life. This is because they take an interest in what we do, what we think, and how we feel. We feel a sense of attachment because having connections with others validates our own existence. Relationships can bolster our self-concept because we feel better about ourselves when we are appreciated by others.

Relationships make life more meaningful because we share thoughts, ideas, feelings, emotions, and aspirations to gain a different perspective giving them more significance. Our experiences can be more fun when we share them with others. Our ideas are more interesting when others appreciate them. Perhaps these are some of the reasons why nature created us with needs and wants we cannot fulfill ourselves, so that we are motivated to form relationships with others.

Relationships can help improve our self-concept, but they can also damage it. In relationships we disclose information about ourselves that can make us vulnerable. Some people may take advantage of that information and use it for their own gain. They may say or do things that hurt our self-concept. They may be concerned about losing their sense of who they are to another person or to the relationship. Depending upon the nature of the relationship, the other person has a say over what we do giving them some power or control over us. We all have different degrees of how much control we will allow other people to have in our lives. A relationship may be going fine until we feel the other person is getting too much control, which can lead to tension and conflict, or may even end the relationship. In other situations we may avoid relationships altogether if we perceive another person could have too much control over us.

Not everyone looks to form relationships with everyone they meet. Most of the time we are not looking to form relationships, but instead we form them when we have a need or a want we are looking to have fulfilled. There are times when we avoid relationships because they not only won't help us, they could hurt us. We might avoid them out of a fear of what might potentially happen. If we have had a relationship that turned out badly, it could make us more reluctant to get involved in another similar relationship. This is because it is difficult to know what might happen in the future.

We may avoid relationships because of a feeling that others might ambush us, lie to us, have a hidden agenda, or try to manipulate us. We may feel that being in a relationship will make us more vulnerable. We might avoid relationships if we feel they could violate our privacy. When someone doesn't want a relationship with us, it could be perceived as rejection when in reality they may have issues that they are working through, but instead of explaining it, they just avoid the relationship. It is helpful to be aware that when we try to form relationships and others don't seem interested, we don't perceive it necessarily as rejection of us.

Relational Development

All relationships have one thing in common, at one time the people involved did not know each other. This means that relationships go through the process of relational development. This process can be characterized by four phases that are governed by the laws of uncertainty, shared meaning, and investing. Since everyone is different there is no one right way to develop a relationship. A relationship can go through these phases rather quickly or it might take some time. How a relationship goes through these phases depends on the nature of the relationship, the individuals involved, and their desired outcomes.

1. Relational creation is how we form relationships. This is the law of uncertainty phase because we get to know others by reducing uncertainty.

2. Relational growth is how we develop relationships. This is the law of shared meaning phase because we share meaning through the process of self-disclosure to develop commitment to the relationship.

3. Relational maintenance is how we sustain relationships over time. This is the law of investing phase because it is when we invest our time, energy, and other resources in maintaining the relationship.

4. Relational dissolution is how relationships end. This is a return to the law of uncertainty phase because uncertainty in the relationship is increased to the point of breaking it apart.

I. Relational Creation
The Law Of Uncertainty Phase

When we first meet someone we may be unsure of how to communicate with them. So, we rely on familiar patterns of communicating governed by the rules of social reality to tell us how to behave. We use the perception process to obtain information about them in order to help us know how to proceed. Based on the information we have, we try different approaches looking for one that will work. This is why there is often an awkward tension or stiffness when we first meet someone, because we feel self conscious, perhaps even uncomfortable not knowing what to do or to expect from them. Before we can form a relationship, uncertainty needs to be reduced.

The first phase of relational development is motivated by the law of uncertainty. The first time people get together is generally based upon the connections they have with one another. They may communicate with one another because they are in close proximity, have similarities, communicate frequently, or share common interests. They may seek to form relationships in order to fulfill needs and wants they cannot fulfill themselves.

Whenever we encounter a new situation that we are unfamiliar with, we look for ways to communicate with others. If we had to figure out how to communicate in each and every situation it would take too much time and energy. So, as part of the rules of social reality people have developed patterns of communicating that tell them how to act and behave in various situations. These are preestablished ways we communicate with others that work rather like a script works in a play or movie. We use them because everyone knows the lines and what to expect, which reduces uncertainty.

We often use these patterns in unfamiliar situations like a job interview, first date, moving to a new neighborhood, going to the grocery store, or visiting an unfamiliar place. Some patterns are simple greetings and others are more complex ways of interacting. They are commonly used because they meet our shared expectations, which reduces uncertainty making people feel more comfortable. When we hear the same words repeated it gives us feelings of comfort and familiarity. When familiar patterns are not followed, it can increase uncertainty, which is why people might feel uncomfortable if they are changed too much.

In order to use patterns of communicating it can be helpful to be aware of the situation, the people involved, and their expectations. In many situations the expectations of others will determine what we say and do. It can be helpful to be aware of what others are doing and follow their lead. However, there may be circumstances when they will not expect you to behave as they do because doing so may not be considered appropriate. Knowing that you are new to the situation, they may expect you to behave differently.

One response to a new or unfamiliar situation is to try to act like we know what we are doing. While it can be helpful to have some knowledge, when we act like we know what we are doing we could run the risk of making erroneous assumptions. A more effective approach is let others go first and follow their lead. Be honest about your knowledge of the situation. If they know that you are new to the situation, they should be sympathetic to your circumstances and may be willing to assist you. This is because at one time they were new to the situation like you are now, so they may see themselves in you. Clearly asking others for their help or advice is a good way to start. If they do not know you, they may have unrealistic expectations of you and your behavior. If you show an interest in them, they are more likely to be receptive to you.

Behavioral reinforcement.

We use behavioral reinforcement to reduce uncertainty about others in order to invest in relationships with them. We communicate by utilizing the process of communicating to make a connection with them to share our Great Idea. Then we wait for feedback to know how well it was received. Their feedback can shape the nature of the relationship.

When we first communicate with someone we can potentially receive one of three possible responses. Our message is either accepted, rejected, or ignored. If we receive positive feedback then our message is accepted and we are on our way to developing a relationship. If we do something that is successful we are likely to repeat it. When something results in a successful outcome we are more comfortable with it because it reduces uncertainty.

This can make us more likely to take the same approach in other situations because we now have reasonable expectations that it will work again. However, over time things change, so past ways of communicating may become less effective and eventually no longer work. Rather than looking for a new approach, we may keep trying the old ones potentially making things worse. Eventually past approaches may no longer work making us wonder what went wrong. What we need to do is examine our perceptions and expectations, gather fresh information, and create a new approach.

When we receive negative feedback, we might feel that not only is our message rejected, we may also feel personally rejected as well. We may try a different approach and if we receive negative feedback again, we may become frustrated or agitated reducing the likelihood of future contact. This discourages us from communicating or behaving in this way again because it was unsuccessful. It may have a negative impact on our self-concept and we may even feel hurt or rejected. Since these feelings are uncomfortable, we are less likely to repeat them in the future. However, negative feedback can sometimes be perceived as a challenge encouraging some people to try it again, sometimes acting out more forcefully.

Feedback can be ambiguous or unclear. This can motivate us to repeat the original message until we get a clear reply. However, the other person may choose to ignore us by providing no feedback. This can be the most difficult response to deal with because there is no information to interpret. We cannot be sure if the other person was unable to respond or just didn't care. With no information we often provide our own interpretation perhaps deciding it is not worth the effort. If we feel there's something to be gained, we may continue to repeat the message until we get either positive or negative feedback.

How we form relationships.

Think about the people in your past and present relationships. How did you get to know them? Do you remember the first time you met? In all relationships there is some connection that forms the basis of how we get to know someone. While we could potentially meet anyone to develop a relationship, we only make connections with a limited number of people and most of them never develop into relationships because we have a limited amount of time and energy to invest in them. We can not form a relationship with someone without first making a connection. The most common ways we meet people are those who we see on a regular basis through everyday activities such as work, school, church, in our community, or doing errands. The closer their proximity, the greater the frequency, and the more intense the connection, the greater the likelihood of developing a relationship.

These are some of the ways we meet people to form relationships.

- Family. These are the people we are related to and the first people with whom we develop relationships. Because of the close ties, these relationships are often the strongest and last the longest. Family relationships are generally structured and have specific labels such as parent, child, or sibling. These relationships have a formal aspect that carries societal and legal expectations such as a parent, child, or spouse. However, each family can develop their own ways of expressing these relationships.

- Proximity. This is probably the single most important factor in developing relationships. Proximity involves people who are close to us, who share the same geographic or professional space like our family, friends, neighbors, or coworkers. In order to have a relationship with someone, we first have to meet them. We cannot have relationships with people we've never met because we need to make a connection with them. Typically, we meet someone face to face, but we can also develop relationships in other ways such as by mail, telephone, or over the internet.

- Frequency. We not only have to make a connection with someone, we have to keep in contact with them. Frequency is how often we see someone or communicate with them over a period of time. We can develop relationships with people who are not in close proximity, but with whom we have frequent contact. The more we communicate with someone, the higher the likelihood we self-disclose information about ourselves increasing the potential of creating a relationship.

- Intensity. This is the degree of contact we have with someone over a period of time. If we see someone frequently or spend a large amount of time with them, the intensity of the contact can help to create a relationship. Our most intense relationships are often with the people we see where we live and work. We can also meet someone and spent a lot of time with them, however, a short intense relationship tends to not last very long because when the intensity subsides, the relationship is not as sustainable. For example, when we attend camp or a seminar we can develop close relationships with others and promise to keep in touch with them. However, after it is over we may not keep in touch, at least not for very long. This is because when people go back to their normal lives the intensity goes away. The relationship is unlikely to continue unless there is another connection to sustain it.

- Similarity. The law of uncertainty can motivate people to create and maintain relationships with others who are similar to them because uncertainty is reduced. Since we like ourselves, if we perceive someone is similar to us we should like them. Similarity can include many qualities such as similar likes, dislikes, interests, education, or work. It can be with people who share similar values, attitudes, or beliefs. We are more likely to create relationships with people who have similar backgrounds like culture, education, ethnicity, or geographic affiliations. They may have similar tastes in food, clothing, or music. They may have similar experiences, occupation, or participate in the same activities that we do. The more we find someone is similar to ourselves, the more we have to talk about so we can utilize the law of shared meaning to create interest in a relationship.

- Profession. After our family, our closest relationships are often developed through our work. This is because we spend the most time there away from home. We are motivated to create relationships at work to get along with our coworkers to help us do our job better. It is easy to create relationships with people from work because we are in close proximity, we spent a lot of time together, and we often have much in common with them such as similar knowledge and experiences. We develop professional relationships to make work easier, to advance our career, and to earn more money. However, just like relationships created by short periods of intensity, if we leave our job, our work relationships are likely to fade away unless there is another connection to sustain them.

- Relationships in common. We meet new people through people we already know. The people we know also have friends, family, coworkers, and acquaintances. They may introduce us to someone with whom we develop our own relationship. These relationships reduce uncertainty because we both know the same person so we have something in common. The rationale is that relationships should have a degree of transitivity. For instance, if we are friends with person A, and they are friends with person B, then we should be able to be friends with person B. Since relationships are created between the people involved, this does not necessarily hold true. Just because one person we like is friends another, it does not necessarily mean we will like them or they will like us. This is why some people may be reluctant to introduce us to people they know because if it doesn't turn out well, they may be afraid that we will blame them or it could hurt their other relationships. Alternately, their friend may end up liking us better changing or ending our friend's relationship with their friend. It might also change or end our relationship with our friend as well.

- Common ground. When we meet someone for the first time we tend to look for things we have in common to make ourselves feel more at ease and comfortable around them. Finding common ground gives us familiar topics of conversation to make connections with others to share meaning, which reduces uncertainty. This increases the likelihood of developing a relationship because it bolsters our self-concept making us feel more comfortable around others. We are more likely to develop relationships with people we find interesting and can engage in conversation. Conversely, we are less likely to develop relationships with people that are difficult to talk to or we perceive as not interesting.

- Attraction. We form relationships with others we find attractive. We like to be around people we find attractive as well as those who find us attractive. We find others attractive for many reasons other than just physical appearance. Attraction can be intellectual, emotional, professional, or psychological depending upon our needs and wants. We are attracted to others because we find them exciting, interesting, considerate, supportive, or stable. We are attracted to people who like us, who make us feel important, who bolster our self-concept, and make us feel attractive. Attraction is a powerful motivating force because it represents our expectations of fulfilling future needs and wants. The perception of attractiveness can determine whether or not we pursue a relationship.

- Likeability. We like people who like us. We like people who like us because they have good taste. They make us feel good about ourselves and bolster our self-concept. Since our self-concept is enhanced through reflective feedback, when we are liked by others we feel accepted and valued as a person. Having the approval of others who like us is a powerful social reward. When someone likes us it helps to reduce uncertainty and makes us feel more at ease. Conversely, the lack of approval can be used as a punishment. If someone doesn't like us it can increase tension pushing us away from them because no one likes to be around others who don't like them.

- Random chance. Every once in awhile we meet someone by chance and hit it off, becoming friends or perhaps more. When we meet them we may feel a connection, a gut feeling, or intuition that peaks our interest motivating us to pursue a relationship. These types of relationships can surprise us because they tend to go against typical methods of forming relationships due to their high degree of uncertainty.

Meeting people.

In order to develop a relationship we must first meet someone we do not know. Because there is a higher degree of uncertainty, we can feel uptight or apprehensive. We can be overly self aware or self conscious because we want to be liked. We might not consider that the other person may have the same feelings about us and are wondering if we like them.

We come in contact with new people all the time. Whether we are at work, school, church, or the grocery store, we are around other people we don't know. In most cases we do not make an effort to get to know them. We may even try to avoid making eye contact so we don't have to make a connection. We can be motivated to do this by the laws of uncertainty and investing. We do not try to get to know them because we may have the perception that since we know nothing about them the uncertainty is too great, so we don't see any potential benefit in trying to form a relationship.

Whenever we meet someone we can feel a high degree of uncertainty. We may feel apprehensive because we don't know what to expect from them or how they will behave. While there is the possibility that they may be threatening or could do us harm, the more common concern is being rejected. So, we may put up an invisible barrier for self defense to keep others out. However, this could increase uncertainty by making them feel threatened.

When we decide we want to meet someone we need to get their attention. Getting a person's attention is important because we cannot have a relationship with someone we haven't met. We can't meet them without making a connection, and we can't make a connection without initiating one by getting their attention. How to approach someone we don't know to get their attention can be the most daunting part of meeting them. Since there is no one right way to do this, the best approach is not to force the situation, but rather to let the circumstances of the situation work for you.

A good way to make connections is through someone you already know. If you can have someone you know introduce you to them it reduces uncertainty making you less threatening. Having another person introduce you takes the pressure off you to keep the conversation going. This gives you a chance to gain important information in order to maintain the conversation and to determine if you want to pursue a relationship or not.

If having someone else introduce you is not feasible, you might find a reason to talk to them. It could be asking them if they know someone you know, asking what time it is, or for directions. Most people don't like clever opening lines because they can seem phony or manipulating. If you are looking to meet people it is helpful to look friendly and open to conversation. We like to meet people who seem confident, relaxed, open, and approachable because it reduces uncertainty about them. Since we cannot speak to them until we make contact, looking approachable is done nonverbally by smiling a little, making appropriate eye contact, having an open posture, and being aware of those around us.

First impressions can be difficult to change even though we may not actually remember the first thing someone said to us. This is because first impressions are not only about what you say, but how you say it and how others perceive it. Impressions are based on perception and much of what we perceive comes from nonverbal communicating through our body language. Creating a good first impression comes from acting confident, self assured, and friendly. If we are perceived as being relaxed and at ease it makes us appear less threatening, so other people are more likely to be more at ease with us. Conversely, if we are perceived as being uptight, nervous, or forced, other people are likely to respond similarly and might consider our demeanor strange or threatening.

In the process of communicating, we are constantly receiving more information than we can use. So, in order to process it we filter out information that we perceive as not being important to us. The same is true of individuals in relationships because we do not have the time or energy to develop meaningful relationships with everyone we meet. So, we evaluate the potential future return of pursuing a relationship by making a type of on the spot cost benefit analysis to determine if a relationship is worth pursuing and what type of relationship to pursue. We filter out people we don't perceive as having the potential for a future relationship. This may determine if we go up and talk to someone or decide it's not worth it.

For example, when we are around other people during everyday activities, like standing in line, we may consider someone rude because they do not talk to us or avoid eye contact. It is not so much about acting rude, but rather about making an assessment of the value of pursuing a relationship. This is because the situation is temporary and the only thing we know we have in common is that we are all standing in line. Most of the time we determine there is little or no future potential in pursuing a relationship. This is an example of the natural inertia that must be overcome in creating relationships.

There are situations when circumstances override the natural inertia that prevents us from making contact, so we are motivated to talk to someone even though we know there is little or no chance of a future relationship. We might do this out of a need to alleviate boredom by having someone to talk to or to pass the time. We may feel that we are being treated unfairly by having to wait for a very long time, so we might seek to gain support from others to get the line to move along faster. We may want to entertain ourselves in a mundane situation. We may also make contact in order to gain information about something around us.

One exception to this is when we might go up and talk to someone famous or that we find interesting or attractive even though there is little chance of forming a relationship. We do this because if someone we find attractive responds positively to us, it can bolster our self-concept. People might do this because the potential benefits override the inhibiting inertia.

Identity Management.

When you introduce yourself to someone you have never met before, what do you say? What information do you include and what do you leave out? What do you say first, second, or last? Do you talk about your work, family, past experiences, or interests? Do you introduce yourself the same way in every situation? How we choose to introduce ourselves is influenced by the rules of social reality, our inferences about the expectations of the situation, and the people we meet. How we do this is the process of identity management.

Next time you meet someone for the first time, be aware of what you say about yourself. If you have time afterwards, write down as specifically as possible what you and the other person said. This will give you information about how you communicate who you are to others. Writing it down helps us to think about the process as it actually happened rather than how we perceive it later. Doing this can help provide insight into how we perceive ourselves and our expectations about how we would like others to perceive us.

Identity management comprises the choices we make about what we say and how we behave when we communicate with others. It would be extremely difficult as well as rather unwise to try to communicate everything about ourselves because it would be overwhelming and inappropriate. Therefore, we need to make choices about what information we communicate about ourselves, to whom, and under what circumstances. Identity management works like public relations, we make choices about what information we communicate to others that can shape their impression of us and to help us achieve our desired outcomes.

When we meet other people, we communicate information about ourselves whether we choose to or not. We may choose what to say, but we cannot choose to stop communicating nonverbally. How others perceive us, as well is how we perceive ourselves, is partially based upon our individual characteristics. Others use these characteristics to gather information about us in order to reduce uncertainty to determine how to behave. This is due to our natural tendency to want to understand others and their motivations based upon observable characteristics. We make inferences about others based upon many characteristics such as their age, gender, ethnicity, height, weight, clothing, possessions, and appearance.

We make perceptual inferences based upon these characteristics motivated by the law of shared meaning. People look for meaning in what they perceive about others. They do this by comparison, they take what they observe and compare it to their past experiences. People do this because it is an easy way to gain information about others rather than doing the more difficult task of finding things out for themselves.

We all have variable characteristics that are difficult to see and so are difficult to make inferences about. These characteristics can change considerably in relatively short periods of time. They more accurately represent who we are as a person and our self-concept. They can include our attitudes, values, beliefs, preferences, interests, likes, and dislikes. We are likely to communicate some of these characteristics more than others.

Identity management is to some extent based upon the perceptions and expectations of others. Motivated by the law of uncertainty, we may choose to communicate only certain information and alter our behavior in order to be perceived as being like others so we will be accepted by them. If we act too differently from our true selves, identity management might be perceived as manipulation or being phony. Conversely, low degrees of identity management could communicate the impression that we don't care about ourselves or others. Identity management is a matter of balance. It can be helpful to use an appropriate level of identity management to maintain your individuality, while being considerate of the expectations of others.

There are varying degrees by which we manage identity. We use higher degrees when we first meet someone, go on a job interview, or go on a date. We are motivated to do this because we have desired outcomes, so we monitor our behavior to make a good impression. We are careful about what information we share and what we reveal until we get to know the other person better. However, there are times when people could reveal too much or inappropriate information that can make others feel uncomfortable.

Identity management is governed by the law of investing because we invest part of ourselves and our resources to get to know others. We are careful about how much information we share and our level of investment, so that we get what we expect in return. If we do achieve a portion of our desired outcome, we are more likely to share more later. If not, we may be less likely to put ourselves out again in the future.

Everyone manages several identities because we present ourselves in different ways in different situations. This can be based upon several factors like the roles we fulfill such as spouse, coworker, or friend. These identities are based upon the context or situation such as at home or in public. They can be based upon the groups we belong to and their expectations such as work or family. They can be based upon our desired outcomes or the needs and wants we are looking to have fulfilled such as making a living.

In each of the situations, we present a different identity based upon our self-concept and the expectations of others within the rules of social reality. This means that we could have a family identity, a work identity, and a public identity. Each of these represents a part of ourselves that we present to others based upon the demands of the situation and expectations of the other people involved. For instance, we would not behave the same way at home as we might with our friends or at work or in church.

We communicate for a reason so we create identities for a reason. We do this to fit in with the expectations of others to reduce uncertainty, so that they will be willing to invest in relationships with us. People do not want to be around or invest their time in others whose behavior they perceive as unpredictable because there is too much uncertainty. People want to be around others who they perceive as being stable and predictable, so they can trust them because they know what they can reasonably expect in the future.

When we communicate with others we manage our level of self-disclosure through identity management. We do this by making choices about what information to share and what information to withhold. Sometimes we manage our identity by choice, other times we don't think much about it so it happens naturally. We make these decisions based upon the nature of the situation, mutual expectations, the people involved, and the rules of social reality.

These are some options people use to manage their identity around others.

- Agreeable. We want to be liked by others because it makes us feel good about ourselves. No one wants to be around someone who is disagreeable, difficult to get along with, or unpleasant. We like people who are reasonably agreeable, but it is a matter of balance because being too agreeable can be perceived as being phony. Agreeing with others affirms their self-concept making us more attractive because it is a social reward. People who are confident in themselves are more able to agree and disagree while expressing their own thoughts in an honest and friendly way.

- Helpful. We want to be perceived by others as someone who is helpful and supportive because no one wants to be in a relationship with someone who is not. We want to be helpful because it is the right thing to do and we want others to be helpful and supportive in return. Being helpful is good to a degree, however, people who are overly helpful can be perceived as clingy or trying to manipulate others for their own gain.

- Empathetic. We like to be around others who listen and empathize with us by seeing things from our perspective. We like to be around people who are open to our ideas and point of view. We like being around people who are sympathetic, nurturing, and compassionate because it fulfills an important need for support and security.

- Humor. Humor works to reduce tension and makes people feel more at ease. We like people who have a good sense of humor because being too serious is no fun. People are more approachable when they don't take themselves too seriously. However, someone who constantly makes jokes or does not seem to take things seriously can be annoying and may be perceived as covering other problems. Everyone has a different sense of humor, so use of humor can be risky. What one person finds funny another may find offensive. It's best to hold off on using humor until you get to know someone in a more serious manner first, unless something just happens to come up that is naturally funny.

- Etiquette. Etiquette and manners are the behavioral expression of the rules of social reality. Manners govern our behavior and how we use patterns of communicating with others. We use it to manage our identity and make a positive impression on others. We use it in more formal circumstances or where something is at stake when we don't want to take risks. We utilize etiquette by having good manners, being polite, and respecting others. We are motivated to use etiquette and manners by the law of uncertainty because it reduces uncertainty, so others will perceive us as stable and trustworthy enabling them to be more comfortable with us. It demonstrates that we are knowledgeable of the rules of social reality and are willing to abide by them, so that others can invest in us.

- Success. We want to be perceived by others as being successful. We can do this in a variety of ways such as having a good job, income, relationships, family, or being good at what we do. We communicate success by talking about our accomplishments, our family, and things that we have done. We are motivated to do this because we want the respect of others, however, overdoing it can work in reverse by giving others the perception that we are only trying to impress them.

Conversation.

In order to create a relationship, we must first make a connection. One of the most common ways we do this is by engaging in conversation. This makes conversation one of our most important communicating skills. We have many conversations every day with our friends, family, or coworkers. We usually don't think much about these conversations because we have done this many times before and we know what to expect. There are times when having a conversation with someone is natural and easy. At other times it may seem difficult and next to impossible. No matter how comfortable or uncomfortable we feel conversing with others, communicating skills can be developed and improved.

Whenever we meet someone we don't know, there is a natural uneasiness, awkwardness, or tension. This feeling comes from the high degree of uncertainty we feel when we don't know much about someone. We can have a natural tendency to keep our guard up by being careful what we say and do because we do not know what to expect from them. However, we want to meet other people because it is enjoyable and we learn things by talking with them. So, in order to communicate effectively with others and get to know them enough to develop a relationship, uncertainty must be reduced to create an atmosphere that is relaxed and comfortable enough to communicate with others. Developing conversational skills can help ease the tension and reduce uncertainty to create a more pleasurable experience.

We are motivated by the law of uncertainty to communicate with people so that we can find out more about them to feel more comfortable around them. Getting to know someone through conversation is nonthreatening and a way to encourage self-disclosure. This helps reduce uncertainty to build trust and security that is necessary for any relationship. The law of shared meaning motivates us to share our experiences and stories about ourselves, so we can understand and get to know others better. The law of investing motivates us to communicate with others to determine the potential of investing resources in a relationship.

In practically all aspects of life, conversation is an important skill because it is how we meet and get to know others on a more meaningful level. Since relationships have both a task and social aspect, it is helpful that we can communicate not only about the task at hand, but also engage in social conversation. We engage in conversation to develop personal connections that enable better working relationships. Most people do not make decisions simply on the task ability of an individual, they also consider their social characteristics. People want to work with others who not only can do their job, but who are enjoyable to work with as well.

In order to reduce apprehension and develop conversational skills, it can be helpful to practice talking to people you come in contact with while doing everyday tasks. Talk about something that is familiar to you or that you enjoy. This should give you a natural self-confidence because you know something about what you are talking about. This will make you appear positive and upbeat because it's something you enjoy. When you are confident and upbeat the other person should pick up on that and respond similarly. However, if you strain for something to talk about you can appear as if you are closed off or have a problem.

When you first talk to someone there is always the chance that they will not respond. This can put you in an awkward situation. Should you say the same thing again or try something else? Instead of opening with a line, get the conversation going by asking open ended questions. A statement can be ignored, however, the rules of social reality necessitate that reasonable questions should be answered. A person is more likely to answer a question because they want to be perceived as being helpful or polite. The question should not be overly complicated and be related to the context of the situation. Then, if there's no response it is not overly obtrusive to ask them again or ask another question.

A question should be general in nature and not too personal. It should encourage the other person to reply with more than single word answers like yes or no. The purpose is to get the other person to talk about themselves. Asking them what they think or how they feel about something shows that you are interested in them and encourages conversation. Anticipate potential questions others might ask you and have short, to the point answers ready. If you have to think about it for too long they may think you are not being honest or making it up.

Usually the situation or circumstances can provide an opening question like asking for directions or if they know someone you know. This opens up the conversation because they are not threatening questions and people can easily answer with more than just saying yes or no. Have a couple questions in mind to initiate a conversation that can fit various situations. Don't over rehearse what you are going to say or use clever one liners because they could sound phony or insincere.

Start with familiar topics of conversation. Have a few topics in mind so you don't stand there staring at them trying to think of what to say next because the conversation will end if you don't have anything to talk about. Talk about subjects that you know something about and look for ones that you both are interested in to keep the conversation naturally going. Avoid topics that are overly personal, complicated, controversial, or ones the other person may know little about. Let the situation work for you by talking about something close at hand such as why you are there or what's going on around you.

At an appropriate moment in the conversation you might introduce yourself. When we introduce ourselves to other people, we often say things about ourselves like our name, what we do for a living, where we live, or our interests. Ask the other person their name and repeat it once out loud. Saying their name communicates that they matter and helps you to remember it. If you say it wrong they have the chance to correct you. All too often we hear a person's name once when we first meet them and then forget it. After awhile we get to know them, but we can't remember their name and by then it's too embarrassing to ask them.

A good conversation is balanced, it has give and take. It is not a monologue or a soliloquy. No one likes someone who dominates the conversation. Avoid speaking too long without the other person saying anything or saying whatever comes to mind. Instead, think things through before you say them and give the other person time to respond. If you find you are talking too much ask the other person what they think to shift the balance. Never dominate the conversation, let the other person speak. The more the other person talks the less work you have to do. People like to talk about themselves, but do not let that person be you.

Be positive, do not be negative when you first meet someone or you will come across as a downer. Save that until you get to know them better. Don't talk too much about yourself unless you are asked. Then be honest and to the point. Avoid information about yourself that's too personal or intimate. Keep the conversation light by staying away from controversial topics. A good approach is to start with basic information and proceed in small increments based on what the other person says.

Listen when they are talking. It is easy to only think about what to say next and not hear what others say. Actually listening to them should let you know what to say next by following up what they said. If you ask them questions and don't contribute information yourself, you could come across as overly intrusive. By listening and responding to what they say the conversation progresses and begins to flow naturally. If it doesn't, be ready with something to say.

Use positive nonverbal body language. Smile, nod your head, and gesture occasionally to indicate that you are interested and engaged in the conversation. Make appropriate eye contact using moderation depending on your circumstances. Not looking at them can make you seem uninterested or rude and staring can make people uncomfortable. Eye contact indicates that you are interested in them and are listening to what they have to say.

Not everyone will engage in conversation for many reasons. They may be uncomfortable, they may feel they are not good at it, or they may have had a bad experience in the past. We might feel that when people don't talk to us there is something wrong with us and take it as rejection. Some people just won't talk because they are closed off, unreceptive, angry, or rude. There may be nothing you can do to change that because it is just the way they are.

No conversation no matter how amazing lasts forever. It's better to wrap it up when things are going well than to just stand there after the conversation has withered and died. To gracefully wrap up a conversation, tell them that you need to go, to circulate, or see someone depending on the situation. This gives you a chance to make contact with them again.

Have a clear end to the conversation. Since it is the last thing you say they are more likely to remember it than your opening because now they know you. Clearly signal the end of the conversation, but not necessarily the end of the relationship. How this is done depends upon your desired outcome and what type of relationship you want to pursue. A common ending is to say something like, "I have to go, but it would be nice to talk with you again." This gives them an opening to follow up if they are interested. It shows that you value them and are looking to continue the conversation sometime in the future. However, don't say this unless you actually intend to do it.

Gender.

How many relationships do you have that are gender specific? For many of our relationships gender is not a particularly significant factor because they are based upon what a person does or who they are. We develop professional relationships based upon the job a person does. While we may base friendships and close relationships on an individual's personal characteristics, there are some relationships where gender can make a difference. For instance, we may feel more comfortable with a physician of the same gender. We may prefer to develop close personal relationships like friends of one gender over another. We choose partners or spouses based on gender.

Gender can be a source of uncertainty because when we perceive something as different it can create uncertainty. This can motivate us to want to know more, so we spend time and effort trying to understand people based on their gender. We look for ways to understand others by looking at how they are different. We may assume that since there are physical differences, there must be other kinds of differences as well. Since we are motivated to understand them better, we might concentrate more on differences rather than similarities. However, when it comes to communicating and behavior, we may actually be more similar than we are different. We may be finding differences simply because we expect them.

Much of what is considered to be masculine and feminine in behavioral communicating is determined by how people construct social reality. Our perceptions and expectations about gender have been developed over long periods of time. People follow familiar patterns of communicating based upon gender in order to fulfill these expectations. Relationships involve specialization of labor which determines who does what tasks. This specialization has carried through to today's expectations contained in the rules of social reality, even though either gender can perform many of the tasks in a relationship.

Relationships are formed to help fulfill our needs and wants. We often form gender based relationships to fulfill some of our most important needs and wants, giving us higher expectations about what we contribute and receive. These relationships often involve needs of closeness, affection, and intimacy. This means that men and women can be motivated to communicate differently based on their needs and wants. They may have the perception that if they communicate based upon the expectations of others, they are more likely to achieve their desired outcomes. So, we have developed different styles of communicating and behavior based on gender in order to fulfill the expectations of others to fit in their social reality.

When we perceive the behavior of others, we can have a natural tendency to make generalizations in order to reduce uncertainty to make people more familiar. We do this on the basis of many characteristics such as a person's age, education, ethnicity, and gender. Social reality creates societal generalizations about different gender behaviors. A common generalization characterizes men as being aggressive or competitive and women as nurturing or domestic, even though they do not necessarily hold true.

We have expectations about how each gender communicates based upon the rules of social reality and what we consider to be masculine or feminine. These have become familiar, so we don't think much about them. Expectations influence our behavior and how we communicate with others. In order to form relationships and function in everyday activities, we are motivated to meet the expectations of others, so we often communicate with others based upon how we think we should communicate.

Communicative behavior is influenced by the rules of social reality, which exerts pressure on us to follow established patterns of communicating. These influence our perceptions and expectations about how each gender communicates. We communicate based upon those perceptions to fulfill the expectations of others. We are motivated to do this to manage our identity so that we will be accepted and fit in. Much of how we perceive the differences in how gender is communicated comes from others around us and the media. Social reality provides information that can form the basis of our expectations motivating people's behavior. So, do you communicate differently with people based on gender?

The law of shared meaning motivates us to find meaning in many things. We invest gender with meaning including what it means to be a man and what it means to be a woman. We interpret certain behaviors like body language and styles of communicating as masculine or feminine. We have expectations about what is appropriate clothing for each gender. Because our perception of gender is constructed by social reality it can transfer gender characteristics to inanimate objects like cars or boats.

From the time we are born we learn gender expectations from our parents and family based upon our culture, traditions, ethnicity, religion, and geographic affiliation. Different cultures, religions, and geographic areas have differing rules that define the roles of men and women. We learn this behavior by observing and imitating others we see around us. From an early age people communicate with us differently based upon our gender because they are motivated to follow the rules, not only of social reality, but also their culture, ethnicity, religion, and family traditions. Since self-concept is partly developed through reflected communicating, these differences can become part of our self-concept affecting our behavior. These gender differences are often communicated from generation to generation so they can be slow to change.

We are motivated by the law of uncertainty to not deviate too much in our behavior from the expectations of others for fear that they will be less likely to form relationships with us. This is because when we communicate and behave in ways others expect, it reduces uncertainty, so they are more likely to form relationships that help us to fulfill our needs and wants. The perceptions of others have an impact on how we communicate and behave including how we are expected to behave based upon our gender.

People who fit these expectations tend to be perceived with less uncertainty making it more likely for them to form relationships. So, we tend to modify our behavior to meet the expectations of others. Awareness helps us look at what we know in a new way to break typical patterns in how we communicate based on gender to develop ones based upon individual characteristics. Having options gives us different ways to communicate in order to determine the best one that works for each relationship.

II. Relational Growth
The Law Of Shared Meaning Phase

The second phase of relational development is motivated by the law of shared meaning because we need to share meaning in order to grow a relationship. In this phase, the uncertainty that creates the awkwardness and stiffness we feel when we first meet someone is reduced so that a relationship can form. When individuals are comfortable being around each other, they begin to talk about themselves and share stories about their past experiences. The process of self-disclosure helps to develop trust so a relationship can share meaning.

Everyone communicates for a reason and everyone develops relationships based on their perceptions, expectations, and desired outcomes. Having expectations and desired outcomes for relationships does not necessarily mean that we achieve them. Since a relationship is a separate entity created by the individuals involved, each person has only partial control over it. So, it can have characteristics similar to an individual, but function like a separate entity with a unique personality that may differ from those involved. This is one reason why people often talk about a relationship as if it's another person.

A relationship is created through the law of shared meaning based on the connection between people. This motivates people to self-disclose so that they can better understand one another and communicate more effectively. This helps create shared history, traditions, rituals, and behaviors. People create connections with others to communicate about what the relationship means to them and what it means to be in the relationship.

Self-Disclosure.

We create relationships because they are fun, interesting, and help us fulfill needs and wants. In order to do this, we need information about others to reduce uncertainty so that we can invest in relationships with them. Much of what we learn about other people can be rather superficial which won't help us develop very meaningful relationships. Self-disclosure is the means by which we gain the information necessary to develop closer, more personal relationships in ways that general conversation cannot accomplish. It is the way we share meaning to reduce uncertainty, so that we can invest the time and resources necessary to develop a relationship.

Self-disclosure is the process by which we share or disclose information about ourselves with others. It is how we share meaning to develop relationships because it is a more personal form of communicating than conversation. When we first meet someone, we know little or nothing about them creating a high degree of uncertainty. In order to develop a relationship, we need to reduce uncertainty enough to feel comfortable communicating information about ourselves to them. Without self-disclosure, it would be almost impossible to develop meaningful relationships because it helps develop trust. When we know more about others it increases our ability to trust them because it reduces uncertainty by sharing meaning. If this does not happen the relationship may not develop.

Self-disclosure helps us to develop our self-concept because when we self disclose, others provide feedback that helps us to see ourselves as they see us. When others self disclose to us it can make us feel like we are valued and a worthwhile person, which can bolster our self-concept. This can improve our confidence by letting us know more about how others see us. It can be cathartic as a way to release tension by expressing our feelings and emotions. We feel better when we can confide in another person to share information about what is on our mind.

Not all aspects of self-disclosure are necessarily positive. People may try to use self-disclosure to gain sympathy or other benefits. They may encourage self-disclosure in others just to gain information that they can use to control or manipulate them. They may use it to gain information in order to achieve their own goals, bolster their self-image, or give themselves power. Disclosing personal information can give others a degree of influence or control over us. However, by using effective communicating skills to self disclose in a reciprocal, balanced, and appropriate way, we can protect ourselves against unscrupulous use of personal information.

Why do we share personal information about ourselves with others, even with people we don't know very well? We self-disclose because if we try to get others to share information about themselves, they could feel suspicious, defensive, or even offended. The conversation would likely end and a relationship would not develop. In order to encourage other people to talk about themselves, we talk about ourselves with the expectation that they will reciprocate and share similar information about themselves.

Self-disclosure is important to relational development because it helps to reduce uncertainty about others. We expect others to reciprocate by disclosing the same kinds of information that we disclose to them. If they do, we feel more comfortable with them because they are willing to contribute to the relationship. This reduces the level of tension because there is less uncertainty and we feel more safe and secure around them. The nature of the information they share can be a measure of the degree that they trust us and their expectations about the relationship.

Self-disclosure is not always a smooth process, others may be reluctant to share information about themselves with us. They may have concerns about others invading their privacy. They may withhold information for fear that they will be rejected. All of these things could cause problems in a relationship. If others choose not to reciprocate and disclose information about themselves, we might be less likely to continue this process and the relationship could stagnate or dissolve. If they do not share information about themselves, it can make us suspicious about their motives. We might wonder, what are they trying to hide? This can serve to increase the level of tension to undermine the development of trust increasing uncertainty in the relationship.

Sometimes the initial self-disclosure goes smoothly, then it may reach a point where things don't go any further because one or both individuals are unwilling or uncomfortable disclosing any more information. Then the relationship may stabilize, stagnate, or even end. Not all relationships progress steadily to friendship or intimacy. Most never get beyond being a casual acquaintance. It's helpful to be realistic about our expectations of just what others are willing to self-disclose. The rules of social reality regulate how much information is appropriate to disclose in a particular type of relationship.

We self-disclose in order to reduce uncertainty and share meaning about ourselves and others. Self-disclosure can be difficult because we might feel like we are taking a risk. We may be uncertain about how the other person will use that information, which can increase uncertainty. While there's always the chance that they will use the information to their advantage or use it against us, we are more likely to be reluctant to disclose information because we fear we will not be accepted or may even be rejected. This is why we may be reluctant to disclose certain information or be guarded about the information we choose to disclose.

Self-disclosure can be one way that we actualize the law of shared meaning. When we self-disclose we tell stories about ourselves, our experiences, things we have done, and people we have known. This motivates others to relate their own experiences giving our stories additional meaning. When we share our experiences, we create common bonds that help to build relationships. Doing this gives our experiences deeper meaning when we add their perspective to ours.

Relationships involve making contributions to receive benefits. Self-disclosure helps us to assess the future potential of a relationship. We choose to communicate information that creates a positive image of our self while avoiding information that might damage our self-concept or how others perceive us. Self-disclosure helps us know more about others to develop trust, so that we can feel confident investing our time and other resources in relationships with them. This can make us more confident that these investments will provide benefits in the future. We do this because we have limited resources like time and energy, so we evaluate our relationships to determine their future viability. If we have reasonable expectations of future benefits, we are more likely to be committed to a relationship. Conversely, if we have the perception that things will not work out, we are less likely to be committed and may leave the relationship.

Just as everyone communicates for a reason, we self-disclose for a reason. Before self disclosing, consider your desired outcome for disclosing personal information. We tell people information about ourselves to achieve our desired outcomes and encourage others to disclose so we can learn more about them to develop a relationship. All relationships have different expectations and some are more conducive to self-disclosure than others. We may disclose information and then feel like we have made a mistake or feel uncomfortable. This can be because we may have disclosed information without considering our desired outcomes or potential unintended and undesirable outcomes.

Self-disclosure is governed by the rules of social reality. In order for the process to work, it's helpful to be aware of how these rules can help us create positive relationships. It is customary to share basic information about our self with others without going into great detail. As we get to know someone, we share more personal information about ourselves.

Self-disclosure should be communicated in an appropriate way and at an appropriate time. Too much self-disclosure can be as uncomfortable as too little in a relationship. People do not necessarily want to hear your whole life story, but if they talk about some experience that happened to them, they can reasonably expect you to talk about a similar experience.

Whenever we meet someone we have expectations about them and what kind of relationship we want to develop. We utilize the perception process to gain information in order to ascertain the likelihood of developing a relationship. The process of self-disclosure helps us to increase the accuracy of our perception in order to develop more realistic expectations about the potential of a relationship. If they have the perception that a relationship is reasonably meeting their expectations, they are more likely to continue the relationship. If they perceive that it is not meeting their expectations, they may seek to change or end the relationship.

Self-disclosure helps to build trusting relationships, so that we can fulfill mutual needs and wants. It can help others to get to know us well enough to help fulfill our needs and wants. Relationships help us to fill many important needs such as income, career, safety, security, respect, self-esteem, affection, and intimacy. Self-disclosure has risks, but it also has benefits. It helps us to understand ourselves and others. It is the means by which we reduce uncertainty and invest in others so that we can create and maintain relationships.

Degrees of self-disclosure.

What we disclose can range from very basic types of information to our most personal thoughts and feelings. In any relationship disclosure starts out with very basic information and depending upon the nature of the relationship, progresses to consecutively deeper levels.

The following are varying degrees of self-disclosure.

1. Impersonal. Impersonal self-disclosure is what we do in daily conversation. It involves small talk about topics that are of little significance like the weather, sports, current events, or the present situation. This is information that we have no problem sharing about ourselves with others regardless of who they are. This level of disclosure involves very little risk and we utilize established patterns of communicating following the rules of social reality. If things go well, we may decide to share more personal information. While uncertainty is reduced, there is little shared meaning or investing.

2. Casual. As we get to know someone uncertainty is reduced and they become more familiar, so we are more comfortable being around them. We may talk about what we did that day, what we do for a living, hobbies, interests, likes, and dislikes. We might use this information to introduce ourselves to others with whom we share a connection such as communicating with coworkers. This level of self-disclosure allows us to get to know others on a more fully developed level encouraging trust with little risk on our part. Our interactions are more personalized, but they are still cordial and polite following the rules of social reality. This level reduces uncertainty enough to allow some shared meaning so that we can work with others.

3. Personal. This level of self-disclosure usually occurs in relationships with closer friends and family. We talk about our past experiences, personal preferences, thoughts, and feelings. We no longer only follow the rules of social reality, we can develop our own rules to personalize the relationship. We share personal information creating a higher degree of risk. When people know more about us, it creates a deeper level of trust making them more comfortable around us because we are perceived as more safe and predictable. This helps develop common bonds that create a feeling of closeness strengthening their commitment to the relationship. This level reduces uncertainty to encourage shared meaning so there is some investment.

4. Intimate. This is the highest level of self-disclosure. It is usually limited to only our closest friends, family members, and our most intimate partners like our spouse. The other person knows most everything there is to know about us, which can make us vulnerable because if the relationship turns bad they could hurt us. These relationships have the highest degree of commitment because they have the strongest connections. We establish our own rules, which may or may not follow the rules of social reality. This level of disclosure has the potential for the greatest rewards, but also entails the most risk, which is why they often have the greatest tension or conflict. There is a low degree of uncertainty and a high level of shared meaning with the most investment.

It can be helpful to be aware of the following self-disclosure skills to communicate more effectively with other people.

- Appropriateness. This involves how suitable information is to share with others in a given situation. Personal information should be shared in an appropriate manner based upon the circumstances, the other person, and the nature of the relationship. You may have had the experience of meeting someone for the first time who tells you their entire life story. Rather than developing a relationship, you likely felt uncomfortable and just wanted to get away from them because it's an inappropriate degree of self-disclosure with too much information communicated too fast. Start with basic, publicly known information gradually moving to increasingly more personal information.

- The information. It is important to exercise good judgment about what we share because some information may be appropriate to disclose while some is not. Then, there are probably some things about yourself that are better off not disclosed to anyone. In a new relationship we usually start with the basics, utilizing small talk or conversation about things that are commonly known about us. Once we get to know somebody better we can share more personal information. Not everything constitutes self-disclosure. Talking about the weather, traffic, or current events is not necessarily self-disclosure. In some circumstances it may be perceived as way to avoid having a real conversation.

- The other person. We do not self disclose everything about ourselves to everyone we know. We make choices based upon the other person, the nature of the relationship, how close we are, and how much the other person reciprocates. The nature and amount of information disclosed has to be determined by each person based upon how comfortable they are with someone, as well as the effect it may have had on other relationships. For instance, a person might get in trouble for sharing information with their friends about an intimate relationship because it could be seen as a violation of trust. So, it is important to use good judgment when sharing your personal information.

- The location. Where we share information depends upon the type of information shared. Generalized information can be shared just about any place it comes up in conversation. However, personal information should be shared in a more private location where there is no chance that someone else could overhear it. Some of the simplest activities can be conducive for self-disclosure like going for a walk, having a cup of coffee, or making a meal together. Any activity that can be done together which takes little effort or concentration will allow you to focus on the other person.

- The timing. When we choose to disclose information can make a difference in how it's received. The information you disclose should be relevant to what is happening at the time or reasonably soon afterwards. If we wait too long it can be perceived as if we were reluctant to share information or we needed more time to think of a better story. When relationships advance to the next level it is often an appropriate time to share relevant information. Since we are busy it can be difficult to find time to share information. We may feel pressure to self disclose at an inappropriate time like when the other person is not ready to listen. A good approach is to set aside a time for self-disclosure when things are not as stressful and both people can give it their full attention.

- Reciprocity. Self-disclosure works when one person shares information about themselves and then the other person shares similar information about themselves. Awareness is important because there may be an imbalance of disclosure creating the perception of withholding information. Just because one person discloses information about themselves does not mean the other person will share the same information. If one person thinks that they are disclosing more information than the other, they may feel they are doing more to contribute to the relationship and the other person is not doing their part. There may be reasons the other person is not contributing. They may be simply unaware of the imbalance. They may feel uncomfortable sharing certain types of information. They may feel that some information is just off limits and is nobody's business but their own.

- Pacing. This involves how much information we communicate over a period of time. Pacing is based upon a person's degree of comfort with disclosure. It's always good to start with a go slow approach because you can always add additional information, you can't erase information you have already disclosed. More information is not always better for disclosure. Sharing your life story or pouring your heart out does not necessarily increase trust. Instead, it could undermine the relationship because disclosing everything can be scary for others pushing them away. They may think you're going too far too fast or feel pressured making them uncomfortable. Rather than telling you that's how they feel, they may become more distant, push you away, or end the relationship.

- Detail. This involves the degree or detail of information we share with others. There are two dimensions to information, depth and breadth. Depth refers to how much detail or how much information we share about a specific topic. Breadth refers to the extent or variety of topics or information we share. In casual relationships, we may have moderate breadth, but little depth by talking about a number of topics superficially, with few details. In business relationships we may have less breadth and more depth knowing more details about someone, but only about work related topics. In close personal relationships there is likely to be both depth and breadth of information because we know more details about them.

- Awareness and options. Having awareness is important to self-disclosure so we know how we are coming across to others. We can do this by observing their body language and nonverbal expressions to see if they look interested or uncomfortable. Awareness of a person's response is important to gage the appropriateness of the information you share. You always have the option of what information to share, when to share it, and with whom. Or whether to share it at all.

- Responding. Self-disclosure can be difficult or uncomfortable, so it's helpful to show that you support others when they self disclose and let them know you are there for them. This is done using effective listening skills, providing feedback, responding appropriately, using positive gestures such as eye contact and nodding your head, occasionally paraphrasing or restating what they have said, and asking questions to show that you understand what they are saying. Doing this demonstrates that you are paying attention and what they have to say is important to you. You can reassure them that you appreciate their sharing this information with you. Consider their desired outcome. Do they want help, advice, or do they just want somebody to listen and support them? Telling someone they need to self-disclose more or they don't do enough self-disclosure is not a good way to get them to do it or to build a relationship.

- Nondisclosure. While it's important for people in relationships to communicate openly and honestly, the reality is there are potential benefits to nondisclosure. These are things where the potential risk of damaging a relationship far outweighs any benefits of disclosure. This may include information that is no longer relevant to you or the relationship. Information that may be potentially damaging or hurtful to others. It may be information about others who would see it as a violation of their privacy and their trust in you. Or it may serve no useful purpose in the current relationship.

Not everything we think or feel needs to be self-disclosed in order to have a good relationship. Some thoughts and feelings are better kept to ourselves because they have the potential for being misinterpreted. These kinds of thoughts and feelings are natural, everyone has them from time to time. For example, we might wonder if we should be in this relationship or should end it. If these thoughts go away, the consequences of disclosing them may not. The process of self-disclosure helps us feel valued, so how we respond to others and how they respond to us can have long term consequences.

Trust.

One of the most important benefits of self-disclosure in relationships is creating trust. It helps us to develop and maintain relationships. Trust is the actualization of the laws of uncertainty and investing. It is a means to reduce uncertainty, so that we can invest in relationships with others. Trust is an expression of our perception of another person's future behavior meeting our expectations. Trust can reduce uncertainty to create the stability necessary for society to function. Trust is necessary to reduce uncertainty about others so that we can work with them to create relationships. When we trust someone, we know what we can expect from them making the relationship more secure, stable, and predictable. We learn to trust others by sharing meanings, so that we can better understand them and the relationship. In order to invest in relationships with others, we need to have some degree of trust.

We create trust by reducing uncertainty and sharing meaning about ourselves, so that we can invest in relationships with others. We may expect others to trust us, however, we cannot demand their trust, it must be earned. For this to happen there must be a willingness of both people to trust one another. It is through repeated patterns of behavior over time that we learn what to expect from others and they learn what they can expect from us. We make decisions based upon these experiences creating confidence in the other person's ability and behavior. Trust is an expression of our expectations of the future behavior of others. We have confidence that they will behave in a certain manner in the future based on our perception of their behavior in the present. While trust is voluntary, if we are serious about developing a relationship we need to be willing to trust others.

Trust is built up over time by taking incremental steps to see how others respond. As we progress through the levels of relationships, when we see our investments begin to pay off we are more likely to disclose more personal information. When a pattern of behavior is established there is a reasonable expectation of future behavior in the relationship. Trust is established and maintained when our perception of others meets our expectations. When it does not, we may feel that our trust has been violated.

There are exceptions to this process such as in a period of high uncertainty like during a crisis. These are situations where safety and security may be at stake and so we are put in a position where we have to trust someone we may not know well or even at all. There may not be enough time to develop trust as we would like under normal circumstances. These situations often involve people who are in positions of expertise or authority such as law enforcement or medical personnel. We may be injured and need medical attention, so we put our trust in a doctor who we do not know. We do this in order to fulfill a specific need by putting our trust not so much in an individual, but in their position or training.

Just because we make an effort to get someone to trust us does not mean that they will. We cannot control another person's willingness to trust, we can only demonstrate our willingness to trust them and that we are trustworthy. Then the rest is up to them. If someone decides not to trust us we may interpret it as personal rejection, however, it may have nothing to do with us. Instead, their behavior may be based on their past experiences. If they have had their trust violated in the past, they may be unwilling to trust anyone regardless of who they are.

Every day we have to decide whether or not to trust other people and what they say. For example, we trust the news on television to be accurate, we trust the clerk at the grocery store to ring up the right prices, or we trust that the people driving next to us will obey the traffic laws. Trust not only involves relationships with people we know, it also involves people we don't know and have never met. The rules of social reality require a degree of trust in order for society to function properly. Without it, it would be more difficult to make it through our everyday activities. How much people are willing to trust can be a factor of how much uncertainty they feel about the relationship and how much they can accept. Some people might like a higher level of uncertainty because it feels exciting.

Sometimes trust is mistaken for naiveté. Trust can sometimes be seen as being misplaced, making us blind to reality. While it is essential to trust others in order to have relationships, it should be with both eyes wide open. Because someone is trustworthy now, does not necessarily mean that they will maintain that trust in the future. Misplaced or violated trust can seriously damage or destroy a relationship. So, it can be helpful not to take everything at face value. This is especially important with people in positions of influence or power. So, it can be helpful to follow the old adage, trust but verify.

A common source of conflict can occur over issues of trust. Often, we put people in situations to test them that could result in unintended or undesirable outcomes. In order to avoid this, it can be helpful to not put people in situations where they have an opportunity to violate our trust. For example, if your spouse says they will be working late, they should not be offended if you decide to show up at their work with dinner to see how they are doing. Rather than interpreting it as you're checking up on them, think of it as you're showing that you care. They should probably be more concerned if you don't check up on them.

When trust becomes an issue in relationships it can lead to tension or conflict because it involves a degree of control over others. When someone trusts us they have a certain degree of control over our behavior because we need to behave in ways that do not violate other people's trust, which can reduce our options. This means that trust is the degree to which others have influence over us because their actions can have consequences for us. If a person's actions had had no consequences for us, we would not need to trust them.

Lying.

Lying is not good for us or our relationships because, while people do it to reduce uncertainty, it actually increases uncertainty because it undermines trust. It can have a corrosive effect on shared meanings by changing how we perceive them. It can undermine trust devaluing the investments we make in relationships. In many ways lying has become so pervasive in society we don't even think much about it anymore. We have even developed euphemisms to make it sound better such as being misinformed or stretching the truth. It can be helpful to understand how we characterize lying.

These are ways some people lie, in order of severity.

1. The little white lie. These lies generally do little harm because they are relatively mild in nature, so they do not carry serious consequences. This can include social pleasantries like telling someone we are glad to see them when we really are not. They are easier to overcome as they do not undermine trust because we expect people to tell them.

2. Untruths. Stretching the truth, exaggerating, or lying by omission are often used after the fact to cover up a person's actions. These lies are more serious in nature, but are often overlooked. If discovered they carry minor short term consequences, but if they reoccur they can damage a relationship.

3. Deception. Often a lie is created before the actual action is taken. It may be intentionally premeditated to deceive others. It often misrepresents information for personal gain. This carries more severe penalties like conflict, anger, or the end of a relationship. This is because this type of lie undermines the trust people have in one another that is necessary for a relationship.

4. Illegalities. These lies cross the line from social ramifications to having legal consequences because they can cause injuries to individuals and undermine the trust that is necessary for society to function. These include intentionally misrepresenting something for personal gain, lying under oath, and lying about the character or credibility of someone or something.

Just as people communicate for a reason, people lie for a reason. Lying can be detrimental because it undermines the positive attributes of the laws of uncertainty, shared meaning, and investing. Not telling someone the truth increases uncertainty and undermines their trust making them reluctant to invest in relationships. It corrupts the process of shared meaning by perpetrating false information. However, people can be motivated to lie because of the very same laws of uncertainty and shared meaning. There are benefits for people to lie because it can provide a quick and easy way to reduce uncertainty by creating false impressions rather than taking responsibility by telling the truth.

These are some reasons why people lie.

- To be nice. There are times when the rules of social reality consider telling the truth inappropriate. People might lie because they feel that they are actually being kind to others by not telling them the truth. They may feel that if they tell them the truth they may needlessly be hurt. In this case people are substituting lying for being tactful because it's easier.

- To gain rewards. People can be motivated to lie because the potential rewards are perceived as being greater than the potential harm. They might think that if they were honest it might create discomfort or conflict and others may not like them. They may lie because they want to be liked or to avoid conflict. They may lie to fulfill needs and wants or to achieve their desired outcomes. Whatever the reason, people lie to gain something they feel they cannot get in other ways.

- To protect others. People might lie to protect other people from the consequences of their actions. They may even consider lying as being noble by taking the blame for something someone else did in order to protect them from the consequences of their actions. Taking a tactful approach by being concerned with their feelings can be a better approach and is generally more appreciated than lying.

- To protect a person's feelings. People may lie to others to avoid hurting a person's feelings. Sometimes things are said in the heat of the moment that cannot be taken back, so people might lie about their thoughts, feelings, or emotions in order to protect others and themselves from any damage this might cause. It can be better to wait to tell people some things until they cool off and you have time to think it over, rather than trying to fix the damage afterwards. However, there may be some things people are better off keeping to themselves.

- To protect relationships. People may lie, avoid the truth, or omit information that they think may be difficult or unpleasant for others because it could increase tension or cause conflict in their relationships. They may tell people what they want to hear so that it fits in with their expectations and they will accept it to avoid causing problems. People might do this in order to protect others, but also to protect themselves because telling the truth can be difficult or risky. They may be concerned that by being truthful people won't like them or it may damage the relationship.

- To protect themselves. People lie to cover up things they have said or done in order to avoid taking responsibility for them. They are motivated by the law of investing because they may be afraid to lose what they have invested in relationships with others. Telling the truth can be difficult, complicated, and uncomfortable so people lie to make things easier for themselves.

- To get away with it. People make mistakes or do things intentionally that they know they shouldn't do. If they have done something that they know is wrong, they may not tell anyone about it and cover it up. If someone finds out about it they may become defensive and lie claiming they had nothing to do with it. People lie because they do things in hopes of gaining benefits or avoiding negative consequences while ignoring the likelihood of getting caught.

People want to be supportive of others they care about. However, being supportive of others can turn into misrepresentation or even lying to them. This can happen if we give them inflated feedback creating false perceptions and unrealistic expectations. This can give the other person a false perception that their ability is better than it is, while others will see them as they really are. Isn't it better to hear criticism from someone who has their best interest at heart than to have everyone else be aware of it behind their back?

A more effective approach is being truthful, but tactful. This can be done by avoiding broad generalizations and judgmental evaluations like characterizing things as good or bad. Instead, describe specific elements objectively with options for improvement. For example, in the case of a musician, rather than creating a false impression by telling them they sound terrific when they do not, or saying that they sound awful, you might say that they missed some notes or they were out of tune. This is nonjudgmental, it's more accurate, and it's supportive by giving them constructive information they can use for improvement.

While it is not good to intentionally lie, the reality is that there are some circumstances where the truth may do as much damage as a lie, perhaps even more. In these circumstances only you can determine what is the best approach. It can help to have an awareness of the potential consequences of telling the truth or keeping it to yourself. Then you can chose from several options to find the best approach.

Many of the behaviors we associate with lying are based on stereotypes perpetuated by the media. Nonverbal behavior commonly associated with lying includes not making eye contact, shifting back and forth, speaking rapidly, or looking nervous. However, these are not sure signs because nonverbal body language can easily be misinterpreted. If someone does want to lie to you there are methods they might use that can be effective.

They might think through what they are going to say beforehand, so if questioned, they don't have to figure out what to say. They keep their story simple by sticking to a few basic details. They do not deviate or change their story regardless of what questions they are asked or how often they are asked.

People might lie by connecting the lie to the truth, deviating from it only as much as necessary because lies that are too unusual or complicated can be easier to detect. They don't lie about things that can be verified or proven false. They do not offer information that is not specifically requested. They may even believe it to be true because if you believe it, it feels true. They can communicate confidence by using nonverbal behavior to appear credible by acting natural. They can be aware of nonverbal behavior including how they speak and act in order to maintain consistency when speaking to others. They avoid looking like someone who is lying by controlling nervous habits, using eye contact, and avoiding what looks unnatural or out of place.

We may think that we can detect lies because people cannot control their nonverbal behavior like eye contact or facial expressions. But some people can act natural by familiarizing themselves with what they will say so it sounds true. They may have a natural ability, confidence, or trustworthy appearance. Lies can be exposed by questioning assumptions, increasing awareness, sharpening perception, and verifying the information we receive.

Being aware of how people lie is important because lying damages relationships and hurts society. It undermines the benefits of the law of shared meaning by sharing untrue meanings that can erode confidence in people and in society. We make decisions based on our perceptions that are based on the information we receive. Since most of this information comes from others, we have to judge its truthfulness. We can't make good decisions without accurate information.

Excuses.

Whenever we are involved in a relationship we will eventually need to make an excuse. We make them to protect other people's feelings, to avoid taking responsibility, to atone for our mistakes, and because others expect it. We use them to avoid doing things others want us to do that we do not want to do, as well as to do things we want to do that others do not want us to do. For example, we may be expected to attend a family reunion, but we do not want to go. We could be honest and tell them the truth. However, by using an excuse, we do not hurt their feelings and avoid a potentially uncomfortable situation. We do it to reduce uncertainty by protecting ourselves from the potential fallout from being honest.

Excuses can fall into a few basic groups.

- Uncertainty. One of the most common excuses blames things outside our control. For example, the alarm didn't go off or the car broke down.

- Awareness. This excuse appeals to the lack of awareness or information. For example, I had no idea that would happen.

- Blame. This excuse shifts responsibility on to others. For example, it wasn't my fault because no one told me.

- Justification. This excuse uses an explanation to justify what happened. Children and adolescents may use this excuse when they say that everyone else is doing something or that rules were made to be broken.

- Sympathy. This excuse appeals to the sympathetic nature of others or their emotions when more rational approaches won't work. For example, I was only trying to help.

It can be helpful to be aware of how excuses are used to reduce uncertainty to protect our investments in relationships with others. There are times when the rules of social reality call for the use of an excuse. Only you can determine if it is better to tactfully tell others the truth or use a reasonable excuse to avoid hurting other people's feelings that might damage a relationship.

Apologies.

In relationships there will be times when we will need to make an apology. An apology is about taking responsibility for our mistakes or indiscretions. A good way to avoid making apologies is to consider your desired outcome first. There are times when we may act in the heat of the moment without considering the consequences.

By taking time to consider your desired outcome, you can reduce the intensity of the moment to prevent saying or doing things you may regret later. While apologies can be beneficial, we should try to avoid doing things that necessitate making them.

The purpose of an apology is to repair a relationship that others perceive we have damaged. What matters in these situations is the other person's perception. While we may feel we have done nothing wrong, others may feel we did and so we may have to apologize. The nature and the degree to which we apologize tends to be reflective of the nature of the relationship. The more important a relationship, the more we may need to apologize to make things right.

We apologize to people whose relationship we value and are less likely to apologize to those we don't. It is a means to protect our investment in relationships by trying to restore trust that may have been damaged. It is a way that we demonstrate that we care about a relationship and the other person. It may take a simple apology to restore trust or it may take some time and effort depending on the circumstances and the nature of the relationship.

An apology helps to reduce the uncertainty created by seemingly out of place things we do or say by attempting to restore normality. Whether it does this or not depends on how it is received. What constitutes a good apology is contingent upon what meanings are shared between the individuals involved.

It may take just a word or two, a full explanation, or something tangible like flowers. An apology can include expressions of regret, accepting responsibility, an explanation of your behavior, or an offer to remedy the situation. Be clear what the apology is for and avoid bringing up other issues the other person may not have thought about.

Apologies are a verbal mechanism by which we deal with competing desired outcomes. We have a desired outcome to do what we want to do, but also to keep other people's perception of us in good standing. We might make a mistake, have a lapse of judgment, or do something we shouldn't, but we also want people to have confidence in us.

An apology is a means of bridging the gap between two conflicting desired outcomes that can be used to maintain a relationship. We apologize to help ourselves or to clear our conscience about something we have done so we can feel better about ourselves. We apologize to improve other people's perception of us by reducing uncertainty about who we are. And we apologize to restore trust to repair a relationship so others can continue to invest in us.

III. Relational Maintenance
The Law Of Investing Phase

We often hear that relationships like marriage can be hard work. Tasks need to be accomplished and things need to be done in order to maintain a relationship, but should it be hard work? Instead, it could be energizing and invigorating, because if the work is too hard we may decide it's not worth it and the relationship could deteriorate or come to an end. Relational maintenance is the third phase of relational development. It is about making a commitment to keep a relationship together over time. It is motivated by the law of investing because we need to invest in our relationships in order to maintain them.

We do preventative maintenance on our cars, we fix up our house, and we go to the doctor for a checkup. However, it's easy not to give the same attention to our relationships until there is a problem. We may avoid doing this because we are afraid of what we might find. Instead, we rely on indirect means to communicate how we feel until things get to the point that it may be difficult to resolve them. That's when a relationship can become hard work.

Just as there is no one right way of communicating, there is no one right way of maintaining a relationship. Both people in a relationship have to determine how to do that for themselves. Having an awareness of how relational maintenance can help a relationship and the ways that relationships deteriorate can help determine the best options to avoid problems by creating a supportive relationship.

Practicing relational preventative maintenance can help to avoid potential problems. Relationships provide benefits, but they also require our resources like time, energy, emotions, and material things like money. Our relational satisfaction is based upon our perceptions and expectations. People have a perception of their relationships that includes what they are willing to contribute based upon their expectations of future benefits. It can be helpful to talk about your perceptions and expectations and how the relationship is fulfilling your mutual needs, wants, and desired outcomes. Unfortunately, all too often people are uncomfortable talking about their relationship. They may feel that they just know what the other person is thinking or they may feel that the relationship is solid enough that they don't need to do this. However, if they don't communicate their thoughts and feelings, that's when a relationship can become hard work.

The degree of relational maintenance is contingent on the level of the relationship. Lower level relationships like acquaintances require little maintenance because it's not needed as there is little investment. For the most part, all that's necessary is to act cordial and friendly with others and follow the rules of social reality. In professional relationships we may do things for customers or clients, send birthday or holiday cards to coworkers, or go out for an occasional lunch or dinner. More relational maintenance is often necessary to maintain higher level relationships like with our friends and family. This is because we have higher expectations about them and we have more invested. Therefore, the rest of this section is primarily about higher level relationships.

The power of the laws of uncertainty, shared meaning, and investing can be utilized for effective relational maintenance. Developing effective communicating skills can reduce uncertainty to help us feel more safe and secure increasing stability and commitment to the relationship. Some uncertainty can give it excitement to keep it fun and interesting. Individuals use shared meaning to better understand one another by sharing their thoughts and feelings through appropriate ongoing self-disclosure.

They talk about their experiences to give them deeper meaning. The law of investing motivates people to maintain their relationships by investing in one another for their mutual benefit to achieve their desired outcomes. People form relationships to fulfill needs and wants, so how well they are fulfilled has an affect on their satisfaction and commitment to the relationship.

As a relationship develops, needs and wants change. It can be helpful to be aware of these changes so that they can continue to be fulfilled. If not, a lack of awareness can make people dissatisfied undermining their commitment to the relationship.

To increase your awareness, ask yourself what needs and wants do you and the other person have in your relationships. Consider how well they are being fulfilled and how well you are helping others to fulfill theirs. If they are being reasonably met, then the relationship is being maintained. If they are not, then the relationship may possibly be headed for difficulty. If detected early these situations can be remedied by talking about them and taking appropriate action.

Tension is a natural and unavoidable part of life. It can be created by conflicting needs, wants, and desired outcomes. Relationships have their own needs and wants, and some of them may be opposed to one another creating tension. It can be helpful to have a balance of these needs and wants or it could create dissatisfaction that can undermine the relationship.

These are some conflicting needs and wants that can be a source of tension.

- We need to be with others as well as to be by ourselves. We form relationships with others because we need safety, security, closeness, and affection. However, we also need some space and time for ourselves. Since we cannot do both at the same time, these opposing needs are a potential source of tension. We may want to spend time by ourselves when others want to spend time with us. By understanding these conflicting needs, a balance can be established between them.

- We need self-disclosure as well as privacy. We share information about ourselves to reduce uncertainty, create trust, and develop relationships. We do this on an ongoing basis to maintain our relationships. We want to know more about the other person and they want to know about us. However, we also have a need for privacy and to have space for ourselves. By understanding these tensions we can be respectful of others and what they choose to reveal or not reveal about themselves.

- We need to do things with others as well as by ourselves. In relationships we make decisions with another person, but we want to make our own individual choices. We can become dependent on the other person to do things to make the relationship work, but we still want to have our own independence. It's nice to have someone help get things done, however, being too dependent can make us feel helpless. By understanding this source of tension we can find a balance between dependence and independence.

- We need stability as well as excitement. Relationships involve making a commitment to reduce uncertainty creating stability and security. However, we also have a need for excitement, adventure, change, and to try new things. Too much stability can create dissatisfaction or unnecessary unhappiness. Too much excitement can make a relationship chaotic and uncertain. By being aware of these opposing needs and wants we can find a balance between them to maintain relational stability while making it fun and exciting.

Relational commitment.

Relational commitment is the degree to which a person is willing to put the needs of the relationship ahead of their own. It's the degree to which people are willing to make sacrifices and do things for others and their relationship. It is the degree to which someone is willing to stay in a relationship regardless of how difficult things may get. Generally, the higher the level of the relationship, the higher the commitment. However, there are times when this is not enough, even people in close, intimate relationships can breakup.

If commitment is lacking in a relationship it can be improved by doing things that bring the individuals closer together. People in a relationship may slowly drift apart over time because they change, circumstances change, and their needs and wants change. The beginning of a relationship takes effort because it is new and exciting. When it has stabilized it feels secure, so we turn our attention to those things that are more uncertain. This is why over time relationships may have the feeling that one or both people are no longer as interested in the relationship or may take it for granted. However, this is probably not the case, it's more likely that other issues have not been resolved creating tension that takes more time and attention.

This situation can be improved by paying more attention to the needs and wants of the other person and the relationship. Instead of doing an occasional grand gesture, it's helpful to do little things more often that show your appreciation. Showing that you care does not have to be a lot of time consuming work, it can be expressed by doing little things every day.

For example, it helps to remember birthdays, anniversaries, and other important dates. Create and celebrate your own rituals and traditions around the holidays and other significant events. You can maintain a relationship in everyday activities like afternoon coffee or reading the Sunday paper together. These utilize the power of the law of shared meaning by creating meaning in the things you do together.

Support is essential to maintaining relationships and it is through communicating that we show our support for one another. It is more than just being there during difficult circumstances, but being there to help with the ordinary daily tasks that need to be done. Support is not only communicated verbally, but also in our actions like doing something for the other person just because they want you to or for no reason at all. Since time is our most limited resource, we communicate support and caring by spending time with others. In a close relationship, it should not matter what you do, what matters is that you do it together.

Advice in relationships.

A benefit of being in a relationship is being able to ask another person for advice. Giving and asking for advice is one way we show others we support them. When people ask us for advice, it is likely that they want one of two things. First, they want you to listen, but people don't usually say, "I want you to listen," they say, "We need to talk." Second, they want you to tell them that they are right.

What they are looking for is your support by agreeing with them. Giving advice can be risky because if they take your advice and things don't work out, they might blame you. If they don't take your advice and things don't work out, they may also blame you for not being clear enough. If they do take your advice and it works out, they will be happy that they fixed their problem themselves.

Options for giving advice.

- Determine the other person's desired outcome. Do they want you to tell them what they should do or do they want you to tell them they are right? Don't try the fix something before you know what they want because it could make them upset. Most of the time they just want somebody to listen and give them support.

- Determine your desired outcome. Why do you want to give the other person advice? What do you want to have happen afterwards? The answer is often determined by the nature of the relationship. We might give advice to help the other person, to support the relationship, or so the other person will support us in the future. Sometimes people can be motivated by their own desired outcomes like wanting to feel needed or appreciated.

- Give them feedback. Instead of expressing your own opinion, ask the other person open ended questions that needs more than a one or two word answer to encourage them to talk. Stay on track and stick to the point because it's easy to digress or get sidetracked confusing the issue. Sometimes just talking about the problem out loud makes people think of something new, so they can see their situation in a new way.

- Acknowledge feedback. When giving advice be aware of the feedback the other person is giving you. It helps to know that they understand what you are saying and how receptive they are to it. This helps you to better understand their desired outcome and what they really want you to do. When you know what they want and you are aware of how they respond, it's easier to get to the point.

- Don't make it a competition. A common approach is to relate your own personal experiences to show that you understand what they are going through. However, this can become a competition to see who has had it worse. This changes the focus away from them. When someone asks for help or advice keep in mind that it is about them, not you.

- Have a reason or criteria. In giving advice it's helpful to have objective criteria or logical reasons for it. Doing this can make the situation less personal and lower the emotional intensity. This is helpful if we have to tell someone they are wrong or they should do something because it's based upon objective criteria, so it does not become a personal issue.

- Avoid clichés or popular advice. These offer little substantive information, are not very helpful, and can be overly general by not taking into account the individual characteristics of the person or the situation.

- Utilize effective communicating skills. Clarify what the other person is saying to make sure you accurately understand it. Restate what the other person says so they hear it coming from someone else. It can help to hear it from another person's perspective. When they hear what they are saying from someone else they might decide it's not such a big deal after all.

- Awareness and options. Help the other person to see themselves as others see them. This helps increase their awareness of themselves and the situation. Encourage them to consider other alternatives. Considering options helps them to look at what they know in a new light in order to reach a solution. Consider their desired outcome and if the current situation is supportive of it.

- Be honest. If you care about someone be truthful, but also be tactful even when it's difficult. There are times when people want to be told they are right, however, they also need to know when they are wrong. If you want to help them you should be straightforward and tactfully tell them that you think they are wrong and why. No one wants to be told that they are wrong, so it's helpful to have a reason or criteria for your position. Telling them that they are right would be easier, but they may eventually realize that they are wrong and wonder why you didn't tell them the truth.

- Support is not the same as approval. We may be reluctant to support someone or help them because we do not agree with them. Nobody wants to be told they are wrong, however, they may need our support. It is possible to support someone and help them find a solution without approving of what they are saying or doing. For example, if someone quits their job and you disagree with what they did, you can still support them in finding a new job.

- In giving advice, consider that you might be wrong. Whenever we give support and advice we always think that what we do is good and that we have the right solution. Keep in mind that there's a chance you could be wrong.

Criticism.

Eventually we will find ourselves in the uncomfortable position of having to tell someone we disagree with them or that they are wrong. This can be difficult especially if we value our relationship with them. While many types of relationships should be able to take criticism, the reality is it needs to be communicated at the right time in an appropriate manner. Giving criticism can be one of the most difficult things we do. An effective approach is to be straightforward and honest because it's better to hear criticism from someone who has our best interest at heart than to have other people be aware of it behind our back.

A good approach is to ask the other person what they think. Consider what they have to say and after thinking it over, tell them what you think about it. Perhaps after they have had time to vent their emotions and consider the situation they may see it from a different perspective. You might ask them if they have considered other alternatives. It is helpful to avoid broad statements and generalizations, or to characterize things in judgmental or evaluative terms such as good or bad. It is helpful to focus on the specific issues rather than the individual person. Your desired outcome should be to provide straightforward and honest feedback while being considerate and tactful to maintain a positive relationship.

In giving critical or negative feedback, it's helpful to be aware of the following approaches.

- Begin with something positive and try to make the information as positive as possible.

- Be truthful and straightforward, but tactful and considerate.

- Get to the point, avoid dragging things out any longer than necessary.

- Show them support by emphasizing positive aspects of your relationship.

- Tell them that your purpose is to help them if they want help. If they do not, don't force it and consider another option.

- Avoid evaluative words like good or bad as much as possible because they are overly general and can make things worse.

- Avoid overgeneralizations. Keep things in perspective, rarely is something a total disaster.

- Be specific. Stick to the issues. Limit criticism to only what is necessary.

- Think before saying anything. Carefully consider what to say beforehand to avoid saying something you might regret later.

- Limit the amount of criticism because too much can be overwhelming. You may be perceived as just beating them up.

- Stick to the issues by being objective. Avoid making things overly personal.

- Have some criteria for the basis of your criticism that is objective and credible. Be sure to tell them what it is.

- Don't force your criticism on others. Just because you have an opinion does not mean others have to accept it. Consider that you might not always be right.

- Take responsibility for your own opinions, don't just assume others share them.

- Remember the importance of the relationship. Is it worth the controversy?

- Be aware of how the other person is responding and adapt your approach as necessary.

- Know when to quit. There is a point when enough is enough. People either get it or they don't, so don't belabor the point.

- End upbeat. Reaffirm the relationship. Tell them that you support them.

People often talk about constructive criticism, but do we really ever find criticism constructive? We consider any criticism as criticizing and nobody likes to be criticized. However, being in a relationship involves taking criticism. In this sense, criticism should be considered similar to a critique, which is a review or assessment of various qualities.

People have a natural tendency to defend themselves when they are criticized. However, it's better to avoid becoming defensive because the other person may feel that they are trying to be helpful and it could provoke a defensive response in them. If you respond defensively, then you have given them something else to criticize. Be aware of the difference between offering criticism as a critique instead of just being critical.

The following are options for responding to criticism.

- Listen to what they are actually saying. Often we jump to conclusions or make assumptions about what we think someone is saying. Often criticism is not as serious as what we assume it to be. You can't respond to criticism unless you understand what the other person is actually saying.

- Ask for more information to have them clarify what they really mean. It can be helpful to understand the full scope of the criticism before responding. Often criticisms are broad generalizations based on a few bits of information with little detail. Never guess about the specifics and clarify language that is unclear because they may not really know what they are talking about. Sometimes people use criticism to pressure others to say something they want them to say.

- Avoid responding unless necessary. Not all criticism warrants a response. Just because someone criticizes us we don't have to feel obligated to respond. We can just listen to criticism and tell the other person that we will think about it without making any promises or commitments. In responding to criticism, it's easy to use broad generalizations like they don't know what they're talking about. This doesn't really address the issue and can escalate the situation. There may be some truth in what they say and considering that they may be at least partly right can help.

- Ask for feedback. Ask them what they would do in your position. That doesn't mean you have to do what they say, but it helps you understand their point of view and what the real issues are. By asking for more information and feedback you take the emotional intensity out of the situation. When people give criticism they are likely to expect you to be defensive and when you aren't, they may not know how to respond.

- Be open to new ideas. You don't have to agree with everything people say, but be open to the possibility you might be wrong. We often have the perception that agreeing with criticism is a weakness, however, we can benefit from the observations of others even if we do not agree with them. After we've had time to think about it, some of it may be good advice. By looking at something familiar in a new way, we may come up with a better idea.

Communicating bad news.

It's easy to tell others something that's fun or positive, but nobody wants to tell someone bad news. We avoid telling people negative things because we want to be liked. We have a fear that if we do they will get upset at us and it will hurt our relationship. The best approach is to be truthful, but tactful and supportive. Present information objectively and then let others make their own decision what to do about it.

Some common approaches can make a situation worse like ignoring it, bad timing, changing the subject, using clichés, or not getting to the point. We do these things because we feel we are being nice by helping to protect others, however, this might make the situation worse. Not being direct or truthful about a difficult topic may not be fair to others.

Options for giving bad news:

- Think about what you're going to say before you say it. Don't jump in before you think things through so you don't say something you wish you hadn't. Think of the most tactful approach and run it by someone else you trust or practice it out loud where no one can overhear you. Be truthful, but be tactful. Consider your nonverbal body language because it's not only what you say, it's how you say it.

- Stick to the facts. Use descriptive statements and avoid judgmental words like good or bad because they can make people more upset.

- Get to the point. Long explanations or sugar coating things only makes people more upset or angry.

- Limit the scope of the conversation to what's essential. It's easy to get sidetracked and digress into other issues that are better left for another time and may only complicate things making them worse.

- Choose an appropriate time and place when you can have their full attention without distraction and other people will not overhear or interrupt what you have to say.

- Avoid being condescending or giving the impression that you know how they feel. Avoid saying things like, "I've been through this before." While it may be true, it's easy to turn it into a competition.

- Listen to their reply and find something that you can agree with to show support.

- Let the other person know that they are important to you. Assure them that you have their best interest at heart. This can help them be more receptive to what you have to say.

- Think about how you would like to be told the same news. Even though we know that bad news will eventually pass and things will get better, we may need to hear someone else say it. This expresses stability and security to provide them comfort.

- Reaffirm the relationship. Even though people already know you care, they appreciate hearing you say that you care about them, that you are important to them, or that you love them. Let them know that you will be there for them and support them.

Communicating networks.

Our relationships do not exist in isolation. We make connections to communicate our Great Idea to others who provide us with feedback. They in turn have their own connections with others and so on. This creates a series of connections that comprise a communicating network. Communicating networks provide and regulate the flow of information between the individuals within them. These networks determine who communicates with whom, when, in what manner, and about what topics. They are important to us because they create and maintain the connections that people make to communicate with one another.

Networks are formed similar to how we form relationships. They are often formed to fulfill mutual needs and wants. They are often made up of people who share proximity, familiarity, intensity, or similarity. They share a common connection like a workplace, school, church, or community. They are often created and maintained by the mutual need for information. Communicating networks not only share information, they can have an influence over our behavior.

We are motivated to form communicating networks by the laws of uncertainty, shared meaning, and investing to gain information to fulfill our needs and wants. Networks reduce uncertainty because they provide us information we need so we can know what's going on around us, which helps us feel more safe and secure. We share meaning through networks by telling stories and sharing information. Others then add their own information and experience giving them additional meaning. When these stories and ideas circulate within networks they help to form our social reality. By having more and better information we have more confidence to invest in relationships with people in our network. Over time we get to know them and validate the information we receive so that we can trust them enough to invest in relationships with them.

Networks are created based upon our needs and wants for information to achieve our desired outcomes. They can be used to persuade and influence people's perception. They can affect our self-concept and how we see others. They shape our perceptions and expectations. We can't be everywhere or know everything we need to know, so we get information from others through these networks. The better the network, the better the quality of information we get to help us make better decisions. Information we gain from a network goes through the perception process to make the information meaningful and useful for us.

Our communicating networks can have an influence on our view of social reality because we form them based on our perceptions and expectations. If others perceive something as good or bad, it can affect how we perceive it. The quality of the information we receive from these networks is important because we make decisions using the information we have, not the information we would like to have. People communicate these perceptions and expectations with one another through networks. These perceptions create expectations within the network that can combine to develop a larger social reality that may or may not actually reflect physical reality.

To more fully understand networks and the effect they have on you, draw a map of your own communicating networks. Take a piece of paper and draw a small circle in the middle and put your name in the circle. Then draw circles around it like planets orbiting the sun. Write the names of each person that you regularly communicate with in an ongoing relationship in each circle. Draw lines between you and them so it looks like spokes of a wheel. These lines represent the connections you have with others.

Then do the same for each of those people. Draw small circles around them, like moons orbiting each planet and put the names of people you know they communicate with around them. Each spoke end will have its own wheel. Then draw lines to indicate the connections between those people who you know communicate with each other. It may begin to look like a spider's web. Your communicating network likely includes family, friends, coworkers, acquaintances, and neighbors, as well as others. Putting it down on paper can help you see how you make connections with others and where you get your information.

IV. Relational Dissolution
Return To The Law Of Uncertainty Phase

It is said that all good things come to an end and so do many of our relationships. When a relationship comes to an end it can make us feel sad, depressed, upset, even angry. The end of a relationship, especially a close one, can be very traumatic. We spend a great amount of time and effort on creating and maintaining relationships. However, we spend comparatively little or no time considering how our relationships may come to an end. Just as forming relationships is a natural and inevitable part of life, so is ending them. The reality is nothing lasts forever and all relationships eventually come to an end.

The loss of a relationship is a consequence of the law of uncertainty. People may grow apart, their needs or wants may change, or they may have experienced something that is difficult to overcome. Relationships can end suddenly and unexpectedly or slowly drift away over time. While we may have little or no control over some relationships, others may have warning signs that the relationship is in trouble giving us a chance to do something about it. If we are careful about maintaining a relationship, we can recognize problems and deal with them as they occur. If we avoid the warning signs, it can increase uncertainty creating unhappiness, misunderstandings, tension, and even conflict resulting in their deterioration or disillusion.

We form relationships in order to fulfill specific needs and wants. If those needs and wants are reasonably fulfilled, it provides an incentive to maintain the relationship. However, our needs and wants can change over time and so do our relationships. We may form a relationship based upon a specific need or want such as with our coworkers when we get a job. These relationships fulfill our needs at the time, but if we leave our job the need no longer exists. If any of our work relationships have not made another connection or progressed to another level beyond the initial need or want, then there's no longer any need for these relationships to continue, so they may deteriorate or end.

In some intimate relationships we have the expectation for fulfillment of our need for affection, intimacy, or sex. Each person may have differing perceptions and expectations of what constitutes fulfillment. If there are differing expectations one person or both may look for alternatives to fulfill those needs, but may also keep their relationship because it continues to fulfill some of their needs and wants. If one person's needs for intimacy has not been fulfilled it may be motivation for infidelity. Infidelity is not necessarily just physical, it can be fulfilling the need for intimacy, attention, acceptance, or self-disclosure with someone outside the relationship. Emotional or verbal infidelity can be just as damaging as physical infidelity because it can be dishonest or deceptive undermining the relationship.

Changes in relationships can make them more unstable leading to deterioration or dissolution. Things happen to us, people say and do things, and other people might get involved in a relationship that can increase uncertainty. The stronger the relationship, the more uncertainty it can withstand. However, if the uncertainty becomes too great it can cause the relationship to deteriorate or dissolve. Relationships are based on creating common connections through shared meaning. If individuals in the relationship start sharing different meanings with others outside the relationship it could pull the relationship apart.

The power of the law of investing affects all types of relationships. People engage in relationships knowing that they must contribute their own resources to make the relationship work. They do this because they have the expectation that they will receive fair rewards and benefits that will fulfill their needs and wants. One common misconception is that people seek to maximize rewards and minimize costs in relationships, in other words buy low sell high. This approach almost guarantees dissatisfaction and dissolution of a relationship because no one wants to be in a relationship with someone who does as little as possible and expects a lot in return.

Instead, people more often seek fair rewards for fair contributions. They may want to end up a little better than breaking even. This is because if one person's gain is significantly more than the other person it can be a source of dissatisfaction, resentment, tension, or even conflict. This imbalance provides a disincentive to trying to get as much as possible out of others by buying low and selling high. Most of the time people want to treat others fairly because they want to be treated fairly in return.

Relationship deterioration is largely contingent upon each individual's perceptions and expectations with the relationship. If they perceive that they are contributing more than the other person and receiving less, they are likely to become dissatisfied. If this imbalance is not resolved it can hasten the dissolution of the relationship. In some instances if a person perceives that they are getting much more than the other person, but contributing much less they may feel guilty about their role in the relationship. So, it can be helpful to balance the relationship so each person feels that they are contributing and receiving fairly. However, this does not necessarily mean that everything is divided equally as each relationship must find its own economic equilibrium.

Utilizing the perception process, people evaluate the contributions they make and benefits they receive from their relationships compared to others they know. We tend to use other relationships as a comparison in order to judge how well we are doing. We might compare our relationships to friends, family, coworkers, or people we see in the media. We often carry a balance sheet in our head of how well we are doing in our relationships, whether we are aware of it or not. So, why do some people stay in abusive relationships when it is hurting them? It may be because they feel they've made an investment and are afraid they will lose it all if they leave. It may be the fear of the uncertainty of being alone or that they may never have another relationship again. If they're being treated badly, the process of communicating through reflective feedback can give them a low self-concept perhaps making them feel that they are not worthy of a decent relationship.

This could create a cycle of negativity that can be difficult to change. Because they are already experiencing discomfort, any change could be perceived as increasing uncertainty making things more uncomfortable. This can motivate them to stay with what is familiar even though it does them harm. When we know a relationship is in trouble we may be reluctant to confront the issue because we hope that things will eventually get better or workout on their own. We may fear confronting the other person because of what may happen if we do. We might look at other people's relationships and see that they are also having problems to determine if our relationship is better or worse than theirs.

It's easy to overlook problems until they become difficult or impossible to fix because it can be easier to avoid or ignore them than to confront them. It can be easier to find fault and blame someone else for our problems. When relationships do not go the way we expect it can be very difficult. We can invest a portion of who we are in them and they become a part of our self-concept. So, when a relationship comes apart it can be very damaging to our self-concept.

In these circumstances it's helpful to step back for a moment to consider your desired outcome. We form relationships for a reason and we end them for a reason. Consider the reasons and desired outcomes you had when you began the relationship. Are they still relevant? Perhaps not and it's time to reevaluate them or move on. Considering your desired outcome can help you put things in perspective.

There are times when we have to end a relationship and it can be one of the most difficult things we do. It is never easy because we don't really want to hurt another person. We may be reluctant to confront the situation because we fear the consequences. You can utilize the approaches for giving bad news in this chapter by being truthful, but tactful. A direct approach allows everyone to be free to move on and for the healing process to begin. While increasing awareness and having options will not necessarily save a deteriorating relationship, at least you can feel that you have done everything you can do rather than wondering what happened or if there was something else that could have been done.

Levels Of Relationships

The level of a relationship is based on the intensity and frequency that people communicate. The most basic level entails the most superficial and basic means of communicating. In each successive level, we share more information about ourselves. The more personal the information we share, the higher the level of the relationship. For instance, we share very little personal information with a store clerk. We share some things about ourselves with our coworkers, more with friends, and the most with close family members.

When we first meet someone, we generally determine rather quickly what type of relationship we want to pursue. We start out with a high degree of uncertainty that causes feelings of awkwardness because we don't know what to expect of others and they don't know what to expect of us. So, we spend time talking about ourselves to get to know the other person to reduce uncertainty through the process of self-disclosure. As a relationship progresses to a higher level, the nature of how we communicate and interact with one another becomes more complex and individualized.

Levels of relationships originates from the law of uncertainty because we are motivated to reduce uncertainty by getting to know others in order to fulfill needs and wants. All relationships, including higher level relationships, begin at the most basic level and then progress through higher levels of relationships. However, most of our relationships never progress to the higher levels. Instead, they get just so far then they stabilize or fall apart. What level a relationship reaches is contingent on the law of shared meaning which encourages us to share information about ourselves through self-disclosure. It is also determined by the law of investing based on the degree of commitment and trust in the relationship, its needs, wants, and desired outcomes.

Most of our relationships can be characterized by these levels of interaction.

Level I. Acquaintances.

This is the most basic relationship level and how most of our relationships begin. It is the most prevalent and common type of relationship we have. It has a high degree of uncertainty, so we share little meaning and rely on the rules of social reality to govern our behavior. Most of our relationships do not progress beyond this level because we do not have the time or energy to get to know everyone we meet on a personal level nor is it necessary to achieving our desired outcomes.

These relationships are with people who help us to get the things done that we need and want to do. They can include store clerks, bank tellers, and coworkers. These people help us to achieve a specific desired outcome. Their role in helping us to accomplish our task is generally more important than the individual's personal characteristics. We use patterns of communicating that follow the rules of social reality when communicating with people we do not know because it goes easier and faster when everyone knows what to expect. However, if we deviate from what is expected it can catch the other person off guard and they may not know what to say or do.

Level II. Professional relationships.

Professional relationships involve ongoing connections with people through our work, job, or career. They are less superficial than acquaintances, but communicating is often based upon the role that people play such as their job. Relationships are based more on a person's role or job than who they are as an individual. We have a professional relationship with our boss and coworkers whether we want to or not. We share meanings that are related to work and maintaining a professional relationship. These relationships help to fulfill important needs and wants like income, status, and inclusion that can increase our commitment to them. Some of these relationships may progress to the next level, like getting to know a few coworkers more personally as friends.

How we communicate at this level is governed not only by the rules of social reality, but also by the rules of groups and organizations. We invest time and other resources in these relationships with the expectation of benefits now and in the future. Since the rewards are higher and there's more at stake, the rules are more strictly enforced with clear punishments for infractions, like being fired. If we leave a group, like when we change jobs, many of these relationships eventually come to an end. We are unlikely to hear from them because the need that motivated the connection no longer exists.

Level III. Personal relationships.

We develop personal relationships when we reduce uncertainty to get to know someone better than an acquaintance. We share meaning through increased self-disclosure by sharing stories about ourselves because it builds trust so we can invest our time and energy in them. These relationships fulfill many of our social needs and wants such as friendship, companionship, or sharing interests. These relationships are based more on the characteristics of the individual person and are more social in nature.

We develop these relationships based on our interests, proximity, similarity, and things we have in common, which can give them a stronger commitment. The most common personal relationships involve our friends, coworkers, and family. These relationships involve a higher degree of feedback, so they can affect our self-concept. They are governed by both the rules of social reality and rules we create just for this relationship. They are characterized by increased body language and nonverbal communicating including eye contact, facial expressions, and an increase in touch like handshakes or hugs.

Level IV. Close relationships.

These relationships are often with close friends and family. We generally have fewer of these relationships because they take more time and energy. Close relationships reduce uncertainty because they have a higher degree of self-disclosure. We share meaning about our personal information and experiences. This creates a higher degree of trust so we invest more of our time and resources in them. We often do things for one another with no expectation to receive anything in return.

Close relationships generally last a long time, over many years making them stable, secure, and predictable with a higher degree of commitment. It may take years to reach this level. This level has an increased degree of nonverbal communicating including use of touch. We feel comfortable investing large amounts of our time and resources in them because they can fulfill many important needs and wants like closeness, affection, inclusion, safety, and stability. These relationships are supportive, helping us to feel valued and appreciated. They are not so much governed by the rules of social reality as by the perceptions and expectations of the individuals involved. How we communicate with others in these relationships has a significant affect on our self-concept because we value their opinion.

Level V. Intimate relationships.

When we think of an intimate relationship we often think of physical intimacy. However, this is only one aspect of intimacy. Intimacy can also be emotional, psychological, or intellectual. Intimacy can be characterized by the nature of how we communicate and the degree of self-disclosure we have with one another. We can have physical intimacy without sharing any other meaningful kinds of intimacy.

While we may consider sex a part of an intimate relationship, not all intimate relationships are sexual and not all sexual relationships are intimate. We can have emotionally intimate relationships without physical intimacy like with close friends and family. Our closest intimate relationship is generally with a partner or spouse. These people know the most about us. These relationships are characterized by a high degree of self-disclosure and uncertainty reduction, so we trust them the most. We use them to share meaning because we often share many of the same experiences making them more meaningful.

Only a few relationships progress to this level because of the amount of time, energy, and other resources it takes to invest in them. We form them because these relationships fulfill some of our most important needs and wants like nurturing, support, help, and affection. These people know more about us than anyone else increasing our vulnerability, which can be a source of tension or conflict. The closer the relationship, the more we invest in it, so the more expectations we have about it increasing the potential for conflict because we have more to lose. How we communicate can affect our self-concept through reflected feedback. Since this involves people whose opinions we value, they can have a significant influence on our self-concept and social reality.

Family Relationships

At some point two people make the transition from being individuals to becoming a couple. This is a more specialized type of relationship as it is a close, intimate relationship that can lead to creating a family. When two people become a couple they bring their own ways of doing things from their past experiences into the relationship, so some aspects of the relationship may have to be renegotiated. This transition is more likely to go smoother if they have an awareness of each other's needs and wants, perceptions and expectations, and desired outcomes.

When two people become a couple, they go through many of the same things that people go through when they form other types of relationships. They need to reduce uncertainty so that they can feel comfortable and secure with one another. They share meaning through self-disclosure so that they can trust each other. They invest resources like their time and energy to make a commitment to the relationship.

When two people become a couple they will have to make decisions regarding their behavior and how they communicate with one another. They will have to work together to allocate resources like time, space, and money. Each person now has some control over the other, which can lead to tension and conflict. As two individuals become a couple and perhaps a family, it's helpful to develop ways to deal with problem solving, decision making, tension, and conflict. This can give the relationship a better chance of success. Effective communicating skills outlined in other areas of this book can help including listening, language, conflict, crisis, problem solving, and decision making.

A popular shared meaning is that relationships are ordained by a higher power through divine intervention. This can be communicated by characterizing relationships as being "meant to be" or by having a "soul mate." This perception is created by the law of shared meaning, which motivates us to find meaning in our relationships by believing that we are guided by a divine power that will lead us to a relationship that is meant to be. This can help to reduce uncertainty about a relationship because if we feel it's meant to be, it can help us to be more comfortable with it. This works until the relationship breaks up when we might use the same rationale by saying, it was not meant to be.

Relationships have both task and social characteristics. Being a couple can be fun, exciting, and romantic, but there are tasks that need to be accomplished in order for the relationship to function. There's a point where the focus shifts from fun and romantic activities to the more practical everyday tasks necessary to maintain a relationship. This can be disappointing or disillusioning and may result in feelings that the romance has gone out of the relationship because to some extent it has.

There can be tension between competing needs and wants. Daily tasks may be difficult to make exciting or romantic, but if all a couple's time is spent working then the relationship can become less attractive. A couple may feel like things have changed, but they don't know why or what to do about it. Creating awareness of this process can help to avoid potential negative consequences by having options to work out a balance between the task and social aspects of a relationship.

Sex.

One of the ways couples communicate with one another is through sex. Sex is a way that we reduce uncertainty by getting to know another person in a very intimate way. We invest sex with shared meaning based upon our values, culture, ethnicity, family, religion, and past experiences. It's closely tied to things that have meaning to us including commitment, marriage, spirituality, and morality. It can be one of the most valued ways that we invest in a relationship with another person. This makes sex a connection that has the potential to communicate many things in a relationship.

We use sex to fulfill many needs and wants like to feel good, show affection, make a commitment, provide support, and to make the other person feel valued. We need affection and the feeling of closeness. We want to have children and raise a family. Sex can help create connections that strengthen our commitment to a relationship. It creates closeness, a high level of intimacy, and is used to express feelings and emotions. Considering the other person's needs and wants can help us to fairly contribute and benefit from the relationship. Because if one person feels they are unfairly contributing or not benefiting, it can lead to dissatisfaction undermining their commitment to the relationship.

When it comes to sex we have many perceptions and expectations, but may be reluctant to communicate them. We may do this out of fear of rejection or getting hurt. We may think that if our partner loved us they would know what we want. The reality is that if we love them and want them to know what we want, we should just tell them. It's helpful to truthfully, but tactfully communicate our perceptions and expectations so that the other person knows what we would like from them and what they can expect of us. When we know what's expected we don't have to guess and we have a better chance of satisfying them and feeling fulfilled. Effective communicating helps to fulfill our expectations because if they are not fulfilled, we may be motivated to look elsewhere to have them fulfilled.

In a relationship each person can have different desired outcomes creating a source of tension. If both people have reasonably compatible desired outcomes it helps create commitment in the relationship. But, if their desired outcomes are distinctly different it may create unnecessary unhappiness or drive them apart. In order to avoid problems it's helpful to communicate our desired outcomes to work out something that is mutually acceptable.

While there has been a focus on technique and methods when it comes to intimacy, it can be helpful to a relationship to think about sex in a different way. Think of it as making a connection to communicate with another person. So, what message do you want to send, as well as receive? Sex is a unique form of communicating because we make connections using all of our five senses. We see the other person, we hear them, we touch them, we taste by kissing, and we may smell them or their perfume or cologne. Perhaps this is why sex is considered so sensual, because it makes connections using all of our senses.

We use the process of communicating to share our Great Idea with another person. In this instance it's sharing affection, support, pleasure, and caring. It can be helpful to provide feedback by being supportive to let them know what you like and what you would like from them. The nature of the feedback we receive can affect our self-concept, so when it is given in a positive way we feel good about ourselves. If it's perceived as negative, it can hurt us.

It can be helpful to have an awareness of what you communicate and how it's being perceived to know how well your message has been received. Making assumptions is a good way to be disappointed or frustrated. If you want the other person to do something, let them know. If you want to know if they like something, ask them. People may avoid doing this because they may feel apprehensive or embarrassed talking about these things. However, it's better to talk about them beforehand, so they don't create misunderstandings later.

Marriage.

Marriage is the most formalized relationship we have in society because it creates both a spiritual and legal connection between two people. Marriage is the means by which society institutionalizes two people coming together as a couple. It is an institution ordained by the church and sanctioned by the state. It is an institution that is a fundamental part of society shaped by the rules of social reality. There is no other relationship where we pledge publicly before our friends and family to forsake all others until death do us part.

Marriage institutionalizes and legitimizes a couple's relationship according to the rules of social reality, religion, culture, and geographic affiliation. The creation of marriage was motivated by the laws of uncertainty, shared meaning and investing because it serves the societal function of creating and maintaining stability, structure, and security. It is an important means of uncertainty reduction for individuals as well as society. It is a means to share meaning about who we are and where we come from. It is a means to invest in relationships that can last a lifetime.

The law of uncertainty motivates people to get married because marriage can help to reduce uncertainty. It reduces uncertainty about our partner, so we can get to know them on an intimate level, which helps us to become comfortable sharing our lives together. It helps to create a level of trust necessary to do things like living together, sharing financial resources, making joint decisions like buying a house or having children. It creates a formal structure to raise children in a safe and secure environment.

Marriage is one of the most important ways we share meaning with others. It can help us find meaning in life and in our experiences. Marriage is universally recognized by all cultures, ethnicities, religions, and nations. However, each of these groups gives it their own unique set of meanings by having their own rituals and traditions. This makes marriage an example of the law of shared meaning because it marks the transition of two individuals from different families coming together to create a new one. Couples reaffirm this shared meaning when they celebrate their anniversary each year.

Just as people communicate for a reason, they get married for a reason. They want to reduce uncertainty in another person, share meaning with them, and invest in a life together. People are motivated to get married to fulfill many of their most important needs and wants including affection, inclusion, support, and intimacy. It helps fulfill the need for safety, security, and stability to give a relationship structure. People want to share their thoughts, feelings, and experiences with someone. People want to have children, raise a family, and make a home. People want to be in a positive relationship because it can improve their self-concept.

In order to have a more effective relationship it's helpful to understand our needs and wants, and to clearly communicate them to our partner. If each person understands the other person's needs and wants, then they can work together to develop ways to fulfill them to their mutual satisfaction. If we feel our needs and wants are being adequately fulfilled, we are likely to be more committed to a relationship than if they are not. If we feel that we are not getting something we need in a relationship, we may look for it elsewhere.

We make many assumptions about why people get married. We assume they marry for love, but they may also marry for security, money, prestige, self-esteem, social pressure, or to fulfill expectations. When people get married they have the desired outcome of spending the rest of their lives together, however, about half of all marriages eventually breakup. A couple can have different, even conflicting desired outcomes about marriage that may cause tension, conflict, or even dissolution of the relationship. In order to avoid problems, it can be helpful for couples to communicate their true desired outcomes, so that they can work them out in ways that are mutually acceptable and beneficial.

Marriage is one of our most important relationships, so it creates many expectations. How satisfied we are with marriage is based, in part, on how well we perceive our expectations are being met. Our expectations involve practically all aspects of the relationship including what we contribute as well as receive. If our perception is close to our expectations, we are likely to be happy with the relationship. If our perceptions don't meet our expectations, we can become unhappy, frustrated, and may even want to breakup.

In order to avoid this, it's helpful to periodically check your perceptions and expectations by sharing them with your partner to see if they are compatible. It's helpful to have an awareness of the gap between perceptions and expectations because this difference can affect a person's commitment to a relationship without their being aware of it. Through awareness a couple can develop options to keep this from becoming a problem.

We all have perceptions and expectations about how well our needs and wants are being met in our relationships. However, it is easy to be unaware of how these can motivate behavior. So, it can be helpful to increase your awareness by writing down your needs and wants in a relationship. Then rank them in order of importance. Write down your expectations for yourself, your partner, and your relationship. Then write down your perceptions about how well your expectations, needs, and wants are being met.

We think that we may know how we feel, but writing it down and talking about it makes us think it through because we have to communicate how we feel. If we ask somebody if their expectations are being met they probably would just say, yes. Having a list gives a starting point to determine what things are working well in a relationship and which things could use improvement. Once you know what they are you can develop ways to improve them.

It can be helpful to a relationship for a couple to consider these questions.

What are my needs and wants in a marriage?
What are my partner's needs and wants in a marriage?

What are my desired outcomes in a marriage?
What are my partner's desired outcomes in a marriage?

What are my perceptions of our relationship?
What are my partner's perceptions of the relationship?

What are my expectations about myself and my partner in a marriage?
What are my partner's expectations of me and themselves in a marriage?

What are my expectations about marriage?
What are my partner's expectations about marriage?

Are those expectations being met? How can they be better met?
Is there a gap between our perceptions and expectations that could cause tension?

How do we communicate, make decisions, solve problems, and allocate resources?
What are our rules, roles, rituals, traditions, and norms of behavior?

The purpose of these questions is to get a couple talking about important aspects of their relationship. Everyone has expectations as well as perceptions about how well they are being met. If they are not being met it can undermine their commitment to the relationship creating tension.

These questions are not meant to be a comprehensive list, but rather a place to begin a conversation that can continue over time. They can help to reduce uncertainty so that each person has a better idea of what to expect. They can help to share meaning so a couple can come to understand one another better. This process can help to build common bonds so that they can invest in their relationship.

Typical approaches to compatibility might use the same set of standardized questions for everyone that can overlook a couple's unique characteristics. Asking open ended questions helps to get a couple thinking and talking about their relationship. This provides a customized approach so a couple can determine what issues are important to them. They can then talk about the issues they determine are important in more detail.

Increasing awareness can help improve a relationship because no two people perceive everything the same. This approach could be used as a diagnostic methodology to evaluate a relationship to help a couple to better understand how they perceive themselves, their partner, and their relationship.

Children.

One of the reasons for forming and maintaining relationships like marriage is to raise children. A child can be one of the biggest challenges for a couple because it can change their relationship. Their relationship can change because the focus is no longer on one another, but on the children. It changes a couple's roles and responsibilities from being the children of parents, to being parents who are responsible for their own children.

Having children changes the nature of a couple's relationship even before a child is born. This experience can increase uncertainty, so they will be motivated to reduce it by developing relationships with others who have the resources to fulfill their new needs and wants. Pregnancy changes their communicating network by adding new sources of information and support they never needed before, such as medical professionals and other couples going through the same experience. They are motivated by the law of shared meaning to seek out people who share the same experiences to learn from them and because it helps give their own experiences greater meaning.

With the addition of a first child, how a couple communicates with each other can change. When a couple communicates, it is directly one on one with each other all the time. When they have a child, their focus is now on their child. This means that they will no longer be spending nearly as much time and energy on one another and then they may wonder why they don't feel as close as they once did.

With each additional child, a family will adapt their roles, rules, and structures to accommodate their growing family. The nature of their relationship will change because how they communicate will change. It is helpful to be aware of these changes because parents can end up spending the majority of their time and energy with their children leaving little for themselves. Instead, they need to take care of their own relationship first because it's what keeps the family together.

The biggest change to a couple's relationship can be making the transition from being a couple to a having a family with children. So, it can be helpful to have an awareness of how the law of uncertainty relates to having children. Having a child, particularly the first child, raises the level of uncertainty for a couple because it's a new experience. With each additional child there can be new sources of uncertainty, so a couple may have to reassess the rules, roles, and structure in their family. The purpose of parenting is to reduce uncertainty to create stability and structure to provide a safety net when children need it, to share meaning about the family and the world so that they can function in society, and to invest in relationship that will last a lifetime to provide support and security.

When couples decide to start a family, they may assume they have compatible desired outcomes. The reality is that these may differ creating an underlying source of tension or conflict. Just because two people have compatible desired outcomes to get married does not necessarily mean that they have the same expectations when it comes to having a family. In order to avoid unnecessary tension or conflict, it's helpful to clearly communicate them in order to work out desired outcomes that are mutually acceptable.

Having children can be stressful as well as rewarding for a couple, so it can be helpful to understand one another's perceptions and expectations such as who will be responsible for doing what tasks. In this context, the words parents or couple includes a married or unmarried couple, partners, and single parents, as well as biological and adoptive parents.

To help, parents can ask the following questions.

1. What are my perceptions and expectations about myself for having children?
2. What are my perceptions and expectations about my partner for having children?
3. What are my perceptions and expectations for my children?
4. What are my and my partner's desired outcomes for having children?

These questions are open ended so instead of having preestablished topics to discuss, each couple will come up with their own based upon what is important to them. Since everyone is different, each couple's concerns will be different. In raising children we often rely on the experiences that we had when we were children growing up. We may emulate our parents and how they raised us because it's familiar and we are comfortable with it so it reduces uncertainty.

For the first years of a child's life they are totally dependent on their family for all their needs and wants. A family helps to fulfill a child's emotional, social, physical, and material needs. Even when a child gets older and is able to take care of themselves, they may still look to their family to fulfill many of their needs and wants.

Having children is about investing in relationships that last a lifetime. Parents may find themselves focusing on their children, so they can unintentionally neglect investing in their own relationship. Taking care of a child's needs and wants can leave them feeling tired, overwhelmed, or overworked. It can exhaust their resources to a point where they don't have time to spend on themselves. Couples can become focused on their children, so that they neglect their own relationship until it starts to erode or even break apart. Single parents may not have time to invest in a new relationship. It is understandable that they put their children before themselves, however, they may do so to the detriment of developing other relationships.

Having children changes a couples needs and wants from focusing on their own to those of their children. They may put their children's needs and wants before their own because they feel that that's the right thing to do. They may find they have less time and other resources to fulfill their own needs, which can put stress and tension on their relationship. Having an awareness of how needs and wants could change their priorities, can help keep their own relationship strong. Through awareness a couple can develop options in order to maintain or restore their own relationship. They can renegotiate their relationship, so that they can fulfill their needs while still providing for those of their children. It is important for couples put their own relationship first, to keep their family strong.

Children often learn how to communicate and behave in relationships when they become adults by emulating their parent's relationship. However, if the parental relationship is not strong the entire family, especially the children, may suffer. A good illustration of how this works is when before taking off in an airplane, adults are instructed to place the oxygen mask on themselves first before assisting their children. This is because if they try to put the child's mask on first, if they are not be able to breathe, they cannot help their child. By placing it on themselves first, they will be able to breathe, so they can help their child.

In a family if the parents are stressed, frustrated, or angry they may have a diminished ability to help their children. If their relationship is weak or stressed they may not be as effective in their relationship with their children. If the parental relationship feels secure, then there's a much better chance that the parent child relationship will feel secure as well.

In the process of communicating, the nature of the feedback we receive from others has the potential to affect our self-concept. When we are born we have little or no self-concept, it develops as we grow older. It can be helpful to be aware that how we communicate with children can affect their self-concept and how they perceive themselves, potentially for the rest of their lives. Children learn how to communicate by observing family members and these behaviors can be carried on later in life. Parents can help their children to develop effective ways to communicate with others by example.

Parents should talk regularly with their children beginning at an early age because there may come a time when a child has problems and it will become necessary to have a talk with them. However, by this time things may have progressed to a point where dealing with it will be more difficult. The time to talk begins when children are very young. Don't wait until they drink, smoke, try drugs, or something else before talking about it. Sometimes we wonder when is a good time to talk about difficult subjects like sex or drugs with children. If they ask about it, it's time to talk about it. If they don't get the information they need or want from you, they will get it somewhere else. Wouldn't you prefer that they got it from you? It is helpful to engage them in conversation on a regular basis, so they are comfortable talking with you. This should help make it easier for them to talk about difficult subjects. It's easy to get busy and put things off until it becomes a problem, but by that time it may be too late.

It is easy to use the first style of communicating, described in Chapter 1, by only telling them what to do. Instead, try using the third style by engaging them in conversation, which encourages them to talk and give you feedback about what they are thinking and feeling. Take your cues from your children, be honest, keep it simple, and keep the discussion age appropriate. Don't try to cover everything all in one talk. Encourage them to think about things by asking open ended questions. There should be an ongoing series of conversations that parents have with their children over their whole life. Instead of the big talk, start with small talks. This can become a family norm. It begins an ongoing process of communicating with your children so they trust you and feel comfortable talking about these things when they are very young and will feel comfortable talking to you when they get older.

Parents might avoid doing this because they feel awkward or uncomfortable talking about subjects like sex or drugs. But it's better that you talk with them and that they come to you for advice rather than going to someone you don't know. They will seek out information where they feel comfortable getting it. Sometimes we just don't know where to start when talking about difficult subjects. Follow their lead, when they want to know they will ask, so be ready to talk to them. Be truthful, but tactful and don't get bogged down in extraneous details. Keep information on their level and if they want more information, they will ask.

Regularly communicating with your children not only provides information, it also reduces uncertainty about you so they know that they can trust you and can come to you when they need something. It helps to share meaning to make our experiences more significant to help you understand them better. It also makes them trust you more by investing in your relationship. When you know your children, you don't have to worry about what they are doing, because you know what they are doing.

When children go to school it creates a whole new communicating network. Previously, they communicated mostly with family members, but now they have a whole new network of classmates, friends, and adults. It's helpful to prepare them for this by involving them in a variety of activities with others so they are more adaptable to new situations. This can familiarize them with new and different social realities so that they are prepared for them. As children get older, the rules need to change to adapt to changing circumstances because their self-concept is being increasingly influenced by others outside of the family through the process of communicating. Their self-concept can be altered by social pressure and behavioral reinforcement from their peers, friends, or schoolmates. They have needs and wants that they increasingly fulfill themselves or through other people who are outside of their family. This gives outsiders a growing influence over them that can affect their behavior based on how others accept, reject, or ignore them when they communicate.

Adolescence is a time of change in self-concept, perception, and expectations. It is a time of transition from being dependent upon our family to fulfill our needs and wants to doing things for ourselves. It is a time when the primary means of communicating changes from their connections with family members to new connections with others outside their family. It is a time when we negotiate conflicting needs and wants like the transition from dependence to independence and from being a member of a family to becoming an individual.

How well parents have prepared their children for this can make a difference in how well they adjust to changes that can influence their behavior. For instance, if rules or structures are too rigid, adolescents may disobey them to get them changed. If rules and structures are more flexible, they may not see the need to disobey them because they are able to create their own rules within the rules of the family.

By having an awareness of how the process of developing self-concept and behavioral reinforcement works, parents can make choices about how they communicate with their children from an early age. It helps to understand that changes are not necessarily a rejection or abandonment of their family, but that children go through a process of renegotiating their self-concept based upon how they communicate with new groups of people as they mature. This can be a positive and significant development because it is how a child moves from being dependent on family members to become an independent adult.

Both children and adolescents want increasing degrees of independence so they can develop their own self-concept. Parents can provide positive channels and experiences by which they can do this. They can have them make their own rules, establish their own structure, be responsible for their own space, and be involved in activities that can help bolster their self-concept. These things can help their development by providing activities where they can make their own decisions, have adventure, and even take risks while still maintaining the family connection.

We have a natural tendency to want to protect our children from things we think might hurt them. However, by overprotecting them they may become less prepared to deal with problems when they encounter them, particularly when they become an adult and are out on their own. Instead, parents can help prepare their children for what's out there in society by increasing their awareness about how these things work and their consequences.

Children need a certain amount of uncertainty to motivate them, but not so much that it discourages them. Families reduce uncertainty for children by providing stability, so that they will feel safe and secure. However, if uncertainty is reduced too much and everything is taken care of for them, they may not do the things they need to do for themselves to foster their development and independence. Children and adolescents can benefit from a degree of uncertainty where everything is not taken care of by their family, so that they can learn to become reliant on themselves.

Children may have a need for excitement, adventure, escape, or even danger. If this need is not fulfilled within the family, they may look for adventure and excitement outside the family by engaging in risky or dangerous behavior. They may want to be with friends who they perceive as being less judgmental or more exciting because they don't impose boundaries, rules, or structure. Since they have limited experience, they may not consider the potential consequences. To avoid this from happening, families can share activities that fulfill the need for escape, adventure, and risk in a safe and structured manner.

Becoming a family.

Family can be a much overused word. People talk about their immediate family, extended family, work family, and even inanimate objects are characterized as families like a family of companies. For the purpose of this book, family is a group of people who are connected by a stable set of relationships they share for their entire lives. Most of the time a family is defined by the perception of the individuals involved. If people consider themselves a member of a family, then a family exists. At some point in their lives, family members share proximity, frequency, intensity, or similarity. A family can be considered those people who have reduced uncertainty, shared meaning, and invested in one another for a lifetime. You can quit a job, but you can't quit your family.

Family is something we all have in common, it is an unavoidable part of life. Forming a family is a natural part of human behavior, so we don't generally think about it very much. We are born into a family, grow up in a family, and may form a family of our own. It is through our family that we first learn about ourselves, others, and the world around us. It is helpful to understand how families communicate because of the influence they have over our lives. Families affect our self-esteem, shape our perception and expectations, and influence our desired outcomes. They can create their own social reality that affects our thoughts and behavior.

It is through the process of communicating with family members that we develop our self-concept and sense of who we are through reflected feedback. This shapes the person we become because it is part of how we define ourselves as an individual. Our family affects our behavior throughout our entire life. It is where we learn about our culture, ethnicity, religion, and social reality. In a family we are part of a social and task oriented group. We are part of a communicating network that is connected to other families.

Some characteristics of a family.

• Uncertainty. A family helps their members to reduce uncertainty about the family, other members, and the world around them.

• Shared meaning. A family shares meaning about the family and what it means to be a member of the family.

• Investing. A family provides a means for members to invest in the family and in each other as well as protecting that investment.

• Identity. A family has a collective identity. Members know that they belong to the family and each member considers themselves to be a part of the family. A family communicates what it means to be a member of the family including its history, traditions, and rituals.

- Connections. A family has a network of connections between members through which they communicate that does not exist between people outside the family. Members often have a higher degree of interaction that creates an ongoing relationship.

- Desired outcome. Family members generally work together to achieve mutual desired outcomes.

- Needs and wants. Family members work together to fulfill their own, and other family member's needs and wants as well as those of the family. Families allocate resources and make decisions, which gives the people who do this influence over the others.

- Rules, norms, and roles. A family has rules, norms, and roles that govern their behavior. Most often these are informal and communicated verbally. Families have a process by which they get things done, make decisions, and resolve conflicts.

- Structure. A family has many types of structures. These structures create a hierarchy of roles and responsibilities. They determine things like how members utilize shared spaces and allocate their time.

The nature of family.

People are motivated to form families by the law of uncertainty because life can be chaotic and unpredictable. The world is a big place and families help to make it smaller. Families can give our lives structure, stability, and security to reduce uncertainty. Families have structure and boundaries giving us a feeling of stability. We spend a lot of time with our family, so we get to know them very well giving us a sense of security. Our family members are concerned with our welfare and well being giving us a sense of safety. If the family is evaluated based on the context of how groups function it is possibly the most effective kind of group, which is why it is the foundation of society.

Families are brought together by the relational elements of proximity, familiarity, frequency, and intensity. They form our closest, most personal relationships because we often live with them, know them very well, see them often, and care about them. We are motivated to be a part of a family to fulfill many of our most important needs and wants. From the time we are born, families provide for many of our needs and wants, reducing uncertainty until we can take care of ourselves. Families have the means to fulfill their member's needs and wants to create stability, security, and predictability. Because they allocate resources, families can exert influence as a form of social control to regulate members' behavior. This can help everyone know what is expected of them and what to expect from other members.

Families need to reduce uncertainty in order to function, however, they also need some degree of uncertainty to function effectively. When uncertainty is reduced too much, it can reduce the motivation to look for new ideas, information, and ways of doing things. It can create overconfidence making people more reluctant to change. Having some uncertainty can motivate family members to increase their awareness, look for options, question assumptions, and look at what they know in a new or different way. Families need stability, but they also need to be able to adapt to changing circumstances.

How families communicate can be a manifestation of the law of shared meaning. We share meaning with our families from the time we are born. It is from our families that we learn about what it means to be a person and how to function in society. We learn about our culture, ethnicity, religion, and geographic affiliations. Families educate us and help us to develop important skills. It is in our family that we learn about ourselves, others, and the things around us. They teach us what we need to know giving us experience so that we can function on our own out in the world.

In families we share our ideas and experiences with others and they share theirs with us. We get to know our family through the process of self-disclosure, which develops trust so we can live and work together. When we need information and knowledge to make decisions or solve problems, we often seek out the help and advice of our family. We can learn about things from their knowledge and experience.

Families share meaning through their traditions and rituals that are a part of their customs and culture. They may have their own language, symbols, and terms. Families have a history and heritage that is communicated through rituals in which members participate. We share meaning by telling stories about our past experiences and aspirations for the future making them more meaningful. This can give us a sense of where our family has been in the past, where we are today, and what to look forward to in the future. These stories often include what a family has done to overcome adversity and how much they have accomplished giving them a collective identity.

One of the first things people learn about us is our name. We use it when we introduce ourselves to others and it communicates information about us to reduce uncertainty. Everyone has a name that combines their family name with their own individual name, which gives us our individual identity as well as a connection to other family members. A name can share meaning about who we are including our gender, ethnicity, religion, or geographic affiliation. It gives us a connection to the past including our ancestors and heritage. A name gives us a sense of who we are that we use in presenting ourselves to others and influences how others perceive us. Our name has the potential to affect our personality, self-concept, and how other people perceive us.

In our family we feel comfortable investing our time, energy, and other resources with the expectation that we will receive benefits for our contributions. Family members can be more willing to share their resources with other members including their time, energy, expertise, experience, and material resources. We are motivated by the law of investing to create and maintain families because they provide the stability and structure necessary for members to invest in lifelong relationships.

Families are made up of many generations creating a hierarchy that can determine how resources and power are allocated. Families have the means to accumulate many kinds of resources, so they have to make decisions about what resources are allocated and to whom. These resources can include things like how money, space, and time are allocated. This gives the family members who make these decisions a degree of power or influence over the others. This power can be used as a form of social control to influence the behavior of other members to conform to the norms and rules of the family.

We are likely to invest more of our resources in our family than any other relationship because we have expectations of benefits that only families can provide to fulfill many of our most important needs and wants. Families can provide social rewards to their members in ways that other relationships cannot. They can provide verbal praise, reinforcement, acknowledgment, support, respect, status, and prestige. These social rewards can be a powerful force motivating people to make a commitment to their family.

Being valued and accepted by others validates who we are as an individual by making us feel appreciated bolstering our self-concept. This can fulfill our needs and wants for acceptance, affiliation, and support. Conversely, families can use social rewards as a punishment by withholding needs and wants fulfillment from members to enforce the rules. If we feel we are not receiving fair benefits it can be a source of tension and conflict. This is one reason why familial relationships can be the most rewarding, as well as the most infuriating.

Through the process of communicating, families can shape our self-concept by providing us with reflected feedback. We utilize this reflected feedback to see ourselves as they see us. When we receive positive feedback, it bolsters our self-concept. When we receive negative feedback it can be especially harmful because it comes from people we are close to and whose opinion we care about.

We have expectations about our family and perceptions about how those expectations have been met. Tension and conflict can arise when our perceptions do not meet our expectations. In order to avoid this, it can be helpful for family members to communicate their perceptions of how those expectations are being met.

An important part of maintaining a family is sharing meaning by participating in family events like rituals and traditions. Rituals are repeating patterns of communicating and behaviors that can occur at specific times or during certain events. Traditions are ways of doing things that are often passed down over many generations. These can include every day rituals like having dinner together and annual traditions like celebrating birthdays, anniversaries, or holidays. Rituals and traditions are based upon our family's past experiences, culture, ethnicity, religion, and geographic affiliations. These events and the behaviors that accompany them are used to share important meanings about our family, our ancestors, and our heritage.

Family rituals and traditions are often governed by a special set of rules and established patterns of communicating. They have a deeper meaning that is shared by everyone who participates. They have a history that has been developed over long periods of time. Families are motivated to create rituals and traditions by the law of shared meaning because they can help members to make sense of their experiences by sharing them with one another. Participating in these rituals helps to create connections between ourselves and others. They create boundaries between those who participate and understand them, and those who do not.

Rituals and traditions provide an important function for a family because they fulfill a number of needs and wants. They provide for identity needs by letting people know who they are and where they came from. They provide for affiliation needs as people feel closer to others who share the same traditions. They fulfill the need for structure by providing regular recurring activities that give us a sense of stability and predictability. We often look forward to celebrating these traditions every year. They fulfill our need to develop our self-concept by connecting us to others who share these traditions with past generations.

Family structure.

Family structure consists of a family's roles, rules, and boundaries. Structure helps to organize a family to let everyone know who is responsible for what. Structure is essential for families to function properly. Families have many types of structures, the most well known is a hierarchy often based upon age with grandparents at the top followed by parents and then children. This structure is often illustrated in a family tree.

Structure also involves how families communicate, use time and space, and create boundaries. These family structures can be more malleable, which is the degree to which they can be changed, adapted, or influenced by others. They can range from strict to flexible. A strict structure provides stability to keep things together by reducing uncertainty. Flexibility allows a family to adapt to changing circumstances. Having flexibility allows them to have options to choose the best one for their situation.

However, too much flexibility can make life more chaotic and unpredictable increasing uncertainty, which reduces stability. Being overly strict can hinder individual creativity, reduce options, make decisions more difficult, and create tension. A balanced approach between being strict and flexible allows for families to have options that takes into consideration each member's individual nature while maintaining the family structure.

Part of a family's structure is establishing boundaries. All groups we belong to have boundaries that define who is a member and who is not. They fulfill important needs like giving members a feeling of belonging and being sheltered from the outside world. Families create and maintain boundaries to protect their members by fulfilling their need for safety and security as well as having a feeling of being connected to others by belonging to a group. Boundaries can also be open or closed depending on the structure of the individual family. Closed boundaries don't allow people to move across them very easily. They can provide structure, but can also be restrictive. Open boundaries allow people to move in and out more easily, but they may increase uncertainty.

Internal boundaries exist within a family. They can separate some members of a family from others. One of the most common boundaries is between adults and children. Boundaries can have an affect on how family members communicate, share ideas, and interact with one another. Boundaries can influence how individual members communicate with one another and what they communicate about. Some matters are only talked about within the family and are not allowed to be shared with outsiders. Some things like making decisions may only be discussed between adults, while some topics may not be talked about at all. Informational boundaries determine what information members keep to themselves or share with only a few others.

Boundaries create both physical and psychological structure. When we have small children we set up physical boundaries to protect them from things that may do them harm such as childproofing cabinets. We also establish psychological boundaries that regulate their behavior to not only keep them safe, but to develop important social skills. Boundaries can include what they can and cannot do, expectations for their behavior, how to use space, following schedules, and obeying the rules.

Children may try to test the boundaries to find out where they are. They may act out with different behaviors or go places that they know they shouldn't just to see if the boundaries will be enforced. It's helpful to be consistent in defining boundaries so that they understand what is expected of them because if the boundaries keep changing they can become frustrated. Consistency in boundaries, helps create stability and makes it easier to enforce them.

Children need structure because it fulfills the need for stability and predictability. It reduces uncertainty for them by letting them know how things work and what is expected of them. It enables them to learn how to arrange things in their life like how they utilize their time and space to be more organized and effective when they become an adult. If they do not have structure as a child, it may be more difficult for them to adapt to structure later in life. If they grow up with structure, when they are older they will have the experience to give them the ability to make their own choices to establish their own structure.

Structure can take several forms. It can be how time is organized so that the same things, like meals, happen at the same time every day. It can be how their responsibilities are organized like cleaning their room or helping with household chores. Structure teaches skills like being organized and punctual. Structure organizes what happens on which days during the year including celebrating special dates like birthdays, rituals like holidays, and seasonal activities like swimming or skating. This gives children things to look forward to and develops their skills to plan something and see it through. It provides stability and a degree of future predictability while giving them responsibility. It can help them to feel more connected to their family and to others.

A family's power structure is about who has control, makes the rules, makes decisions, and allocates resources. Power is necessary in order to have stability and to get things done. In families, power is often invested in an older adult or shared between parents who have children. As the children get older, they are given more power and control in making decisions. Families can have more needs and wants than they have resources to fulfill, so someone has to make decisions about which ones will be fulfilled and how resources are distributed. This creates a hierarchy of power based on who decides which members get what resources.

A family's communicating structure consists of a series of connections between members as well as with outsiders to form a network. This communicating network consists of who talks to whom, about what, when, and under what circumstances. How information flows through these connections depends upon each member's needs and wants. Most often information comes from the top down such as from the parents or older family members. Some members may serve as gatekeepers because they have connections to outsiders that can provide the family with information or other resources. For instance, the children may get information from people they know at school or in the neighborhood.

A family's time structure determines how family members allocate their time. Time can be a family's most valuable resource and how it is structured communicates what is valued by them. Children need structure, so they learn how to organize time until they are old enough to do it on their own. If they do not have structure, then they will not learn the importance of using time and may have difficulty as an adult. Having a regular schedule teaches children responsibility so they know what to expect, which can help fulfill the need for stability.

Time structure involves how we schedule our daily activities like when to get up in the morning, have meals, and go to bed. It is also how we schedule dates throughout the year like for birthdays and holidays. It gives the family stability and a sense of predictability by creating shared expectations of what the family will be doing together in the future.

A family's spatial structure includes not only how they use physical space, but also psychological space, areas of responsibility, and turf or territory. One of the fundamental functions of a family is to provide shelter, but a family also takes a house and makes it a home. Our home has shared meaning representing safety and security because it is where we spend much of our time. Our homes are a physical manifestation of who we are as a family. How we decorate it, the objects and possessions we choose, and furniture we fill it with reflects our sense of style and preferences creating a tangible and visual expression of who we are. We have many objects and possessions that have a story behind them and invests them with meaning.

We structure our space not only with rooms for specific functions, but also by what is considered public and private space. Public space is open to everyone such as the living room, dining room, and kitchen. It is used for interactions between family members and outsiders who visit. Private spaces are the area of our homes that we have all to ourselves so we can control who has access to them like a bedroom or den. These are not usually open to outsiders. We protect our spaces and if others violate them it can lead to tension or conflict.

Families allocate space for individual members based upon their needs and status in the family. Who controls what space reflects the family power structure. Typically, the more powerful family members control more space. For example, parents control most of the space in their home and perhaps have the largest bedroom. Children may have to share a space in a bedroom and have little say over how much of the family's space is used. As they get older they may want more control over their own space.

Family rules.

Practically all aspects of our lives are governed by some set of rules including our family. Without rules life would be chaotic increasing uncertainty. Rules are necessary to reduce uncertainty so that a family can function properly. We establish rules to govern our behavior, so that everyone knows what is expected of them and they know what to expect from others. We do this to establish structure, security, safety, and a degree of predictability. Having structure in families can make them attractive as a source of comfort and support. Rules are important for children because they provide the structure and boundaries necessary for their development as members of society. If they do not learn how to utilize structure at an early age from their family, it may be more difficult for them to deal with structure later in life when they become adults and have a family of their own.

Families have rules that everyone is expected to follow. Rules communicate and enforce the structure and boundaries necessary for their safety and security. However, some rules can go unspoken so we don't know about them until we break them. So, the rules need to be clearly communicated to everyone so that they understand what is expected of them. When they get older, parents can explain why the rules are important, so that the children will better understand why they are necessary. As they gain more responsibility, children can have a say in making the rules because by having a say in creating them, they are more likely to follow them.

Children will test the rules to see if you are serious and will actually enforce them. This is why it's important to be consistent, to clearly communicate the rules, and fairly enforce them. It's important that children understand what they did wrong so they can correct their behavior in the future. If they ask why they can't do something, instead of saying, "Because I said so," it's better to tell them the reason so that they understand why rules are important. Understanding why makes them more likely to comply, so when they get older they can make their own rules because they understand why families have them.

Having rules creates stability, but rules also need to be flexible so that they can be changed as needed. If the rules are too strict, family members could justify breaking or ignoring them. If they are too flexible they do not serve their intended purpose. Families need balance and a means to change the rules to respond to changing circumstances. In this way they can make changes as needed that do not undermine the family structure, but can respond to changing circumstances. When children get older, they can have a say in creating some of the rules giving them more responsibility.

Rules consist of two types. Constitutive rules govern what constitutes appropriate behavior. Regulatory rules regulate behavior by providing restrictions with a mechanism for their enforcement like punishments for infractions. Doing this is important because without any consequences no one would obey the rules. Rules not only need to be understood, but everyone needs to know that they were established for a good reason. Rather than using clichés or threats, it's helpful to let them know that you don't want to keep them from doing things, but you want to keep them safe. It lets them know you are serious and that you care about them.

Once rules are established they don't do much good unless they are uniformly and fairly enforced. Children learn that when mom says no it does not necessarily mean no, it means keep asking dad until he says yes. Then it's an issue between mom and dad. Having a united front between parents is important, so children don't look for an opening to exploit. This encourages them to abide by the rules creating consistency and structure, which are important for a family's well being. In creating rules it is important to avoid clichés like, "If you live under my roof, you follow my rules." Statements like this provide a loophole because they could reply, "Then I'm moving out." This undermines the rules and creates an unintended undesired outcome. Instead take the approach that the rules are there to help them because you care about them.

Family roles.

Roles in families consist of mutually shared expectations of individual behavior. Families have tasks that need to be accomplished, which means somebody has to do them. Since everyone cannot do the same things at the same time, individual members will specialize by taking on different tasks creating their roles. Families often consist of multiple role relationships each of which have their own set of distinctly different responsibilities like parent, child, sibling, or spouse.

Some roles, like parent and child, are fixed and don't change. Once someone becomes a parent, they are always a parent. Other roles, like who does the cooking are variable depending upon each family's needs and wants, which may change over time. Having stable roles reduces uncertainty because everyone knows what they are supposed to do. Family roles are often based on the mutual perceptions and expectations of family members. When their expectations are similar and their perceptions are realistic, they should feel that things are going well. However, if there are differing expectations of what each person is supposed to do or there's a perception that some people are doing more than others, there can be tension or conflict.

Roles are important because someone has to take responsibility to accomplish tasks and family members need to know who is responsible for what tasks. Many roles are based upon the individual's relationship with the rest of the family such as parent, child, and sibling. We are given responsibility based upon our age and ability. Some roles are based on social position or characteristics like age, gender, or marital relationships. Families have task roles that entail getting things done such as bringing in an income, shopping for food, and doing household chores. The roles that have the most responsibility are typically done by adults and as the children get older they can take on roles with more responsibility.

Roles are fulfilled based on mutual expectations and past experiences. They can be influenced by a family's background, ethnicity, culture, religion, and geographic affiliations. Roles may also be fulfilled based upon each member's interests or ability. Some roles are fixed while others are determined through behavioral reinforcement. When members exhibit a behavior and they receive positive reinforcement from other members, they are likely to continue the behavior. If they receive a negative response they are less likely to continue. This is why it's important to give family members positive reinforcement when they do something helpful for the family.

When they are young, children learn how to behave by watching their family members and then try out that behavior for themselves. As they get older, they may emulate the behaviors of their friends and peers. Through the process of behavioral reinforcement they will try out different behaviors to see the response. When they receive approval, they feel valued and are more likely to repeat that behavior to gain approval again. If the behavior is met with a negative reaction, they can be discouraged from repeating that behavior. If the feedback isn't clear or consistent it may be confusing causing them to act out in negative ways. If they get no response they are likely to repeat it or they may act out to get a reaction. There are times when they may repeat negative behavior just to get attention. If they do something positive and do not get positive response, it can be discouraging reinforcing negative behavior. So, receiving clear and consistent feedback helps to develop positive behaviors.

Families have tasks that need to be accomplished, but they also have social needs. An important function of parents is to socialize their children so that they are able to function in society. This is so that they can take care of themselves when they leave their family to live on their own. Families provide nurturing, emotional support, and encouragement to help them to develop a positive self-concept. They also need to enjoy themselves because no one wants to work all the time. Social roles help fulfill a families need for fun, relaxation, excitement, and adventure. This can include planning activities to have fun or relax to help relieve tension that can build up in families.

It can be helpful for a couple to have a united front to avoid any overlap of authority that could cause confusion or conflict with children. While a common approach is for couples to divide things equally, it may be more effective for each of them to have their own areas of influence. For instance, a couple could determine their desired outcomes, then each would have their own areas of responsibility. This makes it less likely for children to try a divide and conquer approach if one parent says one thing and the other says something different.

Family commitment.

Commitment is the degree to which family members feel close, help one another, and are willing to sacrifice their own needs for those of the family and other members. Families generally have a higher degree of commitment than other groups because they share common experiences, culture, religion, and space. Commitment fosters loyalty, support, nurturing, and caring for one another. These are encouraged because of the high degree of self-disclosure that can reduce uncertainty to create trust and predictability. Commitment motivates family members to identify with their family and consider themselves to be a part of it for their entire life.

Families have a high degree of commitment giving them the confidence to make sacrifices, work hard, and support the family without necessarily expecting anything in return. We are comfortable making long term investments giving our family stability. Families have strong connections so they work together for their mutual benefit. Because of the high level of investment, people often feel closest to their family members. But a high level of investment can also be a source of high levels of tension and conflict.

Family members connect when they spend time together. They can share their thoughts and feelings or get help solving their problems. Doing this helps parents understand what their children are thinking and to check their perceptions and expectations, so that they are realistic. They can ask other family members for their advice to solve problems and help them to make decisions. This is how we show nurturing and support by creating closeness and commitment in relationships through the law of shared meaning. Doing this helps us build a positive self-concept making others feel valued and appreciated.

Family members may wait until there's a problem, emergency, or even a crisis before they talk with one another. They may only talk to each other or altogether as a group whenever something comes up. They may begin by saying, "We need to talk." Everyone knows this means that there is a problem. This approach can make communicating between family members stressful and negative because they wait until they have bad news. In order to avoid communicating being perceived as a bad thing, families can have regular times where everyone gets together to talk.

Families and food naturally go together. Food is an integral part of traditions and rituals like when families celebrate holidays and other important events. Many types of food are associated with a specific culture, ethnicity, or geographic region. This makes food an important part of a family's history, culture, ethnicity, and geographic affiliation. Preparing meals is part of what it means to be a family because it creates connections that bring people closer together. It has become all too easy to eat something out of a microwave by ourselves. Instead, by cooking and baking from basic ingredients, children can learn about how food is made and why it's important.

It can be helpful for families to spend time together preparing meals because doing this can fulfill many important needs in addition to making something to eat. Doing this can help to reduce uncertainty by encouraging family members to talk to each other. It can help them to share meaning because food is often connected to our past experiences, traditions, and heritage. It promotes investing in one another because we are spending time together. Preparing food is an activity that promotes conversation. Cooking and baking teaches children important life skills because everyone needs to know how to take care of themselves and their family. It teaches children how to follow a plan, how to budget, and how to choose and buy ingredients. It teaches them about food and where it comes from. Everyone likes to eat, so cooking together can be a fun family activity. Then the family can sit down to share and enjoy what they made together.

Families can develop activities that bring everyone together. It can be a time for them to talk to one another without the pressure of having 'a talk.' They could make their own greeting cards for birthdays, anniversaries, or holidays. This is one way for children and parents to spend time together. It is something that they can enjoy and be proud of for many years. Another activity is to make a book of rules for the family. All families have rules and children often try to get around them. They may not be aware of the rules or don't understand them. Making a family book of rules can help children to better understand the rules and have input into making them, which can make them more likely to follow them.

Family tension.

Relationships can be perceived as being hard work because they are often a source of tension. Tension can come from differing perceptions and expectations. Each person may expect to do things their way, so they are constantly struggling with each other. Tension may come from unfulfilled or competing needs and wants. It may come from the perception of not getting fair rewards for fair contributions. The feeling that a relationship is hard work may be an indicator of underlying problems stemming from struggles over control, power, or allocation of resources. Developing clear norms, roles, and rules can help to relieve tension to help a family become more effective.

Families can be one of our biggest sources of tension due to conflicting or unfulfilled needs and wants. This is because of the nature of our relationships. We are often very close to other family members not only emotionally, but also living in close proximity. Families, like individuals, have conflicting needs and wants that can be a source of tension. Family members need to spend time together, but they also need their own space. They need to feel a part of the family, but also have their own individual identity. They compete for resources such as having their own room, space, and possessions.

Families allocate resources and there are often more needs and wants than a family has the resources to fulfill. This means that families have to make decisions and create priorities that can be potential sources of tension. It can be helpful to have an awareness of the sources of tension and utilize decision making and problem solving approaches to find one that reduces it. Having family members involved in making the decisions that affect them shows that they are valued. They are more likely to support a decision if they understand why it was made and they are part of the process. When they know the criteria and reasons for making a decision it can help to reduce tension.

An effort should be made to resolve tension before it undermines a relationship. Having awareness of one another's perceptions, expectations, needs, and wants happens when family members communicate on a regular basis. Some things may be difficult to talk about, but talking about them is better than letting them take control of a relationship. Communicating helps to avoid situations where one person feels like they are guessing what others are thinking that can make a relationship feel like hard work. Using effective communicating skills gives each person options on how to deal with difficulties like resolving tension and conflict. By using problem solving and decision making techniques described in Chapter 4, family members can work these things out in a way that brings them closer together.

Family change.

Change is inevitable and unavoidable in families. It can be predictable and can be beneficial or it can be unpredictable and potentially detrimental. It is helpful for families to develop their own mechanisms for change, so that they can make choices about what kind of change they want. Managing change can help create a predictable process that can develop new ideas without undermining the family structure and stability.

Families can change when new members join or they merge with other families through marriage. When two families come together they may have differing social realities based upon culture, ethnicity, religion, geographic affiliation, or other factors that can be a source of tension or conflict. Each family may compete against the other with individual members taking sides in order to gain power to get their way. It can be difficult if one group tries to dominate the others because this can lead to feelings of discontent and even hostility. One approach to resolve this tension is to take elements from different cultures within each family and combine them. A family might develop its own rituals to create new traditions developing its own culture. This gives everyone a say in the process, which helps them to support it.

Popular culture has created the expectation that when a child turns eighteen they should leave home. Adult children who do not leave home or return later to live with their parents are often characterized by the media as losers or social misfits. This is an unrealistic characterization that needlessly undermines family structure and commitment. It increases uncertainty because leaving home can be difficult at any age. Instead, families should determine what works best for them.

Throughout most of history, and even today in many cultures and countries, there are not the same expectations for children to leave home. Instead, they stay a part of a multigenerational family that might include not only grown children, but also elderly parents and grandparents living together in one household. This has numerous benefits including lowering costs for living expenses, which can help save money increasing financial security. This also provides family members support in ways that are more difficult to do if they live apart.

As our parents get older, living with their adult children allows them to be cared for rather than sending them to an institution where they are in unfamiliar surroundings. When families stay together, they are able to provide resources for one another to fulfill mutual needs and wants.

People come together to create families, but they also separate from each other breaking up families. This happens in many ways such as members leaving home, divorce, and death. We are constantly forming and ending relationships throughout our lives. Some end slowly over time as people fade away and some end suddenly and dramatically. Families usually have greater longevity than other relationships. Whenever a member leaves the family, like a child leaving home or a parent in a separation or divorce, the other family members need to renegotiate their relationships because the roles and responsibilities of the member who leaves has to be picked up by the remaining members.

Change can be especially difficult if all the children have left home and a couple is now all by themselves. This can be a difficult adjustment because it changes how they communicate, their roles, rules, and norms. Instead of focusing on the children, they now return to focusing on one another. While this may be perceived as a good thing, it may also become a source of uncertainty, tension, or conflict. So, it's helpful for couples to plan ahead for how things will change so that they can be prepared.

Marital deterioration.

Uncertainty can contribute to the deterioration or dissolution of a relationship. Problems can develop slowly over time until they seem too big to resolve. By then it may be difficult to determine when they began or what to do about them. This is why regular relational maintenance can be helpful in preventing potential problems. All relationships go through rough patches, but if they are lasting longer than usual or feel different it may be an indication that the relationship is deteriorating. If there are more unresolved problems or decisions than normal, it can increase tension and conflict. A couple may be spending more time apart or with other people than together. They may treat outsiders as more important than one another. They may no longer do things like they used to do. They may look to others outside the relationship for needs and wants fulfillment. They might find someone else to talk to, to confide in, or for support.

There can be times when a relationship might feel like hard work leaving people feeling frustrated, angry, or that something is not right, but not knowing why. While anything worthwhile requires an investment of time and energy, it doesn't necessarily mean it has to be hard work. If it feels like that, perhaps it's time to look at what is going on in the relationship from a new perspective. Working harder may not help, it might even make things worse. For example, if you have problems giving a speech in public you don't work harder doing the same things, you learn skills to help you communicate more effectively so it becomes easier. Getting at the source by increasing awareness and utilizing options to develop more effective communicating skills can help.

Relational deterioration can be a time of intense emotions with increased uncertainty. It can create a crisis within a family and crisis strategies in Chapter 4 can be helpful in coping with this situation. Stressing positive messages and avoiding unnecessary negative ones can help create a more realistic atmosphere rather than one of panic or uncertainty. During a time of transition it can be helpful to seek out support from other family members and friends. Regardless of the underlying disagreements or extreme emotions it's important to keep things as stable as possible for the rest of the family.

Separation and divorce can be very traumatic because it increases uncertainty not just for a couple, but also for the rest of the family. It can change the family structure including roles, rules, and norms. It can change the meanings that family members share. It can be stressful creating tension and conflict. So, it can be helpful to talk with other family members about what is going on and what will happen in the future in order to reduce uncertainty. Divorce represents the end of a significant investment in a relationship with another person. This can motivate some people to want material benefits like money, a house, or alimony in return for their investment. They may feel they are entitled because they have contributed years of their time and energy to the relationship.

We get married and form families to help us fulfill many of our needs and wants by making connections with others that divorce can sever. This creates uncertainty as now other sources need to be found to fulfill these needs or they go unfulfilled. We confide our thoughts and feelings in a spouse, so after a divorce we may no longer be as comfortable doing this. This can lead to our feeling that there is no longer the safety and security that once existed in our life. These needs and wants not only apply to couples, but also to the rest of the family who may feel like they are losing something important.

Divorce can affect relationships with others in their communicating networks, like with friends and family. Married couples often have married couple friends. In a divorce they may find these friends more distant and may even lose touch with them. This can be due to increased uncertainty that might make others look at their own marriage in ways they don't want to, exposing their own relational problems. They may feel that if their friends can get divorced it could happen to them as well, and that can be uncomfortable.

As couples and family members get older, uncertainty increases because of the potential for unknown events that may happen. A family faces new issues such as retirement, health concerns, and changing needs and wants. Children can find themselves taking over the role of caregiver to their parents. This changes the nature of the relationship as power and authority moves from parents to their children. As people live longer, more children are facing the responsibility of caring for their own elderly parents. This means that there may come a time when the rules and responsibilities that have been stable for most of their lives now need to be changed creating increased uncertainty and tension. By having an awareness that these things can happen and how uncertainty affects us, options can be planned in advance to reduce uncertainty to make the transition smoother.

Conflict

Conflict has been used to describe everything from disagreements to war. There are personal conflicts, sports conflicts, even armed conflicts. Conflict can be a disagreement where two or more people are at crossed purposes with incompatible objectives. It often involves some kind of struggle, perhaps even taking physical action. Conflict is used as a literary device between two characters who are at crossed purposes overcoming obstacles which motivates their actions to drive the plot forward making the story more interesting and exciting.

There are many different ways that we use the word conflict. For the purpose of this book, conflict takes place through verbal and nonverbal communicating between two or more people. It is more than just a difference of opinion or expression of personal preferences. It involves making decisions and taking action to achieve a desired outcome with some kind of resolution. Conflict is a natural part of all of our relationships, which is why it is in the chapter on relationships. Conflict can happen not only in families, but almost anywhere including at home, at work, in relationships, in groups, in organizations, and in society.

People sometimes say that they have an internal conflict or that they feel conflicted. This is not the same thing as a conflict. An internal conflict is the inability to make a decision. Feeling conflicted can be an expression of a moral dilemma about something we may not feel is right. For example, we may feel conflicted about going golfing when we feel that we should be spending time with our family. This is not so much an actual conflict, but rather a tension between competing needs and wants.

How much time and energy do you spend avoiding conflict? If you are like most people, you probably spend some time and energy trying to avoid conflicts with others. Because of the law of uncertainty, conflict is inevitable and unavoidable. It is a natural part of life created by tension between conflicting or competing needs and wants in our interactions with others. We try to avoid conflict because it's uncomfortable, however, doing so can create additional tensions and problems.

In order to handle conflict more effectively, it can be helpful to understand how it works and what can be done when it occurs. We can better understand how conflicts arise in order to avoid the unnecessary ones and limit the severity of others. Conflict can bolster or hurt our self-concept depending on how we approach it. Having options and communicating skills can help you feel that you have done everything possible to resolve it even if you don't achieve your desired outcome.

Just as there is no one right way to communicate, there is no one right approach to conflict. All conflicts are different because they are based upon the issues, circumstances, and the people involved. We first learn how to handle conflict as children by observing the examples of our parents and other family members. Children might learn how to win conflicts and get their way by throwing tantrums or crying. When they become an adult they learn that these tactics don't work so well. People can learn conflict skills by making mistakes through trial and error, but this can leave them feeling unhappy about how they handled a conflict, even if they got their way.

We may emulate the habits and familiar patterns for dealing with conflict that we learn from our parents and other family members. This is because it is in our family that we will first learn how to negotiate relationships that can establish patterns we might keep for our entire life. We may emulate the example of our parents when we have our own family in how we handle conflict. How conflicts are handled might be contained in the rules that govern our relationships like what topics are off limits, never going to bed angry, or not raising your voice in the house.

Conflict is often a result of the law of uncertainty. It can happen when there is uncertainty about tasks, rules, norms, responsibilities, or how resources are allocated. When a desired outcome is unclear it creates a higher degree of uncertainty about what to do and who should do it. Conflict is a result of unresolved issues so the future outcome is undecided which can be uncomfortable increasing uncertainty. It can be helpful to separate the actual conflict from other types of uncertainty to reduce tension. The need to reduce uncertainty can be a source of motivation for people to work together to resolve their conflict.

When we communicate with others we share meaning with them, however, meanings are not always clear, which can lead to misunderstandings. Conflicts can occur over the meaning of information, the importance of that information, and how it should be used in making decisions. They occur over our priorities, behaviors, and what we value. We look for meaning in people's behavior to explain why they start conflicts and what they really want from them. We invest conflict itself with meaning often characterizing it in negative terms.

The law of investing motivates us to invest in relationships, in groups, and in society. However, there are times when we might feel that our investment is threatened. Conflict often involves allocation of resources and competing interests because we have limited resources to satisfy potentially unlimited needs and wants. This sets up conditions for conflict as to how those needs and wants are fulfilled. Conflict often happens because there is something at stake. People can be motivated to disagree or create conflict because they feel that they have something invested and this is how they can get what they want. They may initiate a conflict in order to protect their investment because they feel that they are losing something.

Conflict can provide a means of investing in relationships. If a conflict is handled well, it can help people feel closer because they overcame difficulties together. Conversely, if a conflict is not handled well, it can damage a relationship resulting in a loss of trust undermining their investment in it. A positive outcome is more likely if the people involved have a process or mechanism by which they can handle conflict while still maintaining their commitment to the relationship.

We all have different needs and wants, many of which are in conflict with one another as well as with those of others. For example, our family may feel that we need to spend time with them when we want to spend time by ourselves creating tension or conflict. Our needs and wants can be a major source of conflict because we have to negotiate with others in order to fulfill many of them and they may not be willing to cooperate with us. Developing skills can help us to handle the tension created by these opposing needs and wants to help us achieve our desired outcome.

How we view conflict is based upon our perceptions and expectations, which are shaped by our past experiences. This can make it easy to have a distorted perception of conflict that does not reflect reality, so we might overreact making the situation worse. If we have the perception that we are not good at handling conflict, it may affect our behavior making us unsure or hesitant, so that our perception becomes a reality.

This makes it important for us to check our perceptions to make sure that they are accurate by seeking out information to clarify the situation. We may have unrealistic, overly optimistic expectations that can make reaching a resolution more difficult. Developing communicating skills helps us handle conflicts with realistic expectations to come to a resolution. Having accurate perceptions helps to create realistic expectations, which can help to reduce the uncertainty and apprehension that is a natural part of conflict.

An important communicating skill is developing options to handle conflict in order to fulfill our needs and wants, and achieve our desired outcomes. Just as we have our own individual style of communicating, we have our own approach to conflict. It can be helpful to have an awareness of how you usually approach conflict. All too often when a conflict arises we go on autopilot and turn into a person we probably would not recognize or want to be. We may jump to conclusions, make assumptions, get angry, or act out against others. While this is a natural tendency, improving our awareness helps us to know how we are coming across to others, so that we can take a more positive and constructive approach. This gives us more options to increase our chances of a successful resolution.

Conflict has an intensity that brings out emotional responses that can make us react less rationally resulting in unintended or undesired outcomes. We can get carried away in the moment defending ourselves or attack the other person escalating the emotional intensity of the situation. It can be helpful in conflict situations to take a moment and pause to consider your desired outcome. Is your desired outcome to escalate the situation and perhaps damage the relationship, or is it to work out a reasonable solution?

By pausing for a moment to consider your desired outcome, you can reduce the emotional intensity of the situation to increase your awareness and consider your options. By not responding to others with the same intensity, you do not give them a reason to continue to fight. Instead, they are forced to actually talk about the issues improving the chances for resolution.

Conflict resolution.

We have all experienced conflict, so it can be helpful to look at it in a new way. While we all want to get our way in a conflict, the reality is that we can't get it all of the time. Sometimes we get what we want and other times we don't. Then there are those conflicts that never seem to go away, so we need to find a way to manage them. Just as we consider the effectiveness of how we communicate, consider the effectiveness of resolving conflict. This helps to avoid thinking in terms like good or bad and win or lose, so we can find something positive in a conflict even if we don't achieve our desired outcome. This does not mean that the issues are necessary resolved our way, but instead the tension surrounding them is resolved or at least reduced.

Conflict is often perceived as something bad to be avoided. We often think that conflicts are something we should not be proud of because it is a personal shortcoming or failing. For the most part these perceptions are not true. Conflict can be constructive or destructive depending on how we handle it, whether we get what we want or not. It can be constructive when it utilizes effective communicating skills because it helps people reduce uncertainty, share meaning, invest in one another, and gain new insights in order to achieve something better than they might have accomplished individually.

Conflict can be harmful when it inhibits us from gaining new insights and information. It can increase uncertainty when it prevents us from changing or finding new ways of doing things that may be better. It can be harmful when it damages our self-concept or hurts our relationships. It can be frustrating when it prevents effective problem solving or reaching the best possible solution or desired outcome. By understanding how we communicate in a conflict, we can minimize its harmful affects and focus on the helpful ones.

We have all experienced conflict and how we feel about it depends upon our past experiences. By understanding how conflict works, we can respond to it in a new way to manage it more effectively. It helps us to question our assumptions, check our perceptions, and evaluate our expectations so they are more realistic. In order to resolve conflict, it can be helpful to consider the other person's point of view to see things their way. We should consider the possibility that they may have a point or may be right. This does not mean that we will agree with them, we do this to gain insights to find a better solution.

Groups and individuals might use conflict with other groups and individuals to increase their members' commitment to the group or to a cause. When one group has a conflict with another, its members can be more likely to work together for the common good to pursue their mutual desired outcomes. Group members can be less likely to criticize one another or their leader if they have a common threat to overcome. If people have a common adversary, they can become more dedicated to the group and the group's goals. They are more likely to work harder and provide more resources to achieve their desired outcomes. This can motivate some groups or leaders to fabricate or exploit a common adversary or conflict that might not otherwise exist, or be as severe, just to motivate their members to increase their commitment and contributions to the group.

Working together in difficult circumstances can be helpful to bring people closer together. This is because shared experiences can create meanings that strengthen relationships. Whether the outcome is positive or not, working through conflict can make people feel more connected. People are motivated by the law of shared meaning to talk about their experiences with others because it helps invest them with meaning. By working through a conflict together, people can develop trust so that they are more likely to invest in their relationship.

When we successfully resolve a conflict it can improve our self-concept. However, if we don't resolve it in a way that we are comfortable with, it can undermine or even damage our self-concept. If we use effective communicating skills, act in a professional manner, and feel that we have done our best even if the outcome is not what we had hoped for, we can still feel good about ourselves bolstering our self-concept because we know we have done the best we could do under the circumstances. We know that not all conflicts will work out the way we want, so when a conflict does not work, we can at least use it as a means to improve our communicating skills.

While we cannot necessarily control the outcome of a conflict, what we say and do can determine whether it becomes destructive or constructive. It can be helpful to utilize confidence and competence. Confidence is the belief that we have in ourselves and our ability. Competence is our ability to utilize effective communicating skills and act in a professional manner. By being confident we can help to avoid feeling threatened, which can lead to emotional responses such as defensiveness or hostility. By being confident and having a positive attitude, we can influence how others perceive us and how they respond to the conflict. By taking a calm and controlled approach, others are more likely to be encouraged to follow our lead because they likely want to be perceived as being professional and open minded whether they are or not.

Conflicts can be created when people are resistant to change or making decisions. If things are going well we may not look for change or try anything new because there's no motivation. Change can be difficult when it increases uncertainty, which is uncomfortable and we do not like being uncomfortable. This is because we do not know for sure what the outcome will be, but we know for sure what the current situation is like making it more attractive. Some conflicts can be more uncomfortable than uncertainty motivating us to resolve it, which can result in our having to make changes that might otherwise not have been made.

Conflict intensity.

Not all conflicts are the same. Some are superficial while others are more intense. The intensity is determined by the nature of the conflict, its source, what's at stake, and the determination of those involved. Conflicts can vary based upon their depth and breadth. Depth is the intensity of the conflict, how deep individual feelings go, or how willing people are to dig in their heels and fight to win. The breadth of a conflict is the scope or number of issues that are involved, which can range from one to many. In determining your options for the most effective approach, it can be helpful to ascertain these two dimensions to determine the scope of the actual issues.

There are different kinds of conflicts that vary depending on the issues involved. Some conflicts are based on a difference of perceptions or expectations. These are common and usually rather easy to resolve. A difference of opinion involves a different point of view including differences of meaning, how to use resources, or what actions to take. These conflicts can usually be resolved with some effort. Disagreements are more intense conflicts that involve issues like needs and wants, perceptions and expectations, and desired outcomes. These may require extra effort and resources to resolve.

More serious conflicts can involve multiple issues. They have a greater depth because those involved are more likely to be motivated to stick to their position and fight it out. These conflicts can last for long periods of time and involve not only individuals, but also groups and organizations. They are usually about deeper issues like values, beliefs, and shared meanings. The most serious conflicts can involve a struggle, litigation, or physical outcomes. These often involve complex issues and may last a long period of time. They often need formal methods of resolution by third parties.

Sources of conflict.

In order to effectively resolve a conflict, it's helpful to identify its source. Sometimes they are easily identifiable and other times they can be difficult to determine. A conflict may start with one issue and then spill over into others. Sometimes people create conflict in one area to cover up the real issue in another. They may be uncomfortable or unwilling to discuss the true source of the problem and may get upset when someone asks them about it. Just as everyone communicates for a reason, people engage in conflicts for a reason. To help successfully resolve a conflict, it can be helpful to know their reason or motivation. Everyone has their own motivation for starting and pursuing conflicts as well as resolving them. While this may not always seem logical or rational, it's because they are motivated by their own reasoning, not yours.

We are motivated by the law of uncertainty to reduce uncertainty, however, we may not agree with others about how to do it. Conflicts can arise from the law of shared meaning. When we get new information we give it meaning to make it useful to us. We may share meaning, but disagree about how to interpret it or use it. Since this is based upon our personal perceptions, these conflicts can be more difficult to resolve as they can affect our self-concept. We might disagree about what we value and what that value should be. Values can be based on deeply held beliefs that can make these types of conflicts difficult to resolve because they are a part of our self-concept and personal social reality.

We have many needs and wants that we are motivated to fulfill and some can be contradictory or conflict with one another. For instance, we want to spend time with others, but we also want to have time to ourselves. We want to work, but also have fun. This makes for conflicts between needs and wants we cannot fulfill at the same time. So, we have to make choices and set priorities that can create a conflict because others may see things differently. This is why we are likely to have conflicts in our relationships over needs and wants fulfillment, allocating material and social rewards, using time and space, and determining roles and responsibilities.

We all have different perceptions and expectations about ourselves and others. Our differences in perception can be a source of conflict including how we interpret facts, definitions, events, and other types of information. Most of the time these conflicts are relatively easy to resolve. Different expectations can be a source of conflict particularly when they involve what we expect of others or what they expect of us. These can be more difficult to resolve because we may be unwilling or unable to meet their expectations or they meet ours. Conflicts arise when others prevent us from achieving our desired outcome. These conflicts can be difficult to resolve because they involve fulfilling needs and wants.

Life is full of decisions to be made and problems to be solved. We can have conflicts over what constitutes a problem, what information is needed to solve it, what methods should be used to solve it, and how to implement it. We often have conflicts over power such as who has the authority to make decisions and who is responsible for carrying them out. For example, we may come into conflict with our coworkers over roles, norms, responsibilities, or how to utilize time or space. These conflicts can be resolved by clarifying who is responsible for doing what tasks and letting others take responsibility for themselves.

If we cannot determine the source of a conflict we might say it's a personality conflict. This might mean that there is not a substantive issue at stake or it's just two people who don't get along. Other times there's no particular reason at all. These conflicts can be emotional in nature making them difficult to resolve because they involve an individual's self-concept. The best approach is to focus on the task at hand and not on individual personalities.

Stages of conflict.

Depending upon the individuals and issues involved, conflicts can go through a series of stages. It can be helpful to be aware of these stages and how they work to determine the best approach for resolution. Generally, the earlier conflict can be recognized and addressed the more likely it is to be satisfactorily resolved. If the conflict is not addressed early on, it can intensify as people may take more entrenched positions making it more difficult to reach a resolution. Because of the law of investing, the more time and energy people invest in their position the more difficult it can be to reach a resolution.

- Preconflict. This is the situation before the conflict is noticed when everything is normal. Conflicts can arise very quickly over a single event or they can build more slowly over time through many events. Since conflicts can begin without our being aware of them, it can be helpful to check our perceptions and expectations from time to time to see if everything is all right. By talking to others, asking questions, and verifying our perceptions and expectations we can conduct a kind of relational preventative maintenance to reduce the potential of a conflict occurring.

• Conflict escalation. At some point in time things go from being normal to not being normal. We may have an awareness or a feeling that there is a problem, but cannot ascertain what it is. There may be a growing dissatisfaction, disagreement, or frustration that can turn into a conflict. One person should communicate that they have a conflict, so that both parties are aware of the conflict and that something needs to be done to resolve it. This is usually the best time to try to resolve it, however, all too often it either goes ignored or it escalates.

• Conflict stabilization. At this stage everyone involved knows that a conflict exists. As soon as you are aware of it, it's helpful to identify the source and the issues involved. It's helpful not to escalate a conflict, but rather to isolate it by determining its depth and breadth. It's helpful to limit its intensity because one conflict can cause others making things more difficult to resolve. Once these are determined, it should be easier to develop an approach to reaching a resolution that everyone can support. The more the people involved are motivated to resolve it, the more likely they are to come to a resolution. However, there are times when conflict benefits people by providing them support and resources which can reduce their motivation to resolve it.

• Conflict resolution. This stage can be reached quickly or it can take some time depending upon how willing everyone is to resolve it. Resolution begins with the mutual awareness of the nature of the conflict and the options available to resolve it. It helps to develop communicating skills so that each party has an increased awareness of the other person's position. In order to resolve a conflict, each person should to be open the possibility that they may be wrong and the other person may be right, at least in part. We often have a personal investment in our positions, so any resolution other than what we want could hurt our self-concept. In order to avoid this, it's helpful to look at the issues without getting personal by discussing them objectively. Have everyone express their position verbally because some conflicts arise out of the need to be heard and acknowledged by others. Decision making and problem solving approaches in Chapter 4 can help.

• Post conflict. Just because a resolution is reached does not necessarily mean that the conflict is over. There are often things that need to be done as part of a resolution. People may have the perception that a conflict is resolved, but then there is no follow up to see that the solution was properly implemented. This can lead to a future resurgence of the conflict. It's helpful to follow up to make sure the conflict is resolved well enough so that it does not reoccur. It can be useful to evaluate the effectiveness of the approach to determine its usefulness in future conflicts. We can improve our communicating skills by evaluating the effectiveness of the resolution to determine what went well and what could be done better in the future.

Approaches to conflict.

We have all experienced conflict. There were probably times you felt good about the outcome and other times not so good. The approach that was taken may be the reason why. Just as we have our own style of communicating, we have our own style of handling conflict. Since there is no one right way to handle conflict, having options can be helpful to achieve an effective outcome. How we respond to conflict can affect how we feel about it. Some approaches we might take in response to a conflict include direct, indirect, and confrontational approaches. Some of these approaches are more effective than others. Some are not recommended, but are included because they are often used so it is helpful to be aware of them. Awareness of these approaches can give you more options to help resolve conflicts.

Direct conflict approaches.

We utilize these approaches when we want to directly address a conflict or its issues. These approaches involve working together with others to find a resolution. While these can be effective approaches to resolving conflicts, it's helpful to be aware that not everyone will respond as you hope they will.

- Accommodating. We often accommodate others when we value our relationship with them. We might do this if someone has a higher status or more power than us, like our boss. We might accommodate someone because we do not want to deal with them. People might accommodate others when they feel a conflict is not worth the time and effort, they may be afraid of them, or they feel they won't get what they want. While this may not achieve your desired outcome, it can be a way to cut your losses and end the issue. You can benefit because the conflict is over and you no longer have the stress or tension associated with it.

- Cooperation. When people cooperate they work together to fulfill mutual needs and wants. They put aside their individual goals and concentrate on achieving a desired outcome for mutual benefit. This approach works best when the individuals involved want to maintain a cordial relationship.

- Consensus. A conflict can be more easily resolved when everyone agrees on a solution. This approach encourages everyone to work out a solution that they can support. It is often used when there is social pressure for everyone to agree because one person would not want to be perceived as going against the others.

- Compromise. This is when everybody gives up something they want in order to reach a resolution. This word can have a negative connotation because it gives the impression that you have to give up something of importance or value.

- Voting. When other methods do not work, the last resort may be to take a vote. While voting is the most democratic means of resolving conflict, it can be the least satisfactory because it can create friction between people who vote against each other.

- Cooling off period. Some conflicts create an emotional intensity that needs to be reduced before it can be addressed. In these circumstances it can be helpful to have a cooling off period to reduce the emotional intensity, so that everyone can look at things more objectively at a later date.

Indirect conflict approaches.

We utilize indirect approaches when we do not want to directly address a conflict. These can involve more posturing than seeking a resolution. While these are not good approaches to resolving conflicts, it's helpful to be aware of how they work because they are widely used.

- Avoidance. While avoidance is not usually considered an effective approach, the reality is that there are some circumstances where it works. It can be used when there is little to gain or the cost of conflict may be too great. Sometimes people use conflict for intimidation, harassment, or manipulation, so avoidance may be the best approach. It may be necessary when a conflict could damage a relationship or where there is little chance of a positive resolution.

- Doing nothing. This is a common approach that results in the conflict not being resolved. If the conflict is not serious, it may eventually die out over time as people lose interest in it. However, doing nothing gives the perception of not caring, which can potentially make the conflict worse. Doing nothing is different than avoidance because avoidance generally involves taking some action to get out of the way of the other person.

- Denial. People may deny that a conflict exists or that there is any problem. They may do this hoping it will go away. They may even act sympathetic. If they do admit there's a problem, they do nothing to help resolve it.

- Ignore. When we want to discuss a conflict, others may change the subject or refuse to talk about it at all. They may do this because they feel if they do not talk about it then it doesn't exist, so they don't have to deal with it. Sometimes people do not acknowledge a conflict or even the other person. Ignoring someone can be used to punish them by not recognizing their existence.

- Apathetic. There are times when people cause conflicts and don't seem to care about the consequences, the other person, and sometimes even themselves. They may do this because they are fearful of the outcome, they may be apprehensive about developing a meaningful relationship, or they may be overwhelmed by dealing with too many problems.

- Delaying. Putting something off is a common tactic to avoid conflict. They might say they want to fix things, but keep delaying doing anything about it. People put things off in hopes that the other person gets tired or forgets about it. The longer it is dragged out, the less likely the other person will invest time to resolve it.

- Confidence. People may not step up to resolve a conflict because they have a lack of confidence, skills, or awareness of their options. They may feel that it is easier just to go along with whatever everyone else decides. They may feel it's better to keep the peace than to fight.

- Abandonment. Sometimes people don't want anything to do with the conflict, so they hand it over to someone else to deal with it or they may walk away. This can happen when someone feels overwhelmed or that they have no chance of getting what they want.

- Humor. This is used as a means to defuse tension or avoid taking responsibility. In some conflicts people use humor to make fun of or joke about someone as a way of communicating their problems or conflicts.

- Placating. The purpose of this approach is to please the other person instead of finding an equitable resolution. It is used in conflicts when one person may have a fear of conflict, rejection, or of the other person. They may do this if they feel they don't have a good case, the other person is more powerful, or they want something else in return later.

- Obligation. This involves motivating others to do something out of a sense of duty or loyalty. They may have done someone a favor and now want something in return. While doing things for others can be a good thing, some people might use it to persuade others to do things they might not want to do.

- Emotion. People use emotional appeals because they engender strong feelings in others to persuade them to do what they want. A common approach is using guilt to make the other person feel that they are somehow responsible for the problem.

- Calculating. This is the opposite of emotional approach because it is characterized by the lack of emotion. Calculating treats conflict as a game and people as pawns, where the objective is to vanquish the opponent to win.

- Blaming. Instead of looking to resolve the conflict, one person blames the other for the problem to shift the responsibility off them on to someone else.

- Martyrdom. This is the opposite of blaming. It is a form of self sacrifice where one person takes responsibility for the conflict and is willing to pay the price. They may portray themselves as unjustly persecuted in order to gain sympathy. While this might be considered manipulation, it can work because it plays on people's good nature.

- Sufficing. This is when people do something easy that suffices for working out a real solution. They take the easiest solution whether it works or not. While this is a poor way to resolve conflict, it is done surprisingly often.

- Bargaining. This approach treats conflict like deal making where people trade one concession for another. They may ask for things they don't want, so that they can give them up giving the illusion of making concessions.

- Distracting. This approach works by creating another problem or crisis that diverts attention away from the real conflict. It is based on the assumption that if another situation is perceived as worse, people will forget about the conflict because they have only so much time and energy.

- Repetition. Some people approach conflict by repeating the same thing over and over until the other person gives up or others start to believe them. When something is repeated over and over, it can take on a validity of its own whether it is correct or not.

- Coexisting. This is when both parties acknowledge the conflict, but it is not resolved. They agreed to do different things for a period of time to see how it goes. This approach can be used when an agreement cannot be reached.

- Covert. When people have a conflict or problem with someone, instead of telling them they go behind their back and tell others, so they may never be aware of it. They may tell others about the problem to gain their sympathy or turning others against them. Since they do not know there is a problem they don't do anything about it, so they might tell others they don't care. If the other person does find out and confronts them, they may act as if everything is fine. Some people do this because they feel they cannot win by conventional means so they try to discredit, sabotage, or hurt others. They may do this to put pressure on the other person to get what they want.

- Subversive. This happens when a conflict has been resolved, but one party refuses to accept that they have lost, so they keep on pressing their case to try to get their way or undermine the outcome. If they can't win on their merit they will try to attack their opponent personally, and if that fails they attack the process. Some versions of this approach includes using protests, boycotts, harassment, recalls, or litigation.

Confrontational conflict approaches.

Confrontational approaches to conflict often use power, control, or manipulation to impose one person's will on others to force them into a resolution. Winning can become more important than working out a resolution or preserving the relationship. This approach is often one sided leaving the losing party feeling defeated. While these are not good approaches to conflict, it is surprising how often they are used.

- Competition. Instead of trying to reach a mutually satisfactory resolution, some people see conflict as a competition they must win. They are out to achieve their desired outcome regardless of the cost. This can be useful when a quick decision is needed like in a crisis, however, it can do more damage or potentially escalate the conflict.

- Ambushing. This is a deceptive approach where one person listens to the other, but instead resolving the conflict they try to get the other person to say or do something that can be used against them.

- Leverage. This approach seeks to deny one person something they need or want unless the other person gets their way. For example, a person in a relationship may threaten to breakup in order to motivate the other person to do what they want.

- Confrontation. This approach uses power to intimidate, influence, punish, or manipulate others to get their way. People might be motivated to do this because they may not want to be perceived as weak or feel that they have something to lose.

- Control. Some people view conflict as a challenge to their authority, so they feel they need to exert control over others to win at all cost. The rationale is that if they compromise on one thing they may be forced to compromise on everything.

- Manipulation. This is the unethical use of power to force or trick people to support them. Manipulation can include appeals for sympathy, guilt, or fear. A series of rewards and punishments can be used in order to coerce others to do what they want.

- Blackmail. This is a specific form of manipulation that uses threats of retaliation to get the other person to do what they want. It can involve threats to reveal potentially embarrassing information. It can be withholding of something of value like fulfillment of needs and wants. It can be preventing them from doing something or achieving a desired outcome.

- Intimidation. This is motivating others to do something by harassing, belittling, or threatening them. It works by creating fear in their mind so they do what others want.

- Aggression. In resolving conflict, aggressiveness can be anything from being obsessive to physically threatening. This can make the other person feel humiliated, embarrassed, or fearful of retaliation.

- Anger. Conflict can become emotionally charged leading to verbal aggressiveness. People may get angry not only to vent their emotions, but to scare others to motivate them into doing what they want. Under these circumstances the best approach may be to stop and get away from the other person until things cool off.

- Self righteousness. Some people feel that they are always right about everything all the time. When faced with conflict, they may see it as a personal attack on them even though they are always concerned with everyone else's welfare.

- Force. Some conflicts are resolved by sheer force. Force can be mental, emotional, even physical. This approach is utilized when people think they can use power to control others to give up their position so they can get what they want.

- Shutting out. This is a more passive means of using force when one person tries to get their way by refusing to listen to others. They get their way by being closed off, shutting out the other person preventing them from doing anything.

- External forces. Some people use forces outside of themselves to justify their actions or to motivate others to give in to what they want. They may take the moral high ground, call on spiritual or religious doctrine, or claim they are doing a higher power's work so they can get their way.

- Panic. This is creating a false sense of urgency so others believe the conflict has to be immediately resolved to avert a crisis or disaster. This approach can force people to make quick decisions before they have the time to think them through. If they had more time they probably wouldn't go along. This approach can be used to manipulate others when they don't have a strong argument.

Conflict for conflict's sake approaches.

There are some instances when people start a conflict just for the sake of having one. Under these circumstances there is little hope of resolution, so it's best to stay away from them.

- Entertainment. Some people might create conflict for fun, entertainment, or excitement. They may have a need for power or control. These conflicts often have little substance, so there is no real solution. If someone is behaving like this, you might let them know how others perceive them. There may be other ways to meet these needs other than creating conflicts. This sometimes happens with adolescents, who may provoke conflicts to get people to notice them or to assert their independence.

- Conflict conflicts. Some people love a good fight, so they create conflicts to feel important or bolster their self-concept. They might use them as a means to prove that they are right, knowledgeable, or accomplished. Resolving these conflicts may be difficult because they never give up. The best approach is to avoid them.

Formal conflict resolution approaches.

When other approaches fail or when directly communicating with the other party is not a good idea, formal third party approaches can help facilitate a resolution. These approaches are a good alternative when our abilities, skills, or resources are not capable of reaching a satisfactory solution.

- Third party approaches. This approach uses intermediaries to reach a resolution. This can be useful in circumstances when direct contact with the other party is not effective. This can be a useful approach when there is emotional intensity or hostility between the parties. It can be used if there is a history of conflict or if the parties are not able to meet face to face.

- Rules approach. This approach uses written rules to resolve a conflict. It can be used when a solution needs to be impartial or objective. To reach a solution, everyone needs to agree on what rules apply and how to apply them. This approach is often used in sports or legal conflicts by using rules and laws for resolution.

- Formal approaches. These approaches to conflict resolution include arbitration, negotiation, mediation, and litigation. They often utilize outside experts who have a specific skill to help resolve the conflict like an attorney or mediator.

Conflict resolution skills.

Conflict resolution means bringing a conflict to an end. It does not necessarily mean that it is resolved the way you want it to be resolved. You may get what you want, only part of what you want, or nothing at all. Sometimes it's better to have it over and done with by cutting your losses and ending the conflict. Even if you don't get what you want, there can be benefits by no longer having to deal with the tension, stress, and frustration that can accompany a conflict. When it's over you can relax and forget about it. This can free up your time and energy to use on more fun and productive activities.

In order to effectively resolve a conflict, it is helpful to have an awareness of how you handle conflict to help identify what has worked and what could use improvement. Knowing this can give you options on how to approach conflict based upon the situation. Having choices of conflict skills gives you a better chance of using the most effective option to fit your situation. No one wins every conflict, but by having a variety of approaches and using communicating skills effectively, you can feel good about how you approach conflict regardless of the outcome.

The following are some approaches to give you options for conflict resolution.

- Utilize the law of uncertainty to reduce conflict. Determine what the conflict is actually about. There are times when people get into disagreements about something only to realize that they are both arguing the same position or about nothing substantial at all. Determine the scope of the issues. Then set boundaries to limit what is going to be discussed. This keeps the conflict from escalating. Determine if the conflict is worth spending your time and energy on before going any further because some conflicts are not worth the trouble.

- Reduce uncertainty by actually listening to what the other person is saying to avoid misunderstandings that can cause unnecessary conflict. Listening to what they have to say does not mean that you have to accept their position or even agree with it. Doing this can give you more information to understand the issues and the motivation for their behavior. If you expect others to listen to you, you must be willing to listen to them. They may know something that you are not aware of, so you might learn something. By clearly understanding their position you are better able to resolve the situation. All too often people assume they know the other person's position and end up fighting about nothing at all.

- Ask the other person questions to get more information to increase your understanding of the issues. This can divert their attention by getting them to talk. They may be taken off guard by this response, so they might not know how to respond. Doing this can help to avoid misunderstandings that could potentially make a conflict worse. Provide feedback by letting the other people know what you are thinking as long as it's positive and helps to resolve the problem. Describe the effects of the situation rather than making accusations or criticizing the other person.

- Reduce uncertainty by being prepared for conflict, so if you are faced with one you can stay calm and avoid the temptation to retaliate or escalate the conflict. It is a natural response to be defensive and respond with the same emotional intensity. However, this might intensify the conflict. It takes self control and practice to stay calm in high pressure situations. We plan for success in other situations, so why not be prepared for conflict. By being prepared you can develop skills that will help you when you need it.

- Have a plan in case conflict comes up unexpectedly. Sometimes people put others on the spot because that's how they think they will get what they want. They may try to take the other person by surprise to get their way. So, have a plan for conflict and be prepared or you may react out of habit or emotion, escalating the conflict. This can put you in a position you would rather not be in, making it less likely you will get a favorable resolution.

- Utilize the power of the law of shared meaning. Shared meaning can help resolve a conflict by making a connection with the other person. Look for shared meaning by finding something you have in common with the other person or something good to say about them. Utilizing shared meaning emphasizes what you have in common and downplays your differences. This can be helpful because coming to a resolution often begins by finding common ground.

- Utilize communicating skills by being aware of what others are saying and how you are coming across to them. Consider shared meanings in your nonverbal body language. We don't just communicate with what we say, but also how we say it. It is helpful to be aware of how you are coming across to others because they interpret your nonverbal information to try to understand you better. Be aware of how you express emotions to avoid saying something you might regret later. Avoid humor, while it can lighten the tension, it can give the impression you are not serious about the issue. Avoid making assumptions or jumping to conclusions about the other person because everyone has different abilities and skills, some people are better at expressing themselves than others.

- Put yourself in the other person's position to see the situation from their perspective. You do not have to agree with them, but it can help you to better understand them. Show respect and treat others the way you want to be treated. It shouldn't undermine your position to be polite and courteous or to show concern for the interests or feelings of others. Doing this can help because finding a resolution is not just up to you, it's also up to them.

- Use the law of investing to reach a resolution. Invest in a resolution by taking responsibility to resolve it. It can be easy to blame others to avoid taking any responsibility. Even if the conflict is not your fault, by being a part of the process you can be part of the solution. Offer leadership to help decide how to proceed, look for potential solutions, and offer a way to reach resolution. Leadership skills that can be helpful are found in Chapter 4. If you don't take an active role, you may find yourself being shut out or pushed into doing things that you do not want to do.

- Encourage others to invest in a resolution by acknowledging their position. This shows that you have listened to them and understand their position. This does not mean that you necessarily agree with them. Avoiding others or ignoring what they have to say can communicate that you do not care about them potentially making them more determined to get their way. By understanding the other person's position, you can appeal to their sense of fairness and what is in your mutual best interest. People can be more likely to reach a mutually accepted resolution if they feel that you are motivated out of concern for them as well as yourself.

- Consider how your relationship may be affected by the conflict. Some conflicts can damage or even destroy a relationship. Consider what you will gain compared to what you may lose. Ask yourself, is it more important to win the argument or preserve the relationship? It can be helpful to work with the other person to develop a means to resolve the conflict without damaging the relationship. A supportive relationship should be able to withstand conflict without damaging it.

- Consider your desired outcome. If someone confronts you they may expect you to react, so they will have likely prepared for you to defend yourself. So, if you don't get defensive, you can reduce the emotional intensity because they may not be expecting it. Consider your desired outcome, is it to escalate or resolve the conflict? It has been said, choose your battles wisely. We do not have the resources to fight every fight, defend every position, or accept every challenge. Consider what is at stake because some things are worth fighting for and others are not. You don't want to take on battles that could be costly with little chance of success. There should be no dishonor in a gracious retreat.

- Avoid the tendency to explain yourself under pressure. Whenever someone confronts us we have a natural tendency to want to explain ourselves to justify our actions. This can be perceived as being defensive or even an admission of guilt. It gives others more information, which is not what you want to do at this time. In more serious situations, do not give information to anyone in authority or who may be able to use that information against you later. Exercise your right to remain silent until you understand the situation and have had a chance to seek counsel or advice. Your desired outcome should be to get more information from them because if you are being attacked you should know why. The more information you can get, the better your chances are of reaching a resolution.

- Avoid stating your opinion as fact, instead express them as opinions or feelings. For instance, instead of saying, "You were wrong" say, "I had a feeling that was wrong." Feelings cannot be proven to be right or wrong because they are your own. Use descriptive rather than judgmental language. Rather than calling something bad use specific examples.

- Avoid getting dragged into other people's problems. Sometimes we get drawn into a conflict we would rather avoid. Just because someone else has a conflict does not mean you have to join in too. We may get involved in a conflict and then discover more serious underlying problems. If things aren't working out, by using communicating skills we can at least feel that we have tried everything possible. You have options when it comes to conflict and one option is to walk away.

- People don't always confront others in private, they can verbally attack others in places where other people are around. Stop to consider what those other people might say about you and what happened because you do not want to be perceived as being the aggressor.

Do not become defensive and attack them back, instead express your concern. Doing this makes you look confident and competent in front of others. If you attack an aggressor, regardless what they did to you, people are likely to sympathize with them because you retaliated even though you had every right to do so.

- Two skills that can help resolve a conflict are competence and confidence. Competence is your ability to communicate with others, having an awareness of the situation, and options for resolving a conflict. It is having an awareness of your skills and the ability to use them effectively. Confidence is having faith in yourself and your abilities. It is the ability to communicate effectively to help achieve your desired outcome. In a conflict, people are more likely to be receptive to someone who shows competence because they seem knowledgeable. People are likely to be persuaded by someone who is confident, because their demeanor helps to reduce uncertainty.

A process for resolving conflict.

It would be great if conflict resolution was always as simple as sitting down with someone to talk it over. While it can be nice when this happens, it is not always the case. There are some situations when it can be helpful to have an organized process to find a solution that is workable for everyone. When faced with a conflict people can have a natural tendency to react out of habit or emotion. By using an organized process to work through conflict, it can be resolved more effectively.

The following approaches can help provide options, so you can choose what will work best for you in your situation.

1. Formal or informal. When faced with a conflict there is a natural tendency to respond impulsively rather than thinking things through. This is not necessarily a good approach. Having an organized process to work out a conflict shows that you are taking it seriously to find a resolution. The approach used should be appropriate for the people involved and the circumstances. For example, conflict between family members could be handled informally around the kitchen table because it fits in with the nature of their relationship. A work relationship might utilize a more formal process in an office or conference room.

2. Agree on the rules to proceed. If there are no rules about how to resolve the conflict, it's easy for things to break down into a free for all where nothing gets done. Having everyone agree on a few rules can make the process run much smoother. For example, some rules can include no derogatory or inflammatory statements or interrupting others. You can establish as many rules as everyone agrees upon, however, the more rules you make the less likely people are to agree to them. Having a few clearly stated rules should be sufficient.

3. Agree to meet. Having a meeting may sound overly formal, but it shows that you take the conflict seriously. It's important to get everyone together at the same time so that no one can say they did not have a chance to participate and have their views heard. Doing this helps avoid indirect and evasive responses like ignoring, avoidance, or denial because everyone has to confront the issues together.

4. Agree on a time to meet. Set aside a time that everyone can get together. Give them time to be in the right frame of mind to work out a solution. Enough time should be set aside so everyone can be heard without being rushed or cut off. There should be a definite ending time to discourage people from dragging things out indefinitely wasting everyone's time. If

the issue cannot be resolved in the time allotted, additional time can be scheduled. If people are given a reasonable amount of time they cannot say they were pressured to give in.

5. Agree on a place to meet. The place to meet should be comfortable so that everyone can relax and focus on the issues, but not so comfortable that they will want to stay for a long time. It should be free from distractions that get people off track or disrupt the process. The location should be appropriate to the people involved and the nature of the conflict. It could be a home, office, or a neutral location. It should be a place that protects everyone's privacy, away from others who may listen in.

6. Agree on an agenda. Even informal meetings should have an agenda to organize the process so that the discussion stays on track. An agenda lets everyone know what is going to happen and what will be discussed. It gives everyone a plan to follow. An agenda is a listing of the items to be discussed in the order they are to be discussed along with the time allotted for each. Everyone should agree on the agenda beforehand so they cannot say that their issues were not considered or that they didn't have time to speak. It's easy to go off on a tangent, so having an agenda keeps everyone together and on track.

7. Agree on the issues to resolve the conflict. Everyone may agree that there is conflict, but they may not agree what the conflict is about. Agreement helps to avoid wasting time on unimportant things. Everyone needs to understand what the meeting is meant to accomplish and how things will be done. Clearly defining the limits and scope of the discussion can help everyone stay focused and on topic. Agreeing on a process to reach a decision keeps everyone from arguing about unimportant procedural problems that can hurt the process and prevent a resolution.

Conducting the meeting.

Having a face to face meeting can help facilitate a resolution. When everyone gets together in the same place they have the opportunity to explain their position so that the others can hear them out and ask questions. This should give them the feeling that they have been heard and what they have to say is valued. Sometimes all people really want is to be heard and acknowledged.

These are things you can do in the following order to have an effective a meeting.

1. Start with a positive atmosphere. Because conflict involves disagreements, it's helpful to create a positive atmosphere to reduce tension so people can relax to be more conducive to finding a solution. This can be done by meeting in a place that's comfortable and free of distractions. If appropriate, providing refreshments, like water or coffee, can help to make them feel welcome and appreciated.

2. Introductions. It can be helpful for everyone to get to know each other, if they don't already. Have each person introduce themselves and talk a little bit about their background to help put them at ease. If they get to know each other through the process of self-disclosure it reduces uncertainty to help find common ground to invest in working together for a common resolution.

3. Describe the process. After introductions it is helpful to quickly review the agenda so everyone has realistic expectations of what the meeting should accomplish.

4. Presenting positions. Have each person present their position without any interruption. Give everyone the same amount of time to be fair and keep things moving. This may be the first time they have all actually heard each other's position. By stating their position at the beginning, they are less likely to change their mind later on. This gets everything out in the open, it clarifies the issues to be considered, and helps to keep everyone on track.

5. Find common ground. After everyone has stated their position, there should be some common ground. In order to reach a resolution, it's helpful to begin with what everyone already agrees upon and then work on areas of disagreement. This can provide some momentum toward reaching a solution by starting with agreement instead of disagreement.

6. Reach a solution. Once everyone has presented their positions, they can present possible solutions. It can be helpful to go around the room and have each person contribute their best idea creating a list of possible solutions from which they could choose the best one or two. The section on decision making in Chapter 4 has several techniques to reach a solution. Some possible ways include compromise, collaboration, or consensus. If one method doesn't work, try another.

7. Once an agreement has been reached, it should be written down and a copy given to everyone so that they will comply with it. This is important because people's memories change over time and they may have different recollections of what was decided. Writing things down shows that it's important to everyone.

8. Evaluating the agreement. The final agreement may have a provision for enforcement that explains what happens if one of the participants fails to comply. Depending upon the nature the conflict, there could be a means for review and revision of the agreement to change it at a later date if needed. It can be helpful to evaluate the effectiveness of the solution such as what worked and what could be improved.

Negotiation

There are times when a more formal or structured process is needed to reach a resolution. Negotiation is a more structured method of conflict resolution and decision making. It can include a written agreement or contract that sets out the terms of the resolution. It is often used when making financial commitments like purchasing a car or a house. When we buy something that costs a lot of money we generally don't just walk in and write a check, instead we negotiate the price, financing, and other terms that are set out in a written agreement. It is helpful to be aware of how the negotiation process works because practically everyone will use it at some point.

Unlike other conflict resolution methods, negotiation involves using a bit of strategy and a bit of subterfuge by not communicating your true objective. Negotiation is often about value and value is often determined by perception. Negotiation strategies often involve shaping the other party's perceptions and expectations to achieve your desired outcome. In a negotiation, each party gives up something to get what they want. This can motivate people to initially ask for more than they really want. Then they can give up something they asked for knowing that they don't really want it. This can give the other party the perception that they are making concessions when they may not be giving up anything at all.

In informal situations a person may often be their own negotiator. We do this to make purchases like a car. In more formal circumstances a third party negotiator is often utilized.

For example, people will use a real estate agent when buying a house or an attorney when negotiating a contract.

Whether we represent ourselves or have a professional represent us is determined by what's at stake, how much money is involved, and the professional expertise needed to negotiate the agreement. Generally, the more money that's involved, the more specialized the field, and the more complicated the issues the more it is in everyone's best interest to utilize a professional negotiator.

To find the most effective approach determine your desired outcome, but have reasonable expectations about what you want because there's only so much the other party is able to do. Avoid making negotiations personal. Show the other party respect and consideration regardless of what they might say or do. It helps to be perceived as being fair, open minded, calm, and rational.

If you are negotiating with someone you know that you have an established relationship with, it's important to put the relationship ahead of the negotiation. You don't want to come across as inconsiderate with someone whose friendship you value.

Formal negotiations are often conducted by a designated leader. However, when you negotiate on your own, like when buying a car, you should take the lead. Determine your desired outcome and do your homework, so that you know as much information as you can about what you want. Leadership is about keeping the negotiation process on track and not letting the other person push you into something you do not want to do.

Avoid any deal that does not achieve your desired outcome. The other person should give you time to think things over. They should let you show any written agreement to someone else like an attorney. If they don't or it doesn't seem right, you might want to walk away.

The negotiation process.

Negotiation often begins by presenting an initial offer. Typically, neither party initially offers what they actually want and the other party rarely accepts. If they did, it would not be a negotiation, it would be an agreement. Their initial position may be different from what they really want because they know they will have to change it as part of the negotiation process. If there are terms to the agreement, these are also presented.

In monetary negotiations, the buyer typically starts lower than they want to pay and the seller starts higher than they are willing to sell. This gives them room to negotiate until they find a price in the middle they can both agree on.

Each person may ask for things they don't really want or more than they want, so they can have room to negotiate. This gives them items to use to make concessions, so they can be perceived as being cooperative while still pursuing their desired outcome. They may use some items as a diversion to draw attention away from what they really want.

This is done to create the perception that they have compromised because negotiation is often about giving something up in order to gain something better. The negotiation process can determine how important each issue is to the other party by testing their willingness to keep it in the final agreement.

Options for effective negotiation and conflict resolution.

- Use the law of uncertainty to encourage everyone to work together for a resolution. Conflict can increase uncertainty because people do not know what to expect. Reaching a resolution lets people know what to expect of one another now and in the future, which can reduce tension and uncertainty increasing stability.

- Share meaning about what a resolution means for everyone. Listen to gain information about the others. Find common values or interests that can encourage a resolution. Use appropriate self-disclosure to build trust. Negotiations need not be only task oriented. Having some social time can help relieve tension and help people to work together.

- Utilize the law of investing by emphasizing that everyone has invested their time and energy in the process and if a resolution isn't reached, they could lose that investment, so it is in their best interest to find some agreement. There is usually some area that everyone can agree on, which can be a first step toward reaching a broader solution.

- Consider the needs, wants, perceptions, and expectations of others. People may not be comfortable talking about their needs and wants, but it's helpful to know if they are not being met. It's helpful to understand their expectations for reaching resolution. This includes expectations they have of themselves, others, and the resolution process. It can be helpful to have everyone take some time to talk about how well their perceptions are meeting their expectations.

- Consider the desired outcomes of others and what they are able to do. Consider your own desired outcomes including not just what you want to gain, but what you are willing to do and what kind of relationship you want to have. Know your limits and stick to them.

- This process can be time and energy consuming leaving everyone feeling tired or frustrated. When people get tired, emotions and tensions may run high hindering progress. Taking a break lets everyone get away from the situation so that they can relax. Breaks can include coffee, lunch, or adjourning for the evening, if necessary. Taking a break can be helpful because it can be better to take a break when things are not going well than to continue. If you feel that you are being pressured or manipulated, ask to take a break to relieve the pressure.

- If nothing seems to be working remember that not everything can be resolved. You can never know everything there is to know about others and what they are able to do. They may not be able to come to an agreement for a variety of reasons. By utilizing communicating skills, you can better understand why some things just don't work out. It's better to know that you tried than to wonder what went wrong thinking that there was something that you could have done.

As much as we do things to keep control of a situation, the only thing that we can really control is ourselves. Regardless of whatever is happening around you, stay in control. Decide what you are willing to do and not do. Have boundaries and stick to them. Do not let others manipulate or maneuver you. Stay focused on your desired outcome. Avoid escalating a situation by saying something in the heat of the moment you might regret later.

When you take this approach, you take responsibility for your behavior and how you communicate with others.

Uncertainty and Relational Communicating

Relationships can be difficult. People might do things for no apparent reason. We might feel that a relationship is not going right, or did not turn out like we had hoped. This can leave us feeling upset or frustrated and we may not know why. By understanding how the laws of uncertainty, shared meaning, and investing affect us, we can better understand how relationships are created and maintained. We can develop skills to communicate effectively with others to improve our relationships.

We form relationships to fulfill needs and wants, and to achieve our desired outcomes. By having a clearer understanding of our own needs and wants, as well as those of others, we can better fulfill them and help others to fulfill theirs to have more satisfying relationships. We can reduce uncertainty by utilizing the perception process to better understand ourselves, others, and our relationships. So, when they do not meet our expectations, instead of causing unnecessary tension and dissatisfaction, we have options to be more effective.

We can reduce uncertainty by understanding how we meet people to create relationships. We can grow our relationships through self-disclosure to share meaning with others to get to know them better. We can invest in relationships to maintain them fostering a commitment to others. We can have options for handling difficult aspects of relationships, so when we have a conflict we can reach a more satisfying resolution.

This approach to uncertainty could be utilized as a diagnostic methodology to evaluate our relationships to improve them so they can be more satisfying. We can identify the relational skills that we have and those that could use improvement as a means to form better relationships. It can help us feel better about ourselves improving our self-concept and giving us more confidence in our relationships. By understanding our desired outcomes in relationships, we can focus on what is really important to us and clarify our priorities in order to achieve them more effectively.

Chapter 4
Professional Communicating

What if you went on a job interview, but you didn't know what the job was for? What would you say? What if you got the job and it was a really good job you didn't want to lose, but no one told you what you were supposed to do. What would you do? After you were there for a while, you still don't know what to do. You don't ask anyone because you don't want to look like you don't know what you are doing and don't want to get fired. Now what would you do?

While this may sound unlikely, you may have experienced something like it without even knowing it. This is because when we join a group or organization it's likely that no one told you the unwritten rules that govern people's behavior in organizations. Following the rules and norms of behavior can be more important to your success and job satisfaction than doing what you were hired to do. All groups and organizations have rules that govern how people communicate and behave. The other members may or may not tell you what these rules are, so you might break them and not even know it. Knowing how groups and organizations work can help you communicate more effectively increasing your chances of success.

Professional communicating is the third level of interaction. It is about how you communicate with others to create and maintain professional and other types of relationships in groups and organizations. It can characterize the connections we make with others including our friends, family, coworkers, and business associates. Groups are important to us because they permeate practically all aspects of our lives. We often define ourselves based upon the groups that we belong to like our profession, religion, ethnicity, culture, and geographic affiliations such as where we live or were born. We identify with groups based on our interests, hobbies, sports, work, and other activities. While many of these activities are based on our individual interests we do not do them by ourselves, but rather in groups with other people.

When you talk to other people, what do you tell them about yourself? You might say something like you play the guitar or are a football fan. You might say that you are a parent, a teacher, or play in a softball league. The first items are about you as an individual, but the second items are about your relationships with others in groups. When we communicate with others, we manage our identity to shape their perception of us to achieve our desired outcomes. We use our group affiliations to define ourselves, to make connections, and to find common ground with others. We do this because groups are a part of our self-concept and how we define ourselves. In order to increase your awareness of how groups can affect you, it can be helpful to write down on a piece of paper all the groups that you have ever belonged to whether you are currently a member or not. Then write down why you joined each group and if that reason is still the same or has changed.

Groups and uncertainty.

You have probably been a member of a group where things went well and you felt good about the group. You have probably also belonged to a group where things did not go well, so it felt like a waste of time. This may have left you wondering what makes some groups more effective than others. Having knowledge of how groups work can affect how you feel about a group because having a good group takes effective communicating skills.

Forming and joining groups is a natural part of life. They are part of how we define ourselves as individuals. It is helpful to know how groups work because of the influence they have in our lives. Groups can provide resources, affect our self-esteem, influence our perception and expectations, and affect our desired outcomes. They can create their own group social reality which gives them power over their members' behavior.

We are motivated to form groups and organizations to reduce uncertainty about ourselves, others, and the world around us. Groups reduce uncertainty by fulfilling many of our needs and wants. They create stability, security, and predictability. They have longevity beyond their individual members. The can acquire and allocate more resources than individuals. They can exert influence as a form of social control to regulate members' behavior. They let members know what is expected of them and what they can expect from others.

Groups share meaning about the group and what it means to be a member. They share meaning through traditions and rituals creating their own customs and culture. They may even have their own language, symbols, and terms. It is by being in groups that we get to know people through the process of self-disclosure. Sharing meaning helps people to reduce uncertainty, so they are better able to invest in the group and the other members. Groups help their members to invest in one another and provide a means to protect those investments.

Much of our life is organized based upon groups such as our family, work, school, church, community, and our interests or hobbies. It is in groups that we feel comfortable investing our time, energy, and other resources with the expectation that we will receive benefits for our contributions. Group members are more likely to share their resources with other group members including their time, energy, expertise, experience, and even material resources.

Members can feel comfortable investing in the group by self-disclosing to other members. By sharing their thoughts and feelings with others, they can make them more meaningful. Groups allow for role specialization, so that each person can spend more time on specific parts of a task and learn specific skills they might not otherwise be able to do when working alone. Groups contribute to our self-concept and affect how others see us. They share meaning about the group and what it means to be a member.

What constitutes a group.

There are many different ideas about what constitutes a group. What makes a group can be thought of in several ways including its purpose, structure, or size. We consider ourselves part of a group based upon the activities that we participate in with others, but not all gatherings of people constitute a group. When we are with others participating in an activity it does not necessarily make it a group.

For instance, it is not considered a group when we go out and cheer for a sports team even though we consider ourselves part of a group of fans. We often do things with others that are loosely organized on a temporary basis that does not necessarily constitute a group. So, for the purpose of this book, simply having a bunch of people gathered together does not necessarily make it a group.

Being a member of a group is a kind of relationship, so it can include many of the same characteristics that comprise relationships including proximity, frequency, intensity, and similarity. Defining what constitutes a group is similar to defining what makes a group of people a family. Most of the time a group is defined by the perceptions of the individuals involved. If people consider themselves a member of a group, then a group likely exists.

The following are some characteristics of a group.

- Uncertainty. Groups help its members to reduce uncertainty about the group and the other members.

- Shared meaning. Groups share meaning about the group and what it means to be a member.

- Investing. Groups provide a means for members to invest in the group and in each other, while protecting their investment.

- Identity. Groups have a sense of collective identity. Members know that they belong to the group and each member considers themselves to be a part of the group. Groups often have names, logos, or perhaps a mascot. Members have a clear idea of what it means to be a member of the group as well as its traditions and history.

- Connections. Groups have a network of connections between members through which they communicate that does not exist between people outside the group. Members often have a higher degree of interaction that creates an ongoing relationship.

- Desired outcome. There is a mutual purpose or desired outcome that the members of a group work together to achieve. In order to achieve their desired outcome, a group has tasks that members need to accomplish. Groups have a sense of collective outcome as they generally succeed or fail together.

- Needs and wants. Groups fulfill many of their members' needs and wants, which motivates them to join the group in order to have them fulfilled. Members work together to fulfill their own needs and wants, as well as those of the group. Groups allocate resources and make decisions, which gives the people who are in charge influence over the others.

- Rules. Groups have rules that govern individual and group behavior. Most often these are informal and communicated verbally. Larger more formal groups might write them down in a handbook. Groups have a process by which they get things done, make decisions, and resolve conflicts. Members understand and utilize this process in order to work together to achieve their desired outcomes.

- Structure. Groups have many types of structures that can vary from formal to informal. They may have a hierarchy of how members relate to one another and who makes decisions. Groups have a shared sense of time and space. They spend time together as a group such as attending meetings or participating in activities. Groups determine how members spend their time in the group. They often control physical space, like offices, and determine how that space is utilized. Members create their own psychological space, like territory or turf, by determining who is responsible for what.

Why we form groups.

Life can be chaotic and unpredictable. People behave in ways that seem unexpected, even threatening. We are motivated to form groups in order to reduce uncertainty about ourselves and others. From the time we are born, groups like our family provide for our needs and wants, which reduces uncertainty until we can take care of ourselves. When we tell others we are a member of a group, it creates a perception of who we are in their mind. Uncertainty is reduced between individuals that belong to the same group even if they do not know one another. As a member of the same group they share a common experience, tradition, and understanding of what it means to be a group member. In order to become a member, they may have had to fulfill some requirements or have some specific skills. This can provide information to help reduce uncertainty about them even if we do not know them personally.

We like to be around people who like us and who are like us. We feel safer with others who we perceive to be similar because it reduces uncertainty. This motivates us to join groups so we can learn more about others making them more predictable. When we choose to join a group, it is often based on what types of behavioral norms we find amenable. We have a natural tendency to join groups when we perceive the others as being similar to us because we share a connection or common bond. We are motivated to join groups with others we find attractive. This can include physical attractiveness, but also other attributes that we find attractive such as likable, knowledgeable, humorous, entertaining, or supportive.

While reducing uncertainty is an important function of groups, having some uncertainty can be good. Groups need some degree of uncertainty to function effectively. When groups reduce uncertainty too much, they might stop looking for new information and generating new ideas because they no longer feel that they have to do so. This creates the perception of confidence that can easily become arrogance, so group members might shut out important information or resist change. Extreme conformity can stifle creativity, originality, and growth. Having some uncertainty can be good for groups, just as it can be helpful for individuals because it makes us think more about our ideas, question our assumptions, challenge what we know, and helps to bring in new ideas so we can look at what we know in a new or different way.

In groups we share our ideas and experiences with others and they share theirs with us. This process of shared meaning gives them greater significance. This is how we convey shared meaning about ourselves to others. When we tell others that we are a member of a particular group, it communicates information about who we are without having to explain everything in detail. Members participate in rituals and traditions that serve to share meaning about the group. These shared meanings combine to create a history of the group that is communicated with other group members. Members communicate what it means to belong to the group. Over time these stories can create a common culture. Society is comprised of many groups and together these create social reality.

Through the process of communicating, groups can have a significant affect on our self-concept by providing us with reflected feedback. We utilize this reflective feedback through the process of communicating to see ourselves as others see us. When we receive positive feedback it can bolster our self-concept. This motivates us to join groups where we will receive positive feedback that validates our perception of ourselves whether it is accurate or not. When our self-concept is validated it makes us feel valued as a person. This is why we can be reluctant to leave some groups even though the group may not be effective or a positive influence.

Sharing meaning can make us feel an important part of a group, we can feel valued and appreciated as an individual. When others accept us it bolsters our self-concept and increases our confidence. Groups can give us a feeling of contributing to others and making a difference. When we help others we can feel good about ourselves. Many groups are organized to support a cause, to help others, or to make people's lives better. In these cases, the act of helping others can be the reward. It can give people a sense of meaning or purpose in life, a feeling of doing something worthwhile, or being a good person.

As a member of a group, when we need information or help to make decisions or solve a problem, we do not have to figure everything out for ourselves. Instead, we can seek out the help and advice of other members who might have done this before to make us more proficient sooner than we could on our own. Because of the law of shared meaning we can understand and learn about things from the knowledge and experience of others without necessarily having to do all the work ourselves. As a member of a group we can seek out advice from other members who have had similar experiences to find out what worked for them to help us determine what we should do.

We join groups because the world is a big place and groups help to make it smaller. They help us make sense of our experiences and the world around us to make life more meaningful. When others share their point of view or insight, we can see things in a new way that can help make our experiences more useful to us. Groups provide meaning to our experiences by developing a culture that explains why things are the way they are. They share meaning through rituals and traditions that can make life more meaningful because we have a connection to others, as well as to the past.

Groups and organizations provide an important means of implementing the law of investing. In relationships, we invest in the other person on an individual basis, so if the relationship ends, so do the benefits. Groups and organizations provide a mechanism that allows us to invest in other people on a wholesale basis, even people we do not know. When one person leaves the group our relationship with the group or the other members does not have to end. This gives us expectations of receiving future benefits for our contributions to the group because groups transcend dependence on individual members. This increases our expectations of stability and predictability about the future.

Groups provide social rewards to their members in ways that individuals cannot. They can provide verbal praise, reinforcement, acknowledgment, support, respect, status, and prestige. These social rewards can be a powerful force motivating people to contribute to the group. Being valued and accepted by others validates who we are as an individual by making us feel appreciated bolstering our self-concept, which can help to fulfill our needs and wants like acceptance, affiliation, and support. Conversely, groups can use social rewards as a punishment by withholding needs and wants fulfillment from its members.

Groups can provide monetary and material rewards. We invest our time, energy, and other resources in the group and each other in order to fulfill mutual needs and wants. Investments are regulated by the group's rules and norms, which determine how resources are allocated to its members. As a member of a group, we make connections with many people providing a means to invest in many relationships instead of getting to know only one person at a time. We are motivated to do this because our contribution to the group may be little more than we would contribute to an individual relationship, however, because there are many people in the group we can potentially receive more benefits and rewards. This saves time by not having to get to know everyone individually like we do when we form relationships.

Being a member of a group shapes our perceptions of ourselves and others based upon how others communicate with us. It also shapes our perceptions of others outside the group because we make assumptions based upon their group affiliations. Many times when we are part of a group we are expected to look, act, speak, and even behave in certain ways to fulfill group norms and rules. We all have perceptions and expectations about ourselves and others. These include what we think we are expected to do for others and what we expect others to do for us. Groups necessitate mutual contributions to achieve common goals by putting the group's interests ahead of the individual.

We have expectations about our experiences in the groups we belong to and perceptions about how those expectations are being met. Tension and conflict can arise when our perceptions do not meet our expectations. In order to avoid misunderstandings, it can be helpful for group members to communicate their perceptions of how those expectations are being met, so that they understand them better. When everyone has an understanding of what is expected of them and what they can expect from others, the group can avoid unnecessary dissatisfaction that can lead to tension and conflict. When we are part of a group we might assume that the other members think like we do, but the reality is they may not. Since everyone is different, all members of a group contribute differently leading to the perception that some people are doing more work than others, which can lead to tension and conflict in the group.

By regulating member's behavior, groups help create a basis for the norms that comprise their social reality. Groups are a means of socialization. It is through groups that we learn about ourselves, others, and the world around us. We learn about society by participating in our family, school, church, and community. It is in groups that we learn the rules of how to behave. Groups are able to do this because we are motivated to conform to the expectations of others in groups because if we behave within the accepted norm we are rewarded. If we behave outside the accepted norm we can be punished. Members who consistently behave outside group norms can be excluded or removed from the group and prohibited from receiving its benefits.

The bank.

We join and stay a member of groups because they allocate resources that fulfill many of our needs and wants. So, when we join a group it could be thought of like joining a cooperative or being approved for a loan by a bank. When we join a group, we can benefit from the resources it has to offer, but first we have to be approved by the members. This motivates us to seek their approval by reducing uncertainty about ourselves, so that the bank will accept us as a member. When uncertainty is reduced about us, it enables the other group members to feel comfortable sharing their resources to invest in us, like having a line of credit to draw on. If the bank does not approve of us, the other members could be less likely to share their resources because investment in us can be perceived as having too much uncertainty.

When you become a member of the bank you agree to follow its rules. This includes the patterns of communicating and rules for behavior that have been determined as acceptable for its members. When members follow the rules, uncertainty is reduced and they are perceived as more stable making others more confident investing in them and in the group. By following the rules we show that we are willing to make a commitment to the group and are worthy of receiving its benefits. Rules help to keep the group together because without them it would break down into chaos. This exerts a form of social control over its members so that they are more stable now and more predictable in the future.

If we do not follow the rules, we can be perceived as less stable and uncertainty is increased. The group may exert punishments for infractions of the rules to keep its members in line. The bank has to do this because if it doesn't, then there's no reason for anyone to follow the rules and it will fall apart. If infractions continue, we may be shut out or asked to leave the group. This can motivate the group and its members to withdraw their investments in us, so that we no longer benefit from the resources of the bank, in effect closing our line of credit. If we leave the bank by quitting the group, we are no longer bound by the rules. So, we may be perceived as more uncertain and will not continue to receive its benefits. This is why people can be motivated to stay in groups that they are not happy with or that they do not agree with because they do not want to lose the benefits they receive from them.

When individual members of a group invest in the group and its members, they are also investing in themselves. This is because when they help the group and the other group members individually, it benefits the group, which in turn benefits them. When the group does well and is successful it can make the other members successful. People are motivated to help one another as part of a group because they have a shared destiny or desired outcome. When the members of a bank do well, then the bank prospers. When the bank prospers, individual members are likely to do so as well. Conversely, if they are reluctant to help one another or invest in other members, the group may not receive the resources it needs which can undermine its success and its members.

Groups and their members often have connections to other groups and individuals. A group may have the added benefit of allowing its members access to the resources of other groups and organizations, and their members. If a member of one group is approved and in good standing, they may also benefit from the resources of another group. For instance, if the group is part of a larger organization, like a department of a company, resources may be available to all the departments within the organization.

You may have had the experience of leaving a group where you considered the other members to be your friends. After you left, you may have found that you now had little or no contact with the other members. They may no longer contact you or even return phone calls or emails, leaving you wondering what happened. Even if there was some contact after you left, they most likely drifted away over time. When a person ceases to be a member of the bank, such as if they quit or are removed, they are no longer permitted the full benefits of the bank. If they were allowed to keep them there would be no reason to join the bank or follow its rules in the first place.

For instance, if a person leaves their job they may find the coworkers they considered friends no longer call or have contact with them. This can be due to increased uncertainty because if a member of the bank communicates with someone who is no longer a member, they could be perceived as more uncertain by the others and could be shut out by the bank so they no longer receive all of its benefits.

Since change can happen through information coming from outside of the group, maintaining connections with former group members may bring unwanted change to the group undermining its stability. When someone is no longer a member they have less in common with the group. There is likely to be less proximity, familiarity, intensity, or similarity to create connections. Since they have communicated through the bank about bank business, they may no longer have much to communicate about. People have many demands on their limited time, so when someone is no longer a member they no longer have the same connection and other members are less likely to have as much time for them.

Some of the remaining group members may be willing to take their place to help fulfill the other members' needs and wants. For example, if a member is fired or has left because they were disgruntled with the group, they might tell the current members who might agree with them creating dissatisfaction in the group. This could reduce their commitment undermining the effectiveness of the group. The perception may be that if current members associate with a member who left, they too may find themselves no longer a member in good standing and unable to receive the full benefits of the bank.

Group needs.

We have many needs and wants we cannot fulfill ourselves that can be fulfilled as a member of a group. Groups are attractive because they have the resources and ability to fulfill many of our needs and wants. Groups save us time and effort by fulfilling some of our needs on a continuous basis. Without groups, every time we had a need or want to be fulfilled we would have to find a way to do so. For example, we work with a group of people in order to provide a regular paycheck to fulfill our monetary needs. If we did not belong to a group by having a job, every time we needed money we would spend time and energy looking for something to do to make it.

Groups can accomplish more to fulfill mutual needs and wants by working together than individuals can by working alone. Groups are able to mobilize resources for their members. They provide for material needs like a salary. We can learn how to do things by benefiting from the expertise and experience of others. When more people are involved in problem solving there's a greater wealth of knowledge, experience, and expertise. Groups have the potential to make better decisions, solve complex problems, and provide the resources needed to get things done.

Groups fulfill personal needs like our need for affiliation by being around other people. They fulfill our need for inclusion because we have connections with others who consider us a part of the group. They fulfill our need for friendship with other people, so we can trust and confide in them. They fulfill our need for closeness by having others who we care about and who care about our well being. We often form our closest and longest lasting relationships with others who belong to the same groups as we do.

Groups are able to convey many kinds of social rewards that fulfill its members' needs. Groups can fulfill our need for prestige, esteem, and status in ways that we cannot fulfill as individuals. Not all groups are the same, we invest groups with meaning depending upon what they do and who belongs to them. Different groups are perceived differently giving them different levels of status and prestige. For instance, a professional sports team can have a higher status than an amateur team. When someone joins a group the status of the group is often transferred to the individual member. Alternatively, if a high status person joins the group, the status of that person can be conferred upon all members of the group. When a sports team signs a high profile player it can raise the status of the team and the other members. Some people join groups because of the status or prestige conveyed by the group upon its members.

The process of transference can work for prestige, respect, and self-esteem. If a group is respected or members held in high esteem, their status can transfer to other members of the group. If a member of the group does well, they may be held in high esteem and respected by other members. This process can also work in reverse, if the group develops a bad reputation it can transfer the lack of status or prestige to its members whether they have deserved it or not. Groups give people the chance to contribute, to feel like they are making a difference, to do something worthwhile, and to develop their talents. Groups often have a hierarchy within the group where members have different ranks or levels of importance. This motivates the members to work for the good of the group so that they can improve their status or rank within the group. The ability to meet needs and wants makes some groups more attractive or powerful than others.

Just as we experience tension as individuals, groups can experience tensions from conflicting needs, wants, and desired outcomes. As individuals, we have tensions between our conflicting and competing needs and wants, such as the need for excitement and stability. Groups can also experience tension between conflicting needs like the need for structure and flexibility. Individual members can experience tension between one another based on their own needs and wants.

For instance, members need to spend time working within the group to accomplish group tasks, but they also need to spend time by themselves away from the group with friends and family. Members may be unaware of these tensions and think there is something wrong with them or the others, which can lead unnecessary conflict. In order to be part of an effective group it is helpful to be aware that these tensions exist to mitigate their effect.

These are sources of tensions that occur within groups and options for alleviating them.

- Decision making. Groups have more resources available to them to make better decisions, but this may not happen because they can get caught up in tensions between competing interests. Members need to make decisions as a group, however, they often make decisions as individuals. Groups can take longer to make decisions than individuals, which can create tension.

  To avoid unnecessary tension, groups can develop a process to solve problems and make decisions. It is helpful to determine the rules for this process and the desired outcome before starting the decision making process, so that it goes smooth and in a time effective manner.

- Conflict. No two people see everything exactly the same, so all members can potentially see things differently causing conflict. These differences can be a source of strength when group members bring different points of view together. However, more people means more potential sources of disagreement and tension. This is why groups should develop a process to deal with conflicts before they occur, so they can be resolved when they do.

  The section on decision making in Chapter 4 and conflict in Chapter 3 provides more details about options on how to do this. Effectively managed disagreements can be good for groups because it tests ideas, so that they can come up with a better solution. However, it can be bad if it prevents the group from reaching a decision that everyone can support.

- Pressures to conform. Groups provide a means of social control because they have rules that regulate behavior. They allocate resources to fulfill needs and wants, so they can exert pressure on their members to conform to group norms. Most of the time we are not a member of just one group, we are members of several groups each of which may have different expectations. This can cause tension between the expectations of one group with the expectations of another. This can make people feel uncomfortable or make it difficult for them to conform in some groups, but they might not know why. It can be helpful to be aware that while rules are important to keep the group together, they could also hinder it from being effective by keeping people from feeling comfortable. By being aware of this, groups can develop norms of behavior that keeps the group functioning while allowing for individual expression to keep members happy.

- Costs and rewards. Groups provide benefits to their members that often come at a cost. Like other relationships, we may keep a balance sheet listing the benefits and costs in the back of our mind based on our perceptions and expectations. The difference between our perception of what we contribute compared to our expectations of what we receive in return can have an influence on the satisfaction we feel and our commitment to the group. While there is a common notion that people maximize benefits and minimize costs, or buy low sell high, nobody wants to be in a group with someone who wants everything and does little in return. Instead, people are likely to seek fair rewards for fair contributions.

If we feel that we are making fair contributions and receiving fair benefits in return, we can feel a sense of satisfaction that will increase our commitment to the group. However, if we feel we are contributing more than our fair share and receiving less than others, we are likely to become dissatisfied reducing our commitment. This could motivate us to look at other groups as a comparison to determine how well we are doing. We may even think about leaving the group and joining another. If enough members feel this way it can undermine the effectiveness of the group creating tension and conflict, which might cause it to breakup. The group can avoid unnecessary tensions by encouraging its members to clearly communicate their perceptions and expectations, so that they can be more in line with reality. Balancing responsibilities and rewards can help group members feel that they are receiving fair returns for fair contributions.

- Individuality and affiliation. When we join a group we give up a certain amount of our individual freedom by allowing the group to make some decisions for us. We do this because groups provide benefits and allocate resources including monetary, social, and status rewards. In exchange, we give up some of our time, energy, and personal freedom. When we join a group for employment we give up some of our freedom to do whatever we choose to do with our time. We do this because we have the mutual expectation that other members of the group will do the same for us. Members contribute their resources and give up some individual freedoms for the benefit of all members of the group. This gives the group power to control the behavior and interactions of its members within the group by establishing norms, rules, and patterns of communicating.

Groups can help alleviate potential tensions between individuals and the group by clearly communicating the group's expectations for behavior and allowing for some degree of individual differences within the rules of the group. They can have group members come up with some of the rules because people are more likely to support rules when they have a say in making them. The group can encourage individuals to take the initiative and support their efforts when they support the desired outcomes of the group.

- Time. This is perhaps our most limited resource and we contribute a lot of our time to groups. We often measure our investment in groups based upon the amount of time we spend in them. The more time we spend, the greater our investment and commitment. Group members may have different ideas about how to best utilize the group's time because it takes time to meet, make decisions, and get things done. How members perceive the group is using time can be a source of tension particularly if they perceive others are wasting it. This can cause members to become impatient or unhappy with the group.

Groups can reduce tension by being aware of how they are using their members' time to make sure that it is as productive as possible because if members have the perception that the group is wasting their time, they may become dissatisfied reducing their commitment or they might leave the group.

- Individual personalities. While we choose many of the groups we belong to, we cannot always choose who else belongs to these groups. This can create conflicts between individual personalities creating tension. In some groups, members get along while in others they can be at odds with one another. Some members of a group may try to dominate or control the group for their own gain, while other members may hold back or withdraw.

While the group is made up of individuals, the focus should be on accomplishing group tasks. If the group is not accomplishing its tasks, members may become unhappy and not contribute to the group making it less effective. In order to reduce tension between members it's helpful to develop behavioral norms, methods of decision making, clearly defined roles, and other structural mechanisms that can help the group to achieve its desired outcomes. These mechanisms help to keep overbearing members at bay and encourage those who may hold back to contribute. A group can balance these things by creating expectations that individuals will work cooperatively for the good of the group.

- Individual responsibility. Groups have a shared sense of responsibility and each group member should assume responsibility for their actions within the group. Differences in individual perceptions and expectations may lead to tension or conflict over who is responsible for what tasks. Members may seek to avoid taking responsibility by claiming something was not up to them or that others were responsible for what happened.

In order to avoid this, clearly communicate who is responsible for doing which tasks and have a contingency plan if things do not go as expected. While one person may cause a problem, the other members may bear the consequences for what another member does, even if they had nothing to do with it.

- Group change. Group members often have differing expectations about what kinds of changes are acceptable and which are not. Some people join a group hoping it will never change and some people join a group to change it. This can create tension between those trying to change the group and others who resist change. This tension can waste the group's time and resources. In order for any changes to be successful, they have to be acceptable to everyone. Members need to be comfortable with change or they may work against it to undermine it. The more people feel something is at stake or that the change will cause them to lose something they have invested, the more they may work against it to try to stop it.

So, it's helpful to communicate the benefits of change and to have a process where everyone can contribute. When people have something to gain and they have a say in making the decisions that affect them, they are more likely to support them and see that they are successfully implemented.

- Desired outcomes. We join groups in order to accomplish things that we cannot do as individuals. Ideally, our individual desired outcomes should be compatible with those of the group, however, this is not always the case. It is more common for a group's desired outcome to come into conflict with those of individual members. There is a natural tendency for members to put their own needs, wants, and desired outcomes above those of the group. If the group is not meeting their needs and wants they are more likely to work for their own benefit rather than for the group. This can be damaging to a group because if everyone pursued their own individual objectives, the group could not accomplish its tasks or achieve much of anything as a group.

In order for a group to function, the group's desired outcomes must take precedent over the individual's. This is because if everyone pursues their own individual desired outcomes there is no longer any purpose to having a group. Conversely, if individual needs and wants are not fulfilled, tension is created and people might leave the group in order to have them fulfilled elsewhere. Putting group goals over your own creates interdependence between individuals because the outcome affects all of its members.

For example, a sports team either wins or loses. All members win or lose together collectively as a group. Because the outcome for all members is dependent upon one another, there is an incentive to work together. This creates interdependence where the desired outcomes of all the members are tied together. While not all groups have such a clear cut outcome, when a group is successful all members should benefit.

Types of Groups.

Since our family is our first experience in a group, it can form our first perceptions and expectations of how groups work establishing the norms for how we act in groups throughout our life. This is where we learn how to make decisions, resolve conflicts, via for resources, and negotiate need and want fulfillment. As we get older, we become members of other groups both spontaneously and by choice. We are a member of some groups because of who we are and join other groups because of the connections we have with others. Groups can be formed naturally or spontaneously as well as deliberately or purposefully.

These are some types of groups you may encounter.

- Naturally occurring groups. People have a natural tendency to get together with others in groups to share mutual interests and activities. We create groups based upon things that we have in common with others who live in our community, go to the same school, attend the same church, share common interests, or work at the same place. We form groups with others with whom we have a connection, live in close proximity, or share a common interest. We do this to make what we do more fun and interesting. Some of these groups develop naturally or spontaneously because of a common connection or shared interest. People have a natural tendency to share information, interests, or each other's company.

- Purposely created groups. Many groups are formed intentionally in order to achieve a specific purpose or desired outcome. These groups are often created with a structure to enable it to do something more than individuals can accomplish alone. They tend to be task orientated like a business that produces a product or service. They can also be socially orientated, so people come together to share a common interest or hobby. We purposely create groups in order to participate in activities and accomplish tasks with others in a way that fulfills our mutual needs and wants, that it is beneficial for everyone.

- Newly formed groups. All groups have the same thing in common, at one time they did not exist. Every group has to be formed, so when a group first forms its initial members all join at the same time. This means that members are likely to be on an equal footing because there is no past history. These groups experience a period of adjustment motivated by the law of uncertainty. This can be characterized by feelings of awkwardness where everyone is uncertain about what to expect from one another and from the group because they have no experience to give them the information they need. If they know little about one another they will need to reduce this uncertainty through the process of self-disclosure to create trust so that they can invest in each other to form the group. Newly formed groups have to reduce uncertainty by determining many aspects of how the group works in order to function including their structure, roles, norms, and rules. Until this happens, they may have a difficult time working together.

- Existing groups. Most of the time we join an existing group where the other members already know one another and have a past history. They have already reduced uncertainty, shared meaning, and have invested in the group. They may have already developed their group's structure, roles, norms, and rules. This puts the new member at a disadvantage because they know less about the group than the other members. Even though the group is established, the introduction of a new member can put the group through a period of adjustment because they need to reduce uncertainty about the new member. A new member must get to know the existing members and how things are done in the group. The new member will probably have little say at first in how the group works, so they need to conform to the group norms and rules.

- Task groups. Just as individuals have needs and wants, groups have their own needs and wants to fulfill. Regardless of the nature of the group or how it is created, groups have tasks that need to be accomplished in order for the group to function. The most common purpose for forming a group is to accomplish tasks, because more people working together can accomplish more tasks faster and more effectively. Task groups can be formal in nature, like in a business, or they can be more social. Even social groups have tasks that need to be accomplished for the group to function effectively.

- Social groups. Some groups are formed to fulfill the social needs of its members. They are often more informal and casual. All groups have social needs because working all the time is no fun and does not make a group very attractive or satisfying for its members. Even if the purpose of a group is to accomplish tasks, it may not feel very satisfying. This can happen when the social relationships are not well developed. Members need to accomplish tasks, but they also need enjoyment, relaxation, or to just have fun. How these needs are balanced depends upon the members of the group.

- Teams as groups. Some groups are referred to as teams and their work called teamwork. A team is always a group, but a group is not necessarily a team. A team is usually a part of a larger organization. They use sports metaphors to transfer the attributes that make sports teams successful to make the group successful. A team is often a specialized type of group formed with a clearly defined desired outcome. They are generally more focused and structured with a strong sense of commitment, loyalty, and group identity. Teams function much the same as groups, so when we talk about groups it also refers to teams.

Whether the purpose of a group is task or social, groups have tasks that must be accomplished by its members in order for the group to function. This means that members give up some of their independence by allowing the group to make some decisions for them in order to gain benefits the group can give in return. Getting things done is one of the primary reasons we form groups. If a group is not accomplishing its tasks, group members will become dissatisfied with the group creating tension. Even groups that are social in nature have tasks that need to be accomplished such as organizing activities or making a budget.

By participating in social activities we get to know other group members through the process of self-disclosure that includes telling stories about ourselves and our experiences. We get to know each other by participating in traditions and rituals like celebrating important dates and events. It is through these activities that we get to know others as individuals as well as to reduce stress and just have fun. This is why it's important to socialize in groups by doing things like getting together for coffee or spending time not doing tasks.

When we get to know others on a more personal social level, we reduce uncertainty, share meanings with them, and develop trust so we can invest in more effective relationships to better carry out the purpose of the group. Without having the social needs of the group met, people can become burned out or dissatisfied with the group leading to tension and conflict reducing their commitment and perhaps motivating them to leave the group.

Every group has to find its own balance between fulfilling task and social needs, but both of these must be addressed for a group to be effective. Some time should be set aside for each because they both cannot be fulfilled simultaneously. This can create a natural tension between the task and social needs of a group. Just as there is no one right way to communicate, there is no one right way to fulfill these needs. Each group needs to find the way that works best for them. Some ways to do this can include scheduling time before and after meetings where members can socialize and talk informally with one another. The group can celebrate rituals and traditions. They can spend time together in activities when they do not have to be concerned about accomplishing the task.

How Groups Are Formed

How do we meet people to form groups with or find groups to join? Sometimes it's by choice and other times it's by chance. Sometimes it's a bit of both. Groups are formed by making connections with others and communicating through those connections. In order to form groups we must first make a connection with others. To do this we have to meet them for the first time.

So, we often rely on familiar patterns of communicating that follow the rules of social reality. People create groups for reasons that can be as varied as the individuals who create them. We are motivated to create groups to help us fulfill mutual needs and wants that we cannot fulfill ourselves. The advantage of joining a group is that they can fulfill needs and wants on an ongoing basis rather than negotiating with others every time we need something.

In groups we get to know people over long periods of time reducing uncertainty increasing predictability and stability. Groups help us to communicate with others by making connections with them. Groups help make life more meaningful by sharing our experiences with others. Groups can provide structure and future predictability enabling us to invest resources in others to achieve desired outcomes. They increase security, stability, and predictability motivating us to form groups in practically all areas of our lives.

We form groups in a similar manner to how we form relationships. However, relationships are generally more social in nature and tend to develop more naturally or spontaneously. Groups are more likely to be intentionally formed and organized to accomplish tasks even if they are also social in nature. Relationships are based upon the unique personality of each individual involved. A group can develop its own personality with its own needs and wants. Groups go through a similar process of initiating contact, self-disclosure, and behavioral reinforcement that relationships go through as detailed in Chapter 3.

A group's identity is not so much about the individual members, but rather the relationships members create collectively with one another. This is why people can act one way in one group and a different way in another group. If members act as individuals, there is not much of a group identity. In order for them to be a group, there has to be connections and some degree of coordination between them. In order to do this, each person must give up something in order to gain something in return.

In relationships, two people communicate directly with one another negotiating everything between themselves creating a balance of power. Groups have a different climate because by adding a third person the balance of power shifts, changing the nature of how they communicate with one another. Each person now divides their attention between the other two. Chances are each person spends more time with one person than the other creating an imbalance.

Since we contribute resources and receive benefits in relationships, adding a third person can change the nature of how they are distributed. With three people there is the potential for two of them to make decisions giving them power over the third person. You have likely experienced a relationship with a friend who then got a girlfriend or boyfriend, or perhaps even got married. Chances are the nature of your relationship and how you communicated with them changed.

Groups usually have more than three people, but when we go from a two person relationship to three people or a larger group, how they communicate with one another changes. There will be people who communicate more with some and less with others. How resources are distributed can create an imbalance in the group.

In order to be part of a group, we have to make a connection with others so that we can meet them. Since we are only able to come in contact with a finite number of people, we have limited options of what groups we can join.

These are some of the connections we make to meet people to join a group.

- Family. Our family is the first group that we belong to, it's where we learn how to communicate and behave in groups. A family usually has a hierarchy of clearly defined relationships and roles such as parent, child, and sibling. A family is a very specialized type of group because it is more dependent upon the individual relationships between members to create the group rather than the group creating the individual relationships between its members. Looking at families as a type of group, families are most likely the most effective form of group because they have the ability to fulfill the task and social needs, wants, and desired outcomes of its members, which is why they are the foundation of society.

- Proximity. In order to form or join a group with other people, we first have to meet them and make a connection. We form groups with people who are in close proximity to us, who share the same geographic or professional space like our neighbors or coworkers. We usually meet them face to face, however, we can join groups in other ways such as long distance or over the internet.

- Frequency. We not only have to make a connection with others, we have to keep in touch with them. Frequency is how often we communicate with other people over a period of time. The more often we communicate with others, the greater the likelihood of forming a group.

- Similarity. We form groups with people who we perceive are like us. The rationale is since we like ourselves, if someone is similar to us then we should like them. We form groups with people who are likely to have a similar background, experience, education, ethnicity, culture, or geographic affiliation. They may have similar tastes in food, clothing, sports, politics, or music. We do this because the more we find someone is similar to us, the more uncertainty is reduced and the more we have to talk about. Motivated by the law of shared meaning, sharing similar ideas and experiences helps give our experiences and interests more meaning. When we hear about the experiences of others, it can make our own more meaningful.

- Intensity. Most of our contact with others is on a superficial basis creating little commitment. In order to form a group there has to be a commitment to the group and the other members. Intensity is created by the time and energy we expend with others, which can increase our commitment to them. We are more likely to form groups with people that share a higher degree of intensity, like family members or coworkers. The intensity of the situation can create needs and wants that are likely to go away when the group returns to a normal state. This is why traditional seminars and teambuilding exercises work in the short term, but can lose their effectiveness over time.

- Profession. Aside from our family, the groups we are most likely to join are associated with work. This is because work is where we spend most of our time away from home. We are motivated to create groups in order to get things done, to make work easier, and to develop our career. We form both task and social groups at work. Task groups help get things done and social groups help make work enjoyable. Groups are sometimes created for a specific purpose such as a company department or team. Some groups are created naturally in order to share similar interests. These groups often form between people who have things in common like work experiences or interests.

- Common interests. When we meet someone for the first time we are motivated by the law of shared meaning to look for similar interests to find common ground. This helps reduce uncertainty because when we know something about them, it gives us something to talk about. We form and join groups in order to share common interests, activities, sports, and hobbies. Forming groups helps us to share knowledge, experiences, and resources to enhance our own experiences by sharing something that we enjoy with others. Sharing information and resources helps group members benefit from the experience and knowledge of others. Having common interests helps to reduce uncertainty between individuals encouraging them to form and maintain groups.

- Connections in common. We join groups because we know the people who belong to them. Since we like them, we may decide to join a group they belong to so we can spend more time with them or with people who we perceive are similar to us. Groups often use their members' connections to recruit new members to join the group.

- Attractiveness. We join groups because we find them attractive. Groups carry status, prestige, and respect. We want to become a part of a group because these aspects are often transferred from the group to the individual members. We join groups because we find individual group members attractive. This can take on many forms including physical, intellectual, spiritual, or emotional attractiveness. We are attracted to them because we want to be around people that have characteristics that we are interested in, such as their appearance, intelligence, thoughtfulness, helpfulness, or because they like us. We like people who like us because it makes us feel valued, bolstering our self-concept. Attraction is a powerful motivating force because it represents the expectation of future needs and wants fulfillment.

- Likeability. We like people who like us because it makes us feel good about ourselves and bolsters our self-confidence. This is one of the reasons we form and maintain friendships with others. Nobody wants to be a member of a group where they feel that nobody likes them. We all like to be liked, it makes us feel good about ourselves because we feel valued and accepted by others. Approval of others by liking them is a powerful motivating force because it is a significant social reward. When someone likes us it reduces uncertainty and makes us feel more at ease because it represents their investment in us. Conversely, disliking someone can be used as a punishment. When someone does not like us it increases tension and pushes us away from the group because no one likes to be around others who don't like them.

- Random chance. Every once in awhile we stumble upon a group of people where we just hit it off. These situations are often unexpected because they tend to not fit in with other typical methods of joining or forming groups due to their increased degree of uncertainty. We may find a group attractive because of a higher level of uncertainty, which gives it a degree of mystery, excitement, or adventure. It may be that we have just come across a group where we feel a connection or gut feeling that catches our interest motivating us to join.

Group Development

All groups have one thing in common, at one time the group's members did not know each other. This means that all groups go through the process of group development. This process can be characterized by four phases that are governed by the laws of uncertainty, shared meaning, and investing. Since every group is different there is no one right way to develop a group. A group can go through these phases rather quickly or they might take some time. How a group goes through these phases depends on the nature of the group, the individuals involved, and the group's needs, wants, and desired outcomes.

Phases of group development.

1. Group creation, the law of uncertainty phase. Individuals come together to form a group motivated by individual needs and wants to achieve mutual desired outcomes. They may know little or nothing about one another, so they need to reduce uncertainty to function as a group.

2. Group growth, the law of shared meaning phase. Once uncertainty has been reduced to a level that members are comfortable with, they share meaning to develop their social reality, which includes the group's structure, boundaries, norms, roles, and rules of behavior.

3. Group maintenance, the law of investing phase. Once group members know more about the group, they begin to feel comfortable investing their time, energy, and other resources in the group and in one another in order to work together to achieve their desired outcomes.

4. Group dissolution, return to the law of uncertainty phase. There are times when a group no longer functions and may cease to exist increasing uncertainty.

I. Group Creation
The Law of Uncertainty Phase

The first phase of group development is motivated by the law of uncertainty. People are first drawn together based upon the connections they have with one another. People form groups for many of the same reasons they form relationships. They may be in close proximity, share common interests, or have similar desired outcomes. They are motivated to do this in order to reduce uncertainty, so that they can fulfill needs and wants they cannot fulfill as individuals.

Every group has one thing in common, at one time it did not exist. Every group member has one thing in common, at one time they did not belong to the group. Every group had to be created and every group member has to go through the process of joining the group. Even if a person was part of forming a group, they still go through the process that new members go through to get accustomed to the group and its members.

When we meet with a group for the first time we want to make a good impression. We use identity management to shape the impressions others have of us by presenting ourselves as we want them to perceive us. We want to be perceived as likable, so they will like us because we like being liked. We want to be perceived as agreeable, so they will get along with us. We want to be perceived as being helpful, so they will help us. We want to be supportive of others, so they will support us. We do this because we want to be perceived as someone who would be a good group member.

We want to make a good impression, so when we first get to know someone we reduce uncertainty by following the rules of social reality. We make a good impression by how we communicate, both verbally and nonverbally. We talk about general subjects to get things started while looking for specific topics that might be interesting to talk about. We use conversational skills to create a natural flow being careful not to talk too much or too little. We utilize positive nonverbal body language such as smiling, facial expressions, and eye contact to make a connection.

In order to reduce uncertainty, we utilize information that is available to us when we first meet someone to develop a first impression. Since we don't know the others we probably have little information about them, so we form an impression based on the information that's available, such as what they say and how they use nonverbal body language. If there is information missing, we fill in the gaps using our past experiences whether it is accurate or not.

When meeting new people we often have a heightened sense of self-awareness giving us a feeling of apprehension or anxiety. Anxiety is an emotional feeling based upon increased uncertainty. We might focus on how we are coming across to others because we want to make a good impression so they will like us. This may create feelings of uncertainty or awkwardness in the conversation because we are searching for common ground as well as trying to determine how others perceive us. We don't usually consider that the others may also be just as concerned about how they are coming across to us. When we feel anxiety we are more likely to communicate on a superficial level.

This level of communicating cannot continue for very long because if there is too much uncertainty, people will not be able to get things done. This means that one of the first tasks a group faces is the challenge of reducing uncertainty in order to decrease individual apprehension so that they can function as a group. This can be done through conversation with appropriate self-disclosure, so that members can find common ground to reduce uncertainty enough to begin to function as a group. When they feel more comfortable with one another, they are better able to communicate in more depth and build common connections enabling them to get to know one another better.

Whenever we join a group we can find ourselves in an unfamiliar situation motivating us to look for ways to communicate with others. If we are not sure what to do, we may fall back on past experience, which may or may not help. If uncertainty is too high, we may hold back and not talk very much letting others do all the talking, which can make us feel like an outsider. In these circumstances it can be helpful to use familiar patterns of communicating that are part of the rules of social reality. Patterns of communicating are preestablished methods of interacting with others that work like a script in a play or movie. They help to reduce uncertainty because we have heard them before. We use them because learning how to communicate in every situation we face would be difficult and time consuming.

We use patterns of communicating to reduce uncertainty in many common situations such as a job interview, first date, going to the grocery store, or meeting people we don't know. These patterns include simple greetings as well as more complex ways of interacting. They tell us what we should say and do to act properly in a given situation. For example, a common pattern of communicating when we meet someone is to say, "Hello, how are you?" And the expected reply is, "Fine, thank you." We are not supposed to actually tell them how we feel. If we did, it would be unexpected and not part of the established patterns of communicating, so they may not know how to respond.

We use familiar patterns of communicating when we first form a group to get things going until the group members get to know each other well enough to develop their own ways of communicating. They may rely on their past experiences in other groups and behave in ways that they have done in the past regardless of the new situation. This can create a feeling of stiffness and awkwardness within the group because everyone is uncertain how to communicate with one another. Some people may hold back by not participating letting others dominate the conversation. While patterns of communicating work initially, a group cannot effectively accomplish its tasks or achieve its desired outcome in this manner. The group needs to develop its own method of communicating between members. By knowing how this process works, you can help a group to become more effective.

Balancing the group.

A group is only as effective as the individuals that comprise it. This makes the choice of who is in a group important to its success. Some groups develop naturally and members have little or no choice over who is in the group. Some groups are open to anyone who wants to join. Some groups are purposely created to achieve specific desired outcomes so there may be criteria that determines who can join. Other groups place restrictions or requirements on who they allow in the group in order to maintain a perception of exclusivity or the professionalism of the group. They may have requirements like earning a degree or passing a test to maintain professional standards and public confidence in the group.

Choosing group members may be the most important single task facing any group. To create a group that works well together takes balance, it takes a form of economic equilibrium. Balancing a group involves balancing the roles people play within the group. It is finding the right combination of experience, skills, and expertise relevant to the task. It takes the right combination of communicating skills. For example, a group made up of all leaders may have a more difficult time working together in a group than one that is more balanced with people who have experience in more supportive roles.

In choosing members for a group consider what they bring to the group. While it is important to give consideration to their expertise and work skills, they also bring with them their communicating skills, behavior, attitudes, and past experiences. Consideration should be given to their social skills and ability to work with others. People may be good at what they do, but they might have difficulty working in a group with others.

Just as everyone has their own style of communicating, everyone has their own style when it comes to participating in a group. In selecting group members, consider how the group handles decision making, problem solving, disagreements, tension, and conflict. Group members should be willing to work for the good of the group by putting their own personal desired outcomes after those of the group. They should be able to plan, prioritize, organize tasks, schedule time, and contribute to the work of the group.

In selecting group members, consider each person's communicating skills, their participation in other groups, the roles they fulfilled, their commitment to those groups, and how well they work with others. It is helpful for members to have a connection so that they feel comfortable with one another to reduce uncertainty. This will help them to work better together to accomplish their tasks. In addition to their ability to accomplish the task, members should have effective communicating skills because it will have a direct effect on the success of the group. It does little good to bring together a group of the best experts if they cannot work effectively together.

Since people join groups for a reason, consider their reasons for joining the group including their needs and wants, perceptions and expectations about the group, and desired outcome for themselves and the group. Everyone joins the group because they have their own needs and wants to fulfill. If they go unfulfilled, it can undermine their commitment to the group. Members whose personal needs and wants are at odds with those of the group may interfere with its objectives potentially making it ineffective. Be wary of people who want to join a group simply for their own gain as well as those who say they only want to help others without any personal benefit, because these attitudes could hinder the effectiveness of the group.

Instead, look for people who acknowledge their own needs as well as those of the group. If people are simply out for their own gain then there could be competition within the group leading to tension and dissatisfaction undermining their ability to work together. If people claim that they are only interested in helping others and are not in it for themselves, they may be ignoring their own needs and wants leading to personal dissatisfaction making them an ineffective group member. They may say they want to help others and are not interested in themselves because that's what they think others want to hear. Some people might use the appearance of altruism to manipulate others.

Much consideration has been given to how to choose the right members for an effective group. Attempts to find an ideal formula to create the perfect group have largely fallen short. There is no one right way to choose the right people to create a successful group. This is largely due to the variable nature of personal characteristics. People can change how they communicate and behave based upon the other members of the group, the nature of the task, and their own desired outcomes. These variable personal characteristics will change depending upon their interactions with others.

We all have fixed characteristics that we cannot change such as our gender, ethnicity, age, or physical appearance. We also have variable characteristics that change or vary depending upon our circumstances. Some of these include our demeanor, nonverbal behavior, commitment, and style of communicating. These characteristics can change from group to group depending upon the other members and the circumstances of the situation. We might act differently depending upon our perceptions and the expectations of others.

It can be difficult to create an effective group based on a formula because these variable characteristics can change each member's behavior depending upon the circumstances. The same person may behave distinctly different in different groups. They may be outgoing and talkative in one group then act withdrawn and quiet in another. This is because groups can change our behavior, how we communicate, and even how we perceive reality.

Group size.

In balancing a group, consider the optimum size to achieve the group's desired outcomes. A group needs to be big enough to accomplish its task, but not too big to detract from it. Size depends on the resources that will be needed, the task to be accomplished, and the individual member's abilities. A workable size allows every group member to communicate directly with every other member. Groups are considered to be three or more people, but a more practical size can be from five to around twenty members. If a group is going to make decisions that involve voting it must have an odd number of people to prevent tie votes.

Group size has tradeoffs as there are advantages and disadvantages to both small and large groups. It's helpful to be aware of these in order to choose the optimal size for your group. Larger groups have more resources, information, experience, and expertise, but this does not mean that they make better decisions than smaller groups. They can handle more work by breaking a task down into smaller tasks and assign them to individual members to get them done more efficiently.

However, large groups may need more structure to function. A few people may dominate the group while others may hold back and not contribute as much. They can fracture or breakup into smaller groups with cliques of members communicating amongst themselves. Larger groups have fewer interactions between members and less time for each individual to have their say. They can be difficult to control and take more time in making decisions, which may necessitate taking a vote. Members of larger groups can be more likely to feel disconnected, be dissatisfied with the outcome, and have less satisfaction with the group.

Smaller groups tend to be more informal because everyone can meet face to face so they are able to communicate directly with one another. They are likely to make decisions faster, have less dissent, and are less likely to have tension or conflict. Everyone tends to participate because they aren't able to hide or go unnoticed. They are more likely to have fewer rules and make decisions based upon consensus. They are less likely to have hierarchies, so everyone is on the same level as everyone else. It can be easier to find a common time and suitable space where everyone can meet.

However, a smaller group has fewer members to bring in information and resources than larger groups. They may need to rely more on connections to other people or resources outside of the group to get things done. They may become overworked leaving them feeling stressed or frustrated. Members may have to take on multiple roles and more responsibility as there are less people to do the work.

New members.

When a new member joins an existing group the current members might expect that nothing will change. However, a new member can increase uncertainty creating feelings of awkwardness. This is because the new person is uncertain what to expect from the group members and the existing members are uncertain what to expect from the new member. They will have to go through the process of self-disclosure and behavioral reinforcement in order to reduce uncertainty to develop trust, so that they can work more effectively with one another. The new member brings with them their past experiences from other groups, so they may expect to do things the way they did before. Even if their role in the new group is assigned such as in a job description, they will need to negotiate their own place within the group through the process of behavioral reinforcement.

When a member leaves the group and no one replaces them, the other members will have to pick up the slack and take over their responsibilities. If a new member is brought into the group to fill the vacant position, they will have to go through the process of behavioral reinforcement. This is how a new member can upset a well functioning group, by increasing uncertainty so it does not function as well. By understanding and supporting the behavioral reinforcement process that groups go through, bringing new members into a group can be a much smoother and more positive experience.

Once a group has been established it may develop procedures to bring in new members. Some groups have restrictive guidelines for approving new members, while others are happy to have anyone join. Some groups allow new members to simply show up if they want to join the group, which means that they may have little or no control over who is a member. Other groups have a choice of who they recruit and criteria for accepting new members.

Choosing new members involves the same considerations as in balancing a group. Consideration should be given to a person's experience, education, expertise, and ability to accomplish the task. Consideration should also be given to their group skills such as their ability to work in a group with others, their commitment to the group, how they make decisions, and how they deal with tension and conflict. These group skills are important because they determine how well they will work with others in the group.

No group remains the same, existing members leave and new members join. The more formal the group and the higher the turnover, the more helpful it will be for groups to develop a mechanism by which new members can smoothly join the group and old members leave. Groups can utilize the laws of uncertainty, shared meaning, and investing to help new members make a smooth transition into the group because they will need to renegotiate roles, norms, and rules to include new members. In formal groups, such as a business, new members may go through an orientation or training program to learn about their group or organization. Even in groups where there are formalized rules that are written down, there are often unwritten rules that a new member needs to learn.

A new member should be given time to get to know the other group members by encouraging self-disclosure to help develop trust. New members can be more easily brought in to the group when they have time to socialize with existing members, so that they can get to know each other on a more personal level. This helps fulfill task as well as social needs of the group and its members. Group members can go through the process of self-disclosure with the new member by taking time to talk about themselves.

Newcomers to an existing group can be at a disadvantage because they do not have the same knowledge about the group that existing members have. So, it can be helpful to learn about a group's history, rules, norms, and ways of communicating before joining it. It can help to listen to stories members share about their past experiences and the group's history because they can communicate the values of the group. They can offer to do little things to help other members because it demonstrates a commitment to the group. They can learn the rules and norms of behavior including verbal, nonverbal, and body language, as well as how they use time and space such as decorating their offices.

Whether you are a part of a group that just formed or are a new member in an existing group, these are characteristics of an effective group member.

- Participate. Be there, show up for meetings, be on time, and stay until the end. The most frequent complaint people have about other group members is that they arrive late, leave early, or just don't show up. This behavior can be perceived as a lack of respect for others and their time.

- Contribute. Groups are about sharing resources in order to get things done. If you want to get something, you usually have to give something in return. Every group has tasks that need to be accomplished so you need to contribute time, energy, expertise, experience, attention, or material resources to benefit the group.

- Be courteous. Be courteous to other group members and show them respect in order to receive it in return. This creates a positive environment so that the group can work well together. It's important to do this whether or not the other members deserve it because being courteous is not about how they behave, it's about who you are as a person.

- Be prepared. Do your homework and be prepared for meetings and activities. Not being prepared undermines the effectiveness of the group and wastes time for group members who are prepared.

- Do your fair share. Groups need to get things done and effective groups share tasks fairly between group members. Group members are willing to pick up the slack when necessary. Know what is expected of you and fulfill those responsibilities because people don't like having to do the work of other members.

- Follow the rules. All groups have rules. Get to know what they are and follow them because without rules, the group could not function effectively.

- Support others. One of the purposes of forming a group is to provide mutual support for one another that cannot be achieved as individuals. In a group you support the other members because you want them to support you. If they don't support you, look for another group that will.

- Acknowledge the contributions of other members. Respond positively to their ideas and agree with them when possible. Support the group process to make and implement decisions.

- Be fair, objective, and open minded. Consider what others have to say. Consider new ideas and new information. Consider the possibility that you might not always be right about everything all the time.

- Be ethical. Avoid being overly critical of others, do not play politics, do not have hidden agendas, and do not act in your own self interest. The group exists for the good of everyone not just to benefit one person or a select few.

- Help the group achieve its desired outcomes. You can do this by putting group goals above your own personal goals. You can keep the group moving forward to accomplish its task by contributing, by evaluating information on its merits, and encouraging the group to make good decisions that will benefit everyone.

- Help individual members fulfill their needs and wants. By helping others get what they want, hopefully they will reciprocate and help you get what you want. If you help them and they don't help you in return, find another group that will.

Difficult group members.

While these are characteristics of an effective group member, not all group members will have them. They may avoid work, be overly negative, criticize others, or upset the group's progress. They may act aggressively and if others disagree with them they might take it as a personal rejection. Their problems can become a problem for the entire group. Sometimes a group member can become detrimental to the group. They may want attention because they feel that no one listens to them or they do not have a say in the group. Their perceptions may not be meeting their expectations or they may feel that they are not getting fair rewards for their contributions. They may feel that the group is going in the wrong direction, making bad decisions, or is not doing what they expect.

People in groups don't exist in isolation, they are members of other groups and have relationships with people outside the group. They may have a problem outside the group and bring it into the group. The problem may have nothing to do with the group at all, so the group may be unable to solve it. By increasing their awareness members may be able to provide support and resources to make the situation better. It can be difficult to know why people behave in ways that damage groups. The only course of action may be to stop it as soon as feasible because if it is not stopped, other members will become unhappy and frustrated with the group potentially tearing it apart. While there is no one best way to deal with difficult group members, it may help to take an incremental approach. Begin with an informal, casual approach to resolve the situation and then increase the intensity as needed.

These are options when working with difficult group members. Start with the more informal approaches and progress to the more formal ones as needed.

1. Talk to them about what's bothering them. Perhaps the group is not meeting their expectations or fulfilling their needs and wants. They may feel that they are contributing, but not receiving what they expect in return.

2. Talk to other group members, but do not go behind their back. They may be willing to speak with the other person about it. Listen to what they have to say and stick to the issue because it's easy to get off the subject. You can validate their importance as a group member without agreeing with them or taking sides. Sometimes people just want to vent and have someone listen to them.

3. Take some time during a meeting to have each member talk about any problems they might have. Hopefully the disruptive member will talk about their problem. This approach

should be managed by someone who can keep the discussion on track, so it doesn't break down into chaos because everyone may feel they have something they want to complain about. The difficult member may not speak up so they may have to be tactfully drawn out.

4. The group may need to let them know what they are doing in a descriptive, nonjudgmental way and give them a chance to respond. They may not be aware that they are causing a disruption and it might help to bring it to their attention. If they see that others care about them they may be willing to change. Doing this gives notice that they have been told on the record that their behavior is disruptive, such as in the minutes of a meeting.

5. Since they have been told their behavior is disruptive, if they become disruptive again you might ask them at a group meeting what is bothering them. Try to address their concerns, but inform them that the group has rules and ask them to not behave in this manner or the rules will be enforced.

6. If the group has done everything it can with the resources it has, then it may be time to get outside support. Many groups have connections to other groups or organizations that can provide assistance in dealing with disruptive members. Businesses often have a committee that reviews employee behavior or may offer counseling or support.

7. If this doesn't work, the group may need to remove the member as quickly and pleasantly as possible. How this is done depends upon the rules of the group. Groups and organizations often have rules for these situations. If your group does not, consider making some.

These approaches give you options, but things may not go well. Some people may become defensive lashing out at other members, perhaps even threatening them. There are some situations where the only solution is to remove the disruptive member for the good of the group. By pursuing other options first, the group can feel that it has made an effort to resolve the situation before taking action. If the group decides to remove a difficult member, they must have a united front because if there is dissent within the group, it could split the group making it unable to function. If the difficult member is not removed from the group, the other members might become frustrated or unhappy with the group. This is necessary for the good of the group because if a difficult group member is allowed to stay, it can undermine the other members' commitment to the group and good members may leave.

In a business, if an employee is having problems, they should be given a chance to correct them. Being fired should not be a surprise. No one should ever be summoned to an office and summarily fired. It's demeaning and it reflects badly on the organization and the person doing the firing. It increases uncertainty undermining employee commitment and investment because they might be let go too. You might utilize these options first.

1. Meet with the employee to tell them what needs improvement and what they need to do, with a time frame to do them. Inform them of the consequences if they don't.

2. If they do, let them know they have improved. If they don't, inform them where they are deficient and with a final deadline to make improvements or they will be let go.

3. If they still do not remedy the situation, then they need to be fired or they could undermine the organization. Meet with them again. Give them the reasons for their dismissal. Be truthful, but tactful, avoid clichés or platitudes. Express regret for having to do this and wish them well. Avoid making it overly personal or drawn out.

When a member voluntarily leaves the group it can also be difficult. If a group experiences a lot of members leaving, the remaining members may feel abandoned or rejected. This is because our self-concept is to some extent connected to the groups we belong to based on how the other members communicate with us. Leaving a group or organization can be more difficult than joining it because when we leave we often leave friendships behind, give up benefits, and make changes that increase uncertainty reducing stability and predictability. We may feel a sense of loss and even go through a period of mourning. If we leave to join a new group, we will go through the process of behavior reinforcement all over again by getting used to a new set of norms, rules, and getting to know a new group of people.

People leave a group either because they choose to or because they have to leave. People may choose to leave groups because the group is no longer meeting their needs and wants, they are looking for a change, or the group has changed from what they expected. People leave groups because they retire, move away, are fired, or they have to leave. We should expect to leave groups and to have other people leave the groups that we are in. While knowing that leaving groups is inevitable and unavoidable, it doesn't always make it any easier.

II. Group Growth
The Law of Shared Meaning Phase

When a group first comes together there is a high degree of uncertainty because people are unsure what to say and how to act creating an atmosphere of awkwardness and formality. Once group members get to know one another, they reduce uncertainty to a level of comfort that enables them to work together so the group can grow and develop. When members are comfortable with one another, they begin to talk about themselves and their past experiences. They share stories about themselves, others, and the group. This begins the law of shared meaning phase of group development. Sharing meaning helps to create a common understanding within the group of what the group means and what it means to be a member.

A group has meaning to both its members and those outside the group. A group can be like a person, it can develop a unique identity separate from the individuals that comprise it. Members may express that identity by giving their group a name and symbols like a logo, mascot, or group colors. If the group has been given a name by outsiders, like in a company or department, the members may put their own mark on it by giving it a nickname.

Shared meaning lets group members know what the group stands for and what it means to be a member. This is often communicated through the stories members tell and the group members' history, traditions, and rituals. Groups can utilize identity management, much as individuals do, to manage what they communicate about themselves with people outside the group to influence their perceptions and achieve their desired outcomes.

Groups, like individuals, have needs and wants that must be fulfilled to achieve their desired outcomes so the group can function. This motivates individual members to take action to accomplish them. Groups have many members to accomplish these tasks, but everyone cannot do the same thing at the same time. This means that group members need to specialize by taking on specific tasks, roles, and responsibilities. Since there are many people doing many tasks, groups need structure in order to coordinate their activities. If everyone did whatever they wanted, the group would become chaotic and nothing would get done.

Developing a group structure includes creating rules and standard operating procedures which members accept as their normal means of behavior, commonly called norms. In naturally occurring groups norms are often not predetermined, so the members will have to create them as they go. In groups that are intentionally created, like in a business, the structure may be established in advance, but the members may still need to negotiate how they will get things done. Behavioral reinforcement is the mechanism by which groups develop and solidify their structures like norms so that they can function effectively.

Self-disclosure.

Self-disclosure encourages investing in groups much like it does in relationships. It is a means by which we make connections with one another. Group members talk about themselves and about their past experiences. Members take turns contributing to the collective experience of the group. Disclosure begins at a very superficial level by talking about commonly known information such as where people live, what they do for a living, and recent events. As people share information they become more comfortable sharing more personal information. As group members get to know one another it reduces uncertainty so that they are more familiar and predictable enabling them to trust each other to contribute their resources to work together.

Self-disclosure is more effective when done in incremental amounts over time, sharing only information that is appropriate to the group. Disclosure should be reciprocated so everyone feels like they are fairly contributing. This way no one feels they are contributing more information about themselves than anyone else. We share information as we feel comfortable and when we feel it's appropriate. Too much disclosure, shared too fast can be considered inappropriate potentially scaring people away. Too little disclosure can be perceived as holding back, being evasive, or being aloof. Individual members can utilize feedback to determine the appropriate level of self-disclosure that itself may become a group norm.

Behavioral reinforcement in groups.

Groups develop their own specialized ways of communicating and doing things through the process of behavioral reinforcement. This process begins by using familiar patterns of communicating as members exhibit behaviors to accomplish tasks based upon their past experience and perceptions. The group selects which behaviors it deems appropriate for the group and seeks to eliminate those it does not. To do this, members may utilize the process of communicating to share their Great Idea with others in the group and then wait for feedback. The nature of the feedback they receive at this early stage can determine the future behavior of the group.

Members communicate in different ways and exhibit different behaviors based upon their past experiences in order to find ones that work for them and the group. This behavior is either accepted, rejected, or met with indifference by the other members. When a group member does something that the others approve of, they are encouraged to repeat it and if it's repeated over time, it can become part of the group's behavioral norms. Agreement is a powerful social reward because it affirms our ideas, bolsters our self-concept, and improves our confidence. Once group behaviors have stabilized, they may be difficult to change. By being aware of this process you and the other members can utilize positive reinforcement to reward useful behavior to help the group become more effective.

However, groups may not always positively acknowledge helpful behavior, but instead reinforce negative behavior. Negative feedback usually discourages detrimental behavior from reoccurring, but there can be circumstances where a negative response can be perceived as a challenge, so the behavior is repeated. There can be times when members might give positive feedback to behavior that could hurt the group because they find it funny or entertaining.

Negative behavioral reinforcement discourages behaviors through the process of communicating. If we receive negative reflective feedback it can hurt our self-concept motivating us to not repeat the behavior. If a member's behavior is met with consistent negative reinforcement it is not likely to be accepted by the group and should not become part of the group's norms of behavior. Negative feedback from the group makes us less likely to repeat the behavior because we do not want to run the risk of rejection. Under certain circumstances this process can work in reverse. A person receiving negative feedback may see it as a challenge and repeat their behavior again perhaps even more forcefully. In some cases, any feedback may be seen as positive no matter how negative it may be. For example, a child may act out in order to get attention from adults even if it is negative.

If the feedback is unclear, the behavior will likely be repeated until clear feedback is received. If there is no feedback, it can be difficult to know what to do. If group members feel they are being ignored they may become frustrated and act out more forcefully leading to tension or conflict. If some members are ambivalent they can be perceived as not caring, which can hinder the group's development. If ambiguous feedback is not clarified, the group will have difficulty stabilizing or getting anything accomplished because members won't know how to act or what is expected of them. By knowing how this process works, we can provide clear feedback during this time in the group's development to reduce uncertainty and establish ways of communicating to help the group accomplish its tasks.

Behavioral reinforcement can contribute to the social climate of the group. When positive behaviors of group members are met with positive feedback, it creates a social climate that makes the group attractive for its members fostering their commitment to the group. This encourages communicating between members and motivates them to contribute for the good of the group.

This also provides rewards by making members feel that they are valued and that they make a difference. A positive climate can be developed by complementing one another, acknowledging other member's contributions to the group, agreeing with them, sharing credit for accomplishments, and recognizing their achievements. Supporting others can involve doing things for others as simple as offering someone a cup of coffee to helping them out when they need it.

If a member disagrees all the time or there is excessive negative behavioral reinforcement, it can create a climate that can discourage the other group members from contributing to the group. This can create feelings of tension, anxiety, and dissatisfaction. It can lessen a member's commitment to the group and the other members. People may put up with a negative climate and stay with the group in order to receive rewards, but they are no longer as committed to it or achieving its desired outcomes.

They may simply go through the motions doing a minimal amount of work just to get by. For example, if the group creates a negative climate of joking and not getting serious, members may stay with the group just to receive its benefits or perhaps out of a need for entertainment, however, they may not take the group seriously making it difficult to effectively accomplish their task.

Group norms.

The process of behavioral reinforcement creates a set of normal standard operating procedures, called norms, for the group. Groups do this because the members have to work together to develop their own ways of doing things. Norms consist of just about anything that is considered normal for the group. Norms refer to a group's normal pattern of behavior consisting of the shared expectations that members have for behavior in the group. They let members know what is expected of them and what they can expect from the others. They often include how group members communicate with one another, how they behave, and how they make decisions, solve problems, and resolve conflicts.

The way that group members first accomplish a task can set a precedent, which if repeated can establish a norm as part of their standard operating procedures. For example, how the group resolves their first conflict may be repeated when conflicts reoccur whether it was effective or not. Precedents work rather like first impressions. They may not be effective, but after they have been established, they can be difficult to change. This is a process that happens naturally or it can be purposely managed. Precedents may be created haphazardly that can hinder the group's success making it difficult to change later on. It can be helpful to be aware of how this process works in order to create precedents early in the group's history that create positive norms to help the group achieve its desired outcomes.

In order to form a fully functioning group, norms need to be stabilized so that group members will share the same perceptions and expectations. They need to know what is expected of them and what they can expect from the other members. People don't like surprises or uncertainty, they want stability and predictability especially in others who are close to them and with whom they share a common purpose. Without norms every group member would do whatever they felt like doing reducing the group to chaos so nothing would get done. Norms provide a means of social control by establishing boundaries for behavior and structure so the group can accomplish its task.

Groups establish task norms based upon the needs and wants of the group. The purpose of task norms is to regulate the behavior of individuals so that the group can accomplish its tasks. These norms regulate how individual group members work together in order to keep them on track to achieve their desired outcomes. This can include procedures on how the group accomplishes its tasks such as setting priorities and establishing deadlines. Task norms can be used to determine the process of how decisions are made, problems are solved, and conflicts are resolved. They can determine how resources are allocated like how time and space are used.

Groups not only have task norms, they also have social norms. People do not just work together, they need to get along with one another. These norms regulate the social aspects of the group including how group members interact with one another. They determine who communicates with whom, about what, and under what circumstances. They can regulate how members communicate with others outside the group. They help to give meaning to the experiences of group members.

Groups often have a history and traditions that are shared between group members to provide a meaningful connection with the past. Social norms communicate how members participate in the activities of the group including rituals and traditions. These can include celebrating birthdays and holidays as well as informal rituals like getting together for coffee.

Group norms need to be stable in order to provide structure for the group, however, groups also need the flexibility to change. As circumstances, tasks, and group members change, norms need a way to change as well. Groups need a mechanism to adopt new norms that are helpful and to discard those that are a hindrance. By having an awareness of how this process works, members can choose to change their norms in a purposeful manner to become a more effective group, rather than waiting until circumstances force them to change.

Group roles.

Norms are the shared expectations that group members have of the group's behavior and roles are the shared expectations members have of each individual member. Groups have needs and wants that must be fulfilled, desired outcomes to be met, and tasks to be accomplished. In order to accomplish them, someone has to do the work and who does what work comprises a role. A role is a specialized type of behavioral norm consisting of the perceptions and expectations that each member has about their responsibilities in the group.

Roles are based on the needs and wants of the group because this is how they are fulfilled. A role in the group is rather like a role of an actor in a play or movie. Each actor knows what they and the other actors are going to do providing predictability enabling them to perform their role. Roles let group members know who is responsible for doing what tasks, so that each person can do their job and the group can function effectively.

Roles in groups can be developed through the process of behavioral reinforcement similar to how norms are established. Groups need to have things done and group members need to do them. Group members take on individual tasks and their actions are either accepted, rejected, or met with indifference by the other members. When the group approves of what a member does the member will fill a role and when everyone has their role, the group's structure will stabilize. If the group responds negatively or ignores a member's behavior their role will not be established because it is not supported. It's helpful to have an awareness of how this process works to help stabilize roles, norms, and rules within the group as soon as feasible, so it can function effectively and get on to accomplishing its tasks.

In this process of determining roles, people do not necessarily choose their own role, but instead they negotiate for it with other members of the group. Without the support of other members a person cannot effectively fulfill their role. If more than one person tries to fulfill a role, there may be a conflict as they vie for the group's approval until one person is chosen. When all members agree who is responsible for doing what tasks, the group structure will be established and the group can accomplish its tasks. If this does not happen, the group structure will not stabilize and things could become chaotic undermining its effectiveness.

While it is important for roles to be well defined in order for the group to function, groups need a mechanism to change roles within the group when necessary. Roles need to be changed in order to account for changing group members, circumstances, and tasks. There may be new duties and responsibilities that need to be allocated to existing members. When a person joins the group, they need to find their place in the group. When a person leaves the group, the other members may need to pick up the slack. Clearly defined roles are important so that everyone knows who is responsible to do what tasks to avoid tension and conflict.

When a member joins or leaves the group or the task changes, the group may need to go through the process of behavior reinforcement again to renegotiate the roles within the group. This can happen even in established groups. If the group is aware of this process and how to deal with it, they can effectively renegotiate new roles in a positive way to get on with their work. If they are unaware of it, it may cause unnecessary frustration with the group that can lead to increased dissatisfaction that may result in the loss of the member's commitment. This is how effective groups can become unproductive after a change in membership. It can also provide a means for getting the group going again if it has problems.

Every group is different, so roles will depend upon the nature of the group and its desired outcomes. A common role is the group leader, who is responsible for keeping the group on task and getting things done. Leaders can have formal titles like manager, director, president, or CEO. Other titles include, a secretary who keeps the record of the group, writes agendas, keeps minutes of the meetings, and sees that information is disseminated to group members to keep them informed. A treasurer handles the finances of the group. A group may have a gatekeeper who controls the channels of communicating between the group and outsiders. A group may have a researcher who gathers and evaluates information for the group. A group may have a critic whose role it is to be critical and test the validity of information to help the group make decisions.

Roles are created to fulfill not only the task needs of the group, but also their social needs. In addition to the group leader, there may be a social leader who promotes positive relationships between members. Someone may play the role of peacemaker who helps resolve tension and conflicts. A group may have a historian who keeps the history of the group or oversees group rituals and traditions. A group may have a social planner who takes care of social activities such as celebrating holidays, birthdays, and other events.

Norms and roles develop because a group has to establish certain behaviors and ways of communicating in order to fulfill its needs and wants, so it can accomplish its tasks. If everyone does whatever they want or if they all do the same thing, then the group will be in disarray increasing uncertainty. Since the law of uncertainty motivates people to take action to reduce uncertainty because it's uncomfortable, group members will be motivated to reduce it by developing group norms and roles. The group has to reduce uncertainty in order to work effectively, so it can accomplish its tasks. How it does this is usually governed by a set of rules so everyone knows what to expect.

Group rules.

In order for groups to function properly, there needs to be a mechanism to regulate behavior. That mechanism helps to establish the rules for the group. Where norms are shared expectations of group behavior and roles are shared expectations of individual behavior, rules are the shared expectations of how both are governed. Rules serve as a form of social control giving them power over the behavior of group members. Rules can be negotiated between group members over time or established when it first forms. When a group first forms it may have no rules, so members look for guidance from the rules of social reality. A group may utilize rules from its members, other groups, or from a larger organization if it is part of one. Even if the rules are established when the group first forms, there is often an informal process by which the unwritten rules are established.

Rules are often created by the process of behavioral reinforcement, so members exhibit different behaviors that are either accepted or rejected by the other group members. Members try out different behaviors based upon their past experience and their perceptions of the needs and wants of the group. When a behavior is deemed acceptable by group members and is repeated over time, it can become part of the norms of the group. For example, when the group first meets and someone wants to speak, they might raise their hand because they did so in a previous group. If others do the same and support that way of doing things, it can become part of the group's rules. However, if a behavior is rejected, it is not necessarily discarded like a norm or role, it may become part of the rules that this behavior is not accepted.

Rules are a means of social control because they regulate the behavior of group members. While this may seem restrictive, it is necessary in order to reduce uncertainty, create stability, and increase predictability so that group members can invest their resources in one another and in the group. Without rules no one would know what to do or how to behave and the group could not function. Generally, the smaller the group, the more informal the rules. The larger the group, the greater the potential for disagreement or conflict, so more formal rules are often needed. Even when there are written rules there are often informal rules that govern everyday behavior that are usually not written down. Members may consider these rules as important as the formal ones. They may not be openly communicated, so members may not even know they exist until they break them.

Groups have basically two types of rules, constitutive and regulatory. Constitutive rules contain information about what constitutes acceptable and unacceptable behavior within the group. However, it seems like there is always someone who breaks the rules, so without an enforcement mechanism they are not as effective. This is done with regulatory rules that regulate the members' behavior. They may also be called punitive rules because they prescribe punishments for those who break them.

Practically all aspects of our lives, all groups we belong to, and every endeavor we are involved in is governed by some set of rules. Rules do not just tell us what to do, they can also give us helpful advice how we should do things. They are meant to help us do things better and are often based on the experience of others. Rules are necessary in order to create structure within groups and within society. For example, members of a musical group cannot play whatever they feel like playing. They have to agree on the rules including what music to play, how to play their instruments, and how to perform together with others in a group. Groups need rules to function properly and to be effective by creating stability because everyone knows what to expect.

When a member joins a group they need to know the rules. Since some rules are not written down, new members learn them gradually from experience over time. It takes time to become adjusted to the norms of the group because all too often current members assume the newcomer will just get it. The most common way a new member learns about the rules and norms of the group is by observing the behavior of others and emulating it. If they are not sure about something, they could ask existing members who may or may not tell them. Often newcomers only learn the rules and norms when they violate them and are punished by the group. To help new members understand the rules and norms, a longtime member could help them by providing advice and answering questions.

Group structure.

Groups need structure because it creates stability to reduce uncertainty. This provides predictability so that people can invest in the group and work together to accomplish its tasks. Structure is necessary for many aspects of the group including its roles, rules, norms, networks, and boundaries. Smaller groups generally have less structure since everyone can communicate directly with everyone else. As groups grow in size, communicating between members becomes more difficult, so more structure is needed for it to function effectively.

Group structure benefits both members and those outside the group by helping them to better understand how it works. How a group is structured can communicate confidence, competence, responsibility, and professionalism to others. This helps group members accomplish tasks by understanding the group and its purpose. Structure helps members understand how they fit into the group and how what they do contributes to the benefit of everyone. Having a formally recognized structure gives groups legitimacy by letting outsiders know who is responsible for what tasks. As a group becomes more formal, it may have more formal positions as part of its structure like president, CEO, secretary, or treasurer. These positions give the group legitimacy and creates the perception of professionalism and competence.

Groups not only have formal structure they also have informal structure. A formal structure is comprised of the ways in which group members are expected to interact with one another. This structure may not have been created by the group members themselves, but by other people outside the group such as a larger organization. The informal structure often reflects how members actually communicate and their everyday behavior. As organizations become larger they need to develop structures to function effectively, but these can also serve as barriers to effective communicating. This can motivate members to utilize informal networks by making connections that get around bureaucratic rules so that they can get things done.

Groups need structure, but they also need to adapt to changing circumstances. This creates tension between having a fixed structure and a need for flexibility. Highly structured groups tend to be less flexible reducing their adaptability to change with changing circumstances. Groups that are moderately structured provide for change within an established structure, but more serious change may be difficult. Flexible groups are able to change rather easily which may increase uncertainty. A group needs to find its own degree of adaptability depending upon its needs and wants, the task to be accomplished, and how comfortable members are with change. For most groups an effective approach falls somewhere in the middle where there is a clear structure that is flexible enough to change as necessary.

However, there are groups that need to be more structured. This approach works because the objective is clear and the method to achieve it is well defined. Conversely, a more flexible structure can be effective for groups where creativity and developing new ideas are important to the group's success, like in the arts. A flexible structure works well in areas like technology where groups need to adapt to new ideas and different styles quickly, but need a structure to keep everyone organized. Most businesses tend to be structured with clearly established norms that allows for some types of change, but it may resist others. When a group grows larger it needs to develop structures to help it function, but over time these structures can become overly bureaucratic or strict reducing flexibility and its ability to function effectively, which is the opposite of what was intended.

Group boundaries.

Boundaries are an integral part of a group's structure. They can be external, formed around the outside of the group and internal, existing within the group. External boundaries define who is a member and who is not by separating insiders from outsiders. They regulate who is allowed to participate in group activities, which gives members a feeling of being part of a group. Boundaries have both positive and negative effects on a group. The stricter the boundaries the more difficult it can be for people to cross them, which can make a group more exclusive. Boundaries can restrict the flow of information coming in and out of the group. The more flexible the boundaries, the more information that can get into the group. However, members may feel less connected to other members.

Internal boundaries are often used within a group to regulate behavior. They can be used to create hierarchies, ranks, or levels of authority by giving some people more status and importance than others. This can provide motivation for members to stay with the group for longer periods of time, so they can move up the ranks to get more benefits. Boundaries can be used to control the flow of information regulating who communicates with whom, about what, and under what circumstances. They can be used to create power within a group by restricting access to certain people. They can be used to help people work more effectively by grouping members together by profession or task like having a sales team.

Not all boundaries are the same. They can be open or closed, and strict or flexible depending upon the needs of the group. External boundaries can be used to regulate how easy it is for people to become a member of the group. If a boundary is open then it's relatively easy to become a member and for members to communicate with outsiders. If a boundary is closed, it may be difficult or impossible for someone to join the group or for outsiders to communicate with people inside the group. Flexible boundaries allow for people to move around as needed to accomplish the task. Strict boundaries don't allow as much movement and are often found in more formal groups or organizations such as defining departments within a company.

How boundaries are constructed can be a matter of degree and balance depending upon the needs and wants of the group. For instance, if the boundary is too large, too flexible, or to open it feels less like a group and more like a crowd of people. If the boundary is too closed, too strict, or too small members can feel constrained or restricted possibly inhibiting them from accomplishing their task. Having a balance means keeping the boundaries open and flexible while allowing the group to adapt to change as necessary.

Language is another kind of boundary groups utilize. The ability to understand or speak a group's language can identify insiders and outsiders. Many professions like the medical, legal, and scientific fields utilize their own specialized language. These groups have their own specific technical jargon in order to increase precision in communicating information. It is important for everyone in the group to understand the group's specialized terms and to be able to speak the language in order to convey information accurately. The people who speak the language are considered insiders, while not understanding the language keeps everyone else out. Using a specialized language can raise the prestige and status of group members who understand them.

Group networks.

Groups do not exist in isolation, they have connections with others outside the group. They are often a part of a larger organization as well as the larger community. People do not communicate only with other group members, but also with people outside the group. Networks help regulate the perceptions and expectations of group members by letting them know how well they and the group are doing. Members make connections outside the group because they may need resources the group does not have to fulfill their needs and wants. They need to gain information in order to make good decisions. The better the quality of the information a group has, the better decisions it should make. This can make the group more effective so group members can feel more satisfied with the group increasing their commitment.

Networks are a series of connections between people that transfers information in, out, and around a group. Groups often utilize strategies in the form of norms to manage their boundaries to maintain their group's integrity rather like countries use borders and customs to control what goes in and out of a country. In a group, not every member talks with every other member the same amount or in the same manner. A network consists of who communicates with whom, under what circumstances, and about what topics. Networks help to fulfill group members need for information. How information flows in and out of the group can tell a lot about the group, its openness, its rules, its boundaries, and its structure.

Formal networks follow an established hierarchy carrying official information for the group or organization. Informal networks generally carry information that people are interested in and want to receive. Networks work because they follow the process of communicating by making connections between people. One person can serve as a liaison or gatekeeper to bring information into the group or keep information out. The more connected a member is to other networks, the more information they are likely to have access to, which can give them more power within the group. Networks can form a chain that goes through the group or organization or they may look like a wheel with one person serving as the hub communicating with others as the spokes.

Leaders and Leadership

A leader is a specific role that is created within a group. It can be the most important role because a leader has power and influence over the other members of a group. They can be responsible for managing the group, assigning tasks, regulating norms, allocating resources, and enforcing the rules. Groups and organizations have different types of leaders that gain their position by a variety of means.

These are some of the most common types of leaders.

• Task leader. They keep the group together so that it can accomplish its tasks to achieve its desired outcomes. They see that all members have something to do and that they do it. They can be appointed, promoted, a founder of the group, or are selected through behavioral reinforcement.

• Social leader. They help maintain the social well being of the group by promoting social activities and interpersonal relationships between members. They help members to fit in, maintain member satisfaction, and encourage commitment to the group. This position is often created through behavioral reinforcement.

• Appointed leader. Groups may have a leader who is appointed or designated by some person or entity outside the group. For example, a workgroup may have a leader appointed by the boss. If that person has not been chosen to lead by the members it may create tension or conflict. If a leader is appointed, they may still need to go through the process of behavior reinforcement to become the group's natural leader to be effective.

• Natural leader. This person becomes the leader of a group through the behavioral reinforcement process. They are chosen by the other group members to lead the group. They may not necessarily be the task or appointed leader.

• Founder. Groups and organizations are created by an individual or group of people. The founders often have special status in the group. They have usually been in the group the longest, so they know the group better than anyone else. They often become the president or CEO. Over time they become part of the group's culture and history.

- Power leader. This is a person who uses power, influence, and control over others to become a leader. Power can come from a person's experience, expertise, charisma, or by force. They may gain power by promising group members benefits in exchange for their position. Some leaders gain power through brute force or unethical use of power. They may use coercion, threats, manipulation, or relationships with other influential people to gain a position of leadership.

- Motivational leader. This person becomes a leader based upon their power of persuasion and their ability to motivate people to follow them.

- Charismatic leader. These people are attractive to others and are often good speakers making them persuasive, which motivates people to follow them.

- Situational leader. There are times when groups face unusual circumstances like a crisis. A person becomes a leader because of their skills or expertise in facing a particular situation, solving a problem, or resolving a crisis.

- Visionary leadership. People will follow a leader who presents a vision of the future that seems better than today. These leaders are particularly effective when people are facing difficult times or a crisis and want things to get better.

- Spiritual leadership. Authority is often based upon appealing to people's spiritual or religious beliefs in a higher power. This form of leadership is attractive when people feel uncertain about other forms of leadership or are looking for answers in life.

- Coaching. Some leaders approach leadership like sports. They might act like a coach who provides their experience and expertise to help the team. However, the coach does not necessarily play in the game. A variation of the coach is the facilitator, someone outside the group who has experience or expertise to help the group facilitate their development or complete a task.

- Manager. Technically a manager manages people as opposed to a leader who leads them. Sometimes leaders downplay being a leader, so they can make themselves appear as if they are an ordinary person who is just one of the group.

- Teacher. Leaders may characterize themselves as teachers helping others to learn how to solve problems for themselves rather than providing answers. They may see part of being a leader as educating other members.

- Military. Some leaders take the approach of a military leader like a general leading their troops into battle. This can be a more direct approach in which they give orders that others are expected to follow.

- Legitimation. In order to be effective, a leader needs a legitimate claim to lead others. Legitimation is the process of uncertainty reduction by investing in authority. It has been used in many societies throughout history. Royalty claimed legitimacy by bloodline, pharaohs claimed descendancy from the gods, and in a democracy leaders claim legitimacy from the will of the people. If a person becomes a leader of any other type they need to legitimize their claim to leadership, otherwise people may become disenchanted and no longer follow them, perhaps even replacing them.

Becoming a leader.

Many types of leaders are chosen through the process of behavior reinforcement. Since the leader is such an important role it may be the most difficult one for the group to select. Not everyone wants or tries to be a leader. Many members are not considered for leadership by the others, so only a few go through the process of behavior reinforcement. If two or more members want to be leaders or the group is unable to select a leader, it can create a schism that impedes the effectiveness of the group.

People find leaders attractive. They not only aspire to be leaders, they like to be around them. Perhaps it's because this can fulfill their need for status, prestige, or to feel important even if they are only around others who are important. It may fulfill a need to have power or exert influence over others. It could be to fulfill a need to receive the social and material benefits that leaders can provide.

Even though we find leaders attractive, people often deny that they want to be a leader. This may be because society can be suspicious of its leaders. People who want to run for public office often deny they want to run until the last moment and when they do, they claim that they are running for the good of the people, not for themselves.

There is no one best way to become a group leader. Becoming a leader often depends upon gaining the support of the other group members. If you want to be a leader you have to act like one and make connections with the other group members.

These are some characteristics of leaders.

- Show up, arrive early, stay late, and don't miss meetings. One of the simplest things you can do is show up. Few things irritate people more than someone who shows up late, leaves early, or misses meetings. To be a leader it takes commitment and dedication to the group above and beyond what is expected of other members.

- Talk. Talk appropriately contributing to the group discussion. Do not dominate the conversation because talking too much can annoy people, but do not hold back either. Keep what you say simple, easy to understand, straightforward, and nonjudgmental. Not saying anything gives the appearance that you are not interested or are aloof. Leaders listen to what other people have to say and then know just the right time to speak up, what to say, and most importantly when to stop speaking.

- Listen. When others speak actually listen to them and show support for what they have to say. Ask questions of other group members to draw them out. Offer your opinion at the appropriate time. Look at the big picture. Don't get bogged down in excessive details or petty squabbles. Listen to what others say and then develop your own ideas to help the group achieve its desired outcomes.

- Feedback. Be warm and friendly to the other members. Provide positive feedback because it bolsters other people's self-concept. Be polite and supportive of other people's ideas. It makes them feel good so they will like being a member.

- Be serious. Joking around and being the center of attention may get people to laugh or to like you, but they are not likely to take you seriously as a leader.

- Be informed. Do your homework, gather information, and be prepared. People who are perceived as knowledgeable have a greater chance of becoming a leader.

- Avoid taking sides. We want to support others, however, you may end up alienating most of the group. Instead, be the peacemaker by bringing all sides together to find a solution that everyone can agree on and that works for you too. Avoid getting locked into one position that may become unpopular. Offer suggestions and alternatives rather than telling people what they should do. Avoid taking positions that others may not support because leaders need support.

- Pick your battles. There will be times when you will have to take a decisive position and that can mean taking sides. The old adage, pick your battles applies here. There will be times when if you don't take a decisive position, others will get the perception that you are incapable of making decisions.

Functions of a leader.

Perhaps you have had experience with leaders who you felt were good while others were not so good. Perhaps you have had the experience of being a leader yourself. It is these experiences that form our expectations about what constitutes a good leader and how to exhibit good leadership.

Group members need to know what they can expect from a leader and a leader needs to know what they can expect from the other group members. To be an effective leader, it is helpful to be aware of and utilize the laws of uncertainty, shared meaning, and investing.

- Leaders reduce uncertainty. People join groups to reduce uncertainty and leaders can help make the group more stable and secure. They can help the group to stabilize its structure, rules, roles, norms, and other ways of doing things. They help keep the group on task to achieve its desired outcomes. They help allocate resources so group members can have their needs and wants fulfilled. They can create a feeling of security to instill confidence in the group by being supportive, helpful, fair, and by doing what they say they are going to do.

- Leaders provide information, allocate resources, and assign tasks so group members can do their work more effectively. They help make plans for the future and follow up to see that things get done. They help structure the group and its procedures to work more effectively to make good use of its resources like each member's time. They delegate responsibility, so that everyone does their fair share and they allocate rewards so everyone feels they benefit fairly. They help the group to make decisions by encouraging everyone to participate, so that they feel they are contributing to the group. They help the group solve problems, work out disagreements, and resolve conflicts. They do this to help increase each member's satisfaction and foster commitment to the group.

- Leaders facilitate shared meaning. Leaders can help facilitate the process of self-disclosure to develop social relationships, so that group members feel comfortable with one another enabling them to work together more effectively. They can help members feel that they are making a contribution and that they are valued as an important part of the group. They help members feel like they fit in with the group and introduce new members to others making them feel comfortable. They can lead the group in rituals and traditions that shares meaning within the group. They can help members understand the history and significance of the group and what it means to be a member. They communicate the big picture and a vision of the future, so that group members know where they fit in, where they are going, and what to expect in the future.

- Leaders encourage investment. It is important to create and maintain the stability of the group by helping to develop rules and fairly enforce them. They help the group to be able to create an atmosphere of trust so members can invest their time and other resources in the group. They see that everyone benefits from the group and receives fair rewards for fair contributions. They help encourage longevity of the group for its members, so they are comfortable investing in the group over long periods of time. They maintain connections outside the group to help bring in information and other resources the group needs.

- Leaders encourage members to participate in decision making giving them a feeling of ownership in the group process, so that they are more likely to support and implement decisions. Leaders set an example to get other members of the group to invest in the well being of the group by putting the interests of the group above their own. They give credit to other members and reward them for what they do. They help to elevate the status and prestige of others and don't worry about getting credit for themselves, but rather share it with others. Leaders bring out leadership qualities in others by helping them to develop their competence and bolster their confidence. They are not threatened by the successes of others, but rather compliment their accomplishments and achievements.

- Leaders help fulfill needs and wants. We join groups to receive benefits that fulfill our needs and wants. Since leaders often allocate many of these benefits they have influence over the behavior of the other members. Leaders can use that influence for the benefit of the group by helping members to get things done. They can provide rewards for those who do well and penalties for those who break the rules. By providing benefits, leaders help to increase member satisfaction and increase commitment by making the group attractive. They can recruit new members to join the group and help them to learn the rules of the group by providing information or serving as a mentor to help them fit in.

- Leaders shape perceptions and expectations. Everyone has expectations about what a leader should be and what they should do. Leaders can help the group by managing the perceptions and expectations of its members. They can clearly communicate their perceptions so that group members have realistic expectations of them as well as of themselves. Leaders can provide current and accurate information about the group and what is happening around them to help keep the perceptions of their members in line with reality. All too often there is a tendency for leaders to portray things better than they really are so that others will like them and follow them. They may do this if they are fearful that by being honest they may lose the group's support. However, by being truthful, but tactful they can help the group to create accurate perceptions and realistic expectations.

- Leaders can be more effective when they have an awareness of their own style of communicating, the style of their members, and the style of outsiders. They need to have an awareness of what is going on both inside the group and outside the group that affects it. They help members to solve problems, make decisions, and achieve the group's desired outcomes. They help to develop individual member's expertise, experience, education, and skills for the good of the group. They can help to create options to avoid potential problems by being proactive rather than reactive. Leaders help to develop leadership skills in others.

- Leaders communicate the big picture to the group by taking the pieces and putting them together, so that everyone knows how they fit in and how they contribute to the whole. People are more committed to groups and organizations when they understand the big picture, know how they fit in, and can see that they make a difference. All too often we do not see the big picture or know where we fit in creating a sense that what we do does not matter. By seeing the big picture, people can feel that they are part of something bigger than themselves and what they do really does matter because they are making a difference. This helps increase individual member's satisfaction and commitment to the group.

- Leaders communicate a vision of the future, which is a comparison of the current situation to what the group could look like in the future. It includes a course of action to achieve that vision. Leaders use vision to help shape expectations, so that everyone will work together for the same desired outcomes. This vision should be attractive and compelling by providing a view of the group that is better tomorrow than it is today. This can motivate the members to invest in the group over the long term, so they will work toward making that vision a reality, whether it is actually achieved or not.

Leadership styles.

There's no one right way to be a leader. Leadership style is contingent upon a leaders individual characteristics, the group's tasks, its members, and their desired outcomes. Approaches vary from hands on to delegating, from analytical to creative, from flexible to structured, and from democratic to authoritarian. Effective leaders are aware of their own leadership style and can utilize a variety of options depending on the circumstances.

These are some basic styles of leadership.

- Hands on leadership is when a leader is involved in many aspects of a group including decision making and helping members with the group's tasks. A hands on approach can be helpful when a leader is engaged in what is going on in the group. However, being too hands on could be perceived as interference or lack of trust in the other members.

- Delegating authority is when a leader puts other people in charge of getting certain tasks done. Leaders can use this style to give group members more responsibility and more of a say in what happens in the group. Doing this can help to develop their leadership abilities. However, some leaders might use this as an excuse to not do their work themselves.

- Analytical leadership looks at things from a scientific perspective, sometimes quantifying things by putting numbers on them so they can be measured. For example, productivity can be measured in numbers or percentages, which can be useful for comparison. However, it can overlook the human aspects of the group.

- Creative leadership breaks out of conventional structures to apply leadership qualities based upon the specific circumstances. It can be helpful to look at a situation in a new way to find different solutions. However, this style can be perceived as lacking structure causing some members to lose confidence in the ability of the group to accomplish its task.

- Democratic leadership allows everyone to have a say in decision making. This gives members an opportunity to contribute to the group. However, decisions may take longer and may be more difficult to reach. There is a greater possibility of disagreement and conflict slowing down the group creating tensions and divisions between members.

- Authoritarian leadership controls group members giving them very little say because decisions are made by the leader. This style of leadership works when a task needs to be done quickly or decisively, or when there are few options and the outcome is clear such as in emergency situations. However, this style of leadership can motivate members to withdraw and not contribute reducing their commitment to the group.

While these represent some styles of leadership, most leaders utilize a combination of them depending on the circumstances. At times they may use authority to make quick decisions for the good of the group. Other times they lead based upon group consensus and support.

Leaders need to provide structure for stability, but also be flexible enough to change based on the circumstances. Some problems need to be looked at analytically while others need a creative solution. The key to becoming an effective leader is having an awareness of your own leadership style, skills, and abilities. Then, having options to choose the right approach in a given situation.

Followers.

We place a great deal of importance on being a leader and leadership skills. There are awards for leadership, there are seminars on leadership, and books are written about leadership. So, what do we do for followers? What would you think if your boss took you aside and said that you would make a good follower? We may not consider the role of followers like we do leaders, but without them there would be no leaders.

We have all seen an orchestra concert. Picture in your mind the conductor leading the orchestra. Now picture in your mind the same conductor on stage conducting without the orchestra. Who would watch a conductor conduct all by themselves in silence? That would look pretty strange. An orchestra can make music without the conductor, but a conductor cannot make music all by themselves.

Similarly, a leader can't lead if there's no one to follow them. You can't have good leaders without good followers. We give credit to leaders for their achievements, but it is often their followers who do the work necessary to get the job done. Good followers make groups and organizations work because they get things done. They need many of the same qualities and have many of the same responsibilities as good leaders. They are responsible, they stay focused on the task, they organize resources, and pay attention to details while seeing the big picture. In order to be an effective leader, it helps to be a good follower.

Many organizations have an organizational chart that starts with the CEO at the top and follows down through the various levels showing where everyone in the organization fits in. At the bottom are the people who do most of the actual work. Picture this chart in your mind and then turn it upside down. Now the people who get things done are at the top with the CEO at the bottom. This is how we can look at leadership in a new way. All too often information flows from the top down to the bottom. When this chart is turned upside down, the information from where the work gets done can get to the leaders, so they can make good decisions.

Some leaders may act as if it is the responsibility of the group members to support them. They utilize the group's resources to gain benefits for themselves. This can undermine the effectiveness of a group or organization. It is the responsibility of a leader to support the group members and to see that their needs are met, so that they can do their job effectively.

The group should not exist to support the leader, the leader should be there to support the members of the group so they can get the job done. Leaders should make sure that the members of the group or organization have what they need to do their job because without them, there is no need for a leader. In order to do this they must get out of their offices and spend time with their employees and customers to really know what is going on.

An orchestra can make music without a conductor and an organization can survive without a leader. However, if a group loses too many members who do the work, a leader cannot do the work of those members, just as a conductor cannot play all the instruments. So, leaders should support group members to foster their satisfaction and commitment to the group.

III. Group Maintenance
The Law of Investing Phase

Once uncertainty has been reduced and group members share meaning to develop the group, they need to invest in the group and each other to maintain the group. Groups provide benefits, but they also require contributions from their members. These contributions can be in the form of time, energy, emotions, attention, and material things like money.

The perceptions and expectations members have of receiving benefits for contributions can affect their satisfaction with their group, their commitment to the group, and what they are willing to do for the group. This begins the law of investing phase of group development, which is necessary to maintain the group over time.

When a group stabilizes, uncertainty is reduced making it more predictable. This gives the group a greater chance of having longevity, which creates value because it motivates members to stay with the group longer to receive benefits. When people have a perception of receiving future benefits from the group, it gives them a reasonable expectation that they will see the investment they make now payoff in the future.

This can make the group more desirable to its members and encourage them to increase their commitment to the group making it more valuable to them and others. Increased value raises the group's status by increasing member commitment. Groups often increase in status when more people are willing to do more to be a member.

Individual members invest in the group when they begin to identify with the group and see it as their own. They may refer to the group as "my group" or "our group." This is an expression of their collective sense of ownership and pride in the group. When they introduce themselves to others outside the group, they may mention that they are members of the group. They may even define their self-concept and manage their identity based upon belonging to the group.

Group satisfaction.

Satisfaction represents the degree to which an individual member is happy with the group based upon their perceptions and expectations. It is often based upon how well they feel their expectations have been met and the extent to which their needs and wants have been fulfilled. The more members feel that these are being met, the greater their satisfaction increasing their commitment to the group. They are likely to do more for the group because they will not want to lose their benefits.

All too often groups become more concerned with getting the task accomplished than with member satisfaction. If the group does not work well together or is not successful, members may wonder what happened. Having awareness of the law of investing phase of group development enables leaders and members to increase group satisfaction without necessarily requiring more resources. The more individual members feel a sense of satisfaction, the more they will be committed to the group and willing to work for the good of the group to make it successful.

Groups and organizations may try to improve the quality and effectiveness of the group, however, when it doesn't work it can leave them wondering what went wrong. If members become dissatisfied with the group they are more likely to contribute less, be less committed, and the group will suffer. If they are dissatisfied enough, they might compare their circumstances to other groups to see if they can get a better deal somewhere else. This can create a climate of dissatisfaction in the group undermining its effectiveness. If enough people become dissatisfied with the group it may deteriorate or fall apart.

Group satisfaction is often based on the perceptions and expectations of individual members. Everyone has expectations of what they want to contribute as well as receive from the groups they join. Most people expect to make fair contributions and receive fair rewards. These perceptions are usually based upon a person's past experiences and what they have received in the past. For instance, what some may consider generous monetary compensation others may see as inadequate.

Group satisfaction is often based upon the degree to which members feel their needs and wants are being fulfilled by the group. We join groups to fulfill needs and wants we cannot fulfill ourselves, which creates expectations about what we feel we should receive as a member of the group. When a member's perception matches or exceeds their expectations, it can increase their satisfaction with the group. So, if members have the perception that their needs and wants are being reasonably fulfilled, they are more likely to contribute to the group increasing their satisfaction with the group. After all, if group members are getting their needs and wants fulfilled, why would they want to leave?

If group members feel that their needs and wants are not being fulfilled, they may be less likely to feel satisfaction with the group. If their perceptions are not meeting their expectations, it can motivate them to look at other groups to see if they can do better. This can create dissatisfaction eroding their commitment to the group. If they become dissatisfied enough they might leave the group.

Each member's investment is based upon their perceptions and expectations. Members are likely to have perceptions of the group and what is expected of them, so they are willing to contribute based upon their expectation of future benefits. People don't usually seek to maximize rewards and minimize costs by buying low and selling high. Rather, they seek fair rewards for fair contributions. This is because no one wants to be in a group with someone who does as little as possible and expects to get as much as possible.

Groups do not work in isolation, members communicate with people outside the group such as customers, clients, friends, family, people in the larger organization, and the community. These people may have the perception that they have an investment in the success of the group. For example, a member's spouse or family may feel they have an investment in the group because they are also dependent upon their salary. This can create their own perceptions and expectations about the group and its members, which can be a source of satisfaction or dissatisfaction. They can be a source of social rewards by providing support, nurturing, self-esteem, and showing respect making group members feel good about the work they are doing and the group.

The people outside the group can form a loose knit network of their own based upon their connections to the group members. It can be helpful to the group's effectiveness to consider the influence that these people have on the group. Members may not be aware of just how much influence they may have on the group, which could potentially be greater than the group members exert on themselves because of how outsiders communicate with group members. Through the process of communicating, members receive reflective feedback from outsiders that can affect the group's self-concept and how they see themselves.

It can be helpful for groups to be aware of how people outside the group can influence their effectiveness. This is because group members don't get all their support such as their needs and wants fulfilled by the group itself. They often depend on others outside the group to fulfill them, which can give them some degree of influence in the group. The support members get from their families can help improve their self-concept and feeling of satisfaction raising the collective self-esteem within the group. A group may have social events that include these people in order to keep them informed about the group and to learn more about their perceptions and expectations.

It can be helpful to be aware of the degree to which group members are satisfied with the group. All too often member dissatisfaction goes unnoticed, ignored, or members keep it to themselves because they don't want to be characterized as a complainer or risk their investment. Members who tell others that they are dissatisfied may be punished by the group to discourage dissent from spreading throughout the group. If members feel they could lose their investment, they could withhold their problems with the group until it builds up to the point where they can no longer deal with the tension, creating conflict or they may quit.

Dissatisfaction can be reduced by encouraging group members to share their thoughts and feelings without the fear of retaliation. Groups may not be in a position to offer more material rewards, however, it is relatively easy to offer social rewards such as acknowledgment, recognition, and respect to bolster members' self-concept. Utilizing these methods is effective because agreement is one of the strongest means of supporting others because it affirms their value to the group. When our ideas are accepted by others it elevates our status with the group.

Group commitment.

Commitment is the degree to which individual group members are attracted to be a member of the group. It is the degree to which they put group goals above their own. It is the degree to which they are willing to stay with the group through difficult times and to resolve conflicts. It is the degree to which they are willing to work hard to complete a task without regard to gaining personal rewards. Commitment can be a measure of how strong the connections are between individual group members.

Groups necessitate making a commitment not only to the group, but also to the other members of the group. An individual member may determine their commitment to a group based on what it stands for or the rewards it can provide. They can have a strong commitment to a group even though they may not get along with the other members. Conversely, people may stay in a group they don't feel very strongly about, but they may feel connected to the other members. For instance, this might happen in a company where members may not be happy with what they do, but they feel they are working with a great group of people. The level of commitment members have to a group can help or hurt its effectiveness. So, it is important for group members to support other members because they in turn would want their support.

The commitment members have to a group can be measured by the degree to which they;

• Put aside their own needs and wants for the good of the group.

• Put group goals and the goals of other members above their own.

• Work through conflicts to resolve them.

• Undergo adversity to keep the group together.

• Defend the group to others outside the group.

All groups have different degrees of commitment ranging from very low to very high. The degree of commitment is contingent upon the nature of the group, the individuals involved, and the task to be accomplished. For many groups, after reaching a certain level of commitment, having more commitment is not necessarily better. Some groups do not need a high level of commitment to function effectively.

For example, a casual social group may be better served by having a low degree of commitment, so that members don't feel pressured in ways that could push them out of the group. They may not have the time or other resources to commit to the group and demanding more could make them quit. Conversely, a more structured group like a sports team often demands a higher degree of commitment to be successful.

A member's commitment can be seen as a measure of their investment in the group and in the other members. Commitment is based upon an individual's perception and expectation of their needs and wants being fulfilled by the group in the short and long term. Investments come in different forms depending upon an individual's needs. Some members may forgo short term rewards with the expectation of greater long term rewards such as working for a higher purpose or a retirement pension.

Groups with a high degree of commitment tend to do more work, help one another, do what is necessary to get the job done, and encourage feedback. They speak up when necessary and work through conflict and disagreement. They have high morale and are less likely to leave the group to join another one. They enjoy spending time with one another often staying after meetings to talk socially.

Groups that have a low commitment tend to be more quiet and polite, tense and uneasy, and have low morale. They avoid conflict for fear that it will hurt the group because it probably will. They tend to hurry through their tasks so they don't have to spend time together. When their expectations are not met, there can be a high degree of turnover. Group members are less likely to stay in the group and are more likely to leave to join another group.

When a group has too little commitment it is more likely that nothing much gets done and members become easily dissatisfied with the group. Too much commitment can make group members overly confident, aggressive, and likely to take risks that can lead to undesired outcomes. If a group is taking up too much time and making too many demands it could burnout group members. Group commitment is a matter of balance that each group has to find for themselves.

Group power.

Groups are attractive because they concentrate power and people want the benefits that power can bring. Power can provide a means to fulfill many of our needs and wants. When people are grouped together they create hierarchies, ranks, or a kind of pecking order among members, which gives some of them power over others.

Power based hierarchies are often expressed by the amount of respect, status, and prestige that is given to fulfill the needs of its members. Groups concentrate power because they are comprised of people who gather and allocate resources, which means that someone has to decide who gets what. Because members have needs and wants they seek to have fulfilled by groups, the people who distribute resources have power over those who want their benefits.

Groups have tasks that need to be accomplished, so people have to do them. Some tasks are more important to the group than others, so they are often ranked or prioritized. Some tasks are more difficult, require more education or expertise, or are done by members who have been in the organization the longest. The law of shared meaning invests these tasks with different values, which creates power, ranks, and hierarchies. This is evidenced by the wide range of salaries organizations often pay their employees.

Groups create power because they have the ability to fulfill needs and wants. This motivates members to do what the group wants them to do so they can have them fulfilled. If they want to gain benefits, they have to comply with the rules of the group. Groups create rules that control member's behavior and provide punishments for those who violate them. Groups can do this because they control and distribute resources by determining who receives them and who does not. These resources help members fulfill both social and material needs and wants.

This works fine as long as the members of a group can create their own rules and control their own destiny. However, there might be times when people with ulterior motives gain control of a group to use its resources for their own benefit to achieve their personal desired outcomes. They may use the resources of the group to reward those people who help them gain and keep power, while denying resources to punish those people who oppose them. It may be difficult to recognize people who do this until they have gained power and by then it may be too late to stop them. This is why groups need mechanisms in order to ensure that power is used fairly for the good of the group.

Power is attractive because of its ability to reduce uncertainty by creating safety, security, and predictability. Power is necessary in society for the protection of its citizens to keep them free from harm. It is a way to get the things done that need to be done in order for society to function. Power is attractive because of its ability to allocate resources and benefits. People want to be around others who they perceive as powerful with the expectation that they will be the beneficiary of some of those resources. They have the expectation of power transference, if they are near others who are powerful they may be perceived as having power and status themselves.

We have a tendency to invest power with shared meaning. We look at power as being some-thing that can be a positive force for good as well as a destructive force. Power is based upon things having value and sharing meaning often gives them value, so power is often based upon what meanings people share. People compete for things they consider valuable giving these things power over their behavior. This means that power can be based on the shared meanings we have about things, people, and groups. It can be measured by how much a person is willing to do to get what they want.

Power is something individuals want, but could live without. However, without power groups would be less attractive and have a more difficult time to recruit and keep members. Without power groups would have difficulty enforcing the rules or getting things done. Groups need power in order to gain the resources necessary to function, to keep members motivated, to accomplish tasks, and to keep the group together. Power makes groups attrac-tive so they can gain and maintain member's commitment to the group over time.

Power is based upon our perceptions and expectations. It is based on our perception of the degree to which others have control or influence over us. Power is the manifestation of our expectation of receiving future benefits for present behaviors. It is important in groups because it keeps them together and motivates its members to behave in ways that helps the group function. Groups can exert power over their members because the members have expectations of receiving benefits that will fulfill their needs and wants. The more people expect to gain, the more likely they are to submit to the power of the group. The degree to which power can be exerted is often the degree to which the group can fulfill their needs and wants.

We allow this control because we expect to receive benefits in return for our cooperation. If we do not want to get something from others then they have little power over us. For ex-ample, we work at our job with the expectation that we will receive a paycheck and perhaps a promotion or a raise in the future. Our employer has power over us because they control our salary and other benefits that we need and want. If we no longer work for them, their power is gone. However, there are some types of power we cannot disregard, such as the power of government over its citizens. So, power is to some extent based upon our willing-ness to accept it in exchange for the expectation of receiving benefits. If you don't want someone to have power over you, don't expect anything from them.

Types of power.

Power can be divided into two basic types; persuasive and coercive. Persuasive power is generally psychologically based, we exchange something we have like our time and energy for things that we need or want like money. It is the ability to control or influence indi-viduals and to allocate resources. We use persuasive power by communicating with others. Coercive power is the exercise of power by force such as that used by government, law enforcement, or the military.

We are motivated by the law of uncertainty to submit to power in exchange for reducing uncertainty like keeping order, ensuring public safety, and maintaining stability in society. Without this power anyone could do whatever they wanted and life would become chaotic and dangerous. Even in countries with oppressive governments, people tend to accept the government's power to keep order. Power generally comes from a specific source that re-duces uncertainty fulfilling needs and wants.

These are some sources of power in groups.

- Persuasion. Power comes from the ability to persuade people to think a certain way or take a certain course of action.

- Information. Power comes from having a particular expertise, experience, skill, or educational background. It is often said that knowledge is power and the more people have to offer that others want, the more power they can exert.

- Resources. Power comes from the ability to allocate and control resources, the most common is money.

- Social rewards. Behavior can be motivated by social rewards because people want to be liked. These include status, prestige, respect, affection, and self-esteem.

- Morality. Power comes form religious and spiritual sources. From tradition, values, and doing what is right.

- Charisma. A charismatic personality can persuade others to do things they might not otherwise do. People like to be around others they find attractive, confident, or likeable.

- Position. Power comes from a person's job or position. A boss or employer has the power to hire, promote, and fire employees. Groups have a hierarchy of power that is often concentrated at the top.

- Competence. This is the ability to get things done, to make decisions, and solve problems. People like others who they perceive as being competent.

- Connections. Having connections can be a source of power because people are willing to do things for others who they perceive as having connections. They might think that their connections will benefit from them.

- The people. Power comes from having the support of the will of the people. Elected officials claim their right to office comes from the people who elected them.

- Force. Power comes from the ability to use force. It can come from the barrel of a gun. Groups like law enforcement and the military have the power to exert force to keep order.

Groups have the ability to exercise power, distribute resources, convey benefits, exert punishments, and expel members. Since these things have a direct affect on the quality of life of the group's members, there must be ethical considerations as to how they are implemented. Groups make significant contributions to the lives of their members, but they also have the power to hurt them. Groups, their leaders, and members should be held accountable for the consequences of their actions and impact they have on the lives of their members. Whenever groups have this kind of power they are open to the possibility of corruption and the abuse of their power.

While no group ever considers themselves corrupt, there needs to be consideration given to preventing a group or individual members from the corrupt use of power. Groups need to have moral standards of behavior and ethics. These are often developed based on past experiences, social reality, and spiritual considerations. This means that the standard of ethics can vary widely from group to group. What is considered normal for one group may be considered unethical in another. Ethics are about the choices we make, what we do, and what kind of person we want to be.

The larger the group or organization, the greater the tendency to become legalistic in order to create a stronger structure to keep order. Groups use rules and ethics to keep order where society makes laws. Ethics deal with morality, with right and wrong and what constitutes acceptable behavior. Law deals with what is legal, what is written down in statutes or has been decided by the courts. Ethical and moral resolutions involve changing behavior. Legal resolutions usually involve monetary damages or punitive consequences.

Groups should develop a standard of ethics that all members follow that sets out guidelines for what constitutes ethical conduct. It should provide for the general welfare of the group and its members by holding them accountable for their actions. The purpose is to enhance the standards of the group and support the welfare of group members. Groups and their members should not be able to hide behind a group identity, but rather be held accountable for their actions and decisions.

Group longevity.

One reason we form groups is because they have longevity beyond its individual members. Over time, a group's founders are eventually replaced with new members. As a group grows older, members eventually leave, so it must attract new members to keep it going or the group will cease to exist. This creates a hierarchy within the group giving members who have been there the longest higher status and more power than new members.

Older members often have more experience, more expertise, and more knowledge about the group. They also know the group better, know how it works, and how to get things done. Groups often rank their members in a pecking order from the highest to the least status based in part on how long they have been a member.

Groups provide rewards to their members based upon how long they have been a member of the group. These can be material rewards such as salary and bonuses. They can be tangible rewards like a bigger office with nicer furniture in a more desirable location. They can also be social rewards like respect, status, influence, and power. Groups often allocate rewards based on how long a person has been with the group to provide an incentive to encourage members to invest their time and other resources over long periods of time.

This helps to ensure the continuation of the group after the founders and other members are gone. It helps to increase the attractiveness of the group because members know they can increase the return on their investment by staying longer. This creates stability increasing the potential longevity of the group by motivating people to make contributions now with the expectation of receiving benefits later. This motivates them to make long term investments rather than seek short term rewards, which should benefit the group.

While there are benefits to promoting group longevity it can also lead to group paralysis. When members keep their position in the group for long periods of time it can discourage others from staying in the group or new members from joining. This is because it could create the perception that the long time members receive all the benefits and resources, so newer members will have to wait a long time before they receive them, if at all. The perception that a few people are receiving most of the benefits may create dissatisfaction, even anger among the other group members. This can lead to stagnation and resistance to innovation, which can be more likely to happen in large organizations.

Group conformity.

Large groups and organizations use power hierarchies to increase their members' conformity to the group. Members are motivated to make a commitment to the group over long periods of time in order to move up the hierarchy to gain increased rewards. In businesses, this can come in the form of promotions and increased salary. The use of differential power and rewards can work in large organizations, but can undermine the effectiveness of smaller groups.

In a small group, everyone knows what the others contribute, so if there is a large discrepancy in rewards those who receive less will be dissatisfied undermining their commitment to the group. Smaller groups can be given group rewards to motivate them to work together for the good of the group. When they receive individual rewards they are more likely to compete with one another undermining their ability to work together.

Groups exert a form of social control that exerts pressure on members to conform to the rules of the group. The more a person wants to be the member of a group, the more willing they may be to change their behavior to belong to it. The degree of pressure to conform is often related to the attractiveness of the group and its ability to fulfill individual needs and wants. The more a group can fulfill the needs and wants of its members and the more their perceptions meet or exceed expectations, the more attractive the group will be and the more likely members will change their behavior to conform to the group.

A group must exert some pressure on its members to conform because otherwise it would not continue to be a group. When a member does not conform to the rules and norms of the group, the other members might exert pressure to get them to comply. If they do not conform, other members may make fun of them, ostracize them, ridicule them, or even quit communicating with them. If a member's actions are serious enough, the others will expel them from the group.

While this sounds extreme, groups must do this or the group will break down into chaos. If a member is perceived by the others as not conforming, but still receiving benefits, the others may begin to question why anyone needs to conform at all. This can motivate other members to stop conforming to the norms of the group undermining its effectiveness and success. Nonconformity can be perceived as a threat to the group because it increases uncertainty undermining a group's stability and future predictability.

Groups have pressures to conform, but they need a mechanism to provide exceptions to conformity to facilitate change. In the larger society, social reality dictates acceptable behavior, however, some people behave outside those rules in order to introduce new ideas or bring about change. For instance, artists, musicians, writers, actors, and celebrities may be allowed to deviate from the norms of society to bring about change such as new styles of clothing, music, art, and new ways of thinking.

This mechanism utilizes the process of behavioral reinforcement. If others find these behaviors acceptable through positive feedback, they may catch on and become more widely adopted. Many types of art and music once considered scandalous are now widely accepted. If there were no such mechanism, society would be less likely to change and could stagnate.

Extreme conformity.

Sometimes groups take over all aspects of their members' lives to increase their commitment to levels that can be detrimental for them. They do this by using communicative methods and other structural devices to make an individual dependent on the group for their needs and wants. The group then replaces their social reality with an alternative social reality created by the group. This group reality can be attractive because it often plays on deeply held beliefs, utilizing activities and rituals so that members become so absorbed in meeting the demands of the group they lose sight of practically everything else.

This can be done by making them dependent on the group to fulfill all or most of their needs and wants. The group might reduce their awareness and options by telling them that they need to make sacrifices to affirm their commitment to the group. They might cut off their connections with others outside the group who could provide information and support. This can make them dependent on the group for all their information. Since information is the basis of making decisions, they make decisions based upon what the group tells them.

These types of groups can give members the perception of receiving more rewards in the future for making sacrifices in the present, to motivate them to immerse themselves in the group even though they may actually gain very little. If they don't comply with the group's demands they may be threatened with sanctions, punishments, loss of benefits, even expulsion from the group. People can be motivated to comply because they don't want to risk losing what they perceive as their investment in the group and future benefits, even when leaving may be in their best interest.

People can be reluctant to leave some groups even when staying is not in their best interest. If their only source of support is through connections with other group members, leaving the group means that these connections will be severed and their support will be gone. Because groups create a shared sense of meaning, the group has meaning to them, which may be lost. Group members can exert a degree of influence over the their self-concept, so leaving the group means leaving a part of themselves behind. Groups provide stability and structure, so leaving the group would increase uncertainty. Since uncertainty is uncomfortable, people can be motivated to stay making it difficult for them to leave, even when they probably should.

IV. Group Dissolution
Return to The Law of Uncertainty Phase

There's an old saying that goes, all good things come to an end, and many groups come to an end. When people create or join groups they probably never considered how the group will end or that it will ever end at all. Not all groups last forever, eventually many come to an end for a wide variety of reasons.

They may have accomplished their task, they may no longer be fulfilling the needs and wants of their members, or they may no longer be relevant. The group may have lost its founder or members who were the driving force behind the group. Since groups are created for a purpose, the purpose it was created for may no longer exist and the group has simply run its course. In these circumstances the time may have come to disband the group and part ways.

Some groups may realize that their time has come to an end, while others may fight on against the odds. We spend a great deal of time with others in groups so when it ends we can feel a loss in our lives. However, it may be better to intentionally end a group that has come to the end of the line rather than painfully trying to keep it going as it slowly dwindles away.

Groups have traditions and rituals that celebrate important events for the group and its members. When someone retires there is often a celebration to commemorate their accomplishments. Instead of letting the group slowly wither away, the group members could have this kind of event to retire the group and bring it to a close. The event can be used to celebrate the accomplishments of the group and its members giving them closure by spending one last time together as a group.

Organizations

We spend a lot of our time in organizations because they make significant contributions to society and the lives of the people who are a part of them. An organization is a group of people brought together by common interests to achieve mutual desired outcomes. They can create their own specialized form of social reality affecting how we see ourselves, others, and the world around us. We are motivated to join them because they have the ability to allocate resources to help us achieve our desired outcomes and fulfill material and social needs and wants. This gives them power to motivate and influence behavior. In many ways groups and organizations can have considerable influence over us.

Organizations have many of the characteristics of a group, but are generally much larger. They can be made up of many smaller groups joined by connections making up networks that regulate the flow of information and resources. They tend to be more formal than groups with well defined rules, structures, and boundaries. They have tasks and desired outcomes that members are expected to fulfill based upon specialized roles. They often have centralized power with clear lines of authority, levels of management, and a hierarchy of importance. They allocate resources, provide rewards, and extract costs giving them power and social control over their members, like The Bank described earlier in this chapter. They have norms of behavior that are regulated by rules enforced with rewards and punishments.

There are many different types of organizations, so for the purpose of this book the word organization can refer to many kinds of entities including, but not limited to businesses, corporations, not for profit groups, government, schools, religious institutions, social clubs, and community groups.

We create organizations because they have the ability to reduce uncertainty in ways that individuals and groups cannot do. They can do this because they have the ability to gather and allocate resources for their members. Organizations can make us feel more safe and secure by reducing uncertainty. They reduce uncertainty by creating structure, so everyone knows what is expected of them and what they can expect of others. By working together with others, we can accomplish tasks that we could not accomplish working alone. They have longevity, the ability to continue to exist long after the founders and current members are gone, increasing stability and predictability for their members. They reduce uncertainty by fulfilling material, social, status, and security needs making them attractive to join.

Organizations are held together by the connections between members that form communicating networks through which they share meaning. Members share meaning about the organization including its history, how it was founded, its values, and common purpose.

They share meaning about what it means to be a member of the organization. They share meaning about the experiences of the members of the organization through the process of self-disclosure. This can help to encourage their members to trust one another enough to be able to work together. They share meaning by participating in traditions and rituals like celebrating important events and special days. An organization's name and logo are invested with meaning telling their members and the public who they are and what they do.

Organizations have structure to provide stability, so that people will be willing to invest their time and other resources in it and in the other members. They utilize boundaries, hierarchies, and levels of authority to create structure that gives the organization and some of its member's power. They develop rules of behavior, so that everyone knows what is expected of them and what they can reasonably expect from others. They allocate resources, provide rewards, and issue punishments to maintain order, so that people will feel comfortable investing in them. Many aspects of an organization are created and motivated by the law of investing to ensure its stability and longevity, without which people would consider it risky and be unwilling to invest the resources necessary for it to function.

An organization can work like a marketplace where communicating is the currency and people are constantly making offers that are being accepted or rejected. Understanding organizational behavior and how its members communicate with one another can work rather like a balance sheet that can be utilized to analyze the effectiveness of an organization. It can measure how willing people are to invest in it and each other, and how much of a return they expect on their investment. The difference between an individual's perceptions and expectations can be an indicator of their commitment. The degree to which their needs and wants are being met can be an indicator of their satisfaction or dissatisfaction, which can affect their commitment to the organization.

An organization can be like an individual with its own needs and wants that must be fulfilled in order to function. It exists for a reason and its members must accomplish tasks to achieve its desired outcomes. If they don't, the organization will not function and might cease to exist. An organization can work like a relationship because it is created by the connections between individuals, so no one person has total control over it. It is a separate entity from the people who comprise it because they create it between them. While members contribute to its existence, it can take on a life of its own with its own personality.

Individual members have their own needs and wants to fulfill that motivate them to join an organization. Organizations are attractive because they fulfill many needs and wants in ways that individuals cannot. They fulfill not only monetary needs, but also the need for inclusion, status, respect, self-esteem, growth, and a feeling of contributing something worthwhile to make a difference. Tension can be created between the needs and wants of the organization and the individual members. However, individuals must put the organization's needs first in order for the organization to function effectively.

Organizations can create their own specialized version of social reality that can serve as a form of social control to regulate individual member's behavior. Members create and nurture social reality when they tell stories about the organization, its history, important events, and its members. Sometimes these are stories about the early days or overcoming adversity. An organization often communicates its own social reality including its history, how it was founded, and why it exists, which can include stories about the founders, what kind of people they were, and their achievements. While these stories are based upon fact, there is often an element of added drama to make them more exciting.

These stories are more than just reminiscences of the past, they have a message for members today about the organization. They communicate organizational expectations about its values and how members should behave. Sharing these stories is motivated by the law of shared meaning because it creates a connection that brings members together for a common purpose. For example, people tell stories about the history of the United States including historical figures like George Washington and Thomas Jefferson. These stories have a message beyond a recollection of events, they communicate a deeper message of communal values and beliefs. They are used to share social reality like what America stands for and what it means to be an American.

Organizational satisfaction.

Everyone has perceptions and expectations about themselves, others, and the organization. They have expectations about what they are supposed to contribute and receive. They have perceptions about how well those expectations are being met, which may or may not reflect reality. Members often have differing perceptions and expectations that can make them feel satisfied or dissatisfied about their role in the organization. Satisfaction helps to increase a member's commitment encouraging them to do their job more effectively. Dissatisfaction can decrease commitment making people unhappy, perhaps even motivating them to leave.

Satisfaction is an emotional response to an individual's perception of the difference between what they are contributing to an organization compared to what they are receiving from it based on their expectations. Everyone's expectations are different because they are based on past experiences, comparisons to others, and their self-concept. When people perceive that they are receiving fair rewards for fair work they are more likely to be satisfied. When they feel they are contributing, but not receiving fair rewards, they can become dissatisfied. This means that member satisfaction is often based upon their perception of how well their needs and wants are being fulfilled, which may or may not reflect reality.

Generally, the higher degree of satisfaction the more an individual is motivated to commit to the organization by contributing their time and resources. The law of investing motivates people to reduce or withdraw their commitment in an organization when they feel they are not getting fair rewards. This is why it can be helpful to understand how member satisfaction works because when members are dissatisfied, it can undermine the effectiveness of the organization. This can reduce their commitment motivating them to withdraw resources and perhaps even leave. While there will always be some dissatisfaction in any organization, if the level becomes too great it may no longer be able to function effectively.

Organizational growth.

Organizations are created much the way groups are created. They can be formed spontaneously out of shared interests or created intentionally to achieve specific desired outcomes. They can grow naturally by people getting together based on their mutual interests that can attract others growing the organization without a definite plan. They can be started by a founder or a group to accomplish specific tasks like running a business. An organization often starts out small and when it becomes successful, it attracts other people and grows larger. When a group gets too large to function as a group, it may divide into two or more groups creating the need for an organizational structure to keep it together.

When an organization grows so large that everyone cannot communicate directly, like face to face, with everyone else, it needs to develop structures so it can function. This increases an organization's needs and wants requiring more people to fulfill them. As an organization grows, the nature of the tasks shift from the original purpose for which it was established to organizing the organization. For example, a person starts a store that is successful, so it expands to other locations. As it grows, the focus shifts from selling things to managing store locations and employees. Employees are no longer hired just to sell things in the store, but also to run the organization doing managerial tasks such as accounting, human resources, and property management. These tasks must now be accomplished, so the organization can function before anything is actually sold.

In smaller groups, one person may fulfill many roles and do multiple tasks giving them more experience and developing more skills. They can get a broader view of the organization, what it does, and how everything works together. As organizations get larger, more tasks need to be accomplished so more individuals are needed to accomplish them. This can lead to role specialization with a division of labor where members devote more of their time to a specific task concentrating on a particular task or skill. In larger organizations many people may be assigned to a specific task. This can unintentionally create boundaries, so members may not understand how everything fits together or how the overall organization works. They may no longer feel that they contribute or they may not know how what they do fits into the big picture because they only communicate with people close to them, who do what they do and not with people in other areas of the organization who may be different. This can make the organization lose focus or compete for resources that could damage it or fracture it into pieces because fewer members know how everything works together.

People can have a feeling of accomplishment when they know how what they do helps the organization. It can be helpful to have a way for members to move around an organization doing different tasks to gain more skills. This benefits the organization because members are can do many tasks increasing their flexibility rather than specializing where they can do just a few. They know how things work together giving them the big picture. This can help facilitate professional growth increasing their satisfaction and commitment. They also gain the ability to know how the organization works which can help them to become leaders.

Organizational structure.

In order to function effectively, organizations need structure including rules, roles, and norms of behavior. Structure usually consist of different types of connections between members. Organizations need to develop structure so that they can accomplish their tasks and achieve their desired outcomes. Structure can be defined by the boundaries that exist in and around the organization. Organizational structure should be clearly communicated, so all members understand what is expected of them and what they can expect of others, because how an organization structures itself can bring people together or it can divide them by pushing them apart.

Rules are the means by which an organization implements its version of social reality. Most organizations have their own set of both formal and informal rules. The formal rules are often written down in the form of official handbooks, guidelines, contracts, and other written documents. The purpose is to regulate individual behavior by conforming to the norms and expectations of the organization to help it to accomplish its tasks. New rules are often instituted after there has been some incident or infraction. Rules tend to be more reactive than proactive, often written in response to a problem. Rules can be presented in the context that they are there to protect the individual members, however, since they are created by the organization, their purpose is more often to protect the organization than individuals.

In addition to the formal organizational rules, groups within the organization often create their own set of informal rules. These rules are rarely written down, but can be more effective in regulating the behavior of its members. They are often created by the members through the process of behavioral reinforcement. Most of the time we only learn about these rules after they have been broken and we are reprimanded. We can learn them by observing the behavior of others or asking a more experienced member.

These are some of the structures that can be found in organizations.

- Power structure. Organizations have official power structures that are often organized along the lines of an organizational chart with power concentrated at the top flowing down through the organization. Power can be thought of as having the authority over others to regulate their behavior. In reality, there are several types of power that have their own sources. Information can be power and those who have it, regardless of where they are in the organization may be able to wield it. People who are gatekeepers, like assistants and secretaries, can have power because they control access to decision makers who allocate resources. Longtime members can have power because they know how to get things done. People at all levels can hold power because of their skills, knowledge, connections, influence, information, or the length of time they have been with the organization. It can be helpful to get to know the people who have power in your organizations.

- Task structure. The task structure of an organization consists of the connections between members that enable them to work together to accomplish tasks and achieve their desired outcomes. Task structures include division of labor, departments, and role specialization. They let people know their responsibilities and what tasks they are expected to accomplish. In organizations people may work in other ways creating their own informal task structures. They are more likely to work and communicate through informal structures based upon their needs and wants, common interests, and areas of expertise. These are the connections between individuals that create networks through which information flows. Formal structures tend to be more static, where informal structures are more likely to be dynamic, flexible, and open to change. This can make informal structures more helpful to people in accomplishing their tasks.

- Social structure. While the primary focus of an organization is to accomplish the task or desired outcome, consideration must be given to the social relationships of the people that accomplish them. The social structure of an organization is who communicates informally with whom about things that are not task related creating communicating networks. People socialize and spend time with others outside the formal structure discussing business and making decisions. People are more likely to work with or provide resources to people who they know on a social basis because uncertainty is reduced. Taking time to develop social relationships reduces uncertainty between members because it shares meaning and encourages self-disclosure to build trust, so that they can invest their time and other resources in the organization and in each other.

- Time structure. Time is a valuable resource in organizations and how they use it communicates their priorities and what they value. Time structure involves how members organize their day, week, and year. Do they spend their time in meetings, at their desk, or with customers and clients? It also includes social uses of time for rituals like coffee breaks and important days of the year like celebrating holidays. Time is prioritized and tasks organized based upon their importance to the organization. The structure of the organization often determines how people spend their time and what activities they value.

- Space structure. Organizations are not just comprised of people, they also include buildings, offices, and other types of space. How organizations utilize space can tell a lot about what is valued and how people communicate with one another. Since physical space is often valuable, organizations make decisions about how to organize and allocate their space based upon their values. Larger offices in nicer locations are often given as a reward for achievement for years of service to the organization. The higher up a person is in the organization, the more space they generally have. People are more likely to communicate with others that are in close physical proximity such as the adjoining work spaces as well as psychological proximity like working on similar tasks. Spatial structure is not just physical, it can be psychological. People often have an area of responsibility or expertise such as their turf or territory, which they are likely to protect from incursions by others.

Nonverbal communicating in organizations.

In order to fit in, it can be helpful to communicate the right messages. While we might focus on what we say, much of what others perceive about us is communicated nonverbally.

These are some ways of communicating nonverbally in organizations.

- Time. How organizations use time communicates what is valuable to them because it is their most limited resource. How individual members use time communicates their values and priorities to others. Different groups have different values when it comes to utilizing time. In some, punctuality is valued above all else. In others, getting things done is valued. If someone is working on a project they may continue to work rather than taking time out for a meeting. They may place value on how people spend social time including coffee breaks, lunch, and other activities like participating in sports or volunteering in the community.

- Space. Since everything has physical limitations, space is another limited resource. Space has to do not only with physical space, but also with territory or turf. Organizations have to place their people somewhere and where they place them in specific locations, buildings, and next to other people communicates what's important to the organization. Consider how offices are physically arranged. Who is next to whom, which are open or closed, and which people are accessible or blocked by gatekeepers like secretaries. People in organizations often stake out their own territory and defend it against intrusions by others. Territory can be seen as allocation of resources, allocation of space, influence over others, and duties or responsibilities.

- Symbols. Organizations have symbols that people invest with meaning. The most common are an organization's name, colors, and logo, which are carefully chosen to present as a form of identity management. Organizations have other symbols that members invest with meaning that communicates their values like badges, uniforms, or artwork. This can include the type of building they occupy, where it is located, how offices and public spaces are decorated, and what people choose to put in the offices. They can include what people wear or the kind of cars they drive. For example, frugality or the environment may be valued, so people drive less expensive or fuel efficient cars. They may value art by having it displayed in public spaces and individual offices.

- Appearance. How we look can be important because of what it communicates to others in the organization as well as outside of it. Organizational norms can dictate how people dress, how they do their hair and makeup, and what accessories they wear including jewelry or watches. Appearance communicates information about a person's job, values, even their income. Many professions have uniforms that communicate their job, position, or rank like the police and military. Groups and organizations use appearance and clothing like uniforms and patches to communicate expertise, competence, and authority.

Organizational networks.

Individuals need information to reduce uncertainty so they can invest in the organization and in one another in order to work together. In order to fulfill this need, organizations have official networks to disseminate information through connections such as emails, memos, and publications like newsletters. However, this may not be enough to fulfill the need for information. So, in order to fulfill that need members create connections with others based on similarity, proximity, intensity, and familiarity to form communicating networks which can become a part of an organization's structure.

In organizations information tends to flow from the top down, but not so much from the bottom up. People tend to be more comfortable communicating laterally with others who are on the same level as themselves. However, in order to make good decisions information needs to flow from the bottom, where decisions are implemented, up to the top where they are made in order to evaluate how well they work.

People tend to talk to others with whom they share space, who they are close to, who they have known for some time, who they see as similar, or who share the same interests. This is much like the way that people form relationships based on proximity, similarity, frequency, and intensity. They are more likely to communicate informally and share information because there is reduced uncertainty based on a common connection. This series of connections creates informal networks in the organization through which information flows. The activity of these informal networks can be a measure of how well the official networks are fulfilling the need for information.

We have a need for information and when it is not fulfilled, we seek out ways to fulfill it. Organizations have networks to communicate information to its members and most of the time these networks provide the information that is needed. However, there are times when they can become inadequate and do not provide the information people want so they seek out other ways to get it through connections with others. This demand to fill the need for information to reduce uncertainty can motivate rumor and gossip.

The laws of uncertainty and shared meaning can motivate us to create and circulate rumor and gossip. When there is a lack of information, uncertainty is increased, so we seek to reduce it. When we experience something we may not fully understand, we can be motivated to make sense out of it by looking for shared meaning in it. These explanations have power because they can motivate people's behavior resulting in tangible consequences.

When normal sources of information do not meet the need for information, people can be motivated to seek out other ways to obtain it. The amount of rumor and gossip in an organization can be an indicator of the difference between the supply and demand for information. This can be a measure of how well the formal communicating networks are fulfilling the needs of its members. If there is relatively little rumor or gossip, then there is relatively little need for more information. If there is a lot, then the formal networks are not meeting the need for information.

Rumors are based on speculation or opinion that is not necessarily supported with facts or truth. They are often about events that might happen in the future. While they may be untrue, they can sound believable. Rumor can be in greater demand when there is a time of uncertainty or crisis in an organization increasing the need for information. The higher the demand for information and the less official information is forthcoming, the more likely rumors will be spread. People also spread rumors in order to gain attention or prestige within an organization because people pay attention to them.

Gossip is usually about the behavior of people we know or who are well known that has happened in the past. It is usually communicated through casual conversation with people who are close to us. Gossip is appealing because it reduces uncertainty about people who are perceived as mysterious or interesting. It is a way that people share meaning by using gossip as a basis of comparison to evaluate their own circumstances. We use it as a subject of conversation to make connections with others to develop relationships by talking about common interests. We don't just gossip about well known people like celebrities, we gossip about people we know like our friends, family, coworkers, and neighbors.

Every organization has some degree of rumor and gossip. We share rumor and gossip so we will be considered part of the group because it creates connections and shares meaning with others. We find it interesting because it fulfills the need for information, entertainment, or excitement. It makes us feel that we know something others don't. It may not even matter that the information is true as long as it is interesting or exciting.

Most of the time this information is relatively harmless, however, there are times when it can do damage because information motivates behavior. By having an awareness of what's happening, an organization can provide information to meet the demand. If damaging rumors or gossip occur, a response may be necessary to mitigate the potential damaging effects of the information. Rumor and gossip is sometimes used as a public relations mechanism to manage and influence perceptions in order to achieve desired outcomes. By increasing interest, people may take notice of someone or something motivating them to take action. They utilize the process of communicating by creating a message that cuts through the noise and interference to get our attention.

Organizational Climate

Organizational climate describes the nature of how people communicate with one another. It is important because it can affect people's state of mind. While it is mostly psychological in nature, it is communicated through the social interaction of people, so it can have tangible results manifested in their behavior. It is an important part of an organization because it can make us feel good about ourselves. A positive climate makes an organization a fun place to be, motivating people to want to be a part of it. A negative climate can reduce an individual's commitment to the organization, so they feel less satisfied, making them more likely to leave. Organizational climate is important because it affects the ability of people to work together and accomplish their desired outcomes. This is because it has an influence on the perceptions and expectations of themselves, others, and the organization.

These are some elements of an organization's climate.

- Emotional. We all experience emotions and everyone is in some type of a mood all the time. Most of the time we are in a generally good mood. Since this is not uncomfortable, we don't think very much about it until something happens that puts us in a bad mood. People can pick up on the emotional intensity of others and transfer their emotions through the connections between individuals that comprise communicating networks. They may have been feeling similarly, but did not act on it until they heard someone else express it confirming their feelings.

- Openness. Climate can include the degree of openness people feel when they communicate with one another. They may share information freely, openly, and honestly. Conversely, a climate may be restrictive so people don't say what's on their mind. People have different degrees to which they are accepting of different kinds of information. Information can be restricted through a narrow frame of reference or filtered out. The degree of openness in an organization involves how people use filters to keep information from getting to others particularly those at the top who make decisions.

- Adaptability. An organization's climate has degrees of adaptability that can vary between strict and flexible. Some have strict standards that people are expected to comply with giving them very little individual choice. This happens when the task to be accomplished is very specific like a sports team where the desired outcome is to win. Others are more flexible so individual choice and creativity is valued. These can be organizations that need to be in touch with ongoing changes in the external environment in order to accomplish their tasks. Every organization has to find a balance between strict and flexible that helps them accomplish their desired outcomes.

- Patterns of communicating. In organizations people tend to follow familiar patterns of communicating. These are the reoccurring scripted patterns we use to talk with one another on a regular basis. Members may create their own specialized patterns of communicating with others in an organization. These patterns can create climates that are positive or negative, warm or cold, and friendly or formal. This is generally determined by the tone of communicating between individuals. This can include their appearance, nonverbal body language, facial expressions, posture, and tone of voice. Most of the time these patterns are meant to create a positive climate, but if they are overly negative it can propagate a climate that undermines member effectiveness and commitment.

- The weather. The climate in an organization can be characterized by terms used to describe the weather. An organization's climate can be sunny, cloudy, or stormy. It can be characterized in terms of temperature like hot or cold, which can be raised or lowered depending upon people's emotional levels. Positive climates can be characterized as warm and sunny, and negative ones can be cold and stormy. These climates can travel through the communicating networks in an organization like storms travel across the countryside. Sometimes you can do something to improve them. Other times, just like the weather, there's not much you can do other than taking cover and riding them out until they pass.

Since climate is comprised of the social atmosphere within an organization, it is open to individual perceptions. People have a perception of the attitudes and emotions of others that may or may not be accurate. If people perceive others are feeling a certain way they may be more inclined to think that they should feel the same way too.

People have expectations about what type of climate they need to do their best work. This is often based upon their past experiences and personal preferences. Some people prefer a climate that is informal, fun, warm, friendly, and open to new ideas and information. Others may prefer a more fixed, formal, and structured climate that values tradition.

Perceptions and preferences create expectations about the climate in which people work. They may expect the organization to be open and flexible or closed and strict. Some climates are based on past traditions that resist change, where others actively pursue change. These expectations can motivate individual behavior within the organization and how members communicate with one another. If people fit in with the organizational climate, they are more likely to feel comfortable as a part of the organization. If the climate is meeting their needs, it can increase their satisfaction and commitment.

If a member does not fit in with the organizational climate they can feel uncomfortable, not accepted, or that their needs are not being met. They may feel like an outsider even though they are in the organization. This can be a source of tension or conflict undermining the effectiveness of the organization. Since the climate is created by everyone together, one person can have a difficult time trying to change it. If people do not fit in with the organizational climate they may only have two choices, to change their behavior to fit in or to leave.

An organization's climate can have a great influence on its members' self-concept, which can affect their satisfaction and level of commitment to the group. If a climate is cold, formal, or overly negative it can hurt people's self-concept because it is affected by reflected feedback through the process of communicating. If people are not receiving feedback that meets their needs, it can harm their self-concept making them less satisfied with the organization lowering their commitment and harming their ability to work effectively with others.

A negative climate can develop when others ignore, interrupt, don't listen, or dismiss our ideas. It can happen when we don't feel that we are getting the respect we deserve or that we are not taken seriously by others. If they feel that they are not appreciated by others it may cause them to withdraw and become detached, breaking down connections between them because people don't want to be around others who are negative or overly critical. This climate can hurt an organization's effectiveness because it increases uncertainty making people reluctant to invest in others.

Negative climates can develop without people being aware of them. By increasing our awareness we can help to keep the climate from becoming too negative or critical and make it more positive and productive. People may be communicating negative messages for a reason, so it can be helpful to understand why they do it. By looking for more information and asking questions, it reduces the emotional intensity and helps make a negative climate more positive. We can respond to a negative climate by being negative ourselves even though we don't have to be. Having an awareness of how climates affect us can help us to not fall into these patterns.

These approaches can be used to make an organization's climate more effective.

1. Awareness. It's easy to be unaware of why we feel the way we do, so we may end up being upset or unhappy, but don't know why. How we feel may not come from our own situation, but from other people because we can pick up the emotions of others around us. Having an awareness of how we feel and where those feelings come from can help us to do something to improve the climate around us.

2. Appreciate. We can begin creating a positive climate by considering how we would like to be treated and then treat others that way. We can be considerate of others, be open to their opinions, and address problems as they happen rather than trying to avoid them. We can appreciate other people's point of view by looking for things we have in common.

3. Attention. We pay attention to others by listening, spending time with them, or simply saying "Hi" to greet them. Listen, ask questions, seek out more information, and provide feedback. People get upset because they may not feel they are getting the attention they deserve, so provide them with appropriate feedback. All too often we can spend time in an organization where no one says anything to us. Organizations can create a climate whereby people are friendly and pay attention to one another making them feel like they belong. This can provide fulfillment for important needs and social rewards by affirming their value as a member of the organization.

4. Acknowledgment. People want to be recognized for their contributions. They want to feel like they are receiving fair rewards for fair work. All too often people are not properly acknowledged for their contributions to the organization. Acknowledgment is a strong social reward, so providing it within an organization can improve its climate. This can be done by providing recognition for what people contribute by giving them credit for their work. Organizations can develop rituals where they reward members for their service and contributions.

5. Agreement. This is one of the strongest social rewards that people can provide because it shows their opinions are valued by others. When we agree with someone, we create common ground. In a negative climate, finding some area of agreement can reduce the emotional intensity of a negative climate. We can agree with the other person's perceptions and feelings validating their self-concept without necessarily validating their position. Agreement does not necessarily mean that we agree with everything.

6. Accuracy. We can't agree with everything all the time or nothing would get done. There needs to be some degree of disagreement in order to test and evaluate ideas so we can make decisions and accomplish tasks. When we have to disagree it's helpful to be truthful, but tactful by considering how others will respond. It helps to be descriptive rather than characterizing things as good or bad. Consider how you would want to be told the same information. Focus on accurate specifics of the situation rather than an individual's characteristics.

7. Adjustment. There are times when a climate calls for direct intervention. Ask group members how they feel about the situation to determine the source of tension that is harming the organization's climate. The better these sources are understood, the better the chance the climate can be improved. Possible sources come from lack of resources, lack of support, lack of cooperation, feeling overworked, or a lack of fairness. By getting these issues out in the open perceptions may become more accurate and expectations more realistic.

Organizational Culture

Organizational culture consists of the reoccurring patterns of communicating and behavior that comprise the rules and norms of interaction between individuals within an organization. This can help facilitate the effective functioning of the organization because it reduces uncertainty by providing structure and stability. It is a means of sharing meaning to facilitate understanding of the organization and its members. The culture of an organization serves a similar function as the culture of a country or geographic region. It can communicate its history, language, customs, rituals, and social reality. This can make becoming a new member of an organization feel like going to a foreign country. It's helpful for members of an organization to know its culture to increase their satisfaction, while fostering their commitment to it.

While organizational climate can change to reflect the emotional intensity of the moment, organizational culture changes more slowly over time. The culture often begins when an organization is created and develops in one of two ways. It can grow spontaneously through the natural interaction of its members over time through the process of behavioral reinforcement. Or, it can be created and developed intentionally to achieve specific desired outcomes. However, when a culture is imposed on an organization the members may try to create their own informal culture. By understanding how culture works, organizations can have options to develop a culture that is the most effective for them.

Organizational culture can be used as a form of social control over its members by using rules, norms, and other structural devices to motivate members to conform to its social reality. An organization's culture can help it to function effectively because without it people would not know how to behave or what was expected of them. Instead, they would do whatever they felt like doing increasing uncertainty making things chaotic. Culture shares meaning between members so they can communicate and understand each other in order to accomplish their tasks. Culture helps to create common ground to develop the social connections that bring people together.

An important part of how we express culture is through rituals and traditions. Rituals are established patterns of communicating or behavior repeated in a similar way over time. They might involve the ways in which members interact and communicate with one another. They may involve regularly occurring activities such as coffee breaks or Monday morning meetings. Traditions are patterns of behavior that an organization's members share based upon their mutual customs or beliefs. For example, an organization may believe strongly in supporting the families of its members, so they have events in which family members are encouraged to participate. Organizations may have rites of passage like having a party or ceremony when a person gets promoted, changes departments, or retires.

These activities reduce uncertainty because members get to know one another on a more personal level. When members participate in rituals and traditions together, it gives them a sense of unity of purpose and a feeling that everyone is in it together. This can be helpful in larger organizations where all members cannot feasibly get together at the same time. By participating in the same events, they are part of the same community. For example, when groups celebrate a holiday, they are unified in a common experience even though they may not all be physically together. These activities fulfill individual member's needs and wants for affiliation and recognition by creating connections between members that can increase their satisfaction and commitment to the organization.

In practically any culture there is the potential for splits or schisms that can divide it into smaller groups. This can lead to tension and competition for resources undermining the effectiveness of the organization. Members can have diverse interests motivating them to group themselves together based upon their interests or expertise. A unique culture can develop around a particular specialization within the larger organization. Members are motivated to do this out of the need to associate with others who they perceive are like themselves to share interests they have in common. Members can be motivated to form informal groups just like they do in society based on familiarity, similarity, intensity, and proximity.

The most common way that people learn about an organization's culture is by experiencing it for themselves. This can take some time and they may make mistakes that can cause unnecessary tension. Organizations can make this process easier by providing a means to inform their members about how their culture works.

These options can help you learn about an organization's culture.

- Awareness. Be observant by paying attention to what is around you. Practically everything has the potential to communicate something. This includes how people talk, behave, dress, what they have in their offices, even the cars they drive. A good way to learn about an organization's culture is to observe and communicate with others. Be aware of the connections between people in both the formal and informal networks including who communicates with whom, about what, under what circumstances, where, and in what ways.

- Power. In every organization there are people who have power and those who do not. Power is the ability to get things done and who has it is not always who you might think it is. A person may have the appearance of power, but in reality they may not have very much. A person who may have a position that doesn't seem significant may be influential within the organization. Often the people who can get things done are those who have been there a long time because they know how the culture works.

- Getting things done. Observe how others get things done. People are constantly making decisions, so look at what criteria they use to make them. Determine what needs and wants people have and how you might be able to help fulfill them. Observe how others communicate, who they connect with, and how. For example, a memo or phone message may not get answered, but people may talk to you informally over coffee. Knowing how others in the organization get things done can help you to know how to communicate in a way that helps you to achieve your desired outcomes. This utilizes the process of communicating to create your Great Idea to communicate it to others through the proper connection to reduce interference that may prevent them from responding to you positively.

- What arguments work. Notice what methods of persuasion work and which ones don't. The people who make decisions have their own needs and wants, so some arguments won't work no matter how valid they may be. It's helpful to know their needs and wants, and the criteria they use for making decisions, so you can shape your argument to meet their expectations. For example, an organization may approve proposals that cut costs or involves health and safety issues. You can learn how to do this by finding out how the last decisions that were approved were presented. Look at what arguments, evidence, and methods of reasoning were successful. Knowing what proposals were turned down can help you know what not to do. By knowing this you can tailor your message to increase the likelihood of it being favorably received.

- Get advice. It can be helpful to find a person who has been in the organization for some time and knows how things work who would be willing to help you and give you advice. Start slow by getting to know people through self-disclosure by sharing appropriate information to reduce uncertainty about yourself. Test the usefulness of any advice and be aware of how others are perceiving and responding to you through their feedback.

- Observe others. Watch how people behave, how they act, how they dress, and how they organize their space and time. Notice who spends time with whom, when, and under what circumstances. Listen to how they communicate with one another and the stories they tell. Who communicates with whom will tell you about the networks of communicating and informal structures within the organization. Observing how people behave and interact with one another will tell you about their norms. How they dress can tell you something about their attitudes and values, such as if they are formal or casual. How they organize their space can tell you about their social traits. For example, if everyone has pictures of their family on display, family values could be important to the organization. Is the décor conservative or innovative, inexpensive or opulent? People surround themselves with objects and symbols that they invest with meaning giving them value, so it can be helpful to understand what these objects mean.

Organizational self replication.

Have you ever noticed that some organizations don't ever seem to change, even over long periods of time. For example, you may have noticed a business or government agency that seems to have the same people working there even though it is many, many years later. They act, talk, perhaps even look the same. You may have even thought they were the same people at first, but after so many years that could not be possible. This could be a business where you worked, a store where you shopped, or a government office. If it has happened to you it can be a strange phenomenon to experience and there is a good reason for it.

In many organizations there can be an internal inertia that resists change. This can be propagated by a self replicating mechanism that works rather like cells in the human body. Our body replaces old cells with new ones that look the same as those they replace. If they were too different, our appearance would change and we would look different. People leave organizations and have to be replaced with new people in order for it to survive. The people who select their replacements often self replicate by hiring people just like those who left or who are like themselves. The law of uncertainty motivates them to hire and promote people who are similar to those already in the organization. They hire them to reduce uncertainty so they will support the existing culture because it promotes stability and security.

An organization is like other living organisms, it seeks to eliminate what it perceives as a threat. If new members are too different they could increase uncertainty that may pose a threat to the existing members. Existing members may be reluctant to accept people they perceive as being too different, because if the new people think too differently, they could challenge the existing members' social reality creating tension. If the new person's way of thinking prevails, the existing members might be perceived as being wrong undermining their power and authority potentially damaging their self-concept. This can provide motivation for organizations to avoid implementing change. This can be one reason why organizations can grow to a point where they cease to innovate and begin to stagnate, or decline.

If the new members are too different than the existing members they may not fit in and could be ostracized, even rejected by the existing members. They might be creative or ambitious showing up the existing members. This could make them feel that they are no longer effective and might loose their power and influence in the organization. This might motivate them to eliminate any threat they may perceive to their position by removing new members who might be considered too different.

If new members do not change to fit in, it could hurt their self-concept making them become dissatisfied and frustrated with the organization, so they may eventually leave. They may feel pressure to change their behavior to fit in with the organization and its culture. If they change, then they may become just like the others and the people they replaced. Organizational culture has the power to motivate people to conform because an organization can fulfill its members' needs and wants. It can also punish members who exhibit behavior outside acceptable norms forcing them to conform or leave. It is this process of self replicating that can make an organization look virtually the same many years later. Having an awareness of this process means it does not necessarily have to happen.

There can be a characteristic of social reality whereby groups and individuals look to punish someone for the actions of others. There may be people who have committed transgressions that go unfettered until uncertainty becomes too high, then the group may need to restore economic equilibrium by targeting an individual or group to be punished for the transgressions of everyone else. This person is often innocent and undeserving of this treatment. They might be very accomplished, so others want them removed because they perceive them as a threat. They may be treated harshly, unfairly punished, even forced out.

Organizational growth and decline.

Organizations can go through the same developmental phases as groups and individual relationships because they are created by the connections between people. They can go through a process of creation, growth, maintenance, and decline. They can become successful and grow until they reach a point where the organization reaches a plateau, so growth and innovation declines or even ends and it goes out of business. So, how can organizations be innovative and creative, grow successful, only to decline and wither away? The answer can be found in the laws of uncertainty, shared meaning, and investing.

When an organization is first created it is in the uncertainty reduction phase and there's a high degree of uncertainty. Uncertainty can work as a motivational influence if it is managed effectively. The people who comprise it are learning how to negotiate their roles, norms, rules, structure, and social reality. They go through the process of behavioral reinforcement trying different things until they are accepted by others. At this point, there is a high degree of uncertainty, so they are possibly the most open they can be to new ideas and new ways of doing things. This flexibility helps them to be innovative and creative.

When an organization becomes larger and older, chances are good that they have significantly reduced uncertainty. They have solidified their roles, norms, rules, structure, and social reality. Rather than negotiating these things, members are expected to conform to the organization's ways of doing things. People with different ideas may be cast as troublemakers to be ignored or removed. Reduced uncertainty provides security and stability, however, it also reduces the flexibility and the ability to adapt to change. It can create an attitude of, "I know what I'm doing," which can lead to arrogance. Arrogance can be one of the leading causes of organizational decline.

Reduced uncertainty is followed by the shared meaning phase. As most of the members are new, they're involved in the process of sharing meaning about themselves, others, and the organization. They negotiate what the organization stands for and what it means to be a member. Since this is a process that is fluid and evolving, it's open to change and interpretation. As an organization grows and becomes larger, it has more established shared meanings between its members about the organization and what it means to be a member. Members have less ability to contribute to changing that meaning, and are expected to conform to it. Members who share different meanings about the organization are more likely to change to fit in or leave.

When an organization is new, members usually have very little invested in it because the organization has not yet developed. It is less likely to have established much structure or hierarchies that can create value in organizations. This means that the members are more flexible and willing to try different approaches to become effective and successful because there is less investment to lose. Structure is developed to help increase stability, but it can also restrict innovation and trying new things that could be successful.

When an organization goes through the investing phase of development, its members can become more cautious about what they do because they do not want to loose the time, energy, and other resources they have invested in it. This can make them less likely to innovate or do things differently because doing so could be perceived as increasing uncertainty. There are often hierarchies and ranks created by the members because they have invested significant amounts of their time there. They are likely to resist change and innovation because they do not want to lose their investment, future benefits, or place in the organization.

The process of communicating will change as an organization grows. In the beginning, it is generally smaller so members can communicate with everyone in the organization more frequently regardless of rank. Information at the bottom can more easily flow to the top where decisions are made. There's less apprehension about communicating across the organization because it is smaller and everybody is closer, physically as well as psychologically. It is more likely that everyone is all in one location sharing the same space. This encourages communicating networks to facilitate the flow of information needed to innovate and grow.

In larger organizations, members can be less likely to communicate across the organization because it is more difficult and can be perceived as increasing uncertainty. The organization's culture may even discourage it. Instead, there are often established formal communicating networks members are expected to use. They can be more distant, often physically separated by offices, different floors, perhaps even different locations. They may be reluctant to share their ideas for fear of rejection, punishment, or the loss of their investment. Members are more likely to communicate with others on the same level or in the same department. This can reduce the flow of information that could help them be innovative and creative, by reducing their awareness leading to poorer decisions. This can encourage some to use information as a means to improve their own position rather than the organization.

Organizations have their own needs and wants, just as individuals do. When an organization is starting out it has lots of needs and wants, but it likely has few resources to fulfill them. This motivates the members to do more with less. It encourages them to come up with new and creative ways of doing things in order to save resources, like time and money. When an organization gets larger, it can have more resources, but there still is a problem of allocation. In order to receive the resources they need, members are more likely to conform to the expectations of those that provide the resources, rather than develop their own means of accomplishing a task. They are more likely to be less innovative and creative. They can be less likely to question their superiors and just do what they're told.

When an organization is new, the members utilize the social reality of society or their past experiences. They may share different social realities that can create uncertainty about the organization and what to expect. As it grows, members negotiate what the social reality of the organization will eventually become. This means that to some extent they have a say in what the organization will look like, how it behaves, how it communicates, and what it does. This can provide more flexibility to create an organization that is highly receptive not only to its members, but also to its customers and the outside environment.

As an organization grows, its social reality solidifies, so individual members have less say in what that means. It can also become more resistant to outside influences. This means that it could potentially develop a bunker type mentality where it not only does not accommodate change, it actually resists it. This can be expressed when they say things like, "That's the way we have always done it." This can make the organization less flexible to respond to changing circumstances necessary for it to function effectively.

Organizations do not have to fall into this pattern of growth, stagnation, and decline. By having an awareness of this process and its causes, an organization can take measures to prevent it. This can happen at basically two points in an organizations history. First, it can happen at the very beginning when an organization is formed. It can happen when its members are negotiating how the organization will function. They can provide a mechanism for the group to bring in new information facilitating change. This needs to be part of an organization's culture on all levels in order for it to function properly. While this is probably the easiest way to do this, it takes an understanding of the process and the foresight to do it in order to instill it into an organization from the beginning.

The second approach is to develop a new culture after an organization has existed for some time. This is more realistic, however, once an organization develops its culture, it can be difficult to change. Change has to begin at the very top and permeate all levels throughout the organization. The new culture should encourage communicating across all levels and with people outside the organization, like customers. This facilitates new ideas and innovation, so people feel safe trying new things that could help the organization without the fear of being penalized or losing their investment. The new culture has to be clearly communicated to everyone in the organization. There also needs to be a means to deal with those who will resist the change because they may see it as a threat to their position, power, or investment in the organization.

Organizational change.

Organizational change is part of the process of how we restore economic equilibrium in groups, organizations, and even in society. One of the functions of organizations is to reduce uncertainty to create stability over long periods of time. However, since change is inevitable, organizations also need a means to change. This can create tension between change and stability. People may say that they want change because they do not want to be perceived as being old fashioned or close minded, while at the same time they might resist it by saying things like, "That's the way we've always done things around here."

Organizational self replication can perpetuate a static culture that resists change because it is perceived as uncomfortable increasing uncertainty. Change takes leadership and a willingness to change, but change should not be done just for its own sake. Even if people want change, actually getting them to change can be difficult. So, organizations may need to develop a means to reduce uncertainty to maintain stability while bringing in new ideas that can facilitate change.

These are some options to help facilitate change in organizations.

- Utilize the law of uncertainty. People are more likely to change when their perception of the current situation increases uncertainty making things uncomfortable. Portray change as a means to reduce uncertainty by making things more stable and secure. If uncertainty about changed is reduced, people are more likely to accept it.

- Utilize the law of shared meaning. People are more likely to change to preserve their values or uphold important traditions that create stability and security. A common argument against change is that it is contrary to existing values. Connecting change to an organization's traditions legitimizes it because it is based upon the group's common values and beliefs. To avoid resistance, emphasize that change does not mean everything will change.

- Utilize the law of investing. Encourage people to invest in change by communicating a vision of a future that is better than today. People may object to change for fear of losing the investment they have in the organization. So, it's helpful to reassure them that their investment will not be lost, but rather will have greater value after the change. They are more likely to support change if they have the perception that their investment today will payoff with greater returns tomorrow.

- Utilize small incremental changes. There is a threshold for change that people are willing to accept. After that, uncertainty increases to the point that they are motivated to resist it. If the change is below that level, they are less likely to pay as much attention to it. People are more likely to accept small incremental changes over time more than a large one all at once. Once people become comfortable with a small change, additional small changes can be added. This creates a series of changes increasing the threshold of what people are able to accept until the entire change has been implemented.

- Utilize influential members to facilitate change. Social reality is negotiated in organizations by its members in an ongoing process allowing opportunities for change. Influential members who are respected or held in high esteem can utilize behavioral reinforcement by sending positive messages and using their influence to convince others to change.

- Offer rewards and incentives to members who are willing to change and impose costs or punishments for those who will not change. Change can be promoted as bringing more resources into the organization to benefit its members with material and social rewards for those who support it. If possible, have members participate in the process because they will be more likely to support change that they feel they had a say in creating. When they feel ownership of the decision making process, they are more likely to see that their decisions are successfully implemented.

- Utilize people's needs and wants by appealing to them. Even though people join organizations to have their needs and wants fulfilled, it is unlikely that they will all be fulfilled. So, present change as a means to better fulfill them. People may feel that they are not being treated fairly, so characterize change as providing them with fair rewards. Chances are people feel that they should be doing better and if change can help them to do that, they will be more open to it.

- Utilize the rules to implement change. People are more likely to resist change if they perceive it as violating the existing rules. In order to reduce uncertainty, change should be implemented using existing rules. Even dictatorial regimes have laws, elections, and parliaments to legitimize their power. This is because those who are against change will look for ways to stop it by using rules because it is difficult to argue against them. As change is implemented these rules can be changed as necessary.

Organizations can also experience organizational infiltration. This happens when a group of people infiltrate an organization by joining it with the express purpose of gaining power to change the purpose or culture of the organization to fit their agenda. Groups and organizations need new members to function and there are those who may join with ulterior motives.

This is a variation of organizational self replication, except that the purpose is to intentionally establish a new culture in an organization by replacing existing members with ones who share the new culture or social reality.

This process of organizational infiltration can happen when a group of people wants to use an organization to achieve their own desired outcomes. They join the organization, then gain positions of influence or power to change the organization's culture and even its values. They may have connections to other people or groups that can exert influence over the organization and influential members. They may bring in others who share the same agenda and will support them. It may take only a few key people to infiltrate an organization. They provide resources and promote those who support them and punish or cut off resources to those who don't. The new changes should let everyone know that they are expected to go along with the new culture or face consequences.

External and internal culture.

External culture is the culture of the society in which an organization exists. Internal culture is the culture of a specific organization. It is created by its members within the larger external culture. Because an organization may be located in or have members from several external cultures, they may have different styles of communicating and norms of behavior. This can make it difficult for members to work together increasing uncertainty because people may feel unfamiliar with one another. This could reduce the effectiveness of an organization because people may be uneasy or unwilling to invest in one another due to increased uncertainty.

By utilizing the law of shared meaning, members can develop an understanding of an organization's culture to reduce uncertainty, so members of different cultures know what to expect of one another making it easier for them to work together. Some professions have a specialized culture so members communicate within the social reality of their profession giving them a common connection. When working on tasks they are likely to communicate utilizing their professional culture.

Organizations are immersed in an external culture, which affects the organizational culture including local cultural traditions and rituals that can be part of the social activities of the organization. An organization can gain knowledge of the local culture by making connections to the local community and by participating in and promoting local community activities and events.

Uncertainty can be reduced by making connections between people of different cultures across the organization, so that they know more about one another. Creating a positive social climate encourages them to communicate with one another utilizing self-disclosure to reduce uncertainty, so that they can work better together.

Organizations that include members from different cultures and specializations can work together more effectively by developing common communicating skills including having a common language. This provides more connections to communicate with one another to reduce uncertainty with problem solving and decision making by letting members know the rules, norms, and social reality.

When they know what to expect, it can increase member satisfaction fostering their commitment to the organization. This helps to develop a common culture so that people from different parts of the organization have an awareness and options to work effectively together. When brought together to accomplish a task, they can get to work without having to figure everything out because they will know what to do.

Culture

Culture is a specialized version of social reality created by groups of people over time to reduce uncertainty about themselves and the world around them. It is a means to share meaning through customs, traditions, behaviors, and ways of communicating. Culture is something that we are all born into and that we all have, making it inevitable and unavoidable. It often originates in a particular geographic area and can be associated with a specific group of people based on their shared history and experiences. They often communicate their culture through their appearance and what they say and do. Culture influences many aspects of life including art, music, literature, clothing, religion, and architecture.

Culture is a significant part of our lives because it shapes how we communicate and how we interact with others. It contains its own social reality consisting of norms of behavior and patterns of communicating. It serves as a form of social control because it has the power to motivate behavior. It creates security through rules that are often institutionalized in laws. It creates power and authority that is communicated through levels of hierarchy. It has its own networks of connections through which people communicate. It reduces uncertainty by communicating important aspects of life so that people can better understand themselves and others.

Practically anywhere we live, we communicate with people from other cultures. Understanding culture enriches our lives by looking at familiar things in new and different ways. Other cultures have faced the same problems that we have and may have approached them in different ways. Understanding culture helps us to avoid misunderstandings that can lead to unnecessary tension or conflict. It can help us see things from other people's point of view.

Culture helps to reduce uncertainty about ourselves because it tells us who we are, our history, our values, and how things came to be the way they are today. When we meet someone for the first time we look to reduce uncertainty about them to make them more familiar, so we utilize information about culture based upon our past experiences to make inferences about them. Culture can also increase uncertainty when we meet others from a culture we know little about because we do not know what to expect from them.

Culture is a manifestation of the law of shared meaning. It is how we share meaning about who we are with large groups of people. People invest shared meaning in art, music, and food based on their culture. People who share the same culture often participate in similar rituals and traditions. Culture invests symbols as well as objects with meaning. It is a means by which we give our experiences a deeper significance. Cultures can develop their own unique ways of communicating to share meaning through language, which is often associated with a specific group of people and geographic area.

Culture provides a means of investing in others without having to know them personally. When people share a culture, they know many things about one another because they share a similar social reality. This helps provide a connection to create and maintain relationships. When people move to another place, like a foreign country they often group together in communities with others from the same culture. They may even move to areas that look similar or have a similar climate. People of different cultures may find it difficult to form relationships and invest in one another because they perceive the cultural differences as increasing uncertainty rather than looking for things they have in common.

Culture is usually associated with geographic affiliation. Geographic affiliation is a geographic area that people have an attachment to giving it a deeper meaning. It could be a country, state, city, or region. It is a place they feel a connection to, are from, live now, or have ancestors. People may feel a connection to a culture and to the geographic area associated with it. Geographic affiliation can play an important part in the development of a culture because culture can be shaped by its typography, landscape, plants, animals, climate, and natural resources. People are likely to live there, but they do not have to have actually been there.

Cultures often develop their own individual characteristics based on the natural resources that were available to them. They used local resources to make food, clothing, and homes creating their own distinctive style. People took inspiration from their surroundings for art and music. Geographic affiliation often determines how people fulfill their needs and wants creating culture. People everywhere have similar needs and wants to fulfill, but they have found many different ways to fulfill them as expressed in different cultures.

Culture is not only associated with nationalities and geographic regions, it can also be a part of groups and organizations. Culture is a way of characterizing a group's social reality including its norms of behavior and how people communicate with one another. Large groups of people, such as an organization or nation, can develop subcultures. These are smaller groups of people that can be a part of a larger culture, but share stronger connections and common characteristics. These subcultures can be affiliated by geographic area, political or religious beliefs, gender, professions, hobbies, activities, and personal interests.

People have many of the same needs and wants, but different cultures have devised different ways to fulfill them. Many of the ways that we fulfill our needs and wants are identified with culture. Learning about how different cultures approach the same problems in different ways helps us to look at what is familiar to us in new and different ways.

Everyone needs food, clothing, and shelter to survive, but they can fulfill them in different ways. Many cultures are known for their unique type of foods that are based on its history and traditions using locally available ingredients. Clothing styles are based upon a culture's needs, climate, history, and available raw materials. Architectural styles are based upon a culture's social reality using locally available materials.

Culture shapes how we perceive the world around us because it is the expression of a collective shared meaning. It provides perspective on how to interpret people's experiences. It influences actions and behavior making it a powerful force because it motivates people to take action and to react to what happens around them. Culture invests behavior with meaning, so people of different cultures can have different interpretations of the same kinds of things. Uncertainty and shared meaning can be a source of misunderstanding, tension, or conflict.

In order to reduce uncertainty we often make inferences about people based upon their culture from information we have gathered in the past. Even though this information may be outdated or inaccurate, we do this in order to make them more familiar. When we do not check if our perceptions are accurate, it can lead to generalizations such as stereotypes that could give us a false impression of someone before we get to know them.

Culture is an expression of social reality, so we may not be aware of how much it affects us. It is helpful to have an awareness of our own culture as well as how others differ. By being more aware of other cultures we gain a respect for them as well as an appreciation of our own.

Different cultures fulfill similar needs in different ways. These are some areas to be aware of where cultures can be different.

- Personal contact. Cultures have rules regarding the use of personal space and what types of personal contact are considered appropriate. Some cultures value following the rules of etiquette where others are more casual and informal. Some hug or kiss on the cheek, while others shake hands, bow, or keep their distance.

- Traditions. Cultures celebrate rituals and traditions that include events from everyday activities, to annual holidays, to special events. The events that people celebrate are often based upon cultural traditions. Common sources for holidays and celebrations are based on the changing of the seasons, religious observances, and significant national days. They can be used to share meaning about important cultural events or well known people. Religion is an essential part of the traditions of a culture because it contains a strong sense of social reality. Many of a culture's holidays, rituals, and traditions are based on religion.

- Time. Cultures interpret how people use time differently. Some cultures value punctuality, when dinner starts at seven, it starts at seven and being late shows disrespect. Some cultures utilize approximate time, when dinner starts at seven it's okay to show up a bit late. Some cultures have more relative time, dinner starts when everyone gets there. It is helpful to be aware of how a culture views time, so you don't unintentionally offend people.

- Humor. What is humorous is often based upon how language and common knowledge is utilized. Humor can be subjective and often culturally based. What may be funny in one culture may be offensive in another. Be careful using humor until you know people better.

- Food and drink. Many cultures have their own unique food and drink. These are generally made from local ingredients and represent long standing traditions that are an important part of special events and celebrations. Guests are often treated to special cultural dishes and culinary experiences.

- Art and music. Cultures often have their own styles of artistic expression based upon their heritage and traditions. This can consist of unique styles of music including traditional and contemporary music. They have their own products and industries utilizing locally available natural resources.

Cultural involvement.

When people become a member of a new organization or move to another country, they can be motivated by uncertainty to keep their own ways of doing things. They may seek out and spend time around others they perceive are like themselves. When people immigrate to other countries they often settle in areas that are geographically similar to where they came from, if one exists. They may avoid the local people making them feel disconnected, ignored, even rejected. Uncertainty can create tension making them apprehensive to make connections with others and then they may wonder why they don't fit in.

Becoming involved in other cultures can help us to appreciate our own. Understanding and showing respect to other cultures should be reciprocal, other people should be as open to understanding your culture as you are open to understanding theirs. It's not only important that we respect other cultures, but for other cultures to respect ours. Cultural diversity often emphasizes differences between cultures, which can be problematic because they rely on generalizations that may not be universally applicable.

The following are several approaches to experiencing a culture ranked by their degree of involvement.

1. Avoidance. In experiencing a new culture, we make few changes and keep our own culture by living just as we did before. We do not adapt to the new culture or any of its rules of behavior. This can create barriers between us and others that can be a source of tension. Not having contact with others can increase uncertainty due to lack of information. There is still a high degree of uncertainty, with little shared meaning and no investing in the new culture or relationships with others.

2. Adventure. We may move to a new culture with a sense of adventure and excitement in order to see new things, meet new people, and have new experiences. We may even live more like a local and less like a tourist. We may immerse ourselves in the culture for a short time, perhaps learning some of the language, but we keep our old culture and old ways of doing things. While we adapt to new ways of doing things in public, in private we continue to do things as we have always done maintaining our previous culture. We have reduced some uncertainty about ourselves, but even though we have some increased shared meaning, there is little investing in the new culture.

3. Adaptation. We find there are things that we like about our new culture and adapt our lifestyles to follow local rules and customs. We adopt many of the ways of the new culture as our own both in public and private. It is becoming more familiar to us, so we find ourselves doing things the new way without thinking about it. We might learn to speak the language and participate in the traditions, rituals, and activities that locals participate in.

We should now be reducing uncertainty about ourselves to others and we should be feeling some reduced uncertainty about the new culture. We reduce uncertainty about ourselves to meet people and begin to have relationships. Life should become more enjoyable as we share meaning with local people to gain a better understanding of the culture. As we develop relationships we share meaning with the new culture and local people. This should encourage us to invest in relationships with others and for them to invest in us, at least as an acquaintance, perhaps friends, or more.

4. Acceptance. This is the most intense degree of involvement. We have adapted to the new lifestyle and do what others do when we are around them. As we meet and talk to people, we share meaning with them because we understand the new culture. We are likely to replace our past cultural norms of behavior with those of the new culture. We have accepted this way of life and methods of doing things as our own.

We participate in the traditions and customs of the new culture, speak the new language, and have made connections and friendships with others in the new culture. We feel like we are part of a community with a sense of belonging. We feel a sense of reduced uncertainty about others and they feel similarly about us, so that we can develop the degree of trust necessary to invest in the local community and the can invest in us.

No matter where we live, people will feel differing degrees of uncertainty, especially if we look or act different than the locals. We are not likely to completely reduce the uncertainty we feel wherever we live, but we have probably reduced it as much at it can be reduced. Sharing meaning is an ongoing process, but we can feel that we can now share meanings like a local. We have chosen to invest in the new culture. We cannot make other people invest in relationships with us, we can only show that we are open to making new relationships. This may be the most difficult part of moving to a new culture, we cannot know how well we will be accepted.

When moving to a new culture, people may not adapt to the new culture. Instead, they practice avoidance by continuing their old ways of doing things. They may form groups with others of their own culture establishing their own structures, rules, and norms. This can increases feelings of uncertainty in those already living there, motivating some people to avoid them because they know very little about them. This can manifest itself in divisions within a community or society creating tension increasing uncertainty.

It can be helpful to take a balanced approach to experiencing a new culture by maintaining familiar cultural traditions, but following the local patterns of communicating, rules of behavior, and participating in local rituals and traditions. Getting involved in a culture can be the most effective way to learn about it and gain a greater understanding of others.

However, we may be reluctant to do this because we do not know what to do. Or we might read about a culture and then act as if we know what we are doing. The problem is even the best information may be out of date or inaccurate. It is better to acknowledge not knowing about a culture rather than trying to act like you do. Being straightforward about your understanding of a culture communicates that you are honest, open minded, and have an interest in it, so people should be open to teaching you about their culture.

Diversity tends to be approached in terms of the differences that make us unique. Emphasizing differences can increase uncertainty and advance generalizations or stereotypes by emphasizing how we are different. By thinking about culture in a new way, we can look for commonalities to make connections with others so uncertainty can be reduced. The purpose of cultural understanding should not create division, but create connections that bring us closer together by emphasizing the similarities that can create shared meanings with others.

We do this to reduce uncertainty about one another, so we can get to know each other better to form relationships. We can utilize the law of shared meaning to understand more about each other as well as ourselves. We can make connections to share meaning with others to understand them better to create common ground. We invest in others to develop relationships with them. While we are culturally different, we are similar in that we seek to fulfill similar needs and wants, and achieve mutual desired outcomes. Rather than adapting to a culture by imitating what others do, we can create understanding to develop a culture that we share.

People of all cultures join groups and organizations in order to fulfill needs and wants, form relationships, and achieve desired outcomes. These are things everyone has in common that can encourage them to make connections to help them understand each other's culture. When people spend time together, they utilize the power of self-disclosure to reduce uncertainty about one another creating connections which builds trust. And when they do, they feel safe and secure enough to invest in relationships with one another, in organizations, and in their community.

Problem Solving and Decision Making

Imagine it's a typical day and your three children are fighting over the same toy. The fighting has been going on for a while now and it's getting quite loud, so you have finally had enough. What do you do? Our natural tendency might be to go over and take the toy away from them. Congratulations, you made a decision. Unfortunately, the problem has not been solved. You still have three unhappy children.

Using problem solving skills you might have looked at why the children were fighting in the first place to determine how to best resolve their predicament, instead of only resolving yours. Perhaps you could find other toys that they would like better. Perhaps there was a game or activity they could play to take their mind off the toy. Perhaps the toy could be shared with each one having it for a specific amount of time. You could sit down to play with all three of them and the toy together for a while until they got tired of it. Or, perhaps they are hungry or tired and need a nap. Considering which approach to take is problem solving, doing something about it is making a decision.

While they are similar in nature and often used interchangeably, problem solving and decision making are two separate processes that can work together. We can solve a problem without actually making a decision or make decisions that do not solve problems.

Just as there is no one right way to communicate, there is no one size fits all approach to problem solving and decision making. There are many options you can utilize to find the one that best fits your situation. It can be helpful to have an awareness of how decisions are made and then have options to choose from to select the most effective approach. Since you know your situation, only you can select the best approach for you.

Problem solving and decision making methods can be used not only in groups and organizations, but also for individuals, relationships, work, and families. They are in this chapter on professional communicating because even though these are important skills for us as individuals, we often use these skills with others to have effective groups and organizations.

These are some options for effective problem solving and decision making.

- Get good information. In cooking, preparing good food takes good ingredients. Good decisions need relevant, accurate, and current information.

- Get organized. It helps to have an organized approach in gathering and using information. When more people work on a problem, it can both help and hinder reaching a successful solution.

- Get outside of yourself. We have a tendency to try to work things out ourselves and not ask for help. However, we have connections with others who can provide information and other helpful resources. Groups can seek help from outside the group.

- Get going. In working through problems there is a tendency for groups to break the work up into small pieces giving it to individuals who work on it alone. Instead, bring group members together by asking for their help and advice to make them part of the process. If people have a say in how decisions are made, they are more likely to support and implement them. This is because they feel they have ownership in the process and therefore a stake in the outcome.

- Get a process. Problem solving and decision making are norms that groups develop. While there's a tendency to fall into one way of doing things, groups can be more effective when they develop a variety of options so they can choose the best one for the situation. Before a solution can be reached, the group has to agree on the process by which it will be reached otherwise there may be dissent over how the decision was made undermining the effectiveness of the group.

- Get to the issue. There's a natural tendency in solving problems to bring in personal or past issues that are irrelevant to the problem at hand. By getting to the issue you can better understand the cause of the problem, limit its scope, and avoid problems that can derail progress preventing you from reaching a good solution.

- Get the group to step back. It's easy to get personally invested in your own solution and try to convince others to agree with you to do things your way. By having the group take a step back, it helps everyone to be objective and avoid getting personally invested in any particular solution. Instead, the group can focus on reaching the best solution that benefits everyone.

- Get the right size. Balance the group to keep its size compatible to its task. More people working on a problem can bring in more resources to solve it, gather more information, and provide more points of view. However, more people provides more chances for disagreement, takes longer, and may not result in better decisions. Balance the mix of experience and expertise in the group, so members complement each other without unnecessary overlap.

Problem solving and decision making options.

The following options provide several step by step approaches for making decisions and solving problems, not only in groups and organizations, but also for individuals, relationships, and families.

Just as there is no one size fits all way to communicate, there is no one best approach to making decisions and solving problems. These methods are meant as a guide, so you can choose what works best for you in your situation. They can be altered or combined as needed.

Consensus.

This is a collective decision making process in which all members generally agree on the best course of action. Depending upon what is to be decided it may be relatively easy for a group to achieve consensus. There may be other times when consensus cannot be reached and the group needs to be prepared to use another method of decision making.

Compromise.

This option is used when everyone gives up something they want to gain something they want in order to reach a decision. Group members may accept less than they want in order to reach agreement. Depending upon what is at stake, this approach can create friction and discontent within the group. When consensus is not achievable, compromise may be the next best choice.

Majority vote.

Voting is used in situations where other forms of decision making may not be feasible or where each member's position needs to be on the record. Voting can be the least satisfactory approach because it might create divisions within the group. Members who are outvoted may feel that they no longer count or are respected in the group. They may withdraw, retaliate, or even leave the group. Voting could create factions in the group.

The scientific approach.

This approach applies methods used in scientific research to problem solving and decision making. It consists of a set of steps to solve problems. These steps can be changed to fit your situation in order to achieve your desired outcome.

1. Identify the source of the problem to determine its cause.

2. Determine your desired outcome in solving the problem.

3. Establish your criteria to evaluate each solution.

4. Identify possible solutions and their workability.

5. Evaluate each solution based on your criteria.

6. Select and implement the best solutions.

7. Review the effectiveness of the solution.

8. If the problem is not solved, try the next best solution, until one works.

While this approach is structured and rigid, variations of it can be used to fit your situation.

The analytical approach.

This is a more flexible variation of the scientific approach.

1. Define the problem. Determine the nature of the problem and if it really exists. Sometimes what is perceived as a problem may not be much of a problem at all if given a closer look. Many times we do not get to the true source of the problem or get bogged down in extraneous issues.

2. Isolate the scope of the problem. Problems are not always as big as they seem, so narrowing its scope to determine what the issues really are can go a long way to solving it.

3. Evaluate the cause of the problem. Collect information about possible causes. Determine what is fact and what is opinion or speculation. The better the information, the better the solution. Knowing the source can provide insight into solutions. If only symptoms are treated, the problem will likely persist.

4. Establish objective criteria to evaluate potential solutions. Having criteria will provide you with guidelines for selecting a solution. For example, a solution may need to fit in a

specific time frame or be cost effective. Your criteria will help you choose the best possible solutions by eliminating those that are unworkable. Having impartial criteria helps keep the outcome objective rather than based upon individual preferences or opinions.

5. Discuss possible solutions. Develop as many workable solutions as possible without being judgmental because they will be evaluated later. Be sure everyone has had a chance to contribute their ideas. If everyone does not have their say, they may feel they were left out and resist implementing the solution.

6. Use the criteria you selected to evaluate possible solutions. Rank them from best to least workable. Consider the resources that will be needed, the cost, the time to implement, and their practical workability. Consider potential consequences of each and develop criteria to evaluate its success after implementation. By waiting to evaluate solutions until now, you avoid hindering creativity and generating ideas that might not otherwise be considered.

7. Implement the solution. Once it is implemented, evaluate it based upon your predetermined criteria to evaluate its effectiveness. If it is not successful, look at other solutions that have been generated that can be implemented until one works. At this point, it can be helpful to evaluate the decision making process to see how well it worked. All too often after a decision is implemented there's little or no follow up to see how well it worked.

The creative approach.

The scientific and analytical approaches use a linear, step by step method. The creative approach uses a more flexible and open method.

1. Begin by looking at similar problems that have been successfully resolved. Considering why they worked can provide inspiration for solving the new problem. It can be helpful to know what has worked and not worked in the past.

2. Ask group members to come up with as many potential solutions as possible. Set a specific amount of time to do this before you begin. As each person comes up with a possible solution, write it down where everyone can see it. Go around the group so that everyone has a chance to participate. Encourage members to modify existing solutions using them as inspiration to come up with additional ideas. The purpose is to generate as many solutions as possible no matter how unrealistic they may sound. Do not evaluate or eliminate any of the solutions.

3. When the group is finished, combine similar ideas and eliminate unworkable ones. Then critically evaluate each of them as to how well they will solve the problem.

4. Workable solutions are put in order from most to least desirable. The best solution is implemented and criteria developed to evaluate how effective it is. If it doesn't work, then move to the next best solution on the list.

The purpose of this approach is to make a decision using two different methods together. The first is to come up with as many ideas as possible. This can encourage the group to be creative by looking at the problem and solution in a new way. It encourages them to come up with solutions they might not otherwise consider. The second method is to critically evaluate the solutions to choose the best one.

The intuitive approach.

This approach is based on the notion that people can get too close to a problem to see it clearly or objectively. They get wrapped up in specifics that prevent them from seeing the big picture. Our mind can become overloaded, so it can be beneficial to take a break by getting away from the problem and thinking about something else for a while. Then we can take a fresh look at it later.

It works like the perception process where we select, organize, and interpret information to fit it in with what we already know. It can take some time to process new information, so by getting away from the problem and doing something different, our mind is cleared and it can work more effectively to process information and reach a solution.

1. The group can identify the source of the problem or the decision to be made. The important issues are identified including the nature and scope of the problem, its causes, and potential solutions. Once all the information is gathered and understood by everyone, the group moves on other things.

2. The group members go away and work on other tasks, so they don't work on the problem. The rationale is that when we are working intensely on a problem, our mind may become overloaded with information and we are unable to process it all. We become too close to the problem to see the big picture. It becomes so familiar that we may overlook important aspects. By setting it aside and forgetting about it for awhile we are able to relax and clear our mind so we can see the problem more clearly in a new light.

3. While we are thinking about other things our subconscious mind continues to process the information using the perception process to interpret and organize the new information with what we already know by giving it meaning. When the process has finished there can be a moment of revelation and a solution becomes clear. This could be an idea we hadn't thought about, and we might even see the situation in a new or different way.

4. After the group members have had time to consider the problem, they get together and present their possible solutions. Then the group works through the solutions to choose the best one based upon its workability and other criteria.

5. The best solution is implemented and evaluated for its effectiveness to determine its success. If it is not successful, there is a list of additional solutions that can be implemented without going through the whole process again.

This approach utilizes the law of shared meaning because new information has to fit in with what we already know so that we can understand and use it. This can take some time to process especially if the new information is different. This method is similar to the perception process of selecting, organizing, and interpreting information to make it useful to us.

When something dramatic happens we may need time to process our thoughts and feelings. If our mind does not process it, then the new information is more likely to be dismissed or rejected. When this process is over, we are more likely to utilize the new information.

Medical approaches.

There are several approaches to problem solving that are analogous to medical treatments.

• Symptoms and illness. Problems can be approached like a doctor would diagnose an illness by looking at the symptoms in order to determine its cause. When the cause has been established, a prescription and course of treatment can be developed in order to cure the illness or solve the problem.

• The holistic approach. In Eastern medicine, like acupuncture, the body is viewed as an interconnected series of systems. Acupuncture points are not necessarily located next to what part of the body they affect. Many points for internal organs are found on the feet or ear. So, problems many originate in places that may not be self evident. For instance, problems with getting deliveries out on time may not be in the department that handles deliveries, but rather in the sales or information technology department.

• The allopathic approach. In Western medicine, the body is broken down into components such as the circulatory or respiratory system. Each system is examined separately and becomes a specialized medical field. Illness is treated with remedies that counter the effects of the symptoms. In this approach, a problem is broken down into smaller parts that are analyzed and resolved individually. They are then reassembled once a solution is been reached. This approach works when a problem is large and needs to be broken down into smaller pieces or systems that can be solved individually in order to reach the larger solution.

The participatory approach.

Not every member of a group contributes equally or in the same way. In groups there may be one or two members that contribute more than the others. They may try to dominate the discussion or force their ideas on the others. There may be some members who are quiet and hold back by not contributing as much as the others. They may have good ideas that the group never gets to hear. The participatory approach is a way to equalize the influence of all group members to encourage everyone to participate.

1. The group identifies the nature and scope of the problem. It identifies the decision to be made. Information is gathered about the problem including its causes and effects. Each member is given time either before or at the meeting to consider the problem and potential solutions.

2. At the meeting the members are given a few minutes to write down on a piece of paper their best possible solutions to the problem.

3. Each member is asked to rank their solutions from most to least desirable.

4. One group member serves as moderator and goes around the group asking each member to tell the group their best solution.

5. As each member tells the group their solutions, they are written down on a board in front of the group so everyone can see them.

6. The moderator goes around the group one or two more times to gather more solutions, if they are needed. Similar solutions are combined.

7. Group members are then asked to look at the list of solutions and write down three new solutions based upon the ones that are on the list.

8. The moderator goes around the group and asks each person to tell the group their best solution. They are written down on the board in front of everyone and the old list is discarded.

9. The group is then asked to discuss and evaluate the list of new solutions. The group is asked to rate the new solutions choosing the best one. This process of going around the group can be repeated as many times as needed to come up with a workable solution.

A common approach is to go around the group and have everyone contribute an idea. However, while one person is explaining their idea, no one else is listening to them because they are thinking about what they are going to say. Giving everyone a few minutes to write down their ideas before anyone speaks gives them time to think about what they are going to say before you begin, so they can listen to everyone else.

This can help everyone focus their attention on what the others have to say and actually listen to them. Having each person write a list of several ideas gives them options to choose from rather than concentrating on just one idea. If a person before them has the same idea they can choose the next item on their list. This makes the process go smoother so no one feels like they are being put on the spot and they don't waste time trying to think of something to say.

The rationale for doing this is that people often have a preconceived notion of what they want to happen. They present their idea and then try to convince everyone else to agree with them. The participatory approach helps everyone work together instead of having each person trying to get their idea adopted, which could harm the group.

The participatory approach encourages everyone to utilize a truly collaborative process to create a solution together. By going around the group a few times, ideas get mixed together and no one has exclusive ownership over any one. It encourages the group to come up with ideas collaboratively as a group rather than as individuals and then fight over whose idea gets chosen. This approach gives all members a chance to contribute equally. When everyone has a say in the process, they feel that they have ownership of it and are more likely to support implementation of the solution.

The long distance approach.

This is a variation of the participatory approach that can be used when time is limited, if the group is large, is separated by long distances, or members are unable to meet together.

1. Everyone is provided information as to the nature of the problem and the decision that needs to be made.

2. When everyone has the information, they do their own research and information gathering to come up with a short list of potential solutions that are ranked in order of workability. Everyone sends their list of solutions to one designated person, perhaps the group leader or secretary.

3. When the solutions are received, the designated person tabulates them and makes a list of the top solutions. This list can contain as many solutions as the group wants to consider. There should be at least four to eight to consider, but no more than twenty or it becomes too time consuming. The tabulated list is sent to the members.

4. Each person is asked to choose their top solution, or top three depending upon the length of the list. Their choices are ranked by which ones get the most responses. Since they only know their own solution, they cannot push the group to choose theirs.

5. At this time the group or a smaller committee can choose or vote for their top choice, which is the one that will be implemented.

6. This process can be repeated as many times as the group needs to reach a decision that is successful. The group should do this at least twice, but not too many more times as people may lose interest.

This process is similar to the participatory approach applying it to a large group that cannot meet all together. It uses a combination of the creative process with voting to choose a solution. It also provides a list of decisions ranked in order of preference to choose from to give the group options and alternatives in case the one chosen is not successful.

The reverse approach.

Most problem solving and decision making approaches begin with the problem and move towards finding the solution. This approach works in reverse because it starts with the solution and then works backward to the problem. This process is used for situations where there is a clearly defined desired outcome, a fixed deadline, or other limitations.

1. Determine what the desired outcome looks like.

2. Determine the criteria for the desired outcome. For example, it needs to be workable or cost effective.

3. Determine what needs to happen just before the desired outcome is reached.

4. Determine what needs to happen just before the last step before the desired outcome is reached.

5. Then work backwards for each step that needs to take place in order to reach the next one.

6. Work backwards through each step until you reach the situation as it exists today.

7. Once all the steps are completed determine how well they meet the criteria.

8. Make a list of the resources that are needed to accomplish each step.

While this process may seem backward, it can be used for decision making and problem solving like when building a house. If you build a house, you do not start with an empty lot, proceed to gather materials like lumber and bricks, determine the best way to assemble them, and see what you end up building.

Instead, you would draw plans of what the house will look like when it is finished. You then work backwards to make a materials list, set time frames for each stage, and determine the cost. If the house needs to be completed by a specific date, a schedule can be established by working backwards from the date of completion to determine when each step needs to take place.

Crisis

Crisis is included in this chapter on groups and organizations because even though how we deal with a crisis involves individual skills, when we experience a crisis we often need the resources and support of groups and organizations to help us get through it. A crisis can happen in many areas of our life including as an individual, in our family, at work, and in our community. In each of these instances, it is often by working together with others in groups that we are able to work through a crisis.

A crisis is usually based around an event or series of events that causes a sudden and extreme shock or change. It dramatically increases the level of uncertainty undermining our stability, security, and even safety. It has the potential to cause emotional as well as physical harm. It often takes priority over everything else until it is resolved. It forces us to make decisions and confront issues we might otherwise avoid or may not even know about. The result can be powerful as well as beneficial. A crisis can be a turning point changing the course of events, even changing our lives.

Crisis is a natural part of life, we all experience some kind of crisis in our lives. What constitutes a crisis depends upon the people involved. It depends on our perceptions and expectations as well as our preparation and training to handle it. What can be a crisis for one person may be another day at work for someone else. For example, emergency responders like police, firefighters, and paramedics respond to crisis situations because they are prepared to respond. Training helps to increase awareness and options that reduces uncertainty. The better we are prepared, the less likely we are to perceive something as a crisis.

These are some characteristics of a crisis.

- Crisis poses a threat to stability that dramatically increases uncertainty. A crisis can threaten basic needs and wants such as our health or physical safety. A crisis can be the loss of something we have. It could be the loss of a house in a natural disaster or the loss of a spouse in a divorce. Many times the restoration of what has been lost is not always possible, so something new may have to be established, which can be difficult. We may have to deal with many different kinds of crisis including personal, relational, financial, emotional, spiritual, and medical.

- Crisis demands a response. There are times when something happens to us and we do not necessarily need to do anything about it. In most cases crisis demands a response where we take a course of action. We have to make decisions and take action in order to protect ourselves, our family, our safety, or our security. We may experience events outside of our ability to cope with them using normal problem solving methods. So, we have to utilize new resources and new ways of doing things in order to respond.

- Crisis affects everyone involved in a similar way. It can affect their well being, state of mind, health, or relationships. It can bring out the best and worst in people because some rise to the challenge while others might try to avoid it or attribute blame.

- Crisis has time limits. A crisis generally lasts for a specific period of time and eventually it passes. However, its effects may last much longer, even a lifetime. There is often a limited amount of time to respond creating urgency and pressure to take action. For example, in natural disasters there can be a limited time to help those affected.

- Crisis creates new norms. Motivated by the law of uncertainty, we want stability in our lives and crisis disrupts that stability. We face daily ups and downs that aren't a crisis because we can tolerate a certain amount of stress and uncertainty. When a crisis happens it increases stress beyond what we can handle, so we must look for support and to develop new ways of handling the situation. After the crisis, we may maintain some of these new ways, so that we can deal with crisis more effectively in the future.

- Crisis necessitates mobilizing resources. When we face problems that we can deal with we use the resources we have available to us. In a crisis, these can be quickly overwhelmed, so we have to find additional resources outside of what we normally use. We look to groups like our family, friends, church, community, or the government for help to provide them.

Crisis is a physical manifestation of the law of uncertainty. It is characterized by a sudden and extreme increase in uncertainty motivating us to take immediate action. It can undermine our feelings of safety and security making the future less certain and predictable. It can make us look for new ways of doing things. It can increase uncertainty long after the crisis has passed. We can reduce the uncertainty it creates by being prepared and planning ahead. However, we often don't do it because we think a crisis will never happen to us, which is why we may not prepare for it until we have experienced it.

The law of shared meaning motivates us to look for meaning in the things that happen to us. We invest them with meaning in order to make sense out of them and to reduce uncertainty. We want to know why things happen because it gives us a deeper understanding of ourselves, others, and the world around us. When we don't understand things that happen to us, we might find meaning in them by saying things like, everything happens for a reason. We may do this in a crisis to find meaning in our experiences. Sharing meaning with others about a crisis can help us to handle the things that happen to us better in the future.

There is a natural inertia that can keep us from planning for crisis because it takes time and energy to prepare for something that might not happen. This natural inertia is due to the many things we have to do every day that takes up our time. We might not realize the benefits of doing something like preparing for crisis until after it has happened. The more we have invested and could potentially lose, the more we are motivated to invest in prevention and preparation. When we have experienced a crisis, we can be more motivated to be prepared for the next time to protect our investments.

The nature of a crisis can be affected by our perception of social reality. A crisis usually involves events that happen in physical reality that we react to based upon how we construct social reality. Crisis is not only physical, it can be psychological existing in the minds of individuals. When things happen to us in physical reality we want to make sense out of them, so we invest them with meaning to determine how to respond. How we utilize social reality to interpret a crisis can make a difference in how successfully we negotiate it. This can make things better as well as worse because how we utilize social reality to interpret our experiences can have ramifications in physical reality.

We evaluate a crisis based on our perceptions and expectations. If something constitutes a crisis or not can be based on what we expect to happen and how we perceive the situation based on our past experiences. For example, if we expected to get a raise because we have gotten them in the past, but were fired instead, we may experience a financial crisis because it did not meet our expectations based on past experience. Some may perceive the loss of a job as a crisis, however, if this has happened before we may see it as motivation to do something different with our career.

In the process of communicating we send our Great Idea through connections across The Great Abyss to others who receive it and provide us with feedback, so we know that our message is understood. In a crisis, this process can break down because of a sudden increase in the need for information that may not be available. Important connections may be cut off blocking the flow of information. There may not be time to get a message to others and receive feedback before having to act. Available resources and methods of decision making may be unable to cope with events, so the entire process may cease to function properly.

Under the best of circumstances the flow of information can be obstructed by the interference of The Great Abyss. In a crisis, there is often a sharp increase in this interference making obtaining reliable and current information difficult. It is likely that more information is needed, but important connections may be shut down so less information may be available. The information that is received may not be what is needed to make good decisions. This means that when critical decisions have to be made that may affect people's lives, they are often made by fewer people, with less resources, with lower quality information, and a diminished ability to evaluate those decisions before they are hurriedly implemented. This is how decisions made in a crisis situation have the potential to make things worse.

It can be helpful to be aware of why poor decisions are made in a crisis so that they can be averted. Having an awareness of potential sources of crises helps to develop options that can be rapidly implemented without the need for connections to provide information that may breakdown. This involves creating a plan of action and gathering resources that will be needed before a crisis begins when there is adequate time to gather information, evaluate options, and obtain feedback. Then if a crisis happens, the plan can be quickly implemented.

Crisis, like conflict, does not need to be all bad. It shows us where our current methods of doing things are inadequate. It can make us do things differently and develop new solutions. It can make us gather new information and seek out support from others. It can make us learn new things and try new approaches that we normally might not have considered. Many safety measures and training we have today originated from the response to crises.

The false crisis.

The law of uncertainty and the nature of social reality can work to create a false crisis. Some people might utilize the power of the law of uncertainty to manipulate public perception to create a false crisis to achieve their desired outcome. In the media we often hear about all kinds of crisis. A crisis can intensify public perception resulting in tangible consequences affecting our physical reality. This can cause anxiety in people's minds motivating them to take action escalating the crisis in physical reality, making it worse than it needed to be.

People make decisions based on information that is available to them and much of it comes through the media. What we are told in the media can motivate people to take action that might make a crisis worse. So, when someone calls something a crisis, it's helpful to consider their motivation. Ask yourself if they are trying to push you into a way of thinking or doing something that under normal circumstances you would not do. There can be times when information communicated in a crisis is based on personal opinion to further a particular agenda.

The perceptions that exist in people's minds can motivate them to take action creating reality. Anything that has been created by people, first existed in someone's mind and was communicated to others in order to become physical reality. This process can work similarly with psychological concepts like a crisis. If people believe that there is a crisis they may be motivated to behave in ways that end up creating one. This is due to the power of the law of uncertainty, which motivates people to respond to alleviate a perceived crisis. People can use the power of this process to further their own personal desired outcomes.

Uncertainty can be created by the law of shared meaning because behavior is motivated by how we invest uncertainty with meaning. When we perceive increased uncertainty, we look for meaning in it to better understand what is happening, so we know what we should do. People notice something is happening, but they may not know what it is. There can be the perception that others know something that they don't know, so they may follow them because they don't want to be left behind or lose out. They may take action because they think it's better to do something now rather than to take a chance on what might happen later. This may happen with few ill effects, however, at other times it can have serious consequences.

How this works is illustrated by old western movies. The cowboys are herding the cattle to market and along comes the cattle rustlers to steal the cattle. They are able to steal the cattle by stampeding the herd. They only need to get a few going and the rest follow. If people have the perception of a crisis they can be motivated to take action to restore stability whether the crisis is real or not. The power of the law of uncertainty can be used to manipulate people to do things they otherwise might not do. They are in effect stampeded to get them to do what others want them to do in a hurry before they can think it through. This phenomenon has the potential to manifest itself in economic and financial crises.

Sources of crisis.

Crisis is important to understand because it potentially affects us all. How much it affects us depends upon how we understand it, how well we are prepared for it, and how we respond when it occurs. If we handle a crisis well, it can increase our knowledge and bolster our self-confidence. Crisis can be caused by a number of sources. It can be a severe single event that happens suddenly and unexpectedly, or it can be caused by a series of events that build up slowly over time. It can be caused by something that we know will happen eventually, but we don't know when. It can be caused by an individual, group of people, or by nature. It can be totally unexpected or predictable. It can be caused by an accident or on purpose.

To help improve our response to a crisis, it's helpful to be aware of its source.

- External crisis. These are caused by events outside of our control. They may be caused by other people or by nature like being fired or a natural disaster. As much as we may plan to avoid a crisis, many of them are brought by outside forces beyond our control.

- Internal crisis. These are crises that are created by us or that primarily affect us as an individual. They can be psychological, such as an emotional crisis. They can be caused by our actions that affect others such as a divorce. They can be caused by decisions that we make or our actions like quitting our job resulting in a financial crisis.

- Unpredictable crisis. These are events that we cannot predict or that can happen without warning. External unpredictable crisis includes things like natural disasters. Internal unpredictable crisis includes things like accidents or medical problems.

- Predictable crisis. These are stressful situations that we can reasonably expect to happen during the course of our life. These occur when we experience different events or stages of life that can upset our stability like illness or old age.

Crisis communicating.

A crisis can increase uncertainty, undermine stability, and threaten our investments. It can elicit feelings of anxiety, anger, frustration, and even fear. We may question our ability and the ability of others to respond effectively. This makes it easy to only communicate negative messages about the negative aspects of the crisis. How we characterize our experiences can set the tone for how we feel about them affecting our thoughts and actions.

How we communicate about a crisis can have an impact on its outcome. Through the law of shared meaning our perceptions can manifest themselves in reality. This is because we look for meaning in the things that happen to us, so how we communicate about them can motivate our actions. Characterizing circumstances in evaluative terms like bad or terrible can make things worse because perception can create social reality. Instead of being overwhelmed with negative messages, it can be helpful to balance them with positive ones.

There is an inherent duality in the nature of crisis. This is expressed in the Japanese word for crisis, kiki, which is written with two characters that separately mean danger and opportunity. When we communicate about crisis, we often talk about danger, but there is also the potential for opportunity. This is because crisis has the power to make us do things and think in new ways to make changes we might otherwise not do, or even consider.

As difficult as it may be in times of crisis, it is helpful to communicate some positive messages emphasizing the opportunity to resolve the situation. It is helpful to communicate these messages because they reduce uncertainty, build stability, reduce anxiety, and invest in relationships. By utilizing the power of the law of shared meaning we can create more positive perceptions about a crisis that can become reality helping us to get through it.

Having a more balanced distribution of positive and negative messages can have a beneficial affect on our perceptions and expectations. When our perceptions are improved, it can improve our expectations, so we will feel better about our situation. Doing this can give us added confidence to act more decisively, so we can feel more assured about the situation, which can help to resolve things more positively.

When we stay positive we can feel better about ourselves and our abilities to do our best to achieve the best possible outcome under the circumstances and overcome adversity. This does not mean that we should be unrealistic or characterize the situation as being more positive than it actually is, but not just focus on the negative. A crisis can make us think in new ways, gain new skills, and challenge ourselves in ways we might otherwise not do.

Phases of crisis.

Crisis can be overwhelming, but it can be easier to cope with if we approach it as a series of events or phases. We can learn from our experiences and gain new knowledge to help us handle a crisis better in the future. In order to reduce uncertainty and increase stability we can develop norms that comprise our ways of doing things. These are often based on our past experiences. We might not think about them until we have to, so it can be helpful to be aware of them because they can affect what we do in a crisis.

1. The law of uncertainty phase. A crisis can begin with a rapid and dramatic increase in uncertainty undermining our stability and security. Everyone involved is aware of the crisis that overwhelms their resources and normal methods of problem solving. There is often a limited amount of time to respond because the longer it takes, the more serious the consequences may be. Circumstances change the normal ways of doing things for everyone involved which may continue once the crisis has passed.

Just what constitutes a crisis may be difficult to define, but everyone involved knows when one happens. They may know the exact moment it happened or it may be difficult to determine because it may have been building up over a long period of time. Much of what constitutes a crisis depends upon how we perceive and interpret events. How we do this is often based upon our past experiences and skills. What may constitute a crisis for one person may not for others. Uncertainty is uncomfortable, but crisis can create feelings of anxiety, anger, or fear because we may not know what to do or what will happen next. This can motivate people to take action to restore normality seeking a state of equilibrium.

2. The law of shared meaning phase. When everyone involved is aware of the crisis, they begin communicating about it. They invest what is happening with shared meaning recognizing it as a crisis. The need to communicate dramatically increases to the point where it may overwhelm the ability of existing networks to handle it. When people communicate, they characterize the crisis in terms that are negative-danger or positive-opportunity. How people communicate about the crisis in its early stages can affect their perception of what is happening to them shaping their expectations. These perceptions and expectations motivate behavior because they can have tangible consequences. How people communicate at this stage can manifest itself in physical reality, affecting how successful the outcome will be.

In a crisis we communicate with people involved in the crisis and others outside the crisis communicate with us in the form of support or advice. We may get information from family, friends, the media, experts, public officials, or professionals who are trained to handle a crisis. We invest what they say with meaning to fit it in with what we already know to make it useful to us. The nature of the messages people send can change the emotional intensity of the situation. Negative messages can increase emotional intensity by increasing uncertainty. They increase the perception of negative circumstances, which can create expectations that things are going badly causing people to become apprehensive or even panic, diminishing their ability to react to their circumstances. Negative messages increase uncertainty undermining people's confidence making them less likely to do what is necessary in a crisis, which could make the situation worse.

Communicating positive messages provides specific information to help give people confidence to do what is necessary in a crisis. This emphasizes stability so that people will remain calm helping them to think clearly to resolve the problem. Positive messages can help to decrease emotional intensity by reducing uncertainty. They show support for others to bolster their confidence increasing their chances of success. If people have the perception that the crisis is something they can handle, they may expect things to work out giving them the confidence to handle them more effectively.

3. The law of investing phase. A crisis is an overwhelming increase in uncertainty that motivates people to take action to return to a normal, stable state. Eventually the level of uncertainty reaches a peak or turning point where it begins to subside either naturally or through the efforts of people to resolve it. Negative-danger messages should be diminishing and positive-opportunity messages should be increasing as people focus their attention

from the crisis itself to what needs to be done afterwards. The emotional intensity should drop as people begin to feel a sense of relief that the worst is over.

In this phase, we seek to restore the previous state of normality or if that's not possible establish a new state of equilibrium. Because a crisis overwhelms old norms or ways of doing things, we can be motivated to find new ways of doing things to resolve the crisis. One of the positive aspects of crisis is that it gets people to think about what is familiar to them in new ways. We look at the causes, at what worked, and what didn't work to resolve it. New norms that proved effective to resolve the crisis can be kept based upon their usefulness. We can learn from our experience to take a bad thing and turn it around to make it better. Even in bad situations, it can be helpful to look for the good things that we can benefit from.

It can take some time to come to terms with the crisis because it takes time to fit the new information in with what we already know. We may need time to think about or process our experiences because we tend to perceive things based upon past experience that can make some things difficult to assimilate or utilize. This works like the perception process where we select, organize, and interpret the information we perceive to fit it in with what we already know so it can be useful to us. We do this to fit present reality into our own personal social reality, which is primarily based upon our perceptions of past experiences. The degree to which we are able to process the information determines how well adjusted we are with the experience to improve our response in the future.

4. After a crisis. How we feel after a crisis can have a significant affect on our self-concept. If we feel that things went as well as they could, it can improve our self-concept making us feel confident about our abilities. If we feel that the crisis has not been effectively resolved or things could have gone better, it can hurt our self-concept. By evaluating our skills before and after a crisis, we can be better prepared for what may happen in the future.

Once uncertainty has been reduced to tolerable levels we may try to establish a stable set of norms. However, things may not return to how they were before, but instead there will be a new state of stability or equilibrium. The degree of difference can be determined by the severity of the crisis and how much it forced us to make changes. Many of the ways that things were done during the crisis may become a part of the new state of normality. In a crisis, we can learn new ways of doing things, making decisions, obtaining information, using resources, and making connections with others for support. It can motivate us to make changes we may have wanted to make, but had put off because they seemed too uncertain.

If a crisis passes relatively quickly people are more likely to return to norms more similar to those utilized before the crisis because they are familiar. If a crisis drags on, they are more likely to get accustomed to the changes crisis brings making them less likely to return to the norms they had before the crisis. As they have time to reduce uncertainty, they become more accustomed to the new norms.

Crisis preparation and prevention.

Because a crisis is over does not mean it no longer has any affect on us. It can have both emotional and physical effects for some time afterwards. By having an awareness of this, we can avoid letting past experiences undermine the present because there can be a tendency to overreact in the wake of a crisis. Before a crisis, adequate preventative measures may not have been taken, so after a crisis people may go to extremes instituting unnecessary new measures that can be costly and burdensome that actually provides little real protection.

When it comes to crisis the old adage, be prepared still applies. Preparation and training helps to reduce uncertainty and improve effectiveness in a crisis. It can help to have an awareness of potential sources of crisis and develop options to respond to them. This helps us to determine what crises we potentially face and what we can do to prepare for them.

To reduce uncertainty and be better prepared in a crisis it can be helpful to conduct a crisis assessment, so you can develop a plan. A plan can reduce uncertainty and be a source of confidence in a time of crisis to help you be more effective. How to prepare depends on the nature of potential crises. Anticipating a crisis can be helpful to avoid ones that can be avoided and mitigate the effects of those that are inevitable.

Important moments for avoiding crisis, as well as unintended or undesired outcomes.

1. Moment of no return. This is when a course of action can't be reversed or stopped. For example, it is when the ship can no longer change course in time to avoid hitting the iceberg.

2. Moment of realization. This is when people know what is going to happen. For example, it is when the crew realizes the ship will hit the iceberg.

It is important which moment comes first. If the moment of no return happens first, the ship will hit the iceberg. If the moment of realization happens first, the ship can change course to avoid the iceberg and will be saved.

Options for developing a crisis plan.

1. What might happen to you? Identify any potential crisis that might happen to you. Determine the sources of the crisis and your desired outcomes during and after the crisis.

2. What will you need? Identify the resources you will need and gather them together, including water, food, clothing, and money. Have any items you may need ready to go at a moments notice. Identify outside resources that you might need such as emergency responders. Consider how much time you will need to get to a place of safety or to get help.

3. What will you do? Create a plan of action. Determine what needs attention now, what can wait, and what is out of your control. For example, a medical crisis needs attention now, a financial crisis might wait, and in a natural disaster all you may be able to do is wait until it passes. Determine which things you can do yourself and which ones need support from others. Have an alternative plan as well just in case the first plan cannot be implemented.

4. Rehearse. Test the plan by practicing it such as conducting a drill or dry run to give everyone the opportunity to know what they are going to do under actual circumstances. Doing this can help make everyone feel more confident when it comes to implementing the plan because it reduces uncertainty, so it will feel more familiar.

5. Communicate. Think about how you will gather information. You may not be able to depend on telephone service, so consider other ways to communicate if necessary. Keep things positive and focus on what can be done to keep everyone calm and focused. Avoid negative messages that can scare people increasing their anxiety or uncertainty.

6. Implement. If it's necessary to implement a crisis plan, start with an awareness of the scope and nature of the actual crisis to avoid overreacting. By knowing exactly what is in-

volved, you can focus on the things that need to be addressed now and put off less pressing issues until you have more time. Having a plan gives you options to select the best one to fit your situation. Keep messages positive to encourage confidence in others and communicate a positive vision of what it will be like when the crisis is over.

We learn how to handle a crisis from our experiences, but it can be helpful to talk about your experiences with others to gain more insight and information. Due to the law of uncertainty a crisis is not a matter of if, but a matter of when. Being prepared gives you a chance to plan and gather the resources necessary to reduce uncertainty before it happens to help you achieve a better outcome. We have a tendency to put off doing this because these things happen to other people. The best time to plan for crisis is right now, before something happens because once it does, it's too late to plan ahead.

Uncertainty and Professional Communicating

What would happen if you no longer belonged to any groups? Many people have spent time on their own, outside the influence of groups. Jesus spent forty days fasting in the desert. Buddha was thought to have spent forty nine days sitting under a tree to find enlightenment and spiritual insight. Other people have gone on spiritual quests. So, if you could get away from all the groups that influence you, what would you do? What new insights could you gain about yourself, others, and the world around you? Would you read, develop a new skill, travel, or sit under a tree?

While we may not be able to get away from others for that long, we can find some time to get away from the influence of groups. It could be for a week or a weekend. Having some time away from groups and organizations can help us increase our awareness of how they influence us. This can help us reflect on what things are working well and what we would like to change.

Groups and organizations provide us with many benefits, but so can spending some time on our own. Doing this can help us to relax, reduce stress, and process information to help us clear our mind to become more focused. We can develop our skills, clarify our perceptions, and manage our expectations to make them more realistic and useful. We can evaluate our needs and wants, and how well they are being met. We can simplify our life by focusing on our desired outcomes and what is really important to us. We can spend time without worrying about meeting the expectations of others.

Some groups seem to get along and things go well, so we don't think much about them. Other times nothing seems to work leaving us feeling frustrated. Groups and organizations can utilize the laws of uncertainty, shared meaning, and investing as a methodological tool to help diagnose problems and find solutions to make them more effective.

By understanding the law of uncertainty, groups and organizations can balance uncertainty with uncertainty reduction to provide stability, yet motivate effective behaviors to foster innovation and avoid becoming overly complacent. The law of shared meaning can be used to create a common culture and positive climate that fosters desirable attributes like commitment and member satisfaction. Understanding the law of investing and how it motivates behavior can help to make groups and organizations more effective. These laws can be utilized to fulfill needs and wants, manage perceptions and expectations, and achieve desired outcomes.

Chapter 5
Societal Communicating

What if your only source of information was from people around you? What if you only got the news from the people you saw face to face? What if you did not have access to any media like television, radio, newspapers, or the internet? How would this affect what you know? How would this affect the decisions you make? How would this affect your behavior and how you communicate with others?

While this is unlikely to happen, there was a time when people obtained information by communicating directly with other people. They lived in communities that were small enough to make public communicating with everyone else feasible. As communities grew larger, it was not possible to directly communicate with everyone, so society needed to find a way to communicate with large groups of people. This need motivated the invention of many of the technologies that makes societal communicating possible.

In most forms of communicating, we make a direct connection with others, so we usually know who we are communicating with and they can provide us with feedback. Societal communicating is different because we are more likely to make a connection using technology with people we do not know. This form of communicating is important to the effective functioning of a society because it provides much of the information that is needed to develop opinions, solve problems, make decisions, and form perceptions and expectations. It can enable us to make connections that create common ground bringing people closer together. Societal communicating is a means by which people take social reality and make it become physical reality.

Societal communicating is the fourth and final level of interaction. It is about how we communicate with others in public and how others communicate with us in society. Societal communicating is comprised of several different methods of communicating. The first section is about how people communicate with others in public, including professional public communicating. The next section is about how others communicate in public with you. This includes the three most prominent sectors of society; the media, business, and government. The final section covers how we as a society communicate and the effect this has on people including creating knowledge, the economy, government, and social reality.

Public Communicating

Public communicating consists of the ways we make connections to communicate our Great Idea with others in society. It could be to a few people or to large audiences. It can include written messages like a memo, email, letter, report, article, or book. It can be verbal like a speech, presentation, or video. It can involve the use of technology that is controlled by others like television, radio, or the internet.

In most forms of communicating, you create your Great Idea and make a direct connection with others you know who can provide you with feedback. In public communicating, we are less likely to communicate directly with others we know. We are more likely to make an indirect connection through a third party to others we cannot see and do not know. We may receive direct feedback, delayed feedback, or no feedback at all. Public communicating often utilizes technology, which can create a disconnect between us and our audience making it more difficult to facilitate feedback. Public communicating tends to be more formal, structured, and planned in advance, before the audience actually receives it. This means that in public communicating, it is helpful to know how to structure and communicate messages to achieve your desired outcome.

Most of the time when we communicate with others we use the third style of communicating described in chapter 1. This is a conversational style of communicating that provides instantaneous feedback. In public communicating, this happens when we speak in front of an audience or give a group presentation. We can read their facial expressions and see their eye contact to ascertain their interest or attentiveness. There may be an opportunity for people to ask questions to provide us with feedback. Through feedback we can know more about our audience and how we are being perceived by them.

Many of the ways we communicate in public falls into the first or second style of communicating. In the first style, you construct your message and then send it to your audience through a connection hoping they will get it. It's rather like shooting an arrow into the air and hoping it hits its target. This happens when we communicate through third party intermediaries such as print, radio, or television.

The second style is like a tennis match where you send your message to others and they may or may not reply by providing feedback or delayed feedback. Whatever the style, public communicating utilizes more indirect connections with your audience, so it's helpful to know as much as you can about them to develop a message that will hit its target. Without public communicating, it would be difficult for people to take their Great Idea and share it with others in order to make it a reality.

Public communicating has the potential increase uncertainty because we don't always know how our message will be received by the public. We don't always know who our audience is or receive feedback from them. People can use the power of the law of uncertainty by publicly communicating misinformation or withholding information. This can increase uncertainty undermining stability motivating behavior with potentially negative consequences.

Much of how we share meaning to construct social reality takes place through public communicating. It is the means by which we share stories about ourselves and others to create a common culture. We can share meaning through creative expression in the arts and entertainment. Public communicating can give society a sense of collective identity making us feel like we belong and are connected to others. It gives us a sense of what it means to be a member of society. It is how we share rituals, traditions, and communal values. It helps us to define who we are as individuals and as a society.

Sharing information through public communicating is essential for people to invest in themselves, others, and in society. This is important because it provides the information we need to make decisions, accomplish tasks, and achieve desired outcomes. Individuals communicate in public in order to encourage others to invest in them and their ideas. This process is necessary to facilitate creativity, invention, exploration, discovery, and self expression that are necessary for society to function and grow.

Public communicating is a means by which leaders inform us about issues that are important to us. It is how we as a society make decisions that affect us. It helps us to reduce uncertainty, so we can invest in one another to create security and stability in society. We determine our willingness to invest our resources like time and money based upon information we receive from others who communicate publicly through the media.

With most types of communicating, you create your Great Idea and communicate it to others by making a direct connection with them across The Great Abyss and then receive feedback. In public communicating, the process of communicating begins with you and your Great Idea. However, connections are often made through third parties and with the use of technology making it more difficult to cross The Great Abyss, because it can be much larger. This means that you may have less control over how your message is communicated and who receives it, because you are more disconnected from your audience and there are more types of interference to get in the way.

We communicate in order to fulfill our needs and wants, which may involve communicating publicly. We may have the need to share information, to persuade others, or to achieve desired outcomes involving large numbers of people. We may have the need to gain the respect of others, bolster our self-esteem, or improve our self-concept by communicating with others. When we communicate with large numbers of people, it can increase our prestige and may even provide us with rewards such as monetary resources.

We use the perception process to select, organize, and retain information that we find useful. People communicate publicly to provide information that can shape the perceptions and expectations of others in order to achieve their desired outcome. You can utilize this process by providing information to others that affects their perception process shaping their expectations.

In doing this, it's helpful to have an awareness of your audience's existing perceptions and expectations. Information that fits within them is more likely to be accepted and utilized. Information that does not fit within them is more likely to be discarded or rejected. This process can be helpful because it provides the information people use to make decisions that influences their actions.

In order to communicate effectively in public, it's helpful to have an awareness of the process of how people communicate with others. It's helpful to have an awareness of your own communicating skills and how you are perceived by others. It's helpful to have an awareness of your audience, their needs and wants, perceptions and expectations, and desired outcomes, so you can create a message that will be understood and accepted by them.

It can be helpful to have options about how you communicate with others, the connections you make, and how you create your message so that it will reach them through the interference of the Great Abyss. Having awareness helps you to choose the most effective approach to reach your audience and achieve your desired outcome.

Everyone communicates for a reason and they communicate in public for a reason. The reason you communicate publicly affects how you will construct your Great Idea and the connections you make to communicate it to others to achieve your desired outcome. Desired outcomes can be to share information, entertain others, persuade them, or motivate them to take action. Your audience also has its own desired outcome for receiving your message, and knowing as much as you can about them can help you to achieve yours. This can also help to avoid unintended or undesired outcomes.

The Process.

Before you can communicate your Great Idea to others, you first need to create it. You might want to give a speech, write a report, or make a video. While these situations are different, the process of creating them has similar elements. Instead of describing each of these separately, this process can be used to create your message to use in many different situations. Like most aspects of communicating, there is no one right way or one size fits all approach. The Process provides options so you can choose what works best for you in your own situation.

The Process of creating a message to communicate in public begins with you. So it's helpful to reduce uncertainty by knowing yourself including your communicating skills, background, experiences, credibility, and competence. It can be helpful to reduce uncertainty in your audience by letting them know something about yourself through the appropriate use of self-disclosure to build trust. You might let them know a little bit about yourself, your experiences, accomplishments, and expertise to communicate confidence and credibility.

Using self-disclosure can help your audience to be more receptive to your message. In circumstances where the audience will see you, like in a speech or video, it's not only what you say, it's how you say it. They will pick up on your nonverbal body language, so if you appear confident they should be more comfortable with you. If they perceive you as uncomfortable, it can increase uncertainty and they may become skeptical of your message.

When you first meet someone there is a high degree of uncertainty motivating others to look for more information about you. When you communicate in public, chances are the audience knows little or nothing about you, so there is a high degree of uncertainty motivating them to want to know more. They may want to know more about your credibility, experience, or motivation for communicating your message. By having an awareness of this, you can utilize self-disclosure to communicate information about yourself that is relevant to your message such as your skills, expertise, or experiences. Reducing uncertainty helps to establish credibility, so the audience will be more receptive to your message.

In most forms of public communicating, your Great Idea needs to be written down first before being put in its final form. The old adage to begin at the beginning is not necessarily the most effective way to proceed. Getting started can be difficult, so don't get bogged down with what to write first. Start with what is important, interesting, or what you know the most about, then fill in the rest later. Everyone communicates for a reason and you are creating a message for a reason, so start with that first.

Consider these options when creating your Great Idea.

- Uncertainty. When you communicate in public there is often a high degree of uncertainty in your audience about you and your Great Idea. Look for ways to reduce uncertainty to make your audience more receptive to your message. This can be done by providing relevant information about yourself and your message.

- Share meaning. Look for ways to connect to your audience by sharing meaning through appropriate self-disclosure such as telling stories about yourself and your experiences.

- Invest. Encourage your audience to invest in your Great Idea by providing information that can be useful or beneficial to them.

- Desired outcome. To create an effective message it's helpful to determine your desired outcome. Your desired outcome is more than just a goal or objective, it is what you want your audience to think or do after they receive your message. In determining your desired outcome it is helpful to have realistic expectations about your audience and what they can do because unrealistic expectations can lead to frustration or disappointment.

- The topic. What one or two things should your audience remember even if they forget everything else about your message? Asking this should give you your topic. Your topic is the subject of your message, your main idea, thesis, or claim. A good topic is something that interests you as well as your audience. Keep it simple and straightforward. You should be able to summarize your topic in a single sentence.

- The claim. If you're making a critical argument, the topic is referred to as the claim. You support your claim with evidence put together with logic and reasoning. All the information in your message should support your claim. The information is structured using reasoning to make it persuasive to the audience. A claim is often used in more formal methods of communicating. For example, an attorney in court makes a claim of guilt or innocence that is supported with evidence.

- Scope. Consider the scope of your message including its depth and breadth. The breadth is how much information you cover and the depth is how specific or detailed you get. The combination you choose depends on your message and your audience. In determining this consider the knowledge of your audience, your knowledge, and the time that is available. It's better to cover less information and have your audience understand your message than to try to do too much leaving them behind.

Your audience.

Connect with your audience by utilizing the law of uncertainty. By reducing uncertainty about yourself and your intentions the audience is more likely to feel comfortable with you and be more receptive to your message. The law of shared meaning helps you to establish common ground, so you can make a connection with your audience. You can use the law of investing to encourage them to invest in you and your message by sharing information about your expertise, knowledge, experience, and that you have a genuine interest in their well being. People are more likely to be open to information that they find useful, interesting, entertaining, or is in their best interest.

To achieve your desired outcome it is helpful to know as much about your audience as you can. This includes your audience's perceptions and expectations, needs and wants, and desired outcomes. By knowing how they form their perceptions, you can create a message that cuts through the interference to get across The Great Abyss. By knowing their expectations, you can create your message to meet them. By knowing their needs and wants, you can focus your message to better fulfill them. And by knowing their desired outcomes, you can create your message to help them to achieve them.

Knowing as much as you can about your audience should help you to determine the best means to reach them so you can communicate more effectively to achieve your own desired outcome. There are several ways to get to know your audience. If you are speaking in front of a group, go and talk to people informally as they are arriving at the venue to get to know more about them. For larger audiences interviews, focus groups, and surveys can be used to learn about their interests.

These are characteristics of audiences to be aware of when you create your message.

- Audience needs and wants. People tend to pay attention to information they think will help them fulfill their needs and wants. The more you know what these are, the more likely they are to pay attention to you. This helps you to get their attention by cutting through the interference making it less likely for them to filter you out. If they are already looking for information to help them fulfill their needs and wants, they are more likely to be predisposed to your message. People tend to pay attention to information that reduces uncertainty because it makes them feel more secure. They look for information that shares meaning for them. And they also look for information that helps them to invest in themselves, others, and society.

- Audience perceptions. It's helpful to be aware of your audience's perception of you and your message. You can utilize identity management and appropriate self-disclosure to affect their perceptions of you to make them more receptive to your message. You can present information that is in line with their perceptions and expectations to make it easier for your message to fit in with what they already know. It can be helpful to be aware of the perceptions they have of themselves to know if their perceptions accurately reflect reality or not. This should help to get through the interference so that they can have a positive perception of you.

- Audience expectations. Just as you are communicating your message for a reason, people have their own reasons for paying attention to you. They have expectations of you and your message. It's helpful to be aware of their expectations so you can meet them as reasonably as possible. Not all expectations are realistic, however, if you know what they are you have a better chance to meet them to make your audience more receptive to you. If their expectations are unrealistic, you may be able to present information that can help them realize this so they can become more realistic. They also have expectations about themselves and just how much they are willing to do. So, be realistic in what you expect them to do because they can only do so much.

- Audience types. In many types of public communicating there are two types of audiences. The first is your primary audience. This is the audience that will actually receive your message. The second, is your secondary audience. These are the people who will likely receive your message afterwards through other connections. Either one or both of these audiences can be the target audience you want to reach with your message. For example, a candidate for political office may speak at a convention. This is their primary audience because they will see and hear the candidate in person. The secondary audience consists of voters who were not there, but may see it on television, hear it on the radio, or read about the speech in print.

- Demographics. These are the traits people have that can be observed or rather easily identified. These include age, gender, ethnicity, geographic affiliation, group affiliation, education, or economic status. Audience research is often based upon demographics to understand the behavior of groups of people. By having an awareness of your audience's demographics you can structure your message to reach them more effectively.

- Psychographics. These are traits that are unique to individuals that are more difficult to identify. They include a person's interests, hobbies, likes, dislikes, behaviors, and psychological makeup. These can be difficult to ascertain, but can be more significant than demographics because they provide information about an audience's needs and wants, behavior, motivation, and desired outcomes. If you know these things, it can help you to create a message that utilizes common ground to cut through the interference to reach them and achieve your desired outcome.

- Group affiliation. It's helpful to know what groups your audience belongs to in order to share meaning because group members often share common interests and groups exert a degree of influence over their members. Utilizing information that is of interest to group members can reduce uncertainty to make them more receptive to your message to achieve your desired outcome.

- Knowledge. It's helpful to know what knowledge your audience has about your topic to determine how much background information to cover so they will understand your message. You want to avoid covering information they already know because they might find it boring. Conversely, you don't want to include information they don't understand. For instance, your message would be crafted differently if you were speaking to a professional organization than the general public. If you are unsure of their level of knowledge, take a middle of the road approach by not being too specific or too general. Clearly define any terms or concepts you use.

- The situation. All communication takes place within a context or situation. It can be helpful to know as much as possible about what is happening that could affect how people perceive your message. This can include people's past experiences and future expectations.

Levels of Response.

Previous approaches to public communicating were often based upon the intention of the creator of the message, like writing an article or giving a speech to inform, entertain, or persuade. However, this approach does not necessarily consider the audience's perspective, needs and wants, or desired outcomes. So, it can be helpful to look at public communicating from their perspective by considering what their potential response might be.

The following are levels of an audience's response with each level representing increased acceptance or commitment to your message. These levels can affect their behavior and how they communicate with others. They start with the most basic and easy to achieve going to the most advanced and difficult to achieve.

Level I. Awareness. This is the most basic level of response. The purpose is to increase your audience's knowledge and understanding of your subject. It is the easiest response to achieve because the audience does not have to do anything more than listen to you and understand your message. Awareness includes informing, defining, explaining, or demonstrating something to make it more familiar to your audience.

Level II. Agreement. We communicate publicly with others to get them to agree with us because it acknowledges the significance of our ideas. When people agree with us, it can make us feel good about ourselves contributing to a positive self-concept. It helps to reduce uncertainty because the other person thinks the same as we do. Agreeing on issues that are part of our values and beliefs can be more difficult because it involves information that may be contrary to our self-concept or social reality. The more something involves our self-concept or view of social reality, the more difficult it can be to change because it may create uncertainty. If you are looking for agreement it's helpful to be realistic in your expectations.

Level III. Action. This level involves motivating people to do something you want them to do. There can be many types of action from buying a product or supporting a cause, to changing a lifestyle. This can also include getting people to stop doing something you want them to stop doing, like smoking. This level includes the other two because in order for them to take action, you must first inform them and they must agree with your idea. Then you can use persuasion to motivate them to take action.

Having your audience take action is a more difficult desired outcome because they may already be doing things that they are comfortable doing. So, change might be perceived as increasing uncertainty making them uncomfortable creating resistance. While it may be comparatively easier to get people to understand or agree, it is much more difficult to get them to take action because instead of just thinking about something, they have to actually do something. Their action can be delayed because they may not do what you want them to do right after they hear your message. This can be a problem because the longer the interval between the message and the action, the less likely people are to do it because everyday activities interfere and they can forget.

Methods that effectively motivate people to take action are generally based upon the law of uncertainty. This is because uncertainty is uncomfortable so it can motivate people to take action. Uncertainty can manifest itself in emotions like anxiety, fear, or anger. While it may seem like a good idea to use positive emotions to motivate people to take action, if the emotion is positive there is little discomfort.

Negative emotions can be powerful motivators because they can increase a person's level of discomfort and uncertainty. When people feel enough discomfort they should be motivated to take action. The more intense the emotion and the more uncomfortable it makes us, the more likely we are to be motivated to do something about it. So, when people want others to do something, they might make them angry or fearful because these emotions can be a powerful motivator.

If you want to motivate people to take action, consider what kind of action you want them to take. Do you want them to take action before, during, or after something happens? These are three options.

- Proactive. Taking action before something happens by getting ahead of the curve such as with preventative medicine.

- Interactive. Taking action while something is happening by riding the curve such as treating an illness.

- Reactive. Taking action after something happens by following the curve such as finding a cure.

Level IV. Actuation. This can be the most difficult level of response to obtain because it involves the most change. It not only involves agreeing with an idea and taking action, but also spreading the word to inform and persuade others about it. This makes it the least likely outcome because it involves adopting a belief, motivating behavior, and sharing it with others. Actuation is often used in social, political, environmental, and religious causes. For example, people may agree with and support a political candidate, and then go out to campaign for them as well.

Persuasion.

The second, third, and fourth levels of response share the common element of persuasion. We use persuasion to get others to agree with us or to motivate their behavior. These are options that are effective in persuading others.

- Reasoning. We persuade others by using forms of evidence organized by reasoning to build an argument to achieve our desired outcome. Our desired outcome can be called the premise, thesis, or claim. We support a claim of evidence based upon established standards and criteria rationally organized to reach a conclusion. This method is persuasive because it is presented as objective and logical instead of being subjective and open to opinion.

- Emotions. Use of emotion appeals to our values and beliefs. Common emotional appeals include empathy, sadness, guilt, anger, or fear. Many emotions can be uncomfortable motivating us to take action. Emotional appeals are a powerful motivating force that can be used when reasoning may not be as effective or there is not sufficient evidence.

- Tradition. Traditions and rituals are an important part of who we are. They are part of our history and how we make connections with others. We celebrate important events by doing things that have been done by other people before us. Upholding traditions can be a powerful motivating force to persuade people because it represents stability and predictability.

- Authority. People can be persuaded based on the advice of a person who is considered an authority or has expertise, experience, credibility, or trustworthiness. We can be persuaded by people whose values we share or who we hold in high esteem. We can also be persuaded by well known personalities with whom we may feel a connection.

- Shared values. It's easier to persuade others when we have something in common with them such as similar values or interests. Shared values form connections between people that can make them feel that we are all in this together. It's helpful to find some common ground between you and your audience because it makes them more likely to agree with you or to take the action you want them to take.

- Needs and wants. People are always looking to fulfill needs and wants, so you can persuade them by providing something they need or want. By knowing your audience, you can tailor your message to include potential benefits for them. If they see that your message has something that will benefit or help them, they can be more likely to agree or take action.

Gathering information.

Once you have determined your desired outcome and developed your Great Idea, you will need to gather information. This can come from a variety of sources and the best place to begin is with what you already know from your own experiences, knowledge, education, and expertise. We gather information through observation, participation, and by talking to others to learn from their knowledge and experience.

It can be helpful to be aware of these types of information.

- Primary sources. This is the best place to get information because it comes directly from the source, so it is the most current and accurate. These sources are usually individuals relating their own experiences and observations. They can also include research like interviews, statistics, and studies. This information can be the most difficult and time consuming to obtain, which is why we are more likely to use secondary sources.

- Secondary. This is information that comes from the original source through an intermediary like a reporter who interviews someone and then reports what they said. This means that the information can potentially be altered, edited, or changed. An intermediary can add their own views potentially changing its meaning. Secondary information is easier to obtain as it is more widely available.

- Quantitative and qualitative information. Quantitative information pertains to quantities, those things that can be measured or expressed by numbers like statistics. Statistics use numbers to measure things or represent information, so it can be used for analysis or comparison. This can make difficult information easier to understand. Qualitative information expresses the unique qualities of something that cannot be easily characterized by numbers, but rather by description, illustration, explanation, or narrative.

- Statistics. Some types of information can be presented in numerical form to make it easier to understand. Statistics and poll data is based on asking people questions, but their answers may not be truthful or accurate. Statistics can be manipulated based upon the questions you ask and who you ask. If you use statistics it's helpful to be sure the information is relevant to the topic, easy to understand, current, and from a credible source.

- Quotes are the words that someone has written or said. When the quote is from an expert or well known person, it can be used to support an argument by providing evidence. It's important that the quotes are accurate and relevant to the topic.

- Opinions are what people think about a topic. This can be an expert opinion, public opinion, or an average person's opinion. An expert can provide an opinion to support a claim whereas an average person can provide an opinion to illustrate public perception.

- Descriptions are based upon sensory information that creates a picture in the minds of the audience. You can use imagery to include impressions based on our five senses of sight, sound, taste, touch, and smell.

- Narratives provide information in the form of a story. We often express information about our past experiences and about people we know in narrative form.

- Illustrations provide an example by telling a story that can be either real or hypothetical.

- Explanations can tell us why something happened, its cause and effect, or how something came into being.

- Comparison and contrast use two things to illustrate their differences or similarities. Contrast works by highlighting the differences between two things whereas comparison works by highlighting their similarities.

- Definitions take words or concepts that are unfamiliar to an audience and puts them in a familiar language.

- Examples are specific instances that can be real or hypothetical about a specific situation that has either happened or might happen.

Communicating an effective message depends on having quality information. This means that it is important to critically evaluate the information you use as well as testing its accuracy and validity. It should be relevant to your topic or support your claim. It should be current and accurate. It should come from credible sources such as a recognized expert or authority. And it should be credible, trustworthy, and used accurately.

Gathering information for a message is like gathering evidence for a court case. In court, you want to prove your claim before a judge or jury who is hearing your case for the first time. So, how do you make your case? You provide evidence that is clear, accurate, easy to understand, and comes from credible sources. The evidence is put together in an organized way that is easy to understand. Reasoning is used to explain how the evidence fits together to support your claim. It is helpful to be aware of any counter arguments that could undermine your claim and be ready to refute them.

Others may try to undermine your argument using irrelevant facts or present alternatives that may sound good, but may not be workable. They may sound reasonable, but they do not hold true. Some of them are used so frequently they are often mistaken for forms of reasoning even though they are not. False arguments are called fallacies and it is helpful to be aware of what they are to avoid them. These are described in greater detail in Chapter 2.

Structure.

Structure involves how you organize and present your Great Idea to others. It includes methods of organization, use of evidence, and reasoning. It includes the major structural elements of your message including the introduction, main points, transitions, and conclusion. It includes how you use language, word choice, sentence structure, and paragraph organization. All these elements are arranged to make the message as effective as possible, so you can make a connection by cutting through the interference for maximum impact on your audience.

Once you have gathered the information you need, it has to be organized in a way that can be easily understood by your audience. Organization deals with the perception process and the mind's ability to select, organize, and retain information. Most of the information we perceive is chaotic, received in random bits and pieces. Our mind organizes information by giving it structure, so that we can better understand it now and utilize it in the future. Organization is important because if people have to work too hard to understand your message they may not pay attention.

You can make it easier for them to understand your Great Idea by utilizing one of several established methods of organization.

- Chronological. Ordering events as they happen in real time.

- Sequential. Presenting events in the order in which they need to happen such as performing a task.

- Spatial. Describing how things are physically related to one another like driving directions.

- Topical. This method organizes things by using standard topics or subjects.

- Numerical. This method ranks information based on a sequence of numbers. This can be done by presenting what things come first, second, last, and so on.

- Classification. This method organizes things by natural groups. Plants and animals are categorized by family and species based upon how they are related to one another.

- Cause and effect. This is used to explain why something exists. It is often used to persuade people to take a course of action to solve a problem based on the source of the problem.

- Problem and solution. This method presents a problem that needs to be resolved and the solutions to resolve it.

- Need satisfaction. A need that must be fulfilled is established and then methods are suggested to fulfill that need.

- Importance. Items are organized in order of importance starting either with the least important to most important or the most important to the least.

- General to specific. Items are organized starting with the most general to the most specific or from the specific to the general.

- Comparison and contrast. Comparison is taking two things and relating their similarities. Contrast is taking two things and relating their differences.

- Complexity. This approach takes a concept or process from the simple to the difficult or the difficult to the simple. For example, learning to play the piano begins simply then moves to more difficult music.

- Structure. This approach takes something that is made up of smaller elements and describing how those elements go together. For example, showing how a house is built by describing how each section is put together.

- Function. This approach looks at how things work or how they are utilized. For example, describing the human body might cover the circulatory or respiratory systems.

- Medical. Organizing approaches to problems like diagnosing an illness by identifying symptoms and prescribing treatments.

- The unknown. When communicating about something that an audience doesn't know about, begin with what they do know then connect it with what they don't know.

- Directions. Whether it's completing a task or traveling some place, we have all given and received directions. It can be helpful to begin by clarifying the terms of reference you are going to use. You could use the compass points of north, south, east, or west. You could use visual information like landmarks, street names, addresses, and distances such as blocks or mileage.

Outlines.

Before setting out to write your Great Idea it's helpful to make an outline. A good outline helps you to achieve your desired outcome by organizing your ideas to clarify details while looking at the big picture. There are basically two types of outlines. The first is to help you construct your message. It is basically a list of your ideas organized in the order they will be presented. An outline makes it easier to make changes and move things around before you fully write them out. It allows you to easily try out different options to see which one works the best because once it's fully written out, it's more difficult to change.

The second type of outline can be used like a script when speaking or giving a presentation. The purpose of this outline is to help you stay on track, so you do not miss any important information. It can be typed in a large easy to read font with lots of open space so that words are not crowded together making it easy to read quickly under pressure. It can be helpful to number each page and perhaps even each line of text to help you keep track of where you are in case you lose your spot.

An outline can consist of the entire text, short sentences, keywords, or whatever combination works best for you. Some outlines are written in full text. When politicians give a speech they are likely to read the full text word for word off of a teleprompter. This is so they do not make any mistakes because each word has been carefully prepared in advance and a wrong word could create problems.

You can use a full sentence outline to keep on track or just keywords to cover basic ideas. Each has its own advantages and disadvantages. The more of your message that is written down the more likely you are to sound like you are reading it. However, it provides the security of having all the information in front of you in case you need it. Using short statements or keywords helps you to speak more extemporaneously to sound more natural and conversational. However, there's less information written down to help you if you forget or lose your place. If you are new to public speaking you might try using the full text until you become comfortable speaking in public before using outlines with less information.

Writing delivery queues on an outline can help you communicate more effectively when giving a presentation or speaking to an audience. Delivery queues work like musical notation or stage directions in a script. Add words to your outline that tell you when to use vocal variety and nonverbal behavior, like gestures. Vocal variety is how you say the words you speak including pacing, pauses, volume, intonation, and the pitch of your voice. It can include nonverbal movements like gestures, facial expressions, moving about, and body language. Be sure to make these queues look different so you do not say them out loud. For example, to begin your speech you might write, "Good evening, (look at audience and smile)." This reminds you what to say and how to say it.

Introduction.

The first element of a message is the introduction. It can serve several purposes which gives you several options, so you can use one or a combination of the following approaches.

- The introduction gets your audience's attention. There are several ways you can begin such as talking about current events, something relevant to your audience, the occasion, why everyone is gathered, something unusual or out of the ordinary, a humorous story, or a problem you propose to solve.

- The introduction reduces uncertainty about you and your message. It shapes your audience's perception of your message. Briefly outline your message, let them know your point of view, and what to expect so that they can follow you more easily.

- The introduction shares meaning to create a connection between you and the audience. Use a greeting or reference about something they are familiar with or interested in.

- The introduction encourages your audience to invest their time and attention in you and your message. Share some information about yourself, your interests, or an experience that you might have in common with your audience to motivate them to listen.

- The introduction creates the appropriate tone. You might use a funny anecdote, a serious illustration, or quote from someone who is well known.

- The introduction creates interest. Make your audience curious about what you have to say. Create a mystery that you will solve so they want to pay attention.

In the process of communicating, in order to share your Great Idea with others you have to cross The Great Abyss, which is all the things that get in the way of others receiving your message. It can include interference, other messages, or past experiences. People tend to look for things that fit in with their frames of reference or what they already know because they are familiar which reduces uncertainty. This can be influenced by their attitudes, opinions, or point of view. People are more likely to filter out information they think they don't need or does not interest them. There may be background or psychological noise to distract them. To effectively communicate your message, it should be presented in a way that overcomes this interference.

The interference of The Great Abyss can be overcome by getting your audience's attention, generating interest, and showing how your message will benefit them. This should help to make them more receptive to your message, so they won't filter it out. Start with the general and go to the specific, give them the big picture first, so they know where each part fits. In a video, start with a wide angle shot to establish the scene, then go to close ups to show detail.

These are some options to cut through the interference of the Great Abyss.

- Reduce uncertainty. People are interested in information that reduces uncertainty that makes them feel more comfortable, safe, and secure. They care about things they know about, that they feel close to, that they are comfortable with, or that are familiar to them. They want to know about things that happen close to them in their community, fit their interests, or that they perceive might affect them. They can be interested in things that might happen to them in the future providing a degree of predictability.

- Share Meaning. People are interested in information that shares meaning that makes their experiences more interesting or significant. They are interested in things that they find unique, unusual, interesting, or out of the ordinary. They are interested in other people and stories about their experiences, such as overcoming difficulties or conflict.

- Invest. People are interested in information they perceive as having value or that is important to them. They are interested in things they perceive might affect them now or in the future. They are interested in information about others who are credible, likable, or trustworthy. They are interested in information that will benefit them or that they find useful.

- Needs and wants. People are likely to be interested in things that fulfill their needs and wants because it can be useful to them. They are interested in things that are new and relevant. They are interested in things that give them a sense of adventure or excitement. They are interested in things they find entertaining, exciting, humorous, suspenseful, or dramatic. They are interested in things that they perceive will increase their status, prestige, or bolster their self-concept.

Main points.

The main points of your message are the key ideas that support your claim or topic. You should be able to summarize each of these in a few words or a sentence. Your main points divide your message into several smaller ideas making them easier to organize, so your audience can follow you. It is helpful to focus your message by using as few main points as you need to communicate your message. Keep them consistent and relate them to one another, so your audience can understand them.

For each of your main points, give your audience the big picture first and then go into detail. This lets the audience know how everything fits together, so when you go into detail they will know where it fits in. Each main point is like a short message with a beginning and end. It often begins with a key idea followed by evidence to support it accompanied by an explanation, illustration, or example. Keep these points flexible so that you can add or remove information if you need to change the length of your message.

Transitions.

Transitions are the links between sections of your message including the introduction, main points, and conclusion. They help structure and organize your ideas making them easier for your audience to understand. Using transitions helps your message flow smoothly from one point to the next.

Transitions can include a summary of the previous section or a preview of what's next. They may provide directions like describing a process. They may provide guidelines for the audience such as chronological, numerical, or spatial references. In a video, transitions are the edits between shots and are generally cuts, fades, or wipes, which sets the tone and pacing. Transitions between scenes help the audience follow the story.

These are options for transitions.

- Time transitions use chronological relationships and words such as: now, then, before, after, sooner, later, or meanwhile.

- Connective transitions bridge ideas using words such as: and, also, moreover, in addition, however, but, instead, or although.

- Sequential transitions follow numerical patterns such as: first, second, third, or last.

- Illustrative transitions set out ideas to illustrate points by using words such as: for example, for instance, or to illustrate.

- Inclusive transitions wrap up ideas by using words such as: to conclude, to summarize, therefore, as a result, or consequently.

Conclusion.

The conclusion is how you end your message. It wraps everything up, but is more than simply restating what's already been said. It's like the end of a movie, where everything is resolved for the audience. It can provide a reward to the audience for investing their time and paying attention to your message. A conclusion can be as simple as thanking them for their time or it could provide valuable information that is useful to them. There are many types of conclusions and some are similar to introductions. You can use a quote, illustration, story, example, personal experience, surprise, or challenge them to do something.

A conclusion should wrap up everything and answer any questions the audience might have. It can be used for emotional effect much like music uses a crescendo where the emotional level builds to the end. You could use a decrescendo where the emotional level tapers off to a quiet ending. A conclusion should include the one or two ideas that you want the audience to remember, not just after you finish, but much later on. This is your last opportunity to get your point across, so let them know what you want them to remember.

Style.

Whether they are spoken or written, almost all messages involve some writing, which means there has to be a particular writing style. Writing style includes the tone, mood, point of view, and style of your message. The tone can range from serious to sad to sentimental to humorous. The mood can range from somber to happy.

Point of view can range from your own, to others, to a detached third person. The style you choose can be based upon your desired outcome, your experience, your topic, or your audience. Styles can range from formal to informal, structured to conversational.

- Mood and tone. Many types of communicating utilize a specific mood that sets the general feeling or emotional level of the message. For example, a mood can be warm and friendly, serious and somber, or scary and threatening. The tone is the general quality or tenor of the message. This is determined based upon you and your audience's attitude toward the topic. This reduces uncertainty and creates expectations the audience wants to have fulfilled.

- Emotional intensity. We feel emotions all the time and when we communicate we often share these emotions with others who may feel the same. In creating a message think about what emotions may be most effective in achieving your desired outcome. Some that are commonly used include happy, sad, sentimental, humorous, fearful, or angry. Emotions are used as a means of persuasion or to gain people's attention. Emotions can have levels of intensity, which includes how vigorously they are expressed. For example, movies often increase in emotional intensity as the plot progresses in order to keep the audience interested and to build suspense.

- Pacing. The rate at which information is presented to an audience can range from fast to slow. If the pacing is too fast there can be information overload because people can perceive and retain only so much information in a given amount of time. If the pace is too slow people might get bored and start thinking about other things. Fast pacing can present more information in a shorter amount of time making things sound dramatic or exciting. Slow pacing can help to facilitate the understanding of difficult material. Changes in pacing can draw out important information and be used for dramatic effect.

- Language. The kind of language we use depends on our message, topic, desired outcome, and the audience. How we use it can influence how others perceive us. Through language we communicate information about ourselves including our expertise, credibility, confidence, and competence. Avoid clichés, slang, and technical jargon that people may not understand. Talk about things as if they are happening in the present rather than the past to make them more interesting. Use descriptive language to help the audience to visualize what you're talking about by creating a picture in their mind. Repeating words or phrases creates a rhythm that can give speech a musical or poetic quality. Language can be artistic, emotional, and inspiring. In order to fully utilize the power of language, it's helpful to have a good vocabulary so you can choose the best word to express your ideas. Language and vocabulary are detailed more fully in Chapter 2.

- Creativity. To effectively communicate in public and cut through the interference it's helpful to be creative. Creativity can come from our own unique individual outlook, experiences, and characteristics. It's about how we express our imagination and individuality. Creativity can be developed by increasing your awareness of your own unique perspective on the things around you by seeing them in a new light. While we often think of creativity as being related to the arts, practically anything can be creative. This is because creativity is about breaking out of old ways of thinking by looking at familiar things in a new way as if you were seeing them for the first time. Often the best ideas come from looking creatively at the most common things.

The first draft.

Most types of public communicating begins with writing a first draft to get your ideas down on paper and getting started can be the most difficult part. Facing a blank page can be a daunting task, so start with what you know. Don't worry about getting it right the first time. Once you get something written down on paper, you can decide what works and what doesn't. Ask for feedback from people whose opinion you value.

Starting at the beginning is not always the best approach. Start with what you know, start in the middle, or start with what's easiest for you to write to get things moving. Don't worry about getting things perfect like writing the perfect opening line. If you get stuck don't get bogged down, skip over what's giving you a problem and write something else. It's more important to keep moving because you can always come back to something and fix it later. Breakup big sections into smaller parts to make them more manageable and easier to write.

Communicating your message to others should be fun. Don't write until you are exhausted because then it's not fun anymore. Taking breaks helps you stop and think about what you have written and what you are going to write. It can help clarify an idea to get away from it for awhile and then come back to look at it with a fresh perspective. It's easy to get discouraged when we don't get as much written as we had hoped. Instead of concentrating on the negative, look at what you have accomplished and reward yourself for making progress.

While it would be nice to be inspired when we want to be, inspiration can come at any time so be prepared. It's helpful to carry a small notebook and pen or pencil, so you can write down your ideas when you think of them. However, you don't always have to wait for inspiration to strike, it can be developed. Begin with what you know, with things that interest you, or things that you have already thought about. Then work out from there. Often ideas don't come all at once, but have to be worked out over time.

Refining your message.

Once all the information has been gathered, organized, and a first draft written it needs to be refined. This is the process of rewriting, editing, and proofreading.

- Rewriting. Once you have your Great Idea on paper take a step back to look at the big picture. Make sure that you have included everything you want to include. Make sure the information and evidence supports your central idea. Remove any unnecessary information that does not fit your topic or support your claim. This is a time to change the organization of ideas, sentence structure, or paragraph organization if needed. Paragraphs should follow in logical order using a method of organization. Transitions should be smooth so that one idea flows into the next. The introduction should properly introduce your subject to your audience and the conclusion should wrap everything up.

- Editing. Once everything is where it should be you can start checking the details. This involves rewriting sentences and paragraphs if necessary. Sentences and paragraphs should contain one clearly developed idea. Paragraphs should begin and end at natural breaks and follow logically in order based upon a method of organization. Each paragraph should clearly relate to the preceding and following paragraph to create a flow of information that people can easily follow. Use a thesaurus to find the best words to express your ideas and a dictionary to check that words and terms are used correctly.

- Proofreading. This is the most detailed part of the editing process, which is why it is a specialized skill. Here you are not so much changing sections or words, but looking for errors. When you proofread you check for errors in spelling, punctuation, grammar, and proper word usage. This is the fine tuning of the message to be sure it's written properly in the proper format. While it's helpful to have correct usage of grammar, some forms of communicating use informal rules to be better understood or sound more realistic.

Methods of delivery.

Once you have crafted your message you need to get it to your audience. In the process of communicating, you take your Great Idea and communicate it to others through connections. The method of delivery is how you send a message through a connection. It can be spoken or written, verbal or nonverbal. Methods of delivery can be helpful to communicate more effectively with others to achieve your desired outcome.

To more effectively communicate with others, it can be helpful to practice and rehearse these skills. Whether you are giving a speech, producing a video, or presenting a musical performance, practice and rehearsal are essential to success. Practice is repeating basic skills to develop a proficiency at something and rehearsal is running through an actual performance. These help to develop important skills by repeating them over and over to become proficient. Doing this can help give you confidence to improve your performance.

Rehearsal is preparing for a performance in front of an audience. A rehearsal should approximate the actual performance conditions as much as possible. For example, before a concert a musical group will rehearse to make sure that everything will go smoothly at the performance. Rehearsing your message helps you to discover any unforeseen problems and reduces uncertainty about a performance. It helps to give you confidence to feel more comfortable during your performance because it will feel more familiar.

When speaking or giving a presentation you can utilize one of these delivery methods.

- Full text. Speakers often use a full written transcript of their speech. Newscasters and politicians read the full text from a teleprompter so they say what is written and don't miss any words.

- Outline. This can be in the form of sentences, short phrases, or key words. This works when you know the material well enough not to need a scrip to keep you on track.

- Memorization. This is giving a speech from memory without using any notes. It can sound more genuine, but can be risky if you forget your lines.

- Impromptu. This involves speaking spontaneously and unrehearsed without an outline or a script. This is the way we generally communicate with others every day.

- Extemporaneous. This is when we know what we are going to say, so we perform without any outline or notes. When we speak this way we sound more relaxed and genuine.

- Conversational. This style involves speaking informally as if you are engaged in a casual conversation with another person.

Vocal elements.

An important part of an effective delivery is pronunciation and articulation. Pronunciation is saying words the right way and articulation is saying them clearly. We add extra non-verbal sounds and intonation to what we say in order to communicate how to interpret our words. We alter our delivery to convey our attitude, mood, tone, and emotions.

Vocal variety is changing how you speak to make it interesting to your audience. This includes changing your pacing, pitch, intonation, and volume to add variety to how you sound. Not using vocal variety can make you sound monotone and boring.

- Pitch. This is how we use the high and low tones of our voice. We use pitch to emphasize emotions or make our voice more pleasing.

- Pacing. This is how fast or slow we speak. Changes in pacing can alter the emotional tenor of what we say. Fast pacing is more exciting and slow pacing can be more dramatic.

- Rhythm. Repeating certain sounds, words, or phrases can be used rhythmically for dramatic effect to sound like poetry or music.

- Pauses. These are periods of silence when we stop speaking between words or ideas. They are used for dramatic effect to emphasize ideas. It can also give us a chance to take a breath and compose ourselves before continuing.

- Volume. This is how loud or soft you speak. This can change based on the size of the room. It can be used to emphasize important ideas or to create different emotional effects. Changing volume helps to make what you say more interesting to your audience.

- Intonation. This is the vocal timbre or quality of your voice. It can vary from rich and full to thin and hoarse.

Nonverbal expressions.

Just as we use vocal variety to increase interest, nonverbal expressions are important to visually maintain an audience's interest. They can be used to establish credibility because if you look confident, people are more likely to perceive you as credible. When you are aware of how nonverbal expressions work, they can be utilized to enhance your message.

- Facial expressions. We use them to communicate emotions like when we are happy, serious, or sad. Facial expressions can be used to emphasize important points. We make inferences about others based on their facial expressions like how they feel and the motivation for their behavior.

- Eye contact. We use eye contact to make connections with others. We use it to make inferences about them. When we are apprehensive we might avoid making eye contact. This can create the perception that we are indifferent, bored, or are not trustworthy. When someone looks you in the eye you feel that they are competent and confident about themselves and their message. Appropriate eye contact is a matter of degree, using too much can be as uncomfortable for others as too little. It's important to make appropriate eye contact with others because of what it can communicate to them.

- Gestures. We use gestures to communicate information and share meaning in addition to what we say. While this can include how we use all parts of our body, it generally refers to how we use our arms and hands. Gestures are useful to emphasize important verbal points in a visual manner. They can serve the same function as underlining or using exclamation marks on printed materials. Many gestures have their own meaning such as pointing, waving, or giving the thumbs up. Using gestures effectively is a matter of appropriateness and balance. Too many will make you look nervous, too few will make you look stiff and uncomfortable. Natural gestures can add a perception of confidence and forced gestures can make you look stiff or unnatural.

- Hands. It can be difficult to know what to do with your hands because they can feel awkward or get in the way. Rest them gently on the podium or table in front of you, if you can. If there's nothing to rest them on, hold them down at your sides with your elbows slightly bent. Doing this can feel uncomfortable because we rarely stand this way, but it looks good in front of an audience or on camera. Sometimes people clasp their hands loosely together in front of them and gesture occasionally. Avoid putting them in your pockets.

- Stance. When you are out in public and have to stand in one place for awhile, like in front of an audience, you want to be comfortable and look confident. Stand up straight with your shoulders slightly back. Place your feet at a 45 degree angle with your heels a couple of inches apart, so your feet are spaced at about the same distance as your shoulders. Your knees and elbows should be slightly bent otherwise you may pass out if you stand too rigid. Stand straight, head up, shoulders back, and arms at your side.

- Posture. Posture is how you hold yourself and bearing is how you stand or move. These are important because people make judgments about you based on what they perceive. Having good posture communicates confidence and credibility. Good posture involves standing straight, keeping your head up, and your shoulders back. Having good bearing means moving about with confidence and authority. Avoid shuffling your feet, rocking back and forth, or leaning up against something like a wall. When people do this we perceive them as lacking confidence or not being trustworthy.

- Movement. Whenever you are in front of an audience you will have to move. You may need to get on and off stage or move around while you are speaking. Movement includes how you do things like picking up your feet when you walk. It looks better to pick up your feet by bending the knee very slightly instead of shuffling them. How much you move depends upon the space available, your message, and the occasion. Some movement is good because it makes you look animated. Too much movement will make you look nervous. Use movement to emphasize important points. If you are telling an emotional story you might move closer to your audience because it's more personal. Afterwards, you will want to move back to a more public distance.

- Appearance. People make judgments about the credibility and competency of others based upon their appearance. The best approach is to dress appropriately for the occasion to enhance the audience's impression of you. When you are in front of other people you are a leader and should look the part. A good approach is to dress conservatively, slightly more formal than your audience. Depending on the occasion, you might be expected to wear appropriate specialized clothing like a uniform or costume.

- Act natural. It may take practice and rehearsal in order to act natural. Use nonverbal behavior to help you, but use it sparingly and intentionally. This can make the difference between looking confident or looking nervous, looking professional or looking like you don't know what you're doing. While we shouldn't judge a person's message by how they look, the reality is people do. People make judgments based upon nonverbal behavior motivated by the law of uncertainty. They are looking for information to better understand and evaluate what a person has to say and their appearance is often all they have to go on.

Anxiety.

When we communicate in public it's natural to feel a certain amount of anxiety. Anxiety has been called many things including nervousness, apprehension, and stage fright. These are all an emotional expression of uncertainty. We become anxious or apprehensive about something because the level of uncertainty is higher than we are used to making us uncomfortable. Because of uncertainty, we are more likely to be anxious about not knowing what might happen than knowing what will happen. This is because we can be better dealing with the adversity we know rather than with the uncertainty we do not know.

We can feel anxiety because of uncertainty about the unknown. If we don't know how others will react to us we can become apprehensive. We may be afraid that they won't like us because we want to be liked. We may be afraid that something might go wrong particularly if we have had bad experiences in the past. We tend to remember bad experiences more than positive ones because they're uncomfortable creating tension.

One of the best ways to reduce anxiety is by reducing uncertainty. We can do this by gaining experience through practicing communicating skills and rehearsing our presentation. We can use feedback to increase our awareness of how we are being perceived by others. We can utilize relaxation techniques like positive visualization or controlled breathing. Professional performers often have things that go wrong, but what sets them apart is how they respond. If a mistake is not obvious, just keep going because chances are nobody will notice unless you tell them. If a mistake is obvious, you might stop and say that you need a moment or acknowledge the mistake and briefly make light of it as if it's part of the presentation, then move on.

Even though it can be difficult at times, try to avoid getting frustrated or upset. It can help to expect that there will be some mistakes, so you can be prepared for them. Everyone wants to give a polished performance, but that can put unnecessary pressure on you. A small amount of anxiety can be good because it gives us energy, heightens the senses, and increases our awareness. It makes us stop and think about what we are doing rather than doing things by habit. It makes us consider others and notice their feedback.

A common source of anxiety comes from making eye contact with an audience. Making eye contact is an important part of making a connection with your audience, so it's helpful not to stare at your notes or the floor because your audience will be less receptive to your message. Avoid looking straight ahead or scanning the audience because it will make you look unnatural. If you are nervous about making eye contact, look at the tops of people's heads moving your gaze slowly around the audience. This gives the impression of making eye contact. Eye contact is important because it establishes a connection and credibility with your audience, as well as providing you with feedback on how you are coming across to them.

We rarely tell people that we are feeling nervous, instead we communicate it through our nonverbal body language. We do this with the lack of eye contact, shifting back and forth, putting our hands in our pockets, jiggling keys or coins, touching our hair, rubbing our nose, crossing our arms, speaking rapidly, using a higher pitch, or speaking softly. While we cannot control how we feel, we can develop skills to control what we do. By being aware of our nonverbal behavior and having options we can do things to avoid appearing as if we are nervous.

When you speak in front of an audience your remarks begin when you start to speak, but your presentation begins the moment you arrive at the event. From the time you arrive be warm, friendly, and polite because people may be forming their impressions of you. How you conduct yourself beforehand can make a difference in how receptive they are when you speak. When you go up to speak, communicate confidence through good posture and bearing. Before you begin speaking take a moment to compose yourself, take a breath to relax, set up your outline, adjust your posture, and take control of the situation. Memorize the first few lines you are going to say so that you can say them with confidence to give you a solid start. If the beginning is solid, you will be perceived as confident. If the beginning is not solid, it may be difficult to recover.

This approach helps you to reduce uncertainty. It gives you a chance to familiarize yourself with your surroundings before beginning your presentation. It gives you a chance to relax and bolster your confidence. Avoid rushing or being in a hurry to begin because it can cause you to be off balance getting things off to a bad start. Avoid saying things like "before I begin" or "my topic today." Avoid meaningless words including ahhh, like, or you know. We use these words because we are nervous or because we are not sure what to say. Practice and preparation should eliminate these problems.

Adapting to change.

You are in the middle of speaking to an audience, however, it's becoming clear that things are not going well. Now what do you do? This is when having awareness and options can help. Being aware of your audience can provide feedback to help you determine what to do. You can change or adapt your message or delivery to be more receptive to your audience. For example, if your audience looks lost or confused you may be going too fast for them, so slow down your pacing. You might review information you already presented by rephrasing it in a different way or provide an illustration or example to increase understanding. If the audience is getting bored or restless move around, use a few more gestures, tell a personal story, wrap things up, or take a break if you can.

Increasing your awareness helps you to be ready for the unexpected. We plan for things to go right, but we don't necessarily plan what to do if they go wrong. By anticipating what might go wrong, you can be prepared to make changes during your presentation. Be flexible by giving yourself options for change, so you are not forced to stick with one approach. Don't be reluctant to change what you have prepared if circumstances warrant.

Practice and rehearsal should include alternatives, so you can have them ready if needed. All too often we get locked into one way of doing things because it makes us feel comfortable. Practicing more than one way of delivering your message gives you alternatives. You can make changes by telling different stories, using different illustrations, or adding new ideas based on feedback from your audience.

Professional Public Communicating

Professional communicating in public can include ways that we communicate for our job or career. It includes verbal skills like public speaking, motivational speaking, and making presentations. It includes written skills like writing a résumé, proposals, presentations, press releases, newsletters, or reports. We use these forms of communicating to create and maintain connections between us and members of the public.

We do this to keep people informed, manage our public identity, and influence public opinion. These skills are important because recruiters and employers constantly rank them as some of the most desirable qualities they look for in new employees and in making promotions. Regardless of the nature of the job, people need to work together with one another so communicating skills are increasingly essential to career success.

Professional writing is generally more formal than other forms of communicating. It has established formats and uses proper form and structure including complete sentences and paragraphs with clear methods of organization. It uses proper grammar, accurate spelling, punctuation, and a professional vocabulary. It uses an appropriate tone that is more formal than speaking.

Professional writing should look professional by using the proper format and avoiding clutter to make it easy to read by having an appropriate amount of open space. Avoid using unusual type fonts, instead use a traditional font like Times Roman or Helvetica, so it looks professional and is easy to read.

Correspondence, like writing a letter, generally includes the heading; senders name and address; date; recipient's formal name and title; salutation or greeting; the body, which is your message; closing or ending; signature; and copies or enclosures. Keep correspondence to one page in length because people may not read any further. Near the beginning write in one sentence the reason you are writing. Near the end write the action you want taken.

A résumé is a form of identity management communicated to others in writing. It is an inventory of your education, experience, and skills that has the desired outcome of getting you a job. Know your recipients needs and wants so you can tailor your résumé to meet them. You can do this by knowing as much as you can about the recipient and by getting a copy of the job description, which is a written set of duties and responsibilities for the position. Your desired outcome in writing a résumé and cover letter is to reduce uncertainty about yourself, share meaning about your qualifications and ability to fulfill their needs and wants, and encourage them to invest in you by giving you an interview and ultimately the job. Since many applications are sent over the internet, omit any information that you feel is too personal, that you don't want on the internet, or made public, like your home address. Use relevant searchable key words and technical jargon to help employers find you.

These are some options for information to include in a résumé and cover letter.

- Personal information. This includes your name, title, and method to contact you. You can use an email address or post office box.

- Educational information. This includes degrees and educational institutions as well as training that applies to the position. Also include relevant honors or awards. Describe any skills or knowledge you gained that is relevant to the job.

- Employment information. This includes your past experience, job titles, dates, accomplishments, responsibilities, and employers. Let the reader know about your skills and accomplishments. Reduce uncertainty by letting them know what you did to encourage them to invest in you by telling them what you can do for them. Use active rather than passive language to share meaning by creating a picture of you in their mind.

- Accomplishments. This includes awards, professional associations, and other honors relevant to the position. Leave out those that don't apply to the job.

- Career objectives. Some résumés include an optional career objective or general statement of purpose. Include this only if it's expected in your field or the job application asks for it. For instance, some professions like teaching might ask you to include your philosophy of teaching.

- References. It has become accepted to put "references provided upon request," so have a separate sheet of references or letters of recommendation you can provide if requested.

- Cover letter. Résumés are accompanied by a cover letter that should state the specific position you are applying for, why you are applying, and what you have to offer. End the letter by requesting a meeting or interview. Limit it to one page unless they specifically ask for more information. The desired outcome of your cover letter is to get them interested in reading your résumé and to reduce uncertainty about you, so that they will contact you to set up an interview.

Interviews.

There are many different types of interviews. These can include applying for a job, performance reviews, or being considered for a raise or promotion. You might be interviewed by the media, for a publication, on the radio, or on television. While each has a different purpose, you can utilize similar communicating skills to achieve your desired outcome. Even though another person will be asking the questions, it is important for you to be in control of the situation. While you cannot control what they may say or do, you can control what you say and do.

These are some things to consider to help you communicate more effectively.

- Reduce uncertainty. Perhaps the single most important thing you need to do is to reduce uncertainty in the mind of the person interviewing you, and the audience if there is one, because it can be the biggest obstacle to achieving your desired outcome. You can do this by using identity management described in more detail in Chapter 3. Consider what aspects of yourself and your experience are most appropriate to present to others in public.

- Share meaning. When we share meaning with others we make a connection that creates a common bond. One of the ways we do this is by talking about our past experiences. This reduces uncertainty because others can relate their experiences to ours. In an interview it's important to fully consider what you want to talk about beforehand. It should be appropriate to the situation and not be overly personal. In a job interview, you might talk about your experiences in other jobs. In a media interview, you want to share meaning with the audience, so they will understand your message.

- Encourage investment. In order to achieve your desired outcome it's helpful to give the other person an incentive to invest in you to encourage them to hire you. In a media interview, you want the larger audience to invest in your message. You can encourage others to invest in you by reducing uncertainty through appropriate use of self-disclosure. For instance, in a job interview you might talk about your responsibilities, problems you overcame, or your accomplishments. The person interviewing you may relate to your experiences and share their own stories creating shared meaning.

- Perceptions and expectations. Whether it is for a job, or for the media like being on television, the interview process is a means by which we manage other people's perception of us. We communicate in specific ways in order for others to have a perception of us that supports our desired outcome. Others use the perception process to develop expectations of who we are and what we will do in the future. If they feel that we will fulfill their expectations, they can be more receptive to our desired outcomes, like hiring us for the job.

- Personal appearance. Find out what is expected for the situation and dress appropriately. This could mean work clothes, a suit, or uniform. You want to communicate that you care about others because you made an effort to look good for them. Your appearance communicates information to others nonverbally, so be aware of what you communicate. Appearance and nonverbal communicating are covered in more detail in Chapter 2.

- Speaking. It's not just what you say, it's how you say it. Speak in a relaxed, conversational, and purposeful manner. Speak with normal pacing, slightly lower the pitch of your voice, and use vocal variety to sound interesting. Avoid speaking too fast or too slow or raising the pitch of your voice. When people ask questions, be ready with answers. Waiting too long to answer can give the impression that you are not being totally forthcoming. Keep answers short, honest, and to the point. Do not say too little or too much. More information about speaking and nonverbal behavior is covered earlier in this chapter.

- Nonverbal body language. Your nonverbal body language can communicate confidence and professionalism or nervousness and inexperience. Communicate confidence by moving in a purposeful manner using proper posture and good bearing. Make appropriate eye contact and orientate your posture toward others to show that you are interested in them. Avoid communicating nervousness nonverbally by fidgeting, shuffling your feet, jingling keys, not making eye contact, or touching your clothes or face.

- Awareness. By having an awareness of how the process of communicating works, you can use reflected feedback to infer how others perceive you through their verbal and nonverbal behavior. Awareness of what they say and do can work as a kind of mirror that lets you know how you are doing. However, doing this is a matter of balance. Having too much self-awareness can make you seem self absorbed and having too little can make you seem out of touch or self centered.

- Anticipate their questions. Before any interview, write out a list of potential questions that you might be asked so you can be prepared with your answers. Practice interview techniques and rehearse questions out loud to help you sound relaxed and confident, so you will be perceived as competent and professional.

- Answering questions. Whether it's a job interview or interview in the media, keep your answers to the point and avoid getting off topic. You may not know the questions they will ask ahead of time, but you can prepare some potential questions and practice your answers beforehand. If you are asked a question you don't know the answer to, don't lie or make it up. There's nothing wrong with saying that you don't know or that you would have to get back to them with more information. Don't feel pressured to say something you shouldn't that you might regret later.

In an interview it is helpful to do the following.

- Arrive early, so you have time to relax, check your appearance, and review what you are going to say. They may show you around so you can talk to others and ask questions that can provide helpful information.

- Be polite, friendly, and courteous to everyone including the staff such as receptionists and security personnel. Use self-disclosure to your advantage by sharing little bits of information that are relevant and appropriate to the situation. Opening up and sharing a little bit about a common interest may improve your chances of success and put everyone at ease.

- Be flexible, but always stay in control of yourself even when things don't go as you expect. If the other person does not speak don't feel compelled to talk to fill the silence. This is a technique that can be used to get people to talk and say things they otherwise might not say. If this occurs you might ask them if they have any other questions.

- Ask them questions. At the end of an interview you may be asked you if you have any questions. Always have a few questions ready to ask. This is your opportunity to gain insight that can be useful whether you get the job or not. It's a way for you to give them positive feedback and get some about yourself. They may do this to test you. If you not ask any questions, it could seriously damage your chances of success because it communicates indifference and that you are not really interested in them, whether it's true or not.

- Know your boundaries ahead of time including what you are willing to talk about or do and what you are not, then stay within them. If they ask you something you consider inappropriate, ask why they consider it relevant or politely decline to answer. Be aware of what questions they can and cannot legally ask you. Stay within the prearranged time even if they do not. If they go past it, say that you don't want to keep them.

- Thank them and express your appreciation for taking time to meet with you when you first meet and at the end of the interview. When you are finished ask them what happens next. This is an open ended question to encourage them to tell you their plans and perhaps about other interviews. If they seem receptive, get them to talk about the interview process and the criteria they use to make a decision. Ask them when you can expect to hear back from them. Then if you do not hear back it's an opportunity to contact them again.

• If you are serious about creating a professional relationship, mail a hand written thank you note. Keep it simple, plain, classy, and to the point. If you don't hear anything, you might follow up by asking them where they are in the decision making process. They may be waiting to see if you are interested enough to follow up.

• If you don't get the job you want, consider it a good experience to help you gain important information into the process and how others perceive you. This can give you another opportunity to contact them by sending a follow up letter or call expressing your disappointment and asking them about other opportunities.

Presentations.

A useful communicating skill is the ability to prepare and present a report. There are several options for doing this including writing a report, making a presentation, responding to questions, and using visual elements.

• The written report. A written report can be comprised of several parts. It can include a table of contents, background information, the methodology used to collect information, the criteria for analyzing the information, the process of preparing the report, and lastly the findings, conclusions, or recommendations. Some reports begin with an executive summary, which is a short description of the most important parts of the report. It may also include a cover letter that introduces the report.

• The presentation. When a report is completed it may be accompanied by a presentation. The purpose is not to read the report, but to summarize important points. The report and any accompanying materials such as the cover letter, executive summary, and any visuals or appendices should be distributed to everyone before the presentation so they have time to read them. A presentation can be made by one person or a group. It is written beforehand and rehearsed so it sounds professional. It can cover additional issues that may not be addressed in the report and often allows time for the audience to ask questions.

• Question and answer time. Part of the time allotted for the presentation may be set aside for the audience to ask questions. This serves two purposes. First, it gives the audience an opportunity to provide feedback about the presentation and the report. Second, it gives the audience a chance to learn more about the report. The presenters should anticipate possible questions and practice answers beforehand, so they can be prepared for them. Questions should be answered honestly, concisely, and professionally within the framework of the presentation. If you don't know an answer, you might say that you will have to get back to them with more information.

An important professional skill is being able to write, coordinate, and make a group presentation. Group presentations are created and written using The Process as outlined earlier in this chapter. This can be challenging because instead of one person doing everything the tasks of gathering information, organizing, writing, and presenting are divided between several people. Having several people give the presentation means that the work can be shared, more information can be gathered, and more ideas can be generated.

However, it can be difficult coordinating everyone, making decisions takes more time, and there may be conflicts. Things can run smoother with clearly defined responsibilities, a timetable, a process to make decisions and resolve disputes, and a desired outcome that everyone agrees on. The work should be divided so everyone feels they are making a fair contribution.

Rehearse the presentation as if you were really giving it before you actually give it. This is a good way to work out any problems so they don't happen later. Have a checklist to be sure nothing is missing or falls between the cracks. Group work can be done collectively with everyone making decisions together or it can be divided up with tasks assigned to specific individuals who work on them on their own. Then, everyone comes back to the group to put their individual work together. Most groups work in some combination between the two like dividing the workload, but making decisions together.

Visual elements.

There are times when the written or spoken word does not provide the necessary information to communicate your message. So, you will need the help of visual elements because they provide another way to share meaning with your audience. People are more likely to remember something when it is communicated through more than one connection. You can communicate information with a written report that is presented verbally and illustrated graphically.

Numbers printed on paper or statistics read aloud may be difficult to comprehend, but depicting them visually in a chart can make them easier to understand. This is because people perceive information in different ways. Some people are more receptive to listening, some to what they read or see visually, and others to what they experience.

When you communicate with others utilizing more than one connection they are more likely to understand you. Visual elements provide an additional connection to reinforce your message. Visuals help to share information that can be difficult to communicate in other ways.

For instance, we can describe how our circulatory system works, but it is not as effective as a photograph or diagram showing what it looks like. Visual elements make presentations more interesting for the audience. Professional looking visuals enhance your credibility and can make people more receptive to your message.

In order to communicate more effectively, it can be helpful to be aware of the following options for visual elements. They can be used in many forms of communicating like a speech, video, television show, on the internet, or in a presentation.

- Audio video equipment. This includes electronic equipment like a video projector, slide projector, film projector, overhead projector, audio tape, videotape, or a computer. These items need access to electricity, so they should be set up and tested ahead of time.

- Standalone. These visuals can be seen on their own so they need no electricity or additional technology. They include charts, graphs, maps, diagrams, schematics, and enlarged photographs. They are often put on an easel or hung on a wall. They should be easy to read and use.

- Impromptu. These are visuals that are created during the presentation such as writing on a marker board, chalkboard, or flip chart on an easel.

- Handouts. An alternative to large visuals is to provide handouts. The advantage is that everyone has their own copy they can look at, write notes on, and take with them afterwards. This can include an outline, charts, graphs, visuals, or photographs.

- Tangible. These are tangible items that you can use to demonstrate or show your audience. They can include physical three dimensional items like the actual item or a model representing the item. If the item is small enough you might pass it around the audience. If it's too big to pass around, place it where everyone can see it.

- Living beings. There are some times when it can be helpful to bring a living being as a visual element. For example, using a person to model clothing or a dog to demonstrate dog training.

Any visual should look professional and be interesting to gain and keep the audience's attention. It should be large enough to be seen by the entire audience. Use bright colors, a simple typeface, and plenty of open space to make it easy to read. It should be concise, to the point, and support the topic. It should be easy to understand so you don't have to spend a lot of time explaining it. It should be designed for maximum impact on the audience, but not distract from the message or the speaker. It should be easy to access and use.

Arrive early to set up the visuals before any of the audience arrives. Place them so they are easy for you to reach and everyone can see them. Test them out ahead of time to make sure they work. Items like slide projectors and audio or video tapes should be queued so they are ready to go. Rehearse with your visuals beforehand and have a backup plan in case of unexpected problems like an equipment malfunction.

Spoken public communicating.

Spoken public communicating includes forms of communicating in audio visual media like video, television, and the internet as well as a personal appearance in front of an audience like a speech or presentation. For example, giving a speech involves both writing what you are going to say and then saying it in front of an audience.

In spoken public communicating, your desired outcome is to reduce uncertainty about yourself and your message, so your audience will be receptive to what you have to say. Then, you will want to share meaning with them so that they will understand your message. You may even want them to invest in your message by agreeing with you or taking some action afterward.

You craft your Great Idea and then make a connection to communicate it to others to achieve your desired outcome. The process of creating your message outlined earlier in this chapter provides options on how to write a speech.

Consider your audience's desired outcome by acknowledging them and why they are there in your remarks. Be aware of their expectations and why they are listening to you, so you can fulfill them. Set the proper mood and tone for the occasion. Mention any connections between yourself and your audience, the significance of the event, and why everyone is gathered.

These are some common formats for speeches.

- Ceremonial speeches are given on special occasions like birthdays, weddings, anniversaries, and other important events. They can be used to commemorate a person, place, organizations, or important date. Mention the significance of the occasion, the people involved, the circumstances around it, and why everyone is there even though everyone may already know this.

- Inspirational speeches or sermons are usually spiritual in nature often based upon a religious text. Motivational speeches have the desired outcome of encouraging people to take action. They are often based upon real life experiences such as overcoming adversity. Their purpose is to inspire or motivate the audience by utilizing the power of shared meaning to communicate shared values and beliefs.

- Tributes remember and share mutual experiences about a person or event. They are warm and sincere because they celebrate and acknowledge the contributions of others.

- Dedications commemorate some type of structure like a building, statue, or other monument often named after an individual who has made a relevant contribution. Recognize the significance of the event, the reasons for the dedication, and the audience. This can include historical references, anecdotes, or the reason for the dedication.

- Eulogies are usually given at a memorial service or funeral. They can include the positive attributes and accomplishments of the person being honored. They are generally serious and somber in tone, but can be lightened with personal stories.

- Toasts are a short tribute to a person given at a dinner. Everyone is asked to raise a glass to the person being toasted. They can include positive attributes about a person as well as humorous anecdotes.

- An after dinner speech is a humorous speech given after a dinner or banquet that can include entertaining stories about the experiences of the speaker and people in attendance.

These are several different types of speeches that can be given on separate occasions or they can take place during a single event like a convention or seminar.

- Convention speeches are usually given during an organized event attended by large numbers of people, such as a business or political convention. They often involve a variety of speeches including a welcome address, introductions, keynote speech, awards, and nominating and acceptance speeches.

- Welcome remarks are often given at the beginning of an event to establish a positive tone by recognizing the nature of the occasion, why everyone is there, and to thank everyone for attending the event.

- Introductions are a short speech to introduce another person. Be brief, accurate, acknowledge the occasion, include important information about them relative to the occasion, and say their name pronouncing it correctly. The purpose is to inform your audience about the person you are introducing, to create a positive atmosphere, and get the audience ready to hear what they have to say. You can tell good things about them that they cannot say themselves.

- Being introduced. When someone introduces you, be sure to thank them for their kind introduction and the audience for being there. This creates a positive atmosphere to help make them more receptive to your message.

- A keynote address is the most important speech at an event. It is often given by a noteworthy person to encourage people to attend. It is important to be positive and uplifting because it can set the tone for the event.

- Awards consist of two parts. First, the presenter tells about the award, why it is being given, and why the recipient is receiving it. Second, the recipient should thank those who may have helped them achieve the award. Be brief, to the point, and be humble.

- Nomination speeches recognize an individual for a position, to receive an honor or award, or to run for public office. They include describing the position, honor, award, elected office, or reason for the nomination.

- Acceptance speeches are given to accept a nomination, thank the people who helped them, tell why they are running for office, or what they will do if elected.

Meetings.

You may have attended meetings that left you feeling good with a sense of accomplishment, while other meetings felt like a complete waste of time. What made the difference was probably how the meeting was conducted. Meetings serve an important function because they do more than just making decisions or accomplishing tasks, they help people work together more effectively provided they are properly run. Meetings can create personal connections between people, so they can get to know one another reducing uncertainty. Meetings allow people to share meaning when they talk about themselves and their experiences. Meetings help people to invest in one another and the group, so they can share resources to get the task done.

Meetings help to negotiate the responsibilities of the participants, determine how things will be accomplished, and encourage members to take action to implement decisions. This is when people solve problems and make decisions together. Meetings facilitate the process of behavior reinforcement to help the group accomplish its tasks while developing its norms and roles. They help to develop the skills and abilities of the participants. They are a means to communicate and enforce the rules. How a meeting is conducted can help to increase member satisfaction fostering their commitment to the group. Many tasks could be accomplished by phone, email, or memos, but these don't have the same benefits as meeting face to face.

There are many types of meetings based on the group's desired outcome. Meetings can be used to accomplish a task, make decisions, solve problems, make plans, or disseminate information. Social meetings can improve a group's social climate, provide entertainment, mark significant events, and celebrate rituals and traditions. Creative meetings come up with new and innovative ways of doing things. Committee meetings are often a group of appointed members who make decisions for a larger organization. An annual meeting conducts the business of an organization, such as selecting a board of directors. A conference is a series of meetings with presentations and speeches. A seminar involves providing information, education, or training.

For an effective meeting, utilize the following elements.

- Purpose. A meeting should have a clear purpose that is understood by everyone who attends. Before scheduling a meeting determine if it is actually needed or if things can be done in other ways like with a phone call. Determine a clear desired outcome for the meeting because some meetings are held out of habit or just to show that something is being done. Unnecessary meetings can be a source of frustration by wasting people's time that undermines their satisfaction and commitment.

- Location. The proper location helps ensure a successful meeting. The purpose of the meeting will determine where it should take place. It should be a place that optimizes achieving a group's desired outcomes. Having a professional looking space encourages a professional mindset rather than being in a space that is cluttered. The room should be free from distractions like extraneous noise. It should be the right size to accommodate the group so everyone is comfortable including having enough chairs, tables, and space to work. It should be suited to address specific needs like having a podium, microphone, easel, or flip charts if needed. On the day of the meeting, be sure the room has everything the participants will need like pens and paper, water and glasses, or refreshments like coffee.

- Agenda. This is a written list of all the items that will be discussed at the meeting in chronological order along with the time allotted for each. An agenda is essential to a successful meeting because it reduces uncertainty to help keep things on track and establishes the same expectations for everyone. Avoid putting too many items on the agenda or people may feel overwhelmed. Stick to the allotted time or people may feel that their time is being wasted. The agenda should be written and distributed before the meeting so that everyone can be ready to get the work done. Without an agenda, a meeting can become a discussion without a purpose.

- Meeting time. Finding a time when everyone can meet may be one of the biggest challenges to setting up a meeting. A successful meeting starts and ends on time. Keeping it as short as necessary helps keep the energy levels high maintaining everyone's attention. If the meeting runs long, schedule breaks so everyone can stretch and walk around. If a meeting runs too long or does not end on time, it can make people feel frustrated. Instead, consider adjourning and take up the remaining items at another time.

For an effective meeting, participants should do the following.

- Come to the meeting prepared. Read the agenda and any attachments beforehand. Be prepared and informed about what is going to be discussed. If you have any questions call beforehand to clarify them so you don't waste time at the meeting.

- Arrive at least ten minutes early, so you can help with any last minute preparations. This gives you a chance to talk informally with others or take a few minutes to relax and compose your thoughts. Few things undermine how people perceive you as much as arriving late because it communicates that you don't value their time, even though you do.

- Participate. Talk during the meeting, but have something substantive to say. Avoid dominating the conversation, but don't just sit back either. Come to the meeting prepared to contribute your ideas and ask questions. Organize your thoughts so you are clear and succinct. Before the meeting, write down a few things you want to bring up so you don't ramble using up valuable time.

- Support and encourage others. If you think someone has a good idea, tell them. Utilize positive nonverbal behaviors like smiling and eye contact to show others that you are interested in what's going on.

- Listen to what others have to say. Because you have come prepared, you can listen to what they are saying rather than only thinking about what you are going to say next. Take notes of what others say so that you can respond to them at the appropriate time. Listening helps us make good decisions because we are better informed.

Conducting a meeting requires many of the qualities of being an effective leader as detailed in Chapter 4. The following items provide a plan that can be adjusted or modified depending upon the type of meeting and your desired outcomes. Being a leader requires many of the same responsibilities as a participant, but there are a few other things to do.

To have an effective meeting, it can be helpful do these tasks in the following order.

1. Arrive before everyone else does. Make sure that the room is set up so everything is in place before the other participants arrive. Have the tables and chairs set up, pens and pads in place, water and refreshments available. Be sure that everyone can see everyone else. Check the room temperature so that it is not too hot or cold and the lighting so that it is adequate. Arrange any visuals so everyone can see them. Test any electronic equipment to be sure it is working properly. If there is a speaker, be sure there is a podium and microphone properly placed in working order.

2. Set up your place to sit. The person who conducts the meeting typically sits in the power position. It is at the head of a boardroom table, the center of a long table, and at twelve o'clock for a round table. Place your agenda in front of you to easily see it. During the meeting, check off each item as it is accomplished. Bring a clock that is unobtrusive and easy to read. If you have a wristwatch, take it off and set it on the table next to your agenda. Then you can look at both at the same time to keep the meeting on schedule and no one should notice you checking the time. Looking at your wristwatch when it's on your wrist could be interpreted to mean that you're feeling bored or have someplace better to be.

3. Have someone welcome everyone as they arrive because people rarely arrive all at the same time. You can do this, but you will probably be busy with last minute details. It's discouraging to show up for a meeting and no one talks to you. Welcoming everyone lets them know you're glad to see them and that they are valued. This sets a positive tone for the meeting and develops the social aspect of the group.

4. Allow social time. Schedule a few minutes of social time at the beginning and end of the meeting so participants can talk informally with one another. This utilizes the power of shared meaning and self-disclosure to reduce uncertainty by helping everyone to get to know one another so they can work better together. This can be a time to introduce newcomers to the other members.

5. Start the meeting on time. It's frustrating to show up on time and then wait for a meeting that starts late. Announce to everyone that the meeting is starting and they should take their seats. Once everyone has been seated, call the meeting to order.

6. Begin with a welcome to let everyone know you appreciate them being there. Take a few minutes for everyone to introduce themselves. Write down their names in the order they are

seated or pass around a sign in sheet so you can use their names when you call on them at the meeting. State the purpose of the meeting, expectations, and desired outcomes.

7. Briefly review the agenda to focus everyone's attention on the tasks ahead. An agenda helps you to keep the meeting on task and on time. Check off each item as it is covered. Make notes to keep track of what has been accomplished. Depending upon the type of meeting, you may need to follow parliamentary procedure including calling the meeting to order, roll call, reading of the minutes, committee reports, old and new business, making motions, and voting.

8. A record should be kept of what transpired at the meeting. This is usually done by some-one other than the meeting leader. Groups often have a secretary who writes the minutes of the meeting that includes the date, beginning and ending times, items that were discussed, motions and decisions that were made, and actions taken.

9. The leader makes sure that everyone contributes and no one dominates the discussion. Encourage everyone to talk by going around the room and asking each person to contribute an idea. If decisions need to be made, utilize the decision making processes described in Chapter 4.

10. Keep the group on task to achieve the desired outcomes for the meeting. Wrap up dis-cussions when they have gone on long enough by providing a summary of what has been decided so far. This will help members who may not have been paying attention know where they are and gives everyone a feeling of accomplishment because they are making progress. You can get the group moving to the next item by saying something like, "The next item on the agenda is." If they are reluctant to move on remind them of the time limita-tions. Doing this should motivate them because nobody wants a meeting to run long.

11. When the meeting has concluded, summarize what has been done so everyone feels a sense of accomplishment. Review what actions are to be taken so everyone knows what they are supposed to do after the meeting. If possible, determine the date for the next meet-ing. Be sure to thank everyone for their time and good work. Then officially adjourn the meeting.

12. Allow some time after the meeting for members to socialize. If they feel they are pushed out of the room immediately after the meeting, they may not feel as good about it. Some may want to stick around and talk about the meeting while others may leave right away. This can be a good time to get some feedback from them about the meeting. People may be more willing to say what is on their mind because it is not in front of everyone else and the meeting is still fresh in their mind.

13. After the meeting, have the minutes typed up and a copy sent to everyone who was in attendance and any members who were absent. Include the date of the next meeting or pos-sible dates for it. Send a handwritten thank you note to any guests or speakers.

14. Once you have had a chance to relax and get some perspective, analyze the events of the meeting. Determine how well it went, review any feedback, and review the meeting minutes. This helps you to critically evaluate how well the meeting went. Identify things that went well and things that could be improved.

Media Communicating

Most of the time when you communicate, you create your Great Idea and make a connection with others across The Great Abyss. In media communicating, this process works in reverse. Others create their Great Idea and try to communicate with you as part of a large audience. They have to cross The Great Abyss to make a connection with you by overcoming the interference of filters and frames of reference, so you can receive their message. Media communicating utilizes connections that are often provided by organizations employing large numbers of people such as print media, broadcasting, and the internet.

In the past, people lived in smaller communities making it possible to communicate more directly with one another using methods like public speaking. As populations grew, these methods became less effective increasing uncertainty. People needed new ways to communicate more effectively with a growing population. They were motivated by the law of uncertainty to develop technologies like printing and broadcasting. This reduced uncertainty by making communicating to share meaning with larger audiences possible.

The media is a means by which we reduce uncertainty by gathering and disseminating information about people, events, and the world around us to large numbers of people. It provides the information we use to form opinions and make decisions. While we do not always know the accuracy or validity of this information, we use it because it helps to reduce uncertainty about what is happening around us.

The media is a means by which we share meaning with large groups of people. These shared meanings can become part of a common culture and shape social reality. Media communicating provides a way to share information and persuade others to think different or take action that can motivate behavior.

Our society has become so large that many of our most common connections are through the media. This has made it an influential and important part of our lives. It helps us to know more about other people and society, so we can invest our time and other resources in one another. The media provides much of the information we use in the perception process to develop expectations for ourselves, others, and society. The media provides a connection by which we get the information we need or want about current events, news, entertainment, government, and many other things necessary for society to function, so we can invest in it.

The media can fulfill many of our needs and wants. It fulfills our need for information and knowledge. It can show us how to do new things. It fulfills our need for entertainment, excitement, and adventure. It provides a means for relaxation and escape. It can take us places we want to go without having to actually go there. It can communicate emotions such as happiness, sadness, excitement, and fear. It can provide a means to experience things vicariously through the actions of others without actually having to do them for ourselves.

There has been much debate about the degree of influence that the media has on public opinion and individual attitudes. Do people develop their views on their own or does the media influence them? While people are influenced by the information around them, including what they receive from the media, they have the free will to form their own opinions as evidenced by people frequently disagreeing with those in the media.

However, our view of social reality including our values, attitudes, beliefs, and personal opinions are constructed from our experiences based on the perception process. We use perception to select, organize, and interpret information based upon our past experiences to make them useful to us. Through the process of communicating we receive information from others including the media that can be altered by our filters and frames of reference. What information we select to utilize is based upon our needs, wants, and desired outcomes.

While the media may not directly affect our opinions, it provides much of the information that does. Information provides the basis for our opinions, values, perceptions, and expectations. Because we use the information communicated in the media, it can have a significant influence on us.

Much of how we develop culture and construct social reality is communicated through the media. It provides much of the information we use to form our perceptions and expectations from which we develop the attitudes and opinions that motivate our behavior. It's helpful to be aware of this influence, so that we can verify the validity of the information we receive before accepting it. It's helpful to be aware of this process, so that we do not simply adopt the opinions of other people as our own.

Evaluating media.

There was a time when the media consisted of book, newspaper, and magazine publishers, and later radio and television broadcasters. These organizations were run by editors, publishers, managers, and owners. They were often located in the communities they served, so you could walk through their doors and meet them face to face. They were accountable for what they said or wrote, not only to their audience, but also to their community. The information people relied on had to be written, edited, and published providing the time to check its accuracy and validity. It was clear who created it and they were responsible for this information.

Today, things are very different with global companies and instantaneous information. Misinformation and personal opinion can be communicated as fact. People may have their own agenda to try to get us to think the way they do. So, it's important to not just take someone else's word for something or let them tell us what we should think. We should verify the accuracy and validity of the information we receive for ourselves, so we can separate what is fact from what is opinion. Instead of listening to what others say, look for the original source to verify information for yourself. Instead of simply accepting the information you receive, critically evaluate it to develop your own ideas and opinions.

Whenever anyone communicates in the media, they make choices about what to say, how to say it, what connections to use, and how to present that information. They do this based upon their motivation and desired outcomes. By critically evaluating the messages we receive we can better understand them and the affect they have on us. Consider the motivation of the person behind the message and what they want their audience to do. By having an awareness you can evaluate the information you receive to think for yourself and make choices that are in your best interest.

These are some options to critically evaluate information in the media.

- Consider the creator of the message. This can include the writer, presenter, or group that develops or communicates the message. Consider relevant characteristics like their background, expertise, credentials, trustworthiness, and competence. Consider their motives and desired outcomes.

- Consider the audience for the message. Who are they trying to reach and how do they reach them? Is the message tailored to the audience's interest, needs, and wants? What was the audience asked to do? Was it reasonable or workable?

- Consider the message. This includes the topic, evidence, reasoning, organization, and structure. Was the purpose clear? Was the information true, accurate, and the facts verifiable? Did the evidence support the claim? What method of persuasion was used? Was it logical or did it appeal to emotions like fear? Was the method of reasoning valid or was it false reasoning?

- Consider the connection and method of delivery. How was a connection made with the audience? What method of delivery was used and was it appropriate? Consider who provides the money to communicate the message and if they have a vested interest in the outcome? Are they independent or are they part of a group that has its own special interests? Consider who stands to benefit and what they stand to gain.

- Consider the overall general effect of the message. Was it effective in reaching the audience? Was it in the audience's best interest? Did it help to fulfill needs or wants? What was the desired outcome and was it achieved? Could there be unintended or undesired outcomes? What were you being asked to think or do? Was it reasonable within your values and beliefs? Were you asked to do something you wouldn't ordinarily do?

Doing this can be helpful for both important and not so important decisions. When we purchase something expensive like a car, we often do our homework. We do research, read reviews, and compare models. But we may not do this with other important decisions. Being a member of society is like being a good group member or leader, it requires work and taking responsibility. It means doing research, which takes time and energy. It takes looking to see what people in the media actually say and do rather that listening to what others say about them.

Business Communicating

So, how does a business, or other organization, communicate with you, as well as with the larger public? A business can be like an individual with needs, wants, and desired outcomes. Like other types of groups and organizations, a business needs to communicate with people in order to survive. They need to create and maintain relationships with customers, clients, and suppliers to stay in business. How effective they are in communicating with the public can be an important determinate to their success. There are several ways that businesses can do this.

A business must reduce uncertainty in the minds of the public, not only about their products or services, but about who they are as a business as well. They can do this by sharing meaning with the public. This is why they often communicate how they were founded, their history, and their community involvement. They encourage employees, customers, clients, and suppliers to invest in their business in the long term to help them to be successful.

Identity management is the method by which we shape how others perceive us by controlling the information we communicate to them. Our desired outcome is to create a positive impression, so that others will like us. We do this to reduce uncertainty, fulfill our needs and wants, and achieve our desired outcomes. Businesses and organizations use public relations and advertising as a means of identity management with large groups of people. Their desired outcome is to manage public perception and expectations of them by managing the information that is communicated publicly about them. This is often accomplished through advertising, public relations, logos, use of color, architecture, and typefaces.

Public relations relies on indirect connections through generally free media like written articles or radio and television programs to communicate with the public. These can be perceived as more creditable, but there is less control over the message possibly creating unintended or undesired outcomes. Advertising utilizes paid media so that the message can be controlled, but it can be more difficult to cut through the interference because people tend to tune it out unless it fits their needs and wants.

The purpose of public relations and advertising is to reduce uncertainty in the minds of the public about an individual, product, businesses, organization, or idea. This can help them manage their identity by controlling the information the public receives about them. By reducing uncertainty, the public should feel more comfortable and be more receptive to their message. They may also use a public persona like a person or mascot to represent them to make it easier for people to relate to because this can give them more likable qualities.

Public relations and advertising use the law of shared meaning to create connections between individuals, groups, business, organizations, and the public. They may use tradition and history by telling stories about significant people and events to create connections with the public. They often use familiar symbols, words, and colors by investing them with meaning about the organization. These symbols can have a deeper meaning that is representative of the organization's purpose and what they do. For example, educational institutions use academic symbols like shields, lamps, or books that are associated with learning, so when we see the logo we recognize it and know its meaning.

Public relations and advertising is a means by which businesses and organizations encourage the public to invest in them by managing the dissemination of information about them. They do this to reduce uncertainty and share meaning through a managed type of self-disclosure to create trust, so that people will invest in them to buy their product, promote their program, or support them in other ways. This is done to achieve a desired outcome that involves members of the public taking some kind of action. It can be challenging to persuade large numbers of people who have little or no contact with them to do what they ask.

Public opinion as feedback.

In the process of communicating, you create your Great Idea and communicate it to others who provide you with feedback. In public communicating, public opinion serves as one of the ways that large audiences can provide feedback. Public opinion can be measured through research methodology like surveys, ratings, polls, or focus groups. It can also be expressed in emails, letters, or phone calls. This can help to reduce uncertainty by better understanding what the public needs and wants.

Many businesses and organizations spend time and resources to find out what the public thinks. They do this to reduce uncertainty about what they do and to help them make decisions. Public opinion can become part of the larger social reality because it provides a way to share meaning that can influence how we think about ourselves, others, and the things around us. It can be a way to invest in society because it motivates people's actions and behavior.

Public opinion and polling can be used to determine the effectiveness of many kinds of public communicating. It can be used to measure public satisfaction with many things like products, television programs, elected officials, or public issues. Public perception can affect the success or failure of a product, company, individual, or policy. Because it can have the power to motivate behavior, there are some who may try to change or manipulate public opinion to achieve their own desired outcome.

Public opinion can be gathered through research including surveys and polls. However, there are some issues to be aware of about how public opinion is gathered and reported. Surveys measure a person's response to a question, but not their honesty. People may answer questions the way they think they should, to be perceived as a good person, or because they feel the truth is nobody's business. How questions are phrased and the order in which they are asked can influence how people answer them.

Surveys can reduce complex issues to oversimplified questions. Questions may contain words that are selected to encourage a specific response. Surveys can be skewed which means that they might over represent a particular demographic altering the results. How a survey is constructed and implemented can change the outcome to get whatever results someone wants them to be. They can also be used to alter public perception.

Public opinion is only accurate if the information gathered represents the group being surveyed. Asking everyone's opinion is impractical because there are too many people. Only the census reaches everyone and that's done every ten years. So, a small group has to be selected that has the same characteristics as the larger group you want to know something about. Representativeness is when a small group represents a larger group as accurately as possible. For example, if we are making soup, we taste a spoonful because it represents what all the soup tastes like, so we don't have to eat all of it.

Sampling is when we want to know something about a large group, but it is easier and cheaper to survey a small sample of that group. The challenge is in selecting a sample that represents the larger group so the results are accurate. The sample has to be large enough to include all the characteristics we want to know something about. If it's too small or the wrong group is sampled, then the results will not be accurate. So, if we sample soup to see how it tastes, the spoon has to be the right size so we are sure we get all the ingredients in our tasting. Whenever you hear someone report the results of a survey, it's helpful to know how they chose their sample, its representativeness, who was surveyed, and the methodology for doing it because these factors can alter the results.

Public opinion is often reported in the media in the form of polls and surveys. It can be helpful to critically evaluate them by having an awareness of how they are conducted because they can be made to show any desired result. In order to prevent bias, the sample should be large enough and selected to accurately represent the general public. The questions should be worded and ordered to prevent bias, and any potential biases are recognized and controlled to have minimum impact on the questions, participants, and the outcome.

Potential interviewer bias should be controlled, so that people do not feel compelled to answer in a particular way. Questions with positive-negative or agree-disagree responses should be equally balanced and have a neutral option. Asking open ended questions provides better information even though it is more difficult to convert to statistics. The criteria for the survey, how the sample was selected, and how the information was gathered should be published along with the results, so people can judge its validity for themselves.

A New Style of Public Communicating.

Chapter 1 outlines three styles of communicating. This includes sending a message, receiving feedback, and using a conversational style. Many organizations like businesses communicate with the public in the first two styles. They create a message, product, or service then make connections to sell it to the public. In some circumstances they receive unsolicited feedback or they may seek it out. Businesses can be successful by utilizing the third style of communicating, where they engage in ongoing conversations with their customers, clients, and the public.

In the process of communicating, feedback is used to measure the effectiveness of a message in order to improve it. When people communicate through the media, how do we provide them with feedback? How do they know that their message is getting across? And how do they determine how to improve their message to make it more effective?

Businesses and organizations can intentionally and unintentionally create physical and psychological barriers to interfere with feedback from the public. These can include buildings, security guards, receptionists, managers, assistants, and other gatekeepers who keep the public away from those who make decisions. This means that the people who make decisions may be receiving information through the fewest connections, hindering their awareness and limiting their options.

There are basically two kinds of feedback; solicited and voluntary. Solicited feedback is feedback that the creator of a message solicits or goes out and gets to see how well their message has been received. This form of feedback can include surveys, interviews, focus groups, questionnaires, and phone calls. Surveys are often quantitative in nature because they are easier to administer and evaluate. They convert concepts into numbers that can have a propensity to be simplistic and potentially inaccurate. Qualitative feedback like interviews and focus groups are more time consuming and difficult to analyze, but can be more accurate with more detailed information.

Voluntary feedback is the information individuals provide on their own without being contacted by anyone. This is more difficult to obtain because it takes members of the public time and energy to find out who to contact and then contact them. This type of feedback may be dismissed as coming from troublemakers who are often ignored or pushed away. However, people who provide this type of feedback are often very knowledgeable, motivated, and could potentially provide valuable insight that might otherwise be overlooked.

While complaints can be viewed as a type of feedback, they should be more than just criticizing. Communicate complaints objectively by describing the problem and then offer a solution. Keep a complaint short, to the point, provide evidence to support it, and stay positive avoiding name calling or bad language. While it may seem logical to contact customer service, it may be more effective to contact a manager, supervisor, the president, or CEO of a company because they have more power to take action. Consider asking for help from professional associations, consumer advocates, or regulatory agencies.

To reduce uncertainty, businesses and organizations should consider new approaches to how they obtain and utilize feedback. The old way involved creating a product or service and then advertising it to create a need or want for it with the public. The new way involves bringing the customer into the process by assessing their needs and wants first to help develop a product or service before it is brought to market. This way customer feedback can be used to help improve the product or service in the early stages. Instead of creating a product and persuading people to buy it, it will be customers who will tell companies what they want and they will provide it or risk going out of business.

In businesses and organizations, information often originates at the top where decisions are made and then filters down to the lower levels. However, in order to communicate more effectively they will need a mechanism by which information flows in all directions to all levels. Particularly from the bottom levels, where the work is done, to the top where decisions are made. This will help to provide the best quality information to make good decisions.

Since employees are expected to listen to their superiors, superiors should be expected to listen to their employees as well, without fear of recrimination or retaliation. Those in charge need to listen to those who do the work to improve the effectiveness of the organization. This not only provides important information, it makes people feel like they matter. The more people have a say, the more likely they are to show a commitment to the organization. Those running an organization can benefit from spending time communicating with their employees and customers.

How a business or organization treats its employees and customers can have a significant affect on its effectiveness and achieving its desired outcomes. How it does this is often a reflection of its culture and climate. This can make courtesy an important part of an organization's culture because it affects how members communicate with each other and the public.

Courtesy is more than just being polite or having good manners, it is an attitude that people have towards one another. Courtesy can motivate behavior because people are encouraged to be thoughtful and considerate, and show respect for others. There is a culture of civility and graciousness. It encourages an organizational climate that is cordial, warm, and friendly making it a pleasant place to work, that can increase satisfaction and commitment.

Integrated teams.

An example of how businesses and organizations can think in new ways to foster making connections with the public is with integrated teams. Many organizations, like businesses, are structured by function based on their own needs and wants rather than their clients' or customers' needs and wants. While this may work well for them, when a customer needs help it is often up to the customer to find the right place to get the help they need.

For instance, a customer's initial contact might be with the sales department when making a purchase, but if they need support they have to contact another department. Customers can spend a great deal of time trying to find the right place to get something done or have their problem solved. If their needs and wants are not fulfilled it increases uncertainty so that the next time they want to purchase something they are more likely to go somewhere else.

In order to effectively communicate with others, it is important to have an awareness of their needs and wants. Instead of thinking from your own perspective, it is more effective to think from their perspective. Unfortunately, too many businesses and organizations approach communicating with their customers from their perspective to fulfill their own needs and wants instead of those of their customers.

A new approach to how businesses and organizations can be structured is based on the needs and wants of their customers. Businesses and organizations can do this by forming integrated teams that put a representative from each department like sales, credit, tech support, and customer service together in an integrated team. So, when a customer buys a product or service they become a client of an integrated team. When they need help instead of being put on hold or endlessly passed around between departments, they call their integrated team directly without going through endless menus or transfers. It should not be up to the customer to find the right place to solve their problem, it's up to their integrated team. Now a customer makes only one call to their integrated team who will find a solution for them.

These work teams are integrated in the sense that they are formed to combine functions that are normally considered to be separate, so that they can work together more effectively for the customer. This approach can provide better service to the customer and will save the company time and money handling misplaced inquiries, angry customers, and lost business. This can be a more effective approach to customer service. Instead of organizing support based on the company's perspective, it is organized based on the customer's point of view.

The success of any business or organization is about making connections between itself and the public, as well as between management and employees. Businesses that will be successful in the future are those that make these connections to reduce uncertainty for their customers and employees. What causes a business to become very successful, only to fail or go under later? There are numerous examples of this happening. Businesses may plan for the future, but do they plan for uncertainty?

Doing this can be helpful because one thing that we know for sure about the future is that people will be motivated by uncertainty. Businesses and organizations can benefit from identifying sources of uncertainty, how it can affect their business, and how it might motivate public behavior. Uncertainty can have a wide variety of implications ranging from customers going elsewhere to undermining the economy. In the future, organizations like businesses can benefit from planning for uncertainty as part of their future planning.

Governmental Communicating

One of the great debates throughout history has been the role of government in society. This debate goes beyond the question of what form a government should take or how its leaders are chosen. It is also about determining what the roles and responsibilities of government should be and the nature of the relationship a government should have with the people it governs. This debate has manifested itself in a wide variety of governmental forms from authoritarian where everything is decided by the state to democracies with a higher degree of individual freedom.

The creation of government is motivated by the law of uncertainty. Life is chaotic and things can happen that overwhelm our ability to cope with them. Government has the ability to acquire and allocate resources to accomplish tasks that individuals and groups are unable to do. It provides a means to share information, debate issues, and make decisions that reduces uncertainty in society. It is the nature of government to reduce uncertainty by creating a structure, that provides safety and security for its citizens.

Conversely, having some degree of uncertainty is necessary for society to function. This creates a tension between uncertainty and uncertainty reduction. How people resolve this tension has been the motivation for many different types of government. While we may feel democratic forms of government are best, they have an inherent degree of uncertainty that can make some people feel a need for more structure. This need may explain why there has been socialist, communist, and even dictatorial forms of governance. However, many of these forms fail because they can reduce uncertainty to a point where it damages society by limiting creativity and innovation.

Government utilizes the law of shared meaning by communicating with the public to create and sustain its social reality. Government creates and shares meaning about what a nation stands for and what it means to be a citizen. It shares meaning about its past, rituals, and traditions that are communicated during national holidays and events. It shares meaning about significant people and events in its history. It shares meaning about the institutions of government that are charged with carrying out government functions. Government invests symbols with shared meanings that can be physically embodied in items such as the flag, currency, coat of arms, official seals, national colors, and other symbols that represent important qualities of a nation and its people.

Governments and the people they represent have a shared history, traditions, and culture that were created over a long period of time by people communicating with one another motivated by the law of shared meaning. This is often accomplished by sharing stories about the nation's past and important individuals that serves to share meaning creating a common history and purpose. Government helps to maintain these shared meanings by creating and maintaining institutions that preserve their history. Meaning is shared through the public discourse of policy debates, decision making, and election campaigns. It is an important function of government to foster and share meaning with its citizens.

In order for a group to function, its members have to be comfortable investing their time, energy, money, and other resources in it and in one another. Similarly, government can motivate its citizens to participate and contribute to society by providing for economic activity. But people need to be able to trust that if they make investments, they will have reasonable expectations of a fair return in the future. In order to do this, government must maintain structures that protect these investments by providing safety and stability to increase predictability, so people can invest their time, energy, and other resources with confidence. Government can establish rules that govern behavior along with punishments for violating the rules, so that people will abide by them.

The law of investing provides the impetus for government to create structures to help people invest in themselves, others, and society. These include legislative, regulatory, monetary, legal, and judicial institutions. These institutions are able to transcend the individuals who create them, so that they can be maintained over long periods of time. In order to facilitate investing, it's helpful for the government to create policies that change slowly to encourage stability.

Stability motivates people to have faith in government because it provides reasonable predictability of what they can expect in the future. Since most governmental systems are created by the mutual perceptions and expectations of the people involved, they only work when people believe in them. If government does not enforce the rules or makes changes inconsistently, it can erode the system discouraging people from investing in it.

Throughout history people have sought to reduce uncertainty and fulfill their mutual needs and wants in a variety of ways. They formed groups and organizations to do this, however, the most effective means of accomplishing many of these things proved to be by creating some form of government. How this was done has varied widely throughout history and around the world. The government people created was often based upon a society's view of social reality. There have been many forms of government including monarchy, dictatorship, communist, and democratic. Leaders have utilized various mechanisms in order to rule their people including divine right, birthright, and the will of the people.

Government can be a reflection of the people it governs based on their social reality. This can work like the process of communicating. People communicate to form their own social reality and government provides them with a type of feedback. This means that government can be reflective of society's values, attitudes, beliefs, culture, and behavioral norms because it needs the approval of its citizens to exist. No government, no matter how repressive can exist without the consent of at least some of the people it governs. If people do not support their government, they will find methods to replace it as has been evidenced by changes in governmental structures throughout history. When people no longer accept the legitimacy of the government it will fail.

As a society we have collective needs and wants that would be difficult or even impossible to fulfill without government. An important function of government is to fulfill the needs and wants of its citizens that other groups or organizations may be unable or unwilling to provide because they lack the resources or the authority to do so. Many of these can be logistically difficult or impossible to fulfill outside the role of government.

As individuals, we have tension between conflicting needs and wants like our need to work and to have fun or relax. These are needs that cannot be fulfilled simultaneously, so we have to make decisions about how to balance them which creates a natural tension. The debate about the role of government is based upon tensions between conflicting needs and wants. This tension leads to policy debates between the role of government and individual freedom. Society needs structure, rules, and a means to enforce the rules, but it also needs to allow citizens freedom of expression, association, and commerce. Each of these tensions can be resolved through economic equilibrium.

The role of government in society has come to reflect the tensions between the conflicting needs and wants of its citizens. Each has become its own social reality with some believing that power should be concentrated in government and the public sector, while others believe that power should be invested in the people and the private sector. In the private sector, a business is successful when it is productive and profitable. When a business loses revenue, it has to cut costs or risk going under. The law of uncertainty motivates businesses to improve their productivity and increase their profitability or it will cease to exist.

However, government is not subject to the same forces because it cannot go out of business. Since it doesn't make a profit, its success is often based on growth such as bigger budgets, more employees, larger programs, and increased spending. This is evidenced by politicians promoting increased funding to programs like education instead of asking questions like, what are we really getting for what we are currently spending. This can motivate government to increase spending even when it's not covered by revenues resulting in growing deficits and debt.

The private sector is motivated by the uncertainty of going out of business, so it reduces uncertainty by providing products and services people want to fulfill their needs and wants. Since government cannot go out of business, it is not subject to the same influences from uncertainty. Like other organizations, government has its own needs and wants that can conflict with those of its citizens creating tension. This can motivate it to fend off what it perceives as potential threats. So, while its purpose may be to represent the people, it can be motivated to act in its own self interest to reduce uncertainty.

Businesses create economic equilibrium by cutting costs or increasing productivity, however, there are few incentives for government bureaucracy to do the same. There can be a greater incentive to ask for budget increases every year, whether they are needed or not because money that's not spent is likely to be taken away. Government departments generally receive funding from an elected or appointed body, so rather than competing in the marketplace, all that is needed is a majority vote to provide the funding. This changes the nature of uncertainty as a motivating factor of behavior. Bureaucracy does not need to be concerned with productivity, customer relations, or cutting costs to survive. Instead, their constituency could be considered the people who vote for their funding.

Individuals, groups, businesses, and organizations have checks and balances that provide natural limitations to their growth that affects their behavior. As individuals we can have virtually unlimited needs and wants, however, we have limited resources to fulfill them. Businesses are subject to economic limitations because if they are not able to obtain the resources they need to sustain themselves, they will cease to exist. This means that they are motivated by the law of uncertainty to find methods to reduce uncertainty such as adapting to the market and their customers needs and wants in order to survive.

Government does not have the same limitations that are created by the law of uncertainty. Individuals and organizations must earn their income, where government need only pass a law by a majority vote. Individuals and organizations must abide by the rules and laws of society, government can vote to change them. Individuals and organizations must satisfy the needs and wants of their clients or customers in order to survive, government does not. From a naturalistic perspective, government has no natural predators. Individuals may quit, groups disband, organizations go out of business, but government is enduring.

The nature of government gives it the potential to reduce uncertainty to the point where it inhibits motivation for innovation. Like individuals, government bureaucracy can have virtually unlimited needs and wants, however, unlike individuals its needs and wants could potentially continue to grow unabated. This likely contributes to the failure of socialism, communism, progressivism, or any system where uncertainty is significantly reduced by the government.

Legitimation and The Law of Uncertainty.

One of the most significant sources of uncertainty for any governmental system is legitimation. In ancient times, rulers claimed descendancy from the gods or ruled by divine right. Monarchs claimed legitimacy by birthright. As civilization progressed, the means of legitimation changed as well. However, the need for leaders and governments to prove their ability to lead has changed little. Few governments today refer to supernatural forces to support the political order, however, the fundamental principle remains the same.

As kings and courts gave way to presidents and parliaments, the people had a more direct influence in the choice of their government through the elective process. This established the notion of a government's legitimacy by popular mandate as being conferred directly by the people. Today, many governments claim legitimacy based on a constitution, the nation's founders, or the will of the people. The importance of legitimation is evidenced by nondemocratic governments including dictatorial, theocratic, and communistic regimes holding elections and having parliaments to legitimize their political power. The absence of a clear mandate to lead or the loss of legitimacy can lead to confusion or even anarchy.

The need for legitimation in society is motivated by the law of uncertainty. Without legitimacy, anyone could claim it was their destiny to lead and tell others what to do. This could result in multiple parties claiming it was their right to govern potentially creating chaos, conflict, even civil war. In order to avoid this, society developed several methods by which political power to govern can be legitimized. Legitimation is the method people have developed to invest the right to govern in those who are perceived as the rightful leaders based on social reality to reduce uncertainty in society. If a government and its leaders are perceived by the public as legitimate, the right to govern is accepted by them. If not, they may be rejected and have difficulty governing or be removed from office.

Legitimation is the implementation of the law of shared meaning between those who govern and the people they govern. It is about determining what it means to govern and to be a citizen. It is how we communicate and create shared meanings about our culture, history, and traditions. It is the process by which we reinforce or change the rules of social reality. It is how we create expectations about our government and its leaders. Leaders legitimize their right to govern by using the law of shared meaning about themselves through the process of self-disclosure.

Candidates for public office participate in traditions and rituals like giving speeches, attending public events, and shaking hands with the voters. They participate in events that have little to do with their qualifications for office because they must demonstrate that they share the values of the voters. They must create common ground by participating in communal rituals and traditions. If they do not do this, they could be perceived as being aloof, out of touch, or not caring about the people.

Legitimation is the process of how citizens invest power in their government and its leaders giving them the authority to govern. This process works rather like being a member of a group that extracts costs in exchange for providing benefits. People agree to give up some of their rights and freedoms in exchange for benefits gained by legitimizing their government. Legitimation creates the necessary structure and rules to provide safety and stability, which encourages citizens to invest in the government. If a government's leaders have not undergone the process of legitimacy, then they can have a difficult time governing because the people may be more reluctant to invest in them due to increased uncertainty.

Legitimation helps to instill confidence in the government and in its institutions. It reduces uncertainty, so that people will feel comfortable supporting the government and investing in society. However, if a leader increases uncertainty, it can motivate people to reduce their investments because they are no longer as sure of what they can expect in the future.

Legitimation can be characterized as the process by which a government and its leaders are invested with the power to govern by the members of a society. The relationship between a society and its leaders is constantly changing. Since governments are not entities unto themselves, but are joint ventures comprised of many individuals, both the government and individual leaders can be subject to this process gaining or losing legitimacy concurrently or separately. The result of this problem can be manifested in the overthrow of political regimes through military coups or populist movements. No less significant are the gains and losses of political influence by leaders in democratic governments that can affect their ability to govern.

A leader or government is rarely perceived as having absolute legitimacy or having no legitimacy at all. Instead, there is some intermediate degree of legitimacy, which can be perceived as a function of the ability to foster people's faith in the government. The degree to which a leader is deemed to be legitimate is determined by the degree to which the citizens accept the rule of the government. This is often reflected in approval/disapproval and favorable/unfavorable poll ratings. For instance, Congress can suffer the loss of legitimacy while that of individual members can remain high. A president can suffer a loss of legitimacy that hampers the ability to govern or move legislation through Congress.

Poll data can be utilized in new and creative ways to determine the effectiveness of how leaders share meaning with the people to establish their legitimacy. One measure is their approval rating, which measures the percentage of the people who approve or disapprove of how they are doing their job. Other poll measures include favorability and unfavorability ratings, which can be used as a measure of a their legitimacy. The people are asked who do they support and if their support is strong or weak. Specific issues are measured to determine their importance. The extent that public opinion reflects a candidate's dramatic narratives provides an indication of how well the voters were sharing meaning with their version of social reality.

Legitimacy can be considered the inverse of uncertainty. Legitimacy can be a measure of the degree to which uncertainty has been reduced. When a leader or government reduces uncertainty, it often increases public faith and its legitimacy. When uncertainty increases, it can reduce legitimacy as people have less faith in the government. Legitimacy reduces uncertainty because people need to know why things happen and what to expect in the future. They want to know what to expect from their leaders and how the government will affect their lives. So, people look for explanations, and they look to their elected leaders and the government to provide them. When there is a low degree of uncertainty it creates stability because it gives us a feeling of security. When we don't know what to expect, there can be a high degree of uncertainty creating apprehension and tension.

It can be beneficial to measure the degree of public uncertainty with an uncertainty index. This could be done for many aspects of society including elected officials, public institutions, and the economy. An uncertainty index is important because public uncertainty has the power to motivate people's behavior. When people experience something unfamiliar to them it can create tension making them uncomfortable, which can motivate them to take action to reduce it. This tension is often resolved through the construction of a social reality driven by the characterizations of real life events and experiences. For instance, people want to know why the economy is bad and when it will improve, so they look for explanations. And they often look to the government and their leaders for those answers.

Legitimacy involves people accepting the authority of their government, but this usually means some form of representative democracy. Since government represents a reflection of the social reality of a society, how does it manifest itself? Different cultures have different ways of structuring society based on their individual social reality. This raises the question, can people legitimately choose a form of government other than democracy?

The process of legitimation occurs through several sanctifying agents that are utilized to legitimize elected officials and governments. Many of these sanctifying agents have been part of the political process since government was first created. The pharaohs claimed that they were descended from the Sun God. Monarchs claimed legitimacy by birthright. In democracies, the government is legitimized by popular vote.

However, governments and leaders also utilize these other sanctifying agents.

- The people. The right to govern is conferred upon a leader by the will the people. They do this by claiming popular support or previous election to office. Leaders often avoid saying they want to lead for personal reasons. Instead they become leaders to help the people even when it means great self sacrifice.

- Personal experience. Politicians legitimize their right to lead because of who they are as a person, what they stand for, their history, and traditions. They do this through the process of self-disclosure and identity management by talking about their past experiences like why they went into public service. This can serve to reduce uncertainty about them in the minds of the voters.

- Shared values. Politicians communicate traditional values they share with the people they seek to represent by presenting themselves as an average person just like anyone else. They often go around wearing plaid shirts, eating hamburgers, drinking beer, and doing things to make them look extraordinarily ordinary. If a politician is perceived as being smarter or more skillful than the people they seek to lead, then the people are more likely to not accept them or even reject them as not being one of them.

- The middle class. Politicians run for office to help support what they refer to as the forgotten middle class. They often characterize middle class as being under attack by government, so the next generation will not have the same quality of life as the last. Perhaps they refer to the middle class because it comprises the largest segment of voters.

- Heroes and villains. In any good drama there are heroes and villains. Politicians may portray themselves as a hero fighting for the people against shadowy villains who are hurting the people, ruining the country, or destroying the American dream. These can be their opponent, as well as generalized groups like lobbyists, special interests, Washington insiders, Wall Street, big banks, as well as others.

- External forces. While politicians do not claim divine right, they utilize external forces outside themselves. These include endorsements from influential people like business and government leaders, celebrities, experts, and ordinary citizens. They frequently characterize elections as being at a crossroads or at a pivotal moment in history.

- Internal forces. Many governments have been led by charismatic leaders who hold onto power through their own personality or public persona. Just as people like to be around others they find likable or attractive, people support leaders they perceive as likable or attractive because of their speaking ability, persona, charisma, or popular appeal.

- The rebirth. Candidates often tell the story of how they came to dedicate their life to public service. They may claim that they were living an aimless life, then they had a dramatic moment of revelation that changed their life devoting themselves to public service. While this is based upon actual events, it is often embellished as a kind of spiritual rebirth shaping their destiny for a higher purpose in government.

- Their record. Politicians who have served in office use their record as evidence that they can get things done to serve the public. Their opponents use the same information to show that they are not fit for office because they have not served the public very well or have not done what they said they were going to do. If things have gone well, an incumbent will focus on their success as evidence that they should be reelected. If things have not gone well, they may claim that the work they started has not been finished, so they need another term to get the job done.

- Incumbency. An incumbent may say that now is not the time to elect someone untested and inexperienced, so we must stay the course. This increases uncertainty about their opponent because the public knows the incumbent, so why risk voting for someone they don't know. However, many incumbents have made the mistake of assuming that people would vote for them because they are already in office, thinking that voters will elect what is familiar rather than taking a chance on someone new.

- Change. This is the fundamental method of persuasion for any newcomer because if people cannot see the need for change, they are not likely to choose the uncertainty of a new candidate over the familiarity of the incumbent. People naturally resist change because it represents uncertainty, which is uncomfortable. In order to get people to change, they have to be convinced that it is necessary and unavoidable. They must make people perceive the current situation as more uncomfortable than taking a risk on the unknown. In reality, campaigning based on change can be meaningless. Since they haven't been in office anything they do potentially constitutes change. Politicians who do this are often short on specifics about what change means, the reasons for change, how things will be better, and what steps they are going to take to make change happen. This is because the more specific they are, the less people are likely to support them. And once they are elected to office the reality is that they often change very little.

- Perceptions and expectations. In order to vote for change, people have to change their perceptions and expectations. There are several techniques that are used to do this. The most effective methods for politicians are to demonize their opponent or utilize the uncertainty of a crisis. If there isn't one, a false crisis could panic people creating fear. This motivates people to vote for change because it is perceived as preferable to the status quo. Consider how many politicians have run on change, yet things have changed very little.

- Negative campaigning. Everyone complains about negative campaigning, but it is used because it works. It works because of the power of the law of uncertainty. People are motivated to take action when a situation is uncomfortable or something makes them upset or angry. If the candidates for office are relatively acceptable, people are less motivated to vote for them or may not vote at all. When a candidate is criticized by their opponent, they often accuse them of negative campaigning to portray them as unfit for office. They do this to motivate their opponent into discontinuing their criticism of them and to deflect attention from their own weaknesses or negative campaigning. Accusing an opponent of negative campaigning can be used as a form of negative campaigning.

- Their agenda. Politicians must communicate their agenda to the public in order to control it. If they do not, their opponent will try to define them on their own terms. This includes how they define themselves, their policies, and what they will do in office. This utilizes the law of shared meaning to shape public perceptions and create positive expectations. In an election campaign, it is a candidate's responsibility to point out their opponent's weaknesses and shortcomings. When they do this, their opponent will likely respond by accusing them of negative campaigning. However, this is an important part of the electoral process because it is how we scrutinize a candidate's fitness for office. Since candidates do not advertise their own shortcomings, it is their opponent's responsibility to question their fitness for office because if they do not, no one else can be counted upon to do so.

- Getting it. All too often politicians do what they feel is right, but fail to clearly explain what they are doing and why. They may feel that the public will just, "get it." This is a risky assumption because people are very busy, they have very little time to do their own research, and there is a lot of information competing for their attention. Politicians can run into trouble because of the interference of The Great Abyss in the process of communicating. People filter out information they are not looking for or want. They interpret information using their own perception process. This may change the meaning of the message resulting in unintended and undesired outcomes. Politicians need to be able to clearly communicate and articulate their ideas so the public understands them because people don't necessarily just, "get it."

- Repetition makes right. In order to cut through interference to get people's attention, politicians have to repeat their messages many times. Being consistent gives the impression of confidence, whereas constantly changing a message increases uncertainty giving the impression that they are unsure of themselves. However, repeating misinformation that is untrue can work to create the impression that it might be true, legitimizing its validity.

- Identity management. Politicians seek to control the public's perception about themselves through identity management. They seek to shape public perception of who they are to achieve their desired outcomes. They use identity management to define their opponent in order to change the public's perception of them by providing selective information.

- Social reality. When politicians seek to legitimize their right to govern, they develop their own specialized form of social reality. In order to reduce uncertainty with the voters, it is usually a selected version of the larger societal social reality. They do this by taking facts and giving them their own particular interpretation. They are likely to stay within acceptable limits of the greater social reality because if it's too different, the voters may reject it as increasing uncertainty.

- Vision of the future. Politicians seek to legitimize their policies by presenting a vision of the future that portrays tomorrow as better than today if they are elected. They may contrast their vision with an alternative vision where the people will be worse off if the current politicians stay in office. This is designed to increase uncertainty to motivate people to support them. This means of legitimation utilizes the power of the law of investing because if people see future benefits, they are more likely to support it.

Delegitimation. In order to have a functioning society, people must be able to make collective decisions. Society has always held that once a decision was made by a legitimate process, like a majority vote, everyone would abide by it whether they agreed with the outcome or not. This is a fundamental principle that makes democracies and society work for the benefit of everyone. However, there have been instances when some people and groups have not accepted the decision of a legitimate process, instead pursuing their own agenda. This can create tension in society that can lead to divisiveness.

So, when do we abide by decisions that are reached through a legitimate process even though we disagree with them? When do we continue to fight for what we believe is right? Decision making processes are established to make tough decisions, however, they only work if everyone respects the outcome. When we do not respect the decision and circumvent a legitimate process to pursue an alternative decision, it could work to undermine stability in society potentially increasing uncertainty.

Social Reality and Dramatic Narratives.

When people communicate, they talk about themselves often telling stories about their past experiences. When they do, they might edit these stories to make them more interesting and exciting to the listener. When people understand and can relate to these stories, they share meaning. They have the same understanding of what they mean and possibly share their own stories about similar experiences. This can create a connection, so they feel that they have something in common. This can make people seem more likable, even creating feelings of empathy.

The process of sharing meaning deals with the human tendency to want to understand the motivation for people's behavior to reduce uncertainty about them. Shared meaning is how a person makes a connection with other people, so that they see things in a similar way. This is how a politician gains and maintains people's support. Shared meaning can help to recall familiar stories for those who share them. If a specific story has not been shared, it would not make sense and the entire story would have to be explained.

In order to gain legitimacy, a leader must create and share their version of social reality with other people. So, they often create stories about themselves and their experiences to share meaning with the people. They do this to make themselves appear more personable and likeable to motivate people to support them. Social reality is how people make sense of the world around them. Life can be chaotic, things can happen for no apparent reason and social reality is how we organize and make sense of these things that happen to us. Social reality is important to us because it determines how we interpret our perceptions and what we do about them creating tangible consequences.

A leader's version of social reality is usually comprised of selected portions of the larger societal social reality because it has to be compatible with it in order to be accepted by the public. If not, they may be perceived as too extreme or out of touch. Then, they must make a connection with the people and communicate their message to them so that they will understand it. This is commonly done through the use of dramatic narratives.

It could be said that forms of communicating fall into two categories, fact and fiction. There is the inherent assumption that if a person is not telling the truth they are lying. So, if fact comprises those things that are verifiably true and fiction is an imaginative creation that does not represent actual reality, people who share meaning through dramatic narratives utilize neither fact nor fiction. Instead, they take an inherent reality, like the economy or health care, select a few pertinent items, and present a dramatic narrative that is their characterization interpreted to fit into their version of social reality. This maneuvering between fact and fiction falls within the realm of dramatic narratives.

In dramatic narratives, events are explained to create and sustain shared meaning with other people and to support a specific version of social reality. Much of political social reality is constructed through dramatic narratives that are communicated to help legitimize a politician or to undermine their opponent. They are often given a dramatic, persuasive, or emotional quality to make them more interesting or dramatic. This helps to cut through the Great Abyss, so that people will pay attention to them.

Dramatic narratives can also include heroes and villains, along with characterizations of their actions as being good or bad. A person might cast themselves in their own dramatic narratives as the hero who will save the people from a villain who is out to destroy everything the people hold dear. These dramatic narratives are often action based in order to involve the public who must take action, along with the hero, to save them from a terrible fate if nothing is done. This action can be to support a cause, a politician or policy, donate money, or vote.

Over time, many dramatic narratives can form a recognizable and meaningful view of society that helps to create social reality. The power of social reality lies in its ability to explain our experiences and the world around us reducing uncertainty. It can be used to explain the motivation for people's behavior. The sharing of social reality is a way of creating a common understanding of the world and how it works. The shared meaning contained in dramatic narratives can create a social reality for people. Even though it may or may not accurately reflect actual physical reality, it may be no less real for them. The creation of social reality is motivated by people's need to reduce uncertainty by explaining events in order to make sense of them.

Social reality is created because people want to reduce uncertainty. They want to know about the world around them and social reality can be used to explain and predict physical reality. For instance, people want to know why the economy is bad and when things will get better. They want to know what they can expect from their government and what the government expects from them. These issues are often explained through social reality. This means that social reality can be as important to society as physical reality because much of human interaction and public institutions are socially constructed.

Social reality can be powerful because it tells people how to interpret physical reality and what to do about it. It can be used to explain events by telling people what is happening to them and how they fit in. It tells them what behaviors are accepted and which ones are not. It can serve as a comprehensive explanation of how things work in society. It can also facilitate public confidence in a government by reducing uncertainty about it. People often prefer a reality they have created themselves because it is more comfortable when made up of familiar elements.

Conversion of Social Reality

In order to share their version of social reality, a person must make it attractive to others. There may be some people who are predisposed to them, however, others may share a different version of social reality. When people have a different social reality, they must first be separated from their attachments to the version they currently share. In order to do this, their current shared meanings are often attacked as repugnant, bigoted, racist, or outdated, so that they can be shown how wrong or misguided they really are. When their old social reality is attacked, a person may feel lost, angry, disturbed, or upset.

Once people are persuaded that their old beliefs are wrong, they may feel the need to find a new version of social reality. They may experience a period of uncertainty or struggle. This is when a new social reality is presented to them. This new version is often characterized as fair, just, doing what's right, or open minded. After a period of time, they may come to a new awareness when the new social reality falls into place, so they now see things in a new way reducing their uncertainty. When the conversion process ends, they may feel relieved that their conflict is resolved and uncertainty is reduced. They may be asked to show their commitment to the new social reality with some kind of public action such as volunteering, giving money, or voting.

After a version of social reality has attracted followers, there is the problem of maintaining their commitment. Some groups are able to keep their social reality stable over long periods of time, while others suffer from decline and decay, or may abruptly come to an end. People who have fallen away might be criticized and pressured to return to the new social reality. This can be accomplished by comparing an individual's undesirable behavior and bad character to the ideals contained in the new social reality. The objective is to encourage recognition of their shortcomings, followed by repentance and a renewed commitment to the new social reality. This can help people conform to the demands of the new version of social reality. This helps to keep the people who share the vision committed by maintaining their adherence, as well as to bring back those who have fallen away.

How widely a person or group's social reality is shared can be reflected in their dramatic narratives. One method of observing how well they are shared is though repetition of a particular story. For example, during the course of a campaign, candidates try to reflect on how their messages are being received by the voters. When one catches on, it tends to be repeated and when they do not, they are likely to be dropped. It is the weaving together of many dramatic narratives that share meaning with the public that determines electoral success.

Social reality has a larger, more important function, it can influence who we are as an individual and what kind of person we want to be. It can determine who we are as a people and what kind of nation we want to be. At one time our government and social institutions were only an idea shared by people. It was their vision of what society should be that shaped the world we live in today. It is the shared meanings we have today that will determine what kind of world future generations will live in tomorrow.

Campaigning and The Law of Uncertainty.

An election campaign can be seen as a series of persuasive attempts by both sides to undermine their opponent's legitimacy, while bolstering their own. So, candidates often draw upon forces recognized by the people including traditions, values, beliefs, and popular mandates. Political fortunes seem to be derived from what dramatic narratives candidates utilize to support their legitimacy and convince the people to vote for them. As part of a campaign, candidates create and communicate dramatic narratives in order to make a connection to share meaning with the people. The process of shared meaning is essential to a campaign because it is how a candidate motivates voters not only to vote, but also to support them by campaigning, donating money, or volunteering for them. Sharing meaning is a powerful process because it has the potential to change perceptions and expectations, as well as motivate behavior.

Candidates often utilize established dramatic narratives because the people are familiar with them. This helps to make a candidate's version of social reality more easily understood since these dramatic narratives are ones that the people already know. Candidates need to create their own dramatic narratives that tie into the social reality of the larger society. They accomplish this by affirming common values and beliefs connecting their version to those of their audience.

These are some dramatic narratives that candidates utilize.

1. Restoration. There are times when people feel that in order to move forward to a better future, they need to go back to the past in order to restore something good that has been lost. The restoration dramatic narrative begins in the past when times were good and people

were virtuous. Then there comes a time of troubles that brings on the problems that exist today. They may feel that their problems are due to the people losing their way or that their leaders have become corrupt, so things can be resolved by returning to the values of the past. The attraction of the restoration dramatic narrative is in its ability to maintain previously shared meanings by keeping them intact, while calling for change.

The restoration dramatic narrative has both sacred and secular versions. The religious version is based on the Garden of Eden, which was an idyllic paradise that was lost when Adam and Eve succumbed to temptation and were expelled to live a life of hardship. So, at various times in history, when people suffered a time of hardship they interpreted it as a divine message that they had lost their way and must return to their original values. By restoring their lost values, they will resolve their problems and improve their present condition.

The secular version of the restoration dramatic narrative is based on the values and principles established by the original founders of the nation. The subsequent failure of the government or society to uphold those principles was seen not as a failure of the system of government, but rather a falling away from the true principles upon which the nation was founded. What was needed was to change current values, but this was not a change that turned its back on the past, nor was it a change to something new or foreign. Rather, it was change that returned to traditional values and principles that had been forsaken.

A variation of restoration is the founding. In many groups there is a founding dramatic narrative that tells the story of how an organization, a people, or a nation came into existence. It includes dramatic narratives about how and why it was formed, and the notable people in its history. The founding is important because it is more than just a recounting of the past, it communicates what a group of people stands for, what kind of people belong to it, and how they are expected to behave. For example, the American founding dramatic narrative tells how America was founded, the qualities of the people who founded it, and what it means to be an American. When groups, organizations, or nations find themselves in difficult times, they might utilize restoration as a means of returning to the values and principles of their founding and its founders to restore what made it great.

In an election, candidates may utilize the dramatic narrative of restoration as a means of legitimizing their candidacy and undermining their opponent. A challenger may characterize the incumbent or the party in power as corrupt, having fallen away from the values of the people. If the challenger is elected, they will restore the government to the values that made it great before the current government was elected. In this manner, a challenger seeks to drive a wedge between their opponent and the voters by asserting that their opponent been corrupted or is no longer consistent with the values of the people and must be removed.

2. The rebirth dramatic narrative has a long history in secular and religious rhetoric. It focuses on a person who experiences a defining moment in his or her life that changes or moves them in a new direction. It often begins with their living an aimless life. Then comes a dramatic experience that is characterized as a defining moment, which changes the course of their life. The circumstances of the moment of their rebirth are often recounted in detail and are characterized in an emotional, dramatic narrative style. The rebirth is important to a candidate because it can help to legitimize their candidacy.

3. The persecuted victim dramatic narrative is an old and familiar one in American rhetoric. Many individuals and groups have characterized their problems as the consequence of being unjustly victimized by the system or persecuted by villains out to harm them. These

villains are often characterized as dishonest, unjustly persecuting others for their own personal gain, but it is the people who will ultimately suffer. These villains could not win an honest debate, so they must resort to underhanded tactics abhorrent to the people's values.

4. The American Dream is an old and powerful dramatic narrative that characterizes America as the land of opportunity where anyone can realize his or her potential. It originates from the Declaration of Independence that proclaims all men are created equal and have the right to the pursuit of happiness. The American Dream is about everyone having the opportunity to be successful and prosper. America is a place where everyone is equal regardless of who they are or where they came from. It is about an upwardly mobile society where the next generation will be better off than the last. It is often used because it is familiar to practically everyone, including people all over the world. The American Dream is so powerful that it motivated millions of people to leave their homes and seek a new life in America.

5. A Vision of the Future. Politicians seek to gain legitimacy by presenting a vision of the future that portrays tomorrow as better than today. They may contrast their vision with an alternative vision where the people will be worse off if things do not change. This is designed to increase uncertainty to motivate people to support them. This method of legitimation utilizes the power of the law of investing because if people see future benefits, they are more likely to support them. During an election, a candidate must create and communicate their own vision of the future. Because it represents their purpose for seeking office and what they hoped to accomplish if elected. If they do not clearly articulate a vision of the future, people will be more likely to question their legitimacy. The creation and sharing meaning about a vision of the future is important because it reduces uncertainty about a candidate in the minds of the public.

Election campaigns serve the important function of determining who will govern and the policies they will pursue. However, they also serve larger functions that can be less obvious. Campaigns create and sustain social reality, they both reduce and increase uncertainty, they provide a way to share meaning, and they can encourage or discourage people to invest in society.

The campaign process utilizes the law of uncertainty because it can temporarily increase uncertainty during the campaign and then when the election is over, uncertainty must be reduced because people need to know what to expect from their government. Campaigns temporally increase uncertainty to create separate competing social realities that emphasize the differences between candidates to motivate people to support their candidate.

Campaigns can be thought of as a form of identity management, much like we do as individuals. The desired outcome of an election campaign is for candidates to reduce uncertainty about themselves in the minds of voters. This is often done through a form of controlled self-disclosure, similar to what we do when we meet someone. Candidates use identity management to self-disclose information about themselves utilizing the law of shared meaning, so that the people will become familiar with them to reduce uncertainty motivating them to vote for them.

A candidate must increase uncertainty about their opponent, so that the voters are motivated to vote against them. Negative campaigning is effective because it utilizes the power of uncertainty to make voters angry or fearful, so that they will vote against their opponent. People are more likely to be motivated to vote against a candidate they perceive as unqualified or harmful to them than an average candidate.

Candidates and political parties are often concerned about elections with a low voter turn-out because of how much it can affect the outcome. Perhaps a low or tolerable level of uncertainty explains why there can be low voter turnout in some elections. Rather than the popular conception of voter apathy, voters may not be uncomfortable enough with either candidate to be motivated to vote for any of them.

They may have the perception that either candidate will result in a similar outcome. When uncertainty is tolerable, people may turn their attention to other more pressing concerns and may not be as likely to vote. So, low voter turnout may not necessarily be an expression of apathy, but perhaps a manifestation of reduced uncertainty.

Getting people to turn out to vote can be a significant factor that encourages the negative climate of election campaigns. Negative campaigning can be a powerful motivating force because people are more likely to vote against someone that makes them uncomfortable, angry, or fearful than to vote against someone who may be an average candidate and all right person. The more intense the emotional feeling, the more motivated they may be to support and vote for a candidate. While this approach can be successful, it can increase uncertainty and divisions within society making governing more difficult.

There is a popular belief that many voters wait until it gets close to election day before they decide who to vote for giving candidates time to make a last minute push to get votes. However, voters are likely to form their impressions of the candidates when they first become aware of them much earlier in the campaign. They interpret the verbal and nonverbal messages that come from the media and the candidates themselves that get through The Great Abyss past their filters to form their perceptions.

Political affiliation can be difficult to change because it is a part of a person's social reality. It consists of a person's set of perceptions and expectations about government, current events, and other issues. People subscribe to it because it reduces uncertainty and provides answers to many important questions. It can explain why things are the way they are, even if it is not accurate or based on actual reality. It affects how people select, organize, and utilize information to fit in with their past experiences.

Political affiliation is important because voters can be predisposed to a candidate who shares their own version of social reality. This works similar to how people share social reality in groups, organizations, and communities. In the process of communicating, frames and filters help to determine what information voters pay attention to because they are more likely to utilize information that supports their existing perceptions and expectations.

Voters select, organize, and interpret information that fits in with their expectations, whether it is accurate or not. This means that by the time the campaign gears up and candidates increase their advertising, a significant segment of voters are likely to have formed their perceptions of the candidates and expectations of how they will vote. They will pay attention to information that confirms their perceptions and expectations rather than information that might change them. This may be why much last minute advertising and debates seem to make little difference.

People can be motivated to vote for a specific political affiliation that is congruent with their own version of social reality rather than for the candidate and who they are as a person. They vote for policies and programs they perceive are in their own best interest. This means people can be more likely to vote for concepts, labels, or ideology instead of the individual person because it serves to reduce uncertainty. People may not take the time to develop their own perspective because it can be easier and more socially acceptable to share one of the accepted versions of political social reality.

People may do this for many of the same reasons they form groups such as affiliation, inclusion, or to bolster their self-concept. They are motivated to do this in order to reduce uncertainty and share meaning with others close to them based on proximity, similarity, frequency, and intensity. They take what they perceive and fit it in with what they already know. Candidates and politicians can counter political affiliation influences by being aware of how the laws of uncertainty and shared meaning work to increase awareness of people's needs and wants and how social reality fulfills them.

Governing and The Law of Uncertainty.

From the moment a candidate takes office, they must create a new social reality. After an election, a leader must communicate a new version of social reality that is inclusive of all the people, especially those who voted against them. This new social reality serves to bring people together to reduce uncertainty, so the public can have confidence in their leaders and the government. This helps a candidate make the transformation from a candidate to becoming a leader. Failure to do so can result in political divisions not healing.

Governing and campaigning are different processes. Campaigning is about motivating support, so people are motivated to vote for a candidate, give money, and support their campaign. This often entails being divisive, negative, and casting the opponent as a villain, so that people will be motivated to vote against them. A candidate campaigns to increase uncertainty in the minds of the voters, so their version of social reality must be divisive, critical, and negative, at least in part, because people are more likely to be motivated to vote by feelings of discontent, uncertainty, anger, or fear.

Governing is a different process than campaigning. Governing is about unity, creating consensus, and considering the good of the people. It is about being gracious, consolatory, and working with people including those who disagree with them. A leader needs to build consensus to do what's right for the good of the nation, so they will need a different style of communicating. Rather than increasing uncertainty to garner support, they need to reduce uncertainty in order to make an effective transition from campaigning to governing and from candidate to leader. This transformation is the process of political development that will further a politician's career.

Politicians can go through these levels of political transformation.

1. The campaigner. When a person enters politics they have to find their role like when someone joins a group. They go through the process of behavioral reinforcement in order to get the support of others. Newcomers often utilize the law of uncertainty to capitalize on public discontent with government. They characterize themselves as an outsider who will change things for the good of the people. A campaigner achieves their desired outcome by being divisive increasing uncertainty about their opponent and utilizing conflict to garner support and motivate voters.

2. The politician. Once in office, a politician has to negotiate with several new groups of people in order to get things done. These can include the other members of their elected body like Congress, as well as with staff, committees, bureaucracy, and their political party.

They are likely to go through the process of behavioral reinforcement to negotiate their role in these groups. In order to do this, they will be encouraged to conform to the rules and norms of the group to receive their resources and benefits. This encourages them to go along with others like elected officials and bureaucrats in order to gain their support. A politician is more likely to achieve their desired outcomes through compromise and consensus.

3. The leader. In order to advance politically in government a politician will have to demonstrate that they are a leader who has leadership qualities. They will have to get the support of others to follow them in order to achieve their desired outcomes. They need to bring people together, but they may also need to fight for their supporters to get things done. In order to become a leader, they must demonstrate many of the leadership qualities outlined in Chapter 4.

4. The statesman. This is a leader who has gained widespread respect and esteem from others. They have demonstrated that they have the ability to put the public's interest above their own political interests. They have experience from years of public service. They are more concerned with doing what is right than what is politically advantageous. They have the ability to bring people together to get things done. They tend to stay above the political fray by focusing on the big picture.

Much consideration has been given to why government, particularly in Washington, is broken and doesn't seem to work. A common theme for candidates running for office is to break the gridlock, work across the aisle, and change business as usual. While this persuades people to vote for them, once they are elected little seems to change. So how does this happen?

This can happen because of the power of the law of shared meaning, the law of investing, and the process of behavioral reinforcement. Since an elected body is made up of people, it is subject to the same forces that affect any group or organization. This can occur not just in national government, but in any level of government.

Before candidates run for office, they are a member of groups and organizations in their community. They go through the process of behavioral reinforcement in these groups motivating them to follow the rules of social reality consistent with their community. Once someone is elected to office, they are a new member of a long established group with its own history, rituals, and traditions. This group, whether it's Congress, a legislature, or other elected body will have its own rules of behavior, roles, responsibilities, and norms. There are expectations that comprise a new group social reality that they must adapt to in order to function as a member.

Elected bodies often work much like The Bank as described in Chapter 4. As long as members are accepted by The Bank and abide by its rules, they are allowed to receive its benefits. So, new members of an elected body are likely to go through the process of behavioral reinforcement. They will likely need to negotiate with other members of the group for their place in the group and the resources necessary to do their job. If their behavior is within the acceptable standards, they will receive the benefits and resources of the group.

If it is not, they are likely lose benefits or be reprimanded by the group. This can serve as motivation for members to adapt their behavior from what is considered acceptable by the community that elected them, to what is now considered acceptable as a member of the new group. How this process works is elaborated in more detail in Chapter 4.

Much attention has been given to the influence of lobbyists or special interests on politicians, however, as outsiders they are not able to exert the type of social pressures for conformity exerted by insiders. This is because when a person joins a group, they are dependent upon the other members of the group for many of the resources they need. Because a politician's primary contact is with other politicians and members of the bureaucracy, these groups are able to exert pressure on politicians because they can provide or withhold the resources and connections they need to do their work.

This enables the new group to exert pressure motivating politicians to conform to the expectations and behavior of the group. Since the new group provides resources and rewards, members are likely to change their behavior rather than changing the government. This means that the other members have influence over the behavior of the new members because they must work with them. Since they establish and enforce their own rules, they are the only ones who can effectively change them.

Nelsonian Economics and The Law of Uncertainty

At the dawn of time there were basically two economic activities, hunting and gathering. The development of agriculture created a new economic force in society. Wealth became based on the land and those who had land had wealth. As agricultural methods improved, people had more time to pursue other interests and activities creating economic growth.

Because of the law of uncertainty, economic growth can happen haphazardly and is not always sustained. There may be periods of growth followed by periods of decline. In order to reduce uncertainty, society found ways to sustain economic growth increasing stability through production, reproduction, destruction, substitution, valuation, and legislation.

These are some of the ways society creates economic growth.

- Production. Economic growth occurs through increased productivity, which includes innovation and invention to create new or improved products and services. This can include improvements to existing products or developing more efficient ways to produce them. The motivation for production is to meet the needs and wants of people by providing something of value that is useful to them. This is a preferred method because it encourages sustained economic growth and wealth creation. However, it can be the most difficult way of growing an economy because it takes imagination and hard work, which is why other methods are commonly utilized.

- Reproduction. Economic growth occurs when the population increases to create more consumers. When the population grows and everything else is constant, the economy should grow because more people are buying more things which means more economic activity. This is the easiest way to grow an economy because you don't necessarily have to do anything else. This method of growth occurs through birthrates and immigration. Birthrates increase the size of a population when couples have more than two children. Policies have been favorable to families with children to encourage growth. Some countries have negative birthrates creating concern over their economic future. Growth can also come from people immigrating from other countries. This can be a faster means to increase the population than birthrates, which encourages favorable immigration policies.

- Destruction. This is the process of replacing what we already have with something new. Destruction works in two ways. First, practically everything naturally becomes old, so it may deteriorate, cease to work, become obsolete, or be outdated. The properties of the physical world promotes the law of uncertainty because things get old and naturally decay. Things may also be destroyed through natural processes like extreme weather, so they need to be repaired or replaced with something new. Second, rather than waiting for things to deteriorate, economic growth can be increased by the intentional destruction of what already exists. For example, an existing building is demolished and replaced with a new one. This creates economic activity that is not dependent upon population growth or increasing productivity. At various times in history, war has served this function with increased economic activity to support the war effort followed by periods of economic growth fueled by rebuilding after it's over.

- Substitution. This is replacing something we already have with something else. In order to foster economic growth we either need to create new needs and wants or find new ways to fulfill them. This is done by motivating people to buy new or different things they don't necessarily need. Economic growth can also happen when a want becomes a need. One of the most successful examples of this is the personal computer. It wasn't that long ago that no one had, or even needed a computer. Today, having a computer is considered a need even though it does many things that we could do before having them. Before computers people wrote letters, made phone calls, listened to records, ordered from mail order catalogs, and used film in still and movie cameras. Computers became a necessity by offering new and cheaper ways of doing familiar things.

- Valuation. This involves increasing the value or price of things. The value of things can be based upon people's perceptions and expectations. We invest things with meaning, which gives them value to us. If more people value something, the more willing they may be to pay more for it raising its price. As things become more valuable, they can generate more economic activity. Increasing valuation is a manifestation of the law of shared meaning creating competing needs and wants that are based upon our perceptions and expectations. If our needs are mostly fulfilled, our wants tend to continue to increase. When we fulfill one, we generally move on to another and some wants can become needs. Our expectations of what we should have and the wants that should be fulfilled tends to increase. Managed inflation can provide another means of increasing valuation giving the perception of growth. At times the housing market has provided this kind of growth.

- Legislation. Government often attempts to stimulate economic activity through legislation and spending. It regulates the financial sector, creates monetary policy, sets interest rates, and utilizes other economic measures. Government takes money out of the economy with taxation and redistributes it through spending. This can be the least preferable method of economic growth because of how economic filters work, as described later in this chapter. It can leave fewer resources available for other means of growth.

Wealth creation.

Wealth creation consists of those things that have value, increase value, or create prosperity. It is not necessarily equated with being wealthy, as in having an abundance of money or possessions. A person of any income level can create wealth. Conversely, a person who has an abundance of money or material possessions does not necessarily create wealth. Wealth creation helps people create stability and security in their lives where an abundance of material possessions does not.

Economic activities could be thought of in two ways: making money and creating wealth. While these two may seem similar in that they generate economic activity, they are distinctly different in their outcome. For example, when a person builds a house they make money, but doing so also adds value at each stage of the process creating wealth. This is because the motivation for building a house is based on fulfilling needs and wants to achieve desired outcomes.

The process of wealth creation begins with someone who has land. They grow and harvest trees, which adds value to the land because it provides a useful marketable product. The trees are made into lumber, which adds value to them because lumber is more useful than logs. The builder uses the lumber to build a house along with other materials like bricks, shingles, windows, and appliances. Each of these items goes through a value added process beginning with extracting raw materials from the land to making a finished product that can be used in the house. Value is added at each step along the way as each item is made more useful to fulfill needs and wants creating wealth.

The finished house adds value to the materials that comprise it because a house is more useful to people than a pile of bricks and lumber. The house is built on land that adds value to the land because it fulfills the need for shelter, security, and status. The house attracts more people to live in the area. More houses are built nearby encouraging more people to want to live in the area increasing its value, so the house increases in value. The family borrows money from a bank to buy the house. The bank borrows this money from people in the community like the builder who deposits the money earned from building houses. The family pays interest to the bank, which is used to pay interest on the money deposited by the builder and others.

At each step of the process someone made money because they added value along the line increasing the value of the house. Value is added because each item was changed to make it more useful to fulfill people's needs and wants. As more people need or want these things it makes them more valuable. After several years when the loan is paid off, the house should be worth more than the family paid for it adding value for them.

The second type of economic activity is making money by getting paid for something that does not necessarily add value. For example, after some time has passed, the bank that holds the family's mortgage decides to sell the mortgage to another bank that bundles it with more mortgages into securities and sells them to investors. Each of them receives a fee at each step along the way and everyone makes money. However, this doesn't create wealth because nothing has been done that would add value to the house. It does not make the house any more useful in fulfilling the needs or wants of the family. This difference between making money and adding value is one that encourages wealth creation promoting economic stability and growth.

There are many sources of wealth creation that are used to add value. Land was the first means society used for wealth creation. Wealth came from the land and the products it produced by farming, ranching, logging, and mining. The development of agriculture eliminated the need to hunt and gather so people could stay in one place to fulfill their needs and wants. They invested their time and effort into making improvements to the land by farming, building homes, and creating businesses.

This led to the establishment of property ownership. In some societies much of the land was owned by the aristocracy making it a source of power as well. Increasing numbers of people wanting land and the products that came from it increased its value. Thus, the first methods of wealth creation were based upon working the land and developing its natural resources in order to fulfill needs and wants to reduce uncertainty.

As society advanced, changing needs and wants motivated people to fulfill them not just by working the land, but also by inventing, manufacturing, and selling products. This meant that wealth creation was shifting from the land to manufacturing, trading, commerce, and industry. The law of uncertainty motivates people to make life easier by providing products to fulfill their needs and wants.

To reduce uncertainty people developed manufacturing which utilized raw materials from the land to produce products on a large scale. The growth of industries created jobs, which attracted people to growing cities. This new means of wealth creation added value to the land, the raw materials, and the labor utilized because they were useful to people in fulfilling their needs and wants.

As people were having more of their basic needs fulfilled, they developed new needs and wants, and looked for new ways of fulfilling them. New methods of wealth creation were developed based on intellectual pursuits such as innovation, services, information, and artistic expression. Innovation shifted to not just fulfilling needs and wants, but also creating new ones. Modern conveniences gave people more time to develop more specialized pursuits. As society became more advanced, there was an increasing degree of role specialization as people were spending more of their time on more specific types of tasks. This allowed society to grow and prosper by accomplishing many more different types of things.

Wealth creation became less contingent upon the land and manufacturing, and more on developing new ideas and new ways of doing things. Wealth was not just created by producing something tangible, it was also created by intellectual pursuits and ideas. As economies grew and production methods improved, fewer people were needed to produce the food, raw materials, and products people needed. As people do more things, they need and want more information. So, wealth creation shifted to include areas that created and distributed information.

Job creation as wealth creation.

Economic policy can be a means to encourage job and wealth creation. However, a company can't just simply create a job, because the person hired has to do something that people are willing to pay for, like providing goods or services. It has to be financially supported to add value or create wealth. So, what does it take to create a job? It takes a business or organization that has tasks it needs to accomplish. If there is not a need or want to be fulfilled, then there is no reason to create a job.

Job creation could be thought of in two ways, jobs that are artificially supported or naturally supported. Artificially supported jobs are generally funded by the government or other organization like a foundation grant. Since they do not necessarily create income to support their existence, when the funding ends, the job ends. The money to support publically created jobs is taken from those who might otherwise spend it to buy goods and services that create naturally supported jobs, so they can inhibit economic growth.

The second type of jobs are naturally supported. They are naturally supported because they generate income by producing a product or service people need or want and are wiling to pay for. However, they are subject to uncertainty. If people are not willing to pay for them, there is no need to have the goods or services, and thus no need to have the job.

So, what encourages people to spend money on goods and services that create jobs, so that the people who do them can afford to buy their own goods and services? Uncertainty reduction. Economic uncertainty is reduced when people have reasonable expectations of either getting a return on the money they spend or that they will have enough money in the future to cover what they spend now.

Uncertainty reduction stimulates economic growth and creates jobs because by having a secure job, uncertainty is reduced. People know they will have money in the future, so they may be more willing to spend it now. People's perceptions are formed through the law of shared meaning, by the information they share with others. If people perceive economic uncertainty is high, they are more likely to save more and spend less slowing the economy, whether it is actually bad or not. If they perceive a low degree of uncertainty, they may be more likely to spend and invest more because they have reasonable expectations of getting that money back through income or investments, if not now, in the foreseeable future. This is why an uncertainty index can serve as a vital economic indicator.

Economic uncertainty.

Economic systems can be driven by the power of the laws of uncertainty, shared meaning, and investing. Society has needs and wants that must be fulfilled creating uncertainty as to how this will be accomplished. This motivates people to fulfill them, however, one person cannot do everything and everyone cannot do the same thing, so people specialize by developing a specific vocation or skill.

Through the process of behavioral reinforcement, people develop skills to produce what others need or want. Encouraged by the law of investing, people use their time and resources to create a marketplace that sets the value of these things through negotiation by communicating. This means that communicating could be viewed as a form of economics. People have limited resources like time and money, so they make choices about how to utilize them to achieve economic equilibrium in their lives.

Throughout society, people share meaning about their perceptions and expectations of the economy. They have perceptions about the economy and how well they think they are doing that may or may not reflect actual reality. People have expectations of what they think is a fair return for their investments including not only money, but also their time and energy. When people have reasonable expectations of receiving a fair return and uncertainty is reduced, the economy should benefit. As uncertainty increases, people will share meaning about their perceptions and expectations that can cause them to lose faith reducing the likelihood of investment, and the economy is likely to suffer as a result.

People make choices based upon their perceptions and expectations. Sharing meaning creates social reality that can motivate them to take economic actions. If we expect something to happen, we may look for evidence to support our expectations through the perception process to give meaning to information that may or may not be valid. In the process of communicating, we might filter out information that doesn't fit in with our experiences and we frame perceptions based upon our needs and wants. So, we might only look for information that fits in with what we already know to confirm our expectations. This is how social reality can create physical reality.

The economy can be affected by tension created between the law of uncertainty and the law of investing. It is helpful to have a balance or economic equilibrium between uncertainty reduction and investing rewards in order to create sufficient motivation for people to invest by offering enough of a return to attract them. People are willing to take risks by investing if there is a tolerable level of uncertainty, but they need to feel that they will receive a fair return for their investment.

If uncertainty increases, people are likely to withdraw from the market because they perceive it as potentially too uncertain. This can create an imbalance, disturbing the equilibrium of the market. Public perception of reality can be a more significant motivating factor for behavior than economics because perceptions and expectations can override other considerations such as economic data. This is due to the perception that equilibrium has not yet been achieved, making them unwilling to invest regardless of the potential return.

Interest rates can be perceived as a tangible manifestation of the law of uncertainty, which can affect economic equilibrium. If rates are significantly lowered, such as a means of stimulating the economy, they could instead serve to be a drag on it. This is due to the imbalance and uncertainty they create.

They communicate that the economy is not doing well, so people are more likely to respond by reducing their economic activity. Low rates discourage investors from risking their money by investing. Instead they are likely to withdraw their money waiting for rates to increase. The rationale is that they wouldn't make enough of a return to justify the uncertainty.

This is because low returns do not justify the high level of uncertainty. This means that economic equilibrium is out of balance, so investors are motivated to restore balance by cutting spending. This is how low interest rates could be detrimental to the economy and growth. The balance between uncertainty and investing can be restored through economic equilibrium by setting interest rates at a level that provides a worthwhile return to promote investing, yet is still affordable.

Economic Equilibrium and The Law of Uncertainty

The law of uncertainty motivates how people spend their money, what they spend it on, what they save, and how they invest it. The higher the uncertainty, the more likely people are to cut spending or put their money in safer investments because they don't know what to expect in the future. This can slow down an economy and growth. As uncertainty is reduced, people are likely to feel more comfortable spending and investing more.

The degree of uncertainty people feel can have tangible consequences. There can be times when economic indicators look good, yet economic activity is sluggish making people wonder what is going on. This can be due to the level of uncertainty inhibiting investment. The creation of an Uncertainty Index could be useful to help understand and explain many aspects of public behavior like the economy or consumer sentiment. This could be a national poll of public sentiment used to gauge the level of public uncertainty, degree of shared meaning, and level of investing in many aspects of society including the economy, the president, Congress, and government policies.

People can be motivated by the law of investing to save their money and invest, so that they will have economic security in the future. The higher the uncertainty, the more likely they are to invest in more secure investments. The lower the uncertainty, the less they are likely to think about saving for the future, so they may spend more now. Since people cannot both save and spend the same money, this creates tension between conflicting needs and wants. This tension can be resolved through economic equilibrium.

The law of shared meaning is an important force in economics because public perceptions and expectations can manifest itself in physical reality. If people believe the economy is good, then they are more likely to spend and invest, so it will likely prosper. If the perception is that the economy is bad, they are more likely to reduce or withdraw their investment. They may reduce or stop spending to protect themselves from what they perceive as economic uncertainty.

People make economic decisions based upon the information that they have available to them. Much of the information they utilize comes from people they know and through the media. This information is filtered through the perception process creating expectations that motivates behavior. The gap between perceptions and expectations can be a source of satisfaction or dissatisfaction that can increase or decrease uncertainty. These perceptions and expectations can be based upon reality or their perception of reality to determine their economic activity.

It's helpful to be aware of how our expectations can influence our perceptions because they have the potential to create their own form of social reality. Economic equilibrium is not just about balancing income and costs, it's about what actions people take in order to reduce economic uncertainty. If there's the perception of high uncertainty, people may look for evidence to confirm it.

They can be motivated to do this because the information they perceive makes them uncomfortable and being uncomfortable motivates them to take action. If they think that they may be at risk, they are likely to look for information to confirm their expectations. They may overlook or filter out information that contradicts their expectations because it does not fit in with what they think they know.

We can avoid this happening by keeping our perceptions in line with reality and going to the source of the information. By finding out for ourselves what someone actually said or what the numbers really are, we do not have to rely on what others tell us. Getting information for ourselves takes time and energy, so all too often people listen to what others say rather than finding out for themselves.

There are times when people might disrupt their economic equilibrium and live beyond their means by spending more than they make. They may do this because they have the expectation that their economic behavior in the present will be balanced by future benefits. This is often done when a person gets an education, buys a house, or starts a business. They may have the expectation that their income or the value of their house or business will continue to increase in the future, so they will be able to balance what they are spending and borrowing now with what they expect to gain later.

This means that they are willing to make an investment by going into debt now because they have the expectation that it will work to their advantage and they will be better off in the future, which can create economic equilibrium.

Types of spending.

Practically everyone has some income and how they spend it can determine their future economic viability. Consider the following types of spending.

1. Consumable. These are goods or services that are intended to be used up or discarded. They have little or no value soon after we purchase them. They can include things that fulfill many of our most fundamental needs like food and energy.

2. Durable. These are things that lose value, but at a slower pace. They generally fulfill needs and wants for many years, at the end of which they have significantly less value. These can include items like vehicles, clothing, and appliances.

3. Appreciable. These are items that tend to gain value over time. They can be a major investment like a house or smaller ones like antiques or collectibles.

4. Speculative. These are assets that can gain or lose value over time. They can include stocks or commodities like gold.

5. Static. These are assets that are relatively stable with little appreciable gain or loss over time. They may collect interest to keep pace with inflation. The most common are cash and savings accounts.

We all have to make purchases to fulfill our needs and wants. What we buy and what percentage of our income goes for what kinds of purchases affects our economic well being. While we would like to buy appreciable assets, most of the things we buy to fulfill our needs and wants are consumable, followed by durable items. In times of economic distress we may have to sell appreciable assets to buy consumables, reducing future economic security. This makes it important to purchase appreciable items, like a house. We all need shelter and buying it turns rent, a consumable, into an appreciable expenditure. This helps to maintain financial stability by creating wealth, so we can keep more of the money we earn.

Economic filters.

We have needs that must be fulfilled in order to live. Since we have limited resources, we have to prioritize how we use them. This creates tension between our needs and wants, and the resources we have to fulfill them. Economic equilibrium is how we resolve this tension to reduce economic uncertainty.

The following economic filters determine how this is done.

1. Fulfilling needs. We all have needs that must be fulfilled in order to live. These include things like food, shelter, clothing, health care, insurance, transportation, and utilities. If all our money goes to pay for these things we have nothing left for anything else. While we might try to budget for these, how much they cost can often be out of our control.

2. Paying taxes. Most of the time we have little control over how much this costs because government sets the rates. Taxes not only include federal income tax, but also state, corporate, property, and sales as well as many other types of fees. It can also include health care. While federal income tax is the most debated, it is just a portion of the taxes people pay.

3. Fulfilling wants. After fulfilling needs and paying taxes, we use some of the money that is left over to fulfill our wants by purchasing goods and services. This includes consumer spending that often drives the economy and economic growth. So, the more money that is left in the economy at this point, the more there is to create jobs and create wealth.

4. Donations to charity or causes. If we have money left over, we might use it to help others and the more we have left, the more we can help them. Sometimes people put helping others by making donations before fulfilling their own wants.

5. Savings and investments. Once people have met their basic needs, paid taxes, and bought what they want, the money they have left over has to go someplace. Since few people put their money in their mattress, this money is saved or invested in bank accounts, stocks, real estate, businesses, and other investments. The more people have by this level, the more that is available for wealth creation. So, maximizing this level by reducing the other levels is important for economic growth, job creation, and wealth creation.

The less money that is removed by each filter, the more there is available for the rest. We often have little choice of how much we spend for the first two filters, but we have more control over the last three. Removing as little money as possible in the first two filters can benefit the economy and economic growth because the last three items involve how much people have left to spend on goods and services, to donate, and to invest, which stimulates the economy and wealth creation.

Considering the nature of how economic filters function, liberals should be promoting conservative policies to encourage economic growth because this can provide the increased income necessary to support progressive programs. Conservative policies can exist without liberalism because they promote economic growth, but progressive programs cannot exist on their own because they do not necessarily add value or foster the wealth creation necessary to finance them. It doesn't make sense to promote job creation, while increasing taxes and regulatory burdens on those who create them costing jobs.

In order to meet the cost of fulfilling needs, people need a minimum income. If they have a low income, they may have trouble meeting their basic needs leaving little left over for everything else. At this income level, any taxes a person pays would erode their quality of life by making them less able to fulfill their needs, increasing uncertainty.

There could be a baseline set at the median income level under which people would pay no income taxes. This means that half of all households would pay no taxes. This would not have a serious negative impact on revenue because the bottom half of all taxpayers pay a negligible amount of federal income taxes. The rationale is that paying even a small amount in taxes has a more serious negative impact on the quality of life of lower income taxpayers than taxpayers making over the median income paying higher taxes.

It might seem that raising tax rates would increase tax revenues, however, the result has often been the opposite. Due to the law of uncertainty, when tax rates have been raised revenues have often declined because people will seek to reduce uncertainty in order to restore economic equilibrium. This is because increased taxes motivate people and businesses to find ways to shelter their income to avoid paying them. Upper level earners and big corporations can afford to structure their investments to utilize tax shelters to reduce the taxes they pay.

In a global marketplace, capital looks for economic equilibrium. This motivates it to move away from high tax areas to those with lower tax rates. Companies move to states or countries with the lightest corporate tax burden. Their primary desired outcome is survival, so they will make economic decisions that are in their best interest or risk going under.

Tax policy could be used to restore economic equilibrium to foster economic growth. Corporate rates should be cut and indexed. Small and new businesses should pay little or no tax for the first few years to help them get started. A high number of businesses fail in the first few years and reducing their tax burden should help them succeed. Capital gains should also be reduced to foster economic growth and wealth creation. Social Security could be reduced and indexed, and the income cap removed. Benefits should also be indexed, so high earners receive no benefits because they don't need them. Low earners would receive full benefits because Social Security should be a safety net for those who truly need it.

Increasing taxes can be counterproductive to economic growth because higher earners and big corporations can afford to utilize tax shelters or move to lower tax locations, which reduces revenues. Given how economic filters work, this also reduces the capital available for growth, job creation, and wealth creation. Since this lost revenue must be replaced, it will certainly place a greater burden on middle and lower earners who are the people who can least afford them, as well as increasing deficits and the national debt.

Reducing the tax burden on everyone has a benefit to society because there is a balancing point of economic equilibrium where people and corporations make a decision between paying high taxes or actively lowering their taxes by pursuing tax shelters. Above this point it's more cost effective to take action to pay less in taxes. While doing this may come at a cost, it is done because it will ultimately save money.

Below this point the cost of sheltering income to reduce taxes is no longer cost effective, so it becomes cheaper to simply pay the taxes. This is the point of economic equilibrium, which is based on people's perceptions of what they believe is fair and their expectations of a fair return on their investment.

Society and the Law of Uncertainty

How do you know what you know? How do you know what is true? In the past people developed knowledge that they believed to be true, which we now know is not. Consider that, a second century astronomer determined that the sun and all the planets revolved around the earth. In medieval times, it was thought that alchemy could turn lead into gold. In colonial times, some women were thought to be witches. More recently, it was thought that cigarettes had health benefits because they were both a stimulant and relaxant.

So, how do we know that what we believe today is true? How do we know what we consider to be true today might be proven to be not true in the future? Since people utilize the law of shared meaning to create knowledge as a part of their social reality, this raises an important question. If enough people decide that something is right, does that make it right? Some societies thought that human sacrifices or the burning of witches was right. So, what are we doing today that we consider right because some people perceive it's right, but may not be in the future?

Throughout history people of different cultures from different geographic regions had similar experiences, faced similar problems, and accomplished similar tasks. They often had the same needs and wants that they sought to fulfill. How a society creates and disseminates knowledge can determine how they solve problems to fulfill their needs and wants. Even though they have many similarities, they developed distinctly different solutions often based upon their own unique social reality.

So, how do we come to know what we know? We all have our own way of obtaining information to know what we know. Much of what we know we learn through our education and experiences. This can make it difficult to change what people already know because they may resist new information, perhaps even becoming defensive.

Rather than spending time and energy trying to convince them to change what they know, challenge them to think beyond what they know to gain new knowledge. This can help motivate people to think beyond what they perceive as true. People may resist changing what they believe to be true, but they are less likely to want to be perceived as being unwilling to learn something new. Do they feel that they already know everything there is to know, so they don't need to know anything new?

When we want to know something, how do we find out about it? We might ask others who have experience. We might look to the past to see how it was done before. We may look to forces larger than ourselves to gain inspiration through spiritual revelation. Some societies gained knowledge from sacred texts that looked to the knowledge of the past. We may look at what's available to us in the present using methods like trial and error. We could utilize the scientific method to create new knowledge in the future.

We create knowledge in these ways to help us understand the world around us.

- Perceiving. Gaining knowledge through our five senses; sight, sound, touch, taste, smell.
- Doing. Gaining knowledge through experience by participating.
- Thinking. Gaining knowledge through education, rationality, logic, or scientific inquiry.
- Believing. Gaining knowledge through religion or faith by trusting in something unseen.
- Realizing. Gaining knowledge through instinct or revelation.
- Feeling. Gaining knowledge through intuition, emotions, or empathy.

Knowledge is not just about how we gain information, it's also about how we use it based on our social reality. Gaining new knowledge works like the perception process where we select, organize, and interpret information to give it meaning so it fits in with what we already know. How this happens is influenced by the law of uncertainty. When we feel uncertainty, we are more likely to be open to new knowledge.

When uncertainty is reduced, people can feel more sure about themselves and what they are doing, so they may not be open to new ideas or different ways of thinking. When someone is overly certain, they are not necessarily open to other ideas. Throughout history, many people were certain about things they believed to be true, which has sometimes resulted in disastrous consequences.

Society and social reality.

Throughout history many societies have risen and fallen. Some became great while others never developed. Some still have an influence on us today hundreds, even thousands of years later. Some became great for only a short time while others existed for hundreds of years. Great societies throughout history have shifted geographic locations around the world. So, how does a society make great advances only to fall into decline? Consideration has been given to pivotal moments in history, prominent individuals, discoveries, inventions, and the availability of natural resources.

The power of social reality can be a significant motivating force that influences the development of society. Social reality is driven by the law of uncertainty because it motivates people's behavior exerting pressures to conform as a means of social control to cope with physical reality. It does this by creating expectations of what is acceptable behavior, enforced with rewards and punishments. Social reality can be a positive force encouraging people to develop new ideas, inspire creativity, encourage innovation, motivate people to take action, and communicate ideas with one another.

Examining how uncertainty drives innovation and creativity can help us understand how to improve society and our quality of life. The process of communicating can be applied to examining the means by which people's ideas become physical reality. Discoveries and inventions are facilitated by the social reality we share because there first has to be the right conditions to encourage people to think differently about things and then communicate their Great Idea to others. Innovation can create a great society when social reality encourages people to develop new ideas and new ways of doing things to make them a reality.

Throughout history, changes in social reality have changed the nature of society. In the Middle Ages, social reality was based on The Church and religious texts of the past. This social reality was changed by The Reformation and The Renaissance. Changes in social reality allowed the introduction of the scientific method, which created of new knowledge through research. This resulted in changes in physical reality that were so useful in advancing society they are still utilized today.

When an idea is communicated and accepted by the members of a society it is more likely to become a reality. This makes the conceptual process that precedes the creation of physical reality especially important. How information like your Great Idea is communicated through connections between people can determine how it can manifest itself in physical reality. Advancements in society are motivated by the law of uncertainty because it makes people look beyond what they already know to understand what they don't know.

How society reduces uncertainty can be a critical factor in how that society advances and if it becomes a great society or not. There have been many ideas and inventions that existed as a Great Idea long before social reality allowed them to gain the acceptance necessary to become a reality. People refer to this when they say things like, it was ahead of its time.

Excessive uncertainty can be detrimental for society. If uncertainty is too high, people may be less able to get things done because they are more concerned about their own safety and stability. This can discourage people from investing in one another or themselves. Conversely, excessive uncertainty reduction can also be detrimental because it can lead to arrogance and overconfidence creating a lack of awareness. It can remove the motivation to act and do things that increased uncertainty would provide.

Excessive uncertainty reduction can be harmful particularly when everything is decided at the top such as by government. It reduces the motivation for innovation and creation by inhibiting people's motivation to take action to do things. This is why some forms of government such as socialist, communist, and authoritarian cease to function effectively and often fail because they have reduced some types of uncertainty to a point that it inhibits innovation by reducing the motivation for people to develop new ideas and ways of doing things. This balance of the tension between uncertainty and uncertainty reduction is a part of establishing economic equilibrium.

Advancements in society can be motivated by the law of shared meaning because it facilitates the creation and dissemination of ideas between people. Societies that are able to share meaning encourage understanding, foster creativity, and promote innovation because they share a sense of common identity and commitment.

However, if a society is unable to share meaning, it can inhibit them from communicating with one another and creating a shared social reality. This might happen when they do not share a common language or common culture. When people have difficulty communicating with one another, society can become fragmented creating competing social realities.

When a society becomes removed from the social reality that made it great, it can begin to fragment leading to competing factions that can cause it to deteriorate. When increasing numbers of people become more disconnected, they are less able to communicate or share meaning. When they have fewer connections with one another, social reality can break down hastening its decline. When segments of society try to impose their specialized version of social reality on others, it can lead to societal fragmentation, which can undermine a great society so it declines and decays.

Fracturing social reality.

The story of the Tower of Babel tells how the whole earth was of one language and the people were one. Nothing was restrained from them and what they imagined to do. Nothing they planned to do was impossible for them. In response, God confounded their language so they would not understand one another and scattered them all over the earth. Now, they were no longer able to work together and did mistrust one another. When people share a common social reality they can foster creation and innovation. When it fragments, society can cease to function as effectively.

In order for a society to function, people must be able to communicate with others. They need to build trust in order to invest their resources in each other and in society. One of the mechanisms that allows people to do this is social reality. When there is a clear unified social reality, society has a basis for making the connections that helps it to function effectively.

However, as society developed people engaged in increasing role specialization. While this can be helpful in furthering the development of specialized expertise, people are more likely to spend increasing amounts of their time communicating only with people who are like themselves to the point where they no longer have connections with others outside their network. This change has the potential to make society fragmented.

Role specialization and advancement can fragment society as people do more kinds of things. For instance, there was a time when the majority of people lived in rural farming communities. They shared similar experiences and communicated about things that were familiar to them creating a shared social reality. Most of their social reality was created by communicating directly with people who they knew. They had the knowledge and skills to be self reliant, fulfilling many of their needs and wants in their own communities.

This self reliance helped them make it through the Great Depression and win two World Wars. As times changed, more people moved to the cities and suburbs, worked in increasingly specialized jobs, and got the things they needed from others like from a store. They became less self reliant becoming increasingly dependent on a system where others provide almost everything needed for their survival. This changed their social reality.

Social reality can potentially change in two ways, people change it or events change it for them. Throughout history there have been many pivotal moments that have changed social reality affecting people's behavior. A few of these include the rise of Ancient Greece, the fall of Rome, the Magna Carta, the Reformation, the Renaissance, and self determination embodied in the American Revolution. It is through people's experiences that help build culture providing the basis for shared meaning that forms social reality.

The law of uncertainty has a way of changing social reality. Sometimes it can happen abruptly, while other times it happens more subtly with change going practically unnoticed. One method of change is through a crisis. In a crisis, people make changes to adapt to their new circumstances in order to restore economic equilibrium. The Great Depression was an economic and agricultural crisis that motivated people to change their behavior in order to survive.

The longer a crisis persists, the more likely changes will become comfortable making a return to past ways more uncomfortable after the crisis ends. Returning to the ways of the past can be perceived as increasing uncertainty because they may be perceived as having contributed to creating the crisis. If the new behaviors helped alleviate the crisis, then they will be perceived as reducing uncertainty and are more likely to be kept. The Depression was a long term crisis that motivated the behavior of the people it affected for a very long time after it was over, creating a social reality of hard work and saving that still exists today.

If a society does not share meaning through common experiences that they invest with meaning, then two or more competing social realities could develop. While society is motivated by the law of uncertainty to create social reality, there can be two or more competing social realities. When a society has competing social realities, it has the potential to become divided.

For instance, the nature of social reality would significantly change again during the 1960's with the Vietnam War, which was another long term crisis. Instead of uniting society with a single social reality, it would divide society creating two competing social realities. Many decades later this legacy has manifested itself in the liberal and conservative divide in society.

Since then, no one single shared social reality has fully emerged to replace the one of the Great Depression and the World Wars. Intervening events fractured the old social realities creating several competing new ones. Conservatism and liberalism are two well known competing versions of social reality. When there are two competing social realities there needs to be a release of the tension that is created. Social reality does not develop overnight. It can take years, perhaps decades for it to manifest itself in physical reality.

Social reality has changed in the past, so it will change in the future. When the existing social reality changes, what will take its place? Since the law of uncertainty can motivate us to take action or events will make us change, if this tension is not resolved there is a high likelihood of a crisis occurring to change social reality again.

Changing social reality.

Throughout history people have changed their social reality including the structures and institutions of society. Even today, we see different cultures and countries taking very different approaches to how they structure society. As social reality changes, people change how they do things including how they fulfill their needs and wants.

When change is implemented, it's important that it reduces uncertainty by providing stability and structure. There have been times when change has made circumstances worse leading to chaos, even anarchy. Populist revolts may overthrow a dictator, but then what takes its place? This can leave a power vacuum that may be filled by a government even more repressive than the one it replaced.

There are some ways that people create and change social reality.

- Restoration. This is the need to return to a former state that existed in the past. For example, we need to restore our country to the ideals that made it great.

- Preservation. This is the need to keep something we have that we are in danger of losing. For example, we are in danger of losing The American Dream, so we need to keep it strong for future generations.

- Construction. This is the need to create and build something new. For example, we need to create a new tax system that is fair for everyone.

- Destruction. This is the need to get rid of those things that hold us back or have harmed us because they are no longer useful. For example, we must eliminate wasteful regulation that costs jobs.

- Conservation. This is the need to hold on to what we have for the future. For example, we need to save the environment and conserve our natural resources.

There can be some people and groups who try to change social reality to achieve their own desired outcomes by motivating others to do what they want them to do. In order to change social reality, they will first try to detach others from their current social reality. This can be done by characterizing the old social reality as outdated, backward, or out of touch. They may try to demonize people who represent the old reality by characterizing them as selfish, evil, corrupt, or not having people's best interest at heart. More extreme approaches might characterize the old social reality as repugnant, elitist, racist, or discriminatory.

Once people have been shown how they have been deceived or were misled in the past (even though they have not been) they should be open to making amends, which means that they must change their behavior. If they can be detached from their old social reality, then there will be a void created by the law of uncertainty that they will feel motivated to fill.

When people are looking for answers is when they can be more open to an alternative social reality. This is when some people, who are out for their own gain, might try to convince them that their way is the right way by providing them a new social reality. It might be one that furthers their own agenda or desired outcomes. The new reality is often characterized in positive terms like being fair, just, fashionable, environmental, affordable, or equitable.

If there is dissent, it can be characterized in negative terms to suppress it and punish those who might object. If a person's argument cannot be discredited, then their opponent will try to discredit their character as an individual, so that others will be reluctant to listen to their message. This can include calling people close minded, bigoted, haters, or elitist. These methods can be effective because they alter people's perceptions. They are often used when there is the lack of a valid argument because people do not want to be perceived as having these negative characteristics or associating with people who do.

The following are some methods that have been used to change social reality in groups, organizations, and society to achieve specific desired outcomes. Some of these could be helpful, while others could be considered manipulative or unethical. They are included to increase your awareness of how they can work because they are often utilized.

- Communicate the need for change. How much people are willing to change depends upon their needs and wants, perceptions and expectations, and the amount of uncertainty they will tolerate before they are motivated to resolve it. They are unlikely to risk increasing uncertainty by changing something that is familiar unless they perceive doing so will improve their situation or relieve tension. People can be more likely to change if the need for change is communicated along with the reasons why the current situation is undesirable, and failure to change it will result in serious consequences.

- Provide evidence. Providing evidence for the need to change helps to motivate people to change. Practically any position can be supported by some evidence depending on how it is perceived and communicated. This has been done by using false arguments or fallacies, which are described in more detail in Chapter 2. Sometimes they take evidence used by the opposing position and turn it around to support their argument. Some evidence may be contrived by being selectively chosen to support a specific desired outcome. Statistics, testimony, experts, and eyewitnesses can be altered to provide evidence to fit practically any argument. If people feel that they are thoughtful, rational, and intelligent they are likely to be persuaded if evidence is presented in a rational manner. So, careful consideration should be given to determine if evidence presented is skewed, altered, incomplete, obsolete, or manipulated to achieve a specific desired outcome.

- Get people involved in making the change. Giving people something to do helps them to feel that they have an investment in the process, which can make them more likely to support it. One of the main reasons that programs and policies fail or don't get support is that the public is not given a role with something to do. Utilize the law of investing, if the outcome is linked to their self-concept then they have a stake in its success and are more likely to work for a successful outcome. It's easy to criticize what others do, but it's more difficult to criticize something when you are a part of it.

- Characterize change as temporary. When something is temporary it can be more acceptable because it is less threatening. Once people get used to the new temporary situation or forget about the change, uncertainty will be reduced making it more likely that they will accept the change, so it can be made permanent.

- Set achievable goals. People have an easier time making small incremental changes rather than large ones. The degree of change that is acceptable to someone is based upon their perception of the current situation before the change and their perception of the situation afterwards. If the difference is small, it is less perceptible making it more acceptable. Small changes made slowly and quietly over time should not increase uncertainty enough for people to become concerned. Since the degree of change is based upon perception of the comparisons of the two states, the closer they are the less likely people are to notice. Everyone knows that things have to change and most change takes place within reasonable limits. If the change is too big, it is more noticeable increasing the likelihood of it being resisted because it raises uncertainty above what is tolerable.

- Communicate a vision of change. Engage people's imagination by creating a view of the future that is better than today. This can motivate people to change by portraying it as reducing uncertainty to fulfill needs and wants by providing people with benefits. They may create a sense of urgency by characterizing the present circumstances as intolerable or unsustainable. They might contrast their positive vision of the future with a negative vision where everyone will be worse off if there was no change. This can help to reduce feelings of uncertainty about what change will be like in the future.

- Present change as an opportunity. The law of investing can be a powerful motivator for change because people want others to invest in relationships to help them fulfill their needs and wants. People want to improve their self-esteem and how others perceive them to gain respect and prestige. So, present change as an opportunity for people to demonstrate their intelligence, courage, altruism, or open mindedness. It can be used as a means to improve their personal or professional life, social status, or material benefits.

- Move the furniture. People are more likely to communicate with those who are in close proximity, who share similar backgrounds, are involved in doing similar tasks, or with whom they come in frequent contact. In order to control power in groups, the connections that determine how people communicate can be altered by utilizing spatial relations and frequency of contact to change behavior. Changing the physical or communicating structures forces people to communicate within that structure changing their behavior. For example, in order to reduce the power of a group, move them around or break them up so that they have more difficulty communicating with one another.

- Utilize social pressure. Encourage change by creating social pressure because people want to get along with others in order to fit in. When a person's behavior fits in with the norms of a group or society, others are more comfortable investing their resources in them because of the perception of reduced uncertainty. This works rather like The Bank described in Chapter 4. People can be motivated to change by appealing to their need for acceptance and inclusion. They are more likely to change and engage in behaviors that are considered socially acceptable because they perceive that by conforming they will have needs and wants fulfilled and achieve their desired outcomes.

- Utilize allocation of resources. Change can be motivated by pressuring individuals and organizations that provide resources to withdraw their support for those who resist change. If they cut off their resources like money, it can provide a strong motivation to change. If a group or individual resists change, they may be persuaded by identifying their needs and wants and either fulfilling them or cutting them off from others who fulfill them.

- Appeal to fairness and open mindedness. This approach can be used to motivate well meaning people to get them to do what others want them to do for their own gain. People like to be perceived as being reasonable and open minded rather than disagreeable or closed minded. When people are reluctant or resist doing what others want them to do, they may try to motivate them by characterizing them as closed minded, unfair, disagreeable, obstructionist, discriminatory, haters, or troublemakers, even though they are not.

- Create a diversion. Magicians use sleight of hand to divert our attention to perform their illusions. In the movies, when a character wants to do something that they don't want others to notice, they create a diversion to distract attention from their actions. Change can be a matter of perception, people filter out information that they do not find useful. They make choices about what information to perceive. To help implement change, some people may create an issue that gets attention, so people will be distracted and not notice the change.

- Uncertainty can intentionally be created to give the perception that there is a need for change. The law of uncertainty can motivate change by making people uncomfortable. If people perceive there is increasing instability due to uncertainty, they are likely to become increasingly uncomfortable motivating them to take action. They may even want government or some other authority to restore stability.

- People may be motivated to change by their perceptions based upon false information created to manipulate perceptions to achieve a specific desired outcome. This can motivate people to focus on the danger of an impending crisis that must be resolved. This can make people more open to change because they may now perceive that they are faced with a potential threat that could undermine their safety and security, even though it may not be true.

- Present a plan. If there is the perception that the current situation is unsustainable, it can increase uncertainty motivating people to want to take action to reduce it. They are likely to support a plan that reduces uncertainty if it makes things easier for them. Some people might take advantage of this to achieve an ulterior desired outcome. They may present it before others have time to think of one for themselves. They present several alternatives, all but one are either unpleasant, unworkable, or variations of the same plan. This leaves only one workable solution, which is their ulterior desired outcome giving the impression that there is a choice, when there is really none. If there is opposition, they might say that the time for talk is over, it's time to take action. This is done so people do not have time to form their own ideas.

- Use negativity. Characterizing something as negative can be more motivating than as positive. This is because if circumstances are perceived as being positive, uncertainty will likely be reduced so there is little discomfort to motivate people to change. Negativity can make people feel more uncomfortable increasing uncertainty making circumstances less tolerable motivating people to do something about it so that they will feel more comfortable. One way people motivate others to change is to make them angry or uncomfortable by increasing uncertainty to the point where it's no longer tolerable. This can be done by portraying circumstances as increasingly uncertain and unstable, so the desired change must be implemented. People are more likely to change things they perceive as intolerable, unacceptable, or harmful, whether they are or not.

- Use emotion. Emotion can be a powerful motivating force for change. People are more likely to be moved by emotion than logic because it appeals to personal needs and wants. We all want to feel good, that we can make a difference, and that we are a good person who does the right thing. Some people might use these needs and wants to manipulate others to take action through use of emotion. Emotion is often utilized when rational appeals do not work or are not as effective. Common emotional appeals include sympathy, empathy, anger, and fear. Using these methods can be risky because they could make people feel that they are being manipulated.

- The ticking bomb. Movies create drama and tension by showing a ticking bomb while the hero tries to find it and disarm it. In social reality, some people may use a false crisis or an impending artificial deadline to create tension or drama to provide motivation for change. Change is presented as the only way to diffuse the perceptual 'ticking bomb.' If the prescribed change is not implemented as rapidly as possible or before the false deadline, dire consequences will result. For instance, programs are more likely to be supported if the fate of the world is at stake rather than if it's a good thing to do. This approach is meant to create an emotional visceral reaction, rather than a rational analysis of the situation.

- Give them a push. Some people might use extreme methods to motivate people to change. Most people would never jump out of a window, yet if a building was on fire people might jump. So, to motivate people there are some who might figuratively set the building on fire. They do this by making people feel that they are in imminent danger to motivate them to do things that they otherwise might not do. They are motivated because the danger is usually more extreme than the potential consequences of the action they take. This could be very real danger such as a crisis or could be false danger created by perception. People may create a sense of urgency to take action so there isn't time to verify the information or to come up with alternatives. This can make them more likely to take the solution presented to them.

Once change has taken place, people may not like it. They may find it difficult or uncomfortable and want to undo it by going back to the past or previous situation. Other people might want to make the change permanent. These methods have been used to keep them from undoing change or doing what they want to do.

- Use the law of uncertainty. The past can be more familiar making it attractive increasing uncertainty about future change. So, people may try to alter perceptions casting the old way in negatives terms or as unsustainable. They will try to reduce the perception of uncertainty about the new way. They may characterize it using attractive qualities such as being innovative, environmental, open minded, progressive, or cost effective whether it is or not. This can increase uncertainty about the old way and anyone who supports it.

- Use the law of shared meaning. Traditions and rituals are a way that we share meaning to keep the past relevant today and for the future. Shared meaning tells us what is important in society, it helps share mutual expectations, and it creates common ground. It utilizes the law of shared meaning to communicate what is important and valued by society. It is the means by which we invest words, symbols, and behaviors with meaning. While most of these things develop naturally over time, they can also be artificially created or altered to facilitate change.

- Use the law of investing. Some people may utilize the power of the law of investing by giving people the perception that they have a say in the decisions that affect them. When others feel that they have a stake in the outcome, they can have a greater investment in maintaining and enforcing change. If they have a stake in the outcome, they can see it as part of their self-concept making them more likely to stay with the change in order to keep the respect of others whether they actually like it or not. Putting their self-concept at stake increases the likelihood they will make the change permanent.

- Use needs and wants. People are motivated to take action to fulfill needs and wants, so they are more likely to respond positively to change if they have the perception that it better fulfills them than the ways of the past. Change can be made permanent by fulfilling these needs and wants. If people feel that they are receiving fair rewards that meet their expectations, then they will focus less on the negative aspects of change. If that's not possible, the perception can be created that they will have their needs and wants fulfilled at some unspecified time in the future. This is because if the perception of future rewards is strong enough or the current situation is uncertain enough, people will be encouraged to implement change without expecting immediate rewards.

- Traditions and rituals help to reduce uncertainty by sharing meaning about what it means to be a member of society. They help us to make connections with one another by sharing common values, experiences, and emotions to invest them with meaning. Traditions and rituals may be used to motivate people to take action to fulfill specific desired outcomes because they provide rewards. They can help people let go of the way they did things in the past by replacing them with something they perceive as beneficial in the future, making them more receptive to change.

- Once change has been made, some people may argue that the old ways of doing things may need to be removed or destroyed so others are unable to return to them. Past structures or institutions may need to be discarded so they cannot be reused. This is because if change is perceived as not going well, people may be motivated to return to their old ways. If uncertainty is perceived as being too high after the change, there will be motivation to reduce the uncertainty by returning to the ways of the past because they are familiar. In order to keep people from doing this, the destruction of the ways of the past ensure that they cannot be returned to in the future. This helps to make change permanent because no one can easily undo it once it's done.

Not all change has to happen in this manner. These are some examples of how some people and groups force their version of change on others to achieve their own desired outcomes.

Changing social reality can be for the good to benefit everyone if people are aware of what is happening and have a say in what it will become. Rather than approaching change as negative, it can be a positive force for good to help people and improve their quality of life.

Perhaps the most famous example of changing social reality occurred with the American Revolution. When the American founding fathers declared independence from Great Britain, they did not march on London or camp out in Trafalgar Square. They did not go around looting English shops or overturning and burning carriages.

Instead, they prepared a plan to legitimize the new nation and its governmental structure. They formed the Continental Congress and wrote the Bill of Rights, the articles of Confederation, and the Declaration of Independence, which clearly defined their plan for a new nation.

Everyone knew what the new nation stood for and what they were going to do reducing uncertainty. They shared meaning about freedom and democracy that people the world over have invested in for themselves and their families. It was so well thought out it created a stable structure that has provided a model for many nations and has endured for over two centuries.

The Decade of Uncertainty

The first decade of the new millennium could be known as the decade of uncertainty be-cause of the pivotal events that shaped and defined it. Never before in the history of man-kind have so many people experienced such a high degree of uncertainty. Political, social, environmental, and economic uncertainty encircled the globe and affected all of us.

Even before the decade began, Y2K created a significant increase in worldwide uncertainty over the fear of what might happen just after midnight on January 1, 2000. It was feared that computer systems around the world would crash causing destructive events like bank ac-counts to be wiped out, planes and trains to crash, electricity and water to shut down, even nuclear missiles to launch. While none of these predictions materialized, it created a high degree of uncertainty that motivated people to take action like stockpiling food and water.

In November 2000, for the first time in history the U.S. Presidential election did not deter-mine who would be the president of the United States. For over a month, no one knew who would be the leader of the free world. Even after it was resolved, many people questioned the legitimacy of the election increasing uncertainty. The next year marked an unprec-edented terrorist attack that sharply increased global uncertainty motivating extraordinary actions including increasing security measures around the globe and two wars.

The decade was marked by increasing uncertainty from natural and environmental disasters including earthquakes, hurricanes, tsunamis, an oil spill, and a nuclear disaster. Uncertainty was dramatically increased when established protocols for dealing with these emergencies failed, making people question their effectiveness and the government's ability to cope. The decade was capped with a financial crisis, falling home prices, bank failures, business bankruptcies, and the stock market crash. The government's response including economic stimulus efforts failed as well. People experienced escalating fuel and food prices.

As the decade was ending and the new one was beginning, global uncertainty remained high. Government debt in countries around the world increased uncertainty about their economic viability to provide for their citizens prompting concerns over their defaulting on their debt. Increasing deficits left the US government deadlocked and its credit rating down-graded. Public unrest toppled governments in many countries creating uncertainty about their future stability. An unprecedented nuclear meltdown raised uncertainty about its ef-fects, the ability of government and technology to cope, and even the future of the industry.

In order to reduce uncertainty about the future, much time and effort is expended in the planning, researching, even portraying what the future might be like both in reality and in works of fiction. We are motivated to know more about the future even though much of what is predicted doesn't happen. We are all familiar with predictions of driving hover cars and flying around in jet packs. People would live under the ocean and take vacations on the moon. Yet, many of these predictions didn't materialize. Many events that increased uncer-tainty were not foreseen like the fall of the Soviet Union, terrorism, and the financial crises.

We make plans for the future, however, by doing this we may be planning based on cer-tainty. Many times we have seen planning for the future fail resulting in unexpected and undesired outcomes. Utilizing the law of uncertainty to evaluate the future relies more on how needs and wants could motivate future behavior. It can be helpful to consider how the law of uncertainty will motivate behavior and shape social reality in the future, just as it has shaped and changed society in the past.

Society has created many institutions that have helped to reduce uncertainty. However, they are subject to many of the factors described in this book including climate, culture, self-replication, growth, stagnation, and decline. As they change in scope and influence, they create structures, bureaucracies, and hierarchies that can make them vulnerable to uncertainty. This means the next great crisis is not a question of if it will happen, but when, and how devastating will it be. If we understand the power of the law of uncertainty, we can mitigate its negative effects and find the positive ones. So, how ready will we be for future uncertainty and the next great crisis?

Despite society's efforts over thousands of years to reduce uncertainty, never before in the history of mankind have so many people been so thoroughly affected by uncertainty. In the pursuit of reducing uncertainty, has it actually been increased?

Uncertainty and Societal Communicating

The last hundred and fifty years has seen more advancement in daily life than ever before in history. Yet, people used to be more self reliant for many of their needs and wants, with most of them fulfilled by people in their own community. Now, most people are dependent on others to fulfill most of their needs and wants, with many things coming from outside of their community, even from the other side of the globe. While this can provide more options, it can make people more vulnerable to uncertainty. Society has made great advancements to reduce uncertainty, but has it also made us more vulnerable to the law of uncertainty?

Much of human activity throughout history has been motivated by the law of uncertainty. The pursuit of reducing uncertainty should have resulted in a significant decrease in the amount of uncertainty people experience. However, in the first decade of the second millennium, more people experienced greater uncertainty than ever before in history. Perhaps it is because the more complicated our systems become, the more vulnerable they are to uncertainty. Perhaps we should be looking at building social institutions to foster independence and self reliance in order to flow with uncertainty rather than try to control it.

Life is uncertain. The world can be chaotic. The purpose of this book is to explore how uncertainty affects us because it is always present. It influences how we think and motivates our behavior. Throughout history, most of human activity has been motivated by uncertainty. Uncertainty affects all of us and most everything in our lives. This makes it a topic that is difficult to cover in one book. It is a topic that could be examined and discussed for some time to come. So, this book focuses on how uncertainty affects how we communicate and our behavior.

This is not meant to be the last word on the topic, but instead a beginning. While this book is designed to be comprehensive, it is not meant to be all encompassing. It is meant to increase awareness in order to provide a place to initiate a discussion of how uncertainty affects us all.

In an increasingly interconnected world, how do we protect ourselves from the potential affects of increasing uncertainty? While we may never fully control or even understand the nature of uncertainty one thing is certain, absolute uncertainty will be a part of our lives now and in the future.

Uncertainty and Future Research

Science has sought a unified explanation of how the physical world works. The laws of uncertainty, shared meaning, and investing have demonstrated the potential to provide a unified explanation of the nature of human communicating and behavior. The law of uncertainty suggests that on a deeper level there is an underlying chaotic state that creates energy, which motivates everything it supports to seek a state of stability, providing the structures we have come to know. These laws have the potential to be useful as an analytical methodology in many fields.

This book was designed to be comprehensive by demonstrating the practical application of the laws, processes, and elements of communicating to real life circumstances. In scientific research, a hypothesis is formulated and then it is tested to prove its validity. If it cannot be disproven, it can be considered to be true. The laws and concepts in this book were applied to virtually all areas of behavioral communicating in order to find an area where they did not apply or where they did not hold true. Such a case was not found. Instead, they held up and worked in all areas of communicating and behavior affirming their truth and validity.

The laws of uncertainty, shared meaning, and investing were applied in the context of the field of communication, however, the following are suggested fields for potential future research about the nature of uncertainty.

Uncertainty and anthropology. Throughout history people have faced similar problems, but have solved them in different ways. All people have the same basic needs yet, they developed very different ways to fulfill them. Different societies have created different social realities that affect how they view themselves, others, and the world around them motivating them to create distinctly different physical realities. The law of uncertainty has motivated people throughout history to reduce uncertainty providing a driving force that has moved society forward. Using the laws of uncertainty, shared meaning, and investing could provide insight to examine and analyze people's behavior, culture, and development of society.

Uncertainty and sociology. Throughout history, people have had the need to reduce uncertainty motivating people to create and develop structure in society such as rules and institutions. Different societies have developed distinctly different rules and institutions to reduce uncertainty based upon their social reality. These were created to fulfill mutual needs and wants, reduce uncertainty, share meaning, and invest in society. Utilizing these elements as a methodological approach could help us know more about the development of society and the behavior of the people within it.

Uncertainty and political science. Society has needs and wants that must be fulfilled that cannot be fulfilled by groups or individuals. The law of uncertainty motivates people to reduce uncertainty in order to create security and stability, so that society can function. Government and political systems provide many of the structures and institutions that enable society to do these things. All people have faced similar needs yet, they have developed distinctly different political and governmental structures to fulfill them based upon their own social reality. Utilizing the law of uncertainty as a methodological approach could provide insight into the creation, maintenance, and evolution of governmental systems in society.

Uncertainty and international relations. Just as we as individuals have relationships with others, nations create relationships with one another. These relationships may function similar to those within a group or organization. They seek to fulfill their own needs and wants and are motivated to achieve their own desired outcomes. They can develop their own social reality that may be manifested in physical reality. So, the law of uncertainty could be utilized as a methodology to help examine this behavior.

Uncertainty and theology. Society has many institutions that share meaning and one of the most significant is religion. This is an important part of society because it fulfills many important needs and wants. It creates its own social reality, which motivates people's behavior and creates physical reality. It reduces uncertainty by answering some of the most important questions about life. Throughout history people have shared similar spiritual needs, but have fulfilled them in distinctly different ways. They shared meaning about their experiences and sought to explain what they observed around them. This reduced uncertainty, increased understanding, and made life more meaningful. It helped people to invest in themselves, others, and society. Utilizing the law of uncertainty can help to understand how theology developed to motivate behavior.

Uncertainty and economics. Economics can be a physical manifestation of the law of investing. However, it is also a means to reduce uncertainty by providing structure and predictability. We use economics to share meaning because by giving something meaning, we give it value. Economics is not just about numbers, it's about perceptions, expectations, desired outcomes, and individual needs and wants. The perception of social reality can motivate behavior that can create tangible economic realities. The law of uncertainty, shared meaning, and investing could be utilized as an economic methodological approach to facilitate understanding of economic behavior.

Uncertainty and medicine. The laws of uncertainty, shared meaning, and investing could potentially help to diagnose and treat physical and mental health issues. For instance, in diagnosing illness we look for the cause or symptoms in order to find a treatment. However, there could be a deeper, underlying cause from increased uncertainty. This has the potential to be an underlying cause because our mental state has the potential to manifest itself in out physical state. Increased uncertainty or lack of investing in relationships can result in increased stress, hypertension, or heart issues. When we treat physical symptoms, it could help resolve them by finding ways to reduce uncertainty, share meaning, and encourage investing. Our perceptions and expectations can also have an effect on our health. They can make us feel sad, depressed, or even angry, which can affect our mental as well as physical health. Treating health issues can include addressing psychological issues that can originate in uncertainty, perceptions and expectations, and needs and wants fulfillment.

Uncertainty and biology. People are distinctly different from all other forms of life because they have a complex set of needs and wants they cannot fulfill themselves. What sets people apart is they are motivated to reduce uncertainty, share meaning, invest, and create social reality. They negotiate fulfillment of mutually exclusive needs and wants that can be a source of tension, which needs to be resolved. So, people seek a state of equilibrium or stability combined with growth and change. Uncertainty and the need to reduce it could be viewed as the big bang of human development that motivates our behavior. Utilizing the law of uncertainty can provide insight into our development, behavior, and history.